ANCIENT LEGAL THOUGHT

This is a study of what constituted legality and the role of law in ancient societies. Investigating and comparing legal codes and legal thinking in the ancient societies of Mesopotamia, Egypt, India, China, Greece, the Roman Republic, the Roman Empire, and of the ancient Rabbis, this volume examines how people used law to create stable societies. Starting with Hammurabi's Code, this volume also analyzes the law of the pharaohs and the codes of the ancient rabbis and of the Roman Emperor Justinian. Focusing on the key concepts of justice, equity and humaneness, the status of women and slaves, and the idea of criminality and of war and peace, no other book attempts to examine such diverse legal systems and legal thinking from the ancient world.

Larry May is Professor of Philosophy and Law, Emeritus at Vanderbilt University. He has published 37 books, including *Limiting Leviathan: Hobbes on Law and International Affairs* (2013), *Proportionality in International Law*, with Michael Newton, (2014), *Contingent Pacifism* (Cambridge University Press, 2015), *Necessity in International Law*, with Jens Ohlin (2016), *International Criminal Tribunals*, with Shannon Fyfe (Cambridge University Press, 2017), and is editor of *The Cambridge Handbook of the Just War* (Cambridge University Press, 2017). His books have won awards in law, philosophy, and political science and he has advised the US State Department, the CIA, the NIH, and the International Committee of the Red Cross.

Ancient Legal Thought

EQUITY, JUSTICE, AND HUMANENESS FROM HAMMURABI AND THE PHARAOHS TO JUSTINIAN AND THE TALMUD

LARRY MAY
Vanderbilt University, Emeritus

CAMBRIDGE
UNIVERSITY PRESS

CAMBRIDGE
UNIVERSITY PRESS

University Printing House, Cambridge CB2 8BS, United Kingdom

One Liberty Plaza, 20th Floor, New York, NY 10006, USA

477 Williamstown Road, Port Melbourne, VIC 3207, Australia

314–321, 3rd Floor, Plot 3, Splendor Forum, Jasola District Centre, New Delhi – 110025, India

79 Anson Road, #06-04/06, Singapore 079906

Cambridge University Press is part of the University of Cambridge.

It furthers the University's mission by disseminating knowledge in the pursuit of education, learning, and research at the highest international levels of excellence.

www.cambridge.org
Information on this title: www.cambridge.org/9781108484107
DOI: 10.1017/9781108670012

First published 2019

Printed and bound in Great Britain by Clays Ltd, Elcograf S.p.A.

A catalogue record for this publication is available from the British Library.

Library of Congress Cataloging-in-Publication Data
Names: May, Larry, author.
Title: Ancient legal thought: equity, justice, and humaneness from Hammurabi and the pharaohs to Justinian and the Talmud / Larry May, Vanderbilt University, Tennessee.
Description: Cambridge, United Kingdom; New York, NY, USA: Cambridge University Press, 2019. | Includes bibliographical references and index.
Identifiers: LCCN 2019002337 | ISBN 9781108484107 (hardback) | ISBN 9781108705769 (paperback)
Subjects: LCSH: Law, Ancient – Social aspects. | BISAC: LAW / Jurisprudence.
Classification: LCC KL147.M39 2019 | DDC 340.5/3–dc23
LC record available at https://lccn.loc.gov/2019002337

ISBN 978-1-108-48410-7 Hardback

Contents

Acknowledgments

This book concerns nearly 3,000 years of ancient legal writings. I consider codes of law, edicts, decrees, and court opinions from ancient Mesopotamia, Egypt, China, Greece, India, the Roman Republic, rabbinic writings, and the Roman Empire. Throughout I aim to analyze the legal thought on such concepts as justice, equity, humaneness, responsibility, status, gender, and the rules governing war. This large book on ancient legal thought will be followed by similar books on Medieval legal thought, and also on modern legal thought. This is my retirement project, and I suspect it will indeed consume my retirement years.

I am very grateful to many people who read parts of this book in manuscript or who listened to me present my views in public discussions. They are too numerous to list but the following stand out as having been especially helpful: Scot Aikin, Pamela Barmash, Lena Bohman, Peter Borrok, Ronny Borrok, Eric Brown, Jeff Brown, William Bubelis, Emily Crookston, Shannon Fyfe, Frank Lovett, Zach Hoskins, Sunita Parikh, Eric Ritter, Brian Tamanaha, Steve Viner, and Kit Wellman.

Marilyn Friedman has talked me through nearly every section of this work and has made incalculable good suggestions along the way. My daughter, Elizabeth May, constructed one of the maps and helped me select the other one. The second map is taken from: J. A. Cook, Andrew Endicott, Elizabeth Rawson (Eds.), *The Cambridge Ancient History, Vol. 9: The Last Age of the Roman Republic, 146–43 BCE*, second edition, Cambridge University Press, 1992. My editor, John Berger, has been very encouraging and supportive over the many years it has taken me to complete this volume. I owe him, and the Cambridge staff, especially Danielle Menz, an enormous debt of gratitude. I am also grateful to Helen Flitton and Claire Bell for outstanding work on copy-editing.

General Introduction

Nearly 4,000 years ago, kings in various ancient societies, especially in Mesopotamia (contemporary Iraq), faced a crisis of major proportions. Large portions of the population were horribly in debt, many being forced to sell themselves or their children into slavery to pay off their debts. The laws and customs seemed to support the commercial practices that allowed lenders to charge 20–30 percent interest, and the law protected the lenders and gave no recourse for the indebted. Strict justice called for the creditors to receive what they were due. But another legal concept, the emerging idea of equity, seemed to call for a different result – the use of law as a vehicle to free people from economic oppression. Debt relief edicts were instituted – "clean-slate laws" as they were known – and are of obvious relevance today as well where crushing debt is a major issue underlying social inequality.

It is likely that in every literate society there is some sense of legality, even if it is deeply entwined with morality or religion. Law is one of the main foundations of stability in society, as well as the source for resolving conflict, and for protecting the weakest members of society. And where there is law, there are people who think about law and who discuss both what the law is and what it should be, discussing for example whether or not law should disrupt contracts to help the oppressed at the risk of creating social instability. We will see throughout this work that these topics were very much on the minds of people in ancient Mesopotamia and Egypt, long before the Greeks and Romans.

In this book I will argue that the earliest written law displays a sense of humaneness so that it is at best misleading to think of ancient laws as "primitive" – as somehow inferior for supporting oppression rather than aiding the oppressed. The conceptual focus of the various parts of *Ancient Legal Thought* is the ideas of justice and equity, and especially their interconnection from the earliest writing about law. It is often claimed that ancient (and even modern) law is about an elite exerting power over, and thereby oppressing, subordinates. While there is evidence for this view, I will direct our attention to other evidence for thinking that law was at least presented and discussed in the earliest written texts as providing justice and equity to those who are, for instance, the widows, orphans, poor, and strangers (or aliens) in ancient societies, much more so than seeing law as a vehicle for oppression.

This book concerns the very early history of the legal ideas of justice and equity. In ancient times not only was there law but there were people actively thinking about the nature and application of law. Already with the great codes of law of Mesopotamia from 3,800 years ago we can see a concern for the stabilizing effect of law but also the role of law in protecting the weak. At the beginning of his code of law, Hammurabi declares:

> the gods Anu and Enlil, for the enhancement of the well-being of the people, named me by name Hammurabi, the pious prince, who venerates the gods, to make justice prevail in the land, to abolish the wicked and the evil, to prevent the strong from oppressing the weak, to rise like the sun-god Shamash over all humankind to illuminate the land.[1]

This code of law from 1750 BCE sets several goals for the laws that then follow including serving justice and especially protecting the weak from oppression by the strong. This latter goal is a constant theme in the ancient laws we will examine, displaying the truly humane attitude that ancient lawmakers had toward the laws they instituted. The overarching thesis of the four parts of my work is that humaneness often characterized ancient law as much or more than even the goal of stabilizing the societies.

AUTHORITY

One of the currents we will explore in this book is the idea that law can obligate people to act simply by the law's commanding that such acts be committed. The idea underlying such obligation creating commands is that of legal authority. Here is how Hannah Arendt characterizes authority:

> Since authority always demands obedience, it is commonly mistaken for some form of power or violence. Yet authority precludes the use of external means of coercion; where force is used, authority itself has failed ... even the most draconian authoritarian government is bound by laws. Its laws are tested by a code which was made either not by man at all, as in the case of the law of nature or God's Commandments or the Platonic ideas, or at least not by those actually in power ... [it is] this external force which transcends the political realm, from which the authorities derive their "authority," that is, their legitimacy, and against which the powers can be checked.[2]

1 *Laws of Hammurabi*, in *Law Collections from Mesopotamia and Asia Minor*, second edition, translated by Martha T. Roth, Atlanta, GA: Scholars' Press, 1997, pp. 76–77.

2 Hannah Arendt, "What is Authority?" in *The Portable Hannah Arendt*, edited by Peter Baehr, NY: Penguin Books, 2000, pp. 463, 467.

Legal authority is the authority of laws, where the laws themselves have an origin which allows even the rulers themselves to be checked by reference to the laws.

We will see that in ancient times there were various sources of legal authority. And contrary to Arendt's claim, even if the laws are made by a ruler, in many cases the ruler is also subject to those laws – the laws are recognized even as binding the lawmaker. Indeed, this idea – often called the rule of law – will be seen to be present in quite ancient societies, predating the Romans who are generally thought to have initiated the modern idea of authority, which itself derives from the Latin word *auctoritas*. While civil law is often grounded in the commands of a god or the natural law, we will see that it is also often grounded in the pronouncements of a ruler who claims legitimacy from the people.

Unlike previous works, my focus is not solely on Western legal thought; indeed many chapters will focus on non-Western legal texts and theories especially of ancient China and India. And the entirety of the first part is properly non-Western (if that term can be used) since it is almost completely taken up with Mesopotamia and Egypt, with certain chapters also concerning ancient Israel. Of course, much attention is paid to ancient Greece and Rome, but an attempt is made to bring these great societies into conversation with their non-Western neighbors – indeed the conceptual and practical problems concerning law will be shown to be often very similar across societies.

Also, unlike the many books that treat of only one ancient society, the parts of this work span the time from the very first written laws and discussions of law in Egypt and Mesopotamia, through the Greek and Roman times, covering approximately 3,000 years of recorded laws and analysis of law. Because of the sweep of this book, not all ancient legal texts can be covered. Nonetheless, we will see a reasonably representative sample of the best legal writings of the ancient period – that is, prior to the sixth century CE.

Each part is roughly divided into four sections on the following topics: (a) procedures and trial practices; (b) legal status, freedom, and equality; (c) crime, responsibility, and punishment; and (d) rules of war and peace as well as international justice. In these parts of this work I will pay special attention to the legal status of women over time, and also will confront the changing status of minorities from the earliest treatment of slaves.

We will consider legal texts from as early as 2100 BCE, and writing about law from at least 1000 BCE. Ancient theories of law develop later, but still date from at least 500 BCE to 500 CE. The legal texts I focus on are primarily of three kinds: codes of statute law, summary reports of legal trials, and treaties, in the ancient societies of Mesopotamia, Egypt, Greece, China, India, Rome, and of the ancient rabbis. Of course, I will also examine philosophical writing about law but there is much less of this material than the writing of and about law itself.

My method is straightforwardly comparative in two ways. First, ideas from one society are compared to ideas from that same society at a somewhat later point in time. I will then assess the change of legal ideas over time, say, in different periods of ancient Greece. Second, ideas from one ancient society at a certain time are compared to ideas on a similar topic from another society at about the same time, comparing, say, ideas from ancient Greece with those of ancient China. I then assess the differences between societies.

The comparative assessments are made based on ideas shared widely today. For example, ancient ideas on debt or punishment are here presented through legal texts such as ancient codes of law, debt relief edicts from the second millennium BCE in the Near East, and ideas on punishment in philosophical writings of the ancient Greeks. In assessing ideas of debt or punishment I make no assumptions that an idea being like our view today makes the ancient view better, or worse. I merely work from the perspective of what I bring to an understanding of the law of debt and punishment. I also make no assumptions about whether views show progress broadly over time – although the texts examined may show ideas that progress over time locally in terms of the ability to solve various problems of concern at that time.

It is important to point out that this work is not meant to be a systematic or comprehensive history. Rather this work is a series of studies (or snapshots) on certain ideas that can be found in the writings of these ancient societies that are distinctive of these societies or are presented in greater detail in these societies than before. My focus is conceptual and normative throughout. In this respect I do not aim at a comprehensive account of ancient law, but at an understanding of some of the most prominent and interesting ideas about law in ancient societies.

A very valuable analogy can be drawn from the Pre-Socratic philosophers for whom we have only fragments of their work, leaving later philosophers to reconstruct and infer what their philosophical views were. Like the Pre-Socratic philosophers, the legal texts that are left to us from ancient times are often only fragments – both only parts of texts, and only parts of ideas. The task of the philosopher and legal theorist is to try to discern what these fragmentary texts tell us about the "legal thought" of ancient times. I have chosen to title my book "Ancient Legal Thought" to indicate that the texts examined range more widely than typical texts in legal philosophy would encompass, just as is true of many of the texts of the Pre-Socratics, for we are examining a time when the written law is not always clearly distinguished from other forms of writing.

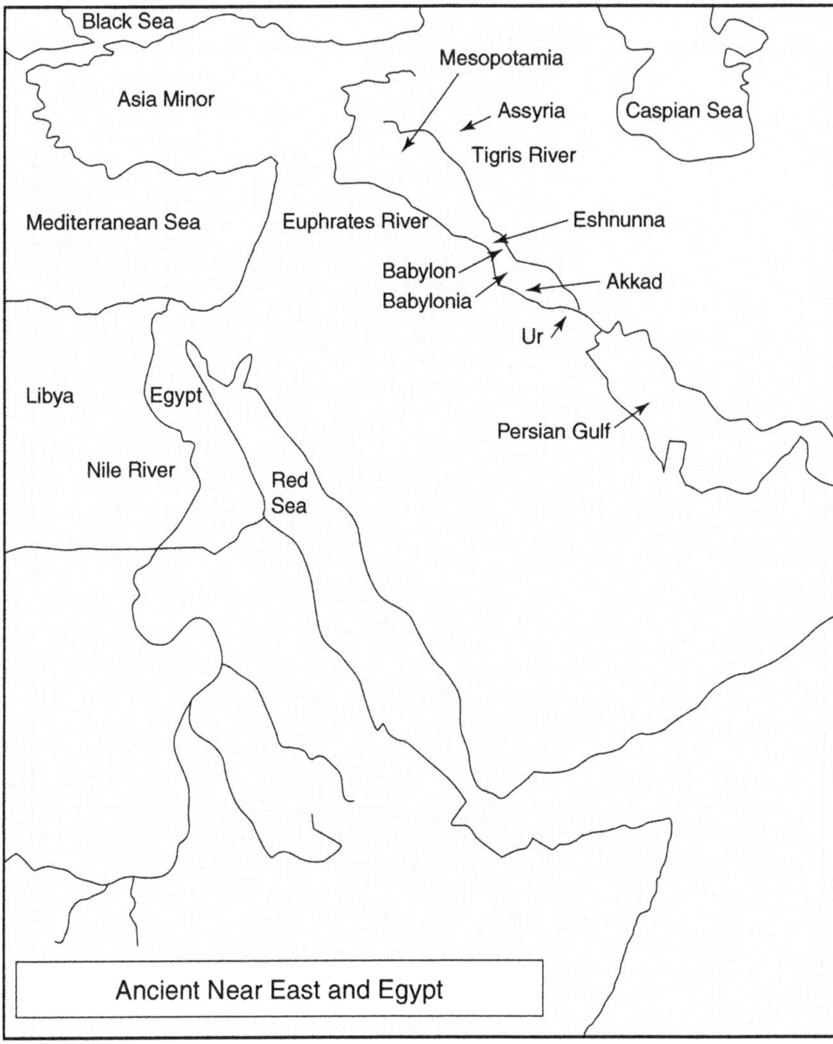

MAP 1 The Ancient Near East

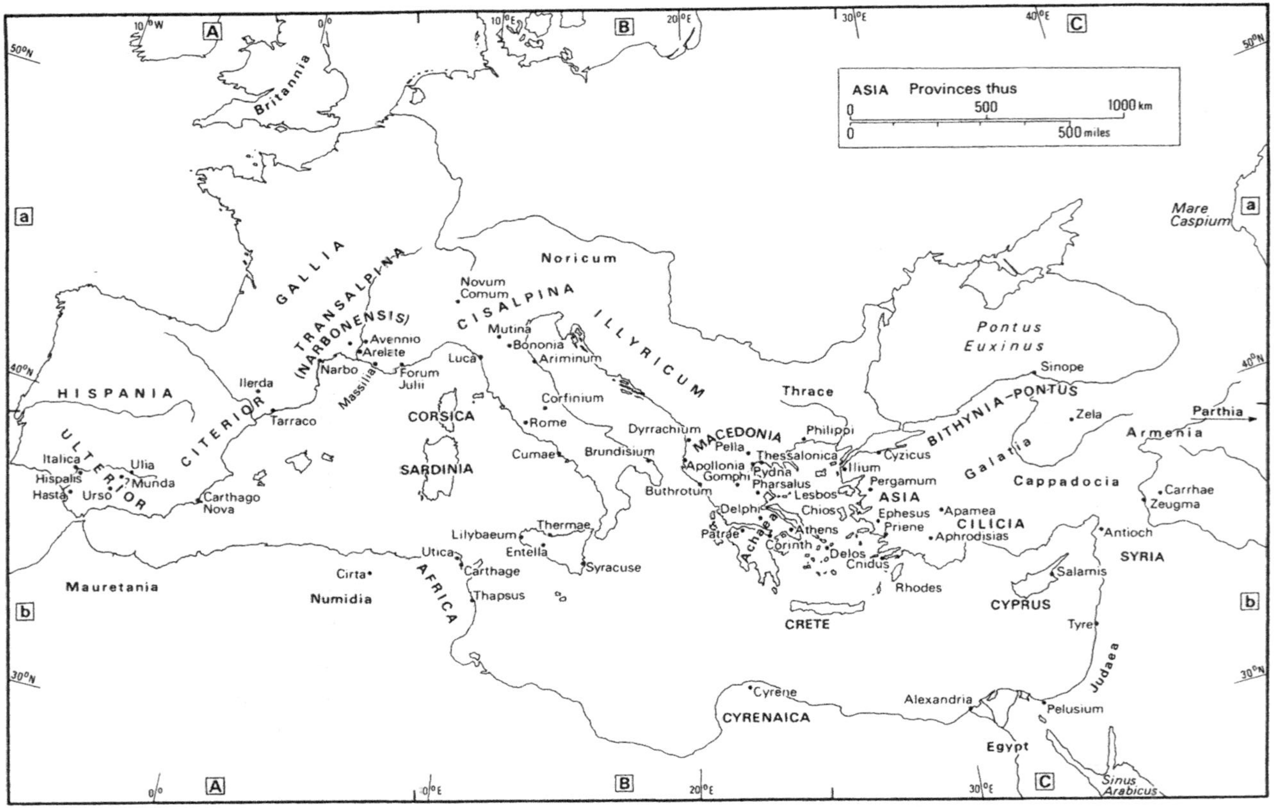

MAP 2 The Roman World at 50 BCE

PART A

Ancient Mesopotamia and Egypt

INTRODUCTION FOR PART A

This first part of my work on ancient legal thought is about the legal thought of certain ancient peoples in the Near East, principally in Mesopotamia and Egypt, and to a lesser extent Anatolia (contemporary Turkey) and Israel. Mesopotamia and Egypt share the reputation of being the oldest civilizations to use writing. And so in my project in examining the history of legal ideas, I will begin with the two societies where writing was first employed. The main reason for starting with literate societies is that there are texts to examine – an institutional recording that can be examined and matched against what seems to be the thinking about law at the time.

What is fascinating is how extensive a written record has survived of ancient legal thought that preceded the Greeks and Romans. The Code of Hammurabi is well known, and has been on display in the Louvre for many years. But there is now much more ancient written material than anyone could possibly master in a lifetime. Since I assume that most of my readers will be unfamiliar with this written record, I will provide many examples of these texts, along with my own attempt to draw inferences from the texts, in the chapters that follow.

In ancient Mesopotamia, the most famous legal text, and the one I will most often refer to, is the Babylonian Code of Hammurabi from roughly 1750 BCE. But there were similar, if shorter, "codes" as far back as the late third millennium that I will also examine. In ancient Egypt records have survived of trials that are very relevant for this part of my study. In addition there are texts, especially treaties, from the Hittites in Anatolia and there are important texts from ancient Israel, especially the Code of the Covenant. We have second millennium BCE texts from Assyria as well, which will play a part in what follows.

Theoretical writings about law develop late in most societies. So, the question emerges of whether we can infer legal thought in societies that had just recently developed a written code or collection of laws. And can we meaningfully discuss legal thought in societies that did not have theoretical writings about law? Much of what follows in this first part of my work attempts to develop arguments to show that we can infer significant legal thinking in societies long before there were treatises by legal theorists or political philosophers. While we do not find lengthy arguments, we do find reasoning and attempts to justify various laws and treaties. Indeed, some of the earliest writings are treaties and statements of how prisoners are to be treated, even though millennia will go by before treatises are written and discussed in humanitarian or international legal thought.

As we will see in more detail as this part of my work proceeds, legal thought in ancient Mesopotamia and Egypt fits several of the categories of legal thought. There certainly are edicts issued by ancient kings extending nearly as far back as writing itself. There are codes that seem to be issued top-down. Yet there is also evidence that assemblies made law, or at least there was discussion of law in assemblies, not just in the court of kings. Law does not seem to be autonomous from other norms in ancient society, especially moral norms. But the question remains, and is the first we will consider, of whether there is abstract thinking about law, perhaps a necessary condition for legal thought.

SECTION I

Ancient Procedural Law

1

Ancient Legal Reasoning

In this chapter I argue that ancient law of Mesopotamia and Egypt employs a conception of law and a type of reasoning that is easily characterizable today as a form of *legal* conceptualization and reasoning. Ancient thought is often characterized as primitive in that magical thinking was at its core. The world was full of gods and spirits who could influence the affairs of humans in ways often unfathomable to most people. There was thus, in this view, a constant search for ways of making sense of the mysteries of life so that some sort of control could be had over the supernatural forces. Today we seemingly know better, and this has been true since the time of the Greeks and Romans, although even for them there was at least lip service paid to the view of the world as controlled by supernatural forces. Some Greek and Roman thinkers pushed back in favor of a secular worldview – giving accounts of this-worldly phenomena in naturalistic terms. The idea was that in later societies, but not in Mesopotamia or Egypt, there were laws of nature that were not a matter of menacing or benevolent spirits but simply the way the world is. And the task was to understand the natural order so that it could be controlled. I will dispute this idea as the chapter develops.

In this first chapter I will introduce the main texts I will rely on from ancient Mesopotamia – the "codes" of law, the collections of laws from this period, as well as the edicts of kings. The texts do not appear to be religious or magical texts. In Section 1.2 I will begin to explain why I do not see law in Mesopotamia and Egypt, after the development of writing, to be primitive. In Section 1.3 I talk about legal reasoning "by example" in ancient times and show its similarity to that of today. In Section 1.4 I then move on to discuss how ancient ideas of justice influenced the conceptions of law extant in ancient times. I also point to the even richer accounts of equity that we can glean from ancient legal texts – not at all a primitive account. And in Section 1.5 I set out some reasons to think that ancient legal thought was at least in part understood as secular rather than religious, as down-to-earth, not overly dependent on what is spiritual – indeed Hammurabi is pictured on the cover of this book as giving his laws to the gods, not receiving laws from the gods.

1.1 "CODES," EDICTS, AND DECREES

The most striking sources of law that come down to us from ancient Mesopotamia are the law "codes" of various kings. Throughout the chapters that follow, these will be often the main sources that I refer to in order to understand ancient legal thought about various matters, such as slavery or debt forgiveness. As many scholars have noted, one of the most intriguing puzzles about these "codes" is that judges do not seem to have referred to them in their decisions. And in addition, they are hardly comprehensive or systematic, but seem, at least at first sight, to be almost random collections of laws.

Here are the first few laws of the earliest of the "codes," the Laws of Ur-Namma (2100 BCE):

> LU #1 If a man commits a homicide, they shall kill that man.
> LU #2 If a man acts lawlessly, they shall kill him.
> LU #3 If a man detains another, that man shall be imprisoned and he shall weigh and deliver 15 shekels of silver.[1]

All of the law collections employ roughly the same form as these Laws of Ur-Namma.

A rough consensus has emerged that the collections of laws, Hammurabi's being the best known because of the magnificent stone stela upon which they are now displayed in the Louvre in Paris, are not properly statutes. In their commentary, *The Babylonian Laws*, the British scholars, Godfrey Rolles Driver and J. C. Miles, provide three different but related ways to view Hammurabi's laws:

> The Laws must not be regarded as a code or digest, but as a series of amendments to the common law of Babylon …
>
> it is a series of amendments and restatements of parts of the law in force when he wrote.
>
> [They are] mere super-structures on a much larger base of custom.[2]

Here is a way to connect unwritten customary law with the law "codes."

Coming from a very different legal tradition to that of Driver and Miles, the French scholar, Jean Bottero, argues:

1 *Laws of Ur-Namma* [LU], *Law Collections from Mesopotamia and Asia Minor*, second edition, translated by Martha Roth, Atlanta, GA: Scholars' Press, 1997, p. 15.

2 Godfrey Rolles Driver and J. C. Miles, *The Babylonian Laws*, Oxford: Oxford University Press, 1952, Vol. I, pp. 41, 45.

> in the eyes of its author the "Code" was not at all intended to exercise by itself a univocal normative value in the legislative order. But it did have value as a model; it was instructive and educative in the judicial order. A law applies to details; a model inspires – which is entirely different. In conclusion what we have here is not a law code, nor the charter of a legal reform, but above all, in its own way, a treatise, with examples, on the exercise of judicial power … it is clearly centered upon the establishment, not of a strict and literal [written] justice, but of equity that inspires justice but also surpasses it.[3]

And so here we have a connection suggested between equity and natural law on the one hand and the "codes" of law on the other.

My own view is similar to that of Marc Van De Mieroop, who argues that there is no reason not to regard these "codes" as law codes in various important senses of that term.

> The code represents the culmination of developments that had started centuries earlier. It is the high point of a tradition in which kings asserted that they protected their people from legal abuse, a tradition that started with Ur-Namma and ended with Hammurabi, some three hundred years later.[4]

As will be clear, I also support the following conclusion reached by Samuel Jackson:

> We cannot rule out the possibility that the legal cases presented in collections such as LH [Laws of Hammurabi] were discussed in the courtroom or at least influenced the reasoning of judges in making their decision. It may be that this reasoning process has not been recorded. Whatever the situation was, it could be unwise to make too many conclusions based on the lack of citations to LH.[5]

The codes were not statutes but rather either past judgments or models for use by judges (much like the US Model Penal Code), and for the training of students. And it is also likely that the codes were records of additions or changes of the customary law.

Regardless of how exactly they functioned at the time, the codes are the best source we have of how ancient Near Eastern rulers thought about law, both specific laws and law in general, and they will be the most important source I will refer to in the chapters that follow in the first part of this work.

In addition to the codes of law we also have good evidence of edicts issued by various ancient rulers. Specific edicts were issued by kings in ancient times in

[3] Jean Bottero, *Mesopotamia: Writing, Reasoning, and the Gods*, translated by Zainab Bahrain and Marc Van De Mieroop, Chicago: University of Chicago Press, 1992, pp. 167, 183.

[4] Marc Van De Mieroop, *Philosophy Before the Greeks*, Princeton, NJ: Princeton University Press, 2016, p. 148.

[5] Samuel Jackson, *A Comparison of Ancient Near Eastern Law Collections Prior to the First Millennium* BC, Piscataway, NJ: Gorgias Press, 2008, pp. 77–78.

order to address a specific issue, such as debt forgiveness. Westbrook gives us the following account: "The constitutional convention was that the king issued decrees in the form of personal orders, although that authority was sometimes delegated to subordinates."[6] If ancient law is thus a matter of many decrees issued for very particular reasons, one can see how the law codes would fill a needed role of providing judges as well as the general populace with more generalized guidance. It is my view that the ancient law codes are like such things today as the Model Penal Code in the United States. The edicts that we will examine in this section seem to have served a more specific purpose in guiding the work of judges.

Here is an account of the very earliest records of an edict, issued by Irikagina, ruler of Lugash in the middle of the third millennium in Mesopotamia.

> He cleared the prisons of indebted children of Lagash, of those having committed *gur-gub-* and *se-sig*-offenses [tax or rental payment offenses], of those having committed theft or murder. He established their liberation (*ama-r gi*). Irikagina made a contract with (the god) Nin-girsu.k, that he will not deliver to the powerful the orphan or the widow.[7]

This edict lists very specific cases where an amnesty is declared for child offenders, an especially humane thing to do even in our own times.

Next consider the best known of the ancient edicts, the Edict of Ammisaduqa in Babylonia several centuries after Hammurabi's reign.

> Section 4. Whoever has given barley or silver to an Akkadian or Amorite as an interest bearing loan or as fees, and had a document drawn up – because the king has established equity in the land, his document is voided; he may not collect the barley or silver on the basis of his document.[8]

Here past debts incurred through loans extended by certain public sector creditors, and perhaps also some "private" individuals, are cancelled.

The Irikagina edict from the third millennium BCE and the Ammisaduqa edict from the second millennium BCE thus address very specific conditions that are to be covered according to their amnesty measures (the *misarum*). Claus Wilcke urges that we regard these edicts as if they were pieces of legislation insofar as kings "issued edicts binding the commoners and officials of their state or city-state."[9] Wilcke

6 Raymond M. Westbrook, "Introduction" to his edited book, *A History of Ancient Near Eastern Law*, Vol. 1, Leiden: Brill, 2003, p. 27.

7 Translated by Claus Wilcke, "Early Dynastic and Sardonic Periods," in *A History of Ancient Near Eastern Law*, Vol. 1, edited by Raymond M. Westbrook, Leiden: Brill, 2003, pp. 142–143.

8 Translated and quoted in Jacob Finkelstein, "The Edict of Ammisaduqa," *Ancient Near Eastern Texts Relating to the Old Testament*, third edition, edited by in J. B. Pritchard, Princeton, NJ: Princeton University Press, 1969, pp. 526–527. I have revised the translation from justice to equity since the term in question is *misharum*.

9 Wilcke, "Early Dynastic and Sargonic Periods," p. 147.

calls them "legislation" and he is right insofar as the edicts and decrees of kings in Mesopotamia and Egypt are the closest ancient equivalents to legislation.

1.2 PRIMITIVE LEGAL REASONING

Many scholars now believe that the invention of writing gives us some of our best evidence for thinking that ancient legal thought advanced to involve abstraction. As Jack Goody has argued, when people move from a largely oral society to a literate one, there is inevitably also a move to more abstract thinking. When a rule gets written down it already is removed from the particular circumstances that gave rise to the initial articulation of the rule.[10] Writing something down fixes it and moves it out of a particular space and time. This is clearly already an abstraction. Here is part of Goody's argument:

> written statements of law, of norms, of rules, have had to be abstracted from particular situations in order to be addressed to a universal audience out there, rather than delivered face-to-face to a specific group of people at a particular time and place. The communicative context has changed dramatically both as regards the emitter and as regards the receivers, with consequent implications for the nature of the message. In written communication a universal injunction "thou shalt not kill" tends to replace the more particular phraseology of "thou shalt not kill other Jews," or perhaps "thou shalt not kill except under the orders of leader, party or nation."[11]

In this and later sections we will explore more fully why this abstraction is so important.

As I said, it is important to note that there are no theoretical treatises on law, as in the texts of the ancient Greek and Roman philosophers. And it is also important to note that many scholars think that ancient Mesopotamia and Egypt suffered from a paucity of abstract reasoning – hence making it odd to think that there was legal thought in these societies where writing was first invented. In addition, what laws there were are often characterized as inhumane, because of the extensive use of cruelty (such as, in the form of *lex talionis*, "an eye for an eye") and death sentences. I will argue though that there was significant legal thought in Mesopotamia and Egypt, and that the laws were more humane than what seems true at first sight.

At the end of the very impressive book, *Before Philosophy: The Intellectual Adventure of Ancient Man*,[12] the Frankforts argue that ancient Near Eastern people, such as those in Mesopotamia, were incapable of abstract considerations because of

[10] See Jack Goody, *The Logic of Writing and the Organization of Society*, Cambridge: Cambridge University Press, 1986, especially chapters 1 and 4.

[11] Ibid., pp. 12–13.

[12] Henri Frankfort and H. A. Frankfort, "The Emancipation of Thought from Myth," in *Before Philosophy: The Intellectual Adventure of Ancient Man*, edited by Henri Frankfurt, H. A. Frankfurt, John A. Wilson, and Thorkild Jacobsen, Baltimore, MD: Penguin Press, 1949. Also see F. M. Cornford,

their inability to break free from "the prescriptive sanctions of religion."[13] They base this conclusion on the examination of myths and hymns, not legal texts. And Henry Sumner Maine, in his monumental book *Ancient Law*, likewise says that ancient peoples did not conceive of law as distinct from religion and morality, and hence law remained in its infancy.[14] While I will not take a stand on what is primitive and what not, I will dispute the idea that ancient people before the Greeks failed to think abstractly about the law.

Abstraction, or abstract reasoning, admits of several meanings and so it is important to get clear on precisely what the charge is against the ancient legal thinkers of the Near East. The kind of abstraction that is involved in abstract reasoning is not necessarily ruled out when conducted in the context of religion. The relevant sense of "abstract" is "withdrawn or separated from matter, from material embodiment, from practice, or from particular examples." And the idea of abstractness then is "the quality of being … withdrawn and separate from the actual, the concrete or the common."[15] It is the inability to think beyond the concrete case in front of one that is thought to be the hallmark of those who cannot engage in abstract reasoning. Or, to put it in a slightly different way, those who cannot engage in abstract reasoning fail to be able to move beyond the particular to the general or universal.

The abilities to form abstract ideas and engage in abstract reasoning are supposed to be what characterizes a development out of the primitive society. There is the sense that primitive people are irrational or at least do not act on the basis of reason but on the basis of superstition and magical thinking. And yet superstition and magical thinking can be abstract in the sense that they are somewhat divorced from the concrete and particular insofar as the irrational could involve a belief in an omnipresent force that was not particular or concrete at all.

There is here also only a loose connection between abstract reasoning and nonreligious thinking. Religion can recognize a god that is not merely a personification of a particular being – indeed there is a Greek idea of the world as being full of gods – which seems to make the gods not particular any more. We will see some ideas of this sort predating the Greeks by nearly a thousand years.

What is the object of this attack on so-called primitive societies is the idea that they are somehow insufficiently developed mentally and hence incapable of understanding the world the way it is, in terms of laws of nature for instance. And in the legal domain, the critique is supposed to be that ancient legal thinking is also incapable of generalizing in a way that moves away from the specific facts at the moment

From Religion to Philosophy: A Study in the Origins of Western Speculation (1912), New York, NY: Harper & Row Publishers, 1957.

13 Ibid., p. 262.

14 Henry Sumner Maine, *Ancient Law*, London: John Murray, 1861, chapter one.

15 OED.

to consider what the larger categories are that are at stake and on the basis of which truly general laws can be built to address more than just one case at a time.

It is my view, and I will provide much evidence for this view, that early Mesopotamian and Egyptian laws display a rich sense of abstraction from the particular set of facts to encompass a broad array of cases, indeed cases that have not yet been encountered. What will be harder is to show that people actually were not just thinking abstractly but thinking about abstract categories, that people were not just employing legal categories that were general and not merely unique to particular cases, but also reasoning about these abstract categories. We do have evidence from which we can reconstruct that such reasoning was occurring but we generally lack explicit evidence that the abstract categories were themselves being discussed.

Raymond Westbrook has mounted a major challenge to the way that I will read the legal texts of the ancient world, and he has focused on the lack of explicit terms for abstract categories and definitions of those categories. Westbrook, who spent his career examining ancient legal texts, nonetheless also claims that ancient law in Mesopotamia is primitive in that it is not abstract in the way that legislation is, at least when compared to the ancient Greeks.[16] He argues that for there to be a non-primitive system of jurisprudence, there must be more than individual judgments – there must be rules that are "reasonably predictable and their results mutually consistent."[17] Yet, he finds that ancient law in the Near East lacked three features, discussed below, which are necessary for a system of non-primitive jurisprudence. I will comment briefly on these three features. I will leave aside the question of what is meant by "primitive," a generally pejorative term, as well as why law is thought to be somehow better when it is more "modern."

The first feature indicative of a system of non-primitive jurisprudence for Westbrook is "division into theoretical categories and definitions of abstract concepts." Westbrook argues that in ancient Mesopotamian texts we do not "find anything remotely like" these features, at least as they are understood typically today.[18] Westbrook is looking for something in ancient Mesopotamian legal texts that matches the tradition that arose from Aristotle's logic. This point is the most interesting of his three points. It is indeed a question to be answered what sort of logic was employed in ancient legal thinking. And if not Aristotelian logic then what

[16] Raymond Westbrook, *Ex Oriente Lex: Near Eastern Influences on Ancient Greek and Roman Law*, edited by Deborah Lyons and Kurt Raaflaub, Baltimore, MD: Johns Hopkins University Press, 2015, especially chapter twelve.

[17] Raymond Westbrook, "The Early History of Law: A Theoretical Essay," reprinted in Raymond Westbrook, *Ex Oriente Lex: Near Eastern Influences on Ancient Greek and Roman Law*, edited by Deborah Lyons and Kurt Raaflaub, Baltimore, MD: Johns Hopkins University Press, 2015, p. 228.

[18] Ibid., pp. 228–229.

sort of logic was employed in ancient Mesopotamian and Egyptian legal thinking? I aim to answer this question as this chapter proceeds.

Categorization is important in legal thinking, at the very least as a way to determine what cases are relevantly like other cases, and what cases are different from one another, in order to determine whether basic fairness exists, so as to follow the principle: treat like cases alike and different cases differently. But as we will see, there does indeed seem to be categorization occurring in ancient Mesopotamia in the way that cases were presented in the law codes with several variations attempting to illustrate what was relevantly similar and dissimilar. Here is one of many examples:

> LH #218 If a physician performs major surgery with a bronze lancet upon an *awilu* [member of the upper class of freemen] and thus causes the *awilu's* death, or opens an *awilu's* temple with a bronze lancet and thus blinds the *awilu's* eye, they shall cut off his hand.
>
> LH #219 If a physician performs major surgery with a bronze lancet upon a slave of a commoner and thus causes the slave's death, he shall replace the slave with a slave of comparable value.[19]

Here what is relevant is the person who acts and the person who is acted on, and the penalties are differentiated according to this categorization.

Second, Westbrook argues that "another basic feature of modern law that is missing: citation of authority whether statute or precedent." In his view, by the time of the Greek, Roman, and Rabbinic jurists, "there was an orgy of citation."[20] It is interesting that Westbrook singles out citation as being especially important for jurisprudential legal reasoning. It is true that the ancient law codes are hardly ever referred to in the decisions of various trials. But if it is true that the law codes were used to train people in how to make legal decisions, as many scholars think is plausible, then there is no straightforward inference from the lack of citation to the conclusion that ancient legal thought was significantly different from Greek, Roman, and even modern legal thought. Referring to the sources of law is important, but of course it need not occur in the written documents – and in any event the written documents concerning ancient trials are not by any means exact renderings of what was said at those trials. My argument does not directly refute Westbrook, but the matter is now more unsettled than he indicated.

Third, "among the long lists of professions – doctor, soothsayer, priest," Westbrook says "there is one missing: lawyer. Or to be more exact, the jurist, the expert in the interpretation of the law."[21] But as we will see, there are many references to judges

19 *Laws of Hammurabi* [LH], *Law Collections from Mesopotamia and Asia Minor*, p. 123.
20 Westbrook, "The Early History of Law," p. 229.
21 Ibid.

and other court officials, such as various scribes. And there are a few rare examples of lawyers from ancient times such as that discussed by Klaas R. Veenhof:

> An "attorney" could be hired in Assur by a plaintiff after authorization by the ruler and the City Assembly. He was hired "to assist" the plaintiff and "to win his case." He was promised a wage plus compensation for travel expenses and food. He received half in advance, to be returned if he abandoned the case before his mission was completed.[22]

But it may be technically correct that the "profession" of lawyer is not yet known in the ancient texts we will examine. Yet, it is not clear that it matters that much if the profession is not named as long as there are people who make their living as various kinds of experts in the legal systems of Mesopotamia and Egypt, as there seems to have been.

1.3 LEGAL REASONING "BY EXAMPLE"

Edward Levi begins his canonical book on legal reasoning in the contemporary Anglo-American context, where case law is crucial, with this observation: "The basic pattern of legal reasoning is reasoning by example."[23] Levi goes on to say that "it cannot be said that the legal process is the application of known rules to diverse facts. Yet it is a system of rules; the rules are discovered in the process of determining similarity or difference." Picking out "key similarities" and then reasoning "from them to the justice of applying a common classification" is the key.[24]

It will be my contention that much of ancient Mesopotamian legal reasoning proceeds in just the way Levi describes and we can see it in operation in the law codes. The codes discuss a particular kind of case. A penalty is then attached to the offense. And then the case is varied. Here is an example that turns up in surprisingly many ancient codes, the ox that gores (the Laws of Eshnunna (LE)):[25]

> LE #53 If an ox gores another ox and thus causes its death, the two ox-owners shall divide the value of the ox, and the carcass of the dead ox.
>
> LE #54 If an ox is a gorer and the ward authorities so notify its owner, but he fails to keep his ox in check and it gores a man and thus causes his death, the owner of the ox shall weigh and deliver 40 shekels of silver.

22 Klaas R. Veenhof, "Old Assyrian Period," in A *History of Ancient Near Eastern Law*, edited by Raymond Westbrook, Leiden: Brill, 2003, Vol. 1, p. 473.

23 Edward H. Levi, *An Introduction to Legal Reasoning*, Chicago, IL: University of Chicago Press, 1949, p. 1.

24 Ibid., p. 3.

25 See J. J. Finkelstein's monograph, "The Ox that Gored," *Transactions of the American Philosophical Society*, Vol. 71, part 2, 1981, pp. 1–89.

LE #55 If it gores a slave and thus causes his death, he shall weigh and deliver 15 shekels of silver.

LE #56 If a dog is vicious and the ward authorities so notify its owner, but he fails to control his dog and it bites a man and thus causes his death, the owner of the dog shall weigh and deliver 40 shekels of silver.[26]

These laws vary the context starting from what is probably an abstracted real-life case and then proceeding through a host of hypothetical cases. Contrary to what many scholars have said, this is legal reasoning, reasoning by example, and as I will next explain, it is reasoning that involves a fair amount of abstraction.

For legal reasoning not to admit of abstraction it would have to concern certain highly specific edicts only – where, for instance, a law set a penalty for a specific act for a specific named person. Law is often seen as a matter of commands, and there can be quite specific commands that seem to be law or law-like. But law can also be a matter of commands in that what is provided for is that people are obligated to obey because of the inherent authority of the law. One of the questions we will take up throughout the various parts of this work concerns how legal authority is viewed when law is made by a single person, and yet the commands are abstracted so that they apply even after the single ruler's death.

Yet, even in the construction of the law by a single person, considerations of what factors seem relevant and what factors seem irrelevant will have to be made – otherwise it is not a law at all but just a personal statement. This of course is also true of the laws of the codes of Hammurabi and Eshnunna that we have seen examples of. But in applying these laws someone else had to decide what was relevant – what was relevantly similar, what was relevant to the purposes of the lawgiver, etc.

In ancient Mesopotamia, one common method was to construct lengthy word lists of such things as divinatory signs, omens, and professions, as well as laws. There is considerable debate about what the rationale was for the collection of these lists, but there certainly do seem to be organizing principles that display a fair amount of abstract reasoning. Marc Van De Mieroop cites one example that is illustrative: "they divided domesticated animals into sheep, goats, and cattle, and subdivided each group according to sex, age, color, and other criteria."[27] Here examples of domesticated animals are listed and categorized just as were laws concerning who owes recompense for damage caused by a goring ox, or by a dog. This method, while it depends on writing, is not merely fanciful or divorced from reality, especially in the law lists.

[26] *Laws of Eshnunna* [LE], in *Law Collections From Mesopotamia and Asia Minor,* second edition, translated by Martha T. Roth, Atlanta, GA: Scholars' Press, 1997, pp. 67–68.

[27] Van De Mieroop, *Philosophy Before the Greeks*, p. 65.

Van De Mieroop has recently proposed that the lists took on a reality of their own, in a way similar to the writings of some contemporary post-modernists. I will not follow Van De Mieroop quite so far, although I acknowledge that the lists sometimes include cases that concern facts that could not exist or are very likely not to exist. But, as is true of the Anglo-American method of teaching law, the lists of examples of various kinds of case can be presented to students as a way of training them in the law, especially in how to decide cases by reference to examples that are in some ways similar and other ways dissimilar from real-life cases. The stress on similarity and difference can be best understood as a way to move from the unique case to a version of that case that can be abstracted and potentially applied to many other cases.

So, I admit that there is a sense that the example cases in the ancient law codes were sometimes fantastically unrelated to actual reality, as is often seen in the very idea of "hypothetical cases." Some of these cases are illustrative, when taken together with other cases, of a method of reasoning that is not necessarily about reality. We can get a sense of how this might work by realizing that a student of American law today would find some hypothetical cases as very close to real-life cases, but some other cases as meant to push the student to see patterns rather than what judges have actually decided.

Importantly, though, an American law student would not cite a hypothetical case to describe the state of the law, for the actual state of the law is not composed of hypotheticals. But the student would use the hypothetical case as a way to think about how the law might be understood when applied to a new set of facts. This can help us explain why the extensive law codes of ancient Mesopotamia are not referred to in the real-life judgments at the time. Yet it is true that the written cases that the students are exposed to are "legal" texts nonetheless. They tell us about how people thought about legal cases and how students were educated to think about the law. And this is obviously related to our task: to try to understand legal thinking in ancient societies, especially in ancient Mesopotamia and Egypt.

1.4 THE TERMS FOR LAW AND JUSTICE

It is the way that the terms for law, justice, and equity are employed in the languages of the ancient Near East that tell us whether and to what extent these terms stood for categories that were the subject of abstract legal thinking. It is my view that this comes out clearest in cases where justice is contrasted with equity, not quite as was true for Aristotle, but in a way that also displays ancient legal thought. Just as in scholarship about the Pre-Socratics, much reconstruction and inferring must be done to understand how the ancient Greek concept of *to apeiron* (the unlimited, infinite, indefinite) was understood, so in ancient legal scholarship much reconstruction and inferring must be done to understand how the concepts of law and justice, as well as equity, were understood.

In ancient times, as far as we can tell, law began to be "written about" once there were written laws. Once law is written, then matters of law are often seen as interpretation and application of the written law to particular cases. Law comes to be understood narrowly as application of general rule to particular case. But as Aristotle put it so well, there is sometimes a gap that opens when law covers a case that is ill-suited to be covered in its particular details, as we will see.

Aristotle uses an image to present the idea of equity that is highly relevant for our discussions: "like the leaden rule used in making the Lesbian moulding; the rule adapts itself to the shape of the stone and is not rigid, and so too the [equitable] decree is adapted to the facts."[28] Sometimes, there is a mismatch such that unfairness, or inequity, results. In the initial movement from individual oral decree to general written law something can be lost that then calls for the occasional new corrective decree, now primarily in written form, to correct an unfair legal decision, which in other respects was legally just. The unfairness is in the result of the application of the law, not in its formal promulgation.

Unlike for the Greeks, justice broadly construed enters into ancient Babylonian legal thought as a variation of a word that otherwise meant "straight," *misaram*. Even kings were supposed to act in a straight way, dealing fairly, equitably, with people, especially those who are least powerful. And Hammurabi says that he has set out his "code" of laws to show people the straight way. But there is another term for justice in ancient Babylonian, *simdatum*, which seems to mean justice understood more narrowly in terms of the particular application of a written law.[29]

Some scholars have tried to sort out these two senses of justice. The term *misaram* is used in some of Hammurabi's letters to indicate "a law creating a remission or moratorium of some kind."[30] Moratoria and amnesties are generally considered acts of equity rather than justice properly or narrowly conceived. As was true for Aristotle, these decrees are seen as corrections of the law due to the particularities of the case. But the correction is not seen as an exception so much as a straightening out of the law. In this sense, what is straight means that which is right, in the sense of the straight justice of equity for a particular case, even if it violates a general rule.

It is not completely clear that the Old Babylonian terms *misaram* and *simdatum* correspond exactly to Aristotle's understanding of equity and narrow legal justice respectively. But what is clear is that early Mesopotamian legal thought is struggling with a distinction that would be very important later, especially for the ancient

28 Aristotle, *Nicomachean Ethics*, 1137b69.
29 Driver and Miles, *The Babylonian Laws*, p. 19.
30 Ibid., p. 22.

Greeks and Romans. The images used by Aristotle seem different in the sense that he sees a sense of straight justice opposed to equity, which is molded to the particularities of the case. Mesopotamians seem to think of the straight as more like the idea of the right (*misaram*) – so right for the Mesopotamians is closer to the Latin *ius* (broad justice as equity) whereas *simdatum* is closer to the Latin term *lex* (properly narrow legal justice).

In ancient Egyptian we find several terms also used for law and justice that provide us with another wrinkle on how to start understanding legal thought at the beginning of civilizations. Indeed at least one scholar has proposed that there is a distinct philosophy of law that we can uncover by looking closely at the terms for justice employed by ancient Egyptians. The chief judge, the vizier, is referred to as the "prophet of Maat," and so we have a close connection between judges and justice in ancient Egypt.[31] But the question becomes how to best understand this idea of Maat.

Henry Frankfort gives us a good start here in a chapter of his book, *Before Philosophy*:

> for the present the reader must accept our word that Maat means "justice," one of the essential attributes of the Egyptian state, and that this justice does not appear to have been codified in statutes or precedents but was expressed in right-dealing in relation to persons and situations. The ruler who dispensed justice was urged to dispense it in relation to need, indeed, to give more than was due …
>
> Daily the king offered up justice to the god … By this fact of daily ritual offering, justice did tend to become a mere form, which might be delivered through literal conformance to law or ritual. But there was also a constant insistence that justice is something more positive than mere neutral conformance, that it lies in doing more than is required … Insistently through these texts ran the obligation of the ruler to render on the basis of need and not on the basis of *quid pro quo* trade.[32]

Giving more than was due is also discussed in some detail in ancient Greek society under what came to be known as *meionexia*, as contrasted with the vice of *pleionexia*, giving less than was due.

The contemporary debates about justice after law ends, especially with the idea of restorative justice, mirror this ancient debate today.[33] If we stick to what is required by strict justice, then all wrongdoers must be prosecuted, and yet to achieve reconciliation sometimes means to be more lenient – not to prosecute in certain cases so that a society can have a better chance of healing. Here again is the interplay of justice and equity.

[31] See Henry Frankfurt et al., *Before Philosophy*, Chicago, IL: University of Chicago Press, 1946, p. 104.

[32] Frankfurt et al., *Before Philosophy*, pp. 92, 94–95.

[33] See my discussion of these ideas in my book *After War Ends*, Cambridge: Cambridge University Press, 2012.

In ancient Egyptian, one of the terms for justice as I said is Maat, a term which has proven very hard to define. Maat is best translated in general as "truth and justice." In one sense, it seems that Maat is more like equity than narrow justice in that it is often translated as righteousness. Maat is also the god whose white feather is placed into the scales opposite a person's heart (and soul) in the final judgment as can be seen for instance in Chapter 125 of the so-called *Book of the Dead: The Book of Going Forth by Day*.[34]

Indeed, there is a very long list of things that one should not have done if one hopes to be worthy of being judged pure. In this list we can find a rudimentary code of conduct that is stipulated by the god Maat. And this list is perhaps the kind of customary set of norms that stood in for a written code of law in ancient Egypt. Here is just a partial list from Book 125 of the *Book of the Dead: The Book of Going Forth by Day*:

> Hail to you, great god, Lord of Justice ... I have brought you truth, I have repelled falsehood for you. I have not done falsehood against men, I have not impoverished my associates. I have done no wrong in the Place of Truth. I have not learnt that which is not, I have done no evil, I have not daily made labor in excess of what was due to be done for me, my name has not reached the office of those who control slaves. I have not deprived an orphan of his property, I have not done what the gods detest, I have not calumniated a servant to its master, I have not caused pain, I have not made hungry, I have not made to weep, I have not killed, I have not commanded to kill, I have not made suffering for anyone ...[35]

This list is clearly the kind of account of customary norms of justice that not only the divine judges would use to judge the purity of those at the end of their days, but also that earthly judges would employ in ancient Egypt in deciding cases. But of course what is missing here is the exact penalty on earth for those who engaged in various impurities.

Harkhuf, a jurist who served pharaohs Mernere and Pepi II, left these autobiographical lines on his tomb:

> I gave bread to the hungry,
> Clothing to the naked,
> I brought the boatless to land ...
> I was one who spoke fairly ...
> Never did I judge between two [contenders] in a manner
> which deprived a son of his father's legacy.[36]

34 *The Egyptian Book of the Dead: The Book of Going Forth by Day*, translated by Raymond O. Faulkner and Ogden Goelet, Jr., edited by Eva von Dassow, San Francisco, CA: Chronicle Books, 1994, Plate 31.

35 Ibid., p. 115.

36 *Ancient Egyptian Literature*, edited by Miriam Lichtheim, Berkeley: University of California Press, Vol. 1, 1973, p. 24.

Here Harkhuf presents the idea of a good jurist or just ruler in terms of providing for those who are most vulnerable, just as had been true of Mesopotamian rulers as well.

In a very controversial book, Anna Mancini has as one of her less extreme claims that Maat is really not at all like justice as understood today concerning distributions. Rather Egyptians "were not familiar with abstractions and dogmas" and did not write down their laws as did later Western peoples. Rather, she says that justice was a matter of righteousness that carried with it both internal and external prosperity.[37] Since, as we will see in subsequent chapters, Egyptian viziers are to rely more on their own conception of what is right than on the written law, we do have a significant difference between ancient Egypt and Mesopotamia. Yet, considerations of right do certainly matter for Mesopotamian judges as well, especially when these judges are dealing with hard cases where the written law does not appear to be properly applicable to the case at hand.

For the Mesopotamians, equity unlike justice is grounded in the law of the gods or the law of heaven. And while today most legal theorists would generally prefer a secular rather than a theological conception of universal and objective morality, theological ways of understanding something like "natural law" have a somewhat advantageous position over those conceptions, like many Greek and Roman ones, that were based on the character of nature that somehow grounded norms – hence the charge of "spooky metaphysics." It is not clear to me that today's grounding of equity or natural law in the character of human nature fares much better than the Greek and Roman conceptions did. I am not here proposing that we today embrace a theological grounding, but rather that we follow one clear sense of such things in Hammurabi's "code." For Hammurabi, equity as *misaram* is grounded in the idea that rulers are protectors of their people, especially the most vulnerable.[38] Here is a possible grounding for equity in a kind of humanitarianism. The ruler as shepherd is supposed to make the law humane by protecting the most vulnerable from harm, "the poor, the widows, and the orphans" as is often said at this time.

As we have been exploring so far, when we go back far enough in time we can find the first societies that developed a written language. In such societies there is already at least a rudimentary system of law. So, the origins of law as custom predate written records, and this seems also to be true of legal thought. Positive law is invented as a written means of settling disputes, as well as an institution that both promotes and also restricts the coercive power of rulers. Equity is then "discovered" or "rediscovered" as an important correction of written law.

37 Anna Mancini, *Maat Revealed: Philosophy of Justice in Ancient Egypt*, Paris: Buenos Books, 2004, pp. 9, 79.

38 It is of interest that some commentators talk of the gods as having been invented by the Mesopotamians, reversing the way the derivation is understood in Mesopotamian texts.

Looking at equity as a matter of "straight justice," rather than as a concept adapted in form to fit specific cases, makes sense if equity is linked to something as sophisticated and abstract as natural law. For the Mesopotamians, I would argue, there is a sense that equity returns to a kind of justice that is what the gods would have had in mind – and hence it is straight insofar as it goes directly back to the gods, not mediated through the written texts of humans. The decrees of equity are often decrees of fair treatment, and the source of such decrees is the idea of a form of justice that is different from the formal justice of the written law.

In any event, there is a clear sense that written law needs to be adjusted in some cases so as to achieve fairness, where the adjustment could include the outright disregard of the written law as in a legally enforced moratorium on debt or an amnesty for those who had been captured in open rebellion. The conceptual point of interest concerns what sources there are for the "law" to which a judge can refer in overruling the clear written law. In many cases Hammurabi for instance refers to the law of the gods as overruling the written law, thus setting the stage for the later development of equity as a form of natural law.

1.5 RELIGIOUS AND SECULAR LAW

The final consideration in this chapter that shows the turn toward recognizable legal conceptualization and reasoning concerns the secularization of law. C. J. Gadd, writing in the *Cambridge Ancient History*, says that it is clear that Hammurabi effected a secularization of what was previously a matter of regulation by priests and the temples:

> a tendency to secularization had already shown itself, and this was accelerated and confirmed under the reformer of his country's laws. His official letters reveal him as hearing many pleadings from suitors, and afterwards sending directions to his local officers bidding them make arrangements on the basis of his decisions. From this it was but a step to appointing district judges in various regions, who now bore the name of "king's judges," and kept in their own hands the administration of justice leaving to the older temple officials only the subsidiary function of administering the oaths, when that final criterion had to be applied.[39]

Ancient legal texts show a mixture of religious and secular influences, but the secular seems to dominate in Mesopotamia.

In Hammurabi's stela containing his law "code," there is a large graphic representation of Hammurabi and the god Shamash, with the god seated and Hammurabi

[39] C. J. Gadd, "Hammurabi and the End of his Dynasty," *Cambridge Ancient History*, third edition, Cambridge: Cambridge University Press, 1973, Vol. II, Part I, Chapter V, p. 204.

standing before him seeming to give the laws to the god. We also find in the prologue, mention of the god Marduk. Here is Driver and Miles' interpretation:

> Although, however, these two gods are mentioned a number of times, they are not said to be the authors of the Laws: Hammurabi himself claims to have written them. Their general character, too, is completely secular, and in this respect they are strongly to be contrasted with the Hebrew laws: they are not a divine pronouncement nor in any sense a religious document.[40]

Moses is given the laws by God; Hammurabi gives his laws to the god. But even as Hammurabi says he has authored the laws, he also seems to feel that the laws must be given to the gods for the laws to attain legitimacy.

Dominique Chapin adds another layer of interpretation that helps explain why Hammurabi is depicted with the god Shamash:

> The king is represented standing in front of the god Shamash, who is recognizable by the rays coming from his shoulders. It is not by chance that Shamash is also the god of divination, designated the "master of judgment and decision" (*bel denim u purussim*). This is not a question of inspiration but of imitation: just as Shamash judges in heaven and decides human beings' fate, so the king on earth must judge trials and render a verdict to all his subjects.[41]

Here the secular rulers and laws are imitations of the divine rulers and laws, inspired by the divine but nonetheless secular.

As in nearly all ancient societies, the gods played a large role in the life of the people. The gods are seen as intruding into the lives of humans, but primarily in predictable ways – according to the divine law. Here the authority of the secular laws was connected to the gods, but the laws themselves were clearly seen as made by the humans who were then bound by them. In ancient Mesopotamia it appears that the lawgivers were early-on thinking about the interplay of divine and human law.

Things were somewhat different in ancient Egypt, since the pharaoh was considered a god – thus the ideas of divine and human law were not as clearly separated as in Mesopotamia. Yet, there is also strong evidence that Egypt was not very different from its neighbors until late in the reign of pharaohs. Here is the assessment of Aristide Theodorides:

> The Nile valley has given us no code, nor any copious theoretical treatises, but the application of law is coherent, despite peculiar features of procedure, with laws to organize it ... The history of ancient Egypt does not present an example of the "secularization" of law. On the contrary – and this is what is miraculous – it attained

40 Driver and Miles, *The Babylonian Laws*, p. 39.

41 Dominique Charpin, *Writing, Law, and Kingship in Old Babylonian Mesopotamia*, translated by Jane Marie Todd, Chicago, IL: University of Chicago Press, 2010, p. 82.

> from the outset, during the Old Kingdom, a high level of institutional and juridical development, which was subsequently distorted by the intrusion of religious practices.[42]

It was only when the pharaoh declared himself to be a god that the secular laws of Egypt were seen as fused with divine law.

This claim that law is secular at the beginning is similar, I believe to Thorkild Jacobsen's claim that ancient politics was democratic at the beginning. But just as primitive democracy was not what we would call democracy today, so secular law in ancient societies is not quite what we would think of secular law today. Even as he embraces the idea that primitive law is largely secular, Hoebel is forced to admit that:

> Every single primitive society without exception postulates the existence of spirit beings and supernatural powers. Each of them attributes emotional intelligence to the spirit beings and holds to the belief that they respond with favor or disfavor to the specific acts of men … Such presuppositions are universal. Their influence is universally felt in the legal realm with the result that elemental postulations of the supernatural also appear as jural postulates …[43]

And the place where the supernatural powers were most often referred to, as we will often see, was in the incentives that were provided for people to obey the law, not necessarily in the authority of the law.[44]

In Chapter 3, we will see the importance of ordeals as well as oath-taking that involve the gods as ultimate punishers of those who do not tell the truth at trial. Yet we can also see the remnants of the ancient legal thought today in this respect when we remember that each witness who appears before American or English courts today must place his or her hand on a Bible and "swear to tell the truth so help me God." This is an oath, as in ancient times, which is at least partially enforced by fear of divine retribution for the witness who fails to tell the truth. Religion, or perhaps superstition, enters into the law in this way today in a perhaps similar way to how religion entered into law in ancient times. Yet, this does not mean that the content, or authority, of law is religious, either then or now.[45] Before turning to that subject, we need to get a clearer sense of how law was interpreted by judges in trials.

[42] Aristide Theodorides, "The Concept of Law in Ancient Egypt," in *The Legacy of Egypt*, edited by J. R. Harris, Oxford: Oxford University Press, 1971, pp. 320–321.

[43] E. Adamson Hoebel, *The Law of Primitive Man*, Cambridge, MA: Harvard University Press, 1954, pp. 260–261.

[44] See ibid., Chapter 10.

[45] Ibid., p. 259.

2

Judging, Trials, and Assemblies

This chapter will argue that there is an emerging idea of a rule of law in the legal thought of ancient Mesopotamia and Egypt. Six aspects of the rule of law, under three headings, will be the focus of this chapter as well as Chapter 3:

(A) separation of powers between assembly and king
  (1) where there was trial by one's peers; and
  (2) where there was restraint on the king by reference to the law
(B) fairness of legal process
  (3) where impartial and transparent decision-making occurs; and
  (4) where the punishment fits the crime
(C) the use of written law
  (5) where law protects the weak from oppression by the powerful; and
  (6) where divergence from written law requires a rationale.

Ancient Mesopotamia, especially Babylonia, as well as ancient Egypt, developed a legal system that involved several key elements of the rule of law.

In Section 2.1, I will discuss how judges did apply various sources, and in Section 2.2 I examine what were considered the virtues of judicial decision-making. In Section 2.3, we see the importance of assemblies, and in Section 2.4 I look at the ancient trial. In Section 2.5 I consider the developing idea of the rule of law in ancient Mesopotamia and Egypt. And in the final section I discuss to what extent it was important that the citizenry participate in justice proceedings in ancient times.

2.1 JUDGES AND JUDGING

The most important official in ancient Egypt after the pharaoh is the vizier, a person who is most clearly associated with the role of judge, although the vizier was an administrative officer with other responsibilities as well. In the earliest of times the vizier operated as a judge without the benefit of written law in ancient Egypt – sources are not in agreement about how long this lasted, largely because whatever written laws there were have probably been destroyed since they were written on relatively fragile papyrus. This provides us with our puzzle for this chapter as we attempt to understand ancient legal thought from our own modern perspectives, namely, how ancient judges conceived of their role as decision-maker and how these judges regarded the various sources of law.

In the instructions delivered at the appointment of the vizier, we can begin to understand how the chief judge and other judges are to understand their tasks. Here in ancient Egypt's 18th dynasty is how Rekhmire the vizier of Thutmose III is instructed:

> Behold, he is not one setting his face toward officials and councilors ... Mayest thou see to it for thyself to do everything after that which is in accordance with law; to do everything according to the right thereof ... It is an abomination of the god to show partiality. This is the teaching: thou shalt do the like, shalt regard him who is known to thee like him who is unknown to thee, and him who is near to – like him who is far – an official who does like this, then shall he flourish greatly in the place. Be not enraged toward a man unjustly, but be thou enraged concerning that which one should be enraged; show forth the fear of thee; let one be afraid of thee, (for) a prince is a prince of whom one is afraid. Lo, the true dread of a prince is to do justice.[1]

Notice the central place of impartiality in the list of judges' virtues. And most significant is the central place of justice in the judge's deliberations.

The idea of impartiality is well presented in the admonition that ancient judges should ideally treat the person unknown to the judge the same as the person known to him, and treat the person who is far from him no different from the person who is near to the judge. This admonition could easily be given today to judges, and even in the same terms. Here is a cornerstone of the rule of law presented in this early ancient legal text. Despite the fact that in ancient Egypt there was no democracy, the rule of law was already becoming firmly established.

In addition we find this fascinating account of the kind of criminal records and also records of how prisoners are to be kept, perhaps similar to such documents as the English Medieval Magna Carta that gave voice to the idea of habeas corpus. Here are more instructions to an ancient Egyptian vizier:

> He who has not disproved the charge at his hearing, which takes place, then it shall be entered in the criminal docket. He who is in the great prison, not able to disprove the charge of his messenger, likewise; when their case comes on another

[1] *Ancient Records of Egypt*, Vol. II, translated and edited by James Henry Breasted, Chicago, IL: University of Chicago, 1906, p. 269.

> time, then one shall report and determine whether it is in the criminal docket, and there shall be executed the things concerning which entry was made, in order to expiate their offense.[2]

The requirement of meticulous record-keeping of who is charged, who is in prison, and who has been convicted, could also easily be advice to judicial officers today.

In the eighteenth century CE, William Blackstone described the idea of habeas corpus, where prisoners had the right to be brought into the light of day to have the charges against them publicly proclaimed, as the greatest bulwark for maintaining the rule of law. No other rights were thought to be secured when this one right was not recognized, since people could be hidden away and hence deprived of any of their rights. Yet, we can find ancient Egyptian texts expressing some of the same ideas as those of Magna Carta, 3,500 years before Blackstone.

From some of the earliest of times, ancient Egyptian law was settled not by the pharaoh but by a council (*qenbet*) of respected members of a given community, and also by a Great Council that directly advised the pharaoh about how to deal with cases of great importance, such as matters of treason. After Egyptian became a written language, each of the councils had a scribe assigned to them. The court scribes not only recorded the proceedings but also performed many other tasks such as investigating and even enforcing judgments.[3]

In their commentary on Hammurabi's "code" Driver and Miles similarly discuss the role of judges in ancient Mesopotamia as follows:

> Such a ward as that described then may, perhaps, have been represented by the mayor and aldermen, who will have met as a court to settle disputes arising in their precincts ... The persons acting as jurors or judges of fact would be members of the ward selected partly for their mature wisdom and partly for their special knowledge of the facts of the case before them. So, in [LH] #5 the "judges" (Bab. *daiyanu*) are part of the "assembly" (Bab. *puhrum*).[4]

And here is where the Babylonian judge reached decisions:

> Where the judges held their courts is not always clear. In #5 they seem to have sat "in the assembly" (Bab. *ina puhrum*), but the documents usually show them sitting in the local temples, since there are numerous references to judicial proceedings "in the temple of Samas" (Bab. *ina bit Samas*). Otherwise the place of the court is mentioned only very rarely, but one passage definitely refers to "the house of judgment," ... while another very obscure text speaks of this place and of "the

2 Ibid., p. 276.

3 See S. Allam, "Egyptian Law Courts in Pharaonic and Hellenistic Times," *The Journal of Egyptian Archeology*, Vol. 77, 1991, pp. 109–127.

4 Godfrey Rolles Driver and J. C. Miles, *The Babylonian Laws*, Oxford: Oxford University Press, 1952, Vol. I, pp. 242–243.

> house of the judgment of the land." … There is no direct evidence to show that they sat anywhere else, for example "in the gate," where Oriental justice was so often administered … Sometimes the "assembly" (Bab. *puhrum*) of a town, for example, of Nippur and Dilbat and elsewhere or a "merchant-guild" (Bab. *karum*) alone or with the judges, is found acting as a court of law, though not in [Hammurabi's] Laws.[5]

The place where courts of law convened seems to be constant in each Mesopotamian jurisdiction.

Constancy of the place where judicial decision-making took place was a key to transparency in these early times. Indeed, like the Greeks to come later, there is evidence that the earliest of trials occurred outside so that no one could be prevented from observing the way that justice and equity were administered. As we will see there is good evidence for thinking that the jury developed out of the ancient assembly – in both cases there is the idea of openness and publicity that are also crucial components of the rule of law.

Switching back to Egypt, Marc Van De Mieroop gives us more detail of proceedings of the judges:

> The viziers' recorded actions were mostly judicial in that they settled disputes, answered petitions, and authorized transfers of property. In four Theban tombs appears a long list of what we call The Duties of the Vizier, a standardized description of the man's wide-ranging responsibilities.[6]

The vizier as chief judge seems to have had, ideally, the same virtues as the regular judge.

We have three accounts of judging in ancient Egypt that are especially evocative. The first is from the ancient Greek historian, Diodorus:[7]

> the chief judge … wore suspended from his neck by a golden chain a small image made of precious stones, which they called Truth; the hearings of the pleas commenced whenever the chief judge put on the image of Truth. The entire body of the laws was written down in eight volumes, which lay before the judges, and the custom was that the accuser should present in writing the particulars of his complaint, namely, the charge, how the thing happened, and the amount of injury or damage done, whereupon the defendant would take the document submitted by his opponents in the suit and reply in writing to each charge, to the effect either that he did not commit the deed, or if he did, that he was not guilty of wrongdoing, or if he was guilty of wrongdoing, that he should receive a lighter penalty. After that the

5 Ibid., pp. 492–493.

6 Marc Van De Mieroop, A *History of Ancient Egypt*, Oxford: Blackwell Publishing, 2011, p. 180.

7 Diodorus, *History*, Bk. 1, Chs. 75–76, Loeb edition, Cambridge: Harvard University Press, Vol. 1., pp. 261–262.

> law required that the accuser should reply to this in writing and that the defendant should offer a rebuttal. And after both parties had twice submitted their statements in writing to the judges, it was the duty of the thirty at once to declare their opinions among themselves and of the chief judge to place the image of Truth upon one or the other of the two pleas which had been presented. This was the manner, as their account goes, in which the Egyptians conducted all court proceedings, since they believed that if the advocates were allowed to speak they would greatly becloud the justice of the case, for they knew that the clever devices of orators, the cunning witchery of their delivery, and the tears of the accused would influence many to overlook the severity of the laws and the strictness of truth; at any rate they were aware that men who are highly respected as judges are often carried away by the eloquence of the advocates, either because they are deceived, or because the emotion of pity has been aroused in them; but by having both parties to a suit present their pleas in writing, it was their opinion that the judgments would be strict, only the bare facts being taken into account.[8]

Here is an account which gives a good indication of how judges were viewed in ancient Egypt. Many of the elements of the emerging rule of law are listed by Diodorus.

Second, consider "The Eloquent Peasant," a well-known tale from ancient Egypt which gives an account of a crooked judge who has harmed the peasant by a wrongful sentence, which contains valuable evidence of the practice of judging in ancient Egypt:

> Is it not wrong, a balance that tilts,
> A plummet that strays,
> The straight becomes crooked?
> Lo, justice flees from you,
> Expelled from its seat!
> The magistrates do wrong,
> Right-dealing is bent sideways,
> The judges snatch what has been stolen.[9]

Once again we find the image of what is bent as an injustice and what is straight is the just or equitable. The judge is to follow the straight path and in so doing to serve justice and equity.

And third we also have the Egyptian pharaoh, Amenemope, explaining what makes a man a good judge as follows:

> Do not move the scales nor alter the weights,
> Nor diminish the fractions of the measure;

8 Diodorus, Bk. 1, Chs. 75–76 (Vol. 1., pp. 261–262).

9 *Ancient Egyptian Literature*, edited by Miriam Lichtheim, Berkeley: University of California Press, Vol. 1, 1973, p. 173.

Do not desire a measure of the fields,
Nor neglect those of the treasury …
Do not go to court before an official
In order to falsify your words;
Do not vacillate in your answers,
When your witnesses accuse.
Do not strain [with] oaths of your lord,
[With] speeches at the hearing;
Tell the truth before the official,
Lest he lay a hand on you …
Do not confound a man in the law court,
In order to brush aside one who is right.
Do not incline to the well-dressed man,
And rebuff the one in rags …
Do not make for yourself false documents
They are a deadly provocation.[10]

Egyptian, as well as Mesopotamian, legal thought, from the earliest of times, was concerned with inspiring an unbiased judge who applied the law fairly to all. We next take up how the judge was to consider the many sources of law and what that might tell us about the ancient understanding of the rule of law.

2.2 JUDICIAL DECISION-MAKING AND ANCIENT LEGAL THOUGHT

One distinguished scholar of ancient Egyptian law, Jean-Marie Krutchten, has argued:

> The important thing is that Egyptian legal documents always refer to a rule (*hp*); whether they concern proceedings or the way judgments were passed: for example … the obligation under which the vizier was laid to judge the claimant "in close accordance with this *hp* which is in his hand." Moreover, it is the basic principle of what the pharaoh stated first when solemnly addressing a newly promoted vizier; "You shall see to it to do everything according to the *hp*, and to do everything according to its own righteousness." As I interpret it, he had to treat each case (a formulation large enough to comprise judgments as well as administrative decisions) according to the established rule, but without sticking to the letter of the law and being unfair.[11]

[10] *Ancient Egyptian Literature*, edited by Miriam Lichtheim, Berkeley: University of California Press, Vol. II, pp. 156–158.

[11] Jean-Marie Krutschten, "Law," in *The Oxford Encyclopedia of Ancient Egypt*, Oxford: Oxford University Press, 2001, p. 9.

Here the legitimacy of independent judicial decision-making and perhaps also discretion is directly recognized. We see once again the importance of equity or fairness, which will also occupy us in Chapter 4.

In one of the earliest references to a judicial proceeding, the Egyptian king Pepi I in Dynasty 6 (c. 2570 BCE) appointed a special judge to hear the case concerning a conspiracy by the queen to kill Pepi I. Here is how the special judge describes the uniqueness of his appointment:

> When legal procedure was instituted in private in the harem against the queen, Imtes his majesty caused me to enter, in order to hear (the case) alone. No chief judge and vizier at all, no prince at all was there, but only I alone, because I was excellent, because I was pleasant to the heart of his majesty; because his majesty loved me. I alone was the one who put (it) in writing, together with a single judge of Nekhen; while my office was only that of superior custodian of the domain of the Pharaoh.[12]

This singular role of the judge seemingly left large scope for discretion. To guarantee fairness, a decision-maker must be given wide latitude in deciding what is the best result in terms of the peculiarities of each case.

Weni, who served Kings Teti, Pepi I, and Mernere, also left this autobiographical statement:

> his majesty made me senior warden of Nekhen, his heart being filled with me beyond any other servant of his. I heard cases alone with the chief judge and vizier, concerning all kinds of secrets. [I acted] in the name of the king for the royal harem and for the six great houses … When there was a secret charge in the royal harem against Queen Weret-yamtes, his majesty made me go in to hear (it) alone. No chief judge or vizier, no official was there, only I alone, because I was rooted in his majesty's heart … Only I put it in writing with one other senior warden.[13]

As we will see, this account of judicial decision-making takes into account special knowledge in determining the characteristics of a good judge.

Of crucial importance is that judges are not acting arbitrarily when they seek equity or justice. Ancient Egyptian viziers and other officials recognized that "*hp* or righteousness," rules but also equity, was their main guide and a given edict needed to be interpreted in such a way that righteousness or equity prevailed. Some have interpreted this ancient Egyptian position as the equivalent of arbitrariness, as have some today who argue for a very strict construction of the law by judges. But judges

[12] *Ancient Records of Egypt*, Vol. 1, translated and edited by James Henry Breasted, Chicago, IL: University of Chicago Press, 1906, p. 142.

[13] *Ancient Egyptian Literature*, Vol. 1, p. 19.

in ancient Egypt did not conceive themselves as entitled to act arbitrarily – since *maat* (justice and truth) could not possibly be served in this way.

In ancient Egyptian legal thought equity is one of the chief sources to which judges should be guided. Yet it sometimes turns out that principles of equity conflict with other sources of law. There are better or worse answers to how to reconcile seemingly conflicting sources. But judges who decide what the law is in such cases are not exercising unbound discretion. It is my view that the ancient ways of understanding the role of judges are best understood in terms of equitable decision-making.

One of the things learned from the ancient sources we have considered is that following a rule and acting righteously were linked. For Egyptian judges acting righteously meant acting in a straight way, and that meant following a rule. The seeming discretion that judges had was due to the lack of written codes of law. But judges must do the right thing and that meant following rules of righteousness, what today we might call rules of equity. There was an objectively right way for judges to decide cases, and so the judges were not free to rule any way they wished. And judges were selected due to their ability to ascertain the objectively right way to decide cases.

From Mesopotamia we can learn that the codes of law provided models of how to judge. Judges in Mesopotamia, as in Egypt, viewed themselves as bound to decide cases justly, according to the straight path. In Mesopotamia, it is very clear that judicial decisions should also conform to equity as a natural law principle. In this respect, Hammurabi's Code was considered the preeminent model for training judges in how to look at cases and find the righteous path to pursue. Justice and equity were viewed as objective legal concepts that were the proper domain of judicial decision-making. Judges had discretion insofar as they could interpret the customary or written law fairly widely, but that discretion was severely limited in the sense that the interpretation and application of law must follow an objective and knowable path.

In ancient Egypt, the vizier was supposed to put himself in the position of the pharaoh – and the pharaoh was a god. So the vizier was supposed to decide like the pharaoh, that is, like a god. For some legal theorists today, a judge is supposed to decide cases from the most reasonable position he or she can imagine, perhaps like a god would. In any event the objectivity that is the paradigmatic character of judicial decisions is not something new or even something that is all that mysterious.

2.3 ANCIENT MESOPOTAMIAN ASSEMBLIES

According to Thorkild Jacobsen, most early trials in Mesopotamia did not involve elaborate debate about the facts – the facts were part of the "common knowledge" of the people who heard the case, otherwise the case would probably not have risen to the level of being heard at all. But even concerning two of the best preserved records of very early Mesopotamian trials, the line between what is a matter of fact and what a matter of law is not clear and so there remains a dispute about the facts that has to be dealt with. Yet Jacobsen is right that one of the most important reasons why kings seem to have emerged from primitive assemblies was to establish an executive authority that could enforce decisions in legal cases, especially in capital cases.

In a series of articles in the 1950s Thorkild Jacobsen argued that what he called "primitive democracy" epitomized the earliest forms of government, especially in ancient Mesopotamia. Jacobsen drew on mythology and epics in ancient Mesopotamia to establish that there was a primitive assembly that ruled in the city-states of very early Mesopotamia.[14] While it is controversial, I find Jacobsen's position persuasive on the earliest form of government in ancient Mesopotamia.

Some of the earliest evidence for the existence of "primitive democracy" in ancient Mesopotamia comes from the epics such as Gilgamesh, probably the oldest epic known. Here is a passage from this epic that probably predates Homer's Iliad by a thousand years.

> Gilgamesh … bolted the sevenfold gates of Uruk,
> he convened the assembly, the crowd gathered around,
> … in the street of Uruk-the-Town-Square,
> Gilgamesh seated himself on his throne …
> Thus Gilgamesh spoke to the elders of Uruk-the-Town-Square …
> Let me start out, I will cut down the cedar,
> I will establish for ever a name eternal![15]

In this passage, we see that Gilgamesh, the king, must go before the assembly and ask for permission to go on his venture to conquer enemies of his land. And we also find that there are elders who have special status within the assembly. It might be conjectured that the ancient assembly of this epic is similar to the assembly that we learn plays a large part in legal proceedings in ancient Mesopotamia, where there is a jury that has special status within the assembly.

Thorkild Jacobsen argued that texts like the Gilgamesh Epic give us evidence of what he called a "primitive democracy." Jacobsen was aware of the seeming incongruity of having a state that was "singularly autocratic in outlook" in the way that kings functioned and yet a "judiciary branch of government" that had a "distinct

[14] Thorkild Jacobsen, "Early Political Development in Mesopotamia," "Primitive Democracy in Ancient Mesopotamia," and "An Ancient Mesopotamian Trial for Homicide," all reprinted in Thorkild Jacobsen, *Toward the Image of Tammuz and Other Essays on Mesopotamian History and Culture*, edited by William L. Moran, Cambridge, MA: Harvard University Press, 1970.

[15] *The Epic of Gilgamesh*, Y170-Y185, translated by Andrew George, NY: Penguin Books, 1985, p. 20.

and democratic character."[16] As his first example he cites post imperial Assyria of the Isin-Larsa period where "the highest judicial authority was not vested in any one individual but resided in a general assembly of colonists, 'the colony young and old,' as it is called."[17] Concerning Old Babylonia, Jacobsen says: "The cases tried by the assembly were, as shown by the records which have come down to us, both civil and criminal cases."[18]

In the record of Hammurabi's law collection we also find a reference to assemblies as having a role in the legal system:

> LH #5 If a judge renders a judgment, gives a verdict, or deposits a sealed opinion, after which he reverses his judgment, they shall charge and convict that judge of having reversed the judgment which he rendered and he shall give twelve-fold the claim of that judgment; they shall unseat him from his judgeship in the assembly and he shall never again sit in judgment with the judges.[19]

Driver and Miles give a gloss on this law:

> What exactly the "assembly" (Bab. *puhrum*) was, however, is not yet certain, but it was apparently a larger body than the bench of judges or "the members of the ward" (Bab. *maru babitum*) who were perhaps the free burghers of a district or ward of a city, possibly it was the assembly of the free burghers of a town or city, over which the judges presided in virtue of their technical qualifications when it met for purely judicial purposes …[20]

This evidence suggests that judges answered to a larger political assembly.

There is also evidence that comes from the documents unearthed at the ancient Mesopotamian city of Mari. Daniel Fleming writes:

> The Akkadian word for "assembly" may be derived easily from the common Akkadian verb "*paharum*" ("to assemble") and appears frequently in the Mari correspondence, but it covers a range of gatherings. No text in my reading used *puhrum* with a town name to represent an urban assembly … Tribal gatherings may be assigned this name without limitation to any particular group … This may be what is going on also in Urgis … No institution is named, but a meeting is called for the town as such.[21]

Fleming summarizes his search of the Mari archives by saying:

16 Jacobsen, "Primitive Democracy in Ancient Mesopotamia," p. 159.
17 Ibid.
18 Ibid., p. 161.
19 *Laws of Hammurabi*, in *Law Collections From Mesopotamia and Asia Minor*, second edition, translated by Martha T. Roth, Atlanta, GA: Scholars' Press, 1997, p. 82.
20 Driver and Miles *The Babylonian Laws*, Vol. 1, pp. 78–79.
21 Daniel E. Fleming, *Democracy's Ancient Ancestors: Mari and Early Collective Governance*, NY: Cambridge University Press, 2004, p. 206.

> Most of the references to collective decision making in towns or tribal groups suggests some level of limited representation rather than full assembly of the population, or at least of free men. A few texts however make clear that a much more inclusive gathering was in view. In some cases it seems that an entire town was called together for proclamations of a royal decree.[22]

There are though some cases where certain residents of a town, perhaps as heads of households, gathered "to speak for the group."[23] The evidence seems strong that there were ancient assemblies and that such assemblies were intimately connected with a kind of rudimentary jury, as we will next see.

2.4 ANCIENT TRIALS

We can find evidence of ancient trials in the third millennium BCE in ancient Mesopotamia. Here is how Benjamin Foster characterizes these ancient trials:

> disputes over property or social status were adjudicated in the first instance at the local level, using neighborhood, temple, or community authorities or notables, the last called "elders" or "mayors" in Akkadian times … There was also a formal court procedure before judges, but this cost money, so was presumably resorted to only by people with means … The court procedure entailed appearing before a judge or judges, who may have been paid for hearing the case, and hiring a bailiff whose task was to schedule the trial and assemble the parties and witnesses at the right time and place …[24]

Trials could be informal in that they were simply adjudications in a community, and there is some evidence that assemblies were where appeals could be raised, as we next see.

Let us consider the complete record of a case that has come down to us from the eighteenth century BCE where we encounter the ancient assembly as a judicial body.

> Nanna-sig son of Lu-Enzu
>
> Ku-Enlila son of Ku-Nanna the barber
>
> and Enlil-ennam slave of Abba-kalla the orchardman
>
> killed Lu-Inanna son of Lugal-uru-du the nishakku.
>
> After Lu-Inanna son of Lugal-uru-du had been put to death
>
> they told Nin-dada daughter of Lu-Ninurta wife of Lu-Inanna

[22] Ibid., p. 233.

[23] Ibid., p. 234.

[24] Benjamin Foster, *The Age of Agade: Inventing Empire in Ancient Mesopotamia*, NY: Routledge, 2016, pp. 38–39.

that Lu-Inanna, her husband, was killed.
Nin-dada, daughter of Lu-Ninurta, opened not her mouth, covered it up.
Their case was taken to Isin before the king.
King Ur-Ninurta ordered their case to be accepted for trial
in the Assembly of Nippur.
Ur-gula, son of Lugal-ibila, Durdu, the birdcatcher, Ali-ellati, the client,
Puzu, son of Lu-Enzu, Eluti son of Tizkar-Ea,
Shesh-kalla, the porter, Lugalkam, the orchardman, Lugal-a-zida,
son of Enzu-andul, and Shesh-Kalla, son of Shara-HAR,
addressed (the assembly):
"As men who have killed men they are not live men,
the males, (all) three of them and that woman
before the chair of Lu-Inanna, son of Lugal-uru-du, the nishakku,
shall be killed," they said.
Shuqalum, the Erin-GAL-GAL, sergeant of Ninurta, and
Ubar-Enzu, the orchardman, addressed (the assembly) as follows:
"Nin-dada, daughter of Lu-Ninurtas, may have killed her husband;
but what can a woman do in (such a matter) that she is to be killed?" they said.
In the Assembly of Nippur it (the assembly) addressed them as follows:
"A woman who values not her husband
may give information to his enemy and thus
he (i.e., the enemy) may (be able to) kill her husband.
That her husband is killed he (i.e., the enemy) may (then) let her hear
– why should he not thus make her keep silent about him? –
her guilt is greater than (theirs:) that they killed a man" they said.
In the Assembly of Nippur, the matter having been solved,
Nanna-sig, son of Lu-Enzu, Ku-Enlilla, son of Ku-Nanna, the barber,
Enlil-ennam, the slave of Adda-kalla, the orchardman,
and Nin-dada, daughter of Lu-Ninurta, wife of Lu-Innanna,
were delivered up to be killed.
Case accepted for trial in the Assembly of Nippur.[25]

This case has a number of important features for showing us how to understand ancient trials especially in relationship to kings and assemblies.

[25] Jacobsen, "An Ancient Mesopotamian Trial for Homicide," pp. 190–201.

Initially notice that the case was first taken to a king, the king of Isin, and this king then referred the case to the assembly at Nippur. Isin and Nippur are different ancient cities – with Nippur having the reputation of being one of the holiest of cities but also as a place where kings would go to consult with religious officials to decide about important matters such as whether to go to war and where to build temples. So, there is some reason to think that the assembly at Nippur might have had a special role to play across Mesopotamia concerning the resolving of disputes or the granting of advice about how to solve problems requiring careful judgment.

It is also of interest that the jury is here presented as a subset of the assembly at Nippur and as having nine members, all apparently common people, not members of the elite or experts. I don't know whether there is any earlier evidence of trials having nine-member juries, but it would not be surprising if this trial at Nippur is one of the very earliest recorded trials to have one of this size.

From this evidence, it seems that the earliest form of government in ancient Mesopotamia was a popular assembly that was open to all citizens, although probably not to women and slaves, and also that this assembly chose a leader in times of crisis, such as when war needed to be waged or a natural catastrophe needed to be dealt with. The king emerged then as someone initially selected by the people because of his superior leadership or administrative skills. And while the king came to assume supernatural status over the next millennium, and thus became someone with a divine right to rule, it seems that the origins of the king's authority were in the popular will of the assembly. As Saggs says, "the Assembly retained a real function in the administration of justice after the last shadow of its political authority had passed away."[26]

The ancient Mesopotamian judicial assembly seems to have grown out of the political assembly. In this sense justice is a matter initially of popular will, not of pronouncement from on high. Even kings could be subject to the will of the assembly, and in the earliest of times it seems that the kings were dependent on the will of the assembly even concerning such decisions as whether and when to wage war. Insofar as the assembly is itself governed by what is the common law at the time, there is a strong sense that these most ancient societies are already governed by a rudimentary rule of law.

The functions of the ancient precursors of the jury seem to be these: to hear testimony and to assess the credibility of that testimony, to investigate the factual background of the case, to assess these facts in light of the commonly known law, and to prepare a recommended judgment that is submitted to the assembly for approval. We see some of these functions in play in the homicide case just examined, as well as the paternity case we will consider in a later chapter. It is clear that there is not

[26] H. W. F. Saggs, *The Greatness That Was Babylon*, NY: Hawthorn Books, 1962, p. 216.

a jury in the modern sense here. But there are enough elements of something like a modern jury to think that ancient legal thought contemplated the idea of a precursor of the modern jury.

2.5 THE RULE OF LAW IN MESOPOTAMIA

As we have seen, in some of the very earliest known trials, it is not the king who is the judge but the assembly, or the subset of the assembly – the jury. It is true that the king is often the one to assign the case to the assembly for decision, and it is also true that it is the king who is often the executor of the decisions of the assembly or jury. But the king sees that it is best left to the assembly to rule in judicial matters, and this is not merely on matters of fact but also on matters of law, insofar as these two can be disentangled from each other in ancient Mesopotamia.

The "code" of Ur-Namma (2100 BCE) in the prologue declares that providing justice for the weakest in the society was one of this king's main duties:

> I did not deliver the orphan to the rich. I did not deliver the widow to the mighty. I did not deliver the man with but one shekel to the man with one mina (i.e., 60 shekels), I did not deliver the man with but one sheep to the man with one ox.[27]

The ruler saw that providing justice was a duty and that this involved making sure that there were procedures protecting the weakest in the society against those who would seek to oppress the weak.

In the Epilogue of the Laws of Lipit-Ishtar (c. 1930 BCE), we find again a statement of the king's recognized duty to establish justice:

> In accordance with the true word of the god Utu, I made the lands of Sumer and Akkad hold fair judicial procedure. I made truth shine forth and I brought well-being to the lands of Sumer and Akkad […] all humankind. When I established justice in the lands of Sumer and Akkad, I erected this stela.[28]

Here we have a specific reference to the importance of fair procedures, not merely to fair outcomes, and it is this reference to procedural justice that is also today seen as a cornerstone of the rule of law.

The reliance on the assembly as the ultimate determiner of justice is also a strong indication that ancient Mesopotamia was the first or surely one of the very first societies to establish the rule of law, not the rule of "man." We can turn to Hammurabi to get a good indication of how a ruler saw his relationship to the law, and especially

[27] *Laws of Hammurabi*, p. 16.

[28] *Laws of Hammurabi*, pp. 33–34.

to what the law is to serve – justice. Here is a portion of the prologue of Hammurabi's "code" of law.

> at that time, the gods Anu and Enlil, for the enhancement of the well-being of the people, named me by the name Hammurabi, the pious prince, who venerates the gods, to make justice prevail in the land, to abolish the wicked and the evil, to prevent the strong from oppressing the weak, to rise like the sun-god Shamash over all humankind, to illuminate the land. (I 27–49)[29]

Hammurabi makes it clear that he sees himself as doing the work of the gods in protecting his flock, especially in guaranteeing justice for the weak.

There is also evidence from Hammurabi's correspondence that he took an active and personal interest in many legal matters, especially in making sure that justice was done when the problem had been caused by one of his own ministers.

> Thus saith Hammurabi. Ilisu-ibi, the … merchant, hath informed me, saying "I lent thirty Gur of corn to Sin-magir, the governor, and I hold his receipt for the same; for three years I have besought him and he will not repay the corn." After this manner hath he informed me. I have beheld his tablet, and Sin-magir shall pay the corn and the interest thereon, and thou shalt give it unto Ilisu-ibi. (Letter XIII)[30]

Policing corruption of government officials is one of the hallmarks of the rule of law.

Thorkild Jacobsen sets out one of the main issues concerning the rule of law that Hammurabi and the earlier kings of Mesopotamia epitomized when he says:

> It is to be noted that the originally rather amorphous role of the ruler with respect to justice: as judge … [then becomes one] of executing judgments … This particular role seems dictated by the difficulties in less developed legal systems of persuading courts to accept cases in which there was no guarantee of execution if the court found for the plaintiff. It is this need for a guarantor of execution which the king meets.[31]

The execution of the law is increasingly seen as the duty of the king and with this development we have a set of features of Mesopotamian law that epitomizes the rule of law.

To summarize, the features of the rule of law that we have seen in the ancient Mesopotamian legal documents are the following:

(A) separation of powers between assembly and king
  (1) where there was trial by one's peers

[29] Ibid., p. 76.

[30] L. W. King, editor and translator, *The Letters and Inscriptions of Hammurabi*, Vol. 3, London: Luzac and Co., 1900, p. 32.

[31] Thorkild Jacobsen, "Early Political Development in Mesopotamia," in his *Toward the Image of Tammuz and Other Essays on Mesopotamian History and Culture*, note 50.

(2) and where there was restraint of the king by reference to the law

(B) fairness of legal process

(3) where impartial and transparent decision-making occurs

(4) and where the punishment fits the crime

(C) the use of written law

(5) where law protects the weak from oppression by the powerful

(6) and where divergence from written law requires a rationale.

The second of these features of the rule of law we see in the legal decisions, especially in the way the king feels under restraint to send cases to the assembly (and juries) for adjudication and then feels bounds to help enforce the decisions so reached.

One last consideration that we can see emerging in the legal thought of ancient Mesopotamia is that of the king himself being subject to the law in a way that would potentially override the king's decisions. We find this aspect of the rule of law seemingly present in the epics and myths in ancient Mesopotamia, such as when Gilgamesh the king feels that he must get the permission of the assembly before going off to make war even though he has already decided that this is indeed the right thing to do to protect the people.

The rule of law is supposed to be the state where law rules over individuals, especially individuals who are in powerful positions. While the kings of ancient Mesopotamia came to take on more and more power, they seemingly did not forget that they owed their power to the will of the people, understood best as the will of the assembly. The strongest remnants of the assembly can be seen throughout the several thousand years of ancient Mesopotamian history most clearly in the way that the assembly continued to play a strong judicial role. One thing that can be inferred from the homicide case examined in an earlier section of this chapter is that the jury and assembly members could question the way that the law was understood and could even disregard the law when it looked to them like justice would not be done otherwise. It was in this manner that the jury decided to condemn to death the wife of the man killed for her complicity even though she had not herself killed her husband. We might wonder though whether "jury nullification" is contemplated here and ask whether such an idea was seen to be consistent with the rule of law, a topic of great importance today.

2.6 PARTICIPATION IN JUSTICE

If we understand ancient legal thought concerning trials the way I have suggested, in ancient Mesopotamia there is not the idea that the law is a matter only for specialists to decide, although I would mention the fact that in some cases there is the possibility of appeal and there the experts may have had a stronger hand in the proceedings.[32] But the idea seems to be that the people should be the ones to decide matters of justice on the ground as it were.

Of course, the rule of law involves other dimensions as well. Prominent among these are procedures that maintain a sense that all are treated as at least rough equals before the law. In ancient Egypt there is evidence that similar struggles with procedural fairness were part of the legal thought of this society. Yet, one scholar to analyze a case from the 6th Dynasty of the Old Kingdom in Egypt concludes: "the case between Sobekhotpe and Tjau shows sophistication in procedure, the allocation of the burden of proof and the certainty of principle."[33] And at this time, as we have seen, there were rudimentary juries as well.

Today, in the Anglo-American tradition, juries play a prominent role in many legal cases, but that is not true in international law or in the domestic cases in countries that follow the Continental system of jurisprudence. Nonetheless, the idea that a person should be judged by his or her "peers" has remained a very important idea. The question is how much of a legal case should be decided by one's peers. Here we can begin by speculating how the Mesopotamian trial for homicide proceeded. First, the king in Isin to whom the case was originally brought assigned the case to the assembly in Nippur. Presumably, the assembly then selected a jury to investigate the case and make a preliminary ruling. But what is unclear is how much of the case in terms of the facts and the relevant law was left to the decisions of that jury.

To begin, here is the relevant part of the trial that was translated by Thorkild Jacobsen:

> Ubar-Enzu, the orchardman, addressed (the assembly) as follows:
> "Nin-dada, daughter of Lu-Ninurtas, may have killed her husband;
> but what can a woman do in (such a matter) that she is to be killed?" they said.
> In the Assembly of Nippur it (the assembly) addressed them as follows:
> "A woman who values not her husband
> may give information to his enemy and thus
> he (i.e., the enemy) may (be able to) kill her husband.
> That her husband is killed he (i.e., the enemy) may (then) let her hear
> – why should he not thus make her keep silent about him?

32 See Ronald Veenker and J. Cale Johnson, "The Appellate Process in the Legal Record [di til-la] from Ur III Umma," *Altoriental Forsch*, Vol. 36, no. 2, 2009, pp. 349–364.

33 Andrew H. Ganley, "The Case of Sobekhotpe and Tjau – Principle, Practice, and Legal Procedure in the Sixth Dynasty," *Discussions in Egyptology*, Vol. 53, 2002, p. 34.

She (more than anyone else) killed her husband,
her guilt is greater than (theirs:) that they killed a man" they said.
In the Assembly of Nippur, the matter having been solved

One interpretation of what happened here is that the jury members were unsure what to decide concerning the guilt of the wife of the victim. We are told that her only role in her husband's murder was that she had remained silent, and it seems unclear to the jury whether this is sufficient for establishing her guilt for homicide. This is why the jury returns to the larger assembly for guidance.

Apparently as a matter of Babylonian law, to be guilty of homicide one had to have a direct participation in the killing. And it seems that the jury is not at all sure that being what we would today call an accomplice after the fact was sufficient to make one guilty of homicide. The grounds for the claim then made by the assembly that "her guilt is greater than (theirs)" is not immediately clear. Is it her silence only or is it her role as wife that is the trigger for the assigning of guilt?

In my view the most likely explanation of the grounding for what the Assembly declared was that they were employing a moral rather than a legal analysis concerning the victim's wife. Perhaps it was thought that a virtuous wife should have been concerned about the welfare of her husband and should have immediately notified the authorities of the identities of the killers of her husband. Or perhaps, although there is little evidence of this, the assembly thought that the wife must have known in advance about the plot and should have warned her husband rather than remaining silent. In any event it seems that the assembly is making a decision on moral rather than on legal grounds, since the jury did not see how to hold her guilty as they understood the law and facts of the case.

Indeed, Jacobsen says: "in these centuries common opinion of right and wrong had moved ahead of the formalization of the common law to demand capital punishment for this particular offense."[34] There is a well-known problem with convictions that are not based in law – namely that the defendants lacked notice that what they were doing at the time was a crime that could put them at risk of prosecution and punishment. It may be that ancient Mesopotamians were unbothered by such a problem since there was obviously a much closer connection between morality and legality for these as with many ancient peoples. As a result, the issue of notice is effectively dealt with if the norms that the jury acts on are indeed public norms, since it can be assumed that people should be aware of what immoral acts might cause them to be put at risk of prosecution and punishment. Equity can provide grounds for trial just as likely as strict justice considerations.

34 Jacobsen, "An Ancient Mesopotamian Trial for Homicide," p. 213.

Second, there are then questions about how best to understand equity in a case like this in Mesopotamia at a time when other manifestations of equity such as debt forgiveness, as we will see in Chapter 4, were not terribly controversial. The problem with the extension of equity to cover cases such as immoral acts of complicity, which are not recognized as illegal acts, is that there is a disconnect between equity and the idea of mercy. When juries acquit despite the law, this is often due to considerations of mercy for the defendant. But when juries convict despite the law, equity is differently understood than its normal close relation to mercy.[35]

The court seems to act on the basis of a moral judgment about the character of the wife of the victim. Here we come back to an issue discussed in an earlier chapter – how equity relates to morality, especially to conscience. Yet, here we have an example of where conscience or morality and mercy diverge, calling into question whether equity's gap-filling capacity is always for the good.While I do not have space to discuss this in greater detail, it should be noted that the conception of equity employed in ancient legal thought does not always track mercy, and may even be opposed to mercy – rather it is a kind of moral fairness that seems to be the basis of equity.

Third, there are questions about how complicity was thought of in ancient Mesopotamian legal thought that this case raises. Complicity is most commonly a matter of aiding or abetting the principal perpetrators of a crime. There is the assembly's claim that:

> A woman who values not her husband
> may give information to his enemy and thus
> he (i.e., the enemy) may (be able to) kill her husband.

But this claim is not consistent with the main claim that the wife kept silent. If she did give information to the killers then this would be a straightforward matter of aiding them and would fall squarely under the contemporary legal concept of complicity. But if the evidence only clearly shows that she kept silent, then, while she may today be considered to be guilty of a lesser charge she would not be guilty of homicide for this omission.

It is also noteworthy, or perhaps notorious, that the assembly and jury treat the wife differently than they would presumably treat a husband who plays a role in the killing of his wife. There is imbedded in this recitation of the issues by the jury and assembly a worry about what constitutes proof of the various charges against the wife of the victim. In the above quotation it appears that the mere possibility that she might have given information to her husband's enemies is enough to

[35] See Alan W. Scheflin and Jon M. Van Dyke, "Merciful Juries: The Resilience of Jury Nullification," *Washington and Lee Law Review*, Vol. 48, 1991, p. 165.

establish this fact. But it remains a serious problem of proof to establish that from a person's silence there was something conveyed or that the lack of silence could have prevented someone's death. Here the idea is that claims about a lack of action are much harder to find proof for than claims about an action. And in claims about complicity, which seems to be what the wife is accused of, the question of proof should loom larger than it appears to have done in this case.

Fourth and finally, there are questions that circle back on the idea of a rule of law, for example, can disregard for the law be consistent with the rule of law? This issue is especially complicated because of the different ways we, as well as the Mesopotamians, could understand the "law" in the rule of law. If we understand law in a broad sense as encompassing equity as well as narrow justice, then equity-based nullifications of law narrowly conceived are not clearly contrary to the rule of law.

The ancient Mesopotamian homicide case illustrates the fact that rulings based on equity that are clearly contrary to law open up the possibility for serious abuse. The jury and the assembly seem to have formed judgments on the basis of how they think that wives should behave – and such legal thought is bound to be open to bias and abuse since it is potentially discriminatory toward women. When criminal proceedings are conducted in such a way that mercy is shown, there are fewer worries than when such proceedings are conducted not from mercy but from a society's collective sense of revenge or retribution. And as we will see, when the questions of proof are added into the mix there is considerable cause for concern.

3

Oaths, Ordeals, and Truth

In this chapter I will argue that the use of oaths and ordeals in ancient Mesopotamia and Egypt can be understood as aimed at solving the enduring problem of ascertaining whether or not a witness or a party at a trial spoke truthfully. In Medieval Europe torture was often employed before any testimony was solicited to make sure of the veracity of the testifier. Perhaps surprisingly, torture was not as widely employed in ancient societies as in Medieval Europe. The two most common methods used as proof of veracity in ancient societies were oath and ordeal, where ordeal typically meant having to float and not drown after being thrown into the river. The ordeal was also employed throughout Medieval history, but has come into disfavor today and is very rarely employed. Oaths were employed extensively and have survived as one of the chief means of testing veracity in trials today, especially in the Anglo-American systems of law. Methods of proof aim to solve various problems with trials that we will explore in this chapter.

There are two problems concerning proof that concern the integrity of a system of law that relies on trials to determine justice. The first problem concerns how to make sure that what people say – how they testify – is indeed truthful. The second problem concerns the need to make the parties in a trial believe in the trustworthiness of the trial – that the outcome will indeed be fair. These two problems, truthfulness and trustworthiness, are addressed in the way that standards of proof are constructed in even the most rudimentary trial.

Truthfulness itself concerns all of the parties in a trial. It is important that the person be truthful who alleges that a wrong or breach has occurred; and it is similarly important that the alleged perpetrator of an illegal act also be truthful. Of even more importance, in some respects, is that the various witnesses to the wrong or breach not merely side with their kinsmen or kinswomen but accurately represent what occurred concerning the facts and even the legal issue at stake. If one side alleges one thing and the other side alleges the opposite, a trial comes to a standstill unless it can be determined that one or the other side is misrepresenting what occurred.

There is also a problem in any system of law about how to make sure that people who are subject to various legal procedures will indeed feel bound by the rules and the outcome of those procedures. Today this is especially a problem in international law where there is a lack of clear enforcement power. In ancient times the enforcement was often left to the people themselves. But in the way the ancient law develops there came to be a priority to avoid pure vigilante justice and instead hope that the procedures provided would be acceptable to those who are subject to them. The river-god ordeal and the administration of oaths seem to have had this feature by design. And at least one commentator links the two modes of proof: "Beside the river-ordeal there was also an ordeal by oath."[1] Both the river-god ordeal and the swearing of oaths were considered ordeals that tested the truth of a person's statements.

In Section 3.1, we will first examine evidence of ancient use of ordeals in legal proceedings. Then in Section 3.2 we will look at similar evidence for the ancient use of oaths in trials. In Section 3.3 we will analyze reasons for the reference to gods and religion in both forms of proof: oaths, and ordeals. In Section 3.4 we consider who it was who determined the interpretation of the oaths and ordeals as evidence. And then in Section 3.5 we consider what were the implicit views of human nature that were at play in the understanding of proof in ancient trials.

3.1 PROOF BY ORDEAL

The divine river-god ordeal was often used to satisfy disputes of proof. In Saggs' wonderful commentary, *The Greatness That Was Babylon*, we are told: "In Babylonia, the Ordeal was the river, and the rule – opposite to that found in Medieval England – was that the guilty person sank and the innocent was saved."[2] The required swearing of oaths before gods was a more common form of dealing with disputes between parties. But the river-god ordeal is mentioned prominently in the various "codes" of ancient law. I am especially interested in this legal procedure since it seems so hard to justify, and yet it was employed in the spirit of trying to find a process that could secure "a decision accepted by all parties as just and binding."[3]

It is not an accident that in both the use of ordeals and the swearing of oaths the gods were said to play a crucial role. Indeed, we find the same procedure concerning oaths having survived in our contemporary Anglo-American justice system, even

[1] Godfrey Rolles Driver and John C. Miles, *The Assyrian Laws*, Oxford: Clarendon Press, 1935, p. 90.

[2] H. W. F. Saggs, *The Greatness That Was Babylon*, NY: Hawthorn Books, 1962, p. 219.

[3] Ibid., p. 220.

with the use of laying one's hand on the Bible to show that one risks divine retribution if one were to lie or otherwise provide false evidence. The ordeal though has not survived and it is to this phenomenon to which I wish to direct our attention in what follows in this section – and in the next section I will discuss oaths in more detail.

The divine river-god ordeal is mentioned in Mesopotamian written legal documents in the early second millennium BCE. One of the earliest laws to mention the river-god ordeal is the Laws of Ur-Namma (LU):

> LU #13. If a man accuses another man of ... and he has him brought to the Divine River Ordeal but the River Ordeal clears him, the one who has him brought (i.e., the accuser) shall weigh and deliver 3 shekels of silver.
>
> LU #14. If a man accuses the wife of a young man of promiscuity but the River Ordeal clears her, the man who accused her shall weigh and deliver 20 shekels of silver.[4]

We are not told here whether other forms of proof had first been tried and found wanting, but it is clear that the river-god ordeal can be traced at least to these laws that were promulgated in approximately 2100 BCE.

Another good example comes from the Laws of Hammurabi, three and a half centuries after the Laws of Ur-Namma were promulgated:

> LH #2. If a man charges another man with practicing witchcraft but cannot bring proof against him, he who is charged with witchcraft shall go to the divine River Ordeal, he shall indeed submit to the divine River Ordeal; if the divine River Ordeal should overwhelm him, his accuser shall take full legal possession of his estate; if the divine River Ordeal should clear the man and should he survive, he who made the charge of witchcraft against him shall be killed; he who submitted to the divine River Ordeal shall take full possession of his accuser's estate.

Here we see that the outcome of the ordeal will make a huge difference in one's fortunes and should not be taken lightly. Indeed, this law of Hammurabi calls for death for the person who accuses someone but where the accused survives the ordeal.

There is evidence from as late as approximately 1076 BCE that the divine river-god ordeal survived in the Middle Assyrian Laws (MAL). Here one law is especially interesting:

> MAL #A24. And if he should deny (that he knew of her status), he shall declare, "I did not know," they shall undergo the divine River Ordeal. And if the man in whose

[4] *Laws of Hammurabi*, in *Law Collections from Mesopotamia and Asia Minor*, second edition, translated by Martha T. Roth, Atlanta, GA: Scholars' Press, 1997, p. 18.

> house the wife of a man resided should refuse to undergo the divine River Ordeal, he shall give "triple"; if it is the man whose wife withdrew herself from him who should refuse to undergo the divine River Ordeal, he (in whose house he resided) is clear; he shall bear the expenses of the divine River Ordeal.[5]

Here, among other things, we see that one of the consequences of subjecting someone to the divine river-god ordeal is that the "loser" may have to pay for the expenses of administering the ordeal. And since the river-god ordeal seems most commonly to be administered in cities like Nippur, it will thus matter quite a lot how far away one is from this city in terms of how much money the loser will have to pay to have had the ordeal administered.

As far as can be told, there was no uniformity in how the river-god ordeal was administered over time in Babylonia – indeed there seem to have been ways to ameliorate the drastic consequences of the ordeal. As Lafont says:

> though it is clear that the process was used to safeguard certain legal principles, it is no less true that a wide margin of maneuver seems to have existed in the way of application and the results.[6]

Substitutes could be used, such as a mother substituting for her daughter. And there is evidence that one's servants and friends could also substitute.[7]

Here is a letter from Mari, at roughly the time of Hammurabi, describing a team of substitutes in a river-god ordeal who eventually declared that they were not telling the truth.

> To my king, my lord, letter of Meptum, thy servant. Regarding the people who were to dive for Haya-Sumu ..., to begin with, a woman was thrown in, and she emerged. After her, an old man; he swam a distance of 80 cubits "in the heart of the god," was successful and emerged. After him, a second woman went in, and emerged. After her, a third woman; the river "married" her. Given that the old man had proved his rights over a distance of only 80 cubits, and that the river had "married" the third woman, Haya-Sumu's people refused to let the last three women be subjected to the water. They agreed: "Town and land are not ours."[8]

Of course substitution still put people's lives at risk, but there is something lost in terms of testing for truthfulness if the witness or the accuser is not the one personally put at risk for providing false testimony.

5 *Middle Assyrian Laws*, in *Law Collections From Mesopotamia and Asia Minor*, second edition, translated by Martha T. Roth, Atlanta, GA: Scholars' Press, 1997, p. 162.

6 Bertrand Lafont, "The Ordeal," in Jean Botero et al., *Everyday Life in Ancient Mesopotamia*, translated by Antonia Nevill, Baltimore, MD: Johns Hopkins Press, 2001, p. 208.

7 See ibid., pp. 206–207.

8 Translation of letter from Volume XXVI of the *Archives Royales de Mari*, to King Zimri-Lim (from correspondence dating from 1775–1760 BCE), in ibid., pp. 205–206.

Here is another important piece of evidence of how the divine River-god Ordeal functioned, again taken from a letter that is from roughly Hammurabi's time:

> Speak unto Zimrilim: saying: Thus says Yatar-Ami thy son: Now lo! these two men whom I have sent with Napsuna-Adad – these men have been mentioned in this report which has been read relating to the town of *Irrid*, saying:
>
> "They have spoken with Sippisa the slave of Bunuma-Adad; they are acquainted with the affair."
>
> And now I am having them sent to the river-god, and their accuser is detained here in prison. Let one of thy slaves, a *kallum*, with Napsuna-Adad escort these men to the river-god. If these men are saved, I will burn their accuser in the fire; if the men die, I will give their houses (and) their folk here to their accuser.
>
> May my father send back an account of their affair to me myself.[9]

Driver and Miles comment that this letter from Mari shows that the river-god ordeal mentioned in Hammurabi's laws is confirmed as in use, since the letter uses nearly identical language as that employed in Hammurabi's laws as well as the Middle Assyrian Laws.[10] The divine river-god ordeal seems to have been used in the most serious cases (perhaps corresponding to our criminal cases – although the categories of civil and criminal are not yet clearly separated), where getting to the truth was the most pressing.

It is not hard to find grounds to criticize the practice of the divine river-god ordeal or any other trial by ordeal. But I wish to use the discussion of the river-god ordeal to set the stage for the seemingly much less severe swearing of oaths. The commonality here between the river-god ordeal and the swearing of oaths is that the accuser or the testifier puts his or her life at stake either by risking drowning caused by the river-god or the wrath of the gods at having their name taken in vain. And the supposed success of this procedure is seen in the evidence of how the people who participated in it, like the team of substitutes from Mari, spoke the truth from fear: the fear of the wrath of the gods, or perhaps just the fear of death by drowning.

Legitimating compliance with the procedures of a legal system depends ultimately on more than fear – the bulk of the people must believe that the procedures will indeed bring justice. Hence the prologues of the various law "codes" in ancient Mesopotamia maintain that the kings who provide the laws are shepherds of the people who care about the fair administration of justice. And the kings like Hammurabi make it clear that they are looking out for those who are weakest and poorest and hence most easily oppressed by those who are strong and wealthy. But

9 Translated in Godfrey Rolles Driver and J. C. Miles, *The Babylonian Laws*, Oxford: Oxford University Press, 1952, Vol. 1 p. 64.

10 Ibid., p. 65.

the river-god ordeal must have evoked very strong reactions in the imagination of the people at this time in much the same way that it does today, bringing together the ideas of serving justice and also worries about divine retribution.

Before leaving our topic of ordeals, let me present a Middle Assyrian Law that mentions both the river-god ordeal and also the use of oaths.

> MAL #A22. If an unrelated man – neither her father, nor her brother, nor her son – should arrange to have the man's wife travel with him, then he shall swear an oath to the effect that he did not know that she is the wife of a man and he shall pay 7,200 shekels of lead to the woman's husband. If [he knows that she is the wife of a man], he shall pay damages and he shall swear, saying "I did not fornicate with her." But if the man's wife should declare, "He did not fornicate with me," since the man has already paid damages to the man (i.e., husband) he shall undergo the divine River Ordeal; there is no binding agreement. If he should refuse to undergo the divine River Ordeal, they shall treat him as the woman's husband treats the wife.[11]

Driver and Miles say:

> In #22 the ordeal is not voluntary; the suspected man must go to the ordeal if he wishes to escape the same punishment, probably death, as that of the guilty woman. The law holds that such a case is not one for agreement [as in property cases] and itself decides the consequence of success or failure in the ordeal.[12]

Driver and Miles also point out that the oath of the woman is not considered dispositive.[13] The upshot of #22 of the Middle Assyrian Laws is that oaths are regarded as dispositive in some cases but not where more serious charges are pending. The river-god ordeal seems to be used more commonly for serious charges – but oaths were used frequently also. We now turn to a fuller examination of oaths in ancient Mesopotamian law.

3.2 PROOF BY SWEARING OF OATHS

The more common form of proof than river-god ordeals in Mesopotamia concerns the swearing of oaths – and like today the oaths are sworn in the name of gods, thereby making the one who swears liable to the punishment of the gods in the case of false testifying. Driver and Miles say that the oaths and river-god ordeals "exhibit to a certain extent the same terminology."[14] There is some dispute about what occasions in Mesopotamia produced the need for people to swear an oath to

11 *Laws of Hammurabi*, p. 160.
12 Driver and Miles, *The Assyrian Laws*, p. 101.
13 Ibid., p. 103.
14 Driver and Miles, *The Assyrian Laws*, p. 86.

the gods – Roth thinks that it did not need to be merely when there were facts or the testimony of parties that were in dispute.[15]

I will now give some examples of how the oath functioned in ancient Mesopotamian legal procedures. First, oaths were used when there was a need to make sure that both parties accepted the final ruling of the jury or assembly.

> Nergal-aha-iddin son of Ahjea, Karea son of Bel-le'I descendant of Ahutu and Nuptaya, his mother, swore to each other by Bel, Nubu, and the oaths of Darius king of Babylon and the lands:
>
> "We shall not reconsider regarding anything we have done."[16]

The general form of the oath not to reopen the case is referred to by the term "*tuppi la ragamin*" and occurs commonly in trial proceedings from Old Babylonian to Neo-Babylonian times.[17]

When there are conflicts in the evidence, oaths were required by both parties in order to attempt to settle the matter. Here is an example:

> Tablet in connection with the house in New-wall of A daughter of X.
>
> B daughter of Y made a claim against A …
>
> The judges in the Shamash temple gave judgment that A should take the oath by the life of the god. A took the oath by the life of the goddess Aya, her Lady and rebutted her [B's] claim.
>
> Since she [A] did not turn back (from the oath), B shall make no claim to A's house, paternal inheritance, property, or inheritance from her husband, as much as they may be, from straw to gold.
>
> She [B] has sworn (to accept this) by the gods Shamash, Aya, and Marduk and (king) Sumu-la-ilum.[18]

Sometimes one party or the other refused to swear and thus gave up the case. But sometimes the mutual swearing of oaths left the conflict still unresolved and then the parties might be submitted to the river-god ordeal.

I now wish to give a sense of how trials proceeded in Mesopotamia by looking at a civil trial concerning disputed paternity that we can contrast with the case

15 See Martha T. Roth in "Reading Mesopotamian Law Cases PBS 5 100: A Question of Filiation," *Journal of the Economic and Social History of the Orient*, Vol. 44, no. 3, 2001, pp. 243–292.

16 Trial from December 1, 513 BCE, translated by Shalom E. Holtz in his book, *Neo-Babylonian Trial Records*, Atlanta: Society of Biblical Literature, 2014, p. 64.

17 An even earlier document referred to as "*di til-la*" can also be found, but that text is kept by an administrative officer, whereas the "*tuppi la ragamin*" "was held by the party that eventually won the verdict." Ronald Veenker and J. Cale Johnson, "The Appellate Process in the Legal Record [*di til-la*] from Ur III Umma," *Altoriental Forsch*, Vol. 36, no. 2, 2009 (349–364), pp. 357–358.

18 Translated and quoted in Saggs, *The Greatness That Was Babylon*, p. 218.

concerning homicide that we examined earlier in the book.[19] In both cases it is an assembly that considers the case – in the latter case the king asks a jury of nine drawn from the assembly to make a judgment, and in the former the king relies on the assembly to make the judgment.

Here is a presentation of the main issues as discussed at the beginning of a contested paternity case and then some of the selected testimony.

> Ninurta-ra'im-zerim, the son of Enlil-bani, approached the sut teretim and the judges of the city of Nippur, he made a deposition as follows:
>
> "My father Enlil-bani, the son of Ahi-sagis, died while I was still in the belly of my mother Sin-nada. Just before my birth, Habannatum, my father's mother, informed Luga the herdsman and Sin-gamil the judge. She fetched a certain midwife and she delivered me. After I grew up in the 'Year in which King Samsuiluna, foremost king, overthrew the enemy countries which were disobedient to him and smote the troops of Esnunna," thus he declared.
>
> [Ninurta-iris and] Ili-ismeanni, [the sons of Ahi-sagis] and of Habannatum, [approached the sur teritim and the judges], they made a deposition as follows:
>
> "Ninurta-ra'im-zerim [is indeed the son/issue] of Enlil-bani. When [the tablet] to the effect that he is the son of Enlil-bani was executed before the divine Udbanuilla (emblem of the god Ninurta), it was written without witnesses so confirming by oath of the god. At this time, let witnesses confirm him by oath of the god!" Thus they declared.
>
> The sut teretim and the judges investigated their matter; they heard (read out loud to them) the earlier tablet with the oath of the god; they questioned their witnesses; they deliberated about their testimony; and as a result because their witnesses (said), as follows:
>
> "We know that Ninurta-ra'im-zerim is the son of Enlil-bani,"
>
> thus they declared –
>
> they ordered the presence of the divine Ubdanuilla (emblem of the god Ninurta), the confirmation by oath of the god of the witnesses who know of the filiation ("son-ship") of Ninurta-ra'im-zeerim, and the return of the report to the Assembly.[20]

19 The categories of civil and criminal are not from Mesopotamia – and there is no evidence that I have found to think that Mesopotamian law recognized anything like this distinction, except that cases where the death penalty was at stake were ones that had to involve the king. See *Laws of Eshnunna*, 48: "And for a case involving a penalty of silver in amounts ranging from 20 shekels to 60 shekels, the judges shall determine the case against him; however a capital case is only for the king," in *Law Collections From Mesopotamia and Asia Minor*, second edition, translated by Martha T. Roth, Atlanta, GA: Scholars' Press, 1997, p. 66.

20 Translated by Martha T. Roth in "Reading Mesopotamian Law Cases PBS 5 100: A Question of Filiation," *Journal of the Economic and Social History of the Orient*, Vol. 44, no. 3, 2001, pp. 257–258.

There then follows the testimony of nine male and female witnesses all of whom swear before the "divine Ubdabuilla (the emblem of the god Ninurta)." This gives us a fascinating example of the use of oaths for those who are witnesses and testify during trial proceedings.

It is interesting here that women were allowed to testify and that they seem to be held to the same standard of proof – the swearing of an oath before a god. Also, once again we see that the assembly is the ultimate body that will make the decision in the case. And while there is evidence for thinking that women were not included in the assembly, they can be the subject of trials and also trusted to give truthful testimony, at least on the condition that they do so with an oath to the gods.

The taking of oaths played a large role in the evidentiary proceeding in ancient Mesopotamia. Oath-taking is a form of self-enforcement that fits well with a society that did not have a clear institutional system of enforcement. The king was beginning to play a larger role in this respect but during the time when the assembly was still the dominant force. The people's will was the crucial component of government and this seems to have extended into the legal domain in how proof was established in these ancient trials.

3.3 THE DETERMINER OF TRUTH

As we noted in an earlier chapter (Chapter 2), judges came over time to replace the assembly. And much later juries would be added, which to a certain extent is a return to the assembly model. What was needed was a determiner of truth that was not one of the parties or connected to one of the parties at trial. Here we have another example of how the components of the rule of law emerged in these most ancient of times. But there was not always an objective determiner of the truth of alleged facts.

In cases of vigilante justice, as when the people who witness a rape immediately kill the rapist, an objective determiner of proof is largely missing. It is as if each person who is a witness to the rape becomes a determiner of proof – testing whether his or her own eyes had indeed seen a given person rape another. But such proof determiners are not objective since the witnesses normally have some relation to one of the parties, the one raped or the one accused of raping. And their determination is final in several senses, most importantly in that the punishment will be swift and normally lethal.

In cases where there are trials, especially public trials, there is often an impartial determiner of proof, or at least this is the ideal upon which trust in the trial process is placed. Time has elapsed since the event in question and calm has returned. As we will see in Chapter 11, there are similar problems of trust concerning treaties – for trust to be placed in a treaty it is hoped that there will be some entity that will oversee the process and determine whether the parties are indeed acting in good faith. In both cases, trials and treaties, some scholars have talked of "self-help" methods to try to assure trustworthiness. Oaths and ordeals are seen as self-help in that an appeal is made to the gods to help the fallible judges determine the true facts.

The Babylonian term for the river-god ordealis *hursan*, and this test of truth was employed predominantly in property disputes as well as in the various assault cases we have been examining. Driver and Miles give this account of the documentary evidence from the time of the Babylonian and Middle Assyrian Laws:

> These documents show that the *hursan* was invoked in Babylonia at least from a period contemporary with that of the Assyrian laws onwards in disputes concerning land, and in all of them it is the king or some public officer who acts as judge and prescribes the ordeal for one or other of the parties.[21]

We find here that normally some official acting as a judge is the determiner of the truthfulness of the parties.

The methods of proof, such as ordeals and oaths, were used by the determiner of truth since the judge was not typically present at the event in question. In addition, the judge must have been aware of the risks that he took in passing judgment in matters that were contested and for which the judge could be blamed by one of the parties and their family members. When the determination of truth is relegated from the judge to a procedure that appeals to the gods, it is the gods not the judge who ultimately are to blame if anyone is. Indeed, the idea that "the god has spoken" is the implicit, and sometimes explicit, underlying idea behind ordeals.

We may extend this inference to the king who delegates judging to officials who are trusted to act in his behalf, but who also somewhat distance the king from judgments that might be perceived as very unpopular. In ancient Egypt it is clear that some of these officials were given independence to act on their own by the king, and who were sometimes judges of cases involving the behavior of the king and the royal family, which was the case of the members of the harem who conspired to kill the pharaoh, as we will see in Chapter 8. There is a very long history of the judges gaining independence of the kings who appointed them, that extended well into the twentieth century CE in England and elsewhere.

The conceptual and practical problem that oaths and ordeals seem to have been instituted to solve is that many legal trials turn on what can be called "he said, she said" predicaments, where the parties cannot both be telling the truth and yet it is hard for a judge to tell who to believe. Property cases are notoriously of this sort, and this might explain why the use of oaths was so prominent in ancient times in property dispute trials. Property disputes could easily concern matters that happened

[21] Driver and Miles, *The Assyrian Laws*, p. 89.

before a judge or many litigants were even born. Of course, more was at stake when the dispute was about an assault, a killing, or a rape.

It is interesting that the institution of objective fact determiners can be traced back so far – to the beginning of recorded legal thought. But as I have been suggesting those associated with these institutions did not necessarily understand how important the institutions were for the rule of law. Indeed, it could be said that there was just as much recognition of the importance of bringing secular law into line with religion as there was about a need for the rule of law. We will explore this issue in much more detail in the next sections of this chapter.

3.4 RELIGION AND PROOF

It is often said that ancient law is infused with metaphysical and religious views that are too distant from our own even to be comprehendible by us.[22] Indeed, one well-known scholar of ancient Mesopotamia has argued that there is a close connection between judgments reached through divination and judgments reached through trials.[23] In both cases there is an attempt to get the gods to reveal the truth to humans. One could get closer to the gods by divination and also by reference to oaths and ordeals. I will pursue the larger issue in another forum, but not here. The point is just that ancient thinking may not be as transparent to us moderns as we may think. Yet, it also seems to me that the attempt to get closer to the gods was not unique to ancient societies. For more than 3,000 years after the time of Hammurabi, trials attempted to employ the gods' aid.

In late Medieval England, the trial by ordeal was eliminated and replaced by a system of trial by jury. Because the ordeal was so intimately connected to the hand of God in determining truth, when the change to trial by jury occurred it was said that the change was to the *vox populi* from the *vox dei* – to the voice of the people from the voice of god.[24] Yet, the change was not one that moved away from God, since the jury trial made extensive use of oaths, which invoked God here as well. Rather one form of proof that relied on gods, or religion was replaced with another. In this section I will consider the relationship between religion and proof at trials.

As I have indicated, both proof and ordeal are intimately connected to ideas of divine intervention and retribution. And yet there is ample evidence that the earliest trials were largely secular not religious, or if there was a close contact between religion and trials these religious trials were marked off from normal trials. In the case of

[22] Here one can note some of the things that are said in Marc Van De Mieroop, *Philosophy Before the Greeks*, Princeton, NJ: Princeton University Press, 2016.

[23] Ibid., p. 136 and elsewhere.

[24] See the discussion of this change in James Q. Whitman, *The Origins of Reasonable Doubt*, New Haven, CT: Yale University Press, 2008, p. 54.

ordeals, Medieval legal practice employed "frightening proceedings" which "were understood to be judgments of God," and these were characterized as "efforts to induce God to decide the case by giving his 'divine testimony.'"[25] Indeed, the forms of the ordeal in ancient times, especially in the Middle Assyrian Laws, were almost as severe as in the Medieval period, of which James Q. Whitman has said: "These frightening proceedings were understood to be 'judgments of God,' efforts to induce God to decide the case by giving his 'divine testimony.'"[26]

Whitman has argued that we should separate two uses of proof: as providing *moral comfort* for those who are reluctant or afraid to pass judgments on others, and as providing *factual proof* in those few cases where the facts were not evident to everyone who was a member of the small communities of what he calls "pre-modern" times.[27] As to factual proof, the idea is that taking an oath is intended "to make the man give evidence" that is likely to be true since the appeal to the gods in the oath indicates that "he must bear his iniquity" if he lies.[28] As to moral comfort for the judge, as well as for the king, the testimony that leads to a judgment of guilt, with the ensuing harsh punishment, is in the hands of the gods not something for which the judges can themselves be held responsible.

Judges and witnesses were held responsible in some cases, especially when there had been some abuse of authority. And at least one significant reason here was that the administration of justice was under the purview of the gods, indeed a specific god had this task. The witness or party to a law suit was treated as someone who was not to be believed unless there was some assurance, and the introduction of the gods created that assurance, both for factual proof important to the integrity of the legal system and for the moral comfort of those who judged.

The larger issue is that an ancient system of law could be a secular system and yet could still retain a religious element. One scholar has argued:

> The code was not just a confirmation of royal justice, but also a work of the king's wisdom … Hammurabi thus expressed the idea that justice and wisdom are closely related many centuries before Plato stated it in his *Republic* … Importantly, the laws were not god-given but human creations. Hammurabi acknowledged later in his epilogue that he received insight into truth from the sun god Shamash (xlviii 95–98), but the laws were his pronouncements. His role was thus very different from that of Moses, who was said merely to have passed on to the people of Israel the laws that the biblical god had given to him.[29]

[25] Ibid., p. 51.
[26] Ibid., p. 53.
[27] Ibid., p. 6.
[28] Driver and Miles, *The Assyrian Laws*, p. 124.
[29] Van De Mieroop, *Philosophy Before the Greeks*, p. 175.

Marc Van De Mieroop here contrasts a Mosaic model with a Platonic one. Both provide an important role to the gods and religion. But the difference is quite important conceptually. In the Mosaic model, God gives the law to humans and then aids these humans in administering that law. In the Platonic (and Hammurabian) model, the gods give the humans wisdom to see what the laws should be, and then the gods aid in the law's administration.

Another model comes from ancient Egypt. Here the pharaoh was literally seen as a god, and so law-making and law-administration was perhaps even more deeply religious than in Mosaic or Platonic models. John Wilson ends his chapter on the function of the state in ancient Egypt by saying:

> Perhaps the answer is that perception, authoritative utterance, and justice were godly characteristics, which were retained by the godly pharaoh … the king was the point of contact between men and gods as the divine ruler vested with concern for the state … His officials were more constrained to law and precedent, but the king's divine qualities permitted him a discretion in the effecting of proper rule.[30]

These ancient models of law and religion all have the idea that the gods play a role in the administration of justice. And as we have seen, standards of proof were an important point at which religion and ancient law overlapped.

3.5 ANCIENT PROOF AND TRUTH-TELLING

If all people were angels, it seems that proof would not be needed to determine the veracity of witnesses and testifiers. Or perhaps it should be said that if we all thought that all of us were angels then proof would not be an issue in trials. Yet there is a tendency to distrust people who are testifiers, especially if the testifier will stand to lose or gain by being believed. In the mistrust there is an implicit acknowledgment that we are not angels. When torture is employed in early Medieval cases, there is for Medieval legal theorists an even stronger implicit assumption – that we are all liars who must be severely treated and threatened with more of the same before anything we say is to be believed. Yet, Hammurabi seems to have ended the practice of deification of the king.[31] The Mesopotamian king does not call himself a maker of divine retribution, and so the river-god ordeal, as well as swearing of oaths to the gods, is necessary.

So we come to the main problem of factual proof – mere mortals are not good at telling when someone is lying and when he or she is telling the truth. In addition,

[30] John A. Wilson, "The Function of the State," in *Before Philosophy: The Intellectual Adventure of Ancient Man*, edited by Henri Frankfurt, H. A. Frankfurt, John A. Wilson, and Thorkild Jacobsen, Baltimore, MD: Penguin Press, 1946, pp. 100–101.

[31] See Driver and Miles, *Babylonian Laws*, Vol. 1, p. 82, note 1.

humans often have strong incentives not to tell the truth. So, how are people to be made more likely to tell the truth? And how can determiners of fact tell when it is likely that truth is being told? This is one of the basic questions of evidence that extends from the beginning of ancient legal thought until today.

In contemporary trials, witnesses are caused to present themselves before judge and jury, and to swear that they are telling the truth, before they testify. Those who testify are often then grilled by a lawyer to ascertain whether they are credible witnesses. Several strong disincentives to lie are also present: the lying witness can be prosecuted for a crime – perjury; the lying witness can face divine retribution due to having sworn falsely; and there is a judge and jury and other members of the public who are present and who will remember if a witness lied. And yet, testifiers still lie.

In the ancient world, as with all legal systems, the assumption has to be that the witness could well be lying – for then precautions can be taken for the worst case scenario. Incentives are introduced to increase the likelihood that witnesses and parties will tell the truth, or are more likely to do so than to lie. As I have reconstructed the ancient legal thought about oaths and ordeals, I have sought to explain why the ancient ideas, especially of the ordeal, can be seen as rational, at least to a certain extent. In the remainder of this section I will be more critical than I have been of such practices, while I continue to investigate what the alternatives were, such as vigilante justice and torture.

Vigilante justice, where those who are on the scene and then punish the perpetrator without a trial, is often excoriated. But there is one clear advantage of such "justice" – there is no need to rely on the fallible memory of testifiers or to try to prevent bias and lying of testifiers from corrupting the system of justice. Indeed, avoiding a trial altogether seems to have been often preferred in ancient times, where trials were only held when the wrongdoing was not witnessed and punished immediately.

Yet vigilante justice, as I have briefly indicated above, is problematic because along with the concurrent time of the wrong, the capture of the alleged wrongdoer, and the punishment of the alleged wrongdoer, there is also a likelihood that is fairly high that other biases will intervene to taint the "process." Most important of all, there is no room for correcting mistaken judgments, intentional or unintentional, since many of the vigilante punishments involved death to the purported wrongdoer. Adding an institutional layer of process between when the incident occurred and when the punishment was meted out leads to less worry about bias.

Torture has been thought for a very long time to make it likely that a person will tell the truth. Torture was employed in ancient times, especially in ancient Egypt, but probably not as often as in Medieval Europe. In Egypt it was common for anyone coming before a judge to be tortured, and sometimes more than once.

Indeed, if a witness has not first been tortured it is sometimes alleged that the witness is not allowed to present evidence to a judge. Tortured testimony is seen as the gold standard of believable testimony.

Yet studies today indicate that during torture people will say what they would not have said otherwise. But what they are more likely to say is what they think the torturer wants him or her to say, not necessarily what the torture victim believes is the truth. This highlights the fact that people differ in what they regard as the truth as well as about the best way to come to the truth, and this fact affects trials in significant ways, especially if in the end there is no consensus about what the facts are – "fact-finding without facts" to quote the title of a recent book.[32]

Marc Van De Mieroop has challenged the idea that a Western conception of truth can be imposed on ancient Near Eastern legal thought. His main contention is that we will do better by looking to post-modern understanding of epistemology than to modern understandings in order to grasp pre-modern ideas in the ancient world. Van De Mieroop's thesis is interesting and provocative – but as we will see perhaps there are less radical, and more plausible, ways to understand the pursuit of truth in ancient legal thought.

Here is a bit of the argument that Van De Mieroop employs in support of his claim for a different way of understanding ancient Mesopotamian truth:

> Only the written word held all information, and reading it correctly and in all its aspects was the Babylonian philosopher's task. That is why god *wrote* messages to humans using the universe as their writing tablet. That is why kings *inscribed* laws onto stone monuments in order to communicate the truth to their subjects. Writing was not imitative of thought and secondary to the presentation of knowledge, it was central to it: it created knowledge by adding unsuspecting levels and nuances. Thus the Babylonians need a grammatology rather than a semiology to understand truth: the written sign was not the signifier or something else, it shaped its own meaning ... This process was facilitated and encouraged by the use of lists, the essential form of Babylonian writing.[33]

According to this view, finding truth was not a matter of seeking a correlation with reality. Rather truth was internal to the written words of a text – and in this sense truth could change, even radically, by the invention of new signs and words.

Van De Mieroop is cautious about the application of his thesis to the area of legal knowledge and truth. Yet, he postulates that the same is true in this domain as in the domain of divinations.

[32] Nancy Combs, *Fact-Finding Without Facts: The Uncertain Evidentiary Foundations of International Criminal Convictions*, Cambridge: Cambridge University Press, 2010.

[33] Van De Mieroop, *Philosophy Before the Greeks*, p. 219.

> The Babylonians did not create order in the universe by investigating its component parts; they created order in lists and applied the order to the universe. The text preceded reality … In law, the list-making behavior may have been more sober but the same underlying principles governed, and entities were created within the codes according to their internal logic … After this was accomplished, the Babylonian scholar turned to reality to observe what had been established in the list.[34]

In the end, the claim is that "Writing preceded reality" and reality was in effect invented by the use of writing. This explains why the law codes were not quoted in judicial judgments, a fact still mysterious to many scholars. But it does not help very much in understanding why Babylonians developed elaborate mechanisms to provide incentives for witnesses and participants in law suits not to lie. Indeed it is unclear what lying would mean if truth is disconnected from reality.

There are indeed important insights to be gained by considering the list-making "obsession" of ancient Mesopotamians. There are very puzzling combinations of things, especially in the divinatory lists that had such things as "a solar eclipse at midnight" or the legal lists that had such things as "a goat threshing grain." But, at least in law, these nonrealistic listings were by far the exception not the rule. The vast majority of list items in the codes can be easily understood as originating in the reality of the times, not constructed by the terms of the list themselves.

As we have seen, there was extensive use of oaths and ordeals in ancient Mesopotamia, both in the codes as well as in other writings about the law. And when the oaths and ordeals were employed it was in the service of eliciting the truth about the reality of the facts of what happened, not merely elicited for creating the truth. One can criticize the use of the ordeal of the river-god as being not humane, but it is difficult to even understand it if it bears no relationship to preventing lying about the reality of an assault or an ownership title.

Oaths and ordeals were already employed as a due "process" to test for veracity and to provide incentive against lying. These methods of proof are the earliest recorded forms of proof. They were administered more humanely than in Medieval Europe, for instance. And these forms of proof indicated that the ancient lawgivers were concerned about the integrity of trials as well as the pursuit and conviction of the perpetrators. It was vitally important that punishment be inflicted on the persons who perpetrated the crimes of manslaughter and assault as well as other illegal acts such as claiming as one's own the property of another person. Uncertainty about testimonial truth-telling was a central concern and several strategies were employed to reduce the uncertainty.

[34] Ibid., p. 221.

SECTION II

Freedom, Equality, and Legal Status

4

Debt Forgiveness and Equity

This chapter is primarily about debt relief and forgiveness. The thesis is that looking at this concept from the earliest of times will give us a fresh perspective on how important humanitarian concerns were to ancient legal thought. In this chapter, the relationship between equity and debt forgiveness will be explored in reference to some of the very oldest texts known, those in Mesopotamia and its neighbors.

In Section 4.1, I will provide a few examples of debt forgiveness in Mesopotamia to motivate our discussion of ancient legal thought in this period and its relevance today. In Section 4.2 I will discuss the idea, from both ancient Babylonia and ancient Egypt, that the state or municipality where a robbery has occurred owes to the victim compensation from the treasury of the municipality or state, and I will attempt to connect this idea to the doctrine of debt forgiveness. In Section 4.3 I will explain the ancient Mesopotamian debt relief edicts and connect these acts to the emerging idea of equity in legal thought in ancient Mesopotamia. In Section 4.4 and Section 4.5 I will draw out some implications of the Mesopotamian case, so many millennia ago.

4.1 THE "CODE" OF HAMMURABI AND THE EDICTS OF AMMISADUQA

In Hammurabi's Code of Laws, there are many examples of merciful treatment of his people, but there are also sometimes very harsh penalties as well – somewhat in keeping with the idea of *lex talionis* (the subject of my Chapter 9). Ammisaduqa, the great-great-grandson of Hammurabi, was a later king of Babylonia who issued an edict on debt forgiveness that is the most complete document of its kind to have come down to us. In this first section I will provide a few examples of the legal writing of these kings in ancient Mesopotamia to give a sense of the form of these very early written legal pronouncements. I will also begin to explain the puzzles that I will then attempt so solve, or at least shed light on, in the rest of the chapter.

At the end of the prologue to his laws Hammurabi says this about what motivates him:

> When the god Marduk commanded me to provide just ways for the people of the land (in order to attain) appropriate behavior, I established truth and justice (Babylonian-*misarum*) as the declaration of the land. I enhanced the well being of the people.[1]

The term "misarum" is what many scholars translate as righteousness or as that form of justice called equity. Equity is the stated impetus for why Hammurabi propounded his laws and I will say more about this issue shortly. Some of the provisions of Hammurabi's laws are especially relevant to the issues I want to discuss in this chapter.

There are several provisions in Hammurabi's Code that aim at debt relief, but are primarily addressed to illegal acts of unscrupulous lenders. Here are three examples that are in Hammurabi's Code:

> LH# 117. If an obligation is outstanding against a man and he sells his wife, his son, or his daughter, they shall perform service in the house of their buyer of the one who holds them in debt service for three years; their release shall be secured in the fourth year.[2]

This example is of a permanent release of people from debt slavery after the fourth year, but says nothing about debt enslavement for less than four years:

> LH #w. If a merchant … should take … interest and … then does not deduct the payments of either grain [or silver] as much as [he received, or] does not write a new tablet, or adds the interest payments to the capital sum, that merchant shall return two-fold as much as he received.[3]

Here is a law that penalizes what is effectively fraud on the part of merchants, where the penalty seems intended to deter such activity without interfering with legitimate creditors.

> LH #124. If a man gives silver or gold, or anything else before witnesses to another man for safekeeping and he denies it, they shall charge and convict that man, and he shall give twofold that which he denied.[4]

Here again there is a kind of fraud that is the subject of the law. In each case, Hammurabi, who calls himself a shepherd, seeks to protect the weakest of his flock

1 *Laws of Hammurabi*, in *Law Collections from Mesopotamia and Asia Minor*, second edition, translated by Martha T. Roth, Atlanta, GA: Scholars' Press, 1997, pp. 80–81.

2 Ibid., p. 103.

3 Ibid., p. 98.

4 Ibid., p. 104.

from oppression at the hands of those who are powerful. And the laws that are propounded seek to curtail fraud as well as sharp dealing – and to do so permanently.

Hammurabi's legal protections arc motivated by equity in one sense, as we see from the prologue, but there is also another set of problems that operate more subtly and also oppress the people, calling for equity in a different sense. Here issuing a general prohibitory law would not be wise since the practices in question, mainly related to charging interest on loans, are not in themselves things that it would make sense to outlaw. Yet, Hammurabi recognized, as was also true of his successors, that debt, especially debt enslavement, could be so crushing as to need periodic forgiveness – a "clean slate" act. We do not have the full texts of the debt relief edicts that Hammurabi issued, but there is good evidence that at least four times during his 40-year reign such temporary debt relief measures were proclaimed, and issued at least eight more times by Hammurabi's immediate successors.

We do have a complete text of such an edict of debt forgiveness from the reign of Ammisaduqa, Hammurabi's relative and also subsequently king. And while there are some provisions that call for permanent ending of certain practices by unscrupulous lenders, there are also provisions that provide periodic debt relief even though the debts were incurred through legal processes.[5] Here are two of the provisions of the edict:

> Section 1. The arrears of the farmers, shepherds, knackers, and people working in the summer pastures, and [other] tributaries to the palace, in order to strengthen them and treat them equitably, are cancelled: the collector must not take any legal action against a tributary's house …
>
> Section 4. Whoever has given barley or silver to an Akkadian or Amorite as an interest bearing loan or as fees, and had a document drawn up – because the king has established equity (*misarum*) in the land, his document is voided; he may not collect the barley or silver on the basis of his document.[6]

Here past debts incurred through loans extended by certain public sector creditors, and perhaps also some "private" individuals, are cancelled.[7]

And for our purposes, it is noteworthy that certain forms of debt that involve servitude are nullified by Ammisaduqa:

> Section 20. If an obligation weighed upon an inhabitant [of the regions] of Numhia, Embutbalum, Idamaras [or of the cities] of Uruk, Kisurra, or Malgum, and he had

5 Dominique Charpin, *Writing, Law, and Kingship in Old Babylonian Mesopotamia*, translated by Jane Marie Todd, Chicago. IL: University of Chicago Press, 2010, p. 93.

6 Ibid., p. 84.

7 Translated and quoted in Jacob Finkelstein, "The Edict of Ammisaduqa," in *Ancient Near Eastern Texts Relating to the Old Testament*, third edition, edited by J. B. Pritchard, Princeton, NJ: Princeton University Press, 1969, pp. 526–527, I have partially revised this translation.

> to place his own person, his wife, or his children in servitude for debts in exchange for money, or as a security, as a result of the king's instituting redress [*misarum*] for the country, he is liberated: his *andurarum* [return to previous status] will be carried out.[8]

In this provision the practice of debt enslavement for those who could not pay their debts was cancelled and the previous free status of the debtor was restored.

> Section 22. The lieutenant of the military governor of the country who constrains the family of a soldier-*redum* or a soldier *barium* to accept grain, silver or wool in exchange for [labor at the time of] the harvest or a[nother] job, shall be put to death. The soldier-*redum* or the soldier *barium* shall be able to take [without repayment] everything that he gave.[9]

Soldiers were thought to be especially vulnerable to be victims of sharp practices.[10] The cancelling of all of these debts, a so-called "clean slate" edict, was retrospective not prospective and hence the debt forgiveness was only temporary in the sense that it forgave past debts but not those debts acquired after the date of the edict.

There are various puzzles that have arisen about the debt forgiveness edicts that were propounded in ancient Mesopotamia. Why was debt forgiveness considered an equitable remedy given that the creditors had not broken any laws and were not accused of any crime? Why were these edicts only retrospective and what effect did the periodic issuing of these edicts have on the status of credit practices? What is the underlying legal theory that is served by such edicts and how does it square with the possible undermining of respect for the rule of law that is occasioned by having the ruler penalize merchants for operating within the law? I will explore these issues in what follows. But I want first to look at somewhat similar laws concerning who has the duty to replenish stolen goods when the perpetrator cannot be found or identified.

4.2 THE LAW OF REPLENISHING STOLEN GOODS

In both Mesopotamia and Egypt there were laws dictating that if a thief stole property from a fellow citizen (or from a foreigner) and the thief was not quickly caught, the political entity where the thief resided should pay compensation to the victim. This idea will be the subject of this section as I attempt to explain how the thinking

8 Charpin, *Writing Law*, p. 89.

9 Ibid., p. 89.

10 See Michael Hudson, "Reconstructing the Origins of Interest-Bearing Debt and the Logic of Clean Slates," in *Debt and Economic Renewal in the Ancient Near East*, edited by Michael Hudson and Marc Van De Mieroop, Bethesda, MD: CDL Press, 2002, pp. 7–58.

behind it could be related to the thinking behind the debt forgiveness laws that are the main subject of this chapter.

Hammurabi propounded a law that was clearly aimed at victim compensation in cases of robbery.

> LH #23. If the robber should not be seized, the man who has been robbed shall establish the extent of his lost property before the god; and the city and the governor in whose territory and district the robbery was committed shall replace his lost property to him.[11]

In this law we see the government held responsible for victim compensation, at least when victims have indeed been harmed and the perpetrator cannot make compensation. And in another law Hammurabi addresses those who would try to take advantage of his law concerning the replacement of stolen property:

> LH #126. If a man whose property is not lost should declare, "My property is lost," and accuse his city quarter, his city quarter shall establish against him before the god that no property of his is lost, and he shall give to the city quarter twofold whatever he claimed.[12]

In this case of a fraudulent claim by "victims," Hammurabi sets a stiff penalty.

There was a similar provision in ancient Egypt in the 11th century BCE in "The Report of Wenamun." Here is a part of that report:

> When a man of my ship fled because he stole a vessel of gold ... I set out for the place where the (local) ruler was, and I said to him: "I have been robbed in your harbor! Now, you are the ruler of this land and you are its judge, so search for my money!"[13]

But the local authorities are unwilling to pay compensation to the victim because the perpetrator of the crime was not a citizen of the town.

In addition Driver and Miles report that there were also similar provisions for compensation of victims or their families in other ancient societies.

> the Babylonian rule that the city or local officers are responsible for paying compensation for offenses committed in their districts is illustrated by a tablet from Nuzi recording that a court has condemned the men of the city to replace the complainant's ass, which has been struck and killed "within the city." It is further illustrated by the Hebrew law of Deuteronomy: this provides that, if a dead body is found in the open country and the slayer is not known, the leaders of the nearest

[11] *Laws of Hammurabi*, p. 85.

[12] Ibid., p. 105.

[13] James E. Campbell, "A Cuneiform Legal Presence in 'The Report of Wenamun,'" *Journal of Ancient Egyptian Interconnections*, Vol. 1, no. 3, 2009, p. 2.

> town shall make expiation for the unsolved murder. So, too, in ancient Arabia the responsibility for a "homicide might be put on the nearest homestead."[14]

The ancient legal practice of providing compensation to victims from city or state coffers is, in my view, closely related to the practice of debt forgiveness, especially when the creditor is itself a public institution. In both cases it is the king who is responsible for going to the aid of those who are poor and suffering.

In the ancient legal texts we have been examining, debt forgiveness and victim compensation are seen as public obligations of the king where the interests of creditors and other citizens-taxpayers are overridden for the common good of the society. The idea underlying these practices is that people should not be made destitute when funds can be found to aid them from the public institutions of crown and temple.

It is possible that debt forgiveness was motivated by the desire to return debt slaves to the status of tax payers, although this seems to be highly implausible as the sole motivation. Indeed, it is hard to see why a Mesopotamian city would pay compensation to victims except at least partially from a concern for fairness and mercy. And the same is true of debt forgiveness, as we will see in the next sections.

When we move out of the ancient period, we find some cities, and non-governmental institutions that have continued into the present age to set up victim compensation funds for situations where victims would otherwise be uncompensated. Indeed, Driver and Miles discuss cases from Asia and Europe, including states that have:

> the practice of imposing collective fines on town or villages for offenses committed within the limits of their jurisdiction when the actual offenders cannot be found; these are contributed in equal shares by every member of the group so penalized.[15]

And the International Criminal Court has in our day established a victim compensation fund for similar purposes. I have elsewhere proposed that this fund and similar ones concerning the victims of war should be established by taxes on the wealthy countries of the world.[16] I will return to other contemporary parallels in the final section of this chapter.

Some have argued that the various reforms with which we shall concern ourselves in this chapter are not good examples of moral reform. Raymond Westbrook has said:

14 Godfrey Rolles Driver and J. C. Miles, *The Babylonian Laws*, Oxford: Oxford University Press, 1952, pp. 110–111.

15 Ibid., p. 111.

16 See Larry May, *After War Ends*, Cambridge: Cambridge University Press, 2012.

> social justice was regarded in the ancient Near East as the preservation of the status quo – as the privileges owed to each citizen as member of a family unit with a recognized socioeconomic status. Where those privileges were lost through an act of oppression, certain mechanisms were available to restore the balance ... Mesopotamian kings boasted of having fulfilled their mandate, but evidence from the Bible suggests that the practice of kings sometimes failed to live up to the ideals of social justice.[17]

This criticism is one I will take seriously in what follows. It is a critique of what actually happened when ancient Mesopotamian kings sought to show that they were supporting social justice in the way they ruled. This criticism is different from that of saying that there was little altruism in the motives behind Mesopotamian rulers. In the section just completed I have tried to indicate that the motives were indeed good – it is up to us next to look more closely at the practices and their indebtedness to the emerging idea of equity.

4.3 DEBT RELIEF AND EQUITY IN ANCIENT LEGAL THOUGHT

Hammurabi uses the term equity (*misarum*) both in his account of why he promulgated the laws and why he had them written on his stela. Commentators are in agreement that some of the most unusual laws and edicts were for debt cancellation. Somewhat later there were similar edicts in Egypt, and the Bible makes reference to some as well.[18] The initial idea of debt relief can be found not very much later than the idea of interest-bearing loans themselves.

It seems that there have been recorded interest-bearing loans as well as forgiveness of such loans since at least 2400 BCE in Mesopotamia.[19] The first recorded instances of interest-bearing loans were public sector loans, and several centuries later there are examples of debt forgiveness edicts for public sector loans as well. Later, in the Old Babylonian period, personal interest-bearing loans became common. Indeed, some commentators have argued that the very point of loan agreements was often to obtain indentured labor, not to obtain a profit in monetary terms. And here, due in part to there being an agrarian economy with many people living in subsistence,

[17] Raymond Westbrook, "Social Justice in the Ancient Near East," in *Social Justice in the Ancient World*, edited by K. D. Irani and Morris Silver, London: Greenwood Press, 1995, p. 161.

[18] See Deuteronomy 15.1–2. On the connection between debt slave forgiveness and other forms of relief of slavery in the Bible see N. P. Lemche, "The Manumission of Slaves – The Fallow Year – The Sabbatical Year – The Jobel Year," *Vetus Testmentum*, Vol. 26, Fasc. 1 (Jan. 1976), pp. 38–59.

[19] Marc Van De Mieroop, "A History of Near Eastern Debt?" in *Debt and Economic Renewal in the Ancient Near East*, edited by Michael Hudson and Marc Van De Mieroop, Bethesda, MD: CDL Press, 2002, p. 63.

debt slavery became a major social problem, affecting "a significant portion of the whole population."[20]

Debt relief measures in ancient Babylonia had two different forms. Most commonly they were temporary measures to alleviate oppressive conditions that had developed legally. But there were some other debt relief measures that were permanent. Many of these concerned practices that were either illegal, such as using weighing scales that had been rigged, or practices that were highly suspect in all cases, such as practices that put undue influence on people who were in need of special protection, such as soldiers returning after battle.[21]

Marc van de Mieroop claims that one of the causes of the need for debt relief was that a "partial 'privatization' of the economy" had taken place. Various "institutions started to contract out work and services." "Administrative tasks were also assigned to independent contractors … the institutions asked private entrepreneurs to act as intermediaries between themselves and the citizenry, collecting dues, issuing payments, and organizing the collection and distribution of resources." "The private businessmen who were contracted for their services did not owe political allegiance to any dynasty, and were left alone to function in politically uncertain times … Ultimately its effects on Babylonian society were disastrous … the level of indebtedness was high."[22]

There are two types of equity underlying debt forgiveness edicts that one can see operating in ancient Babylonia. The first is equity as a kind of fairness that demands equal treatment of the laws. It is this consideration that Hammurabi said led him to propound laws against deception that allowed the evasion of the law, and to have these laws inscribed on stela for all to see in solving their own problems. The second is equity as fairness in allowing for exceptions to the written law so that oppression can be overcome, such as when a man is forced to sell his children into slavery to satisfy his creditors, when there is not a fit between a given law and a set of facts. This second type of equity could perhaps arise because the lawmaker had not foreseen debt slavery as resulting from laws allowing for interest-bearing loans, where such a case would arise and be covered under the law – here Ammisaduqa also uses the term "equity" (*misarum*) for his debt forgiveness edict.

What is curious is that the remedy for oppression of debtors by creditors is an amnesty to all debtors of a certain type (such as those who were debt slaves) granted

20 Piotr Steinkeller, "Money-Lending Practices in Ur III Babylonia: The Issue of Economic Motivation," in *Debt and Economic Renewal in the Ancient Near East*, edited by Michael Hudson and Marc Van De Mieroop, Bethesda, MD: CDL Press, 2002, especially pp. 110–111, 124.

21 See J. J. Finkelstein, "Ammisaduqa's Edict and the Babylonian 'Law Codes'," *Journal of Cuneiform Studies*, Vol. 15, 1961, pp. 91–104.

22 Marc Van De Mieroop, A *History of the Ancient Near East c. 3000–323 BC*, second edition, Oxford: Blackwell Publishing, 2007, pp. 93–94.

on a particular day, not an amnesty that was for all of the people who were indeed suffering from massive debt – certain commercial loans remained in place. And the amnesty wiped out all debt of a certain kind on a given date but it did not extend into the future. Yet, there was no change in the financial laws that had allowed for massive debt to be accumulated. Hence, amnesties had to be granted again in a few more years. So, there are two oddities: why was debt not relieved for all those who were being oppressed by their debt? And why didn't the remedy include a change in the financial laws, or an addition to them, for instance outlawing the charging of 20–30 percent interest, which was common at the time.

The financial laws were fairly minimal at this time, but they certainly could have been strengthened. Yet it might have been thought that the problem of debt, even of debt slavery, was not such as to warrant a radical change in the financial laws. In agrarian economies there is a long period from the time of tilling and planting until crops can be sold. A loan to buy seed (repaid later from the harvest) is an obvious way to solve this problem, and being allowed to charge interest is an obvious way to encourage loans to be advanced.[23] But as with any kind of financial law there can be unintended adverse consequences for the debtors. And this is especially important when the inability to repay a debt leads to selling one's children or oneself into slavery.

We can also look at ancient Egypt for a few examples of debt forgiveness that are somewhat similar to the Mesopotamian cases. In the 24th Dynasty, a pharaoh came to power who is known for being a good lawgiver. Diodorus of Sicily, in his *History*, describes legal reforms of the Egyptian ruler, Bocchoris:

> Their laws governing contracts they attribute to Bocchoris. These prescribe that men who had borrowed money without signing a bond, if they denied the indebtedness, might take an oath to that effect and be cleared of the obligation … And whoever lent money along with a written bond was forbidden to do more than double the principal from the interest. In the case of debtors the lawgiver ruled that the repayment of loans could be exacted only from a man's estate, and under no condition did he allow the debtor's person to be subject to seizure, holding that whereas property should belong to those who had amassed it or had received it from some earlier holder by way of a gift, the bodies of citizens should belong to the state, to the end that the state might avail itself of the services which its citizens owed it, in times of both war and peace. For it would be absurd he felt, that a soldier, at the moment perhaps when he was setting forth to fight for his fatherland, should be haled to prison by his creditor for an unpaid loan and that the greed of private citizens should in this way endanger the safety of all. And it appears that Solon took

[23] See Marc Van De Mieroop, "Credit as a Facilitator in Old Babylonian Mesopotamia," in *Debt and Economic Renewal in the Ancient Near East*, edited by Michael Hudson and Marc Van De Mieroop, Bethesda, MD: CDL Press, 2002, pp. 163–173.

> this law also to Athens, calling it a "disburdenment," when he absolved all citizens of the loans secured by their persons, which they owed. But certain individuals find fault, and not without reason, with the majority of the Greek lawgivers, who forbade the taking of weapons and ploughs and other indispensable things as security for loans, but nevertheless allowed the men who would use these implements to be subject to imprisonment.[24]

Here we find an account of debt relief in ancient Egypt that occurs when certain forms of collateral are employed, especially when a person has put up his body as collateral and once unable to pay the principal is then either enslaved or imprisoned. Despite being different from the Mesopotamian edicts in several important respects, this evidence points to Egyptian debt forgiveness focused on prohibiting the creation of debt slavery.

In general though there seems to be little evidence in Egypt of anything like the "clean slate" edicts of Mesopotamia. Richard Jasnow says:

> Perhaps in part due to the chance of preservation, but perhaps also partly because the Egyptians felt little need as a rule to document such transactions, the quantity of relevant texts from Pharaonic Egypt is inconsiderable in comparison with the vast number of tablets from Mesopotamia. Similarly, the lack of surviving systematic law codes in Egypt until the Hermopolis Legal Code, written in Demotic, removes another potentially rich source of information regarding debt and loans.[25]

Yet, Jasnow then mentions two examples that are especially relevant for us.

> The family of a fugitive may be imprisoned to compel an absconder to return to corvee-labor [compulsory unpaid labor] in the Middle Kingdom, an example of distraint [the seizure of someone's property to pay a debt]. In the school texts of P. Lansing, the farmer's family is seized as security because the unfortunate cannot pay his taxes.[26]

And Jasnow also quotes the New Kingdom Wisdom text of Amenemope:

> If you find a large debt against a poor man,
> Make it into three parts
> Forgive two, let one stand
> You will find in it a path of life.[27]

[24] Diodorus of Sicily, *The Library of History* I, Book I, Chapter 79, translated by C. H. Oldfather, Cambridge: Loeb Classical Library of Harvard University Press, 1933, Vol. I, pp. 271–273.

[25] Richard Jasnow, "Pre-Demotic Pharaonic Sources," in *Security for Debt in Ancient Near Eastern Law*, edited by Raymond Westbrook and Richard Jasnow, Leiden: Brill, 2001, p. 36.

[26] Ibid.

[27] *Ancient Egyptian Literature: A Book of Readings*, edited by Miriam Lichtheim, Berkeley: University of California Press, 1976, Vol. II, pp. 155–156.

Here we certainly have the sentiment if not the legal grounds of debt forgiveness in ancient Egypt.

Edward Bleiberg, a scholar of ancient Egypt and Mesopotamia, points out that "Mutual aid was a widely accepted Egyptian ideal included in the concept of *maat* [justice]."[28] He then says:

> Egyptians living prior to the first millennium did not have a clear concept of abstract value. As Janssen has demonstrated, individual objects had only use value. A bed was for sleeping; grain was for planting or eating. The barter process consisted of objects that were needed. In the same way, loans and credit were never conceived as means of making a profit. They were concrete mechanisms for allowing barter to proceed and for ensuring survival in times of need.[29]

There were debt relief measures in ancient Egypt even if they were not as developed as in Mesopotamia.

In addition, equity played an important role in ancient Egyptian ideas of rulership, even if not so central as equity was understood in Mesopotamian societies. Aristide Theodorides, points out:

> the tomb of Rekhmire, dates from the Eighteenth Dynasty. There we find first a veritable ethic of viziership, in which it is laid down that justice is to be rendered in public and in such a way that every individual shall always secure his rights. To this end, appeal is made to a sense of equity and also, by implication, to jurisprudence: "judge every case with the correctness which is proper to it, [giving every person] his rights."[30]

Debt forgiveness seems to be grounded in equity considerations for at least some Egyptian rulers.

There were also debt relief acts listed in the Bible and also in the laws of Solon in ancient Greece. Here are several laws from the Bible dealing with debt enslavement:

> Deut. 15:12: If a fellow Hebrew, man or woman, is sold to you, he shall serve you six years, and in the seventh year you shall set him free.
>
> Exod. 21:2–4: When you acquire a Hebrew slave, he shall serve six years; in the seventh year he shall go free without payment.

And there was a regular cleaning of the slates as well:

28 Edward Bleiberg, "Loans, Credit and Interest in Ancient Egypt," in *Debt and Economic Renewal in the Ancient Near East*, edited by Michael Hudson and Marc Van De Mieroop, Bethesda, MD: CDL Press, 2002, p. 257.

29 Ibid., p. 269.

30 Aristide Theodorides, "The Concept of Law in Ancient Egypt," in *The Legacy of Egypt*, second edition, edited by J. R. Harris, Oxford: Oxford University Press, 1971, pp. 307–308.

Deut. 15:1–3: Every seventh year, you shall grant a remission of debts.

Lev. 25:8–10: You shall count off seven weeks or years – seven times seven years – so that the period gives you a total of forty-nine years … You shall proclaim release throughout the land for all its inhabitants.

Samuel Greengus, a scholar of ancient Biblical texts, writes that in the Bible, "Omission of interest was envisioned as an act of humanity."[31]

We also have an often overlooked discussion of debt relief by Aristotle in *The Constitution of Athens*, VI, 1–3:

When he had taken power, Solon freed the people both then and for the future by making loans on the security of a person's freedom illegal; he passed laws and instituted a cancellation of debts both private and public which men called *seisachtheia*, for they shook off their burdens. Some try to attack him in this context; it happened that when Solon was about to introduce his *seisachtheia* he told some of the leading citizens and then (according to the democratic version of the story) he was outmaneuvered by his friends, while those who wish to blacken his reputation say that he was a party to fraud. These men borrowed money and bought large areas of land; shortly afterwards, when debts were cancelled, they became rich. This is alleged to be the origin of those who later appeared to have been wealthy for generations.[32]

Aristotle is here critical of the debt relief measures of Solon on grounds that some today might support as well, as we'll see.

In the Mesopotamian *misarum* cases of debt forgiveness, there is no hint that there has been a problem with the *process* of the loans. The key consideration behind the forgiveness edicts is that the *result* of the loans is oppressive to the debtors. Yet, of course the fairness of result is a matter of interpretation and many creditors complained about the debt forgiveness edicts since they apparently saw the result of the edicts to be serious impediments to their businesses. Yet, while there is evidence that the creditors complained, these debt forgiveness edicts were not stopped for this reason.

4.4 EQUITY AND DEBT RELIEF

An example today that is related to the debt forgiveness edicts in ancient Mesopotamia is the contemporary idea that if contracts are unconscionable, they should not be enforced. It has proven to be exceedingly difficult to give a single

31 Samuel Greengus, *Laws in the Bible and in Early Rabbinic Collections*, Eugene, OR: Cascade Books, 2011, p. 103.

32 Aristotle, *The Constitution of Athens*, VI, 1–3, translated by J. M. Moore, Cambridge: Cambridge University Press, 1966, p. 214.

definition of unconscionability that covers all of the various cases that have been said to fall under this category. So today there has been a determination that there are both procedural as well as result-oriented ways to understand the concept of unconscionability. Unconscionability in terms of *process* may occur when there is deception that does not rise to the level of fraud, but which means that there was never a true meeting of the minds, or where the bargaining power between the two parties is greatly unequal. Unconscionability in terms of *result* may occur when one party benefits exorbitantly and the other party loses greatly from the contract.[33] We do not have debt slavery in Western democracies, but there is a troubling trend toward debt prisons, where unconscionability, understood in equity terms, seems to be just the right kind of concept to which to appeal for reforming these debtor prisons.

In the various types of unconscionability the remedy is to nullify, or at least not enforce, the contract. But it is normally not part of the remedy that the underlying laws that gave rise to the possibility of unconscionability are themselves reformed, or determined to be unconstitutional. However, it often turns out that after several courts have ruled that a particular type of contract, such as a rent-to-own contract with exorbitant interest rates, is unconscionable other courts tend to follow suit.[34] So, in some cases there is a de facto if not a de jure change in the law due to the operation of precedent or merely similarity of judgment.

Today, the general idea of the government, rather than private companies, issuing debt relief measures, partially relieving student debt, for instance, is not unknown. But the idea that the government would issue a "clean slate" amnesty forgiving all the debts of private citizens seems radical, although, as I will argue, not without merit. Creditors will of course be horrified, and not without some justification, and yet such things as enormous student indebtedness is a terrible drag on the humane progress of the whole economy.

One thing to note initially is that most of the debt that was erased in earliest times was that debt arising from interest-bearing loans conveyed by the two large public institutions at this time: the temple and the state. The temples and the crown held vast lands and resources that provided capital for the loans to the people who were largely farmers, shepherds, and traders. So, when Hammurabi or the other Old Babylonian kings forgave debt it was often the temple or the crown, as a public institution, which was the creditor.

[33] See Alan Wertheimer, "Unconscionability and Contracts," *Business Ethics Quarterly*, Vol. 2, no. 4, 1992, pp. 479–496, and reprinted in *Philosophy of Law*, edited by Larry May and Jeff Brown, NY: Blackwell Publishers, 2010, pp. 487–499.

[34] See *Williams* v. *Walker-Thomas Furniture Co.*, 350 F.2d 445 (1965); and *Murphy* v. *McNamara*, 38 Conn. Super. 183, 416 A. 2d 170 (1975); as well as *Henningsen* v. *Bloomfield Motors*, 32 N.J. 385, 161 A. 2d 69 (1960).

Today, a lot of the debt also has the creditor being the government – I am thinking here of student loans and mortgage loans, which are at least backed by the government if not with the government as the primary creditor. And so, as in ancient times it is not such a worrisome thing to have the public sector loans forgiven as it would be for the private sector loans. If the creditor is a public institution, debt forgiveness is less problematic than if there is a private creditor since the public sector is in effect offering forgiveness of its own debts,[35] whereas there is something at least in need of justification when the public sector forgives debt that the public sector does not own.

It is interesting that some of the debt forgiven in ancient Mesopotamia was debt enslavement that arose once private entrepreneurs had been assigned the task of administering debt owed to the public sector institutions of crown and temple. Today, the outsourcing of debts that individuals owe to public institutions, such as municipal and traffic courts, has resulted in what some are calling debt imprisonment.[36] Relieving these debts that are intermediate between public and private debt also seems much easier to justify than purely private sector debts.

The relief of people from debt servitude in ancient times, and from debt imprisonment in our own times, is a different order of magnitude from relieving simple monetary debt. In ancient times, debt slavery amnesty is portrayed as clearly in keeping with the mandate of the early Babylonian rulers to protect the weak and oppressed, especially the poor, the widows, and the orphans. Today, it is more controversial than in ancient times that debt relief is one of the chief tasks for any ruler, but it is still sometimes recognized that such debt is a drag on the economy as well as being inhumane. And in the case of debt imprisonment there is something especially odd about forcing someone out of the paid workforce for inability to pay, where the remedy of imprisonment seems destined only to make it much harder for the debt ever to be repaid. Of course, if some of the Mesopotamian scholars are right, and the whole point of lending to people who are unlikely to pay it back is eventually to take the liberty of those people and force them to be your labor slaves,[37] there is of course a perversely rational practice here.

The temporary debt forgiveness edicts in ancient Mesopotamia were seen as consistent with an economic system that allowed for entrepreneurs as well as something like modern private property. And debt forgiveness was thought to be one of the chief "shepherding duties" of the ruler, not something that was merely a matter of

35 Of course, taxpayers might be upset by the government relieving debt that originally was loaned from the tax coffers.

36 Associated Press, "Lawsuit: Court Illegally Jails People Who Can't Pay Fines," October 13, 2015: "The lawyers say indigent people must be offered a chance to perform community service or else jail equals a 'debtor prison.'"

37 Steinkeller, "Money-Lending Practices in Ur III Babylonia," especially pp. 111–112.

charity. We see this in the way ancient Mesopotamian kings bragged about these relief measures as showing that they protected the poor and vulnerable.

It is noteworthy that debt amnesty edicts were regularly declared at the beginning of each new king's rule, so they were not unforeseeable. And at least one scholar has claimed to show that the likelihood of debt forgiveness edicts being issued did not dissuade creditors from continuing to make interest-bearing loans.[38] It is also worth noting that the ancient rulers seemingly did not want their debt relief edicts to have an adverse effect on the general availability of credit. If these rulers had wanted to eliminate interest-bearing loans, then the debt relief measures would have been permanent rather than temporary.

As to the rule of law, one thing to consider is that crushing debt, enforced through the legal system, has the effect of making people less inclined to adopt strong fidelity to that legal system as well as to that ruler. The debt forgiveness edicts have been criticized for being merely safety valve measures, not real reform.[39] I would put the point differently. When a system creates widespread hardship, even oppression, it either must be reformed temporarily or permanently.[40] Temporary reform is still reform if it alleviates hardship and oppression. And such measures can have a longer-lasting effect especially once the private creditors see that "gaming the system" will only result in the need for more amnesties down the road.

The same people who feel oppressed by their current debt are often the people who also want to have credit available in the future. So, permanent restrictions on extending credit may not be the best solution even for the people currently living under crushing debt. In ancient Mesopotamia, the thought at the time, as far as can be determined from the documents, seems to be that "freeing" a person from crushing debt is the best way to help the oppressed.

Up to this point I have been pursuing largely consequentialist reasons to favor debt forgiveness. And one might naturally object that I have not considered such issues as that the creditors might deserve to receive the interest that is contractually owed to them – to say nothing yet of the principal that might also be forgiven by debt forgiveness edicts. Surely there is also a fairness concern for the creditors, in terms of what they deserve, which arises when debt is forgiven, an issue that I have not yet addressed. And matters of what is deserved are not easily pushed aside by simple consequentialist concerns. Or to put the point in terms of the topics we have been discussing, one could argue that creditors should not have their justifiable claims nullified merely by considerations of overall societal well-being.

38 Charpin, *Writing, Law*, Chapter 6.

39 Ibid., p. 94.

40 Of course, the debt arises also because people borrow more than they can repay. But it seems that like cases of unconscionable contracts today, in ancient Mesopotamia lenders were also responsible due to unscrupulous lending practices.

In general, creditors have a right to be repaid, and debtors have a duty to make such payments. Debt forgiveness comes up against this seemingly immovable rock. Yet, these rights and duties are of course not absolute, since clearly we wouldn't condemn the society to ignominy because of a focus on debtor-rights. A state allows creditors to operate in the first place because it is thought that there will be economic gain for the whole society by allowing interest-bearing loans. In some circumstances, and hopefully very few, when such overall economic gain is not forthcoming, creditors' rights may need to be infringed. And in addition, in those few cases where there has been a process problem, such as when creditors have extended loans to people known to be unlikely to be able to repay the loan, the law should not protect these creditors.

Let me next say just a bit about the issue of the generality of law in debt forgiveness edicts. Edicts and other equitable remedies are sometimes seen as not proper laws insofar as the edicts address themselves to particular (often specially named) individuals. As a result, edicts such as the one in Sophocles' *Antigone*, issued by Creon that no one was to bury the body of Polynices, are a legally dubious instrument since they lack generality in much the same way that bills of attainder were condemned by the Founding Fathers in the US Constitution. But the temporary debt relief edicts do not seem to fall prey to these problems, since they are certainly general in form. The debt forgiveness edicts concerned a general group of people, not merely one person.

Nonetheless there is a seeming randomness to the way the ancient Mesopotamian debt forgiveness edicts were promulgated that raises another type of fairness concern. Debtors who are not caught up in a particular amnesty, even though equally deserving as those whose debts are forgiven, will be treated unfairly. The lack of a more sweeping generality to the debt relief measures raises these quandaries. But as I have suggested, more sweeping debt relief measures than the ones we have considered are likely to have too strong a detrimental impact on the whole system of debt and credit in a given society.

4.5 FORGIVENESS, EQUITY, AND DEBT RESTRUCTURING

We might ask why debt forgiveness rather than debt restructuring should be preferred. From the ancient texts examined earlier several answers can be given. First, the middle-men who were given the task of collecting the debts owed to the crown and temple seem not to have been trusted to deal fairly with the debtors. Several provisions in the law codes deal with the fraud of the debt collectors. The second reason is closely related to the first reason to prefer debt forgiveness to debt restructuring: debt forgiveness is less intrusive in the economy than is debt restructuring. Debt forgiveness can be accomplished with a simple legal edict. Debt restructuring requires long-term interference by the government in the economy.

The third reason is also closely related to the first two: there has often been complicity on the part of creditors in that they have encouraged people to take on more debt than they are likely to be able to repay and so it is not unfair to penalize the creditors by allowing debt forgiveness rather than debt restructuring. In ancient times, there is evidence that loans were made with the expectation of default and then with the ensuing enslavement of the debtor. Debt forgiveness seems to be a not unfair response to this situation.[41]

Finally, the ancient texts especially from Mesopotamia portray debt forgiveness as especially in keeping with the humanitarianism that kings are supposed to display toward their people. There is a close link between humanitarianism and mercy that can be traced back into ancient times and clearly is still alive and well today. As in the ancient Greek times, mercy and equity are closely aligned. Indeed, one of the words relating to the amnesty edicts (*misarum*) is the same as the word for equity.

In various recent philosophical debates, the idea of forgiveness has received attention. One point of contention concerns whether forgiveness, as a virtue, could also be a duty. Jeffrey Murphy has defended an account of mercy as a virtue that is never an obligation.[42] For mercy or forgiveness to be an obligation, in Murphy's view, would mean that they are not virtues. The merciful ruler who pardons as a way to display mercy is to be praised not for what he or she has done as an obligation. Others have also argued that even for rulers, merciful acts of forgiveness can not be moral requirements.

As I have interpreted the writings of Mesopotamian rulers, issuing edicts of forgiveness is seen as both an obligation and a virtue of these rulers. And the key component of this view is the link to humanitarianism. And humanitarianism is linked to equity in that equity calls for taking account of the special circumstances of the people who are subject to the laws. In this sense, considering the humaneness of subjects involves treating them for who they uniquely are, including their special vulnerabilities. Showing mercy by for instance forgiving oppressive debts is a humanitarian obligation of the ruler, at least at Hammurabi's time, and when

[41] There remains the problem of whose debts should be forgiven. Ancient Mesopotamian rulers seemed most concerned with the least well off members of the society and directed their edicts at those groups. One might wonder then about the fairness of not relieving the debts of the next lowest groups in the society. Indeed, perhaps the ancient Biblical idea of debt relief across the board is easier to justify, although apparently harder on the creditors than the practices of the Mesopotamian rulers.

[42] Jeffrey Murphy and Jean Hampton, *Forgiveness and Mercy*, Cambridge: Cambridge University Press, 1988, p. 166. Also see Jeffrey Murphy, *Getting Even: Forgiveness and its Limits*, Oxford: Oxford University Press, 2004.

Hammurabi described his acts of forgiveness he saw them as displaying his virtue as a ruler.

Here at the end, it is worth adding that debt forgiveness measures, as well as other amnesty programs, are not necessarily radical matters. Relieving suffering and harm is of course a good thing in any society, and is an uncontroversial role for a ruler who already in ancient times was often seen as a shepherd of his or her flock, protecting the most vulnerable. And debt relief is not necessarily a bad thing for creditors, especially if the alternative is permanently to disadvantage creditors by outlawing usury altogether, or to have heavy-handed, long-term interference by the government in the economy.[43] These debt forgiveness measures are conservative in that they preserve the status quo with only a temporary change.

Issuing amnesty edicts like those in ancient Mesopotamia can be seen as a conservative not a radical practice, despite how counter-intuitive this sounds. The edicts create a temporary fix – a reshuffling of the cards as some commentators have called it – that allows for the continued existence of laws that are highly favorable to business interests. The cards may be reshuffled, but the card game goes on, yet now in a more equitable manner. But it is the considerations of equity that make these debt forgiveness edicts truly matters of reform, even as it is also true that the edicts conserved the status quo.

43 Of course these are sometimes not the only alternatives. Today garnishing wages would be an option – but this would be very difficult in Mesopotamia since there was not a centralized recording of wages.

5

Freedom and Slavery

In this chapter I will discuss the various ways that slaves were understood to be different from freemen and freewomen in the legal texts from the ancient Near East.[1] It is clear that some slaves were regarded as chattel, as is true in contemporary times. But even as chattel, slaves seem to have had more freedom, or freedoms, than is true today.[2] And in any event there were categories of slavery that were not at all like chattel slaves insofar as the "slave" sometimes had the right and sometimes the means to end the enslavement. In any event, I will argue that in the ancient Near East it is not true that legal thought conceived "freedom as the opposite of slavery," as has been proposed by some contemporary theorists.[3]

In Section 5.1 I will survey the various types of "slave" in the ancient Near East commenting briefly on to what extent they were free. I will primarily look at ancient laws as my guide here. In Section 5.2 and Section 5.3 I will discuss in more depth first chattel and then non-chattel "slavery." Here I will engage with Isaac Mendelsohn and other commentators on slavery in the ancient Near East. In Section 5.4 I will discuss various degrees of freedom, and attempt to sketch an ancient conception of freedom that is different from the two dominant understandings of the concept of freedom in political theory today. In Section 5.5 and Section 5.6 I will continue to sketch an ancient conception of freedom and defend it as a plausible conception of freedom contrary to what commentators often claim about ancient societies and their lack of a conception of freedom.

1 I will draw extensively on Isaac Mendelsohn, *Slavery in the Ancient Near East*, NY: Oxford University Press, 1949.

2 Throughout this chapter I am mainly thinking of how slavery is understood by such theorists today as Phillip Petit and Orlando Patterson.

3 Philip Pettit, *Republicanism: A Theory of Freedom and Government*, Oxford: Oxford University Press, 1997, p. 31.

5.1 TYPES OF SLAVERY IN THE LAWS OF THE ANCIENT NEAR EAST

As Mendelsohn tells us, "The earliest Sumerian terms for male and female slaves are the composite signs *nita+kur* 'male of a foreign country,' and *munus+kur* 'female of a foreign country,' indicating that the first humans to be enslaved in Ancient Mesopotamia were captive foreigners."[4] It is commonly believed that the first slaves in the ancient Near East were those who were captured on the battlefield, or during a military raid on a foreign town. In the case of prisoners of war, there seems to be a sense that by having their lives spared, which could have easily been snuffed out, the captives owe something to those who have spared their lives. What is of interest is that these captives had been, just hours before, adversaries who saw themselves on a relatively similar plane – fellow humans who are forced to fight by their military and political leaders. It is also the case that while one might feel that sparing a person's life gives one a claim on the person's life, nonetheless that life is surely seen as a fellow human life and that situations could have been reversed. Perhaps because of this recognition, the master is generally not granted the legal right to kill the slave in several ancient societies.

We also find that some people became slaves out of indebtedness, as we saw in the last chapter. Either a person could not pay a debt and was forced into enslavement until the debt could be paid off, or a person could not support his family and had to sell his children, wife, or even himself into slavery, or debt servitude, in order to obtain the necessities for survival. Here is one of Hammurabi's laws:

> LH #117 If an obligation is outstanding against a man and he sells or gives into debt service his wife, his son, or his daughter, they shall perform service in the house of their buyer or of the one who holds them in debt service for three years; their release shall be secured in the fourth year.[5]

This case is more like what we might call indentured servitude, although it is entered into "freely" and no matter what the terms were, the slavery was to come to an end after three years, as we saw in the previous chapter. In the Bible the term was seven years. Here are several other Laws of Hammurabi:

> LH #53 If a man neglects to reinforce the embankment ... the man in whose embankment the breach opened shall replace the grain whose loss he caused.
>
> LH #54 If he cannot replace the grain, they shall sell him and his property ...

4 Ibid., p. 1.

5 *Laws of Hammurabi*, in *Law Collections of Mesopotamia and Asia Minor*, second edition, translated by Martha T. Roth, Atlanta, GA: Scholars' Press, 1997, p. 103.

These are two of several laws that speak of a person being sold into slavery because of his poverty.

Mendelsohn says: "Lack of employment, or debts, drove people to sell first their children and then themselves into slavery, even though there are no legal documents concerning self-sale." Nonetheless, Mendelsohn cites documents from Nuzi where a free man "caused himself to enter" into slavery "of his own free will" in exchange for life's necessities.[6]

Also in Hammurabi's laws we find an early reference to different types of slave based on who the owner of the slave was:

> LH #15 If a man [*awilum*] should enable a palace slave [*warad ekallim*], a palace slave woman [*amat ekallim*], a commoner's slave [*warad muskenim*], or a commoner's slave woman [*amat muskenim*] to leave through the main city-gate, he shall be killed.[7]

Here it appears that slaves were either owned by a public institution, the palace of the king, or by a private individual. We also have evidence that slaves were owned by the temples, which like the palace had vast property holdings that needed laborers for their lands to be tilled, planted, and harvested.

It is especially interesting that commoners [*muskenum*] could have slaves since the commoners were not themselves fully free – it was the *awilum*, or upper-class person, who was fully free in ancient Mesopotamian societies, as we will see in the next chapter. So we have the oddity, at least to our ears, of someone who is not fully free being able to own a slave. Indeed, even stranger to contemporary ears, we find slaves who could own other slaves, thereby providing evidence among other things that some slaves could own property. And this sets the stage for thinking that there were people who were called slaves [*warad/amat*] who would not be recognized as slaves today. Indeed, one commentator has said that the Babylonian term that is translated as slave in other contexts merely "denotes a subordinate relationship."[8] A commentator has also suggested that the idea of "serfdom" might better capture some of those people who were called slaves in ancient societies, although this would not encompass all of those called slaves since serfs are those who are attached to the land, and some slaves in Mesopotamia were house slaves.[9] Yet, as we will see later, one of the most significant books on slavery today, that by Orlando Patterson, has seen a continuity of the use of the term slave from these ancient times until the present.

6 Mendelsohn, *Slavery in the Ancient Near East*, pp. 14–17.

7 *Laws of Hammurabi*, p. 84.

8 H. D. Baker, "Degrees of Freedom: Slavery in Mid-First Millennium BC Babylonia," *World Archeology*, Vol. 33, no. 1, June 2001, pp. 18–26, especially p. 20.

9 Ibid.

There appear to be many different forms of slavery or serfdom in the ancient Near East where the terms of the enslavement and the conditions for release from slavery differed widely. As I said, at the beginning of this chapter, slaves initially were foreign fighters who often looked just like the people who were their owners. Indeed, over time, because of debt or poverty, most slaves came from the very same society as their owners. In some cases the slaves had once been fully free. Again with the passage of more time, some slaves produced children who were thus born into slavery and for whom it was not true that they had once been free, although these children could be freed in various ways. Just as there were different types of slavery there were also perhaps different conceptions of freedom in the ancient world as compared to the modern age.

The importance of the fact that many slaves were once free, and could return to being free after a fixed period of time or after paying off their debts, is that the way these slaves were regarded was similar to the way that some free people were regarded – slaves could marry non-slaves for instance. It is also true that often the slaves worked side by side in the fields or in a craft with their owners, where the differences among slave and free person would be not be very great.

There was thus a contrast, evident for the owner of the slave, between the slave who was chattel just like an ox, and the same slave who seemed not very different than a free man. But even here, there remained this dual aspect to being a slave, as someone who was partially free and partially unfree. Mendelsohn has championed the idea that slaves in the ancient Near East were in this half-way position because of the humanitarianism of the people at the time.

> The slave was generally of the same "race," color, speech, and religion as his master. Furthermore, the great majority of the slaves were not even of foreign birth, but came from the ranks of the defaulting debtors, originally free members of the same community. In forming an opinion of the character of Ancient Near Eastern slavery we must keep in mind two factors that caused the system to operate on a level quite different from the institutions of slavery in Rome and in America: (1) slavery was chiefly the result of poverty; and (2) the slave lived and toiled shoulder to shoulder with his master in the field and shop. As a consequence the transition from freedom to slavery and vice versa was fluid. A man could be sold into slavery one day and freed the next, and once freed, all ties with his former master were cut off.[10]

We will explore this curious idea, finding evidence that makes the relation between ancient slavery and freedom even more complex, in what follows.

[10] Mendelsohn, *Slavery in the Ancient Near East*, p. 122.

5.2 FOREIGN SLAVES

In the ancient Near East, some foreign slaves looked more like what we would recognize today as slaves than non-foreign slaves. Most of these people were originally members of enemy armies. Foreign slaves were sometimes obtained by capture in war, or by sale. The sales seem to concern persons who were already slaves in the foreign country. But most foreign slaves were those who were captured and enslaved rather than killed on the battlefield. Once the prisoners were transported back to their captors' city-state, the prisoners became slaves who were owned by the crown or the temple. In this situation the prisoners were effectively chattel property. In some cases, the prisoners were awarded to the victorious soldiers as spoils of battle and became the private property of these soldiers.

In Hammurabi's laws we see that captive soldiers had a right of ransom – a right to buy their way out of enslavement.[11] In this respect even those slaves who most resembled contemporary slaves were in a decidedly different status. Here is one of Hammurabi's laws:

> LH #32 If there is either a soldier or a fisherman who is taken captive while on a royal campaign … if there are sufficient means in his own estate for the redeeming, he shall redeem himself, if there are not sufficient means in his estate to redeem him, he shall be redeemed by his city's temple, if there are not sufficient means in his city's temple to redeem him, the palace shall redeem him …[12]

Practically, the redemption or ransom did not always occur, indeed it seems to have rarely happened. But what is of interest is that Hammurabi seems to have believed that it was a "right" of the captured soldier that he be redeemed if funds could be found.

The idea that a slave had the right to redeem himself is significant for how we understand ancient conceptions of freedom. As we will see slaves in the ancient Near East had various freedoms, such as the freedom to marry or to start a business, but only with their owner's permission. Such freedoms were thus qualified by the restriction that the ultimate authority was the owner. But the right to obtain one's release, even in the case of the chattel slaves who were obtained as prisoners of war, does not seem to be so qualified, at least in Hammurabi's law #32 examined above.

We see another indication of the status of the slave in terms of manumission in the Laws of Lipit-Ishtar (LL):

> LL #25 If a man's slave contests his slave status against his master, and it is proven that his master has been compensated for his slavery two-fold, that slave shall be freed.[13]

[11] *Laws of Hammurabi*, see laws #32 and #133–135, pp. 87, 106–107.

[12] Ibid., p. 87.

[13] *Laws of Lipit-Ishtar*, in *Law Collections From Mesopotamia and Asia Minor*, second edition, translated by Martha T. Roth, Atlanta, GA: Scholars' Press, 1997, pp. 28–29.

Here the slave can obtain freedom contrary to his owner's wishes. It is not clear that the Laws of Lipit-Ishtar grant full freedom of manumission to the slave since the law above does not say that the slave himself can pay the compensation, but this possibility is certainly not ruled out either. In his commentary on the Laws of Lipit-Ishtar, Francis Steele goes so far as to say that "There is no analogue in (Hammurabi's laws) ... we have here provision for a slave to purchase his freedom."[14] As I said, it seems to me that there is at least a suggestion of such a possibility in Hammurabi's law #32. The difference between Hammurabi's law #32 and Lipit-Ishtar's law #14 is that Hammurabi's right of redemption applies only to soldiers who have been captured on the battlefield, whereas the earlier Lipit-Ishtar's law of redemption is not so restricted but seems to apply to all slaves.

The right of self-redemption in these very early legal texts calls for us to consider a very different institution of slavery from what exists in the modern age. Slavery, especially when we are talking of chattel slavery, is defined today as having one's life totally under the authority of the owner of the slave. Freedoms are allowed to the slave, but only at the permission of the owner. Insofar as remaining a slave in ancient times is a freedom left to the slave, slavery here looks more like today's indentured servitude. Indeed, we will see in the next section that this is also confirmed by the fact that other types of slavery were restricted by law in terms of length of servitude and other significant factors that the slave owner did not retain control over.

We find in ancient Biblical texts that manumission was regulated by the provision of the sabbatical or jubilee year – slaves were released from service every seven or 50 years. These Biblical provisions concerned chattel slaves, and the redemption of freedom occasioned by these laws makes of slavery a temporary status[15] (although 50-year intervals will often encompass the entire life of the slave). But these provisions in at least one way are not as important as the self-redemption of the Old Babylonian Laws of Lipit-Ishtar and Hammurabi. The institution of slavery is not only temporary, but the control over the slave's life is much more restricted in the Old Babylonian Laws than in the Biblical provisions because of the control over manumission being in the slave's hands. The idea of self-manumission is highly significant conceptually.

[14] Francis Steele, *The Code of Lipit-Ishtar*, Philadelphia, PA: The University Museum of the University of Pennsylvania, 1948, p. 25 [reprinted from the *American Journal of Archeology*, Volume LII, Number 3, July–September, 1948].

[15] See N. P. Lemche, "The Manumission of Slaves – The Fallow Year – the Sabbatical Year – the Jobel Year," *Vestus Testamentum*, Vol. 26, no. 1 (January 1976), pp. 38–59.

The number of chattel slaves that could buy their freedom was probably not very large, and in any event it is not at all clear that a slave could at any time decide to end his or her own slavery. But there is this possibility, and we need to realize that, as we will see, non-chattel slaves could run their own businesses, so there were at least some slaves who could plausibly be in a position to end their own slavery by redemption garnered from their own earned funds. The salient consideration here is that even in what is often called chattel slavery by the commentators, the slave master did not have full domination over the slave. Laws regulated, and restricted, the relationship between master and chattel slave from some of the earliest recorded periods.

There is also the fact that slaves seem to have been branded for life in Mesopotamia, which tends to count against the freedom of the slaves. Yet, while some of the texts, such as those by Hammurabi, seem to talk of a tattoo or other branding mark, there are also references to the removal of the tattoo. And most significantly, there are some scholars who claim that the branding should be understood metaphorically, and they cite evidence for thinking that the slave's branding was merely that the slave was forced to wear a clay tablet around his or her neck, which of course could be easily removed.

There is also evidence for thinking that the tattoo, even if literal, could be and was often removed, and that certain members of the society were given the task of doing just that.[16] This leads to the conclusion that the idea that even chattel slaves could attain their freedom was something that was common in ancient societies. Indeed, even the chattel slave was in many respects half-free and half not. As we will see, this conclusion is born out even more so in the case of people who were voluntarily or involuntarily enslaved for debt or subsistence reasons.

5.3 DEBT SLAVES AND ADOPTION SLAVES

Another main source of slaves in the ancient Near East is debt. Here we can find several important circumstances that tell us quite a bit about the relation between slavery and freedom in ancient societies. People could find themselves as slaves involuntarily because of failure to pay a debt. Indeed, they could be seized by their creditors and forced into slavery in the creditor's home. People could also voluntarily become slaves as when they sold themselves so as to provide subsistence needs for themselves and their families. Here a person would find someone who was willing to support that person and he or she would then agree to be someone's slave in exchange for such support.

[16] See Mendelsohn, *Slavery in the Ancient Near East*, pp. 42–50.

We also need to consider the ancient institution of adoption that effectively allowed for a form of slavery as well that had an even more open-ended arrangement than did debt slavery or chattel slavery. In some cases the legal enslavement arrangement was called "adoption," in which a member of a family could be taken into another family. But this "adoption" was surely a misnomer since the adoptee was made a servant of the adopter and sustenance was the only thing that was provided for the adoptee. Various ancient laws deal with adoptees and other slaves who declared that they no longer wished to be slaves.

Of perhaps greater interest is that slaves could marry non-slaves and the legal status of the children of such marriages is discussed in the ancient laws. Mendelsohn says that "marriages between freeborn women and slaves were common in Ancient Babylonia."[17] If a slave and a free woman decide to wed it is unclear whether the master of the slave must give his permission. And the children of the marriage are sometimes considered free and sometimes not. Consider one of Hammurabi's laws:

> LH #175 If a slave of the palace or a slave of a commoner (*muskenum*) marries a woman of the *awilu*-class and she then bears children, the owner of the slave will have no claims of the children of the woman of the *awilu*-class.[18]

If the master has complete control over the life of the slave one would have thought that he also has control over the offspring of the slave, but this seems not to be the case.

Hammurabi's law #176, is especially interesting in that it contemplates the situation where the free woman marries a slave and "enters the house of the slave" where they "establish a household and accumulate possessions."[19] This gives us the curious picture of a free woman who lives in slave quarters but where she and a slave have the freedom to accumulate possessions, and this is seemingly not up to the arbitrary will of the master of the slave. Indeed, any children that the free woman brings into the household cannot be taken as slaves and must be allowed to go free after the free woman dies or leaves the household, although not before. This also seems to hold true of a marriage between a free man and a slave woman.[20]

If a slave and her master produce children, the status of the children is up to the master, but the master has the curious ability to make these children equal to his free children. Here is another of Hammurabi's laws:

> LH #170 If a man's first-ranking wife bears him children and his slave woman bears him children, and the father during his lifetime then declares to (or: concerning)

17 Mendelsohn, *Slavery in the Ancient Near East*, p. 55.
18 *Laws of Hammurabi*, p. 115.
19 Ibid., p. 115.
20 Mendelsohn, *Slavery in the Ancient Near East*, p. 56.

> the children whom the slave woman bore to him, "My children," and he reckons them with the children of the first-ranking wife – after the father goes to his fate, the children of the first-ranking wife and the children of the slave woman shall equally divide the property of the paternal estate ...[21]

Here we find the possibility that the children of a slave woman could be regarded as not only free but as having equal rights to the children who are born free. And while the determination of status is by the master, the change in status effectuated by the master remains true after his death.

In connection to the discussion of the previous section, debt slaves were slaves as long as they could not pay off their debts. For both kinds of debt slaves, those who were forced into slavery and those who chose it, their slavery could be ended by paying off the debt that had caused their involuntary enslavement or that had accrued for providing their sustenance. In the case of voluntary enslavement, manumission could be obtained when they paid back what had been provided to maintain them over time.

In various respects, the whole idea of debt slavery is very different from slavery in the twentieth century CE. While one is a debt slave it may be true that the slave is exposed "to the arbitrary will of another."[22] But in at least many cases of debt slavery in the ancient Near East, the slave master did not have the right to hold a slave in servitude after the slave had met certain conditions – ending slavery was not "up to the arbitrary will of another." And the children of slaves were not necessarily made slaves, despite what the slave owner may desire.

In addition, while the compensations for injury to a slave were less than that for an injury to a free person, the slave was in many ways considered like a free person. And punishments of slaves for injuries caused by these slaves were often harsher than the punishments for those same injuries caused by free persons. But even concerning such differential punishments, Mendelsohn says the following:

> This fact, namely, that the manner of punishment was prescribed by law and custom and was not left to the discretion of the master, shows that the slave was considered a human being and consequently the master had no power over his life and could not kill him with impunity.[23]

Indeed, Mendelsohn says he is forced to the contradictory conclusion that "on the one hand, the slave was considered as possessing the qualities of a human being while on the other hand, he was recognized as being void of the same and regarded as a mere thing."[24]

[21] *Laws of Hammurabi*, pp. 115–116.

[22] Pettit, *Republicanism*, pp. 31–32.

[23] Mendelsohn, *Slavery in the Ancient Near East*, p. 66.

[24] Ibid., p. 64.

The kind of service that many slaves occupied in ancient societies made it difficult for them to be seen as mere chattel in all respects. This is especially easy to see in the case of *muskenum*, someone who was himself (or herself) only partially free, owning slaves. Here the master was not himself (or herself) fully free. And the types of service of the slave, such as tilling fields, were not different from what the master was also doing – indeed, as indicated earlier, they apparently worked side by side doing the same jobs in the small-scale agricultural economy of ancient societies.

We also find that some slaves were allowed to become craftsmen and even to own and operate their own businesses – apparently resulting in some slaves becoming quite wealthy. By the Neo-Babylonian period (middle of the first millennium BCE) "slaves appear as lessors and lessees of land" contracts, and there is some evidence in the Late Assyrian period that slaves "could themselves own slaves."[25] At this point, slaves seem even freer than they were in Hammurabi's time. So, it is not possible to argue that the idea of being a slave came to have more and more restrictions on the slave's freedom over time, at least in ancient Mesopotamia. Instead it appears that the ancient ideas of slavery were simply quite different from later conceptions of slavery.

Finally, adding to the conclusion that in Babylonia some slaves' status was that of being both free and unfree, we saw in the previous chapter that there were institutions of debt forgiveness in ancient Babylonia that were aimed at freeing especially those debtors who were in debt enslavement. For more than a hundred years in Babylonia, during the first year of a new king's reign it was common that an edict was issued freeing debtors, especially debt slaves. And we also confront the fact that slaves in ancient times, while they were able to be bought and sold as chattel, could also, in effect, buy themselves, thereby throwing open the relation between slavery and freedom in ancient times. It is certainly not true that all forms of ancient slavery were the antithesis of freedom.

As a conceptual matter we are presented with ways of thinking of slavery that are very different from the way we think of slavery today. I am not suggesting that we should form institutions today on the model of ancient slavery. But I am suggesting that the way we think of freedom may be enhanced by considering models of slavery that do not hold that slavery is the antithesis of freedom. My suggestion is that there may be models of understanding freedom that are more subtle and variegated than the dominant models we have today, especially those retained from nineteenth century CE liberalism and seventeenth century CE neo-Republicanism. I next turn to these models before contrasting them with the ways that slavery seems to have been understood in ancient times.

[25] Mendelsohn, *Slavery in the Ancient Near East*, pp. 68–69.

5.4 TWO MODERN CONCEPTIONS OF FREEDOM

A free person has sometimes been seen as one who is not constrained by the will of another and can act as he or she wishes. Modern conceptions of freedom have focused, on the one hand, on the lack of restraint and, on the other hand, on the lack of domination. At first sight this idea is true in the ideal rather than in reality since no one is truly able to do whatever he or she wishes. There are two broad conceptions of freedom in the modern age that theorists have identified: the neo-Roman and the liberal. In this section I will explore these ideas and their variations.

In the modern era, the best known conception of freedom is that put forth by John Stuart Mill. Mill described "the appropriate realm of human liberty" as encompassing:

> first, the inward domain of consciousness; demanding the liberty of conscience in the most comprehensive sense; liberty of thought and feeling; absolute freedom of opinion and sentiment on all subjects, practical or speculative, scientific, moral, or theological ... Secondly ... liberty of tastes and pursuits ... Thirdly ... freedom to unite for any purpose not involving harm to others ...[26]

Mill also gave us the famous formulation of when society can legitimately restrict individual freedom:

> the sole end for which mankind are warranted, individually or collectively, in interfering with the liberty of action of any member, is self-protection ... the only purpose for which power can be rightfully exercised over any member of a civilized community, against his will, is to prevent harm to others ... In that part which merely concerns himself, his independence is, of right, absolute. Over himself, over his own body and mind, the individual is sovereign.[27]

This is the Millian theory of freedom as self-legislation and encompasses the idea that freedom is action which is not interfered with.

It has been a matter of debate whether the Millian theory of freedom is purely episodic, where freedom is measured day by day and action by action, or whether there is a more holistic understanding of freedom expressed by Mill which would mean that a life is not free if it can be interfered with. Answering this question has proved difficult and has spawned a different way to understand freedom.

Several contemporary theorists have recently articulated a different conception of freedom, which is said to owe its origin to Roman times, the idea of freedom as non-domination. As Philip Pettit has said:

[26] John Stuart Mill, *On Liberty* (1859), edited by Stefan Collini, Cambridge: Cambridge University Press, 1989, pp. 15–16.

[27] Ibid., p. 13.

> in the republican tradition, by contrast with the modernist approach, liberty is always cast in terms of the opposition between *liber* and *servus*, citizen and slave. The condition of liberty is explicated as the status of someone who, unlike the slave, is not subject to the arbitrary power of another: that is, someone who is not dominated by anyone else. Thus, the condition of liberty is explicated in such a way that there may be loss of liberty without any actual interference: there may be enslavement and domination without interference, as in the scenario of the non-interfering master.[28]

This model of freedom as non-domination is said to be found in its rudimentary form in the work of Roman legal theorists, and then formulated in its neo-Roman form in the 17th and 18th centuries CE.

Freedom as non-domination is freedom understood in terms of social or legal status; whereas freedom as non-interference is freedom understood in terms of a lack of restraints on action. In some respects these views differ concerning what they think is the object of freedom: the isolated individual or the embedded citizen. So, the views do not stand as completely opposed to one another. Millian freedom is social freedom whereas neo-Roman freedom is largely political freedom. Yet, as we will see in this section, both of these conceptions of freedom are useful in understanding how to characterize freedom in ancient legal thought.

The neo-Roman idea that freedom is simply non-domination explicitly linked freedom to the absence of slavery. In this view, the slave was not in any way free because he was constantly subject to the arbitrary will of the master. Quentin Skinner helpfully qualifies the central claim of the neo-Roman conception of freedom: "What the neo-Roman writers repudiate *avant la letter* is the key assumption of classical liberalism to the effect that force or the coercive threat of it constitute the only forms of constraint."[29] So Skinner then characterizes the liberal position of Hobbes, Blackstone and the utilitarians as defining liberty in such a way that liberty is infringed only by the force of "imprisonment or restraint."[30]

It is today assumed that liberal theory could allow for slaves to be free; neo-Roman theory could not. Yet, what we have seen is that slaves in the ancient Near East seemed to be both free and not free, seemingly suggesting that there is a conception of freedom that lies in between liberal and neo-Roman conceptions of freedom. In order to begin to understand what the ancient legal conception of freedom might be like let us explore in more detail what is involved in the claims about slavery attributable to liberal and neo-Roman theorizing.

[28] Pettit, *Republicanism*, p. 31.

[29] Quentin Skinner, *Liberty before Liberalism*, Cambridge: Cambridge University Press, 1998, p. 84.

[30] Ibid., p. 97 n.95.

For the neo-Roman theorists, a slave might appear to be free insofar as his master was lenient and even benevolent in treating the slave. Skinner refers to a comedy by Plautus, where: "Due to the fact that his master is benevolent and usually absent, Tranio [the slave] is able to boast that he has never suffered any direct oppression at all."[31] The neo-Roman theorists see this slave as unfree despite his boasts. Tranio is "'subject to the jurisdiction of someone else' and ... consequently 'within the power' of another person." The slave, even when able to act seemingly in all he does as he wishes, and never suffers restraint at the hands of his master, is still not free because of being in the power of another person and not within his own "jurisdiction."[32] Given what we have seen of slavery in ancient Mesopotamia, we should note the strong counter-intuitive sound to the claims that the true slave cannot be free at all.

For the classical liberal theorist, a slave could be free in a wide array of contexts. Indeed, slavery and freedom are compatible concepts for the liberal theorist. Most of the types of freedom that Mill regards as core freedoms are those of the inner life of the individual, such as freedom of conscience and thought. But there are also freedoms of action, and these would seem at least sometimes to be constrained in slavery. But for our purposes the most interesting of the Millian ideas is that "over his body and mind the [free] individual is sovereign." The slave may have control of his mind, but his body is not his, at least in terms of restraints placed upon the exercise of his body.

Yet, if the slave is in control of whether he lives or dies, and even whether he remains a slave or not, the liberal theorist would provide us with some reasons to think that the slave is free, in that respect. And insofar as the slave remains under the control of the master, even if the master does not exercise such power, the slave is not free. So, we have come to the point where there might be a conception of freedom that is neither defined exclusively in terms of restraint or in terms of domination. We will have come to a conception of how we can have partial freedom, perhaps exhibited by the kind of slavery that existed in ancient legal thought.

5.5 ASSESSING ANCIENT CONCEPTIONS OF FREEDOM

The neo-Roman (Republican) conception of freedom that is supported by Quentin Skinner and Philip Pettit does not easily embrace the idea of freedom expressed in ancient legal texts. In the ancient view I have sketched, there is a sense that the slave is constrained by the will of another person, and yet that constraint is itself limited by the laws of the society that specify:

[31] Ibid., p. 40.
[32] Ibid., p. 41.

(a) that there is a limit of the range of that domination, expressly excluding the taking of the life of slave by his master;
(b) that manumission can occur, even contrary to the wishes of the slave's master;
(c) that the master is required to end the enslavement at certain times, as when a debt amnesty is declared;
(d) and that the children of the slave and the property of the slave can, in certain circumstances, be controlled by the slave even contrary to the explicit wishes of the slave's master.

The laws of the society constrain the will of the slave's master in these, and possibly other, ways. So while the slave can be sold as if he or she were an ox or a sheep, the slave retains freedoms that the master is not empowered to countermand.

Yet, the classical liberal (Millian) conception of freedom also does not capture the freedom of the ancient slave. Freedom, as seen in the ancient conceptions of slavery, is not a matter of not having impediments to one's action either in terms of physical restraint or coercive threats. It is perhaps harder to see what is at stake here than in the neo-Roman conception of freedom.

Like the liberal theorist, the ancient legal thinker seems to conceive of freedom as a bundle of "rights," not as a matter of one overwhelming condition. Unlike the liberal theorist, the ancient legal thinker recognizes that the slave would not be fully free if concerning a large part of his life his or her master legally could, but normally does not, interfere.

But unlike some liberal and neo-Roman conceptions of freedom, the ancient legal thinker does not think that either one was free or one was not. Freedom for the ancient legal texts we have considered is not merely a matter of being dominated or not. The slave's life could be very similar to the free man's life, or the commoner's life. The freedoms that the slave could pursue, such as the freedom to marry or to start a business were real freedoms, although they were constrained by the need to seek permission from the slave-holder to do these things. Having to seek permission to do such significant things as marry or start a business were important limitations – perhaps so important as to make us think that the ancient slave was unfree.

Yet, the one salient freedom, to redeem his free status and stop being a slave, was not constrained by the slave's master in many cases. Ultimately, in these cases, redemption was a matter of legal right. This was at least partially due to the fact that the master did not have a right over the slave's life. And in all cases, the slave's master had no right to kill the slave or to prevent the slave from redeeming his status as a free man. The master could not continue to restrain the slave if the slave had met the terms of such redemption – normally accomplished by compensating the master for the cost of providing sustenance for the slave and any previously accrued debts the slave owed to the master.

It was true that the slave was at the beck and call of the master, and over most of the slave's life the master could exert his or her arbitrary will. Even though this seems rarely to have happened, the neo-Roman theorists are correct to say that this made the slave, in this respect, unfree. But as noted above the master was also constrained by the laws, especially concerning two of the most important aspects of the life of the slave, his continued existence and his legitimate attempts to become free. The master was in this respect unfree in terms of what he could do to the slave concerning what was most important in the life of the slave. And in this sense the slave was free in respect to the disposition of his life and the length of his enslavement. From the perspective of the neo-Roman theorist today it also matters that the slave was not a participant in the process that made, interpreted, or applied the laws. So, in this respect the slave was also unfree, but so were many other people in ancient societies. Importantly, the ancient slave was not the antithesis of freedom but also was not fully free. Falk says:

> We might gain insight by looking briefly at how slaves were regarded in Biblical times. We find that by law, a slave was entitled to his freedom if he had lost a limb by his master's act. A female slave was likewise freed, if her owner failed to make her his wife or the wife of a member of his family, although he had purchased her for this purpose.[33]

The Biblical law here extends further the idea that masters were restricted in what they could do to their slaves. Not only could they not kill their slaves, but also they could not cause a slave to lose a limb. This is to say that the slave's body, concerning many matters, was his or her own even as the slave was the "chattel" of the slave's master.

Slaves could be sold and bought in very similar ways to any other property. One might then think that slaves had no freedom – for freedom is a human trait yet slaves were treated like oxen and sheep. But such a view would run up against the restrictions we have discussed on how slaves could be treated by their masters. There were no laws on the killing or maiming of an ox or a sheep, and certainly not on their release from captivity. It is thus perhaps not appropriate to think of ancient slaves as chattel in the way we have understood them in contemporary times.

I should mention a seemingly unique law in the Bible that seems to say that runaway slaves are not to be returned:

> Thou shalt not deliver unto his master the servant which is escaped from his master unto thee:

[33] Ze'ev W. Falk, *Hebrew Law in Biblical Times*, Provo, UT: Brigham Young University Press, 2001, p. 117.

> He shall dwell with thee, even among you, in that place which he shall choose in one of thy gates, where it liketh him best: thou shalt not oppress him.[34]

This passage has had many quite different interpretations over the years, but it is undeniable that the slave is here said to have two freedoms: the right to run away, and the right to choose where to live afterward. Here it is even less appropriate to think of slaves in ancient times as theorists do today.

What we have in the ancient legal conception of freedom is a model that seems to occupy a position in between the neo-Roman and classical liberal conceptions. Freedom was a bundle-concept not a concept that was simply either present or not. And so the decision of whether to call the slave free or not depended on which freedoms one was referring to. The point is that the bundle of freedoms of the slave is significant and leads to the conclusion that ancient slavery was not the antithesis of freedom. Freedom and also slavery came in degrees.

For ancient legal thought, freedom seemed to mean that in certain situations and relative to certain constraints, one could choose as one wished. Freedom did not mean that one was unconstrained. More importantly it made sense to think of freedoms, rather than freedom simpliciter, of a slave or of a freeman or of someone who was in between these two social statuses, the commoner (*muskenum*). Similarly women were free in various domains and in various circumstances, even as they were constrained by their husbands or fathers, and even as they were constrained by the law. It is perhaps obvious by now that ancient legal thought expressed a view of freedom that is different from those of the modern age. And it was different enough so as to make it hard for us today to understand such institutions as that of ancient slavery if we try to pigeon-hole it into our modern conceptions. At the same time, the ancient conception of freedom, especially concerning the slave, is not so different from our own understandings of freedom so that we are left utterly mystified. Rather, hopefully we can look at freedom anew, through the eyes of these ancient texts.

5.6 THE RELATIONSHIP OF ANCIENT FREEDOM AND SLAVERY

Orlando Patterson has written important works on the concept of slavery and its relationship to freedom. Here is his assessment of the period we have focused on:

> What genuine slavery existed in the ancient Near Eastern societies was mainly the personal and household kind, although in various periods temple slaves did perform important economic tasks. Significantly, it was precisely slaves of the temple

[34] Deuteronomy 23 15–16. See Richard H. Hiers, *Justice and Compassion in Biblical Law*, NY: Continuum Publishers, 2009, pp. 203–204 for a commentary on this passage.

> who were never manumitted. There is no evidence that a freedman class ever existed in any of these ancient civilizations.[35]

Here Patterson raises an interesting question of whether what was called slavery in the ancient Near Eastern legal texts was really the same as slavery understood today. Patterson is justly famous for arguing that true slavery involved "social death," the complete elimination of the person who was the slave, with no legal rights at all.[36] As we have seen, "slaves" in the ancient Near East were afforded rights, including the right not to be killed by their masters. So, maybe there were no true slaves in the ancient Near East.

But Patterson argues that there were true slaves in the ancient Near East and that while there was a very limited right of manumission, slaves rarely exercised this right:

> The legal evidence clearly indicates that slaves could be manumitted and that running away was sufficiently important a problem to justify harsh, and repeatedly enacted, laws against harboring them. The desire for personal freedom, then, was as much a fact of life as slavery … However, the evidence is equally conclusive that personal freedom never became a value *of any importance* in any of these societies … It would seem that an additional factor explaining the extraordinary absence of records on manumission was the unwillingness of wealthy slaves to be manumitted. They did not want freedom, because there was no social space for the ambitious freedman, and it was not a valued state; indeed, being free involved a loss of status and power.[37]

Again, assuming that there were "slaves" in the ancient Near East, what Patterson here says about them conflicts with what I set out earlier.

There is evidence that slaves were freed, and that evidence, while not abundant, seems clear enough – if not, why were so many of the codes of laws concerned with manumission? Perhaps more importantly, there seems to be evidence, contrary to what Patterson alleges, that some former slaves attained a secure place in ancient societies. In fact, in ancient Egypt some former slaves attained high status. There is also evidence that we will examine in the next chapter that those who were not in the class of freemen, those who were commoners (*muskenum*) but not slaves, had limited and valued freedoms.

As to the claim that freedom was not a valued state for the slave, we can look to the Laws of Hammurabi where a disobedient son or daughter was punishable by being enslaved, certainly not a state that one would want to attain if it were thought that it was a punishment. And we can also note that injuries to slaves were valued

35 Orlando Patterson, *Freedom, Vol. 1: Freedom in the Making of Western Culture*, NY: Basic Books, 1991, p. 34.

36 See Orlando Patterson, *Slavery and Social Death*, Cambridge, MA: Harvard University Press, 1982.

37 Patterson, *Freedom*, pp. 34–35.

less than the same injuries to freemen or commoners. There was a clear social hierarchy especially in ancient Mesopotamia, and those at the top of the hierarchy were in valued positions because of the extent of their freedom.

Moving to the conceptual realm, Patterson argues that some may have valued a free status but this was not the same as valuing freedom:

> valuing the status of being a freeman did not necessarily entail valuing freedom as an ideal to be *actively* pursued. And it was a far cry from identifying it with the right to participate in the running of one's community. The freeman in simple and archaic society valued his free status, but not his freedom. The free group was a merely collective status; it never became a positively active group.[38]

Patterson here denies what seems obvious from our analysis of the evidence: that slaves wished to be free, since in many cases freedom was a state the slave had known prior to enslavement.

Yet, the point Patterson is making is more subtle than one might think from what I have quoted so far. Indeed, the idea of personal freedom contains a fairly stringent set of conditions that, as with Pettit's view examined earlier, seem not to be easily, if ever, realized. Patterson claims that:

> Personal freedom, at its most elementary, gives a person the sense that one, on the one hand, is not being coerced or restrained by another person in doing something desired and, on the other hand, the conviction that one can do as one pleases within the limits of that other person's desire to do the same. Both aspects, negative and positive, lie and have always lain at the heart of the common, and commonsense, conception, whatever philosophers may think.[39]

In addition to being too strict a requirement, there is also no reason to think that the "slaves" we have examined in ancient legal thought could not attain some degree of freedom.

Patterson's conception of slavery as social death seems unlikely to be realized very often in ancient, or modern, societies. And the underlying conception of freedom does not help us understand ancient slavery and its relationship to freedom. The ways slaves were treated in the laws of Babylonia as well as in the laws of the Bible, were manifestly humane in many respects, especially in granting to slaves the right that their masters not kill them. The freedom to live and not to be threatened with death turns out to be very important and does not sit well with Patterson's theory of slavery as social death.

It remains to consider again whether slavery of the ancient Near East legal texts is truly slavery, especially since some freedoms were legally guaranteed to slaves.

38 Ibid., p. 42.
39 Ibid., p. 3.

When Patterson considered one of the main texts I have consulted, he dismisses the abundant evidence from the legal texts by pointing out that we nonetheless lack evidence that these laws were applied. Granting the lack of such evidence is a fact, Mendelsohn suggests, however, that the lack of evidence of manumission in the ancient Near East is due to the fact that slaves were too poor generally to record their manumission status in documents that were likely to be preserved for posterity. It is also true that there is very little evidence of the application of any of the laws of these ancient "codes" to particular cases. Yet, as I have argued in an earlier chapter, in trying to understand ancient legal thought, the textual documents of the law "codes" give us a very good idea of how people thought about legal matters, even if it may be that it does not necessarily give us a good idea of ancient practices.

6

Class, Legal Status, and Equality

It is often said that the Babylonian laws, especially the Laws of Hammurabi, are not as humane as other ancient laws such as the laws of the Bible, because Hammurabi's laws track hierarchical social status rather than treating all equally before the law.[1] And reference is made in particular to the way that the Laws of Hammurabi differ significantly if the person in question is a member of an upper class (*awilum*) as opposed to a lower class (*muskenum*).[2] The suggestion is that the Laws of Hammurabi treated the *awilum* class better than the *muskenum* class. In this chapter I will discuss this issue and argue that while there is class differentiation in Hammurabi's laws, there are often explanations that refer to humane reasons.

In Mesopotamian legal codes there is a distinction among three legal status categories. Driver and Miles summarize matters thus: "Clearly, then, the *muskenum* is inferior in rank and circumstances to the ordinary free man but superior to the free man's slave."[3] The *muskenum* was under the protection of the crown, even perhaps "a servant of the palace" but was able to make a marriage of the ordinary type and even to own slaves.[4] This category of legal status is relatively unique in ancient societies. In this chapter I will survey the various ways that the *muskenum* was understood to be different from freemen and from slaves in Mesopotamian legal texts.

Conceptually, this chapter focuses on the idea of equality before the law, an idea often said to be missing in ancient legal thought. Equality before the law does not

1 See Hans Jochem Boecker, *Law and the Administration of Justice in the Old Testament and Ancient East*, translated by Jeremy Moiser, Minneapolis: Augsburg Publishing House, 1980, p. 123: "The most striking point about these prescriptions is the fact that the penalties differ according to the social standing of the injured party."

2 The idea of class I will employ in this chapter is a modern notion. There were categories of differential social standing in ancient times, but the association with economics is not found. Rather there is something closer to caste in ancient times, although even here the fit is not precise.

3 Godfrey Rolles Driver and J. C. Miles, *The Babylonian Laws*, Oxford: Oxford University Press, 1952, Vol. 1, p. 92.

4 Ibid., p. 93.

mean that everyone is treated exactly the same. It is the hallmark of a legal system that it deals differently when differential treatment is merited. The problem is that if there are class-based differentiations, they appear to be unfair since class is not a relevant difference to warrant differential legal treatment. And while this idea is largely correct, I will argue that certain cases are justified, such as when a person has a status as a member of an oppressed group and is treated better at law than non-oppressed class members. We might initially also realize that sometimes group identification is merely short-hand for collections of people who have similar merit or demerit that the law should address by differential treatment.

Another theme of the chapter is that Mesopotamian legal thought recognized that some people could be formally free and yet not free in substance. In giving these people their own category, Mesopotamian legal thinkers may appear to be doing something wrong in consigning these people to a lower status. Yet, it is my contention that the forthright legal recognition of this intermediary class is more honest, and ultimately more progressive, than thinking that people who were formally free, were truly free, even though their lives were greatly encumbered by social norms and practices.

This chapter is related to the previous chapter on slavery and a later chapter on *lex talionis*. In the chapter on slavery I argued that in some ancient societies the slave was not deprived of all freedoms, in contrast to what seems to be true in later societies. And in the chapter on *lex talionis* I will argue that the talionic punishments seem to be reserved for the *awilum* class, whereas the *muskenum* class punishments were compensatory not talionic. The current chapter is on the legal status of the *awilum* and *muskenum* classes and continues one of the main themes of my work in discussing possible humanitarian understanding of ancient Babylonian law.

6.1 THE *MUSKENUM* IN ANCIENT BABYLONIA

Driver and Miles have said of the *muskenum* of ancient times, that "if he was not a slave, he was also not a freeman."[5] Let us begin by looking at one of the Laws of Eshnunna, propounded just a few years before Hammurabi's laws:

> LE #50 If a military governor, a governor of the canal system, or any person in a position of authority seizes a fugitive slave, fugitive slave woman, stray ox, or stray donkey, belonging either to the palace or to a commoner (*muskenum*), and does not lead it to Eshnunna but detains it in his house and allows more than one month to elapse, the palace shall bring a charge of theft against him.[6]

[5] Ibid., p. 94.

[6] *Laws of Eshnunna*, in *Law Collections from Mesopotamia and Asia Minor*, second edition, translated by Martha T. Roth, Atlanta, GA: Scholars' Press, 1997, pp. 66–67.

Here the member of the *muskenum* class is associated with the palace. Indeed, notice that the palace is entitled to bring charges against the thief for itself but also for the *muskenum*, thereby indicating an even closer connection than merely that the *muskenum* worked for the palace.

In the Laws of Hammurabi we also find a close association between *muskenum* and the palace:

> LH #15 If a man should enable a palace slave, a palace slave woman, a commoner's (*muskenum*) slave, or a commoner's slave woman, to leave through the main gate, he shall be killed.[7]

In light of these passages, Albrecht Goetze says that the *muskenum* is a class of people "attached to the palace."[8]

There is a controversy about how to understand the Babylonian class of the *muskenum*. Everyone agrees that the *muskenum* was a lower class than the freeman (*awilum*), and that the *muskenum* was somewhat above the slave (*wardum*) in the social hierarchy. But there is significant disagreement about to what extent the *muskenum* was free and to what extent he was like the slave. Some, like Martha Roth, use the broad term "commoner" to translate *muskenum*. This is similar to those like Reuven Yaron, who translates *muskenum* as simply "subject."[9] Others use such terms as "crown dependent," and "villein,"[10] giving *muskenum* a narrower meaning. The Encyclopedia Britannica seems to me rightly to employ the narrower sense of *muskenum* as "persons employed by the palace who could be given land in usufruct without receiving it as property."

The term "*muskenum*" is thought to be derived from a "rare Sumerian verb *sukenum* – 'to bow, to kow-tow.'"[11] It also seems to be that the term is associated with some kind of "duty or service."[12] Perhaps as a result of having duties that tie the *muskenum* to the palace's lands, the *muskenum* "is a protected person closely associated with the state." One text specifically mentions that the state took measures to keep the *muskenum* from starving – possibly indicating that the *muskenum* was a "retainer" of the palace.[13] Finkelstein says that the members of the *muskenum*

[7] Ibid., p. 84.
[8] Albrecht Goetze, "The Laws of Eshnunna," *The Annual of the American Schools of Oriental Research*, Vol. 31, 1951–1952, pp. 1–197, p. 131.
[9] Reven Yaron, *The Laws of Eshnunna*, second revised edition, Jerusalem/Leiden: The Magnes Press, E. J. Brill, 1988, p. 133.
[10] Driver and Miles, *The Babylonian Laws*, Vol. 1, p. 91.
[11] Yaron, *The Laws of Eshnunna*, p. 133.
[12] See Driver and Miles, *The Babylonian Laws*, p. 91.
[13] E. A. Speiser, "The *Muskenum*," *Orientalia*, Vol. 27, no. 1 (1958), 19–28, pp. 23–24.

class "were personally 'free' but were economically dependent on the Crown either wholly or in large part."[14]

There are two very intriguing suggestions made by scholars writing half a century apart. Here is a turn-of-the-century (nineteenth to twentieth century CE) author:

> There is no legal disability on the part of the *muskenum*; he is merely a person of less consideration. Whether or not his ranks were recruited from the children of slaves is not clear, but it is very probable that they were.[15]

Fifty years later we find this account of a middle class in the Hittite Laws, which the author says must have been similar to the *muskenum*.[16] Here is his account of this middle class of persons:

> The half-free men, or, rather, the middle and lower classes, must have comprised the semi-free persons who did not belong to the class of free men nor to the slave class. Among them partly must be counted the liegemen, soldiers, and ex-servicemen (who were frequently given plots of land for cultivation on their discharge); semi-free peasants, semi-free tenants, and people in a similar position. The status of all these men may have been legally identical; they seem to have been owned by their masters, in practice their position differed greatly from that of the mass of ordinary slaves and thus they can reasonably be regarded as half-free men.[17]

Both of these scholars suggest that the *muskenum* was attached to the palace and also that perhaps some of the *muskenum* were the offspring of slaves. This could help us solve a problem from our previous chapter about whether there was a social place for manumitted slaves. Although we should note that Greengus claims that a different social group, the "*hupsu*, seem to have been manumitted slaves."[18]

In ancient Egypt, there was also a "commoner" (*rekhyt*) class that included serfs as well who were attached to land and hence not free but rather "unfree" at least as compared to the higher classes.[19] It is unclear whether the laws of ancient Egypt were graded according to these social class distinctions. At least in part, this unclarity is due to the paucity of written legal texts from ancient Egypt on this topic.

Despite what some have said in comparing the classlessness of the ancient Israelites to the class-based laws of Mesopotamia, there is good evidence to think

14 J. J. Finkelstein, "The Ox that Gored," *Transactions of the American Philosophical Society*, Vol. 71, part 2, 1981, p. 32.

15 C. H. W. Johns, *Babylonian and Assyrian Laws, Contracts and Letters*, Edinburgh: T & T Clark, 1904, p. 75.

16 E. Neufeld, *The Hittite Laws*, London: Luzac and Co. Ltd, 1951, p. 119.

17 Ibid., p. 120.

18 Samuel Greengus, "Legal and Social Institutions of Ancient Mesopotamia," in *Civilizations of the Ancient Near East*, edited by Jack M. Sasson, NY: Charles Scribner's Sons, 1995, Vol. 1, p. 477.

19 See David Lorton, "Legal and Social Institutions of Pharaonic Egypt," in *Civilizations of the Ancient Near East*, edited by Jack M. Sasson, NY: Charles Scribner's Sons, 1995, Vol. 1, pp. 345–362, pp. 351–352.

that there were classes in the ancient Israelites that were reflected in law. Various laws distinguished between Hebrews and non-Hebrews. While these social categories are predominantly identified religiously there was a strong sense of social class differentiation here as well. One major difference between ancient Mesopotamia and ancient Israelites is that class was a matter of "blood ties" and "kinship ties" in the ancient Israelites, whereas in Mesopotamia class divisions, especially those recognized at law, were largely not based on blood or kinship.[20] But that there are class divisions in the laws is not a matter of serious debate once the term class is slightly expanded to encompass blood or kinship groups. The ancient Biblical law treated people differently based on their class, but we do not have a clear sense that there was anything like a *muskenum* class in the ancient Israelites. If, though, one thinks of the broader category of "the poor man" there are laws in the Bible that address this "class" of people.[21]

6.2 PROTECTING THE *MUSKENUM* CLASS?

If we think of the members of the *muskenum* class as being specially protected by the palace, we can make sense of some of the disparate treatment of the *muskenum* and *awilum* classes in Hammurabi's laws. Let us consider some of the laws that displayed *lex talionis*.

> LH #196 If an *awilu* should blind the eye of another *awilu*, they shall blind his eye.
>
> LH #197 If he should break the bone of another *awilu*, they shall break his bone.
>
> LH #198 If he should blind the eye of a commoner (*muskenum*), or break the bone of a commoner (*muskenum*), he shall weigh and deliver 60 shekels of silver.
>
> LH #200 If an *awilu* should knock out the tooth of another *awilu* of his own rank, they shall knock out his tooth.
>
> LH #201 If he should knock out the tooth of a commoner (*muskenum*), he shall weigh and deliver 20 shekels of silver.[22]

Notice that the talionic penalty is reserved for the case where a member of the *awilum* class blinds, breaks a bone, or knocks out a tooth of a fellow *awilum*. These penalties, or punishments, are much more severe than the penalties for inflicting these injuries on a member of the *muskenum* class.

[20] See Pamela Barmash, *Homicide in the Biblical World*, NY: Cambridge University Press, 2005, p. 49. Also see Hector Avalos, "Legal and Social Institutions in Canaan and Ancient Israel," in *Civilizations of the Ancient Near East*, edited by Jack M. Sasson, NY: Charles Scribner's Sons, 1995, Vol. 1, pp. 615–631.

[21] See Stanley A. Cook, *The Laws of Moses and the Code of Hammurabi*, London: Adam and Charles Black, 1903, Chapter 8.

[22] *Laws of Hammurabi*, p. 121.

It is often remarked that the penalties are more severe when the victim is an *awilum* than a *muskenum*; but I wish to focus on what the victim gets for his injury. If the victim is a *muskenum*, he will get compensation; if he is an *awilum* he will not get anything except perhaps the satisfaction of seeing his assailant injured. There is thus a sense that the Laws of Hammurabi provide a level of protection to an injured *muskenum* that is not afforded to an injured *awilum*. Because of his dependent status, a *muskenum* can ill afford to have a lost limb – and the compensation will help him to keep afloat economically. No such protection is offered to an *awilum* in these laws.

Another indication of how Hammurabi's laws might seem to protect the dependent *muskenum* is in the laws concerning divorce:

> LH #139 If there is no bridewealth, he shall give her 60 shekels of silver as a divorce settlement.
>
> LH #140 If he is a commoner (*muskenum*), he shall give her 20 shekels of silver.

This case is of mixed results. The divorced woman gets less if she is a *muskenum* than if she is an *awilum*. But the man divorcing has to pay less if he is a *muskenum* than if he is an *awilum*. In the latter case, there seems to be recognition of ability to pay, as we see more clearly in the next set of laws.

Perhaps a better indication of how Hammurabi's laws protect members of the *muskenum* class are the laws concerning fees doctors can charge for their services.

> LH #215 If a physician performs major surgery with a bronze lancet upon an *awilu*, and thus heals the *awilu*, or opens an *awilu*'s temple with a bronze lancet and thus heals the *awilu*'s eye, he shall take 10 shekels of silver (as his fee).
>
> LH #216 If (the patient) is a member of the commoner class (*muskenum*), he shall take 5 shekels of silver (as his fee).[23]
>
> LH #221 If a physician should set an *awilu*'s broken bone or heal an injured muscle, the patient shall give the physician 5 shekels of silver.
>
> LH #222 If he (the patient) is a member of the commoner class (*muskenum*), he shall give 3 shekels of silver.[24]

One might think that these laws value the health of the member of the *awilum* class more highly than that of the member of the *muskenum* class.

However, it is noteworthy that the poorer *muskenum* is asked to pay less than the wealthier *awilum*. This differential fee schedule, enforced at law, treats the two classes differently but not necessarily to the disadvantage of the *muskenum*, or that makes the *muskenum* less honored. Instead, it seems that the law recognizes the

[23] Ibid., p. 123.

[24] Ibid., p. 124.

different economic positions of the different class members and treats them differently, and fairly, on that basis. It is fair to expect less of someone who has less, if the having of less is not his fault but is rather due to the social hierarchy, and especially the fact that a *muskenum* has specials duties and services owed to the state. Next, we will consider laws that seem to treat the member of the *muskenum* class worse than the member of the *awilum* class. Then we look at the relation between equality and equity before then turning to how equality before the law was understood in ancient legal thought.

Reuven Yaron would disagree with the above conclusions. He steadfastly denies that "the law gave special protection to the *muskenum*."[25] Indeed, this is how he views the legal status of the member of the *muskenum* class:

> Altogether then, the picture of the *muskenum* which emerges from these sections is fairly clear and generally accepted: his is a lower class, financially weaker. His injuries are cheaper to settle, he pays smaller medical fees, and incurs less expense in divorcing his wife.[26]

Notice though that the law can recognize class differences without reinforcing them. Yaron focuses on passages that, he thinks, are so clear that they "explode the 'special protection theory' of the *muskenum* and dispose of it."[27]

Let us examine the laws that seem clearest to Yaron to count against the "special protection thesis."

> LH #175 If a slave of the palace or slave of the commoner (*muskenum*) marries a woman of the *awilu*-class and she then bears children, the owner of the slave will have no claims of slavery against the children of the woman of the *awilu*-class.
>
> LH #176 And if either a slave or a commoner (*muskenum*) marries a woman of the *awilu*-class, and when he marries her she enters the house of the slave of the palace or of the slave of the commoner (*muskenum*) together with the dowry brought from her father's house, and subsequent to the time that they moved in together they establish a household and accumulate possessions, after which either the slave of the palace or the slave of the commoner (*muskenum*) should go to his fate – the woman of the *awilu*-class shall take her dowry, furthermore they shall divide into two parts everything that her husband and she accumulated subsequent to the time they moved in together, and the slave's owner shall take half and the woman of the *awilu*-class shall take half for her children.[28]

[25] Yaron, *The Laws of Eshnunna*, p. 142, also see p. 137.
[26] Ibid., p. 142.
[27] Ibid., p. 139.
[28] *Laws of Hammurabi*, pp. 115–116.

Here it looks like members of the *muskenum* class are treated in the same way that slaves are treated. Being treated like a slave does not seem compatible with the idea that one has a protected status. This seems to support Yaron's view.

However it also seems that in many of the laws of ancient Mesopotamia, where the *muskenum* class is mentioned, the law does not further the unequal position of a *muskenum* but instead the law seeks to reduce or eliminate inequalities. Let us examine law #176 of Hammurabi above. Notice that the children of a slave or commoner who is married to a member of the *awilum* class is protected by having half of the accumulated wealth of their parents reserved for their care.

In the Laws of Eshnunna, a neighbor of Hammurabi's Babylonia, we find the following accounts of how the law dealt with thieves on a *muskenum*'s land:

> LE #12 A man who is seized in the field of a commoner (*muskenum*) among the sheaves of midday shall weigh and deliver 10 shekels of silver …
>
> LE #13 A man who is seized in the house of a commoner (*muskenum*) within the house, at midday, shall weigh and deliver 10 shekels of silver …[29]

These are very harsh penalties for theft, or attempted theft, and trespass. It should be said that not all scholars agree that these Laws of Eshnunna should be seen as providing protection for the *muskenum* class.[30] I would agree that the evidence from the Laws of Hammurabi offers clearer examples than the Laws of Eshnunna, since there we have a more straightforward comparison of penalties for a *muskenum* and an *awilum*.

This discussion indicates that there are at least two different meanings of protection for class members. One type, which Yaron is exclusively concerned with, is a matter of deterrence of those who would harm the class members; whereas what I have been concerned with is protection primarily in terms of compensation, and only secondarily deterrence. The case of the intruder, who may or may not have stolen, is best understood in terms of protection when the penalties are quite stiff; but if there is a definite loss, then the best protection is for there to be a monetary equivalent allotted, for those whose losses would put them in serious economic jeopardy without compensation. The laws seem to show a concern with equalizing effects rather than further entrenching inequality among the social classes.

6.3 THE WEAK AND THE POOR

The protections that the Laws of Hammurabi provide to the members of the *muskenum* class are also to be understood in the context of the association of

29 Ibid., pp. 60–61.

30 Yaron, *The Laws of Eshnunna*, pp. 141–145.

the members of that class with the palace, the source of the service duties of the *muskenum*. A *muskenum* is vulnerable to economic problems in ways that the members of the *awilum* class are not. Indeed, there is evidence that starvation among the *muskenum* class was a serious worry at the time of Hammurabi.[31] Protecting the lands of the *muskenum* was in some respects to protect the lands of the palace, since at least some members of the *muskenum* class were fief holders of these lands.

If many of the members of the *muskenum* class were linked to the lands of the crown, then we can understand why it was especially important for the laws of the crown to protect the *muskenum* members. This is so for two reasons. First, the service that the *muskenum* members performed was very important and in need of special protection. But in addition, as I will stress, protection was also important because of the disabilities that the *muskenum* faced due to being so closely tied to land that the *muskenum* did not own.

It is well established that ancient Mesopotamian rulers saw themselves as having a duty to protect the weak and the poor. The *muskenum* were relatively poor, indeed discounting slaves the *muskenum* were what would have been referred to by the category "the poor," or "the weak." In the Preamble of the Laws of Ur-Namma we find the following dedication:

> I did not deliver the orphan to the rich. I did not deliver the widow to the mighty. I did not deliver the man with but one shekel to the man with one mina (i.e., 60 shekels), I did not deliver the man with but one sheep to the man with one ox.[32]

And what we know from the preamble of Hammurabi's laws is that he set out his laws to protect the weak:

> the gods Anu and Enlil, for the enhancement of the well-being of the people, named me by my name Hammurabi, the pious prince, who venerates the gods, to make justice prevail in the land, to abolish the wicked and the evil, to prevent the strong from oppressing the weak, to rise like the sun god Shamash over all of humankind to illuminate the land.[33]

These statements by ancient Mesopotamian kings show that the task of protecting the worse off in the society was an important goal.

We also find similar sentiments recorded in ancient Egypt and among the ancient Israelites. In 1321 BCE, Horemheb propounds his famous edict in which he seeks to end various corrupt practices in the administrative and legal systems of Egypt. In the conclusion the edict declares:

[31] See E. A. Speiser, "The *Muskenum*," *Orientalia*, Vol. 27, no. 1, 1958, p. 23, citing ARM III 79 rev. 8 f.

[32] *Laws of Ur-Namma*, in *Law Collections From Mesopotamia and Asia Minor*, second edition, translated by Martha T. Roth, Atlanta, GA: Scholars' Press, 1997, p. 16.

[33] *Laws of Hammurabi*, pp. 76–77.

> May you hear these commands which My Majesty has newly issued so as to set the whole land in order, after My Majesty had taken to heart these acts of oppression which are being committed in this country.[34]

And in another part of the edict we find this admonition:

> But for any lay official or any priest (concerning) whom one shall hear "He sits (there) to administer justice, and yet he violates justice therein," it shall be (reckoned) to him for a great capital crime.[35]

In general, Horemheb describes himself as a ruler who takes into account the good intentions of the people, especially the peasants, and acts to relieve them of their oppression. At the end of his edict, there is this telling declaration:

> My majesty has taken great pains over Egypt in order to assure that the life of the inhabitants may prosper while he appears every morning upon the throne of Ra. Behold the courts have been set up all over the country to judge everyman living to hold court in the town according to the excellent plans of My Majesty.[36]

In pledging to assure the prosperity of all Egyptians, Horemheb was especially concerned with those who were weak and preyed on by the powerful, even by members of his own government.

For the ancient Israelites, various parts of the Covenant Code seek to provide "justice to widow, orphan, and the poor."[37]

> Deut 14:28–29: At the end of three years thou shalt bring forth all the tithe of thine increase the same year, and shall lay it up within thy gates: And the Levite (because he hath no part or inheritance with thee) and the stranger, and the fatherless, and the widow, which are within thy gates, shall come and shall eat, and be satisfied.[38]

Here those who are weak or poor are provided for out of the tithe. Another Deuteronomy provision also mandates that the poor be cared for.

> Deut: 15:7–11: If there is among you a poor man, one of your brethren, in any of your towns within the land which YHWH your God gives you, you shall not harden your heart or shut your hand against your poor brother, but you shall open your hand to him, and lend him sufficient for his need, whatever it may be … You

34 Kurt Pfluger, "The Edict of King Haremhab," *Journal of Near Eastern Studies*, Vol. 5, no. 4, October 1946, p. 267.

35 Ibid., p. 265.

36 Translation by Charlotte Booth, in her book *Horemheb: The Forgotten Pharaoh*, Stroud, Gloucestershire: Amberley Publishing, 2009, 2013, p. 150.

37 F. Charles Fensham, "Widow, Orphan, and the Poor in Ancient Near Eastern Legal and Wisdom Literature," *Journal of Near Eastern Studies*, Vol. 21, no. 2, April 1962, pp. 129–139, p. 135.

38 Deuteronomy 14: 28–29.

> shall give to him freely … I command you, You shall open wide your hand to your brother, to the needy and to the poor, in the land.[39]

This is a legal command to give aid to the poor and others who are weak.

Charles Fensham documents that there is a common understanding in the ancient Near East concerning the weakest:

> The attitude taken against widow, orphan, and the poor is to be looked at from a legal background. These people had no rights, no legal personality, or in some cases possibly restricted rights. They were almost outlaws. Anyone could oppress them without danger that legal connections might endanger his position. To restore the balance of society, these people must be protected.[40]

The class-based penalties of the Mesopotamian laws were aimed at just such a restoration.

It could be argued that the various pronouncements about aiding the widows, orphans, weak, and poor are just propaganda aimed at making the rulers look good, just as there was also a custom of making pronouncements about victories in battles that often were highly exaggerated. Perhaps the reality of the conditions of the weakest of the society was also exaggerated to enhance the reputation of the ruler. There are two things to be said in respect to this critical point before ending this section of the chapter.

First, it should be said that my purposes are to understand the legal thought of the ancient societies of the ancient Near East (primarily, ancient Mesopotamia, Egypt, and Israel). Legal texts are examined to shed light on and allow us to infer what that legal thought was. I am not primarily interested in what was the reality of the conditions faced on the ground by the peoples of the ancient Near East. This is an interest of my study, but not a primary one largely because it is so difficult to tell what were the actual practices by examining the existing evidence.

Second, as we will see in the following sections, there is some evidence for thinking that people were actually aided by the laws of the rulers who claimed to be aiding the weakest members of the society. But this evidence is difficult to sort out, and like everything else from so long ago, the written texts often provide the best evidence even if it is somewhat flawed.

6.4 CLASS INEQUALITY AND CLASS INEQUITY

In *The Creation of Inequality*, Flannery and Marcus argue that in the most primitive of times there were no social hierarchies. In addition, they argue that inequality

[39] Deuteronomy 15:7–11. See Richard H. Hiers, *Justice and Compassion in Biblical Law*, NY: Continuum, 2009, Chapter 8.

[40] Fensham, "Widow, Orphan, and the Poor," p. 139.

is created by political leaders. In Sumeria a strong state was created that "decided what men were allowed to do" that was enforced by "a system of judges and bailiffs" and codified laws that were instituted to "give the appearance of fairness."[41] Social classes arose when people moved into the cities and left behind far simpler forms of association.

In this view, one of the causes of inequality was the rise of "achievement-based societies" but "they ended with a return to egalitarian behavior." While members could attain greater status or wealth because of their achievements in "entrepreneurial exchange" but also in warfare, they did not pass on their higher status to their offspring. Social stratification required the addition of hereditary advantage or for a rank society, which was to arise later and crystallize inequality. The overarching claim of Flannery and Marcus is that some of the advantages not only created inequality but also unfairness.[42] In their view, the ancient legal systems that develop provide only the appearance of fairness.

In this section I want to explore the underlying conceptual issues in some of the accounts of how law facilitated inequality and also how the fairness of legal systems is only an appearance of fairness. As I have already indicated, ancient Mesopotamian society is often singled out for the way the laws reinforced, or perhaps even created, social classes by the differential treatment at law based on whether one was a member of the *awilum* or *muskenum* classes. Yet, some social inequality is not unfair as we will see.

One of the first things to note is that equality and equity are different and sometimes competing values. Equity, understood here as fairness, can often call for the unequal treatment of people. Of course, it is often the case that equality is understood not as an absolute value, so that equality concerns the similar treatment of those whose cases are relevantly similar, *and* the treatment of cases that are relevantly different not as the same, for fairness' sake. Not treating people the same can be consistent with equality of treatment if the people are relevantly different from one another.

Class may be based on such matters as the perceived differential accomplishments of people over time. Hereditary class membership can certainly be reinforced at law in ways that are both unequal and unfair. But if, for instance, there is a lower social class whose members are likely to be oppressed in a society by members of a "higher" class, it may be fair in law to treat the members of the lower class better than the members of the "higher" class to offset the potential oppression. In addition, it may be that members of one class have been assigned duties that are crucial for

[41] Kent Flannery and Joyce Marcus, *The Creation of Inequality: How Our Prehistoric Ancestors Set the Stage for Monarchy, Slavery, and Empire*, Cambridge, MA: Harvard University Press, 2012, pp. 476–477.

[42] Ibid., pp. 551–557.

the well-being of the society, and that it is fair to reward the members of this class with better treatment. It may be that the members of the *muskenum* class in ancient Mesopotamia fit both of these descriptions.

Differential and unequal treatment at law can be justified by concerns about fairness that are rooted in the way that members of various social classes have come to be treated customarily. Insofar as law compensates for past unequal treatment, it does not merely provide the appearance of fairness. Of course, when law reinforces and adds to the advantaged status of the members of a "higher" class, the law is typically understood as promoting unfairness. For equity, it matters significantly if the law advantages those who are disadvantaged as opposed to advantaging those who are already advantaged.

And as I have been arguing, it is especially important to see that the members of the *muskenum* class have been disadvantaged, at least in part, because of the service they were required to perform for the palace or crown. What the specific duties were has been a matter of dispute, as with many other matters in Mesopotamian law, but it is not disputed that there were special duties that sometimes created hardships for the *muskenum* members. One set of documents indicates that the *muskenum* was to perform four days of public service a month.[43] And the land that the *muskenum* farmed was not his own land but that of the palace that had been assigned to the *muskenum* to be worked – where the muskenum got to keep only part of the proceeds of the harvest, the rest going to the palace.

Even if the *muskenum* class did not have service duties, as some scholars have argued, it is nonetheless undeniable that the *muskenum* class was impoverished and disadvantaged compared to the *awilum* class. Because of this latter fact, if not also because of the former fact, the differential treatment of the *muskenum* class in Hammurabi's laws could be justified on egalitarian grounds, assuming it is true that the laws advantaged the members of the *muskenum* class. Thus, the fact that the Laws of Hammurabi treated members of different classes unequally is not necessarily an indication that those laws were inspired by some form of inegalitarianism.

Amartya Sen has argued that to understand whether a certain theory or perspective is egalitarian we must ask the question: equality of what? Theories or perspectives that contain inequalities of some goods, such as income, may still be egalitarian in other terms, such as welfare.

> We are deeply diverse on our internal characteristics (such as age, gender, general abilities, particular talents, proneness to illness, and so on) as well as external circumstances (such as ownership of assets, social backgrounds, environmental

43 See D. G. Evans, "The Incidence of Labor-Service in the Old Babylonian Period," *Journal of the American Oriental Society*, Vol. 83, no. 1, Jan.–Mar., 1963, pp. 21–22.

> predicaments, and so on). It is especially because of such diversity that the insistence on equality in one field requires the rejection of egalitarianism in another.[44]

This is because the two perspectives, internal and external, on which variables are most important might conflict, with a perspective being inegalitarian with respect to one variable and egalitarian with respect to another.[45]

Sen is especially helpful concerning the topic of our chapter when he says the following:

> Even though such rhetoric (e.g. "all men are born equal") is typically taken to be part and parcel of egalitarianism, the effect of ignoring interpersonal variations can, in fact, be deeply inegalitarian, in hiding the fact that equal consideration for all may demand very unequal treatment in favor of the disadvantaged. The demands of substantive equality can be particularly exacting and complex when there is a good deal of antecedent inequality to counter.[46]

It seems reasonable to think that at least some of the seemingly inegalitarian Laws of Hammurabi concerning a person's social class can be seen as egalitarian with respect to the attempt to ameliorate inequalities in wealth and well-being among the lower classes.

There is a complex relationship between equality and equity. In many situations, radical equality is not compatible with equity understood as fairness. The reason for this is that radical equality, where everyone is treated exactly the same in respect to a certain benefit or burden, fails to take account of relevant differences among people even in the very same situation. As we will see, this does indeed seem to be an idea recognized in the earliest of law "codes" that we have been examining.

6.5 EQUALITY BEFORE THE LAW

In ancient Greece, one model for the law was the image of the god Themes, who stands blindfolded holding the scales of justice. Everyone who came before the courts was to be treated the same in terms of their citizenship. The ancient code of Hammurabi seems to stand opposed to the classical Greek model of equality before the law. But it seems to me that things are more complicated, and that at least some of Hammurabi's laws can be understood as egalitarian. Having laws with differential penalties based on social classes is not necessarily inegalitarian, especially if the laws benefit the lower class rather than the upper class members.

44 Amartya Sen, *Inequality Reexamined*, Cambridge, MA: Harvard University Press, 1992, p. xi.

45 See ibid., p. ix.

46 Ibid., p. 1.

Hugo Bedau has argued that "To think like an egalitarian is to consider the degree and range of inequalities among men and to explore ways to remove or at least diminish them."[47] The law is egalitarian or serves equality by providing compensation and differential punishments so as to overcome and diminish already existing inequalities in the society, and this seems to be what Hammurabi's laws sought to do.

There is evidence that the *muskenum* and *awilum* classes predate Hammurabi's laws in ancient Mesopotamian.[48] So, Hammurabi does not seem to have created these classes with the institution of his laws. Instead, it seems plausible to think that Hammurabi was trying to diminish the inegalitarian effects of having these social classes in Babylonia. As we saw in an earlier chapter, Hammurabi issued debt forgiveness edicts to help those who were oppressed. It is my contention that many of the disparate penalties that seem adversely to discriminate among the classes in Hammurabi's law code, like the debt forgiveness edicts, are aimed at providing equity and ultimately ameliorating the effects of inequality in the society.

There are aspects of Hammurabi's laws that are inegalitarian to be sure. Let me mention several here.

> LH #229 If a builder constructs a house for a man but does not make his work sound, and the house that he constructs collapses and causes the death of the householder, that builder shall be killed.
>
> LH #231 If it should cause the death of a slave of the householder, he shall give to the householder a slave of comparable value for the slave.[49]

Here the negligent builder is killed if the collapsing building kills a free man, but if a slave is killed, the builder must simply provide a replacement slave.

Another example of inequality in Hammurabi's laws that is hard to justify concerns the laws of cheek slapping.

> LH #202 If an *awilu* should strike the cheek of an *awilu* who is of status higher than his own, he shall be flogged in the public assembly with 60 stripes of an ox whip.
>
> LH #203 If a member of the *awilu*-class should strike the cheek of another member of the *awilu*-class who is his equal, he shall weigh and deliver 60 shekels of silver.
>
> LH #204 If a commoner (*muskenum*) should strike the cheek of another commoner he shall weigh and deliver 10 shekels of silver.
>
> LH #205 If an *awilu's* slave should strike the cheek of a member of the *awilu*- class, they shall cut off his ear.[50]

47 Hugo Bedau, "Egalitarianism and the Idea of Equality," in *Nomos IX – Equality*, edited by J. Roland Pennock and John W. Chapman, NY: Atherton Press, 1967, p. 13.

48 Yaron, *The Laws of Eshnunna*, p. 145.

49 *Laws of Hammurabi*, p. 125.

50 *Laws of Hammurabi*, pp. 121–122. See also Marth Roth, "Mesopotamian Legal Traditions and the Laws of Hammurabi," *Chicago-Kent Law Review*, Vol. 13, 1995–1996, pp. 13–39, especially pp. 34–36.

We see here differential penalties based on social class, that may disadvantage lower classes, although note that the *muskenum*-on-*muskenum* slap incurs much less penalty than the *awilum*-on-*awilum* slaps.

Yet, the laws that are most clearly class linked, especially concerning those of the *muskenum* class, seem to be remedial and most plausibly to have as their underlying legal thought that those in the *muskenum* class should be penalized less than those of the *awilum* class for basically the same acts. There are several reasons for inferring that the differential penalties were meant to favor the *muskenum* class rather than to disfavor them.

First, as mentioned earlier, the *muskenum* class had special service duties to the palace that generated a need for the *muskenum* class members to be specially protected.[51] Indeed, one well-known scholar, J. J. Finkelstein, otherwise arguing contrary to my approach, nonetheless has argued that the category of *muskenum* "emphasizes not so much his subservient status – although this seems to lie at the etymological root of the term – as the obligation of the crown to pay special attention to the *muskenum* interests."[52]

Second, the penalties for a member of the *awilum* class were more like criminal punishments in that the victim of these crimes was not compensated; whereas in the case of a member of the *muskenum* class there was compensation for the victim. As Speiser points out, "The field and house of the *muskenum* are protected from thieves under the pain of death … And recovered slaves or animals that belong either to the palace or to a *muskenum* must be returned promptly to the capital by the appropriate officials."[53] Here again there is reason to think that the members of the *muskenum* class needed special protection.

Thus, as we have seen, equality before the law may well have been part of ancient legal thought. The concept of equality of treatment was not understood in terms of treating everyone the same. Rather, we can infer that the law was sometimes seen as a vehicle for compensating or relieving inequality in the society. We thus have a fairly sophisticated conception of equality before the law at this very early time. As in the debates today about affirmative action and so-called reverse discrimination, ancient legal thought also seems to have recognized that equality is not merely a procedural but also a substantive requirement at law.

Equality can be seen as a substantive goal in terms of the results of a law, not merely its formal components. Absolute equality can mean either that everyone is recognized as the same at law as a procedural or formal matter, or absolute equality

51 See D. G. Evans, "The Incidence of Labor-Service in the Old Babylonian Period," *Journal of the American Oriental Society*, Vol. 83, no. 1, Jan.–Mar., 1963, pp. 20–26.

52 J. J. Finkelstein, "Amisaduqa's Edict and the Babylonian 'Law Codes,'" *Journal of Cuneiform Studies*, Vol. 15, 1961, pp. 91–104, p. 99.

53 E. A. Speiser, "The Muskenum," *Orientalia*, Vol. 27, no. 1, 1958, pp. 19–28, p. 23.

can mean that everyone substantively gets exactly the same from the law. When less than absolute equality is the norm, we again see this separation of formal and substantive considerations. Laws can embody either of these forms of equality. When substantive equality is the goal of law, and people are substantively unequal to begin with, then absolute equality must not be how equality before the law is understood; rather there must be remediation that often violates strictly formal equality. I have been arguing that the legal thought of ancient times seems to have recognized just this complex idea concerning equality before the law.

It is perhaps surprising that ancient legal thought could have understood that equality can sometimes only be achieved through the strategic uses of inequality. But that is what I have argued is one plausible way to understand how the *muskenum* class was treated in Hammurabi's laws and in some other ancient Near Eastern legal texts. I have also suggested that it is the use of the idea of equity and humaneness, which came to epitomize how some ancient rulers saw themselves ruling, that was what undergirded the complex idea of equality that developed in ancient legal thought. Ancient Babylonian legal thought that assigned differential penalties based on social class is much more intriguing and sophisticated a form of legal thought than has been traditionally recognized.

7

Women's Separate Sphere

It is frequently said that ancient Mesopotamia was a patriarchal society where women were little better than chattel.[1] The various collections of laws of Sumer and Babylonia contain notorious provisions seeming to deny the rights of women and to subject women to sometimes grotesque punishments. Marriage in Mesopotamia is described by some scholars as nothing more than a sale to the highest bidder. This is certainly the view of Mesopotamia taken by the ancient Greek historian Herodotus and this view dominated historical scholarship until quite recently. Yet, there is solid evidence that some women engaged in business, owned their own property,[2] served in various professions, and were often afforded comparable legal status to that of men. So, at very least the record is mixed.

In this chapter I will consider and partially support a relatively new thesis on the legal status of women in ancient Mesopotamia, where women's role was said to be "distinct from that of men and that might best be described as a parallel universe from which they made major contributions to public life"[3] and where "the involvement of women in the economy was usually that of interacting with other women as if in a world parallel to the one where men worked."[4] All scholars acknowledge that

1 See Hans Jochem Boecker, *Law and the Administration of Justice in the Old Testament and Ancient East*, translated by Jeremy Moiser, Minneapolis, MN: Augsburg Publishing House, 1980, p. 105: speaking of a limited right of separation: "this tendency benefitted married women only and not women in general. There cannot either, of course, be any question of the legal equality of men and women." Also see Elisabeth Meier Tetlow, *Women, Crime, and Punishment in Ancient Law and Society*, NY: Continuum, 2004, p. 65 where she says "Babylonian men valued honor more than the lives of their wives," despite citing much evidence for many legal protections for women.

2 Stanley A. Cook, *The Laws of Moses and the Code of Hammurabi*, London: Adam and Charles Black, 1903, p. 73. Despite holding the view that women were "legal chattel," Cook admits that "In Babylonia we find that women could trade and do business whether on their own or in partnership, she could appear independently in the law-courts as witness or as plaintiff, she could hold private property and dispose of it as she pleased" (pp. 71–72).

3 Harriet Crawford, "An Exploration of the World of Women in Third-Millennium Mesopotamia," in *Women in the Ancient Near East*, edited by Mark W. Chavalas, NY: Routledge, 2014, p. 11.

4 Marc Van de Mieroop, *Cuneiform Texts and the Writing of History*, London: Routledge, 1999, p. 158.

the legal status of women deteriorated over the course of ancient Mesopotamian history, but I will focus on the Sumerian and Old Babylonian era since it is here that there is an often ignored status of women in which they seem to occupy separate spheres with a fair amount of equality with men, but where the spheres did not neatly map onto the idea that the private sphere was for women and the public sphere for men.

This reassessment of the legal status of women in ancient Mesopotamia raises the conceptual question of whether, and to what extent, women could be seen as "equal" to men even though occupying separate spheres. In Section 7.1 I will explore some of the evidence for the "parallel universe" thesis, in terms of how women priests and saloon-keepers were regarded. In Section 7.2 I will look at another set of evidence for the "parallel universe" thesis by looking at how inheritance was understood. In Section 7.3 I will consider the contrary evidence concerning rape, marriage, and adultery, admitting that this is hard to parse with the evidence of "parallel spheres" but also arguing that the evidence is more mixed than often recognized. In Section 7.4 I will discuss the role of women by looking at the ideas of honor and pollution in ancient Mesopotamian thought compared to ancient Greek and Roman views of pollution. By the end of this chapter I will ask if the parallel spheres thesis can be compatible with calling ancient Mesopotamia a patriarchal society.

7.1 WOMEN AS PRIESTS AND SALOON-KEEPERS

There is overwhelming evidence that ancient Mesopotamian women played very important roles in society in the upper classes of royalty and temple-life. Two things should be said before looking at some of this evidence. First, the strong role of women in the two "professions" we examine may not be equal to that of men in similar roles. Second, it may be that these were exceptions and that women in more ordinary situations were not granted such status. To address this second point, I will take up some of the evidence for seeing strong roles for women in more ordinary situations. But I will begin by addressing the first point.

In ancient Egypt, as well as in ancient Mesopotamia, there were a few queens who ruled as if they were kings. Indeed, Jean Bottero discusses "a venerable tradition, according to which, around 2500 BC, the town of Kish was ruled not by a king but by an energetic queen called Ku-baba, a former 'tavern-keeper,' about whom we know nothing else."[5] Queens participated in ruling in many other instances, and queens were often instrumental in diplomatic matters as well.

[5] Jean Bottero, *Everyday Life in Ancient Mesopotamia*, translated by Antonia Nevill, Baltimore, MD: Johns Hopkins University Press, p. 125.

Some of the best evidence for the parallel spheres thesis comes from legal texts on how female priests and other female religious leaders were regarded in ancient Mesopotamia. The *naditu* was a religious class of women who mostly separated themselves from the normal life of marriage and family. Bottero says:

> Wealthy and free, they have appeared to have organized an industrious existence for themselves in their retreat, each following her tastes and capabilities. Some, for instance, spun and wove to earn money; but the majority seems to be devoted to business. They sold and bought landed property, and houses, or they rented them out; they lent at rates of interest: money or grain; they invested and formed associations with itinerant business agents to organize a whole export trade in native products, and the import of foreign goods; they bought and sold slaves; they kept an eye on the working of their lands, engaged tenant farmers, growers, day-laborers, and specialists in the cultivation of date-palms, giving orders to some, reprimanding others, demanding reports on the state of works in progress – in short, in the tranquility of their "convent," leading the true life of "business women" adventurous and hectic. The Code of Hammurabi (#40) mentions them alongside the *tamkaru*, business agents who were responsible for virtually all the main commercial activity in the country, and thus suggests that they formed the female counterpart.[6]

Bottero thus makes a strong beginning case for the parallel universe thesis.

Let us take a close look at some of Hammurabi's laws, including the ones that Bottero mentions.

> LH #39 He shall assign in writing to his wife or daughter or give to meet an outstanding obligation only a field, orchard, or house which he himself acquires by purchase.
>
> LH #40 (However), a *naditu*, a merchant (*tamkarum*), or any holder of a field with a special service obligation may sell her or his field, orchard, or house; the buyer shall perform the service obligation on the field, orchard, or house which he purchases.[7]

These laws are embedded in a set of laws concerning restrictions on the purchase or sale of lands that have service requirements attached to the lands, and that have been bestowed on the owner by the palace or temple. In #39 we see that a father cannot even assign such lands to his heirs; he controls only the land that he owns outright due to acquisition by sale.

Yet, a *naditu* can dispose of her lands as she sees fit. This privilege also extended to merchants and certain unspecified others. Driver and Miles suggest that the rest of the group might include: "herdsmen, millers, and bakers, couriers, and

6 Ibid., pp. 122–123.

7 *Laws of Hammurabi*, p. 88.

so on" who are already recognized as entitled to enlist hired substitutes to perform the service requirement.[8] Some commentators think that the juxtaposition of the *naditu* with the merchant and other tradesmen, along with the equivalence of treatment, means that the female priest is treated as an equal to these male professionals.

There are other legal provisions mentioning the *naditu* that show us how independent was her status in ancient Mesopotamian society. Here is another of Hammurabi's laws:

> LH #182 If a father does not award a dowry to his daughter who is a *naditu* dedicated to the god Marduk of the city of Babylon or does not record it for her in a sealed document, after the father goes to his fate, she shall take with her brothers her one-third share from the property of the paternal estate as her inheritance, but she will not perform any service obligation; a *naditu* dedicated to the god Marduk shall give her estate as she pleases.[9]

Here the naditu priest is treated as a normal male heir, even if her father has not set this out in his will.

Let us next turn to saloon-keepers who were not royalty or religious leaders but ordinary women, although, as I said, around 2500 BCE a former saloon-keeper, Ku-baba, became a famous queen who ruled in Sumer as a king. There is something appealing, and also odd, about the way the profession of saloon-keeper, or innkeeper, seemingly occupied exclusively by women, gained such attention in ancient Mesopotamia. Four Laws of Hammurabi deal with this profession:

> LH #108 If a woman innkeeper should refuse to accept grain for the price of beer but accepts (only) silver measured by the large weight, thereby reducing the value of beer in relation to the value of grain, they shall charge and convict that woman innkeeper and they shall cast her into the water.
>
> LH #109 If there should be a woman innkeeper in whose house criminals congregate, and she does not seize those criminals and lead them off to the palace authorities, that woman innkeeper shall be killed.
>
> LH #110 If a *naditu* or an *ugbatu* who does not reside within the cloister should open (the door to?) a tavern or enter a tavern for some beer, they shall burn that woman.
>
> LH #111 If a woman innkeeper gives one vat of beer as a loan(?), she shall take 50 silas of grain at the harvest.[10]

[8] Godfrey Rolles Driver and J. C. Miles, *The Babylonian Laws*, Oxford: Oxford University Press, 1952, Vol. 1, p. 124.

[9] *Laws of Hammurabi*, p. 118.

[10] *Laws of Hammurabi*, pp. 101–102.

In examining these laws some scholars have been critical of the legal status of women,[11] but these are clearly seen as legitimate professions exclusive to women, so let us look a little closer at what these laws might tell us.

There are other references to harsh treatment of business men who engaged in shady practices. But the punishment of being cast "into the water" is especially harsh. There is also a reference to the women priests, who are seemingly not allowed to enter the tavern or inn, despite the fact that it is run or owned by a woman. In both these cases there nonetheless seems to be an underlying idea that women can engage in business activities but are restricted in how these activities are run. This is easiest to see when a woman innkeeper is prohibited from allowing criminals to congregate. Such a practice might violate a separate spheres presumption.

The prohibition on having women priests entering taverns even though they are run by women is harder to explain. Driver and Miles make two points that are relevant to our larger project in this chapter. First, they say that "the point of the law is that a priestess, even though no longer dwelling in a cloister, must live respectably and above all must not keep or frequent an inn." Their second point is related: "the lawgiver assumes that a priestess who commits either offense is in fact guilty of an act or acts of prostitution."[12] Apparently, according to Miles and Driver, ale-houses, taverns, and saloons were closely associated with brothels. And of course, a priest should not frequent a brothel.[13]

The association between a saloon and a brothel in the ancient Near East is something to ponder in connection to the fact that in Mesopotamia these establishments were run by women. From the perspective of the separate spheres thesis, one might think that this is a problem since the brothel, as well as just a normal saloon, would be frequented by men. Yet, the idea of separate spheres I am considering here is not about keeping men and women separate but about treating women and men equally as long as they operate in their own spheres. So, having saloon keeping as a domain for business women or of keeping the industries of the convent for business women, even if men were their customers, is not itself a problem for the separate spheres thesis.

Allowing women to operate in separate spheres from men is an advance over women's subjugation by men, although the idea of separate spheres is ripe for abuse. And if the separate spheres for women were clearly worse than those for men,

[11] Martha Roth says these laws "should be understood to be regulating commerce (rather than regulating women's activities)." But since the saloon-keepers or innkeepers are all women, and since this is the only recognition of a woman's profession other than being a female priest, it seems worth investigating for what it might say about woman's legal status. *Women in the Ancient Near East*, p. 172, note 20.

[12] Miles and Driver, *The Babylonian Laws*, p. 206.

[13] Ibid.

there would still be significant inequality for women. But the spheres of religious life and business do not appear to be insignificant spheres of daily life in ancient Mesopotamia. Having seen a significant role for women in economic and religious matters, in the next section we will see some of the "rights" of women in other significant areas where the comparison with men is clearer, namely in inheritance and to a certain extent marriage.

7.2 MARRIAGE AND INHERITANCE

The laws of inheritance in ancient Mesopotamia are quite revelatory of the status of women in that society. Here is one of the Laws of Hammurabi that shows the concern for the "rights" of women in marriage and inheritance:

> LH #142 If a woman repudiates her husband, and declares, "You shall not have marital relations with me" – her circumstances shall be investigated by the authorities of her city quarter, and if she is circumspect and without fault, but her husband is wayward and disparages her greatly, that woman will not be subject to any penalty, she shall take her dowry and she shall depart for her father's house.[14]

Two of the most significant women's "rights" recognized by Hammurabi's laws are, first, that a wife may divorce her husband, and, second, she gets to take her dowry out of the marriage when she departs. There are other things to note that make this not a radically egalitarian law: the wife has to be without fault and also circumspect; the husband has to be wayward and "greatly" disparage his wife; and the wife must return to her father's house. Yet, compared to many other societies, as we will see later, this is a kind of egalitarianism nonetheless.

Yet, we see some of the inegalitarian features of the marriage laws when in Hammurabi's next law we observe what befalls the wife who is not circumspect:

> LH #143 If she is not circumspect but is wayward, squanders her household possessions, and disparages her husband, they shall cast that woman into the water.[15]

So, in some circumstances a wife who tries to divorce her husband is subject to capital punishment, whereas the husband is not when the circumstances are reversed. Notice though that the circumstances here are quite restricted to a very small class of cases. The law stipulates that all three of the conditions (being wayward, squandering of household possessions, and disparaging her husband) have to be satisfied for such a severe penalty to be faced by a woman attempting to leave her husband.

[14] *Laws of Hammurabi*, p. 108.
[15] Ibid., p. 108.

Here are two other Laws of Hammurabi that are especially interesting for what it tells us about the legal status of women in marriage:

> LH #148 If a man marries a woman, and later *la'bum*-disease seizes her and he decides to marry another woman, he may marry, he will not divorce his wife whom *la'bum*-disease has seized; she shall reside in quarters he constructs and he shall continue to support her as long as she lives.
>
> LH #149 If that woman should not agree to reside in her husband's house, he shall restore to her her dowry that she brought from her father's house, and she shall depart.[16]

Here husbands cannot divorce certain sick spouses and must either support them for life or let them leave and take their dowry with them, and the choice seems to be up to the sick wife.

Concerning inheritance there are laws that mostly protect the "rights" of women as well.

> LH #150 If a man awards his wife a field, orchard, house, or moveable property, and makes out a sealed document for her, after her husband's death her children will not bring a claim against her; the mother shall give her estate to whichever of her children she loves, but she will not give it to an outsider.[17]

Once a wife derives inheritance from her husband, it is the wife's by right and need not be passed on to all of her children at her death. We do see here, though, that her inheritance cannot be gifted out of the family at her death.

Consider next two more Laws of Hammurabi that show how the "rights" of a wife are strongly protected in circumstances of debt:

> LH #151 If a woman who is residing in a man's house should have her husband agree by binding contract that no creditor of her husband shall seize her (for his debts) – if that man has a debt incurred before marrying that woman, his creditors will not seize that wife; and if that woman has a debt incurred before entering the man's house, her creditors will not seize her husband.
>
> LH #152 If a debt should be incurred by them after that woman enters the man's house, both of them shall satisfy the merchant.[18]

The debts of men and women before marriage are here considered solely their own. And the debts that they accumulate after marriage are considered theirs jointly. There is thus an equality of legal status contemplated in these Laws of Hammurabi.

16 Ibid., p. 109.
17 Ibid., pp. 109–110.
18 Ibid., p. 110.

The disposition of the dowry after a wife has died also gives us a sense of how women were regarded at Hammurabi's time in the eighteenth century BCE:

> LH #162 If a man marries a wife, she bears him children, and that woman then goes to her fate, her father shall have no claim on her dowry; her dowry belongs only to her children.
>
> LH #163 If a man marries a wife but she does not provide him with children, and that woman goes to her fate – if his father-in-law then returns to him the bridewealth that that man brought to his father-in-law's house, her husband will have no claim on that woman's dowry; her dowry belongs only to her father's house.
>
> LH #164 If the father-in-law shall not return to him the bridewealth he shall deduct the value of her bridewealth from her dowry and restore (the balance) of her dowry to her father's house.[19]

While these laws seem to treat the dowry as the father's right, the laws are more subtle than that. The dowry only returns to the father in those cases where the marriage produced no children. And such a provision can be interpreted as a protection for the woman in question since the practice of killing or not providing for a wife, who bears no children, with the hopes of keeping her dowry would be strongly deterred by these laws.

These Laws of Hammurabi concerning marriage, dowry, debt, and inheritance show that women definitely had "rights" during marriage, even if those rights were not the same as those of men during marriage. Despite the differences, it cannot seriously be maintained that women were merely their husband's (or father's) chattel or slave. Indeed, it is hard to understand how these laws could be interpreted as showing anything like a strongly patriarchal relation between men and women. We will now examine some of the evidence often cited for such claims in the next section before drawing some conclusions about the legal status of women in ancient Mesopotamia.

7.3 ADULTERY AND RAPE

In her important work on sexual violence, Susan Brownmiller starts her history of how women are treated when rape has occurred by examining the Laws of Hammurabi.

> About four thousand years ago the Code of Hammurabi, chipped on a seven-foot column of diorite stone, made plain by its omissions that a female was allowed no independent status under Babylonian law. She was either a betrothed virgin, living in the house of her father, or else she was somebody's lawfully wedded wife

[19] Ibid., p. 112.

> and lived in the house of her husband. According to Hammurabi, a man was to be seized and slain if he raped a betrothed virgin, but the victimized girl was considered guiltless … A *married* woman who had the misfortune to get raped in Babylon had to share the blame equally with her attacker. Regardless of how the incident occurred, the crime was labeled adultery and both participants were bound and thrown into the river.[20]

In earlier sections we have already seen that there were significant roles open to women not connected to being a daughter or wife, but Brownmiller does have a point here about how rape and adultery were treated.

If a woman commits adultery in ancient Mesopotamian law she is treated quite harshly. Indeed, perhaps the most grotesque of ancient punishments, being impaled on a pole, is reserved for those women who commit adultery and kill their spouses. Such laws are hard to reconcile with the thesis of parallel spheres. Rapists are also treated quite leniently in many ancient Mesopotamian laws, with the victim of rape sometimes punished more severely than the rapist. Again this is very hard to reconcile with the parallel spheres thesis. I will discuss this issue in this section, ultimately admitting that these examples cannot be fully reconciled with the separate spheres thesis, but offering a bit of nuance in understanding ancient legal thought on adultery and rape. Here there are significant differences from one culture to another and one time period to another. And in most cultures, the adverse effects on those who are the victim of adultery or rape do not force upon us the view that women were chattel or property of some other sort.

Let us consider some of the very earliest laws on rape and adultery. Here are two Laws of Ur-Namma:

> LU #6 If a man deflowers the not-deflowered spouse of a young man, with guile: they shall kill that male.
>
> LU #7 If the spouse of a young man on her own initiative pursues a man and has sexual intercourse with him: they shall kill that woman; that male shall be given his freedom.[21]

Here in the very earliest collection of written laws there is a kind of parallel between the man who is a rapist and the woman who is an adulterer: both are to be killed.

[20] Susan Brownmiller, *Against Our Will*, NY: Simon and Schuster, 1975, pp. 18–19.

[21] Martha Roth translation, from her revised translations in *Women in the Ancient Near East*, p. 148. For comparison sake, here is an earlier translation by the same translator, Martha Roth, of law #6:

> #6 If a man violates the rights of another and deflowers the virgin wife of a young man, they shall kill that male.

Notice that Roth now omits the "violates the rights of another" allowing us to decide whether to interpret the offense of rape as violating the rights of a male, or not. Roth translation, in her *Law Collections* volume, p. 17.

One could try to explain the parallel treatment of a male rapist and a female adulterer in terms of loss of property or honor on the part of the husband: the male rapist forcibly takes what only the husband is rightfully to take; and the female adulterer similarly allows for herself to be taken. Yet, this explanation ignores a number of finer points of these laws that I think are important to consider. At the moment I wish just to point out that the circumstances are highly specific: not all instances of male rapists or female adulterers are subject to the death penalty. And as we will see in other law codes not all forms of rape and adultery are treated the same. Yet, in these early laws, we can at least see a concern that women not be forced to, and voluntarily should not, have sex outside of the house of their husbands. The sphere is perhaps as important as the quasi-property interest of the man.

In the Laws of Eshnunna, a century before Hammurabi's laws, the rapist and adulterer are treated as harshly as in the earlier Laws of Ur-Namma:

> LE #26 If a man brings the bridewealth for the daughter-of-a-man, but another without the consent of her father and mother abducts her and deflowers her, it is indeed a capital offense, he shall die.
>
> LE #28 If he concludes the contract and the nuptial feast for (?) her father and mother and marries her, she is indeed his wife: the day she is seized in the lap of [another] man, she shall die, she will not live.

But there it is seemingly contemplated that if the marriage has not been completed, the death penalty will not apply to the female adulterer.

In the Laws of Hammurabi, adultery is still punished severely, but rape is treated quite differently in different circumstances. Here is one of these laws:

> LH #129 If a man's wife should be seized lying with another male, they should bind them, and cast them into the water; if the wife's master allows his wife to live, then the king shall allow the subject (i.e., the other male) to live.[22]

Two things are important here. First, both male and female adulterers are to be killed. This actually looks like men and women are treated the same here. But second, it is the husband who gets to decide whether his wife shall be spared – and if he does so it is required that the male adulterer shall also be spared. This looks patriarchal, although not completely so since the husband cannot decide what to do to the male adulterer, who is the one who violated his wife and seemingly dishonored him.

One of the most notorious of Hammurabi's laws calls for horribly severe punishment for one kind of adultery:

[22] *Laws of Hammurabi*, p. 105.

> LH # 153 If a man's wife has her husband killed on account of (her relationship with) another male, they shall impale that woman.[23]

Of course, this is a double offense, adultery plus murder. Yet, there are no other cases of murder that are treated so severely – although there are no straightforward murder laws in any event in Hammurabi's laws. So there appears to be something especially horrendous about murder motivated by adultery. I will take up this case in more detail in the next section in the context of honor and pollution.

Let us finally look at how rape is treated in Hammurabi's laws. Here we still have the rapist subject to capital punishment as in the earlier laws:

> LH #130 If a man pins down another man's virgin wife who is still residing in her father's house, and they seize him lying with her, that man shall be killed; that woman shall be released.[24]

Notice that the woman must still be a virgin, although presumably betrothed, for rape of her to warrant her rapist suffering the death penalty. Various reasons have been offered for why this restriction is included in the treatment of rape. The woman's worth to her husband and father is greater if she is still a virgin when the marriage is consummated. So, this law seems to be consistent with a patriarchal reading of these ancient laws. But the nuances give one pause in attributing the penalties to strongly patriarchal assumptions. There is also a clear inference to be drawn about women keeping to their own spheres, although it is not merely because of the woman benefitting.

7.4 HONOR AND POLLUTION

Three of the most severe punishments in Hammurabi's laws concern impalement, burning alive, and forced drowning. It is true that these are indeed grotesque, and also inhumane, calling into question my earlier discussions of Hammurabi as a humane lawgiver. In this section I will examine these laws more closely, arguing that they can be related to ideas of pollution and honor deeply engrained in Mesopotamian religious thought. These ideas are also linked, for many scholars, with the idea of patriarchy in Mesopotamia and most ancient, as well as modern, civilizations. I will cast a bit of doubt on this final claim, but I will recognize, in the next section, that we must modify our views about how much equality women were granted in ancient Mesopotamia.

Here are the most severe of the punishments directed against women in Hammurabi's laws.

[23] Ibid., p. 110.
[24] Ibid., p. 106.

> LH #153 If a man's wife has her husband killed on account of (her relationship with) another male, they shall impale that woman.[25]
>
> LH #110 If a *naditu* or an *ugbatu* who does not reside within the cloister should open (the door to?) a tavern or enter a tavern for some beer, they shall burn that woman.
>
> LH #129 If a man's wife should be seized lying with another male, they should bind them, and cast them into the water; if the wife's master allows his wife to live, then the king shall allow the subject (i.e., the other male) to live.[26]

What these three laws may have in common is that a strong taboo has been breached and there is resulting danger to the moral order of the society.

In the first case, impalement is the punishment for a woman who kills her husband so as to continue an adulterous affair. This clearly challenges the separate spheres, in respect to how severely adultery is treated. But we should note that the offense is especially dangerous because of the murder that is related to the adultery. The woman tries to keep her adultery secret, or to prolong the affair, by means of murder.

In the second case, burning alive is the punishment for a woman priest who frequents a tavern or saloon. As I said earlier, some commentators have suggested a connection between saloons and prostitution. When supposedly celibate women expose themselves to brothels there is both a social and religious danger for the keeping of inns, a job that seems to be the prerogative of women. Not all *naditu* women were confined to the convent. This, in itself, is a progressive idea compared with ideas of the Middle Ages about celibate women. But with this liberality came the need to be even more careful with where *naditu* priests went when not in the convent, lest there be religious pollution, as we will see.

In the third case, forced drowning is the punishment for a woman (and a man) for adultery. Like the first case, we have a law aimed at adultery. One could argue, as Elizabeth Tetlow does,[27] that the disposition of this case is based in seeing women as the property of their husbands. But this does not explain why the adulterous man is also killed by forced drowning. There is a danger to the social institution of marriage here, for sure, and that is what seems to be at the heart of the severe punishment.

Elizabeth Tetlow has argued that cases such as the three above are best understood by reference to the Babylonian idea of pollution:

> The Babylonians believed that certain crimes were so terrible that they created pollution and infuriated the gods. Pollution which denoted impurity and separation from the gods, was a danger to the state and to its religion. Pollution was overcome

[25] Ibid., p. 110.
[26] Ibid., p. 105.
[27] Elizabeth Meier Tetlow, *Women Crime and Punishment in Ancient Law and Society*, NY: Continuum, Vol. 1, p. 71.

> by annihilation of the source and the purification by fire, water, and blood sacrifice, of what had been polluted – the state, the temple, persons, or objects. Offenders who committed crimes that engendered pollution were generally put to death by fire or water.[28]

Tetlow also argues that some of the most severe punishments were reserved for cases where a man was dishonored:

> Babylonian men valued their honor more than the lives of their wives. When honor was lost, the alternative was to live in shame, which Babylonian men found intolerable. Honor could be restored through death of the person who had taken it away.[29]

I find Tetlow's first claim about pollution compelling, but I have reservations about her second claim about honor. In part this is because the concept of pollution seems able to explain these cases without a strongly patriarchal concept of honor.

The Mesopotamian social traditions, especially concerning marriage and family, were indeed strongly enforced. This is no doubt because of some patriarchal ideas, but the idea that I have been focusing on in this chapter concerns the role of women in their separate spheres. Perhaps the danger of adultery in particular, but also of women priests entering potentially into brothels, is that the separate spheres will be violated. In the final section of this chapter I will examine in more detail to what extent the ideas of patriarchy can be attributed to Mesopotamia and how strong they seem to have been.

I will end this section with some remarks about how pollution was regarded in ancient societies. Here is a summary of the elements of pollution for Greek thought in the 5th and 4th centuries BC –

(a) a person has acted in a way that violates a taboo, whether intended or not
(b) the person's act makes the person liable to sanction
(c) the person is now dangerous to others because associating with him or her can also make the person's group liable to sanction as well (for example, a plague can befall a city where a polluted person lives)
(d) the pollution can be expiated or mitigated in several ways:
    i. the polluted person dies
    ii. the polluted person goes through a ritual of purification (*katharsis*)
    iii. the polluted person is exiled.[30]

Most of these elements also seem to be present in the idea of pollution in ancient Mesopotamian thought.

[28] Ibid., p. 60.
[29] Ibid., p. 65.
[30] See Chapter 20.

The Romans, like the ancient Greeks and many other ancient peoples, saw pollution as attaching to certain forms of violence, including rape, and had taboos covering even normal bodily experiences such as menstruation, although only extreme violations of taboos were beyond purification. Here is the Roman historian, Livy:

> In that year, the Vestal Minucia, suspected in the first instance because of her dress, which was more ornate than became her station, was subsequently accused before the pontiffs on the testimony of a slave, and having been by their decree commanded to keep aloof from the sacred rites and to retain her slaves in her own power, was convicted and buried alive near the Colline Gate, to the right of the paved road in the Polluted Field – so called, I believe, on account of her unchastity.[31]

Unchastity meant several different things but here seems to have meant having sexual relations with a vestal virgin who had taken an oath of chastity and also was not supposed to have sexual relations with men on consecrated ground.

In Roman culture there were two main sources of pollution: the blood of someone that had been murdered, or the breaking of a taboo concerning sexual practices. And in an intriguing twist on the Greek idea that the furies pursued those who spilled blood, especially of their closest kin, Cicero declares that actually the hounding of the polluted is internal to the person's conscience, not external in terms of physical punishment.

Pollution can also be related to honor, as appears to be the case in ancient Mesopotamia. Discussing the dietary laws in Leviticus, Mary Douglas postulates that "the Hellenic influence allows the medical and ethical interpretations to run together." The taboos here "coincide with what natural reason would dictate for achieving the good life."[32] Douglas also addresses directly the connection between things that are said to be polluted and things that cause or are associated with danger. Indeed, Douglas claims that "pollution is a type of danger which is not likely to occur except where the lines of structure, cosmic or social, are clearly defined. A polluting person is always in the wrong."[33]

The connection between pollution and danger, and the connection between avoiding pollution and achieving a good life, give us a different understanding of pollution than what we have previously explored. Here pollution is explained not in terms of what one's group has done, or about getting one's hands dirty, or about

[31] Livy, *History of Rome*, Book VIII, Chapter XV, translated by B. O. Foster, Loeb edition, Cambridge, MA: Harvard University Press, 1926, p. 63.

[32] Mary Douglas, *Purity and Power: An Analysis of the Concept of Pollution and Taboo*, NY: Routledge, 1966, 2002, p. 55.

[33] Ibid., p. 140.

having blood on one's hands. Here pollution is about violating rules that the society has determined to promote the avoidance of danger. For Douglas, the polluted person is in the wrong because he or she has violated the society's rules that are aimed to protect the society.

And in returning to the Mesopotamian cases with which we began this section, we can also explain much of the harshness of the punishments of women in terms of pollution. Adultery, like unchastity, challenged the social institutions in Mesopotamia. In the next section we examine whether patriarchy was one such tradition concerning women and how strong a role it played. We also ask how the separate spheres thesis is affected by the thesis about patriarchy. In addition we ask about the extent of equality embodied in the separate spheres.

7.5 PATRIARCHY AND SEPARATE SPHERES

When women are said today to be confined to separate spheres it is primarily meant that they occupy the private sphere of home where they raise the children, cook the meals, and cater to the needs of their husbands. Men occupy the public sphere in such an arrangement, where they earn income, participate in political life, and keep their women from harm. Since at least the nineteenth century CE writings of Harriet Taylor and John Stuart Mill, this separate spheres arrangement has been criticized as inherently an unequal arrangement that was unfair to women who were forced to lead stunted lives. Patriarchy, the rule of men over women, has been seen as not only consistent with separate spheres but even promoted by the consignment of women to the private sphere.

Here is a key passage from Mill and Taylor's famous book, *The Subjection of Women*:

> Originally women were taken by force, or regularly sold by their father to the husband. Until a late period in European history, the father had the power to dispose of his daughter in marriage at his own will and pleasure, without any regard to hers … After marriage, the man had anciently (but this was anterior to Christianity) the power of life and death over his wife. She could invoke no law against him; he was her sole tribunal and law … [Today] She can acquire no property but for him; the instant it becomes hers, even if by inheritance, it becomes ipso facto his. In this respect the wife's position under the common law of England is worse than that of slaves …[34]

For Mill and Taylor, the woman's role is worse than that of the slave because at least the slave can achieve manumission under certain conditions.

[34] John Stuart Mill and Harriet Taylor, *The Subjection of Women* (1869), Indianapolis: Hackett Publishing Company, 1988, pp. 31–32.

I have attempted to show in the previous sections of this chapter that if there were separate spheres in ancient Mesopotamia these spheres did not map onto the separation of the private and public, with women in the private and men in the public spheres. In particular, in reference to Mill and Taylor's book, in ancient Mesopotamia (1) husbands and fathers did not have the right of life or death over their wives or daughters; (2) there were laws that women could invoke if they were harmed by their fathers or husbands; (3) women could acquire property; (4) they had rights of inheritance; and (5) they could divorce their husbands under certain conditions. So, women in ancient Mesopotamia were not subjected to men in the way that Mill and Taylor describe the status of women under the English common law.

The separate sphere that women occupied in ancient Mesopotamia was not one where women were subjugated and men were free. Instead, women had roles in public life where they could be said to have some freedom. It is certainly clear that men had a larger set of public roles than did women. But within their separate public and private spheres women also could attain freedom. It is not the case that these spheres were "separate but equal." Yet, because the law recognized women's "rights" in various matters, the status of women was not one of subjugation but of relative freedom, at least for certain women.

So, what can be said about whether or not ancient Mesopotamian society was patriarchal? If patriarchy is what Mill and Taylor said of the male-dominated English society of the common law era, then it does not appear that ancient Mesopotamian society was patriarchal. Yet, as we saw women were betrothed by their fathers and faced rather severe punishments in cases of adultery. As we saw, the men who were convicted of rape also faced very severe punishments, and it was not necessarily because of the harm to men's honor but instead the harm to society's traditions.

It is not anachronistic to say that women had "rights" recognized at law in ancient Mesopotamia. As Jean Bottero has argued:

> the Mesopotamian woman – married or not – could freely possess her own property of any kind, jewel, money, slaves and dispose of them as she wished; she could sell them, have them bought back, give them away as presents in her lifetime or leave them to whomever she wished after her death – because she was completely free to make a will ... A woman similarly had the right to act as witness to a transaction, and legally guarantee its authenticity, in her signature- seal on the relevant deed – for she possessed her own personal seal, the indubitable mark of her legal independence.[35]

[35] Jean Bottero, "Women's Rights," in his *Everyday Life in Ancient Mesopotamia*, translated by Antonia Nevill, Baltimore, MD: Johns Hopkins University Press, 1992, pp. 123–124.

Bottero calls these "women's rights." But he also admits that "it was a constant feature in Mesopotamia that in matters of public authority and sovereign power the foreground was occupied exclusively by representatives of the male sex."[36]

Some scholars have argued that the position of women became more restricted under Mesopotamian Semitic influences, especially by the time of Hammurabi.[37] But we saw above that the position of women was still relatively free during Hammurabi's reign. Some other scholars have seen such a change occurring at the end of the second millennium, during the rise of Assyria. Harriet Crawford has said: "The situation of women seems to have changed and to have become considerably more restricted by the end of the second millennium [BCE], judging from the evidence of the Middle Assyrian Laws." She says it is unclear why things changed but it is notable that by this time there was an "absence of women in public life."[38] Yet, Crawford comments that, just a few hundred years earlier, "women made important contributions to the public, as well as the private, spheres."[39]

It is interesting that the oldest of the legal texts that we have paints a picture of women's legal status that is not a form of chattel slavery. The picture is highly nuanced, where apparently women were able to exercise a fair amount of freedom in various professional roles, as well as within the more traditional female roles as wives and mothers. When women clearly acted outside their spheres, which included private as well as public roles, then they were subject to some of the harshest punishments of their societies. But keeping within those spheres, women had legal "rights" much more extensive than one might suppose in these ancient societies.

So, were women equal to men in ancient Mesopotamian society before the end of the second millennium? The answer is clearly "no," if one means exactly equal in each domain of life. But the answer can be a highly qualified "maybe" when we see a genuine equality between differential but still important roles for both men and women in many areas of life. In some areas of life women were of inferior status to men, but in other areas of life women were equal to men. Separate spheres are problematic in terms of equality when the areas where women are assigned are greatly devalued compared to those areas where men are assigned, but not when the areas of separate spheres are genuinely valued for both men and women.

36 Ibid., p. 124.

37 This is the argument of Elizabeth Meier Tetlow in her book *Women Crime and Punishment in Ancient Law and Society*.

38 Harriet Crawford, "An Exploration of the World of Women in Third-Millennium Mesopotamia," in *Women in the Ancient Near East*, p. 23.

39 Ibid., p. 22.

SECTION III

Crime and Punishment

8

Complicity and Conspiracy

In this chapter I will examine two famous trials in ancient Egypt, and one in Mesopotamia, in order to gain an understanding of how the idea of complicity was conceptualized in ancient legal thought. I will argue that these trials provide a window into a fairly sophisticated understanding of individual and collective guilt that existed in ancient societies. Our first case, the Harem Conspiracy trial, (approximately 1100 BCE in the 20th Dynasty) is fascinating in its own right since it addresses the assassination of Ramses III by members of his royal court. By some accounts Ramses III was the last great pharaoh of ancient Egypt. The second case, the Royal Tomb Robberies trials (also dating from the 20th Dynasty) is wonderful for what it tells about life in ancient Egypt. The trial record shows how palace guards were complicit in that they were enlisted to aid the robberies of very great wealth in the burial tombs of the pharaohs. The third case, which we already began to examine in an earlier chapter, concerns a wife who is tried for homicide in Mesopotamia because she kept silent about a plot to kill her husband.

Among many questions to be considered in this chapter are those relating to liability, especially in terms of how much assistance or omission one needs to have engaged in for one to be held criminally liable? In Section 8.1 I will rehearse some of the most important facts of the Harem Conspiracy case. In Section 8.2 I will rehearse some of the main facts of the Tomb Robberies case. In Section 8.3 I will give a preliminary account of how ancient Egyptian legal authorities conceptualized conspiracy and I will address the question of how important individual guilt was in these trials, and what difference it makes for such liability if one's inactions are connected to one's roles, by examining a case from Mesopotamia. And in Section 8.4 I will attempt to say something about larger issues of conspiracy and complicity.

8.1 CONSPIRACY IN AN EGYPTIAN HAREM

Thirty-two conspirators were executed in 1167 BCE for conspiring to kill the Egyptian pharaoh, Ramses III.[1] We have a written record of the various court proceedings leading up to the executions. In this section I will examine this record and ask how it was that conspiracy was conceived in ancient Egyptian legal thought. In Section 8.2 I will examine another written record of a trial of tomb robbing conspirators that dates from just a bit later in ancient Egypt. Both of these trials are fascinating insofar as they involve not only high-ranking officials, including a queen and her son the prince, but also because of how the common folk joined with the officials in a conspiracy. Of even more interest, and the main interest of this chapter, is the variegated way that conspiracy was conceptualized in ancient legal thought.

In the text called the Judicial Papyrus we learn of the charges that were brought against the first group of conspirators who sought to kill Ramses III. I here give an excerpt that indicates some of the conspirators and what role they were said to have played:

> Persons arraigned for the great crimes they had committed and placed in the Court of Examination before the great magistrates of the Court of Examination … They examined them; they found them guilty; they brought their punishment upon them; their crimes caught up with them.
>
> The great criminal, Paibakaman, formerly pantry chef.
>
> He was arraigned because of his collusion with Teya and the women of the harem. He made common cause with them and began bearing their messages outside to their mothers and their brothers who were there saying: "Get people together! Incite hostilities in order to provoke rebellion against their lord." …
>
> The great criminal, Petewentamana, formerly agent of the harem in the retinue. He was arraigned because of his having overheard the matters the men had plotted with the women of the harem, and he had not come forward on their account.
>
> Wives of the men of the harem gate, who sided with those men who were plotting those things … Total six women.[2]

[1] There has been much controversy among scholars about whether Ramses III was indeed murdered by the harem conspirators. Most scholars doubted that the conspirators succeeded, since there was no record of this fact. But now, the record seems rather clear. Here is what Eric H. Cline says, in his book *1177 BC: The Year Civilization Collapsed*, Princeton: Princeton University Press, 2014, p. 137:"In 2012, Egyptologists and forensic scientists conducted an autopsy of Ramses III's body and reported in the British Medical Journal that his throat had been cut. The sharp knife that caused the wound had been thrust into his neck immediately under the larynx, all the way down to the cervical vertebra … Death was instantaneous … a thick collar of linen had been placed around his neck, in order to hide the stab wound."

[2] Quoted in Susan Redford, *The Harem Conspiracy*, Dekalb, IL: Northern Illinois University Press, 2002, 2008, pp. 13–15.

We have here various kinds of conspirators, which I will more broadly summarize in a moment.

In another text called the Papyrus Rollin, there is a separate category of conspirators mentioned, those who used magic to incapacitate the guards:

> [Name of accused missing] ... He began to prepare magical texts for the purpose of confusing and disturbing, and to make waxen (figures) of some gods and some potions for disabling the limbs of people.[3]

There was a cataloguing of the accused which ranged from those who perpetrated the killing of the pharaoh, to those who facilitated the killing, to those who knew something of the plot but said nothing, to those who were somehow sympathetic with the plotters.

The harem conspirators can be divided into the following groups. First, of course, there were the perpetrators of the conspiracy. We can divide this group into two: those who executed the plan and those who formulated the plan. In the former group there is Paibakamana, who is called the harem's pantry chief and who was incited to plot to kill the king by an unindicted co-conspirator, Teya, the chief wife of Ramesses III. Since the conspiracy is not just to kill the king, but also to replace him with a prince who is not next in succession, there is also a coup d'état which requires military figures as the main perpetrators as well. Here we find Pasai, general of the Egyptian army, and Bonemwese, battalion commander of Nubian soldiers. In addition, there are several members of the inner court: a butler, a scribe, and an overseer of the harem, who plan the killing of the king and the coup d'état. Teya's son, who is to be installed as the new king, is another unindicted co-conspirator who plays a principal role in planning the conspiracy.

Second are those who are collaborators – who aided and abetted the principal conspirators. Included in this group are various religious leaders and magicians who provided black magic and potions to render guards unconscious.

Third, there are those who kept quiet even though they knew of the plot to kill the pharaoh. Here we have various people who may not have intended to aid the principals but who knowingly did so nonetheless by not warning the pharaoh of what they knew of the conspiracy.

Fourth, is a curious group that is referred to as "sympathizers" with the principal conspirators. I am especially intrigued by this group as will become clear since it is so hard today, as well as in ancient times, to prove that someone is indeed a sympathizer rather than a mere bystander.

Let us turn first to these sympathizers. This group has such a tenuous connection to the main conspiracy that we are brought to consider how the larger society is

[3] Ibid., p. 18.

useful to, and perhaps restraining of, criminal behavior in ancient Egypt. It appears that some of the sympathizers are indeed punished for their "roles" in the Harem Conspiracy, although they are punished less severely than the main perpetrators. But it seems also to be true that there were many other sympathizers who were not brought to trial. Those who were tried seem to be those who had positions in the palace or were connected to the functioning of the palace. The idea seems to be that one way a person can be complicit as a sympathizer is if one were in a position where one might have acted to hinder the conspiracy but did not. This group is then opposed to those who sympathized with the conspirators but who did not have a position that would have allowed for more active participation.

It is also of note that the so-called "passive conspirators," the third group mentioned above, were convicted and sentenced to death along with the main perpetrators.[4] This is similar to our discussion in the next section of the Mesopotamian case where the wife of a murder victim, who did nothing except remain silent, was nonetheless sentenced to death. Passive conspirators are in a position to facilitate by failing to stop the main conspirators, perhaps by failing to do their jobs, failing to raise an alarm, etc.

Among those in the second group, those who were aiders and abettors, were some of the members of the royal harem and even apparently the main queen herself. These individuals could have played an even greater role than the main perpetrators insofar as they planned and then incited the perpetrators to kill, or at least attempt to kill, Ramses III. We do not know whether or not the queen was punished for instigating the conspiracy, but we do know that several high-ranking members of the priestly class were convicted and sentenced to take their own lives, rather than to be executed by being burned alive as was true for those participants who were not high ranking.[5]

In addition, some of the conspirators were tried separately and in secret trials. Here is how one scholar accounts for these separate trials:

> The reason some of the defendants were judged separately is clear: the testimony of those five men was directly related to the crimes of the harem women and would reveal in the women's own words the discussions about the king and their desire to overthrow him. Pentawere and the harem women were members of the king's extended family and the family's "dirty laundry" was not a matter for public knowledge. Like Weni of 1200 years earlier, who boasted that only he and a single scribe were allowed by Pharaoh to hear the charges against the royal harem, it would be

4 Redford, *The Harem Conspiracy*, p. 128.

5 See ibid., p. 124. It is interesting that Eric Peet, in comparing the tomb robberies case to the harem case, says that the perpetrators of the former were "not exceptional criminals" but merely "common tomb-robbers." See T. Eric Peet, *The Great Tomb-Robberies of the Twentieth Egyptian Dynasty*, Oxford: Clarendon Press, 1930, p. 27, note 1.

> these high ranking butlers, confidants of the king, who would be entrusted with hearing the sensitive evidence.[6]

The royal prince was also dealt with separately and was the only conspirator not decried as a "great criminal."[7]

The main perpetrators were led by an army general and a battalion commander, who were in charge of the armed rebellion that was to follow the killing of Ramses III. On the inside, there was a pantry chef and a butler who were responsible for actually killing the king. It is interesting that these individuals, while treated quite harshly, were not treated more harshly than some of those who played a less active role in the Harem Conspiracy. Yet, as we will see later, all are tried in a way that brings out their individual guilt within the setting of the larger group crime.

John A. Wilson has this account of how responsibility was determined in the Harem Conspiracy:

> [Ramesses III's] disclaimer of responsibility and his fixing of the onus of impartial justice upon a court of civil officials, instead of leaving vengeance to his son and successor, illustrate the decline of personal power and authority of the pharaoh. The law was fully delegated from the king to magistrates, who normally acted in his name but were actually full arbiters of justice.[8]

Wilson here seems to disapprove of the formality of law that had replaced the customary base of the pharaoh's personal power. Yet, surely this is a development that is crucial in the long history of the rule of law.

Diodorus explained that such conspiracies would have been very difficult to mount in Nubia because of the way the king's court was treated as his extended family:

> [In Meroe] they say that it is customary for the comrades of the kings even to die with them of their own accord and that such a death is an honorable one and proof of true friendship. And it is for this reason, they add, that a conspiracy against the king is not easily raised among the Ethiopians, all friends being equally concerned both for his safety and for their own.[9]

Apparently, the pharaoh also treated his Egyptian court as an extended family as well, which is why the case we are examining is so interesting.

At the end of Wilson's book about ancient Egypt, just a few pages after the discussion of the Harem Conspiracy and the tomb robberies, he expresses support

6 The Harem Conspiracy, ibid., p. 129.

7 Ibid., p. 86.

8 John A. Wilson, *The Culture of Ancient Egypt*, Chicago: U. of Chicago Press, 1951, p. 268.

9 Diodorus of Sicily, *The Library of History* II, Bk III, Ch. 7, translated by C. H. Oldfather, Loeb Library, Cambridge, MA: Harvard University Press, 1953, p. 103.

for the idea of the Old Kingdom which put its faith in the wisdom of the ancient king. He bemoans the "dreary inflexibility" of the later stages of Egyptian rule. But the cult of the wise king still had royal assassinations and tomb robbers. Wilson is right though to note that over time a legal system typically becomes more and more inflexible about matters of justice. But this, as I have been arguing throughout this work, is why there is then a renewed need for considerations of equity. Conspiracies that involve officials are not caused by an inflexible system of law, or even a decline in the moral authority of the law. At the end of this chapter we will seek an understanding that is more subtle and better fits the facts.

8.2 CONSPIRACY AND THE GREAT TOMB ROBBERIES

We now move to a slightly later time – the reign of Ramses IX and his immediate successors at the end of the Twentieth Dynasty of ancient Egypt, which is at the end of the Twelfth Century BCE. In Thebes, there was a vast area known as the Necropolis, the city of the dead, where most of the important pharaohs and their wives had been buried in elaborate tombs and pyramids. As one scholar puts it:

> The great Necropolis of Thebes plays such an important part in the group of papyri here treated, both as the scene of many of the thefts and in virtue of the connection of members of its staff with the perpetration of the crimes and the prosecution of the guilty parties.[10]

The tomb robberies were probably initially motivated by the fact that the workers at the Necropolis were only paid in food and clothing rations, and these rations were often delivered late to the workers. Among the splendor of the tombs, these workers, who were worse off than peasants, saw a chance to gain considerable wealth. And as we will also see, the workers found willing allies among the officials who were responsible for the upkeep of the tombs, and who were also motivated by the chance to vastly improve their own lot in life.[11]

Here is some of the transcript taken from the Abbott Papyrus just to give a flavor of how the crimes and the participants were described at the time:

> The pyramid tomb of King Sekhemrershedtaui, Son of Re Sebkemsaf. It was found to have been violated by the thieves by tunneling in the *nfrw*-chamber of its pyramid from the outer hall of the rock tomb of Nebamun, overseer of the granary of King Menkheperrer …
>
> The tombs and chambers in which rest the blessed ones of old, the citizenesses and citizens on the West of Thebes. It was found that the thieves had violated them all,

10 Peet, *The Great Tomb-Robberies*, p. 9.

11 See ibid., pp. 12–13.

> dragging their owners from their inner coffins and their outer coffins so that they were left in the desert, and stealing their funerary outfit …
>
> Pewerro, Empereramun herald of the West and chief of Mazoi of the Necropolis, placed the list of thieves in writing before the vizier and the notables and the butlers. They were seized and imprisoned: they were examined, they told what had occurred.[12]

The conspirators include those people who did the robbing, those guards who were bribed, and those who aided the robbers, as we will see.

It is clear that the robberies took place because of the paying of bribes to officials and soldiers who were charged with guarding the tombs from the very sorts of robbers that were eventually caught and prosecuted.[13] It is also clear that the conspiracy involved many others including, for instance, a fisherman who "ferried over six thieves and received from them … gold for his services."[14] In addition there are many others who knew about what was occurring and kept silent for a price, as is true of "two men who received some silver when they threatened exposure … 'though they did not go.'"[15] And as the texts make clear, many of those prosecuted were "members of the Necropolis staff."[16]

In one case, it is clear that the stolen goods from the tombs ended up in the hands of two priests.[17] And it is also clear that the priests were discovered by a ferry-man to have stolen treasure and that the priests "bought his silence with the gift of a garment."[18] The ferry-man's son then testifies to these facts in one of the trials. But despite repeated beatings by the members of the court, the ferry-man would not confess and was seemingly released.[19] We never learn definitely what happened to the priests but they seem to have been caught up with the other members of the conspiracy and dealt with harshly by the court.

In these trials, unlike the Harem trials, those convicted were not summarily sentenced to death.[20] In addition, quite a few individuals were acquitted. That there were acquittals as well as convictions is today considered one of the hallmarks of a fair trial procedure – and I can only assume that this was also true in ancient Egypt as well. We will discuss the issues concerning the rule of law later, but here can

[12] Translated in ibid., pp. 38–39.
[13] See ibid., p. 36.
[14] Ibid., p. 53.
[15] Ibid., p. 25.
[16] Ibid., p. 72.
[17] Ibid., p. 142.
[18] Ibid.
[19] Ibid., p. 152.
[20] Ibid., p. 26.

point out that the court seems especially attuned to the specific role each defendant played, and there is an attempt to match the punishment to the specific role of each.

As with the Harem Conspiracy, there were quite a few people who were indicted who had only a very loose connection to the perpetrators of the robberies. In this group is included those who knew something about the robberies but accepted bribes for their silence. These people are acquitted of the main charge, but nonetheless "condemned for receiving silver known to be stolen."[21] It is curious that these people are not convicted for their roles, passive though they may have been, as was true of some of those involved in the Harem Conspiracy. Of course, since these people are punished quite severely for receiving stolen property I suppose the practical difference is not that much – but the conceptual point is important, nonetheless.

There is a fascinating bit of testimony that seems to show that the average Egyptian was quite aware that both direct perpetrators and accomplices are responsible individuals. A ferry-man's son is being examined and he says:

> They said to him … be you silent and we will give you a *daiu*-garment. So said they to him. And they gave him a *daiu*-garment. But my mother said to him. Silly old man that you are, what you have done is committing theft.[22]

This allows us to see something of the legal thought at this time, not of those who were the members of the royalty and royal scribes, but the common people. And the upshot seems to be that there is a recognition of the guilt that attaches to those who are complicit.

John A. Wilson describes an earlier robbery of a temple that adds insight into our understanding of conspiracies in ancient Egypt:

> In other words, over a period of nine years the temple received only 576 out of 6,300 sacks, slightly over 9 per cent. The ship captain could not have engaged in the wholesale robbery without the knowledge and participation of a host of agents, all the way up from the farmers who delivered the grain to his boat in the Delta to the clerks who registered it at the Temple of Khnum at the First Cataract. The sacks which disappeared were reported as the "total of the grain of the Temple of Khnum, Lord of Elephantine, on which this ship captain conspired with the clerks, administrators, and peasant farmers of the Temple of Khnum, and they looted it and made free with it for their own purposes."[23]

Conspiracies of this sort seem to be not all that uncommon in ancient Egypt.

[21] Ibid., p. 25.

[22] Ibid., p. 152.

[23] Wilson, *The Culture of Ancient Egypt*, p. 280.

Wilson gives the following assessment of how common conspiracies to rob tombs had become.

> A certain amount of looting from the richly piled tombs had always been endemic in Egypt. As far back as the Fourth Dynasty the tomb of Khufu's mother seems to have been plundered in his own lifetime …
>
> The acute epidemic of tomb robbery in the Twentieth Dynasty broke out because the state was desperately ill … Most important of all, the recognized sanctions of the sacred state had weakened, so that there was no effective moral feeling against robbery within a government preserve and against the sacrilege of violating the eternal rest of the gods … But the continuation of the looting for a full generation without effective check and the continuance in office of responsible officials throughout the period make it clear that highly placed officials were privy to the activity and probably were enriching themselves from the plundering.[24]

Theft from the pharaohs' tombs was common yet so was the understanding that it was a wrong.

Concerning the trial of the tomb robbers, we find this account of what happened in its aftermath.

> After the trial, we never hear another word about Pa-ser, the Mayor of Thebes. He drops out of the record. On the other hand, his wily rival, Pa-wer-aa, was still Mayor and Chief of Police in Western Thebes seventeen years later, seventeen years in which the tomb robberies in his district continued in crescendo … In all the documents of investigation there was not a single defendant of high position. Only the little men, the stonemasons and coppersmiths and farmers, were caught …
>
> Amon-pa-nefer continued: "Then we crossed over to Thebes. And after some days the agents of Thebes heard that we had been stealing in the west, so they arrested me and imprisoned me at the Mayor of Thebes' place. So I took twenty *deben* of gold that had fallen to me as (my) share, and I gave them to Kha-em-Oper, the District Clerk of the harbor of Thebes. He let me go, and I joined my companions, and they made up for me another share" …
>
> the bribe went on up high enough to choke off any inquisitiveness about the failure of legal procedure. The long and sorry record of the tomb robberies of the Twentieth Dynasty is a story of higher officials evading their duties because they were gaining personal advantage out of such an evasion. It was the cynical rejection of the content of *maat* and a retention of so much of the form of *maat* as would make an impressive documentary show.[25]

[24] Ibid., p. 282.

[25] Ibid., pp. 286–287.

We will now begin to take stock and try to understand how conspiracy and complicity were understood in ancient Egyptian legal thought.

8.3 GUILT BASED ON INACTION AND COMPLICITY IN EGYPT AND MESOPOTAMIA

One might initially think that in ancient times conspiracies would be dealt with by simply executing all of those who were involved, or who were likely to be involved. In this way sufficient deterrence would be accomplished. But this is definitely not what we have found in the trials that occurred for the harem assassination plot and the various tomb robbery cases. Indeed, quite surprising perhaps is the fact that several people were acquitted, and some others were not summarily executed but given sentences of less than death.

Diodorus, writing about ancient Egyptian affairs provides an interesting take on how responsibility was understood in one of its forms:

> if a man, walking on a road in Egypt, saw a person being killed, or in a word, suffering any kind of violence and did not come to his aid if able to do so, he had to die; and if he was truly prevented from aiding another person because of inability, he was in any case required to lodge information against the bandits, and to bring an action against their lawless act; and in case he failed to do this as the law required that he be scourged with a fixed number of stripes and he be deprived of every kind of food for three days.[26]

We can learn here that inaction, similar to action, was thought to be important and that in certain circumstances it could give rise to legal liability.

One of the most striking features of a murder case from ancient Mesopotamia is that the wife of the victim is convicted of murder and sentenced to death for what appears to be a very small role, if that, that she played in the murder. The victim's wife, Nin-Dada, is said to have been told of the plot to kill her husband and to have said nothing about it. Yet, she is said to be guilty of murder and her guilt is said to be greater than that of the actual perpetrators of the murder.

Today it is common to distinguish between those who are merely inactive and those who omit to act. Inaction is not normally thought to constitute complicity except when it rises to be an omission. Omissions are culpable insofar as the person has a duty to act that was unfulfilled by his or her not acting.[27] The legal idea is that only when inaction is in conflict with duty to act is there liability. Such an idea is perhaps older than we normally realize, as I shall argue in this section, before

[26] Diodorus of Sicily, *The Library of History* 1, Book 1, Chapter 77, translated by C. H. Oldfather, Loeb Library, Cambridge: Harvard University Press, 1933, p. 265.

[27] See Christine Sistare, *Responsibility and Criminal Liability*, NY: Springer Verlag, 1989.

returning our gaze to the rule of law. The subtle difference between inaction and omission seems to be present in the Mesopotamian murder case.

As we saw in an earlier chapter, Nin-Dada is indicted and then convicted because she "opened not her mouth, covered it up." The jury asked the assembly, acting as a kind of appellate court, to clear the matter up:

> "Nin-dada, daughter of Lu-Ninurtas, may have killed her husband;
> but what can a woman do in (such a matter) that she is to be killed?" they said.
> In the Assembly of Nippur it (the assembly) addressed them as follows:
> "A woman who values not her husband
> may give information to his enemy and thus
> he (i.e., the enemy) may (be able to) kill her husband.
> That her husband is killed he (i.e., the enemy) may (then) let her hear
> - why should he not thus make her keep silent about him? –
> her guilt is greater than (theirs:) that they killed a man" they said.[28]

Here the assembly speculates that Nin-Dada could have given information to her husband's killers – but there is no evidence offered to support this speculation.

What seems to be most important is that Nin-Dada kept quiet when she could have spoken out about the plans of the killers. It is startling that there is an ambiguity still remaining about whether she simply did not speak and hence "covered up" her mouth, or whether she had the kind of knowledge that when not revealed was instrumental in "covering up" the identities of those who had just carried out the plot to kill her husband. Today we would say that to be complicit in the murder her covering her mouth must be more than a mere inaction on her part, but an omission. Is there evidence of this subtlety in the account of the Mesopotamian case? I think there is and there is also evidence of how to view role responsibilities as well.

The assembly focuses on the fact that Nin-Dada was the "wife" of the victim, and this seems to make her inaction the kind of omission that would make her criminally liable. In this view, wives are supposed to protect their husbands. The question that is asked – "what can a woman do?" – is answered by the claim that a wife must "value her husband." Nin-Dada did not value her husband when she chose to keep quiet about the plot to kill her husband, whether this was after the fact or before. She is thus complicit in his murder for having failed to live up to her duty as a spouse.

Here we have, at least in germinal form, the idea of how to distinguish omissions from mere inactions. The distinction is drawn in terms of one's duties and these in turn are to be seen by examining one's role responsibilities. We might wonder

[28] Translated by Thorkild Jacobsen in "An Ancient Mesopotamian Trial for Homicide," in his *Toward the Image of Tammuz*, Cambridge, MA: Harvard University Press, 1970, p. 201.

whether a wife, for the Mesopotamians, had a greater duty than her husband to value and protect a spouse. It would seem that the wife's duties of "valuing" or "honoring" her husband are seen as very strong here and perhaps stronger than those for a husband in similar circumstances.

What is novel is why the Mesopotamians in this case would see what the wife didn't do as establishing "greater guilt" than what the men did in killing her husband. Here it appears that role responsibility is more important than general responsibility owed to fellow humans. Not only does Nin-Dada's failure to act establish her greater guilt than those who did act, but her failure to value her husband seems to be more significant for matters of guilt than the failure to value a fellow human expressed by the direct perpetrators of the murder.

The rule of law is implicated in these cases in that there is a clear legal duty not to murder in every society whereas the duty to value one's spouse is considerably less clear and probably not a legally promulgated duty at all in most societies. When juries give priority to moral over legal duties there is a problem for the rule of law, especially as we have seen when juries convict rather than exonerate on the basis of favoring moral over legal duties.

Of course, in the end it did not matter that the wife's familial duty was counted more heavily than the duties of humanity of the men who plotted to kill – since after all death sentences were handed down to the men as well as to the woman. But we have in this very early criminal trial evidence that those thinking about law in a conceptual way were already worrying about how to understand differential roles and how to weigh moral versus legal duties. It would seem that the rule of law is better promoted by giving legal duties greater weight in liability matters. But perhaps we have here a recognition that legality and morality are both implicated in questions of criminal liability since the fidelity to law, a paramount concept in the rule of law, cannot consistently ignore people's moral responsibilities. In this sense, there is an ineliminable moral aspect to the rule of law that explains the way those who are complicit and conspire are treated in terms of criminal liability.

We can also explore how these ideas are implicated in the two Egyptian cases with which we began this chapter. There is a difference in terms of complicity in the harem case based on what was one's role within the palace, and hence in terms of one's duties concerning omissions. Those who were members of the royal staff and the extended "family" of the palace were seen to be liable when they did not speak up about what they knew of the mounting conspiracy. Those who were similarly silent but who did not have special duties to the palace were treated much less severely than those who had such role-based duties and failed to meet them.

In the tomb robberies, the person who was a ferry-man, and not a member of the staff of the Necropolis, was treated much less severely than the person who was a member of the guards, for instance, who had duties to protect the tombs, even when what both people did was the same – doing nothing. In all three ancient cases we have examined, some people were tried and punished for doing nothing. We have seen that when a person's inaction is in violation of a duty, so that it is an omission not a mere inaction, the person is punished more severely than if the person had no duty that was violated by his or her inaction. Of course, there had to be some causal link between the inaction and the harm in question, such as the death of the pharaoh, the husband, or the tomb robbery.

8.4 CONCEPTUALIZING COMPLICITY

Today, there has been much debate about how to understand conspiracies and those who are complicit in large-scale crimes. One of the cases that has seemed easy concerns camp guards who did not try to stop genocide or crimes against humanity from occurring in these camps. What has proven more difficult has been the cases where people outside the camps were aware of what was occurring, and did nothing to stop large-scale harm, but had no *special* duty to do anything other than do nothing. These cases are especially difficult because it seems that there is still a *general* duty to fellow humans that has been violated. So, we today face the question of whether to treat differently types of what are essentially bystanders, and on what basis.

In the harem case discussed above, I said that we could distinguish four groups of people who were tried:

(1) Perpetrators
(2) Collaborators
(3) Aiders and abettors
(4) Sympathizers.

And I asked how the last two categories could have been separated and why different liability was assigned to each group of people who did nothing.

In the harem case, it appeared that the dividing line to separate bystanders was whether they worked in (or for) the palace, where the crime against the pharaoh occurred. While no explicit rationale is given, a plausible idea would be that those who had a relationship to the palace, such as the butlers and chefs, had special duties to the palace and especially to the pharaoh. Since it was the pharaoh who was attacked, it would make sense to distinguish those who were silent and inactive who had a special relationship to the pharaoh from those who did not, such as common folks in the nearby village.

One could argue that people who were sympathetic with the killers, and because of these sympathies did nothing, should be treated the same. The inaction of both groups could be said in some sense to facilitate the attempted regicide. But causation is not sufficient for legal liability, even in these ancient times. The question of guilt also arises, and here, perhaps controversially even today, degrees of guilt can sometimes track what duties were unmet. Of course, the duties must be relevant to the inaction, which seems to be true for the "bystanders" who were punished most severely.

In the tomb robbery cases, those who had a special relationship to the sacred tombs, such as the guards, were separated from those who had no special relationship, such as the ferry-man. And the officials from the Necropolis who remained silent are seen as more guilty yet. Of course the case is not quite as clear-cut as the harem case, since the ferry-man while remaining silent also did transport some of the robbers in a kind of get-away. So, the ferry-man is not merely a bystander who did nothing. But his silence was very important nonetheless, and yet it was not treated as severely as that of others who had a stronger attachment to the sacred tombs.

In the Mesopotamian homicide case of the woman who kept silent about the plot to kill her husband, we are faced with an even harder case, but one where it appears that the special duties of the woman, as wife, played a major role in accounting for her death sentence. Indeed, there is even a mention of her role as wife in the meting out of her penalty. The role of wife is not the same as a professional role, such as that of guard or butler or mayor. But there is a sense that one chooses to be a wife, although there is not nearly as much choice in ancient Mesopotamia as in Western countries today. And what is required of "wives" is perhaps not as clear as what is required of people who have taken on professional roles. But a wife's duties to her husband are different than the duties that an unrelated bystander has to the wife's husband.

One could still wonder why the wife who said and did nothing is treated the same as those who were perpetrators and collaborators. Since all are sentenced to death, we would need to understand the use of the death penalty in ancient times, which would take us too far afield in this chapter, but will be the subject of a separate treatment in chapter ten. There we will attempt to untangle the various reasons for the use of the death penalty in ancient societies such as Mesopotamia.

One category today that seems to be quite similar to ancient construals of complicity concerns those who were employees in concentration camps. It is assumed that those who are camp guards knew, or should have known, what goes on in the camps. And it is further believed that the guards have a special set of duties to those who are held in the camps – most importantly to prevent harm to the campmates. In many cases, the camp guards are not proven to have committed violence against any campmates. And the guards certainly did not plan the deaths in the camps – their leaders are clearly responsible for the planning. Yet, it is thought that the guards are complicit largely for omissions to aid.

But as the people in question are in positions further removed yet from a connection to the crime and its direct perpetrators things get much harder for assigning criminal liability. And things are not helped today by the claim that, especially in crimes against humanity, we all have a duty not to be silent in the face of these atrocities. This claim is surely right morally – the question is only how morality here should influence criminality. Is the immorality of not going to the aid of a fellow human who is in danger or who is suffering sufficient to make this a criminal matter with correspondingly harsh punishments?

There has been a debate over the years since ancient times about how much of criminal law should reflect morality. The folk history of criminal law is that the idea of the criminality of an act is deeply enmeshed with the immorality of that act. Murder is often thought to best epitomize this close connection, and we will see in a later chapter that the Biblical laws against murder are in some sense both moral laws and also criminal laws for the ancient Israelites. And discussions of natural law highlight how one school of jurisprudence sees an intimate connection between morality and most areas of law. It is beyond the scope of this chapter to delve into this debate. What is important though is that many theorists believed, and continue to believe, that criminal law only makes sense as an expression of strong moral sentiments against various forms of harmful behavior.

In ancient Egypt and Mesopotamia, the way that complicity was understood seems very much a precursor of the later debates on the relationship of criminality and morality. This is at least in part because complicity comes in so many degrees so that at a certain point what seems clearly, and solely, moral complicity bridges seamlessly into legal complicity. This is especially evident when we consider cases where the role of a professional or of a family member triggers duties that when unfulfilled affect how we will view a person's inaction. Where we draw the line between inaction that is not a matter of legal liability and inaction that becomes complicit omission is framed by moral views on how these roles should be conceived. The three cases we have examined in this chapter show that in ancient legal thought, the issue of complicity was important and treated with perhaps surprising sophistication and nuance.

9

Crime and *Lex Talionis*

As we saw in an earlier chapter, many authors who have written on ancient law, until at least quite recently, have treated "primitive law" as being law in an early stage of development. In this view, our modern laws are mature laws and are significantly different from ancient law, just as an adult is very different from a child. Ancient law had "*lex talionis*" and over time and up to contemporary times law has rid itself of this primitive concept, replacing it with fixed monetary and prison terms. In this chapter we will see that *lex talionis* is not the oldest form of penalty or punishment, and I will argue that there is much to be said in favor of this idea.

The model of humanitarianism, which I have earlier argued arose in ancient legal thought, seems to stand in stark contrast to the understanding of ancient rulers and legal systems that are overly "punitive." This comes out most clearly in the imputation of a punitive model of *lex talionis* (i.e., "an eye for an eye") that was thought, correctly, to epitomize some of ancient Mesopotamian criminal law. One of the most difficult parts of the larger argument of my work is to show that *lex talionis* can have a humanitarian face, or at least that *lex talionis* need not be opposed to humanitarianism. In this chapter, I will propose that the kind of *lex talionis* doctrine espoused in ancient Mesopotamia is based in the idea of proportionality – where the punishment must fit the crime, and be no harsher than that. I will argue that *lex talionis* stands against the idea that revenge could justify utter disregard of the humanity of the wrongdoer. In addition I will argue that the use of *lex talionis* by Hammurabi signals a rudimentary understanding of a criminal law that is different from civil law.

In Section 9.1 I look to those parts of Hammurabi's Code that are often cited as expressing *lex talionis*. In Section 9.2 I then examine parts of Hammurabi's Code that seem to be at odds with, or express a different punitive principle than, *lex talionis*. In Section 9.3 I offer a way to reconcile these matters by reconstructing the ancient Mesopotamian idea of proportionality (that the punishment should fit the crime). And in Section 9.4 I then confront the most important objections that have been offered to the *lex talionis* provisions of Hammurabi's laws and other ancient laws. In Section 9.5 I discuss the idea that Hammurabi's laws express a rudimentary idea of a distinct criminal law.

9.1 HAMMURABI AND *LEX TALIONIS*

One of the first things to note about *lex talionis* commonly understood in the Bible is that the idea had arisen in Hammurabi's laws in Mesopotamia earlier by a thousand years than the Bible. The second thing to note is that *lex talionis* plays only a small part in Hammurabi's laws – approximately a dozen laws compared to almost 300 laws overall. So, as I attempt to reconstruct the legal thought behind the *lex talionis* provisions of Hammurabi's Code, we must realize that the *lex talionis* provisions are in the midst of laws that contain many other types of punishment listed as well. In the current section I will detail the talionic provisions of Hammurabi's laws but will first start with the law codes that preceded Hammurabi in ancient Mesopotamia and begin to examine what the role of *lex talionis* might be in the overall code of law.

Approximately 350 years before Hammurabi propounded his laws, the Sumerian king Ur-Namma set out his laws in an area nearby. Here are some relevant laws:

> LU #18 If [a man] cuts off the foot of [another man with …], he shall weigh and deliver 10 shekels of silver.
>
> LU #19 If a man shatters the … bone of another man with a club, he shall weigh and deliver 60 shekels of silver.
>
> LU #20 If a man cuts off the nose of another man with … he shall weigh and deliver 40 shekels of silver.
>
> LU #22 If [a man knocks out another man's] tooth with […] he shall weigh and deliver 2 shekels of silver.[1]

Here we have monetary compensation rather than talionic punishment, even when it is the loss of a tooth – one of the two paradigmatic wrongs listed in the Biblical talionic laws. This is strong evidence for thinking that compensation did not come later in time than talionic penalties. Indeed, it seems that monetary compensation came slightly earlier than talionic penalties.

Next consider the Laws of Lipit-Ishtar, propounded by another Near Eastern king approximately 200 years before Hammurabi's laws. Here are some provisions:

> LL #34 If a man rents an ox and cuts the hoof tendon, he shall weigh and deliver one-third of its value (in silver).

[1] *Laws of Hammurabi*, in *Law Collections from Mesopotamia and Asia Minor*, second edition, translated by Martha T. Roth, Atlanta, GA: Scholars' Press, 1997, p. 19.

> LL #35 If a man rents an ox and destroys its eye, he shall weigh and deliver one-half of its value (in silver).
>
> LL #36 If a man rents an ox and breaks its horn, he shall weigh and deliver one-quarter of its value (in silver).
>
> LL #37 If a man rents an ox and breaks its tail, he shall weigh and deliver one-quarter of its value (in silver).[2]

Here we have what would be today called civil negligence acts, rather than criminal acts, and there is monetary compensation rather than *lex talionis* here as well. It might be inferred that the tort of negligence arises and calls for compensation earlier than the idea of *lex talionis*, although as we will see, there is one Law of Lipit-Ishtar that has a talionic form.

Finally, consider the Laws of Eshnunna, propounded by a king a bit before Hammurabi's laws. Again we have monetary compensation rather than retaliatory penalties:

> LE #42 If a man bites the nose of another man and thus cuts it off, he shall weigh and deliver 60 shekels of silver; an eye – 60 shekels; a tooth – 30 shekels; an ear – 30 shekels; a slap to the cheek – he shall weigh and deliver 10 shekels of silver.
>
> LE #43 If a man should cut off the finger of another man, he shall weigh and deliver 20 shekels of silver.
>
> LE #44 If a man knocks down another man in the street and thereby breaks his hand, he shall weigh and deliver 30 shekels of silver.
>
> LE #45 If a man should break his foot, he shall weigh and deliver 30 shekels of silver.
>
> LE #46 If a man strikes another man and thus breaks his collarbone, he shall weigh and deliver 20 shekels of silver.

Again, we find monetary penalties for those who cause losses of eyes, teeth, and fingers, not talionic penalties.

It is therefore quite interesting to see how Hammurabi's laws deal with many of the same situations addressed in the Mesopotamian codes of law that preceded, or were nearly contemporaneous with, Hammurabi. Here are the most famous of Hammurabi's laws that seem to have influenced the Biblical laws of the ancient Israelites.

> LH #196 If an *awilu* [free upper class member] should blind the eye of another *awilu*, they shall blind his eye.
>
> LH #197 If he should break the bone of another *awilu*, they shall break his bone.

[2] Ibid., p. 33.

> LH #200 If an *awilu* should knock out the tooth of another *awilu* of his own rank, they shall knock out his tooth.[3]

Here we have what is often referred to as the origin of the *lex talionis* formulation of an eye for an eye, a tooth for a tooth. But notice that the talionic penalties are restricted to the actions of *awilu*, free persons, when their actions cause harm to other *awilu*.

In my view, the most interesting of Hammurabi's laws is rarely recognized as somewhat talionic.

> LH #3 If a man comes forward to give false testimony in a case but cannot bring evidence for his accusation, if that case involves a capital offense, that man shall be killed.[4]

This is like *lex talionis* in that the punishment is exactly the same as what the victim or accused person would have suffered. This law is especially important since there may not be a victim and in any event the wrong is at least as much to the legal system as to a specific victim.

This provision of Hammurabi's laws has a parallel to a provision in the laws of Deuteronomy, and also in the Laws of Lipit-Ishtar, as we just saw. The Deuteronomy law is clearly later than Hammurabi's law, but the Lipit-Ishtar law is nearly 200 years earlier.

> *Deut.* 19: 18–19 And the judges shall make diligent inquisition: and behold, *if* the witness be a false witness, *and* hath testified falsely against his brother. Then shall ye do unto him, as he had thought to have done unto his brother; so shalt thou put the evil away from among you.

The law in Deuteronomy is wider in scope than Hammurabi's law; whereas the Lipit-Ishtar law does not appear to be about physical punishment.

> LL #17 If a man, without grounds, accuses another man of a matter of which he has no knowledge, and that man does not prove it, he shall bear the penalty of the matter for which he made the accusation.

Here, in the Lipit-Ishtar case, it seems that the penalty refers to monetary compensation, not to physical punishment.[5]

Apparently, there was also something similar in ancient Egypt, although it is not at all certain when the practice originated. Diodorus, writing in the first century BCE, says this about much earlier ancient Egyptian law:

3 Ibid., pp. 120–121.

4 Ibid., p. 81.

5 Although see Pamela Barmash, *Homicide in the Biblical World*, Cambridge: Cambridge University Press, 2005, Chapter 6.

> Those who brought false accusations against others had to suffer the penalty that would have been meted out to the accused persons had they been adjudged guilty.[6]

As in the case of Deuteronomy, the Egyptian law was probably much more recent than Hammurabi's laws that employed *lex talionis*.

In Hammurabi's laws, the laws of Deuteronomy, and ancient Egyptian law, providing false witness in a trial is said to merit a punishment that is of the same sort as what an accused person would have suffered as a result of the false evidence. The punishments for false witnessing seem to be a matter of public (criminal) law and not merely private law.[7] In addition, the penalty does not necessarily benefit the victim, but seems directed at some other goal. A compensatory penalty is much more in keeping with the goal of providing satisfaction for the victim, whereas *lex talionis* is better seen as a public rather than a private remedy, as we will see.

It will be of interest for the discussion in the next chapter that ancient Egyptian law treated perjury even more severely than false accusation. Again here is Diodorus:

> Now in the first place, their penalty for perjury was death, on the ground that such men are guilty of the two greatest transgressions – being impious towards the gods and overthrowing the mightiest pledge known among men.[8]

Thus, the link between the idea of *lex talionis* and the imposition of some death sentences emerges in quite different ways than is normally thought.

In addition, there are other penalties that also seem to have as their point the protection of an institution rather than concern for a victim who has been made to suffer. A very curious case is that of desertion in ancient Egypt.

> Among their other laws one, which concerned military affairs, made the punishment of deserters or of any who disobeyed the command of their leaders not death, but the uttermost disgrace; but if later on such men wiped their disgrace by a display of manly courage, they were restored to their former freedom of speech. Thus the lawgiver at the same time made disgrace a more terrible punishment than death, in order to accustom all the people to consider dishonor the greatest of evils, and he also believed that, while dead men could never be of value to society, men who had been disgraced would do many a good deed through their desire to regain freedom of speech.[9]

6 Diodorus of Sicily, *The Library of History* I, Book 1, Ch. 77, lines 4–6, translated by C. H. Oldfather, Cambridge, Loeb Library, MA: Harvard University Press, 1933, p. 265.

7 See David VanDrunen, "Natural Law, The Lex Talionis, and the Power of the Sword," *Liberty University Law Review*, Vol. 2, 2008, pp. 945–967, especially p. 957.

8 Diodorus of Sicily, *The Library of History* 1, Book 1, Chapter 77, pp. 263–265.

9 Diodorus, Book 1, Chapter 78, ibid., p. 269.

Here a specific penalty was devised to fit the crime of desertion, a crime that mainly affects the society as a whole. In the following sections of this chapter I will take up the emerging idea of ancient criminal punishment in greater detail.

9.2 PENALTIES AND PUNISHMENTS IN HAMMURABI'S CODE AND EGYPTIAN LAW

It is important here to note Hammurabi's laws #198, 199, and 201, where the assaulting party is of a different social rank than the victim. In these cases compensation rather than talionic punishment is proscribed.

> LH #198 If he should blind the eye of a commoner [*muskenum*] or break the bone of a commoner, he shall weigh and deliver 60 shekels of silver.
>
> LH #199 If he should blind the eye of an *awilu*'s slave or break the bone of an *awilu*'s slave, he shall weigh and deliver one-half of his value (in silver).
>
> LH #201 If he should knock out the tooth of a commoner, he shall weigh and deliver 20 shekels of silver.[10]

Hence, interspersed between the famous *lex talionic* provisions are non-talionic provisions.

Indeed, it seems that Hammurabi's *lex talionis* provisions concerning assault only apply to people of the same social status. And so even in Hammurabi's Code of Laws there is not an unequivocal embracing of *lex talionis*. This is even clearer when one notices that as in the talionic provisions I quoted in the previous section, namely # 196, 197, and 200, there are few other provisions that could be strictly classified as *lex talionis*, out of nearly 300 legal provisions in Hammurabi's Code of Laws. In this section, I will catalogue some of the seemingly anomalous laws when compared to the supposedly canonical talionic laws.

It is curious that the eye for an eye provision in #196 not only is contrasted with the compensation for an eye of #199. But in addition, there is an example of an eye *not* for an eye:

> LH #193 If the child of (i.e. reared by) a courtier or the child of (i.e. reared by) a *sekretu* identifies with the father's house and repudiates the father who raised him or the mother who raised him and departs his father's house, they shall pluck out his eye.[11]

And we also find another example of a lost eye that does *not* call for a lost eye in return:

[10] *Laws of Hammurabi*, p. 121.

[11] *Laws of Hammurabi*, p. 120.

> LH #218 If a physician performs major surgery with a bronze lancet upon an *awilu* and thus causes the *awilu*'s death, or opens an *awilu*'s temple with a bronze lancet and thus blinds the *awilu*'s eye, they shall cut off his hand.[12]

In part, this law sets a hand for an eye rather than an eye for an eye. And then we also have a case of a lost eye only calling for monetary compensation again when the victim is of a lower social class than the *awilu*.

> LH #220 If he [a physician] opens his (the commoner's slave's) temple with a bronze lancet and thus blinds his eye, he shall weigh and deliver silver equal to half his value.[13]

Seemingly, there is not a consistent application of the *lex talionis* principle to be found in Hammurabi's Code of Laws.

The overwhelming majority of laws in Hammurabi's Code either call for monetary compensation or for a death penalty, not a talionic punishment. For example, of the first seven laws, three laws call for a loss of estate, a monetary penalty, and a loss of judgeship. Here is an example that is telling even if not necessarily representative of the Laws of Hammurabi:

> LH #8 If a man steals an ox, a sheep, a donkey, a pig, or a boat – if it belongs either to the god or to the palace, he shall give thirtyfold; if it belongs to a commoner, he shall replace it tenfold; if the thief does not have anything to give, he shall be killed.[14]

Here, as with the overwhelming majority of Hammurabi's laws, there is nothing like a talionic punishment.

So, the question becomes why Hammurabi included within his laws the few talionic provisions we have seen. There are three types of case where *lex talionis* arises: (1) where a person of the highest social class assaults another member of that class; (2) where a person bears false witness putting in jeopardy someone on trial; and (3) where there is a substitution of one person for another, "vicarious" talon, as when a son or daughter is to be punished for what their parent has done. In the second case, there is an affront against a particular person, the victim of the false testimony; but there is also an affront to the judicial system that must rely on the truthful testimony of the parties that seek adjudication of their grievances. In the first case, there is a potential break-down in the class structure of the society, not merely an assault on a victim who is of the same status as the assailant. In the third case the loss may be so grave that the society at large is harmed (we will spend more time on

[12] *Laws of Hammurabi*, p. 123.

[13] Ibid., p. 123.

[14] Ibid., p. 82.

this set of cases in the next section of this chapter). In all of these cases of *lex talionis* in Hammurabi's laws, there is an affront to an institution beyond the mere affront to a particular person.

Laws that are aimed at protecting institutions, or in some other way aim to protect the society, are at least proto-criminal laws rather than civil laws. Criminal laws are characterized as involving acts which are a distinctly different concern of the state than acts that call for compensation. As George Fletcher says:

> Crimes intrude upon the public sphere as well as damage private interests. True the offender may harm a distinct individual, but the act of killing, stealing, burglary, or rape violates and unnerves the community as a whole. The crime generates a general fear of violence among those who learn about it. Because crime is an assault upon the public, it makes sense to think of punishment itself as an expression of public authority.[15]

It is my contention that the rudimentary idea of crime is first seen in the introduction of *lex talionis*, with its distinct kind of punishment. I do not disagree with Fletcher's characterization of what counts as a crime today. The origin of this idea is not only with the severity of the harm or its anticipated wide-spreadness.

In the case of Mesopotamia at the time of Hammurabi, threats to certain procedural practices satisfied this bill, but so did certain matters that aimed to preserve social hierarchy. The procedural matters that we have seen to be of most importance are those listed as the very first of Hammurabi's laws. We have seen the third of these, and here now are the first two:

> LH #1 If a man accuses another man and charges him with homicide but cannot bring proof against him, his accuser shall be killed.
>
> LH #2 If a man charges another man with practicing witchcraft but cannot bring proof against him, he who is charged with witchcraft shall go to the divine River Ordeal ... if the divine River Ordeal should clear the man and should he survive, he who made the charge against him shall be killed; he who submitted to the divine River Ordeal shall take full possession of his accuser's estate.[16]

Here the institution to be protected was that of truthful accusation and testimony.

In addition, within Mesopotamian society there were three distinct status categories (which was the subject of Chapter 6): those who were free persons (called *awilu*), those who are commoners with only some freedoms (called *muskenum*), and those who were not free at all (called slaves). Whatever we think of this class structure today, and I am certainly highly critical of it, the structure was thought to be integral to ancient Mesopotamian society. The use of *lex talionis* punishments

[15] George Fletcher, *Basic Concepts of Criminal Law*, NY: Oxford University Press, 1998, pp. 35–36.

[16] *Laws of Hammurabi*, p. 81.

was meant, in my view. to help protect that structure. The penalties for people who assaulted a member of the highest class, especially when the perpetrator was also of that class, was much sterner than if the assault was by a member of a higher class against a member of a lower class.

There is also the fact that those lower in status who attack someone of higher status are treated more harshly yet. If *lex talionis*, in one of its iterations, is meant to police social status or economic class it would be seen as doing so in conjunction with other punishments, such as the death penalty for a slave who attacks a free man. I will address the use of the death penalty in the next chapter. Sometimes the death sentence is consistent with *lex talionis* and sometimes not.

The emerging idea, central to ancient criminal law and punishment, is that the society or the state is in need of protection, and that there is a need for punishments to protect society that is different than the need for victims to receive compensation. How the law deals with such societal needs is seen in the use of *lex talionis* in Mesopotamia and other nations of the ancient Near East, as well as how the death penalty is used. There is both a deterrent and retributive aspect to such punishments that is significantly different from the compensatory penalties of these early law collections. Yet it is hard to see a clear line of development here. In my view rudimentary criminal law arose just slightly later than civil law, namely at the very beginning of legal thought.[17]

9.3 PROPORTIONALITY AND *LEX TALIONIS*

If we think about the idea of why punishment might have arisen it seems clear that punishment could follow a principle of simple reactive vengeance – a literal striking back at the person who has violated the norm or who has caused suffering. And there are few reasons not to strike back with as much force as one could muster. Indeed, one could strike back with lethal force even for the smallest infraction or the least harm. Such punishment can be quite effective in deterring the behavior in question, as tyrants have discovered over the centuries. Yet we do not have such laws and punishments in ancient Mesopotamia, in our earliest recorded ideas of law.

By comparison with simple reactive vengeance, *lex talionis* is often a muted form of punishment. Indeed, *lex talionis* is the epitome of proportionate response – the punishment is exactly the same as what the perpetrator caused to a victim. But when

[17] David Daube begins his important study of *lex talionis* by proclaiming: "The most probable inference is that criminal law notions and civil law notions, the principle of punishment and that of compensation, are of equal age." David Daube, *Studies in Biblical Law*, Cambridge: Cambridge University Press, 1947, p. 103.

compared to mere compensatory monetary penalties, *lex talionis* is much more severe. Yet it does depend on the comparison, and compared to "blind revenge" *lex talionis* is easily defensible since it incorporates the idea of proportionality that revenge often omits. Indeed, many have defined retribution in a way that separates it from revenge or vengeance due to the proportionate restraint of retribution.

For those who think that *lex talionis* is barbaric, it may be important to realize that *lex talionis* was probably not often applied literally, and that it would have been hard to provide a consistent *lex talionis* set of punishments in any event. As Jeremy Waldron has persuasively argued, *lex talionis* is best conceived as follows: "The action which constitutes punishment for an offense should possess some or all of the characteristics that made the offense wrong."[18] Waldron argues that the punishment needs to be similar, not identical, to the assault or other wrong. Many acts seem not to be able to be subject to identical punishments in any event, such as a person who committed treason or who committed rape.

Indeed, there are good historical reasons for thinking that *lex talionis* was rarely understood literally. In E. Sidney Hartland's book, *Primitive Law*, he says that "It rests with the chief who has jurisdiction at the place to decide whether the *lex talionis* shall be enforced, or whether a compensation shall be accepted."[19] And there are many Talmudic scholars who have argued over the centuries that Biblical *lex talionis* is not to be taken literally.[20] Scholars have contended that this was also true for Hammurabi's laws that seemingly employed *lex talionis* punishment. As Raymond Westbrook says: "the avenger in Mesopotamia and Anatolia in principle had a choice between actually exercising vengeance or accepting ransom."[21] Here ransom means paying compensation so that one did not have to give up one's life or a part of one's body.

Scholars have also claimed that laws that seemingly followed Hammurabi's laws employ similar although not identical punishments to the offense. Knut Tallqvist has said:

> The principle of retaliation, clearly conspicuous in LH [Laws of Hammurabi] and in the Old Testament, according to which punishment is to be of a similar character as the injury done by the offender or directed against the limb with which the crime has been committed, is traceable in the Assyrian laws also. In #50 he that has beaten a harlot is sentenced to receive "blow for blow." According to #9 the lower lip of a man who has bitten a man's wife shall be cut off. In #52 it is prescribed that the wife of the defiler of a virgin shall be delivered up for prostitution, and #8

[18] Jeremy Waldron, "Lex Talionis," *Arizona Law Review*, Vol. 34, 1992, pp. 25–51, especially p. 35.

[19] E. Sidney Hartland, *Primitive Law*, London, Kennikat Press, 1924, p. 155.

[20] See Jacob Milgrom, "Lex Talionis and the Rabbis," *Bible Review*, Vol. 12, no. 2, 1996, pp. 16–25.

[21] Raymond Westbrook, *Ex Oriente Lex*, Baltimore, MD: Johns Hopkins University Press, 2015, p. 207.

> decrees that a woman who has bruised both the testicles of a man shall lose both her hands.[22]

We may want to question whether the wrong person is being punished regardless of proportionality, as in the case of the defiler, but it is clear that the man who engaged in the defilement could not himself be literally defiled, since at this time defilement could apparently only be perpetrated by a man on a woman, although a Middle Assyrian Law called for a male rapist to be raped as his punishment.

The idea of having similarity of punishment and offense is today understood under the rubric of "let the punishment fit the crime." H. L. A. Hart has provided a careful critique of this idea that can prove useful for us. He points out that finding the exact measure of a given crime is much more difficult than theorists typically acknowledge. He first discusses what he calls the "crude version of the principle."

> In its crudest form it is the notion that what the criminal has done should be done to him … But as Blackstone has pointed out … this idea is incapable of generalization without absurdity … "Theft cannot be punished by theft, defamation by defamation, forgery by forgery, adultery by adultery."

There may appear to be an exact "correspondence" in the case of the assignment of the death penalty for those who have committed murder. Yet, for Hart, the punishment may not be "really equivalent to the crime" where the person killed is "a nobleman in the bloom of his youth" and the assassin is "a needy decrepit."[23]

Hart then discusses various "refinements" on the *lex talionis* model of understanding proportionality.

> The first refinement is the idea that the suffering imposed by the punishment should be in some sense equal to or proportionate to the wickedness of the crime. But in what sense? How measure either wickedness or suffering in the absence of units of either? … there is no natural relationship to be discerned between wickedness and punishment of a certain degree or kind, so that we can say the latter naturally "fits" the former.[24]

Utilitarians have tried to provide a metric for such calculations but they have generally not been sympathetic to retributive views instead of more forward-looking understandings of reeducation and reform of the criminal.[25]

[22] Knut Leonard Tallqvist, "Old Assyrian Laws," *Oversikt av Finska Vetenskaps-Societetens Forhandlingar*, Vol. LXIII, no. 3, 1920–1921, pp. 1–41, p. 7.

[23] H. L. A. Hart, *Punishment and Responsibility*, Oxford: Oxford University Press, 1968, p. 161.

[24] Ibid., pp. 161–162.

[25] And one can see such early calculations in the way compensation tables were constructed from the earliest of times, many of which do display some kind of proportionality as well.

Hart then concludes cautiously by accepting a version of proportionality that is merely the expression that we "treat like cases alike."

> The idea of proportionality interpreted in this way – as respect for a principle of fairness between different offenders – has still a place in an account of the values which a theory of punishment should recognize. But it is a modest place ...[26]

Yet this seems to be too modest since the idea that the punishment must fit the crime has been a major tool used by those who criticize excessively harsh punishments. There can be harsh punishments that are equally applied, and yet are still in need of reform.

The question for us is whether the motto, "let the punishment fit the crime," is a reasonable way to understand the use of *lex talionis* especially in the ancient Near East. As I said earlier, there are three examples of something like *lex talionis* in Hammurabi's laws. First, there are the cases of assault, where the punishment is supposed to be the same as the offense, so that an offender is forced to lose an eye when he has caused a victim to lose an eye for instance. Second, there are the cases of the use of the death penalty where the offender has caused death and where death is sought in return. Third, there are the cases of the substitution of a life for a life, such as the killing of an offender's son or daughter, as a vicarious punishment for the offender who causes the death of a victim's son or a daughter.

These *lex talionis* punishments do at least partially conform to the idea that the punishment should fit the crime. As Hart indicated there is indeed a crude, if often unworkable, proportionality here. And one can see that in searching for a proper penalty such exact punishments make a certain amount of sense. But there was a system of penalties, in terms of monetary compensation, that was already practiced at Hammurabi's time. So, there was not the need for a sometimes cruder form of penalty.

I have suggested that there may be something about the offenses that were thought to merit *lex talionis* punishment that separates them out, perhaps because they pose a special threat to the society, and where the punishment is not for the victim but for the society as a whole. But can such a thesis be maintained across the three categories where *lex talionis* is applied? The second category is the one closest to contemporary use of lex *talionis*: when a life has been intentionally taken, the life of the killer is then taken. Intentional killing is indeed of grave concern to the whole society but there are other punishments available today that seem to be proportionate, such as life in prison without the possibility of parole. Yet, in the ancient Near East the idea of prisons was not generally known. The first category seems to be the easiest to justify as proportionate and the third category the hardest to justify.

[26] Hart, *Punishment and Responsibility*, pp. 172–173.

In the first part of Section 9.4, I will take up the first category, and in the second half of Section 9.4, I will take up the third category.

9.4 DEFENDING *LEX TALIONIS*

So what is to be said then to the many theorists who have argued that *lex talionis* in its purest form of "an eye for an eye" is not only crude but immoral as a part of a legal system? One of the most significant arguments is one that is similar to one rooted in Jesus' Sermon on the Mount.

> Ye have heard that it hath been said, An eye for an eye, and a tooth for a tooth: But I say unto you, That ye resist not evil; but whosoever shall smite thee on thy right cheek, turn to him the other also.
>
> And if any man will sue thee at the law, and take away thy coat, let him have thy cloke also.
>
> And whatever shall compel thee to go a mile, go with him twain.
>
> Give to him that asketh thee, and from him that would borrow of thee turn not thou away.[27]

Here is the famous attack on the *lex talionis* principle by Jesus who favors the principle of "turn the other cheek" rather than "retaliate in kind." So the first criticism is that retaliation is itself the wrong response to those who have done us harm. Harming the one who has harmed you makes you as bad as your attacker and perpetuates a cycle of violence.

From the perspective of reconciliation among parties, retaliation seems to be problematic. But against this proposition must be placed the idea that security and stability of a society may be at stake. It is true that various ancient kings were known for their mercy and were still able to maintain public order, but they did so by having some penalties and punishments for those who were wrongdoers. Here is Diodorus' description of the customary practices of an Egyptian pharaoh:

> the king punished crimes less severely than they deserved and rendered to his benefactors a gratitude exceeding the benefaction.[28]

It is possible to be benevolent, as well as to be lenient, and still punish crimes.

The question is whether benevolence and leniency are compatible with *lex talionis* punishment. Leniency is a comparative concept – some punishment practices are lenient compared to some other practices. As indicated in the previous section of

[27] Matthew 5:38–42. Pope Francis has recently voiced this concern again – "A lack of forgiveness and a return to law of 'an eye for an eye, a tooth for a tooth' could lead to an endless escalation of conflict." Pope Francis, *The Name of God is Mercy*, NY: Random House, 2016, p. 79.

[28] Diodorus of Sicily, *Library of History* 1, Book 1, Chapter 70,p. 243.

this chapter, *lex talionis*, even if interpreted literally, could be lenient when compared to unrestrained vengeance-taking. And while benevolence may not initially appear to be comparative, it is my view that it is difficult to say whether or not someone's act is benevolent without an understanding of the climate of practices extant in the society in question.

Another common objection is that *lex talionis* is applied unfairly in terms of which social class one belongs to. While I had quite a lot to say about social class hierarchies in another chapter, I wish here only to point out that the *lex talionic* penalties are not unique to Hammurabi's laws in setting different penalties based on one's social class, although the use of *lex talionis* in connection to social class may be unique to Hammurabi. In any event, I do not propose to defend the social hierarchy as it existed in ancient Mesopotamia. My only point is that given that such a social hierarchy was thought to be essential to the harmonious life of the nation, using legal penalties to reinforce that hierarchy is not necessarily problematic.

And yet another objection is that there is not a clear distinction between those acts that are unintentional and those that are committed in the heat of passion.[29] This is a significant objection, and yet it is true of all the law collections of the ancient Near East that intentional action is not required for liability. In terms of legal progress, it is clear that later legal thought made progress when a distinction was made, as it was for Aristotle,[30] between those offenders who intended and those who did not intend to do wrong.

One of the most significant objections to the Mesopotamian version of *lex talionis* is that it sometimes included vicarious punishment, where the true perpetrator could not be found or was not alive. We can think of a situation where a builder's negligence caused a building to collapse, killing the resident's daughter, and in Hammurabi's laws the builder's daughter was to be killed. By contrast the ancient Egyptian notion of *lex talionis* did not have such a vicarious provision. Diodorus says this of Egyptian law:

> Pregnant women who had been condemned to death were not executed until they had been delivered ... since they held it entirely unjust that the innocent should suffer the same punishment as the guilty.[31]

And it is often remarked that there is also no vicarious punishment in the Bible despite its more extensive use of *lex talionis* than in Mesopotamian law.

The idea of vicarious punishment can be defended, as I have done in some of my other writings,[32] but it is very difficult to do so if the punishment is death or if the

[29] See Jonathan Ziskin, "When Two Men Fight: Legal Implications of Brawling in the Ancient Near East," *Revue Internationale des Droits de l'Antique*, 1997, pp. 13–42, p. 16.

[30] See Aristotle's discussion of responsibility in Book III of the *Nicomachean Ethics*.

[31] Diodorus of Sicily, *The Library of History* I, Book I, Chapter 70, p. 267.

[32] Larry May, "Vicarious Agency and Corporate Responsibility," *Philosophical Studies*, Vol. 43 (1983), pp. 69–82.

person punished is completely innocent. Today vicarious punishment is assigned when a child who has been left unsupervised causes harm. In this case, the person who was negligent in supervising the child, the parent or guardian, is rightly held liable and punished. There are similar cases where a wrongdoing employee is not properly supervised, and where the employer is held liable. Even more interesting cases are those in which a corporation is held liable for the harmful actions of its members. But in all these cases the person, or entity, held liable and potentially punished is not completely innocent and has some responsibility for what the perpetrator did.

Vicarious liability and punishment of those who are completely innocent can be rarely justified. Of course, in this domain it will matter quite a lot how innocence is conceptualized. There is a long debate about how to understand innocence that extends back to ancient times and the ideas of purity and pollution are central.[33] One is only innocent in this tradition if one has no connection to wrongdoing.

If innocence is understood as merely not being touched by wrongdoing, as opposed to not committing wrongdoing, then the door is open for a defense of a wide array of vicarious punishments. One meaning of vicarious is simply to experience something indirectly. To be touched by a wrongdoing is not to commit the wrongdoing but still to be affected by it indirectly. However, the vicarious punishment assigned to those who experience wrongdoing and also benefit from it indirectly is not punishment of the innocent and is hence arguably defensible.

The form of vicarious punishment in Hammurabi's laws does not appear to be like the easily defensible forms mentioned above. Here are some examples of vicarious punishment:

> LH #229 If a builder constructs a house for a man but does not make his work sound, and the house that he constructs collapses and causes the death of the householder, that builder shall be killed.
>
> LH #230 If it should cause the death of the son of the householder, they shall kill a son of that builder.[34]

Another example of vicarious punishment from Hammurabi's laws is this:

> LH #209 If an *awilu* strikes a woman of the *awilu*-class and thereby causes her to miscarry her fetus, he shall weigh and deliver 10 shekels of silver for her fetus.
>
> LH #210 If the woman shall die, they shall kill his daughter.[35]

33 See Larry May, *Contingent Pacifism*, Cambridge: Cambridge University Press, 2015, Chapter 6.

34 *Laws of Hammurabi*, p. 125.

35 Ibid., p. 122.

Here the son of the builder and the daughter of the assailant are innocent in any reasonable sense of that term.

Seemingly the only way of defending this form of vicarious punishment is to provide a deterrence justification, where one deters horrible risk-taking by threatening even more horrible punishment. Such a practice will undoubtedly make deterrence look bad, unless the punishment is never carried out but only threatened. Yet then there will need to be an explanation of why such a horrific threat is necessary – what is the aim? Builders and strikers of pregnant women seem to have very little in common. The striker of pregnant women does indeed engage in risky behavior that the society might wish to curtail. But the society would surely not be better off if builders were curtailed from building.

If *lex talionis* is a kind of "social self-defense,"[36] namely defense of a society's institutions or traditions, as Morris Fish has argued, one can make sense of both forms of vicarious punishment, but only if the punishment was threatened and not ever carried out.[37] In the face of such a significant threat, builders would be on notice not to be negligent, and assailants would be on notice not to strike pregnant women, and the society will benefit by such protection. Yet, since these are the only vicarious punishments in Hammurabi's Code there is a further problem of explaining why these forms of behavior, proscribed by Hammurabi, are singled out from all of the many things that society is in need of protection against.[38]

I here offer two brief responses. The first is to acknowledge that Hammurabi's laws were probably not complete and were not meant to be complete laws for the ancient Babylonian society over which Hammurabi ruled. It is possible that there were many other laws at the time, and that the ones listed in Hammurabi's stela were only meant to be illustrative of the rest of the laws.

A second response is that these laws were meant to train the lawyers as well as the populace to think in a particular way, and thus to be able to figure out if an act is proscribed or not, or an act that calls for a penalty or not. A scenario is contemplated and then it is varied in several respects. This method is similar to the construction of lists of the various evils that will befall someone under when a given spell is cast, or the conditions under which one would view a particular constellation of stars in the sky.[39] There was no reason for the laws to be complete.

36 Morris Fish, "An Eye for an Eye: Proportionality as a Moral Principle of Punishment," *Oxford Journal of Legal Studies*, Vol. 28, no. 1, 2008, pp. 57–71, p. 65.

37 Ibid., p. 60.

38 Of course, it could also be asked why other forms of punishment did not seem to provide for the security of these institutions. Such a speculative question is beyond the scope of this chapter.

39 For more on this method of thinking see Marc van de Mieroop, *Philosophy Before the Greeks*, Princeton NJ: Princeton University Press, 2016.

9.5 CRIMINAL PUNISHMENT

We now return to the conceptualization of criminal law that appears to first manifest itself in the ancient texts we have been examining. Here is the way criminal law is typically characterized today:

> The aim of the criminal law … is to protect the public against harm, by punishing harmful results of conduct or at least situations (not yet resulting in actual harm) which are likely to result in harm if allowed to proceed further … With crimes the state itself brings criminal proceedings to protect the public interest but not to compensate the victim.[40]

Civil law is a matter of providing compensation, whereas criminal law protects the public by issuing punishments.

To account for the introduction of *lex talionis* penalties into Hammurabi's laws, I have proposed that we think of *lex talionis* in terms of rudimentary criminal punishments. I shall attempt to say more about this claim in this final section of the chapter. I shall attempt to show that some kind of public blame or liability seems to be undergirding Hammurabi's *lex talionis* penalties, not merely a need for compensation paid to the victim. The *lex talionis* penalties do not make the victim whole or advance the interests of the victim. The proportionality exemplified by the *lex talionis* penalties tracks the importance of the aspect of the social good that is thought to be threatened by the offenses. This serves partially to perform a task thought by retributivists to be crucial for criminal punishment – the amount of censure "should reflect the blameworthiness of the conduct."[41] The threat of *lex talionis* can also be seen as a substitute for proportionality of punishment in a time when prisons were not available, although there is a system for assigning value to various kinds of harms.[42]

Consider Hammurabi's law #210 concerning assaults which result in harm or death to a pregnant woman. There is a clear social good that the society is deprived of when a pregnant woman is harmed or killed. When the pregnant woman is killed, the society loses not only the woman and her unborn child but also future offspring the woman may bear. Yet it is very curious that the penalty for the death of the pregnant woman is that the daughter of the assailant is to be killed. In terms of the good

40 Wayne R. LaFave and Austin W. Scott, Jr., *Criminal Law*, second edition, St. Paul, MN: West Publishing Co., 1986, p. 13.

41 See A. von Hirsch, "Censure and Proportionality," in *A Reader on Punishment*, edited by Antony Duff and David Garland, Oxford: Oxford University Press, 1994, p. 125.

42 See James Lindgren, "Why the Ancients may not have Needed a System of Criminal Law," *Boston University Law Review*, Vol. 76, February/April 1996. Lindgren argues that ancient societies did not need prisons because they had "debt slavery, chattel slavery, the death penalty, exile, beating, mutilation, public disgrace, group punishment, and the blood feud," p. 29.

of the society, there is now another potential producer of future offspring who is removed from the society – hardly something that would make up for the loss of the pregnant woman. So, while I think that many *lex talionis* laws can be justified, this is not true of all of them.

But perhaps this is the wrong way to view things from the perspective of ancient Mesopotamian legal thought. Perhaps what is motivating Hammurabi to call for the killing of the daughter of the assailant when a pregnant woman has been killed is to show the extreme seriousness of the offense. The question is why the law does not call for the assailant to be killed, rather than his daughter. Perhaps it is thought to be worse for a relative to have to pay the penalty with her life for what the assailant has done than for the assailant to have his own life taken. It is obvious that the loss of one's child is of extreme seriousness. Again, this point has limited application for defending *lex talionis* laws.

When a set of laws incorporates an extra penalty, beyond what would compensate a victim, there is a first movement toward laws that are rudimentary criminal laws. In part, the extra penalty reflects the idea that a larger social harm has been caused. In addition, there is something beyond compensation that is incorporated into the penalty and transforms the penalty into a criminal punishment. There are other reasons for adding to the compensatory penalty that could justify a greater penalty than what is proportionate, such as the significance of what was lost to the specific victim as compared to normal victims. But strikingly the penalties that are included in the *lex talionis* provisions of Hammurabi's Code seem to require a justification based in terms of the harm to the society, not merely to the particular victim, although such a justification will not help much in the vicarious cases.

I have been arguing that the *lex talionis* provisions of Hammurabi's Code are best understood as rudimentary criminal punishments. In this sense, these provisions are not primitive or barbaric, as they are often characterized, but part of a progressive movement in how law views victims and their harmful acts. Of course, the harshness of the penalties partially offsets the assessment of the progressive character of these penalties. As C. L. Ten has argued:

> The defects of the *lex talionis* are obvious and fundamental. It cannot be applied to many crimes, and even when it is applicable the formula for its application is too crude and sometimes requires forms of punishment which are morally unacceptable.[43]

Criticisms such as these are the norm, but the unacceptable nature of *lex talionis* is only obvious if it is administered as such and not merely threatened, with people

[43] C. L. Ten, *Crime, Guilt, and Punishment*, Oxford: Oxford University Press, 1987, p. 151.

being able to ransom or substitute monetary penalties in exchange, as seems to have been the case in ancient Mesopotamia.

The idea that we have been discussing is how an ancient society might first come to the rudimentary underlying ideas of criminal law and punishment. I have suggested that one of the first insights here is that the society could be harmed in ways that call for more than something like the monetary penalty of compensation, or a very different kind of punishment. The standard way to understand Hammurabi's use of talionic punishments is as a throwback to earlier, more primitive times. Yet there is no evidence to support the view that talionic punishments surfaced any earlier than Hammurabi's time. And then the question is why the talionic punishments arose when a model of monetary compensation was available.

We have seen that three different kinds of *lex talionis* punishment are contained in Hammurabi's laws. The legal thought undergirding these punishments seems to be very similar to what today we would call criminal punishments that have as their main goal to protect society. It is commonly thought that ancient legal systems treat crime in terms of the principle of *lex talionis*. In this chapter I investigated the varieties of penalties and punishments meted out in ancient societies. I argued that punishments, especially those seemingly governed by the principle of *lex talionis*, can be best understood, and at least partially justified, by reference to two considerations. First there are the positive effects on various important social institutions and traditions. And, second, the proportionality in criminal law is understood in terms of the principle, let the punishment "fit" the crime. This principle seems to emerge in ancient times in terms of considerations of equity, especially procedural fairness, as we have seen more generally in earlier chapters. Criminal punishment is an especially difficult issue for ancient societies as they try to find a way for criminal punishment to be effective and also fair. Hammurabi and later lawgivers seem to have struck on the idea of *lex talionis* for protecting their social institutions.

10

Capital Punishment

Like *lex talionis*, capital punishment in ancient legal thought is often seen as a sign that ancient laws were primitive or undeveloped or even barbaric. In this chapter I take up this charge and explore the types of case for which capital punishment was assigned as well as the possible rationales undergirding such punishments in ancient societies. I will focus on ancient Mesopotamia and very early Biblical law (I will have much more to say about Rabbinic law in the fourth part of the larger work). I should note at the outset that the use of capital punishment, and its extent, varied significantly from one ancient society to another, and does not seem to follow a pattern where the older the society, the more capital punishment was employed – in fact there is evidence of just the opposite. I shall, at the end, argue that there were moral and pragmatic reasons for why capital punishment was employed in ancient times.

In Section 10.1 I will look at cases where death was the punishment for having caused death, a relatively small number of the reported cases. Here I will continue the discussion of the previous chapter concerning *lex talionis*. In Section 10.2 I will explore the cases where death is the punishment for sorcery and black magic, a more numerous class of cases than death for death. In Section 10.3 I will explore the cases where death is not the proscribed punishment where it is today so proscribed: especially in cases of murder and rape. In Section 10.4 I talk about how the death penalty was administered and the state of law enforcement and incarceration in some ancient societies. And in Section 10.5 I will look at several possible rationales for having the death penalty and for how and when it was employed in ancient times in contrast to today.

10.1 DEATH FOR DEATH

The earliest record of the death penalty in ancient times comes from the Laws of Ur-Namma (LU) around 2100 BCE. Here are the laws that call for the death sentence:

LU #1 If a man commits a homicide, they shall kill that man.

LU #2 If a man acts lawlessly (?), they shall kill that man.

LU #6 If a man violates the rights of another and deflowers the virgin wife of a young man, they shall kill that male.

LU #7 If the wife of a young man, on her own initiative, approaches a man and initiates sexual relations with him, they shall kill that woman; the male shall be released.[1]

It is not clear how broad the sweep of LU #2 is. LU # 6 and LU #7 have to do with illicit sexual relations, but it is not clear that LU #6 includes rape.

It is striking that the first of the Laws of Ur-Namma concerns the death penalty. From our contemporary perspective it is also noteworthy that homicide calls for the death penalty regardless of whether the act was accidental or intentional. In general, murder is not dealt with in the ancient law collections from the Near East. But from the placement of LU #1, it is an obvious inference that killing was considered a very serious matter.

In the Laws of Lipit-Ishtar (LL) from around 1930 BCE, we also find a reference to the death penalty.

LL #d If a man strikes the daughter of a man and causes her to lose her fetus, he shall weight and deliver 30 shekels of silver.

LL #e If she dies, that male shall be killed.[2]

Here we have a killing that warrants the death penalty. And while the placement is rather early in this code, suggesting greater importance, the case is very restricted and indeed seems to be relevant only for the death of a pregnant woman by a man who strikes her. Nonetheless this is the only Law of Lipit-Ishtar that calls for the death penalty and we should note that it is a case of death for death.

The Laws of Eshnunna (LE) provide us with several more examples of the death penalty, two of which concern the causing of death to the victim. Here are these two laws:

LE #24 If he has no claim against him, but he nonetheless takes the wife of a commoner or the child of a commoner as a distress, detains the distress in his house, and causes her or his death, it is a capital offense – the distrainer who distrained shall die.[3]

LE #57 If a wall is buckling and the ward authorities so notify the owner of the wall, but he does not reinforce his wall and the wall collapses and thus causes the

[1] *Law Collections from Mesopotamia and Asia Minor*, second edition, translated by Martha Roth, Atlanta, GA: Scholars' Press, 1997, pp. 17–18.

[2] Ibid., p. 27.

[3] Ibid., p. 62.

> death of a member of the *awilu*-class – it is a capital case, it is decided by royal edict.[4]

Both of these cases are ones involving special circumstances where death occurred, not easily generalizable to all forms of killing. The first is restricted to cases where a person is seized for payment of a debt, and the second is restricted to only one class and concerns circumstances that are very specific.

When we come to the Laws of Hammurabi (LH), we get many more examples of cases involving the death penalty but only five where the perpetrator caused the death of the victim. Here are those laws:

> LH #116 If the distrainee should die from the effects of a beating or other physical abuse while in the house of his or her distrainer, the owner of the distrainee shall charge and convict his merchant, and if the distrainee is the man's son, they shall kill the distrainer's son ...[5]
>
> LH #153 If a man's wife has her husband killed on account of her relationship with another male, they shall impale that woman.[6]
>
> LH #209 If an *awilu* strikes a woman of the *awilu* class ...
>
> LH #210 If that woman should die, they shall kill his daughter.[7]
>
> LH #229 If a builder constructs a house for a man but does not make his work sound, and the house that he constructs collapses and causes the death of the householder, that builder shall be killed.
>
> LH #230 If it should cause the death of a son of the householder, they shall kill a son of that builder.[8]

These Laws of Hammurabi resemble those of the earlier collections of laws concerning causing a death, except for the vicarious punishment, which is a characteristic new feature of Hammurabi's laws as we have seen in earlier chapters.

In LH #209 we find something close to contemporary laws that call for the death penalty. If a man strikes a woman of the upper class and causes her death then his punishment is death. The twist we would not find today is that it is not that the man should be killed, but that his daughter should be killed. The same is true of LH #116 and 230. Vicarious punishment is hard enough to justify, but vicarious capital punishment seems very far from what today we would consider justifiable. I return to this difficult topic in a later section of this chapter.

4 Ibid., p. 68.
5 Ibid., p. 103.
6 Ibid., p. 110.
7 Ibid., p. 122
8 Ibid., p. 125.

The case that comes closest to our own understanding of when, if at all, capital punishment in Mesopotamia is justified is in LH #153 – what seems to be the intentional taking of a life. But things are complicated in that the wife has someone else kill her husband, she does not kill herself. If the death penalty is recognized today as justified, this case would still fit since the woman is the instigator of the death. The same cannot be said for LH #229. Today where death results from negligence, even gross negligence, the death penalty is not employed (except for China recently where death was the punishment for a death caused when an apartment building collapsed due to the builder's negligence).

In the Bible we find several of the same prohibitions concerning the death penalty as we have just enumerated above from earlier ancient Near Eastern legal texts. Here is the first capital offense mentioned in the Covenant Code found in Exodus 20–23:

> Exodus 21:12–14 He that smiteth a man, so that he die, shall be surely put to death.
>
> And if a man lie not in wait, but God deliver him into his hand; then I will appoint thee a place whither he shall flee.
>
> But if a man come presumptuously upon his neighbor to slay him with guile, thou shalt take him from mine altar, that he may die.

Here we have distinctions between types of killing, which were missing from the earlier Near Eastern accounts.

Capital punishment for people who cause death is not as difficult to justify as many of the other ancient laws that call for the death penalty. Of course, it was not intentional killing that warranted the death penalty but other forms of killing including those that today would be called mere negligence or even vicarious agency. In the next section we look at another set of laws that call for death where no one has died. And then we will take up cases of murder and rape where there is no call for the death penalty in ancient times.

10.2 SORCERY AND FALSE ACCUSATION

Having looked at some cases of ancient laws that punished death with death, I wish next to consider some cases of capital punishment that are harder, especially for modern theorists, namely those concerning sorcery and magic. The second of Hammurabi's laws is of this sort:

> LH #2 If a man charges another man with practicing witchcraft but cannot bring proof against him, he who is charged with witchcraft shall go to the divine River Ordeal, he shall indeed submit to the divine River Ordeal: if the divine River Ordeal should overwhelm him, his accuser shall take full legal possession of his

estate; if the divine River Ordeal should clear that man and should he survive, he who made the charge of witchcraft against him shall be killed, he who submitted to the divine River Ordeal shall take full possession of his accuser's estate.[9]

Notice that this law does not actually condemn to death those who practice witchcraft – rather the person accused of witchcraft is killed by the gods, through the river-god ordeal, if the accusation is true. And if the accusation is false then the accuser is the one who is condemned to death.

The crime that calls for the state to put someone to death is the person who wrongly accuses someone of witchcraft. In this respect we should also note that the first of Hammurabi's laws is this:

LH #1 If a man accuses another man and charges him with homicide but cannot bring proof against him, his accuser shall be killed.[10]

Here it is the false accusation of homicide that calls for the death penalty, and we may think that what is at the heart of these first two Laws of Hammurabi is false accusation rather than either a concern for homicide or witchcraft.

False accusation could be seen as a threat to the system of justice that existed in ancient times. Since there were no finger print or lie detector technologies, it would have been difficult to tell whether or not an accuser, or a witness, was telling the truth. And truth-telling in the law would be seen as so important that the most severe punishment is reserved for those who falsely accuse or engage in false testimony that puts another person in jeopardy. These considerations are important additions to our earlier discussion of proof by ordeal and oath.

There do seem to be laws against sorcery and witchcraft in ancient times that carried the death sentence. Consider these passages from the Bible:

Exodus 22:18 Thou shalt not suffer a witch to live.

Leviticus 20:27 A man also or a woman that hath a familiar spirit, or that is a wizard, shall surely be put to death: they shall stone them with stones: their blood shall be upon them.

But merely consulting with sorcerers is not a crime punishable with death – the reason for this seems to be different from consulting with false gods, which is dealt with more severely.[11] Yet, it appears that he who consults with sorcerers is to be punished, for they should "cut him off from among his people."[12]

[9] Ibid., p. 81.

[10] Ibid., p. 81.

[11] On the general Biblical prohibitions on sorcery see Richard H. Hiers, *Justice and Compassion in Biblical Law*, NY: Continuum, 2009, Chapter 5.

[12] Leviticus 20–6.

Here is Stanley Cook on the topic of how the Bible dealt with sorcery and witchcraft:

> Laws directed against sorcery are general, and are not absent from early Hebrew collections. Among the exhortations accompanying the Book of the Covenant is one aimed at the extirpation of witches (*mekassephah*; Ex. 22.18) and the wording ("thou shalt not let live") may be taken to imply that the witch might be killed out of hand without resort to judicial procedure … That both Israel and Babylonia should have endeavored to protect individuals from sorcery occasions no surprise, and the only question is to what extent the punishments were actually put into practice. That Saul expelled and "cut off" all sorcerers from the land of Israel (1 Sam. 28.3) is a statement due to a writer who was at least contemporary with, if not later than, the Book of the Covenant. In Babylonia too, death by burning was regarded as the only appropriate penalty for witchcraft, but … it cannot clearly be made out whether it was ever put into effect.[13]

And the question to ask is why death was prescribed for practicing witchcraft, magic, or sorcery.

Along with such things as crimes of a sexual nature that violated the basic norms of the ancient society, we find laws against witchcraft that also seem to be based in the same idea. Despite the fact that ancient religions had a mystical dimension that allowed for priests and other temple officials to interpret the will of the gods, certain purveyors of magic and sorcery were roundly condemned. Perhaps the reason for condemning sorcery and magic is because the practitioners were thought to be falsely claiming to be interpreters of a god's will. Or it might be that they were seen as not acting on behalf of the gods but on behalf of evil spirits. Or perhaps sorcerers were seen simply as a challenge to the society's accepted religious beliefs and hence seen as a threat to the social order.

By the time of the ancient Hittite Laws, in the second half of the second millennium BCE, capital punishment seems to disappear to be replaced by compensation even when death has been caused. Here are the first two laws of the Hittites:

> #1 If anyone kills a man or a woman in a quarrel, he shall bring him for burial and shall give 4 persons, male or female respectively. He shall look to his house for it.
>
> #2 If anyone kills a male or female slave in a quarrel, he shall bring him for burial and shall give 2 persons, male or female respectively. He shall look to his house for it.[14]

[13] Stanley A. Cook, *The Laws of Moses and the Code of Hammurabi*, London: Adam and Charles Black, 1903, pp. 243–244.

[14] *Laws of Hittites*, in *Law Collections From Mesopotamia and Asia Minor*, second edition, translated by Martha T. Roth, Atlanta, GA: Scholars' Press, 1997, p. 217.

In E. Neufeld's commentary on the Hittite Laws we learn:

> Humanitarian principles speak often throughout these laws. The spirit which dominates these clauses is just the reverse of the spirit of customary laws ... The penalties are made less severe and fines or punishments are reduced ... The former talionic and corporal penalties were replaced by compensation; and the death penalty by torture was replaced by a religious ceremony.[15]

Neufeld suggests that the customary laws of the Hittites look more like the ancient codes of Babylon and Eshnunna. These customary laws were replaced by what Neufeld calls "statutes" that were considerably more humane, especially concerning the death penalty which seems to have been eliminated altogether.

10.3 MURDER AND RAPE

In contemporary times, capital punishment is mostly restricted, in those few societies that still employ it, to murder or in a few cases to rape. It is therefore surprising that in ancient Mesopotamia capital punishment is not generally prescribed in these cases, as far as we can tell. It is a matter of great dispute why Hammurabi's laws, for example, do not discuss murder at all. Edwin Good says: "What is most surprising about the ancient codes is the paucity of legislation regarding murder."[16] But Good then points out that in the ancient Biblical law, a "near kinsman of the victim, has the right to take the murderer's life." Murder is sometimes mentioned in the Bible and distinguished from manslaughter. When murder is mentioned it is deemed punishable by death.[17]

We can contrast the Laws of Hammurabi with those of the Bible, as Edwin Good suggests. Here again is how the two cases of murder are treated in the Laws of Hammurabi:

> LH #1 If a man accuses another man and charges him with homicide but cannot bring proof against him, his accuser shall be killed.[18]
>
> LH #153 If a man's wife has her husband killed on account of her relationship with another man, they shall impale that woman.[19]

We have seen these laws before and while they can be seen as murder or attempted murder, the more straightforward cases of murder are not mentioned in Hammurabi's laws.

[15] E. Neufeld, *The Hittite Laws*, London: Luzac and Co., 1951, p. 99.

[16] Edwin M. Good, "Capital Punishment and its Alternatives in Ancient Near Eastern Law," *Stanford Law Review*, Vol. 19, No. 5 (May, 1967), pp. 947–977, p. 951.

[17] Ibid.

[18] *Laws of Hammurabi*, p. 81.

[19] Ibid., p. 110.

In the Bible, homicide is much more straightforwardly treated as deserving of the death penalty.

> Exodus 21:12 He that smiteth a man, so that he die, shall surely be put to death.
>
> Exodus 21:15 He that smiteth his father, or his mother, shall be surely put to death.
>
> Leviticus 24:17 And he that killeth any man shall surely be put to death.
>
> Leviticus 24:21 … and he that killeth a man, he shall be put to death.

These laws cover a much wider swath of killings than the few Laws of Hammurabi. And thus, or so it has been claimed, they come closer to our own understanding of when, if ever, the death penalty is justified.[20]

There has been a long debate about whether certain passages in the Bible might be interpreted as prohibiting even the state to take a life. In this respect consider this passage:

> Exodus 20:13 Thou shalt not kill.

Richard Hiers points out that

> Cain, the first murderer, was not sentenced to death. Rather he was condemned to be "a fugitive and a wanderer on the earth" (Gen. 4:14). Moreover as the story is told, YHWH "marked" Cain in some visible manner to protect him from any would-be, self-help avenger (Gen. 4:15). The author of Proverbs 28:17 advised that anyone who was "burdened with the blood of another" should be allowed (or condemned) to "be a fugitive until death." In effect, these texts suggest that murderers were to receive a life sentence as fugitives or exiles.[21]

Hiers also though points to a much larger set of passages from the Bible that call for a death sentence for killers and others.

We should note that in Mesopotamia by the time of the Middle Assyrian Laws (c. 1076 BCE) some forms of murder and some forms of rape were punished by death. Here are a few of these laws:

> MAL B#2 If a man, who has not yet received his inheritance share takes a life, they shall hand him over to the next-of-kin. Should the next of kin so choose, he shall kill him, or if he chooses to come to an accommodation, they shall take his inheritance share.[22]
>
> MAL A#12 If a wife of a man should walk along the main thoroughfare and should a man seize her and say to her "I want to have sex with you!" – she shall not consent

[20] See Good, "Capital Punishment," p. 951.

[21] Hiers, *Justice and Compassion in Biblical Law*, p. 83.

[22] *Middle Assyrian Laws*, in *Law Collections From Mesopotamia and Asia Minor*, second edition, translated by Martha T. Roth, Atlanta, GA: Scholars' Press, 1997, p. 176.

> but she shall protect herself; should he seize her by force and fornicate with her – whether they discover him upon the woman or witnesses later prove the charges against him that he fornicated with the woman – they shall kill the man; there is no punishment for the woman.[23]

These laws are clearer than the earlier Mesopotamian laws, but they do not make all forms of rape subject to the death penalty.

As far as rape is concerned, Edwin Good tells us that it "is punishable by death only when the woman is either married, or betrothed, and when the man uses force."[24] And this seems to be true even in the most brutal of the law collections, those of the Middle Assyrian period. Reuven Yaron makes a similar point: "Near Eastern laws known to us do not regard rape per se, of an 'unattached' woman as a capital delict … Betrothal has created a personal tie, violation of which by an outsider is a capital crime" and this is true of the Laws of Eshnunna and Hammurabi as well as Deuteronomy.[25] In this respect consider some laws of Deuteronomy:

> Deuteronomy 22: 23–27 If a damsel that is a virgin be betrothed unto a husband, and a man find her in the city and lie with her;
>
> Then ye shall bring them both unto the gate of the city, and ye shall stone them with stones that they die; the damsel because she cried not, being in the city, and the man because he has humbled his neighbor's wife: so thou shalt put away evil among you.
>
> But if a man find a betrothed damsel in the field, and the man force her, and lie with her; then the man only that lie with her shall die:
>
> But unto the damsel thou shalt do nothing: there is in the damsel no sin worthy of death; for as when a man riseth against his neighbor, and slayeth him, even so in this matter:
>
> For he found her in the field and the betrothed damsel cried, and there was none to save her.

Some have suggested that these facts make rape a crime against the husband or the parents, not a crime against the woman or girl who has been raped.[26]

Yet, it is not the denial of a person's right to live or the right not to be grievously harmed that is punished with death in ancient times. But other crimes, as we have seen in previous sections are punished with death. In what follows I will nonetheless try to provide some possible rationales for the way the death penalty was employed in these ancient times. And in the end I will argue that practical considerations are

[23] Ibid., pp. 157–158.

[24] Good, "Capital Punishment," p. 956.

[25] Reuven Yaron, *The Laws of Eshnunna*, second edition, Jerusalem/Leiden: The Magnes Press/ E. J. Brill, 1988, pp. 278–279.

[26] See Good, "Capital Punishment," especially p. 956.

paramount, just as is true for many people today who do not support the death penalty because it seems too often to execute people who are in fact not guilty, although of course there are very many people today who are opposed to the death penalty on moral or religious grounds as well. And some of these people turn to the few passages in Bible that go against the grain and seem to call for life sentences or banishment instead of the death penalty even for murderers.

10.4 PUNISHMENT AND LAW ENFORCEMENT

In his commentary on the Laws of Eshnunna, Albrecht Goetze discusses the procedure by which a person (the distrainee or the debtor) can be seized by a distrainor (creditor). He points out that letters at the time indicate that one procedure involved the distrainee (or debtor) ordered to be seized and the order "executed by *redutum*, 'the sheriff and his men.'" And we also find reference to the distrainee, one of which is "'taken to jail.'"[27] At another point Goetze asks: "Do we have to assume that for these cases a kind of 'police court' existed?"[28] This stands in sharp contrast to many commentators, like Russ VerSteeg, who feel confident in asserting: "Mesopotamian laws do not employ incarceration as a punishment."[29] Driver and Miles say: "there was no police, no public prosecutor, no public executioner"[30] and "in the Babylonian laws … there was no mention of imprisonment, which is expensive to the community."[31]

The case Goetze comments on, in the Laws of Eshnunna, calls for capital punishment if a "female seized in distress in" the house of the distrainor "shall die." As I said earlier, this could be a case of "life for life." But another possibility is that we have here a gross abuse of a system of self-help for creditors, which is itself quite important for the maintenance of credit relationships in the society. Once again this would mean that the death penalty was used to protect the most important institutions of the ancient society.

Those commentators, who believe that there were no jails or police in ancient times, sometimes use this as a rationale for defending capital punishment – what else could be done with those who have committed the worst offenses and are deemed to be dangerous to society. As we have seen, death may be administered extra-judicially

27 Albrecht Goetze, "The Laws of Eshnunna," *The Annual of the American Schools of Oriental Research*, Vol. 31 (1951–1952), pp. 1–197, p. 70. On this page, Goetze helpfully defines "distress" as "a seizure of another's property as an involuntary pledge, its purpose being the enforcement of the performance due from the party distrained. In Babylonian law persons as well as property could be distrained."

28 Ibid., p. 123.

29 Russ VerSteeg, *Early Mesopotamian Law*, Durham, NC: Carolina Academic Press, 2000, p. 127.

30 Godfrey Rolles Driver and J. C. Miles, *The Babylonian Laws*, Oxford: Oxford University Press, 1952, Vol. 1, p. 494.

31 Ibid., p. 501.

by a kinsman of the deceased, or by the state, although there seems not to have been an office of executioner. Good reports that: "The custom in Mesopotamian society of giving free rein to kill the murderer may be a reason for the surprising lack of legislation in the codes about murder."[32]

Driver and Miles discuss how and why there was a transition (perhaps a development) from vengeance of primitive times to compensation later.

> The State by degrees enforced composition and restricted the gratification of vengeance, while it still had to give way to the popular desire in such cases as murder and adultery, if the offenders were caught in the act. This process of limitation by the State was slowly extended, and the injured party was only allowed to carry out the execution himself under the supervision of some person in authority and sometimes merely to be present at it ... the injured parties with their witnesses and such other members of the community as were interested, took part in the execution.[33]

But since there was no public executioner, Driver and Miles suggest that the community members were allowed to carry out the execution sentence under supervision – where this is different from blood vengeance which was not mediated by anything like the rule of law.

If we try to imagine a system of law without a corresponding system of law enforcement it is difficult but something that clearly seems to be true at various times and in various societies in ancient times. As we have seen in earlier chapters, there were ancient judges and even juries, and the king often took an active role in enforcing some judicial decisions. But except for a few rare instances, there is no record of a professional police force or of the office of executioner. So, how did the laws get enforced in these ancient times?

We know that there was not a clear line between what we would today call civil and criminal matters. In fact many commentators refer to ancient "criminal" law as the law of delicts, which would today encompass tort not criminal law. Part of what this means is that criminal matters were largely private matters between the parties – although in our previous discussion of *lex talionis* I suggested that this idea might have been the beginning of thinking about crime as a public offense for which the state should exact specific penalties, where the punishment was to fit the crime proportionately.

Prior to the Laws of Hammurabi, penalties were primarily drawn in monetary terms, where collection occurred just as any debt was collected in ancient times – largely by private parties providing their own self-help. But even here, some especially powerful individuals may try to resist paying, and then the community might come together to aid in the collection of the debt or penalty. In part this is done

[32] Good, "Capital Punishment," p. 952.

[33] Driver and Miles, *The Babylonian Laws*, p. 497.

in order to stop a blood feud from beginning where one party's clan would hold a grudge for past offenses that had not been properly assuaged.

The upshot is that for grievous offenses, allowing the private parties to work out compensation was not always successful. Here we find the state inserting itself into the judicial process, not at the level of law-making, law-interpreting, and law-applying, but in terms of law enforcement. Yet, significant hurdles result for law enforcement if there is no jail or prison – and where there is a jail or prison it is extraordinarily costly to maintain a prisoner at state expense within the jail or prison. In such a situation there would be a high premium placed on forms of punishment that were relatively less costly than maintaining a person in jail or prison. For the most serious crimes, where the community wanted to get the perpetrator completely out of circulation so as to decrease the risks of having this person afoot, capital punishment would hold some appeal. As is sometimes argued today, the cost of executing a murderer is considerably less than the cost of keeping him alive in prison for the rest of his natural life, or even for a significant part of his life.

Another form of low cost law enforcement, but one with significantly greater risks for the community, is to let the people who are witnesses to a grievous crime execute the perpetrator on the spot. To give one example, Driver and Miles tell us: "A man caught looting during a fire is cast into it."[34] They go on to claim that the idea here is extended into other domains: "Burning was inflicted by the Hebrews on a man who married a mother and daughter together as well as on the two women."[35] There is a law of Hammurabi that calls for adulterers to be bound together and cast into the river without any due process:

> LH #129 If a man's wife should be seized lying with another male, they shall bind them and cast them into the water ...[36]

But here, the fact that the couple was seized lying with each other is the key that allows for neglect of any court procedure. Administering the death penalty, whether by witnesses to the crime or by the state, is a form of law enforcement that in at least some respects makes practical sense.

Yet, there is a significant risk when witnesses are allowed to "take the law into their own hands." Since there is no due process here, there is the obvious risk that the witnesses will get the wrong result. Even in the case when the witnesses correctly understand the law as well as the facts they see, mistakes can be made due to the biases of the witnesses toward one or another party. There is in addition the worry that people will take the law into their own hands even when they are not

34 Ibid., p. 495.

35 Ibid.

36 *Laws of Hammurabi*, p. 105.

direct witnesses but only hear second-hand what has occurred. Especially in cases where death is the punishment, these worries attain paramount status. Yet, Boecker reminds us "that was hardly such a thing as imprisonment in our modern sense in the ancient east. It is unknown in the Old Testament."[37]

The question, though, is whether a society is better off still having law enforcement in the hands of the people who witness crimes than if there is the likelihood that the perpetrators will not be punished because of a lack of formal law enforcement on the part of the state. And another question to ask is whether capital punishment is made more attractive when there are no jails or prisons into which a killer could be sentenced. And we will ask, in light of the paucity of jails or prisons, if banishment or exile from one's community is a possible reasonable alternative to the death sentence. We explore these questions and others in our final section of this chapter.

10.5 POSSIBLE ANCIENT DEFENSES OF CAPITAL PUNISHMENT

At the beginning of this chapter I posed the challenge of whether capital punishment could be consistent with a humanitarian conception of ancient law or at least one that is not brutal and barbaric. We will here explore five rationales that have been, or could be, advanced to explain to what extent humanitarianism and capital punishment could be justified in ancient societies. We will consider three pragmatic rationales focused on (1) enabling law enforcement, (2) stopping blood feuds, and (3) community self-defense. Each of these rationales will be found to be somewhat plausible and also problematic. We will then consider the ideas of (4) purification and (5) respect for life, as providing a rationale for ancient capital punishment. The successful rationales for ancient capital punishment largely turn on a combination of practical and moral considerations.

Law enforcement in ancient societies was a problem. In contemporary societies the police are relied on for most of law enforcement across the world. There was no professional police force in any of the societies in the ancient world before Roman times,[38] as far as the evidence indicates. The advantage then of capital punishment, especially administered by community members who were witnesses to killing or rape or other serious crimes, is thus obvious. And the deterrent effect is maximized by the immediate killing of the perpetrator – sending an unequivocal message of what will await those who similarly violate the law.

But there are evident problems if the perpetrator is not immediately apprehended. And even if the alleged perpetrator is apprehended soon after the crime, there is the

[37] Hans Jochen Boecker, *Law and the Administration of Justice in the Old Testament and Ancient East*, translated by Jeremy Moiser, Minneapolis: Augsburg Publishing House, 1980, p. 133.

[38] This issue is explored in Chapter 42.

problem that the biases of the community members could color what they "saw" and their judgment of the "correct" punishment. Vigilante justice is too easy to become the replacement for a police force.

In addition, it is not completely clear that capital punishment is the last resort. Taking the prisoner into slavery is another option in many of these societies, since while there is no professional police force there are well-established mechanisms for enslavement for debt that could be employed in cases of serious crimes rather than merely in cases of debt. And in addition, it is not clear why the person captured could not be forced to pay very large fines in order to be released by the community members who have captured the alleged perpetrator. This latter alternative has the advantage that if it later turned out that the alleged perpetrator was not guilty, or not guilty of what the community members initially thought, the injustice can be corrected – no such correction is available once the alleged perpetrator is killed.

A second important practical rationale for capital punishment concerns the need for a society to protect itself, even though it has never been clear that capital punishment had a deterrent effect. Killings of various types are detrimental to the well-functioning of a society. Officials and witnesses who are crucial to well-functioning of a judicial system can be intimidated, or simply eliminated, by the party who is unhappy with the investigation or judgment issued. Even kings can be intimidated by people who are motivated to threaten to attack and kill them. Capital punishment has been understood for millennia as a way to protect the community from such threats so that the community can function as people wish. Indeed, there was an idea of having substitute kings that developed in some of the earliest societies as a way to stymie potential assassins who wished to change the government by killing the leader of that government.

One thing to say about the rationale of societal self-protection is to wonder whether there are not other means that might accomplish the same effect as is desired by the use of capital punishment. Banishment or exile from the community also removes the threat. Indeed, if removal of the threat is the key rationale of capital punishment there are certainly other methods of accomplishing removal. It is true that banishment or exile is not as permanent a form of removal as is the killing of the person who is the threat. But in ancient Greek and Chinese times banishment seems to be preferred because it is more humane.[39]

A third practical rationale often given for capital punishment is that the blood feud is curtailed. This is accomplished primarily if the death sentence is administered or controlled and sanctioned by the state – yet this often requires more of law enforcement officials than ancient societies are equipped to deliver. If, instead, the

39 See Chapter 23.

death sentence is carried out by witnesses to the crime, the blood feud may be instigated rather than curtailed.

A blood feud is stopped when there is no person or clan to take revenge on. So, there is no reason to think that the death sentence is the only way to stop the feud – although there is something deeply resonating about the idea of blood for blood. Once again we can connect this chapter with the previous chapter on *lex talionis*. In the Bible the idea of "blood for blood" is inspired by a kind of divine proportionality. The person who kills has committed "an act of sacrilege" for having taken a life that was made in God's image.[40]

Yet, it remains unclear why people would think that proportionate punishment must be the same as equal punishment. It seems that other forms of punishment could be as severe, such as various forms of torture, and hence that respecting God's creation would not require taking a life. And the blood feud seems to be something that could be stopped also by something not quite as severe as killing – and here banishment seems like it might be such a punishment because it also removes the killer from his clan.

This then brings us to the non-pragmatic rationales for ancient capital punishment, and here we will take up purification and then respect for the inherent value of life. So, the fourth rationale returns us to a discussion of pollution and purification that we discussed in earlier chapters. In ancient times, killing is thought to pollute the killer as well as potentially those around him or her. Here pollution is a kind of moral taint that attaches to individuals because of violating a taboo or other very serious customs of a given society. Once pollution has occurred, there must be some kind of appeasement or placation of the gods, or in the case of the Israelites, God.

Purification is accomplished by various ritual ways of appeasement, and here it matters as much that a life is taken in return for life as how that life is taken. Fire and water are both seen, in various ancient societies, as the medium of purification so that burning or drowning of the killer was called for. But here it would also matter in most cases who did the killing of the killer – priests of the temple are the most commonly cited people who are to carry out the purification rituals. Capital punishment by means of the witnesses who capture the killer or rapist in the act lacks what is thought to be part of ritual purification.

And as we know from various sources purification can take place in many different ways. Ritual purification can employ a water bath for instance, as in ancient Israelite times as well as today, which does not drown the one being purified. Rituals of various kinds can employ a substitute for the person to be purified, such as employing an animal substitute that is slaughtered to end the pollution. Indeed, rituals were

40 See Hiers, *Justice and Compassion in Biblical Law*, especially pp. 122–123.

an important part of all ancient societies, and animal sacrifice featured in nearly all of them. It is not clear that capital punishment would be thought to be necessary or even appropriate for expiating pollution in an ancient community.

The fifth rationale is the most explicitly moral – respect for life. The sanctity of life, or the inherent value of human life, is cited in some texts, especially from the Bible, as a rationale for capital punishment. The taking of human life is seen as the worst thing that a person can do, and it calls for the severest punishment. This is surely the idea behind the life for life provisions in the Bible. It is harder to see in Hammurabi's times, since it is not killing alone that carries the death penalty.

Respect for life seems in the end to be an especially problematic notion if the death penalty is used to show that respect. There is a strong rationale that showing respect for the life of a now-dead victim demands strong punishment of the perpetrator. But the strong prohibition against taking life is at least partially undermined when the state, or especially the members of the community who are on the scene, kill. This is probably why in many ancient societies compensation can often substitute for the death penalty. And today, the death penalty is increasingly unpopular for similar reasons – indeed the European Union and significant international law documents have outlawed the death penalty today.[41]

If there is an overall rationale for the death penalty in ancient times, which speaks to us today, it would have to be an amalgam of the various considerations we have just discussed. Many people today, myself included, think there are good practical reasons for the death penalty but that these are overridden by the practical difficulties on the other side – especially the likelihood that an innocent person would be executed. The moral arguments in favor of capital punishment – principally the retributive ones – seem to pale by comparison with the idea of the state killing or sanctioning the killing of a human being. The debate today is not all that different in the end from that of ancient times as I have tried to reconstruct it.

As we have seen, the oldest legal records we have do not call for the death penalty – it arises only in the eighteenth century BCE, and is then extended over the next thousand years. There is no clear sense in which the more primitive the society, the more the death penalty was employed. And there is no sense that there was a progressive development away from the death penalty in ancient times. I have not sought to explain these curious phenomena, but to reconstruct rationales for the use of the ultimate form of punishment, the death penalty with an eye to the debates that are still ongoing today.

[41] See William A. Schabas, *The Abolition of the Death Penalty in International Law*, Cambridge: Cambridge University Press, 1997.

SECTION IV

International Justice

11

Ancient Treaties and Trust

What is characteristic of some of international law is that there are rules that are seen to apply to most States, at least in a significant region of the world, and the rules have a bindingness that extends beyond the particular borders of those States. The rules of international law need not be binding for all time, and so international law and natural law are conceptually distinct. But international law does not have to issue from a single world ruler and international law does not have to be effectively sanctioned by organized policing. There does need to be a community of States over which the rules apply, but the system of rules can take many different forms.

I will argue that there was international law probably as far back as 2300 BCE, but for sure by the middle of the second millennium BCE. But whether this was law properly so-called will not be my main concern. Instead, I am primarily interested in the normative question of whether treaties and other diplomatic writings provided norms that were recognized as extending beyond a state's borders.

A bilateral state agreement is not sufficient to establish that there is international law between two States. But the terms of the bilateral agreement could be such that there is recognition of international law. There can be natural law operating and yet this fact is not sufficient to establish that there was international law operating. The norms of natural law would have to be ones that concerned the relations of States, especially when those States interacted with each other, or concerning the relations of citizens of States especially when these citizens interacted with foreign citizens. And, although this is not as clear-cut, the kinds of relations must in some sense be bilateral, or multilateral, legal or politico-legal relations, or at least normative relations concerning the operating of rules, norms, or laws that affect States or their citizens. And one of the chief indicators of the existence of such norms is the employment of sanctions, in some form, that makes compliance with these norms more likely than not.

In this chapter I begin by examining some of the earliest legal documents to have been found, vassal treaties from the middle of the third millennium BCE. In Section

11.2 I analyze the most famous ancient "international" treaty: that struck between Egypt and the Hittite Kingdom in the second millennium BCE. In Section 11.3 I begin to explore the idea of compliance to treaties in the ancient world. In Section 11.4 I explore the specific use of oaths and threats as self-help in enforcement of ancient treaties. And in Section 11.5 I discuss how trust was understood and encouraged in ancient times.

11.1 ANCIENT VASSAL TREATIES

Treaties in ancient times begin life, from the earliest records, as vassal treaties, treaties between a dominant state and a state that is in a subsidiary relation to the dominant state, perhaps because the dominant state has attained dominance by winning a war against the other state. These are not really treaties proper because the two States are not truly sovereign. But what will be important for us is that these treaties set a model for how true treaties were established.

Here are some examples of treaties between city-states in Mesopotamia, so-called vassal treaties. First here is a vassal treaty that is now known as the treaty of the Vulcan Stela, between Eannatum of Lagash and the Ruler of Umma in 2500 BCE:

> Enlil, king of all lands, father of the gods, set the boundary by his firm word for Ningirsu and Shara.
>
> Mesalim, King of Kish, at the word of his god Ishtaran, snapped down the measuring line on the field and set up a stela at this place.[1]

This treaty begins by providing a history of how the parties came to make an agreement. A bit later in the treaty text we learn that the ruler of the vassal state has made the following oath:

> I shall use the fields of Ningirsu only on loan at interest. The irrigation dike I shall not dispute. Forever and always I shall not again infringe upon the boundary of Ningirsu! The dikes and canals there, I shall not divert.
>
> The stela set up there, I shall never again uproot.[2]

And we find what will be characteristic of later treaties between sovereign States, curses associated with non-fulfillment of the agreement:

> If I do transgress, then may the great casting-net of Enlil by which I swore an oath be cast down from heaven upon Umma![3]

[1] *Treaty, Law, and Covenant in the Ancient Near East*, edited and translated by Kenneth A. Kitchen and Paul J. N. Lawrence, Wiesbaden: Harrassowitz Verlag, 2012, Vol. 1, p. 3.

[2] Ibid., p. 7.

[3] Ibid., p. 7.

Since this is a vassal treaty, only the vassal state makes an oath with the attached curse.

Next consider part of the treaty, between Naram-Sin of Akkad and [X] of Elam in 2300 BCE:

> the Lord of Akkad, I will not oppose
>
> my envoy/commander will protect the Lord from hostile acts
>
> Naram-Sin's foe is my foe
>
> Naram-Sin's friend is my friend[4]

Notice that in this very early treaty it is a pact of non-aggression and mutual support as well as an agreement to respect the envoys or commanders of each side. So, even though it is a vassal treaty there are binding obligations on both parties.

In the middle of the fourteenth century BCE, we have a striking record of a treaty struck between a Hittite ruler Suppiluliuma I and Aziru of Amurru. This is still largely a vassal treaty that Aziru was forced to sign. But what is interesting is that Aziru agrees to aid the Hittite ruler in both defensive and offensive wars. And what is of importance for us is that the treaty to aid each other in offensive wars is nonetheless couched in the following way:

> If the King of Hatti [Hittite kingdom] goes against the land of Hurri, or Egypt, or Babylonia, or the land of Ashtata, or the land of Alshi – whatever foreign lands located near your borders are hostile to My Majesty, or whatever friendly lands – [that is, friendly to My Majesty] – located near your borders – the land of Mukish, the land of Kinza, the land of Nuhashshi – turn and become hostile to the King of Hatti – when the King of Hatti goes to attack this enemy, if you, Aziru, do not mobilize wholeheartedly with infantry and chariotry, and do not fight him wholeheartedly, you will have transgressed the oath.[5]

Here we have an exchange of oaths to come to one another's aid in offensive wars, but where even offensive war alliances were justified by references to "hostile" and "enemy" forces. This wording was repeated in several other treaties of the Hittites (in Anatolia) and their close neighbors.[6] Notice also that this particular treaty mentions all other powerful States in the region, perhaps showing recognition that all of the major States were somehow linked together. We will later see a letter of Hammurabi as further support for this proposition.

In the Middle Hittite Period, we even see a reference to what today would be called the rules after war ends. The Treaty Among the Elders of Several Anatolian Communities requires that:

4 Ibid., p. 49.

5 Gary Beckman, *Hittite Diplomatic Texts*, second edition, Atlanta, Georgia: Scholars' Press, 1999, treaty 5, pp. 37–38.

6 Ibid., see treaties 7 and 9.

> after the campaign you shall not violate the wife or daughter of a man, [nor] shall you injure them. After the campaign no one shall steal a man, woman, son, daughter, slave, slave girl, sheep, horse, mule, ass, silver, gold, bronze, or copper implements.[7]

Here we have a strong statement of an emerging understanding of the importance of rules concerning after war ends, *jus post bellum*.[8]

As I said, merely displaying bilateral state agreements is not sufficient to establish that there is international law between those two States. But the terms of the bilateral agreement could be such that there is a recognition of international law if there is acknowledgment by other States in the geographical area that are encompassed in the terms of the treaty, as seems true in some vassal treaties and as we will see in the famous treaty between Egypt and the Hittites.

It also seems to me that for there to be signs of international law, the norms of natural law referred to would have to be ones that concerned the relations of States, especially when those States interacted with each other, or the relations of citizens of States especially when these citizens interacted with other foreign citizens. And, although this is not as clear-cut, the kinds of relations must in some sense be legal or politico-legal relations, or at least normative relations concerning the operating of rules, norms, or laws that affect States or their citizens. Here we seem to have examples of just such a background consideration for treaties, as also when "humanity" is appealed to, as in the Epilogue to the Laws of Lipit-Ishtar, dating from roughly the same time as the vassal treaties we just examined.[9]

Also, international law today is no longer merely about the relations of States among themselves but also about the relations of States to individual citizens, both foreign and domestic citizens. And we have an interesting example of such matters in the following ancient text. In a fifteenth century BCE treaty between Idrimi of Alakh and Pilliya of Kissuwatna, probably another vassal treaty, there is this stipulation: "They shall always return their respective fugitives."[10] In several other treaties of this period there is recognition that fugitives and refugees should not be harmed. In the third section we will see why this is itself an important component in an emerging system of international law, after we analyze the most famous ancient treaty in the following section.

7 Ibid., "miscellaneous text," 27a, p. 165.

8 For more on this idea see Larry May, *After War Ends*, Cambridge: Cambridge University Press, 2012.

9 *Laws of Hammurabi*, in *Law Collections From Mesopotamia and Asia Minor*, second edition, translated by Martha T. Roth, Atlanta, GA: Scholars' Press, 1997, p. 34.

10 Kitchen and Lawrence, *Treaty, Law, and Covenant in the Ancient Near East*, p. 305.

11.2 THE HITTITE-EGYPTIAN TREATY OF 1285 BCE

In 1285 BCE, a major battle took place between two states headed by two of the most powerful state-leaders at this time, the Pharaoh Ramses II of Egypt and the Hittite King, Hattusili III. When the battle ended in a stalemate, Ramses II and Hattusili III completed a treaty that is often cited as the first truly "international" agreement for which a record exists. This was not a vassal treaty since the kings were sovereign over their respective States. And the terms of the agreement are specified for each side, written in the two different languages of the parties. The treaty begins as follows:

> The treaty which Ramses, Beloved of Amon, Great King, King of Egypt, Hero, concluded on a tablet of silver with Hattusili, Great King, King of Hatti, his brother, in order to establish peace and great brotherhood among them forever.[11]

Notice that while the agreement is between two specific individual rulers, it is meant to last beyond their reigns – "forever."

In this treaty there is a non-aggression pact that is its centerpiece, making it a kind of peace treaty "so that for eternity he might not permit the making of war between them."[12] Here are the non-aggression oaths:

> And Ramses, Beloved of Amon, Great King, King of Egypt, for all time shall not open hostilities against Hatti in order to take anything from it. And Hattusili, Great King, King of Hatti, for all time, shall not open hostilities against Egypt in order to take anything from it.[13]

The terms that each party agrees to are the same for each party, signifying that it is truly a parity treaty, a treaty of equal sovereign States.

The alliance formed by the treaty is also portrayed as defensive – aiding in the defense of one another against foreign attacks as well as attacks from within each country.

> And if someone else, an enemy, comes against Hatti, and Hattusili, Great King, King of Hatti, sends to me: "Come to me, to my aid against him," then Ramses, Beloved of Amon, Great King, King of Egypt, must send his infantry and his chariotry, and they will defeat his enemy and take revenge for Hatti.
>
> And if someone else, an enemy, comes against Egypt, and Ramses, Beloved of Amon, King of Egypt, your brother, send to Hattusili, King of Hatti, his brother: "Come to my aid against him," then Hattusili, King of Hatti, shall send his infantry and his chariotry, and they will defeat his enemy ...[14]

[11] Beckman, *Hittite Diplomatic Texts*, treaty 15, p. 96.

[12] Ibid., treaty 15, p. 97.

[13] Ibid., treaty 15, pp. 97–98.

[14] Ibid., treaty 15, p. 98.

So, the mutual aiding of each party against foreign threats from other States is a crucial part of the agreement.

The use of the term "brother" to refer to the ruler of another state, with whom an agreement is entered into, was common at this time. The rulers were not truly related by blood or adoption. But the use of the term brother signified that they were now linked in a significant way, and that they would now treat each other as if the other was indeed a brother. As we will see, treaties from this period often were finalized with the sacrificial killing of an animal. Some scholars have proposed that the spilling of the blood of the sacrificed animal is also an indication that the two kings were now bound by blood.

In this treaty we also see that the mutual aiding of the parties is supposed to protect against internal threats as well.

> And if Hattusili, Great King, King of Hatti, becomes angry with his own subjects after they have offended against him, and he sends to Ramses, Great King, King of Egypt, on account of this, then Ramses, Beloved of Amon, must send his infantry and chariotry, and they will destroy all with whom he is angry ...
>
> And if Ramses, Beloved of Amon, King of Egypt, becomes angry with his own subjects, after they committed an offense against him, and he sends to Hattusili, King of Hatti, his brother, on account of this, then Hattusili, King of Hatti, his brother, shall send his infantry and chariotry, and they shall destroy all with whom I am angry.[15]

These kings vowed to prop each other up in the case of rebellion from within, something seemingly unrelated to the non-aggression pact at the center of the treaty, yet something that recognizes each state's sovereignty.

Of special importance is the part of the agreement that concerns fugitives, which was a common feature of the treaties at this time. And while fugitives, including fugitive slaves, were to be returned, "they shall not punish them for their offenses" or "destroy their households, together with their wives and sons."[16] There is here a clear statement that prisoners are not to be punished, and also more importantly a separation between those who were warriors and those who were civilians, with a complete prohibition on destroying the civilians. The return of fugitives is important as a recognition that each state was sovereign concerning the internal matters, including criminal matters, of that state.

The last part of the treaty has been too badly damaged for us to see what the mutual blessings and curses were that would convince each party to keep to the agreement. We do still have the seals of each of the kings at the very end attesting to

[15] Ibid., treaty 15, p. 98.

[16] Ibid., treaty 15, p. 99.

the formal agreement of this treaty as would be true for any contract at the time. We must look to other treaties of this time to see what blessings and curses were similar to those that were used in vassal treaties, namely appeals to the gods to do terrible things to the noncompliant party.

In this earliest of treaties, we find most of the elements of treaties from this point onward. It is especially interesting that the treaty is struck by two rulers who had been warring as mortal enemies just before the treaty was sealed. Unlike vassal treaties, where one party is effectively forced to agree to the terms of the other more powerful party, parity treaties raise questions of why parties agree and what is the reason they have for trusting each other when they clearly did not trust each other just before the treaty was sealed. The question remains of how such a treaty affected the larger society, which clearly it did given its fame at the time.

11.3 ANCIENT COMPLIANCE

Let me next discuss two issues that have bedeviled international legal scholars today that can be addressed from the perspective of ancient legal thought. The first issue that international legal theorists struggle with today is that there is no organized system of coercive sanctions in the international arena. Some positivist legal theorists have said that this means that international law is not really law at all. To help in addressing this issue we can look again to some of the earliest treaties, those between the rulers of ancient Near Eastern and Egyptian rulers, as well as the earliest of "codes" of law where there were no organized sanctions either. At the end of the treaties or codes there are listed both "blessings" and "curses" that will befall those who keep or break the law.

Consider several examples. Here is the ending of the Laws of Lipit-Ishtar (c. 1930 BCE):

> When I established justice in the lands of Sumer and Akkad, I erected this stela. He who will not do anything evil to it, who will not damage my work, who will (not) efface my inscription and write his own name on it – may be granted life and breath of long days; may he raise his neck to heaven in the Ekur temple; may the god of Enlil's brilliant countenance be turned upon him from above. [But] he who will do anything evil to it, who damages my work, who enters the treasure room, who alters its pedestal, who effaces this inscription and writes his own name (in place of mine), or because of this curse, induces an outsider to remove it – that man, whether he is a king, an *enu*-lord, or an ensi-ruler … may be completely obliterated …[17]

[17] *Laws of Lipit-Ishtar* in *Law Collections From Mesopotamia and Asia Minor*, second edition, translated by Martha T. Roth, Atlanta, GA: Scholars' Press, 1997, p. 34.

This is one of the best examples of the listing of both potential blessings and curses, as issuing from the gods, to anyone who either keeps or breaks the laws of this "code."

Another example comes from a vassal treaty between Eannatum of Lagash and the Ruler of Umma (c. 2500 BCE):

> If I do transgress, then may the great casting-net of Enlil, by which I swore an oath be cast down from heaven upon Umma …
>
> If for any reason, for any cause, a leader of Umma goes back on this agreement against Enlil my King; if he opposes or contests this agreement; if he sets aside this agreement; then may the great casting-net of Enlil be cast down from heaven upon Umma![18]

In a world where an oath is taken seriously especially in light of blessings and curses that connect to the oath, having physical sanctions must have seemed not so important as long as there were cosmic sanctions for noncompliance.

To put the point in a more secular idiom, conventions concerning mutual promising may be sanctions enough for compliance to be predicted if there is a community in which those promises are seen as binding. That the gods will benefit a keeper of a treaty or punish the breaker of his oath at the center of a treaty is employed in most ancient treaties. But there is also a sense that humans will have to be the instruments of divine sanctions and so the treaties can be seen as self-enforcing, especially multilateral treaties, where the parties provide both incentives for compliance and disincentives for the noncompliant.

And in a similar vein we also have evidence of the elusive notion of *aut dedere aut judicare* (either extradite or prosecute) as another form of self-enforcement in these texts from the ancient Near East. In a treaty between Suppiluliuma I of Hatti and Tette of Nuhashshi there is this stipulation:

> If someone incites Tette to evil matters, whether a Hittite or his own subject, and Tette does not seize him and send him to the King of Hatti, he will transgress the oath.[19]

This is another form of enforcement of agreements – a form of reciprocal self-enforcement that is today being seen as one possible way out of the problem of lack of organized coercion in the international arena.

The treaty provision that calls for fugitives to be returned is an indication of a rudimentary form of *aut dedere aut judicare*. The return of fugitives is important for the successful prosecution of crime; but it also serves a goal of international justice as it prevents the criminal from fleeing from one locale to another in order to achieve

[18] Kitchen and Lawrence, *Treaty, Law, and Covenant in the Ancient Near East*, p. 7.

[19] Beckman, *Hittite Diplomatic Texts*, p. 57.

impunity. Extradition of fleeing citizens back to their home States, which seems to be recognized in the treaty provisions dealing with the return of fugitives, can be a key component in the kind of self-help that States seek and that forms the basis of a rudimentary form of international law.[20]

A second issue is how a collection of autonomous States can be brought together under a system of law without losing their autonomy and unique cultural heritage. In the ancient world we have several examples of this happening concerning the amalgamation of city-states – perhaps the best known example is the formation of the Roman Empire. But there is an earlier example that is perhaps more telling since it did not arise through coercion, namely the consolidation of the city-states of Asia Minor into the empires of Hammurabi in the Eighteenth Century BCE as well as later in the case of Cyrus the Great in the Sixth century BCE.

While discussing the Egyptian-Hittite treaty under Ramses II, Wilson speaks of a kind of international customary law:

> Apparently there was an accepted code of international law, which protected the person and property of such refugees, although not their former positions or privileges.[21]

And yet Bederman concludes his impressive study of international law in antiquity by stating: "Despite my occasional use of the term 'international law' in this study, the ancient law of nations was conceived only as an instrument of State relations."[22]

Of greatest importance is a very intriguing statement by Hammurabi and several other scattered references in ancient times that seem to suggest that there was some kind of ancient league of States, perhaps as early as Hammurabi's time. King Zimri-Lim wrote to Hammurabi with a draft treaty containing a statement that had Hammurabi withdraw his claims on the settlement at Hit. Here is the writing of Zimri-Lim's emissary: "On the second day I brought to him the treaty tablet that my lord had drafted."[23] In a letter of reply Hammurabi makes the following comment:

> Take Hit out of the treaty text, so that I can swear to it. Then go to your troops and start the campaign. After our goals have been reached, our fellow kings will come together and judge this matter. I will accept their verdict.[24]

20 See M. C. Bassiouni and E. M. Wise, *Aut Dedere Aut Judicare*, Dordrecht: Martinus Nijhoff Publishers, 1995, especially pp. 26–42.

21 John A. Wilson, *The Culture of Ancient Egypt*, 1951, p. 239.

22 David J. Bederman, *International Law in Antiquity*, Cambridge: Cambridge University Press, 2001, p. 279.

23 Quoted in Marc Van De Mieroop, *King Hammurabi of Babylon*, Oxford: Blackwell Publishing, 2005, p. 70.

24 Ibid., p. 71.

Here it seems that kings at this time, in the eighteenth century BCE, came together to discuss matters of war and peace. And it also seems that Hammurabi was pledging himself to accept whatever decision the kings reached. This last point seems to suggest that the kings passed judgments on matters of war and peace and that the decisions reached were meant to be binding on the kings, even those who might disagree with the rulings. This perhaps provides the setting for the first known "international" treaties that we analyzed above.

We also have other evidence that there was a "Club of Great States" that acknowledged the sovereignty of each other. Here is how Marc Van de Mieroop describes a set of letters, found in Amarna, Egypt from the fourteenth century BCE:

> A group of about forty of these letters had been written to the Egyptian king by his colleagues in the other great States at the time: Babylonia, Assyria, Mittan, Hatti [the Hittite kingdom], Alashiya, and Arzawa. The kings saw themselves as equals and addressed each other as brothers. They discussed diplomatic matters, especially the exchange of precious goods and of royal women, which reinforced the ties between them … most of the letters were written in Babylonian … These Amarna letters cover a short period of at most thirty years from ca. 1365 to 1335, but it is certain that this type of correspondence was maintained throughout the period at several locations.[25]

There are clear indications of an incipient international community of States in ancient times where there was a single language used for diplomatic communication and treaties that set the norms for how the States behaved toward one another.

In the two problems that have bedeviled international law scholars discussed above, the lack of organized sanctions and the lack of a world state, we find at the very least an ancient recognition of the problems and an attempt to solve them. And while the solutions are similar to ones that are sometimes employed in international law today, it is interesting to note how old these practices are. But it is also of note that the return of fugitives and refugees, unharmed, was the subject of several important treaties. I will say more about the return of fugitives in a later section of this chapter.

The consolidation of States into international groups of States was supposedly best accomplished by leaving maximum latitude for the unique cultural and religious practices of each state. It is only a very small step from leagues of States to rudimentary international law. Whether or not one accepts this as "international law" proper, there is international diplomacy here and the casting of treaties as at least

[25] Marc Van De Mieroop, *A History of the Ancient Near East c. 3000–323 BC*, Oxford: Blackwell, 2004, 2007, p. 135.

quasi-legal documents among States. We next consider in more detail the sanctions that were employed to enforce treaties, a further sign of an emerging international legal system in ancient times in mid-second millennium BCE in the Near East.

11.4 OATHS AND THREATS

Hammurabi was one of the first Mesopotamian rulers to record a method of a special type of swearing to indicate compliance with the terms of a treaty. In a letter, Yarim-Addu described the procedure that he observed in Hammurabi's court:

> When Hammurabi went to Borsipa, messengers of the lord of Eshnunna joined him there … They took in their hands the little tablet. They will have the lord of Eshnunna pledge [literally "touch his throat"] by the tablet … and here Hammurabi will pledge ["touch his throat"]. After they have pledged by the little tablet, Hammurabi will have a large tablet, a treaty tablet, taken to the lord of Eshnunna, and he will have the lord of Eshnunna swear an oath.[26]

In another account we find that Hammurabi "touched 'the tablet of life of the gods,' containing the treaty text, and then 'touched his throat' while a calf was slaughtered."[27] This is an even more graphic account of the symbolism attached to the oaths taken by the parties to a treaty. Touching the throat was a vivid way of indicating the seriousness of the pledge or oath, signifying that the king would slit his own throat if he did not keep to his word.

Something similar seems to be symbolized when an animal was sacrificed. Here is how one scholar, J. A. Thompson describes the intended effect of animal sacrifices that occurred at the time of treaty signing in the ancient Near East and for ancient Israelites:

> One of the most interesting and most persistent of the details of the treaty and covenant ratification ceremonies was the sacrificial or ritual slaying of a beast. The significance of this act may have varied from country to country and from century to century although there seems to be a fairly consistent interpretation of the act as a sign of self-imprecation, as though the participants in the treaty would say, "If I break the treaty may this happen to me."[28]

[26] Quoted in Dominique Charpin, *Writing, Law, and Kingship in Old Babylonian Mesopotamia*, translated by Jane Marie Todd, Chicago, IL: University of Chicago Press, 2010, p. 109. Insertions are added by Charpin from the sense of the larger text.

[27] Quoted in David J. Bederman, *International Law in Antiquity*, Cambridge: Cambridge University Press, 2001, p. 63.

[28] J. A. Thompson, *The Ancient Near East Treaties and the Old Testament*, London: The Tyndale Press, 1963, p. 25.

The killing of animals seems to have had important symbolic value for demonstrating future compliance.[29] In fact there is one treaty text that adds "The head is not the head of a lamb, it is the head of Mati'ilu."[30] And another text reads: "As this calf is cut up, thus Mati'el and his nobles shall be cut up."[31]

Thompson gives two examples, one from the Bible and the other from ancient Mesopotamia:

> the practice of Judah in the days of Jeremiah … "And the men who transgressed my covenant and did not keep the terms of the covenant which they made before me, I will make like the calf which they have cut in two and passed between its parts." [and] A formula from the eighteenth century BC treaty between Abban of Alalah and Iarimlim of Iamhad seems to reflect the same kind of thinking. When Abban placed himself under oath to Iarimlim he cut the throat of a sheep and declared "(Let me so die) if I take back that which I gave thee."[32]

Cutting the sheep's throat symbolized even more graphically what the touching of one's own throat also symbolized: that death will be the result of violations of a treaty.[33]

It is important that these symbolic acts were made by a party to a treaty concerning his own life, not a threat against the life of the other party. The symbolic act was accompanied by the swearing of an oath. And so the obvious thing to think is that these symbolic acts are something like the contemporary practice of putting one's hand on a Bible as one swears an oath. The act of swearing is given greater credence when the swearer invokes a god or some other source of dire consequences should he or she not comply or be telling a lie.

The other form of self-help concerns the attempt to make the other party take his or her contractual responsibilities seriously. For one representative contemporary international legal theorist self-help means "all unilateral measures of response which infringe upon a right or an interest of the target state and which are taken in reaction to a perceived wrongful and undesirable act."[34] It is my view that this is exactly what was happening in the treaty-related practices of ancient times. And the

[29] But see Moshe Weinfeld, "Covenant Making in Anatolia and Mesopotamia," *Janes* 22 (1993), p. 138, where it is claimed that: "It seems striking, therefore, that in Hittite and Assyrian treaties the sacrificial element is missing. This could best be explained by the supposition that in the formally developed treaty formulation, the proclamation of the oath replaced the sacrificial ceremony."

[30] Reported in Karl-Heinz Ziegler, "Conclusion and Publication of International Treaties in Antiquity," *Israel Law Review*, Vol. 29, nos. 1–2, 1995, pp. 233–249, p. 237.

[31] Ibid., 238.

[32] Ibid.

[33] See Moshe Weinfeld, "Covenant Making in Anatolia and Mesopotamia," *Janes* 22 (1993), pp. 135–139.

[34] Matt Noortmann, *Enforcing International Law: From Self-help to Self-contained Regimes*, Burlington, VT: Ashgate Publishing, 2005, p. 16.

most common form of self-help was to invoke the wrath of the gods upon a party who breaks the treaty.[35]

Bederman has written helpfully about how to understand the reference to the gods in the oaths that were exchanged to finalize an ancient treaty:

> the nature of the obligation arising from the exchange of oaths and the articulation of treaty curses was religious only in a particular way. To the extent that maledictions were invoked – that bad things would happen if the terms of an international agreement were not kept – it was not always clear that it would be a deity who would oversee the punishment. Sometimes this was implied, but in some cases the ancient mind understood that the consequences of bad faith would follow without a necessary divine intervention.[36]

There seem then to be two things the allusions to the gods are supposed to be symbolic of: actual intervention by the gods, or secular rulers acting in the name of the gods.

Jerrold Cooper has argued that the invocation of the gods was meant to have a hybrid status:

> The treaties [of the third millennium BCE] envisage no remedy for breach beyond the intervention of the gods invoked therein. In reality, the remedy employed was self-help, namely, threatened or actual military action. Because military success was inevitably understood as a sign of divine favor, there was no perceived contradiction between the remedies.[37]

And Gary Beckman has also argued for a hybrid view:

> The deities invoked as witnesses to treaties were also the enforcers of the attendant oaths and guarantors of their provisions. But in addition the rulers of the Great Powers made use of more direct measures to secure the obedience of their underlings.[38]

War was clearly the most prominent sanction that loomed in the background as a threat for noncompliance in ancient legal thought.

War was seen as a battle of rivals for the attention and support of the gods. And in addition, war could also be seen as the manifestation of divine retribution for the

35 See Jan Assmann, "When Justice Fails: Jurisdiction and Imprecation in Ancient Egypt and the Near East," *Journal of Egyptian Archeology*, Vol. 78, 1992, pp. 149–162.

36 Bederman, *International Law in Antiquity*, p. 67.

37 Jerrold Cooper, "International Law in the Third Millennium," in *A History of Ancient Near Eastern Law*, Vol. 1, edited by Raymond Westbrook, Leiden: Brill, 2003, pp. 248–249.

38 Gary Beckman, "International Law in the Second Millennium: The Late Bronze Age," in *A History of Ancient Near Eastern Law*, Vol. 1, edited by Raymond Westbrook, Leiden: Brill, 2003, p. 763.

party that had gone against its word.[39] Throughout the Middle Ages and into the Modern Age CE, the side that won a war was seen to have its cause vindicated as a just cause and as demonstrating that the losing side was on the side of the devil.[40] Even today, victors sometimes claim to have won because they were on the side of the angels. In ancient times, the gods were thought to intervene to punish those who violated treaties, and such intervention came either directly or through the intermediary of human agents. But it seems to me that the threat of enforcement of the gods' wrath by the means of war was probably the most significant consideration.

11.5 TRUST IN THE ANCIENT "INTERNATIONAL" COMMUNITY

Annette Baier has said: "Trust, then, on this first approximation, is vulnerability to another's possible, but not expected, ill will (or lack of good will) toward one."[41] The "special vulnerability which trust involves is vulnerability to not yet noticed harm, or disguised ill will."[42] Of course we don't trust everyone nor do we trust in all circumstances. "Awareness of what is customary, as well as the past experiences of one's own, affects one's ability to trust. We take it for granted that people will perform their role-related duties."[43]

In the cases we have been examining, of treaties formed in the ancient Near East, the customs of mutual trust had not yet been fully established. In such cases, punitive sanctions are important as we have seen, but also it is important that there was a developing shared sense of the importance of mutual bonds of security.[44] A rudimentary community is here essential. And as we have seen there were the rudiments of an international community in the ancient Near East. Indeed, there is evidence of the awareness of what were emerging as the customs of international relations.[45]

Yet, the first States to trust each other in an agreement of non-intervention and mutual support, and to memorialize this trust with a formal treaty, took a considerable risk. This is why the curses and invocations of the gods were so important for the parties to these earliest of treaties. It is an interesting question of whether

[39] See J. A. Thompson, *The Ancient Near East Treaties and the Old Testament*, London: The Tyndale Press, 1963, p. 19.

[40] For an especially interesting view of this practice in the Middle Ages, see Helen Castor, *Joan of Arc*, NY: Harper, 2015.

[41] Annette Baier, "Trust and Antitrust," Chapter 6 of her book *Moral Prejudices*, Cambridge, MA: Harvard University Press, 1994.

[42] Ibid., p. 104.

[43] Ibid., p. 111.

[44] Ibid., Baier quotes the writings of David Hume to this effect from his *Treatise*, Selby-Bigge edition, Oxford: Oxford University Press, 1968, pp. 522 and 541.

[45] See Bertrand Lafont, "International Relations in the Ancient Near East: The Birth of a Complete Diplomatic System," *Diplomacy & Statecraft*, Vol. 12, no. 1 (March 2001), pp. 39–60.

and to what extent everyone in these ancient societies believed that the gods would enforce the terms of these treaties. A full answer to this question is well beyond the compass of this chapter. And since there are no critically reflective texts from these ancient times, as there was for the Greeks and Romans who had a robust discussion of how or even whether to believe in the divine intervention of the gods, it is hard to say much in the context of treaty-formation and trust.

Bederman has provided a fascinating view of what made the ancient treaties primitive:

> Ancient international law was not a primitive legal system because of its doubtful dependence on religious belief. It was primitive because the ancient mind could not conceive of norms of State behavior apart from the admittedly diverse sanctions for non-compliance with those rules.[46]

Yet, I will discuss in this final section whether the sanctions of the ancient treaties are really so different from the ones today. Indeed, it is my view that the problem of trust in a time when parties are vulnerable is an enduring problem, not one restricted to ancient or "primitive" times.

Let me summarize what are commonly recognized components of "international" treaties:

(1) a community of States where there are customary norms;
(2) a recognition of the autonomy of these States by the community members;
(3) the mutual exchange of promises that are recognized as binding;
(4) a system of sanctions for noncompliance.

Here are the components of what today is recognized as the basis of treaty-making. I will next summarize and discuss reasons for seeing ancient treaties as something like treaties today.

First, I have tried to show that there was a community of States, at least in the middle of the second millennium BCE. Such a community is seen most directly in the lively correspondence among the rulers of six-to-ten States, where the rulers referred to each other as "brother," and as forming a Club. There was a common language, Babylonian, as the "lingua franca" for this community despite the fact that each state had its own different language. The form of the letters, as well as the form of the treaties as we will discuss below, was virtually identical. And such similarity can be seen extending much more widely to include the ancient Israelites and the emerging Greek city-states as well as the city-states of the western coast of Anatolia.

Communities can be extensive enough for something like "international" law without all States accepting the exact same norms, especially if many other States

46 Bederman, *International Law in Antiquity*, p. 51.

accept similar customary norms. Another important conceptual point is that there can be international law operating at one time and not at another – when international law is established it need not be forever. These may seem like simple points but it is important for the debates today since, when there is resistance to a regimen of international law, some are led to deny that there ever was international law at all. In this sense international law is very different from natural law. Natural law either exists for all time or it doesn't. International law can be episodic.

Second, concerning the recognition of sovereignty by fellow members of the community of States, in part this is about recognizing other States as on an equal footing with one's own state. We have seen that in the middle of the second millennium BCE the most powerful state rulers in the ancient Near East called each other brothers as a sign of their camaraderie but also as a sign of rough equality among them. In addition, these rulers recognized that fugitives from the laws in one state should be returned to that state. And the intermarriage among the royal families of these States also indicated that these rulers saw themselves as roughly equal. In addition, the fact that these rulers were bound to go to the aid of their fellow rulers to put down insurrections showed that these rulers recognized their fellow rulers as sovereign even when sovereignty was questioned at home.

State autonomy can be understood either from an internal or external perspective. From an internal perspective, there must be a wide swath of affairs that are governed by one ruler, and above whom there is no superior domestic ruler. For the purposes of establishing international law, at least initially, it is not important whether a ruler is recognized by all factions internally as sovereign. What matters is how that ruler is regarded externally. This conceptual point is especially important today since many States are indeed challenged by insurgencies, which could topple the state. But what matters is external recognition. This is not to say that States would not count internal stability as a condition on their recognition of another state's sovereignty. Rather, the withdrawing of recognition of sovereignty is not an inevitable result of internal instability. This is why, for many years, international law existed in the twentieth century even as domestic instability was rampant in certain parts of the world.

Third, the mutual recognition of the bindingness of promises is crucial for trust in the international community. One way to establish that the sovereign rulers of various States in the ancient Near East recognized the bindingness of their promises is by looking at how they described themselves, and the critical attitude that they took toward their promises to other States. Unfortunately, there is very little evidence for this type of recognition. But we can turn to how promises were regarded within each state in the laws of these various States. And, we have evidence that there were treaties signed by the great rulers of the middle of the second millennium BCE.

It is not terribly controversial to think that promises in a domestic setting have a parallel status to promises made in an international setting. And it is clear that promises, especially when accompanied by an oath, were well recognized as binding in all ancient societies in the Near East. In Chapter 3 on oaths and ordeals, I set out more evidence for this claim. We can also find some additional evidence in that rulers offered criticisms of one another when they were perceived as not keeping their words.

Fourth, in these ancient societies there is a regime of sanctions that are meant to increase the likelihood of compliance with international treaties. At first glance, this is where international law today seems to be so different from what might be international law in ancient times. Today there are economic as well as military sanctions that can be employed if there are violations of treaties. And yet even so, there are questions raised about whether or not these sanctions are sufficient to undergird "international" law. Nonetheless we have seen that there were sanctions for violations of treaties in the ancient Near East. Here we need to say just a bit more about the relevance of the curses and oaths connected to ancient treaties.

In the ancient Near East there was a common form to the various religions associated with the major States, where religion and morality were linked in a way that produced a strong sense of personal responsibility. Thorkild Jacobsen says this about Mesopotamian religion in the second millennium BCE:

> There is here the beginnings of a searching of the heart: the insight gained in the preceding millennium that the divine stands for, and upholds, a moral law is now bearing fruit in a realization of individual human responsibility, but also of innate human inability to live up to that responsibility … the penitent may have to seek intercession by higher deities.[47]

Similar things seem to be true across the ancient Near East, where people saw that they had responsibilities but were often not able to fulfill them without invoking a god's intercession.

The case of treaty-making is a good example of where the parties in the second millennium BCE would see that they were responsible for keeping their agreements but where they also saw that help from the gods was needed. Hence, we have the treaties at this time with often elaborate curses at the end indicating what the gods would do to the party that broke the agreement. Such appeal to the gods was not only to hold other parties accountable but also to hold themselves accountable, before the gods.

47 Thorkild Jacobsen, "Ancient Mesopotamian Religion: The Central Concerns," Chapter 3 in his book *Toward the Image of Tammuz and Other Essays on Mesopotamian History and Culture*, Cambridge, MA: Harvard University Press, 1970, p. 43.

This brings us back to the issue of trust. One is more likely to trust another if there is a common set of normative beliefs that exist among the parties. And this is especially true if those beliefs concern personal responsibility. Yet, self-help is still needed both to constrain oneself to do what is one's responsibility and also to constrain other parties in a similar way. And something like appeal to the gods aids in the self-help – perhaps today that is the role of the United Nations, which like the gods must rely on individual States to do its bidding.

12

Aggressive War and Necessity

In the four thousand-year recorded history of legal thought, one of the most enduring questions has been "when is it just to engage in war?" The discussion of whether a state should go to war for reasons other than self-defense is as old as recorded history. The answers to this question have been varied and fascinating, including: opportunity, necessity, vengeance (and punishment). Over the centuries, the most commonly recognized just war is a war of national defense, although even in ancient times wars of humanitarian intervention were sometimes recognized as just.

There is an especially interesting perspective on the justness of war that we can find in ancient legal texts, especially from Mesopotamia and the ancient Near East, although I will also refer to texts from ancient China and Egypt as well. I will argue that the perspective on war that is found in these ancient legal texts can be seen to fit into a rudimentary Just War tradition despite the differences between the time of Hammurabi, around 1750 BCE, and now. In particular, we will find that the dominant perspective of humanitarianism of many ancient rulers manifests itself in a strong concern for achieving peace, and a peace that involved minimizing oppression. The emphasis on eliminating or minimizing oppression can give us a model of understanding how wars for national defense or for rescuing those who are oppressed can be justified.

Since there were many wars occurring in these very ancient times, one of the puzzles then, as well as now, is how to reconcile humanitarian motivations with the waging of war. The just war of the ancient Near East, I will argue, involved war that was aimed at pacification. But the peace that just war aimed at was one that diminished oppression in the target States. And so we have the idea that later emerged in humanitarian intervention wars, although these ancient just wars were sometimes inspired by a stronger sense of humanitarianism than is often seen today.

In the first half of this chapter I will look at some of the most interesting ancient responses to the question: when is war just? Then in the second half of the chapter

I will assess these various responses for normative guidance today. I will draw often on ancient sources in order to show how old the controversy is and how often the answers were different from but relevant to our situation today. My thesis is that from the earliest of times the only relatively sure grounding for a just war is defense of those who are oppressed, either oppressed by aggressors from without or oppressors from within.

12.1 OPPORTUNITY

The nearly constant wars in the early history of Mesopotamia and the rest of the ancient Near East are often discussed in terms of one or another city-state seeking to gain advantage over others whenever the opportunity presented itself.[1] But there is an alternative explanation for why there were so many wars in ancient times – various city-states tried to gain control over enough territory so that pacification could be accomplished, thereby putting an end to the previously constant threat of invasion.[2]

The pure desire for increased territory, or for the gain in wealth or resources, is condemned from a very early point in the history of legal thought. We can turn to Hammurabi whose writings take us back to roughly 1750 BCE. Here is how he describes himself in the Epilogue to his stela that propounds his "code" of law:

> I am Hammurabi, noble king. I have not been careless or negligent toward humankind, granted to my care by the god Enlil, and with whose shepherding the god Marduk charged me. I have sought for them peaceful places, I removed serious difficulties, I spread light over them. With the mighty weapons which the gods Zababa and Ishtar bestowed upon me, with the wisdom of the god Ea allotted to me, with the ability which the god Marduk gave me, I annihilated enemies everywhere, I put an end to wars, I enhanced the well being of the land, I made the people of all settlements lie in safe pastures, I did not tolerate anyone intimidating them. The great gods have chosen me, I am indeed the shepherd who brings peace, whose scepter is just.[3]

There is a scholarly debate about whether we should trust Hammurabi's words here, but my point is just that in this very early legal text Hammurabi feels that he should explain that the reason for the many wars he initiated was to pacify a region, between

1 See Alexander Gillespie, *The Causes of War: Vol. 1: 3000 BCE to 1000 CE*, Oxford: Hart Publishing, 2013, Part II.

2 See Benjamin Forester, "Water Under the Straw: Peace in Mesopotamia," in *War and Peace in the Ancient World*, edited by Kurt A. Raaflaub, Oxford: Blackwell Publishing, 2007, pp. 66–80.

3 *Laws of Hammurabi* (c. 1750 BCE), in *Law Collections from Mesopotamia and Asia Minor*, second edition, translated and edited by Martha T. Ross, Atlanta: Scholars' Press, 1997, p. 133.

the Tigris and Euphrates Rivers, which had had very little peace during hundreds of years of war up to his time.

There is a similar statement on a stone cylinder erected by Cyrus the Great of Persia who conquered Babylon more than a thousand years after Hammurabi. In 500 BCE Cyrus says:

> I am Cyrus king of the universe, king of the city of Anshan ... When I went as a harbinger of peace into Babylon I founded my sovereign residence within the palace amid celebration and rejoicing. Marduk, the great lord bestowed on me my destiny the great magnanimity of one who loves Babylon, and I every day sought him out in awe. My vast troops were marching peaceably in Babylon, and the whole of Sumer and Akkad had nothing to fear. I sought the safety of the city of Babylon and all its sanctuaries. As for the population of Babylon ... who as if without divine intervention had endured a yoke not decreed for them. I soothed their weariness; I freed them from their bonds.[4]

Here Cyrus claims that his conquest of Babylonia and much of the rest of Asia Minor was aimed at liberating the peoples of this region from tyranny and oppression.

Indeed, the Greek historian Xenophon tells us of this (probably imaginary) speech of Cyrus:

> Cyrus: "'Now I am going to let you who have been captured go home and consult with the rest of the Chaldaeans whether you wish to have war with us or be our friends. And if you choose war, do not come this way again without weapons, if you are wise; but if you decide that you desire peace, come without arms. I shall see to it that you have no cause for complaint, if you become our friends.' And when the Caldaeans heard this, they commended Cyrus highly, shook hands with him heartily, and departed for home."[5]

Again, there is scholarly support for thinking that Cyrus was not always so gentle and generous to his captives, but what is of interest is how this early legal text, and the commentary by Xenophon writing a generation later, describes Cyrus' conquest: not in terms of opportunity for gain, but in terms of opportunity to defend a population from oppression and to pursue peace.

There are certainly early accounts of war that stress the precious metals and land that is brought into the hands of a conqueror. But in the discussion of conquest, in some of the very earliest legal texts, there is also the expression of the view that the conquest should be conducted for the good of the people, especially for their defense against being the victims of constant war or against oppression by their

4 *The Cyrus Cylinder*, edited by Irving Finkel, London: I. B. Tauris and Co. Ltd, 2013, p. 6.

5 Xenophon, *Cyropaedia* (*The Education of Cyrus*), Book III, Sec. II. paragraphs 13–14, translated by Walter Miller, Cambridge, MA: Harvard University, Loeb Classical Library, 1914, pp. 255–257.

despotic rulers. We can see in the pronouncements of Hammurabi and Cyrus the incipient and controversial idea of humanitarian intervention that has today nearly replaced national defense as the primary basis of a just war. The opportunity to do good is what is stressed even as it is acknowledged that borders were crossed and military might was used to suppress tyrants.

Opportunity looks like a purely consequentialist notion – if more good can be done by waging war than not waging war then it should be pursued. Yet, today such a rationale would not be sufficient, and there is reason to think that it was not sufficient in ancient times either. Indeed, as we see in the next section, there is strong support for thinking that war needed to be seen as necessary, not merely as beneficial, to be considered just.

12.2 NECESSITY

Recourse to war has often been purportedly justified by various forms of necessity. The main claim of necessity over the centuries has had to do with providing defense against enemy soldiers that are crossing the border, and who have not been provoked to do so. I will discuss this just cause to engage in war again by reference to some legal texts from the ancient Near East. Here is a passage from a treaty between Niqmepa of Alalakh and Ir-Adad/Tesup of Tunip from the fifteenth century BCE:

> If someone from my territory enters your territory to survive, you shall certainly keep them (alive) as though they were of your land. (But) you shall surely not detain them within your territory, and must return them to my territory, you may not confine (even) one family within your land[6]

There are several issues intertwined here. First, and most relevant for us at the moment, is that the mere crossing of borders is not thought to trigger a justified war. Indeed, those who transgress a state's borders are not to be killed, at least in part, because it is not necessary to kill them in order to protect the homeland. There is also another necessity issue here as well, namely that in certain circumstances a state has the obligation to provide for the survival of people from another state.

War was not to be engaged in if it were not necessary for achieving a result that would be considered to be just. The terms for justice in the earliest legal writings encompass both strict legal justice and also the more wide-ranging idea of equity as a distinctly moral concept. It is important to note that achieving equity was often characterized in terms of what the gods expected or demanded of their people. And

[6] *Treaty, Law, and Covenant in the Ancient Near East*, Kenneth A. Kitchen and Paul J. N. Lawrence translators and editors, Wiesbaden: Harrassowitz Verlag, 2012, Vol. 1, p. 311.

this is a significant difference between ancient times and our own. But there is also often a secular reason as well that is intertwined with the religious.

Hammurabi speaks of how the god Marduk instructed him to create the stela that lists his laws. This seems to give the laws a religious significance. But Hammurabi also speaks of how he has duties as the shepherd of his flock, especially to protect the most vulnerable members of the society. This secular reason is intertwined with the religious in that Hammurabi sees his role of shepherd also as commanded by the gods. But this aspect of Hammurabi's role could be as linked to considerations of humanity as to any specific god's command.

Again, Hammurabi intimates that he only goes to war when it is necessary to achieve a lasting peace after other measures have failed. We can see this when Hammurabi speaks of showing mercy to those who are not true threats even as they have given cause for his wrath to come down on them.[7] The idea seems to be that even though Hammurabi has had reason to strike against his enemies he has resisted and shown mercy unless these enemies threaten the well-being of his own citizenry. There is no explicit discussion of necessity in these ancient texts but the sentiment of restraint is so powerful that one can easily infer that war was only considered just if it was necessary to wage it to counter threats to the well-being of the citizenry.

Hugo Grotius, writing in 1625 CE, takes a related although differently grounded position. Grotius offers a strong and clear statement of what he thinks necessity requires:

> therefore the Dread … of our Neighbor's increasing Strength, is not a warrantable Ground for making War upon him. To justify taking up Arms in our own Defense, there ought to be a Necessity for doing so, which there is not, unless we are sure, with a moral Certainty, that he has not only Forces sufficient, but a full Intention to injure us.[8]

For Grotius, reasons such as vengeance may be justifying reasons but only if war is the only way that vengeance can be meted out.[9] Indeed, Grotius argues strongly that past injury is not a just cause to go to war; only the mitigation of truly threatening injury can satisfy the necessity condition.

The difference between Grotius and Hammurabi, who seem to hold similar views about necessity despite living 3,500 years earlier, concerns the rationale behind a fairly strict construal of necessity. Hammurabi is motivated, he tells us, by humanitarian ideals concerning the minimization of oppression. Grotius also says he is

7 See the Prologue to Hammurabi's laws.

8 Hugo Grotius, *De Jure Belli ac Pacis* (On the Law of War and Peace) (1625), translated by Francis Kelsey, Oxford: Clarendon Press, 1925, p. 1102.

9 Ibid., p. 1097.

motivated by humanitarian concerns but these are linked to mutual restraint of powerful nations rather than a concern for the oppressed and downtrodden.

Contemporary accounts are not as clear concerning the importance of satisfying a necessity condition for a just war as was true in ancient times. There is not as much discussion as one would now have hoped concerning diplomacy and other non-lethal strategies rather than violently confronting enemy soldiers.[10] If we were to think about such matters from the standpoint of a two-person case, we would want to know if retreat or building up defenses could be engaged in instead. Yet today it is rare to find concern for such humanitarian issues.

12.3 VENGEANCE AND PUNISHMENT

Rulers have sometimes claimed that retaliation, revenge, or the right to punish, give them justification for recourse to war. Indeed, until quite recently some modern Just War theorists have said that punishment is a just cause to go to war. The idea is that in international affairs where there is no sovereign, rulers will think that they are free to engage in aggression unless other rulers express a willingness to punish these aggressors themselves.

Some ancient texts have supported the idea of punishment as a just cause to initiate war. And in some cases it seemed plausible that this should be so. Think of the case of an envoy or emissary who is killed while serving in his official role in a foreign capital. We can find threats of war and actual occasions of war in very ancient times when such officials are killed or harmed. For example, in a letter from the Hittite king to another Anatolian king, dating from around the sixteenth century BCE, there is a threat of war and armed violence if the envoy named Walmu is not returned to the Hittite king, otherwise the Anatolian king who holds Walmu will be "subdued by force of arms" for this transgression.[11] In such cases, there was both a threat of punishment if the wrong was not quickly corrected, and there was the threat used as something to fear if the wrongdoer harmed the nation by killing one of its agents.

The idea that those who are guilty can have wars waged against them is ancient in origin, although it is not always as straightforward as it has seemed to some commentators. The argument was often couched in terms of what is the righteous path. In the treaties of the most ancient times, we find threats of war understood in terms of punishment for violation of the treaty, as we saw in the previous chapter. Here we can look to some of the earliest treaties, those between Sumerian

[10] See Larry May, *Contingent Pacifism*, Cambridge: Cambridge University Press, 2015.

[11] See "Letter from a King of Hatti to an Anatolian Ruler," *Hittite Diplomatic Texts*, #23A, second edition, edited by Gary Beckman, Atlanta, Georgia: Scholars' Press, 1999, pp. 145–146.

and Egyptian rulers. At the end of the treaties (as is also true of certain "codes" of law) there are listed "threats" that will befall those who break the treaty, as well as "benefits" that will occur to those who keep the treaty, as internal mechanisms of compliance that could prove useful to international humanitarian law.

Consider again a representative treaty between Eannatum of Lagash and the Ruler of Umma (c. 2500 BCE):

> If I do transgress, then may the great casting-net of Enlil, by which I swore an oath be cast down from heaven upon Umma ...
>
> If for any reason, for any cause, a leader of Umma goes back on this agreement against Enlil my King; if he opposes or contests this agreement; if he sets aside this agreement; then may the great casting-net of Enlil be cast down from heaven upon Umma![12]
>
> If for any reason, any cause, an Umma leader breaks this agreement [against Ninki] – if he opposes (or) contests the agreement; if he sets aside this agreement; (then) may Ninki, by whom I have sworn an oath, cause snakes out of the earth to bite Umma's feet![13]

And in the following treaty, punishment in terms of the gods exercising recourse to war is something that is clearly threatened for those who break the treaty:

> Anyone who transgresses these words, Adad/Tesup, lord of divination and Shamash, the lord of judgment, the god Sin and the great gods shall destroy his name and his seed ... from the lands, let them bring down his throne and his [scepter].[14]

The parties invoke the gods who will both seek vengeance and administer a kind of divine punishment for the party who breaks the treaty. Of course, it is the parties that will administer the divine punishment. The underlying assumption is then that the aggrieved party may wage war against the treaty-breaking party on behalf of the gods. Yet also in treaties from this period the rationale not to break a treaty comes from a concern for the benefits the treaty promotes, especially insofar as the people of the nations in question are kept safe. So there are humanitarian reasons given along with fear-of-gods reasons.

12.4 HUMANITARIAN INTERVENTION

The history of writing is normally traced back to the first cuneiform clay tablets found in ancient Mesopotamia around 3000 BCE. Legal documents were among the

[12] Kitchen and Lawrence, *Treaty, Law, and Covenant in the Ancient Near East*, p. 7.

[13] Ibid., p. 15.

[14] Treaty between Niqmepa of Alakh and Ir-Adad/Tesup of Tunip (c. fifteenth century BCE), Kitchen and Lawrence, *Treaty, Law, and Covenant in the Ancient Near East*, p. 313.

very first of the written texts to be recovered from this period, including bills of sale and rudimentary contracts. A millennium after the invention of writing, sovereign rulers were putting their agreements in writing.

If the easy case of a just war is war waged for national defense, then one might think that humanitarian intervention in some cases is at least as easy. For in some cases of humanitarian intervention, war is waged to protect another state when that other state cannot protect itself from external aggression by one of its neighbors. But the most common case of humanitarian intervention is not of this sort, but rather the case where a state is oppressing its own people and intervention occurs to protect these people not from invasion but from their own despotic rulers, or from armed groups that attack other, less well-defended groups within the same state.

Ancient legal texts often express strong humanitarian sentiments concerning recourse to war. As I pointed out at the beginning of this chapter, two of the best known rulers of the ancient Near East, Hammurabi and Cyrus, cite protection of the oppressed as the reason for waging war. In addition, in some of the earliest law "codes" of Mesopotamia we see the beginnings of the ideas of human rights and dignity that are so crucial for humanitarianism today. Here is one example from the Epilogue of Laws of Lipit-Ishtar (c. 1930 BCE), which is very interesting:

> In accordance with the true word of the god Utu, I made the lands of Sumer and Akkad hold fair judicial procedure. I made truth shine forth and I brought well-being to the lands of Sumer and Akkad [...] all humankind. When I established justice in the lands of Sumer and Akkad, I erected this stela.[15]

Lipit-Ishtar also says:

> At the time I liberated the sons and daughters of the city of Nippur, the sons and daughters of the city of Ur, the sons and daughters of the city of Isin, the sons and daughters of the lands of Sumer and Akkad, who were subjugated [by the yoke (?)], and I restored order.[16]

The reference here is clearly to waging wars to "liberate" oppressed people in these various city-states, and the justification is couched in terms of concern for humanity, and all of this from nearly 4,000 years ago.

A defense of humanitarian intervention seemingly could be mounted by considering some of what we have already discussed under the headings of opportunity and necessity. The wrongful waging of war for opportunity is for increasing territory or natural resources or access to the sea. These causes for war do not count as just because, among other things, the cost of war, especially its inevitable loss of

[15] *Laws of Lipit-Ishtar* in *Law Collections From Mesopotamia and Asia Minor*, second edition, translated by Martha T. Roth, Atlanta, GA: Scholars' Press, 1997, pp. 33–34.

[16] Ibid., p. 25.

innocent life, is not outweighed by such causes. Here we could consider various ancient roots of the idea of *jus post bellum*, the justice considerations at war's end. In particular, the idea that war is only just if it is likely to lead to a just and lasting peace.[17] But there are less problematic cases of waging war for opportunity, such as waging war to secure peace in a region that had been ravaged by a tyrannical ruler.

The idea of waging war to stop a war or to stop oppression, and thereby restore the peace, also does not seem obviously problematic. Indeed, if war can be justly waged at all, it seems that the Roman cleric, Augustine, was right to say it would be most clearly so for the cause of protecting others who are innocent. In Augustine's view, war was generally suspect on grounds of the killing of the innocent. But in some situations, war was necessary in order to save innocent lives. Some wars can be considered just insofar as the war is waged for what today we would call humanitarian reasons.[18]

In addition to the idea of opportunity to save or protect the innocent, we can add the idea that some wars can be justly waged out of necessity. In some cases of humanitarian intervention, necessity could be satisfied. The cases will be rare, though, since it is often very difficult to calculate what would be successful as well as when it is clear that there are no other non-lethal means available to achieve the humanitarian goal. In addition there will be worries about the spending of lives and treasure to rescue people in a distant part of the world whose condition is not such as would allow the state to say that it was necessary to intervene.

The rationale for humanitarian intervention also runs up against the rationale for national defense. If a state's borders provide a normative reason to allow self-determination wide latitude, then such considerations will also at least partially weigh against crossing a state's borders to wage a humanitarian war. Yet the normal reasons to warrant such invasions – to stop an impending threat against one's own state, for instance – are not typically available in such cases.

It might seem that humanitarian intervention wars are still wars and hence do not appear to be very humane, hence belying the name for this kind of war. There is something odd about mounting the enormous lethal potential of armies in order to engage in humanitarian action. Defenders of humanitarian intervention will again have to contend with the death of the rescuing soldiers that inevitably results from humanitarian intervention. Humanitarian wars have outcomes that are difficult to predict since these wars are often waged when there are no clear military targets.

17 See *Morality, Jus Post Bellum, and International Law*, co-edited by Larry May and Andrew Forcehimes, Cambridge University Press, 2012; and *Jus Post Bellum and Transitional Justice*, co-edited by Larry May and Elizabeth Edenberg, Cambridge University Press, 2013. Also see Larry May, *After War Ends*, Cambridge: Cambridge University Press, 2012.

18 See Augustine, *City of God*, Book 19, Section 6, reprinted in Larry May, Steve Viner, and Eric Rovie, *The Morality of War*, New Jersey: Upper Saddle River: Prentice-Hall Publishers, 2007, p. 16.

But the rescuing of those who are oppressed was seen as so important in ancient legal thought that only the positive aspects of such intervention was seen to be of overriding importance.

12.5 RECONSIDERING NATIONAL DEFENSE AND HUMANITARIAN INTERVENTION

It is often said that in all cases defense of nation is a just cause to go to war. Today it is common for such a defense to be mounted in terms of self-determination of a people.[19] A conquering army deprives the people of the attacked state of their choice to remain unconquered. But of course the right of self-determination is not an absolute value – and things can be especially difficult when there is dispute within a state about what the people want. Various communitarians have tried to argue that what matters is what the majority of people in a state want but this has not been an easy argument to mount, as the case of a majority oppressing a minority within a state makes abundantly clear.

The ancient defense of nation in some Mesopotamian texts is often drawn in terms of protection against those from outside who would oppress the citizenry. The assumption is that people do not want to be oppressed; and it is an unalloyed good for oppression to be confronted.[20] A consideration of the value of confronting oppression gives to the idea of self-determination some extra weight as self-defensive war is justified.

Also, in some cases diplomatically suing for peace might be a reasonable alternative to mounting armed violence when an enemy army is at the gates. Indeed, the enemy may be provoked into invading, as in the case of the Romans who had kidnapped the Sabine women causing the Sabines to invade Rome.[21] And this raises the question of whether the state first to cross another state's borders should always be seen as the aggressor.[22] For some ancient writers and texts, the idea seems to be that aggressors are those who would oppress, not merely those who would cross boundaries.

Another question often discussed was whether it was better to raise armies than to raise defensive structures. In ancient Egypt, huge defensive structures were built

19 See Michael Walzer, *Just and Unjust Wars*, NY: Basic Books, 1977.

20 Oppression is the term used in the various translations of ancient texts. But it is not clear whether or not this corresponds exactly to what is meant by this term today especially in the debates about racial discrimination.

21 See Livy's account of this historical example in his, *History of Rome*, Book 1, Section IX, lines 1–12, translated by B. O. Foster, Cambridge: Harvard University Press, Loeb Classical Library, 1926, pp. 33–37.

22 See Larry May, *Aggression and Crimes Against Peace*, NY: Cambridge University Press, 2008.

all along the Nile, and pharaohs bragged that such actions averted war.[23] Even in cases where war was justified in self-defense, certain texts challenged whether even this cause of going to war was just if non-lethal actions were not exhausted. Today, some theorists have raised similar challenges, wondering whether police actions and deterrent strategies might not be able to avert war in many cases.[24]

Defensive war remains the least controversial just war today, despite the apparent problems with this idea. One of the problems that we saw in some of the historical sources concerns the fact that States claim to be engaging in defensive war when they have mixed motives including gain. And here is where the historical discussion of necessity is so important. The attack of the aggressive state must be imminent before the defensive war that is waged is considered just. This raises various questions about preemptive, anticipatory, and preventive self-defense.[25] And, on the account I have outlined in this chapter, the war is most likely to be just if the invading state seeks to oppress the population of the target state.

Some legal sources from ancient Mesopotamia, as well as from other parts of the ancient world, provide us with a humanitarian conceptual framework for understanding law and politics. By this I mean that rulers and judges saw law as a way for the most powerful members of the society to be held accountable for exploiting the least powerful. The test of being considered a good ruler was that he or she was a good shepherd for the flock – where the shepherd always cared most about those who could not easily fend for themselves.

The humanitarian model contrasts to the way that ancient rulers and legal systems are often understood. This comes out most clearly in the imputation of a punitive model of *lex talionis* ("an eye for an eye") that was thought, sometimes correctly, to epitomize ancient Mesopotamian and other ancient societies' criminal law. As we saw in Chapter 9, one of the most difficult parts of the larger argument of establishing the humanitarianism of many ancient rulers is to show that *lex talionis* can have a humanitarian face. Part of the argument is to show that the kind of *lex talionis* doctrine espoused in ancient Mesopotamia is based in the idea of proportionality – where the punishment must fit the crime, and most importantly, must be no harsher than that. For ancient legal thought of Mesopotamia and the Near East, *lex talionis* stands against the idea that those seeking revenge could justify utter disregard of the humanity of the wrongdoer.

23 See Marc Van De Mieroop, *A History of Ancient Egypt*, Oxford: Wiley/Blackwell, 2011.

24 See Gabriella Blum, "The Dispensable Lives of Soldiers," *Journal of Legal Analysis*, Vol. 2, 2010; and Larry May, *War Crimes and Just War*, NY: Cambridge University Press, 2007.

25 See Yoram Dinstein, *War, Aggression, and Self-Defense*, third edition,Cambridge: Cambridge University Press, 2001.

As we have seen in this chapter, the two clearest cases of just wars in some ancient legal texts were both waged to end or prevent oppression: wars of national defense – wars waged to prevent a state from violating self-determination or causing oppression of a population; and wars of humanitarian intervention – wars waged to stop a foreign ruler from oppressing his own people. For these rulers, the other classic bases for a just war: opportunity, necessity, and punishment were all related to the humanitarian goal of stopping oppression.

The key is to find a similar basis of support, as I have argued in humanitarianism, for humanitarian intervention wars and wars of national defense. The wars of national defense are sometimes under attack as well. And the ancient conceptual scheme helps as well to provide support for these wars as just wars as well, although not all of them. Aggression is to be condemned as unjust when it has the effect of oppressing or risking the oppression of a population – the mere transgression of borders is not sufficient.[26] Here what counts as an unjust war tracks acts that are clearly unjust in terms of violations of equity.

In ancient times, the source of equity was often thought to be the laws of the gods, or as it later came to be understood by the time of the Greeks and Romans, the source was in natural law. In the earliest records of legal thought the idea of humanity is of central importance. In the Epilogue to the Laws of Lipit-Ishtar, which date from 1930 BCE, he tells us:

> In accordance with the true word of the god Utu, I made the lands of Sumer and Akkad hold fair judicial procedure. In accordance with the utterance of the god Enlil, I, Lipi-Ishtar, son of Enlil, eradicated enmity and violence … I made right and truth shine forth, and I brought well-being to the lands of Sumer and Akkad … [and to] all humankind.[27]

And as quoted earlier, in 1750 BCE Hammurabi says that "I have not been careless or negligent toward humankind."[28]

In this chapter I have tried to give a sense of what some of the oldest legal texts tell us about what makes a war just. And the idea that has remained is that the least problematic of just causes to go to war is defense of one's nation from invasion that was not provoked and where the invasion risked oppression of the citizenry. And the second least problematic cause is war waged also for humanitarian reasons, especially to stop oppression of tyrants of their people. For these ancient legal texts, all other causes for going to war were seen to be highly problematic.

[26] See May, *Aggression and Crimes Against Peace*.

[27] *Laws of Lipit-Ishtar*, pp. 33–35.

[28] *Laws of Lipit-Ishtar*, p. 133.

CONCLUDING THOUGHTS FOR PART A

The earliest codes of law are testaments to the far-sighted and judicious character of the early Mesopotamian and Egyptian rulers. Hammurabi in particular has been remembered for his humaneness that comes out so strongly in the code but also in his many letters that have been recently discovered. Having written laws was a sign that one's society was above, or ahead, of other more primitive societies. If anyone wanted to do so, and if one could read written cuneiform script, one could know what the law is more easily than if laws were not written, and this testified to the beginning of a "rule of law," not merely a rule by one person over all the rest. And with the rule of law comes a priority given to the individual litigant, whose complaint needs to be taken seriously even if to do so would create problems for the rest of the society.

There is thus some reason to think that not only did Mesopotamians invent writing and law, they also were the first people to understand the rule of law as opposed to the rule of man (or woman). Decrees and edicts are issued by someone concerning a current issue or problem. Statutes or codes, while also issued by someone or an assembly, "rule" independently of their originating author – indeed long after the issuer is dead. And this is why the Hammurabi code, as well as the earlier codes, point toward a new way of understanding rules that govern people in a given society – a rule by law abstracted from the people who issued it. When rules are written down in a general form they are disconnected to a certain extent from the author of the rules. This is true whether the rules are synopses of past rulings or rules projected into the future. Here the identity of the lawgiver is less important than that the society continues to adhere to the rules, or the spirit of the laws, of the written text long after the death of that lawgiver.

The Mesopotamian conceptual scheme that we can learn from is a philosophical orientation to law and rulership that is humanitarian in that those who are most vulnerable are of greatest concern. And the cornerstone of ancient humanitarianism is the idea of equity, or fundamental fairness, which is thought to stand in contrast to a narrower sense of justice that treats all equally according to the law, not taking account of specific conditions that make one person much more likely to be harmed by a given practice than another person. It is perhaps surprising but not lacking in evidence how thoroughly equity informed law and its interpretation in ancient Mesopotamia long before the idea is often thought to have arisen in ancient Roman legal philosophy.

In the ancient legal thought of Mesopotamia and the Near East, equity called for rulers to protect those who were the most vulnerable members of their societies. The two domains in which rulers most boasted of their accomplishments were the fields of law and war. Ending corruption of ministers and making sure that people did not go hungry were often mentioned as key legal accomplishments. Winning battles where oppression was ended was also often mentioned as key military accomplishments.

Another related point can be cited in understanding how the individual relates to the group in the thinking of ancient Mesopotamian people. It is controversial, although less so now than when first articulated in the 1950s, that the earliest political forms in Mesopotamia were democratic assemblies not individual rulers such as kings.[29] In some of the cuneiform tablets that have been recovered from Mesopotamia, it appears that assemblies of citizens ruled. Only later do the assemblies seem to appoint a military general to help repel aggressors. And later still, the general is asked to take over the administration of the city-state as well.

Of even greater interest is that there appears to be some evidence for thinking that there was a "super" assembly formed with representatives from several of the city-states of Mesopotamia, and that such an assembly decided on rules for inter-city-state relations.[30] This is still highly controversial, but suggestive enough to be worth reporting once again. Of course the assemblies are in one sense groups, but then as now these groups are formed of individual citizens who are the basis of the legitimacy for the individual rulers, the kings, who have been so much more written about concerning ancient times. These views set the backdrop for the ancient Greek and Chinese thinkers who more clearly focused on the individual and his or her place in the society.

[29] See Thorkild Jacobsen, "Primitive Democracy in Ancient Mesopotamia," *Journal of Near Eastern Studies*, Vol. 2, 1943, pp. 159–172.

[30] See Thorkild Jacobsen, "Early Political Development in Mesopotamia," *Zeitschrift fur Assyriologie*, Vol. 18, 1957, pp. 91–140.

PART B

Ancient Greece and China

INTRODUCTION FOR PART B

Ancient Greek and Chinese legal thought is the focus of this part, the second in this volume on ancient legal thought. Unlike the first part, this second part and subsequent parts will focus as much on the writings of philosophers about the law as on legal texts themselves. In this respect, the works of Plato and Aristotle along with Confucius, Mencius, and Mozi loom large for Part B, especially when they are critical of the laws of their time. But we will also examine the works of Antiphon, Demosthenes, and Isocrates, who wrote speeches for the parties at trial. In addition, we have trial records here that will be closely examined, as well as some law codes, from both Greece and China, which will be important.

In ancient Greek and Chinese times, especially in the fifth and fourth centuries BCE – which is the main focus of this part of my work – law is also used as a vehicle of supporting a system of social class. Here there are also parallels with ancient Mesopotamia. But for the Greeks, the idea of citizenship emerges as perhaps the most salient of all status-based legal classifications. Indeed, while it is often thought that it was the Romans who developed a legal system around the idea of citizenship, which is true, the importance of citizenship for the Greeks is often unrecognized. While Chinese legal thought was class-based, and stressed the individual as subject rather than citizen, it was not significantly less humane than ancient Greece. This will be one of the overarching theses of this part of my work.

In keeping with the earlier part on Mesopotamia and Egypt, I will not provide a developmental or evolutionary picture of the law of ancient Greece and China. Rather what seems most striking is how similar the law is over time. Yet, there are intriguing new institutions that arise which provide some of the special character of law in a given society or historical period. That the Greeks understood legal ideas as entwined with customary ideas of pollution and saw a link between impiety and hubris will be of major concern in figuring out the background for ancient Greek legal thought. In China, the centrality of honor and custom, ideas which were found in earlier times, take on a distinctive character when matched with skepticism about rules. The role of the citizen or subject as displaying certain important virtues is one of the key reasons to pair Greek and Chinese legal thought.

Socrates and Confucius were nearly contemporaries (Confucius died only nine years before Socrates was born). Like the Greeks, the ancient Chinese did not put much emphasis on codes of written law but rather on the customs handed down and debated by those considered most wise. Two ancient Chinese ideas, for example, that I will explore are, first, the Confucian idea that rituals rather than explicit rules are to be preferred in guiding people to be virtuous, and, second, Mozi's idea that even most defensive wars are unnecessary if a proper regard is made to non-lethal defensive actions well in advance of any possible acts of aggression. Mozi tried to convince several kings to follow his guidance.

With ancient Greek and Chinese legal thought we see the beginnings of written commentary on the law and also the very beginnings of a profession of lawyers. But for our purposes it is the ideas of equity and crime that are most significant and most significantly developed – or so I will argue in this part of my work in ancient legal thought.

We will also see the rise of one of the most radical democracies of all time in Athens, and yet we will also see that there were many more slaves in Athens than anywhere in decidedly non-democratic China. In some respects the people under democracy, especially those who were not citizens, were worse off in ancient Greece than in places like ancient China that did not believe either in a participatory system of government or of the administration of the laws.

SECTION V

Law, Justice, and Equity

13

Custom and Law in Ancient Greece and China

In this chapter we will explore the ancient ideas about justice and law that we find in Greek and Chinese writings. Of central concern will be to distinguish custom from legal rules. Some have argued that in both of these ancient societies, religion is the ground of legal thought. This is in one sense undeniable but in another sense overly simplistic. Both Greek and Chinese writers who spoke of law did so in a way that connected law to a natural order, but not necessarily one that made of law something divine. Indeed, there is a strong contrast between the realm of human law and punishments and the realm of religion, as we will see. Even more importantly, I will argue that human law comes in various types where customs and statutes are treated quite differently from one another, especially in respect to ideas of justice. There is a debate within both societies concerning whether written statutes are an advance on grounds of justice or not. Indeed, Confucius said that "the state of no litigation was the ultimate end."[1]

The early Pre-Socratic Greek philosopher, Anaximander, speaks of the seasons as acting against justice (*dike*) when one season turns into another: "And the source of coming-to-be for existing things is that into which destruction too happens, 'according to necessity; for they pay penalty and retribution to each other for their injustice according to the assessment of Time.'"[2] For ancient Chinese thinkers, the seasons were also important for understanding when certain punishments could occur. Punishment, especially capital punishment could only be carried out in the spring or summer.[3]

1 Quoted in T'ung-Tsu Ch'U, *Law and Society in Traditional China*, Paris: Mouton & Co., 1965, p. 249.

2 G. S. Kirk and J. E., Raven, *The Presocratic Philosophers*, Cambridge: Cambridge University Press, 1957, p. 117.

3 See Mark Edward Lewis, *The Early Chinese Empires: Qin and Han*, Cambridge, MA: Harvard University Press, 2007, p. 231.

In this chapter we will first examine Sophocles' *Antigone*, where several senses of law and justice are at play in a way that makes it clear how Greeks saw these categories as overlapping but also as sometimes conflicting. In Section 13.2 we examine how law was understood in ancient Greece by lawmakers and by philosophers. In Section 13.3 we will examine writings of Confucius, including some Confucians, as well as writings of the ancient Chinese legalists, especially Han Feizi. In Section 13.4 we will attempt to find commonalities between certain Chinese writings and Greek writings, where the connection between Confucian and Spartan legal thought, but also including Plato, will be of central concern. And in Section 13.5 we will set out some conclusions concerning these early conceptions of law and legal theory.

13.1 ANTIGONE AND LAW

Two Greek terms that meant "law" are important for us. Hesiod spoke of *nomos* as "an order of living" for humans. It seems that for Homer, the term *thesmos* meant law of a different broader sort, as an order of the entire universe.[4] And two Greek terms that meant "justice" are also important for us. *Themis* is a god, but as a concept also "is specialized to man, the social conscience."[5] *Dike*, the daughter of *Themis*, "is the way of the world of nature, of the universe of all live things."[6] As the social conscience of humans, there is a sense that *Themis* is a term for "right" and goes beyond justice as we would understand it today.

In Sophocles play, *Antigone*, we find three types of law sometimes complementing and sometimes competing against each other in this wonderful illustration of Greek legal thought.

> *Creon* – There is no way of getting to know a man's spirit (*psyche*) and thought and judgment, until he has been seen to be versed in government and in the laws (*nomoisin*) ... These are the laws (*nomoisi*) by which I make our city great ... it is proclaimed to this city that none shall bury or lament [Polinices].[7]

Creon has proclaimed an edict forbidding anyone to bury Polinices, who is accused of treason. Two kinds of law on display here are the customs and statutes of Athens on the one hand and the specific decrees of the ruler on the other hand. These two kinds of law are here seen as complementary. But there certainly can be a major

4 See Martin Ostwald, *Nomos and the Beginnings of the Athenian Democracy*, Oxford: Oxford University Press, 1969, pp. 20–21.

5 Jane Ellen Harrison, *Themis: A Study of the Social Origins of Greek Religion*, Cambridge: Cambridge University Press, 1927, 516.

6 Ibid., p. 517.

7 Sophocles, *Antigone* 175–2015, in *Sophocles II*, translated by Hugh Lloyd-Jones, Cambridge MA: Harvard University Press' Loeb Classical Library, 1994, pp. 21–23.

difference since decrees and edicts are very specific, indeed in this case naming a particular person within the law itself, whereas statute laws and customs of a society are normally more general in form.

In *Antigone*, the major plot concerns a conflict between the laws established by rulers and the laws of the gods. Here Antigone's sister, Ismene, tries to convince Antigone not to bury their brother since this would violate the decree of Creon.

> *Ismene* – our two brothers, on one day killing each other, did themselves both to death at one another's hands. And now consider how much worse will be the fate of us two, who are left alone, if in despite of the law (*nomou*) we flout the decision of the ruler and his powers.
>
> *Antigone* – Do you be the kind of person you have decided to be, but I shall bury him! It is honorable for me to do this and die … there will be a longer span of time for me to please those below than there will be to please those here. As for you, if it is your pleasure, dishonor what the gods honor![8]

For Antigone, acting honorably is in this case inconsistent with following the decree of the ruler, Creon. Antigone believes that unless a human law is consistent with the eternal or natural laws, the human law is not binding and disregarding it is not to do wrong.

Antigone is clear that human laws are of much less importance than the laws of the gods, the eternal laws that she chooses to obey rather than Creon's decree.

> *Creon* – And yet you dared to transgress these laws (*nomous*)?
>
> *Antigone* – Yes, for it was not Zeus who made this proclamation, nor was it Justice (*Dike*) who lives with the gods below that established such laws (*nomous*) among men, nor do I think your proclamations strong enough to have power to overrule, mortal as they are, the unwritten and unfailing ordinances of the gods. For these have life, not simply today and yesterday, but forever, and no one knows how long ago they were revealed.[9]

And Antigone also aligns herself with justice writ large, claiming that she does not do wrong if she follows these eternal laws rather than the laws of the ruler.

Creon argues though that he has been given the right to make laws for all of the citizens of the state, and that he cannot be rightly disobeyed.

> *Creon* – One must obey the man whom the city sets up in power in small things and in justice and in its opposite … there is no worse evil than insubordination! This it is that ruins cities, this it is that destroys houses, this it is that shatters and puts to

8 Sophocles, *Antigone*, 57–77, pp. 9–11 of Loeb edition.

9 Sophocles, *Antigone*, 449–455, pp. 43–45 of Loeb edition.

> flight the warriors on its own side! But what saves the lives of most of those that go straight is obedience![10]

Yet, Antigone continues to assert that she is following the law, understood here as ancient customs, and that she cannot be said by Creon to do wrong.

> *Antigone* – with my mother and father in Hades below, I could never have another brother. Such was the law (*nomo*) for whose sake I did you special honor, but to Creon I seemed to do wrong … What justice (*diken*) of the gods have I transgressed?[11]

For Antigone, justice requires disobeying the human law in this case, even though justice is normally aligned with obeying the law. And the point is that there are higher forms of law and justice which are not always associated with conforming to the law of the land.

In ancient Greece, law came to be associated with human-made rules and as we will see law also became associated with democratic governance. But there remained a worry that mere human law could be at odds with the law of gods or with the laws of nature. Indeed, there was considerable attention given to the question of whether law (*nomos*) or nature (*physis*) should have priority. Antigone came to represent the limitation of law, especially when law seemed to conflict with what was required of conscience. We see some similar issues played out in ancient China as well, but first we must say more about the distinctive democratic orientation to law of the fifth century BCE ancient Greeks.

13.2 LAW AND DEMOCRACY IN ANCIENT GREEK LEGAL THOUGHT

In very early Greek times, there were many customs, some of which we would today classify as laws. From the writings of Homer onward there was special attention to such acts as homicide that were contrary to custom and subject to various forms of censure and punishment. Custom is unwritten and in some Greek city-states is then subject to authorization by assemblies. In Athens we have the fullest record of such laws. In Sparta there were specific decisions not to write down customs. Indeed Grote tells us that the Spartan ruler, Lycurgus, "interdicts … all written laws … When disputes are to be settled or judicial interference is required, the magistrate is to decide from his own sense of equity."[12]

Sparta seems to be the exception rather than the rule in ancient Greece, where written laws proliferated in the 5th and 4th centuries BCE. There is perhaps more at

10 Sophocles, *Antigone*, 660–670, p. 64 of Loeb edition.

11 Sophocles, *Antigone*, 908–920, pp. 87–89 of Loeb edition.

12 George Grote, *History of Greece*, London: John Murray, 1888, Vol. II, pp. 306–307.

play between custom and written law than is easy to see. Whether a rule is written or not does not mark the difference between custom and law. Custom is generally seen as something that has been in existence for a long period of time whereas laws can reflect matters at the moment only to be changed relatively soon thereafter. Having a law in writing makes it easier for the populace to understand it, assuming the populace is generally literate.

We should not ignore how written law came to be associated with democracy in ancient Greece. Here is an analysis by J. W. Jones whose work on ancient Greek legal thought is among the very best:

> It seems probable that up to and during the period of Solon the word *nomos*, which is not to be found in the Homeric Epic, had not acquired that political connotation which was to be so characteristic of it in Athenian democracy. Until then, it preserved much of its old sense of any group's way of life.[13]

Solon is known both for establishing the first Greek democracy and for his codification of the laws of Athens. For Solon, there is a close association between written law and democratic governance, where the task of law-making is one that is held closely by the people through its assembly.[14]

The earliest written laws in ancient Greece date from the middle of the seventh century BCE, from 650 BCE on the island of Crete in the town of Dreros. Here is a fragment from perhaps the oldest extant Greek law:

> Thus has the polis decided: when someone has been *kosmos* the same person is not to be *kosmos* (again) for ten years. But if he should serve as kosmos, whenever he should give judgment, he is to owe double, and he is to be without rights as long as he lives, and whatever he should do as *kosmos* is to be void.[15]

The *kosmos* is the leader of the city-state of Dreros, although it is unclear whether the *kosmos* was a civil or military leader, or both.[16] The law here sets the term-limit for the *kosmos* and also assigns a penalty if the law is not followed. It seems that the law makes reference to an assembly having decided on this term-limit, and if so then we have perhaps the first reference in ancient Greek laws to an assembly that makes law. Gagarin and Perlman comment:

13 J. W. Jones, *The Law and Legal Theory of the Greeks*, Oxford: Oxford University Press, 1956, p. 34.

14 But see Martin Ostwald, *Nomos and the Beginnings of the Athenian Democracy*, who argues that it is Cleisthenes who should be credited with establishing the connection between law and popular self-governance through the assemblies.

15 *The Laws of Ancient Crete c. 650–400 BCE*, edited and translated by Michael Gagarin and Paula Perlman, Oxford: Oxford University Press, 2016, p. 202.

16 See ibid., pp. 1–2.

> it is extraordinary that what may be the earliest surviving Greek law forcefully asserts the power of civic authority, and that the thrust of the law is to control one of the community's most important officials by limiting office-holding to at most one term every ten years.[17]

The first known written law in ancient Greece thus concerns a procedural not a substantive matter, but the procedural matter is of such importance that one could say that this was a constitutional law.

Most of our discussion of Greek law will be based in the law of ancient Athens, and here there is a fragment of a law that is almost as old as the one from Crete, namely Draco's code on homicide. We will explore this law in greater detail in later chapters, but here I wish to call our attention to the fact that Draco's law from 621 BCE is about substantive matters, and seems to be the first written Greek law of this sort. Here is a fragment:

> Even if someone kills someone without premeditation, he shall be exiled. The Basileis are to adjudge responsible for homicide ... the one who instigated the killing. The Ephetai are to give the verdict. Pardon is to be granted, [but] if there is a father or brother or sons, by all or one who opposes it shall prevail ... The prosecution is to be shared by cousins, sons of cousins, sons-in-law, fathers- in-law, and members of the phratry.[18]

In this law we have a substantive provision, concerning homicide and its punishment. And we also have procedural matters addressed, concerning how cases of homicide are to be prosecuted and ultimately decided.

It is not clear why the two oldest laws from Greece would be these laws – of course, it is possible that there were other older laws that have not so far been unearthed. Indeed, it is well attested that Draco's homicide law was part of a code of law that concerned many other matters than homicide – Solon, for instance, is believed to have kept Draco's homicide law but replaced the rest with his own code. But despite these considerations, it seems that matters of governance of the city-state, establishing term-limits for the rulers, and adjudicating the most serious of acts, homicides, were some of the very earliest laws that were written down in ancient Greece.

One can conjecture that laws in Crete and Athens were written out in the seventh century BCE to mark the seriousness of the matters at issue and a desire for conformity over time where the people did not have to rely on collective memory of the customs. It has been much debated but it does seem that there was a level of literacy achieved in both Athens and Crete in the seventh century BCE that had not previously been true and which then set the stage for the written recording of rules that

17 Ibid., p. 204.

18 Ronald Stroud, *Drakon's Law on Homicide*, Berkeley, CA: University of California Press, 1968, p. 6.

were the most important. Once again, the exception to this idea concerns Sparta, where there seems to have been a conscious decision not to write out the rules of the society for the very reason for which Crete and Athens did write out the laws, namely a worry that written laws would be fixed and inflexible.

Nonetheless, unlike other ancient societies where written law was not necessarily for the populace at large (although Hammurabi does seem to give this as the reason for his code when he says: "Let any wronged man who has a lawsuit come before the statue of me, the king of justice, and let him have my inscribed stela read aloud to him"[19]), we have a kind of incipient democratic spirit at play that seeks to involve the populace, not merely the elites, in law-making. We will next explore very different considerations that were at play in ancient China at approximately the same time as the events in Greece we have been considering, and that at least at first sight appear to be closer to the case of Sparta than to that of Athens.

13.3 ANCIENT CHINESE LEGAL THOUGHT ABOUT LAW

In ancient China, the term for custom "*li*" is also later somewhat opposed to law (*fa*). And justice is seen to depend on a correct balance between customary and declared law. Most law was associated with "punishment, as the defining aspect of law."[20] This was especially true of the school of Chinese jurisprudence called "legalism." Such theorists as Han Feizi said: "If law does not command respect, then all the ruler's actions will be endangered. If penalties are not enforced then evil will never be surmounted."[21] And he also said: "The enlightened ruler controls his ministers by means of two handles. The two handles are punishment and favor. What do I mean by punishment and favor? To inflict mutilation and death on men is called punishment; to bestow honor and reward is called favor."[22] One thing that some Chinese legal theorists insist on is that law must be a matter of social control through punishments, often very severe, as well occasionally of rewards also. And law is not well distinguished from a system of such punishments.

Confucius and his followers took a very different view, placing them much closer to Spartan than to Athenian Greek legal theorists. Confucius argued that "*li* prevents what is going to happen, while law [attempts to] prevent what has already happened."[23] And his disciples reacted against the severity of the legalists, especially

[19] Hammurabi, "Epilogue" to his Law Collection, 1750 c. BCE, translated by Martha T. Roth, in her *Law Collections from Mesopotamia and Asia Minor*, second edition, Atlanta: Scholars' Press, 1997, p. 134.

[20] Lewis, *The Early Chinese Empires*, p. 242.

[21] *Han Feizi: Basic Writings*, translated by Burton Watson, NY: Columbia University Press, 2003, p. 27.

[22] Ibid., p. 29.

[23] Confucius, quoted and translated by T'ung-Tsu Ch'U, *Law and Society in Traditional China*, Paris: Mouton & Co., 1965, p. 249.

the excessive punishments inflicted and extensive use of the death penalty. One Confucian thinker said: "To put the people to death without instructing them: – this is called cruelty."[24]

One of the salient differences between the Confucian and Legalist approaches to law concerns distinctions in how law operated based on class. As T'ung-Tsu Ch'U has said, "The main characteristic of Chinese law, after it became Confucianized [after the Confucian reaction against Legalism] was its emphasis on the status factor which found expression both in the kinship system and the system of stratification."[25] This status-based scheme of punishments is at odds with the legalists, especially Han Feizi, who had said:

> The law no more makes exceptions for men of high station than the plumb line bends to accommodate a crooked place in the wood. What the law has decreed, the wise man cannot dispute nor the brave man venture to contest. When faults are to be punished, the highest minister cannot escape; when good is to be rewarded, the lowest peasant must not be passed over.[26]

This aspect of the Legalist's jurisprudence makes it closer to the democratic ideas about law in ancient Athens than is true for Confucianism, which as I said resembles the jurisprudence of Sparta, but also that of Plato, as we will see in the next section.

There is some evidence that there was a systematic legal code produced during the reign of King Mu of Zhou, who reigned from 956–918 BCE, but this and other matters concerning his reign are in dispute.[27] Other Chinese legal codes are known from 536 BCE and 513 BCE, although all that has survived are a few references in other writings.[28] It is probably in reaction to these codes that Confucius argued that law was not as good as customary rituals.[29] There is no sense that these codes derived their authority from the gods, and also no sense that these laws could be overridden by higher or natural law.[30] But this feature of ancient Chinese law is also worrisome to Confucians who saw when law (*fa*) was opposed to traditional custom (*li*) it was

[24] Ibid., p. 252.

[25] Ibid, p. 280.

[26] *Han Feizi*, translated by Burton Watson, p. 28.

[27] See Edward L. Shaughnessy, "Western Zhou History," in *The Cambridge History of Ancient China: From the Origins of Civilization to 221 BC*, edited by Michael Lowe and Edward L Shaughnessy, Cambridge: Cambridge University Press, 1999, p. 323.

[28] See Cho-yun Hsu, "The Spring and Autumn Period," in *The Cambridge History of Ancient China*, ibid., pp. 584–585.

[29] See Michael Lowe, "The Heritage Left to the Empires," in *The Cambridge History of Ancient China*, ibid., p. 1007.

[30] Ibid., p. 1004, contrasting early Chinese law with such Greek works as Sophocles' *Antigone*.

too rigid to provide justice. We take up this issue in much greater detail in the next chapter.

In the third century BCE, a code of law was introduced in the Ch'in dynasty that addressed both procedural and substantive matters. Here is one procedural statute:

> If an Overseer is absent, a Master who is "without evil," or a Prefectural Clerk is ordered to fill the office on probation. Do not order office assistants or clerks (to fill the office) on probation.[31]

We find here a not very subtle reminder that officials are to be above reproach and cannot hide behind their subordinates. This statute is consistent with many ancient codes that require officials to be above reproach.

There are also instructions about how to deal with various types of case in the section of this Ch'in code that deals with "Models for Sealing and Investigating." Here is part of one statute that concerns "death by murderous intent":

> Thief-catcher A of post X in his announcement says: "At the place X within (the area of) my post there is the corpse of a murdered (person), with bound-up hair, a man, (I) do not know who. I have come to announce this." Forthwith, an order was given to the Prefectural Clerk X: "Together with the Prison Bond-servant X, I went to A to investigate. The corpse of the man lay South of X's home, fully on its back. On the left corner of his neck there was a wound made with a blade and on the back two (wounds), all vertical to the neck and the back, each four inches long stuck together and each one inch wide, all depressed, resembling (wounds made by) an axe … The ground being hard we were unable to recognize the murderer's footsteps …"[32]

This model of investigation is quite detailed and points to a concern that the right person be prosecuted and properly brought to justice. Notice also the attempt to discern intent from the various circumstances that were discerned.

There are also more straightforward criminal statutes that I will give one example of here:

> In a fight one uses a needle, a long needle, (or) an awl; if the needle, the long needle (or) the awl wound people, how is each (of these cases) to be sentenced? (When this is done during an unpremeditated) fight, this warrants a fine of two suits of armor; when (with) murderous (intent), it warrants tattooing and *ch'eng- tan* (forced hard labor).[33]

[31] *Remnants of Ch'in Law*, edited and translated by A. F. P. Hulsewe, Leiden: Brill, 1985, pp. 77–78.

[32] Ibid., p. 198.

[33] Ibid., p. 142.

Here there are various mental elements recognized as each deserving different punishment or penalty. One can see that the punishments are fairly stiff for intentional wounding, and indeed, it was the generally harsh punishments that were routinely mentioned as one of the main problems with written statute law, as we will see in the next section.

13.4 THE CRITIQUE OF WRITTEN LAW IN CHINA AND GREECE

In Plutarch's *Lives*, we learn of a Spartan king by the name of Lycurgus who lived in the eighth century BCE. After visiting Crete to learn of their forms of government, he was asked by the Spartan people to return to Sparta.

> Returning, then, to a people thus disposed, he at once understood to change the existing order of things and to revolutionize the civil polity. He was convinced that a partial change of the laws would be of no avail whatsoever, but that he must proceed as a physician would with a patient who was debilitated and full of all sorts of diseases; he must reduce and alter the existing temperament by means of drugs and purges, and introduce a new and different regimen …[34]

One of the more revolutionary acts of Lycurgus was to abolish written law as is recounted by Plutarch:

> None of his laws were put into writing by Lycurgus, indeed, one of the so-called "rhetras" forbids it. For he thought that if the most important and binding principles which conduce to the prosperity and virtue of a city were implanted in the habits and training of its citizens, they would remain unchanged and secure, having a stronger bond than compulsion in the fixed purposes imparted to the young by education, which performs the office of a law-giver for every one of them. And as for minor matters such as business contracts, and cases where the needs vary from time to time, it was better, as he thought, not to hamper them by written constraints or fixed usages, but to suffer them, as occasion demanded, to receive such modifications as educated men should determine. Indeed, he assigned the function of law-making wholly and entirely to education.[35]

Lycurgus is thus renowned for thinking that laws should not be written but that it was better to rely on unwritten customs that were memorized by each successive generation of school-boys, and that discretion to resolve disputes be left in the hands of the educated men of Sparta. As we will see, these ideas are similar to some of those of Confucius as well as of Plato.

34 Plutarch, *Life of Lycurgus*, translated by Bernadotte Perrin, Cambridge, MA: Harvard University Press, Loeb edition, 1914, p. 217.

35 Plutarch, *Life of Lycurgus*, Loeb edition, pp. 241–243.

Confucius was concerned that written law would not be flexible enough to deal with many important matters. Here are several things he said that could be interpreted as in the same vein as those of Lycurgus of Sparta, and at odds with such Athenians as Solon. Here are passages from Confucius' *Analects*:

He who exercises government by means of virtue may be compared to the north polar star, which keeps its place and all the stars turn toward it ...[36]

> If the people be led by laws, and uniformity sought to be given to them by punishments, they will try to avoid the punishments, but have no sense of shame. If they be led by virtue, and uniformity sought to be given them by the rules of propriety, they will have the sense of shame, and moreover will become good ...[37]
>
> If a man be without the virtues proper to humanity, what has he to do with the rites of propriety.[38]

For Confucius, people should obey the rules of society out of fear of shame, not fear of punishment. And in this respect written laws were not as good as unwritten custom at morally influencing people to act from virtue.

Today there is a debate about whether certain constitutional provisions should be written or not. England and Australia, for instance, have steadfastly kept the tradition of an unwritten Bill of Rights, whereas the US has seen its written Bill of Rights as the core of its democracy. Here one of the main issues is that written constitutional provisions lack the flexibility needed for fairness to be achieved in societies of newly emerging technologies, for instance.[39] We return to this topic when discussing equity in the next chapter.

Plato shared the sentiments of both Lycurgus and Confucius in favor of unwritten custom, but late in life when he came to confront the realities of a society that has people who act wrongly because they had not been educated well, he came to endorse written laws, at least for such people.

> For him who obeys, the law should be left silent; but for him who disobeys, it sings in a loud voice after the prelude [explaining the point of the law]:
>
> "Whoever is caught robbing a temple, if a slave or a stranger, is to have the misfortune written on his face and hands and, after having been whipped as much as the judges decide, is to be thrown naked out beyond the borders of the country."
>
> Perhaps by paying this penalty he would become better, by becoming moderate.

36 Confucius, *Analects*, Bk. II, Ch. I, in *The Confucian Analects, The Great Learning, and the Doctrine of the Mean*, translated by James Legge, NY: Cosmo Classics, 2009, p. 145.

37 Confucius, *Analects*, Bk. II, Ch. III, ibid., p. 146.

38 Confucius, *Analects*, Bk. III, Ch. iii, ibid., p. 155.

39 See Tom Campbell, *Rights: A Critical Introduction*, NY: Routledge, 2006.

> So, when someone seems to commit an injustice that merits a monetary penalty … The Guardians of the Laws are to inspect the written records to get precise figures in this regard.[40]

Here it seems that Plato is in agreement that laws should not be designed to speak to the virtuous but only to those who have been badly brought up. This would put Plato at odds with the lawmakers of his time.

But later in *The Laws*, Plato offers this rationale for having written laws at all, which seems to support the idea that both the virtuous and the non-virtuous have a need for laws.

> The laws, it is likely, come into being partly for the sake of the worthy human beings in order to teach them the way in which they might mingle with one another and dwell in friendship, and partly for the sake of those who have shunned education, who employ a certain tough nature and have been in no way softened so as to avoid proceeding to everything bad. It is these who have brought about the words that are going to be uttered. On their account the lawgiver would legislate the laws from necessity, wishing that the need for them would never arise.[41]

Plato recognizes a practical necessity for written law that is something that those who followed Confucius also recognized. But he, like Lycurgus and Confucius before him, would rather have a society in which people were educated in virtue sufficiently to obviate the need for written laws.

13.5 THE DEBATE ABOUT THE PROPER PLACE OF LAW

Today there is a renewed interest in the need for "values education" in all levels of schooling. This is clearly consistent with both Confucius and Plato. But such a stress on the importance of virtuous citizens does not regularly spur people to decry the need for written law and punishment. Where there has been such a challenge is among those who think that people can be better convinced not to do wrong by rehabilitation and communication rather than by punishment. Plato also often spoke of the possibility of rehabilitating all but the worst offenders, and again this put him at odds with the lawmakers of his time.

Plato's "official theory" (as Stalley puts it) is that punishment is justified to cure the wrongdoer of a corrupt soul.The foundation of Plato's penology … is the claim that injustice is bad for us and may therefore be likened to a disease. The primary aim of the penal system must be to cure this disease.[42]

[40] Plato, *The Laws*, 854d, translated by Thomas Pangle, NY: Basic Books, 1980, pp. 246–247.

[41] Plato, *The Laws*, 880e, p. 277.

[42] R. F. Stalley, *An Introduction to Plato's Laws*, Indianapolis, IN: Hackett Publishing Co., 1983, p. 143.

Some people are to be punished to cure their souls, that is, for the future, not as a response to the past. And some other people are to be exiled or executed if it looks like curing them will either take a long time or is impossible. But some of the other things Plato says about punishing homicide and wounding cannot easily fit into this scheme. We can again quote Stalley: "in practice [Plato's] Athenian seeks, not only to make the citizens virtuous, but also to make the state unified and orderly".[43] But the question remains whether these two rationales for punishment will explain the variety of punishments of Plato's *Laws*.

Consider the case of *voluntary homicide*. We can turn to the issue of how a person could voluntarily do evil, given Plato's support for the Socratic doctrine that no one does evil voluntarily. "Voluntariness" is due to the perpetrator being overcome by pleasure or ambition – which is a corruption of the soul. It is voluntary in the eyes of the state because it is not externally forced on the perpetrator. But the corruption is not curable – the person has become evil, and in all such cases Plato says they should be executed. Yet, Plato also says that they should not be buried in the city. Here it looks like we need a different rationale than incurability. Perhaps punishment of the voluntary killer is justified by the state as proxy for the family members who are entitled to kill the perpetrator. But we have then moved away from the model of punishing as curing.

Today, the debates often focus on those who seem to be immune to rehabilitation, sometimes referred to, as was true for Plato, as the incurable offender. The law is meant to take that person out of circulation (through long-term prison sentences) or out of the world altogether (by executing him). But if the incurable offender is literally unable to control his or her behavior, then it is hard to see how the law can rightly punish, at least on the model of seeing the law as educative. Some sociopaths or psychopaths are seen today to be like those people that Plato saw as incurable and uneducable.

Medicalized terminology in penology is as prevalent today as it was for Plato. In only a slightly earlier era from our own, some advocated electric-shock treatment to cure the serious offender. Today, it is more common for geneticists and cognitive scientists to suggest that we could "cure" the brains or the DNA of those who are persistent offenders – some suggesting the hunt for the "bad gene." Our discussion in this chapter as well as a later chapter explicitly on punishment is relevant to these debates on "curing" offenders rather than merely deterring them. We will return to this discussion later.

A final point to be made is that whether one is in favor of rehabilitation or deterrence it does appear that there are some offenders who are simply not influenced by the legal institutions. Law can deal effectively with either those who already are

[43] Ibid., p. 149.

predisposed to be lawful or those who have incentive structures that are amenable to the threat of legal punishment. In many respects, custom is better than written law for those who are already predisposed to be virtuous – that is, in our context, to be law-abiding citizens. In some other respects, written law is better than custom for those who are disinclined to obey the law but who are still influenced by threats. Neither custom nor written law is helpful for those who are "incurable." Now, as in ancient times, the question is whether society should be structured primarily toward the law-abiding who are by far the majority of citizens, or toward the minority who are motivated to be law-breakers, or to the small but still significant number of citizens who are in neither category and yet who are often the most dangerous.

14

Justice and Equity

In the long history of legal thought, from the Mesopotamians to today, one common theme is the tension between law as rule-following, sometimes called "strict justice," and law as providing a fair resolution of disputes, often discussed under the label of "equity." These ideas can be in conflict, where achieving fairness may require not following the rule of law. In the writings about law in ancient Greece and China, we see this theme as well, with an emphasis on equity over strict justice, but for very different reasons in Greece than in China. And the reasons for law as an instrument of fairness that we will explore in this chapter are also different than those in Mesopotamia. I will argue that in both ancient Greek and Chinese legal thought fairness came to be distinguished from justice in relatively unique ways. In this respect there is certainly a change from the earliest ideas of equity in ancient Mesopotamia to the idea of equity especially in ancient Greek legal thought. Equity is given a pride of place in such texts as Aristotle's *Nicomachean Ethics*, where we find an account of equity that makes even clearer than earlier that it is often a major source for how law can be humane.

In one sense justice is not opposed to equity, where justice is broadly conceived to include "natural justice," considerations not only of statute but also of "higher law." If justice is conceived this broadly then the conflict just discussed between narrow justice and equity is actually a conflict within justice itself. I will in this chapter confine our use of the term justice to its narrow meaning so as to be able better to see the contrast with equity. In Section 14.1 we will see why justice narrowly conceived was seen as important. In Section 14.2 we explore some of the problems with narrow or strict justice as understood by Chinese thinkers. In Section 14.3 we will spend time with Aristotle's canonical treatment of equity in his *Nicomachean Ethics* as well as in his *Rhetoric*. In Section 14.4 we will then look to the differences in how equity, and justice, were characterized by Chinese and Greek theorists. In Section 14.5 we seek an understanding of equity that connects to the idea of the limits of law.

14.1 JUSTICE AND THE RULE OF LAW FOR THE GREEKS

In the *Republic*, Plato considers various definitions of justice, ultimately settling on the idea that justice is providing to each his own. And in the *Crito*, it becomes clear that Plato believes that for most people, following the law is the best path to leading a just life. Plato has Socrates argue that even if the law seems to be unjust he should abide by it:

> we must examine next whether it is just for me to try to get out of here when the Athenians have not acquitted me … For us, however, since our argument leads to this, the only valid consideration, as we were just saying now, is whether we should be acting justly in giving money and gratitude to those who will lead me out of here, and ourselves helping with the escape, or whether in truth we shall be wrong in doing all this. If it appears that we shall be acting unjustly, then we have no need at all to take into account whether we shall have to die if we stay here …[1]

For Plato, justice is here understood as doing what the law court's judgment requires even in those cases where it appears that the jury has not properly understood the law. Indeed, it seems that the jury that convicted Socrates was passing a just sentence that Socrates had to obey in order not to act unjustly, even though the jury may have committed an injustice against Socrates in issuing its judgment and death sentence.

Aristotle gives the idea of justice a formulation in his *Rhetoric*, which also links justice to following the law, when he says:

> justice is the virtue through which everybody enjoys his own possessions in accordance with the law; its opposite is injustice, through which men enjoy the possessions of others in defiance of the law … "justly" does not always mean "nobly", when a man is punished, it is more shameful that this should be justly than unjustly done to him.[2]

Here we have justice defined in terms of each getting his own, as was true for Plato. And we have the added dimension of "in accordance with law."

In the *Nicomachean Ethics*, Aristotle talks about several kinds of justice, understood more broadly that merely following the law.

> Since the lawless man was seen to be unjust and the law-abiding man just, evidently all lawful acts are in a sense just acts; for the acts laid down by the legislative art are

[1] Plato, *Crito*, 48C-D, in Plato, *The Trial and Death of Socrates*, translated by G. M. A. Grube, Indianapolis, IN: Hackett Publishing Co., 1986, pp. 48–49. I have slightly corrected the translation.

[2] Aristotle, *Rhetoric*, 1366b8–34, translated by W. Rhys Roberts, in *The Basic Works of Aristotle*, edited by Richard McKeon, NY: Random House, 1941, pp. 1354–1355.

> lawful, and each of these we may say is just. … This form of justice, then, is complete virtue, but not absolutely but in relation to our neighbor.[3]

What we owe each other is to do what the law requires.

But Aristotle recognizes that "there is more than one kind of justice."[4] He then sets out several ways to think of injustice.

> The unjust has been divided into the unlawful and the unfair, and the just into the lawful and the fair. To the unlawful answers the aforementioned sense of justice. But since the unlawful and the unfair are not the same, but are different as a part is from its whole (for all that is unfair is unlawful, but not all that is unlawful is unfair) … for practically the majority of acts commanded by the law are those which are prescribed from the point of view of virtue taken as a whole … Of particular justice, and that which is just in the corresponding sense, (a) one kind is that which is manifest in distributions of honor or money or the other things that fall to be divided among those who share in a constitution … and (b) one is that which plays a rectifying part in transactions between man and man.[5]

Aristotle divides the distributable (a) into the involuntary and the voluntary and the rectificatory (b) into those acts which are clandestine and those that are violent. Sales fall into (a) and murder into (b). In matters of distributive justice "the just is the proportional." In rectificatory justice the judge "restores equality."

If rectification is called for, then at least in the short run it may be that injustice occurs in that the judge must take from the undeserving to give back to the deserving and thereby restore equality. In this way, a tension opens between justice as following the rule of law and justice as a matter of rectification. For the taking of something from one person is a kind of injustice for the one from whom it is taken, even if it means that justice in the grander scheme has been done by restoring to the one who is presently without because of the injustice of the one who now has.

Justice as following the law is actually ambiguous, as Aristotle seems to admit, since it could mean doing what a statute calls for or it could mean doing what proportionality, a principle of legality, calls for. And we have now set things up so that we can next say what is equity as fairness and how it relates to justice. The idea is that in acting justly by strictly following the law a person's actions can result in unfairness to the one so treated due to peculiarities of the circumstances.

3 Aristotle, *Nicomachean Ethics*, 1129b12–26, translated by W. D. Ross, in *The Basic Works of Aristotle*, edited by Richard McKeon, NY: Random House, 1941, p. 1003.

4 Ibid., 1130b6–7, p. 1005.

5 Ibid., 1130b8–35, pp. 1005–1006.

14.2 EQUITY AND FAIRNESS FOR ARISTOTLE

One of the great tasks that Aristotle accomplishes is to clearly and firmly explain how acting justly by following the law can actually result in injustice as unfairness. His discussion is fairly brief in both his *Nicomachean Ethics* and in his *Rhetoric*, but it has had a very profound influence on the ideas of justice and equity in the history of legal thought. In the *Nicomachean Ethics*, Aristotle discusses political justice which is salient for our inquiry in legal theory. Aristotle begins by saying that politics arises "among men who share their life with a view to self-sufficiency."[6] Political justice is then divided in two parts: "part is natural, part legal, – natural, that which everywhere has the same force and does not exist by people thinking this or that; legal, that which is originally indifferent, but when it has been laid down is not."[7]

Equity is then introduced in the following way to distinguish it from one sort of justice.

> the same thing is just and equitable … the equitable is superior … the problem is that the equitable is just, but not the legally just but a correction of legal justice … all law is universal, but about some things it is not possible to make a universal statement which shall be correct …[8] To say what the legislator would have said had he been present.[9]

Equity is then defined to be "a correction of law where it is defective owing to its universality."[10]

For Aristotle, political justice, a form of particular justice, has two components. One part, natural justice, is universal ("which everywhere has the same force"[11]), and does not depend on what people think is politically just. The other, legal justice, was "originally indifferent" until it was "laid down." This distinction tracks to a certain extent the criminal law distinction today between *mala in se* crimes and *mala prohibita* crimes. It also is important for various philosophical debates about justice today, where liberal theorists talk of certain "natural duties" that could be seen to be grounded in natural justice. The idea of natural justice also had a powerful impact on the idea of natural law, in the way Thomas Aquinas extended Aristotle's ideas in the Middle Ages. There is a debate about whether Aristotle had something fairly narrow in mind, as is true of the criminal law distinction, or something much broader, such as the natural lawyers would have it.

6 Ibid., 1134a27.
7 Ibid., 1134b18.
8 Ibid., 1137b10.
9 Ibid., 1137b23.
10 Ibid., 1137b27.
11 Ibid., 1134b18.

Various legal theorists have argued that the Aristotelian distinction between equity and legal justice had a significant impact on the development of equity jurisprudence in England and then in the United States. One interesting question is whether or not the kind of fairness that equity concerns, which corrects legal justice, but is not itself legal justice, might be a form of natural justice. Equity seems to be a procedural restraint rather than a substantive one. Yet, there has been an interesting debate in US Constitutional law about whether or not there is a category of substantive due process, an equitable category.

One way to understand what Aristotle is saying about equity is by examining a passage we have already encountered and a helpful analogy he made. Aristotle employs the following analogy to explain how he conceives equity:

> about some things it is impossible to lay down a law, so that a decree is needed. For when the thing is indefinite, the rule also is indefinite, like the leaden rule used in making the Lesbian molding; the rule adapts itself to the shape of the stone and is not rigid, and so too the decree is adapted to the facts.[12]

This is the classical account of equity understood in a narrow sense of fairness that is necessary to correct the law in certain cases where the current facts are not the ones that were originally contemplated by the lawmaker.

Aristotle's image used to present the idea of equity is highly relevant for our discussions: "like the leaden rule used in making the Lesbian mounding; the rule adapts itself to the shape of the stone and is not rigid, and so too the [equitable] decree is adapted to the facts".[13] Sometimes, there is a mismatch such that unfairness, or inequity, results. In the initial movement from individual oral decree to general written law something can be lost that then calls for the occasional new corrective decree, now primarily in written form, to correct an unfair legal decision, which in other respects was legally just. The unfairness is in the result of the application of the law, not in its formal promulgation.

14.3 JUSTICE AND EQUITY IN ANCIENT CHINA

Confucian Chinese thinkers were skeptical of statute law, especially as undergirded by a rule of law that treated all equally before the law. In large part this was because Confucian thinkers recognized the legitimacy of class differences and saw it as an important value to allow discretion to the ruler to treat different classes and different circumstances differently. In this sense equity was valued above justice narrowly conceived. The Confucian Book of Rites (Li Chi) and other books concerning

[12] Ibid., 1137b28–32.
[13] Ibid., 1137b29–31.

custom set out the importance of rank and distinction, which must be recognized for a society to thrive.

> The li (customs) are for the purpose of distinguishing the superior from the inferior, and of discriminating between the noble and the humble.[14]
>
> There is justice between the upper and the lower; there is distinction between the noble and the humble; there are grades between the elders and the young. There is a difference in standing between the rich and the poor.[15]
>
> Li arrange people in their ranks.[16]
>
> [Li are used] to order the upper and the lower, to regulate the ways of human life.[17]
>
> Li signify to respect the noble, to be filial to the old, to be submissively fraternal to the elders, to be kind to the young, and to be gracious to the humble.[18]

All of the relationships regulated by custom are ones of inequality, except for the relationship among friends.[19] And to best serve such relationships much discretion on the part of the ruler was needed. Custom was to govern the best of societies, indeed without following custom peace and stability in a state could not be maintained, according to early Confucian theorists.

For a short time, ancient Chinese legal thought was dominated by a school of thought called legalism, which rejected the Confucian emphasis on custom and replaced it with a strict sense of justice through written law as well as severe punishments. Han Feizi is a good representative of this school of thought. He makes it clear that he does not support the Confucian idea of different rules for the different classes of people.

> The law no more makes exceptions for men of high standing than the plumb line bends to accommodate a crooked place in the wood. What the law has decreed, the wise man cannot dispute nor the brave man venture to contest. When faults are to be punished, the highest minister cannot escape; when good is to be rewarded, the lowest peasant must not be passed over.

Han Feizi then goes on to argue that severe punishment, especially meted out against superiors and officials, is the best way for society to achieve stability.

> For putting fear into the officials, awing the people, wiping out wantonness and sloth, and preventing lies and deception, nothing can compare to penalties. If

[14] *Huai-nan hung-lieh chieh*, 11, 1a, quoted in Tung-Tsu Chu, *Law and Society in Traditional China*, Paris: Mouton and Co., 1965, p. 233.

[15] *Kuan-tzu*, 3, 13b, quoted in ibid., p. 233.

[16] *Tso chuan chu-su*, 14, 13b, quoted in ibid., p. 233.

[17] *Pai-hu t'ung*, 2, 6b-7a, quoted in ibid., p. 233.

[18] *Hsun-tzu*, 19, 4b, quoted in ibid., pp. 233–234.

[19] See ibid., p. 237.

> penalties are heavy, men dare not use high position to abuse the humble; if laws are clearly defined, superiors will be honored and their rights will not be invaded.[20]

Han Feizi argues that rulers need to employ two handles: "punishment and favor" and not to worry about what the Confucian theorists and sages have to say.[21]

Han Feizi and the other legalists believed that justice was the key component of any good government and that justice required a strict enforcement of the law across all peoples and situations.

> The nation at peace may patronize Confucian scholars and cavaliers; but the nation in danger must call upon its fighting men ... Therefore the way of the enlightened ruler is to unify the laws instead of seeking for wise men, to lay down firm policies instead of longing for men of good faith. Hence his laws never fail him, and there is no felony or deceit among his officials.[22]

The legalists were dominant in China for only a few years but they had a profound impact on ancient Chinese views of justice and equity.

Indeed, despite the sternness of their views they believed that over time their policies would have compassionate results. Shang Yang, another legalist, argued that:

> there is no better means of prohibiting wickedness and stopping crime than by making punishments heavy. If punishments are heavy and rigorously applied, then people will not dare to try (how far they can go), with the result that, in the state, there will be no people punished. Because there are no people punished in the state, I say that if one understands punishments, there is no capital punishment.[23]

The legalists sought to replace a rule of custom with a rule of law and punishment, but the Confucians soon regained power. Yet in their return the Confucians incorporated some of the legalists positions, most especially the respect for law. But there was also the important idea, advanced by Shang Yang, that a ruler could change the model of previous law, even to the point of "breaking the mold"[24] to achieve a fair result. This idea of a kind of equity also influenced the Confucians who were reasserting control in China.

The Han Confucians recognized the need for punishment but only as "supplementary to moral influence."[25] Ch'en Ch'ung writing in the first century CE wrote: "What is left by *li* (custom) is covered by punishment. To go beyond *li* means

[20] Han Feizi, *Basic Writings*, edited and translated by Burton Watson, NY: Columbia University Press, 2003, p. 28.

[21] Ibid., p. 29.

[22] Ibid., pp. 108 and 110.

[23] *The Book of Lord Shang*, translated by J. J. L. Duyvendak, NY: Create Space, 2016, p. 59.

[24] See Michael Lowe, "The Heritage Left to the Empires," in *The Cambridge History of Ancient China*, ibid., p. 1008.

[25] Tung-Tsu Chu, *Law and Society in Traditional China*, Paris: Mouton and Co., 1965, p. 271.

to enter punishment. The two are but the outside and the inside of the same thing."[26] The "Confucianization" of law[27] retained the class divisions in the law but now added severe punishments that could be inflicted for a violation of either written law or custom.

The delicate balance between equity and justice narrowly conceived can be seen in the interactions of Confucians and legalists in ancient China. One way to see the role of equity or something very much like it in ancient Chinese legal thought concerns the use of alternatives to the very severe punishments often issued by a judge. It was common for there to be the alternative of payment of moneys in exchange for relief from these punishments. Obviously this only concerned those wealthy enough to pay. But in addition there were amnesties as well as banishments that sometimes took the place of the severe punishment that would have otherwise been due.[28] What is unclear is whether, like Aristotle, these alternatives were envisioned for cases where the severity of the punishment did not seem fair, or there was some other reason at play. Nonetheless, there is evidence that the often brutal punishments of early Chinese law were tempered in various ways in certain cases. So, equitable relief seemed to sit side by side with harsh punishments of strict justice.

14.4 CONCEPTUALIZING ANCIENT EQUITY

It is worth quoting a long passage from Aristotle in his *Rhetoric* to give us a place to start to understand ancient equity in its most sophisticated form.

> There are two kinds of just and unjust conduct toward others ... The second kind makes up for the defects of the written law. This is what we call equity; it is, in fact, the sort of justice which goes beyond the written law. Its existence partly is and partly is not intended by legislators; not intended, where they have noticed no defect in the law; intended, where they find themselves unable to define things exactly, and are obliged to legislate as if that held good always which in fact holds good usually; or where it is not easy to be complete owing to the endless possible cases presented, such as the kinds and sizes of weapons that may be used to inflict wounds – a lifetime would be too short to make out a complete list of these. If, then, a precise statement is impossible and yet legislation is necessary, the law must be expressed in wide terms; and so if a man has no more than a finger-ring on his hand when he lifts it to strike or actually strikes another man, he is guilty

[26] Quoted in ibid., p. 279.

[27] This term was coined by Tung-Tsu Chu, *Law and Society in Traditional China*, Paris: Mouton and Co., 1965, p. 267 following.

[28] Se Mark Edward Lewis, *The Early Chinese Empires: Qui and Han*, Cambridge, MA: Harvard University Press, 2007, pp. 231 following.

> of a criminal act according to the written words of the law; but is innocent really, and it is equity that declares him so. From this definition of equity it is plain what sort of action, and what sort of persons, are equitable or the reverse. Equity must be applied to forgivable actions; and it must make us distinguish between criminal acts on the one hand and errors of judgment, or misfortune, on the other … Equity bids us to be merciful to the weakness of human nature; to think less about the laws than about the man who framed them, and less about what he said than about what he meant; not to consider the actions of the accused so much as his intentions, nor this or that detail so much as the whole story; to ask not what a man is now but what he has always or usually been. It bids us remember benefits rather than injuries, and benefits received rather than benefits conferred; to be patient when we are wronged; to settle a dispute by negotiation and not by force; to prefer arbitration to litigation – for an arbitrator goes by the equity of a case, a judge by the strict law, and arbitration was invented with the express purpose of securing full power of equity.[29]

There are several meanings, or at least several divergent strains, of equity described here. I will set out these various senses of equity and then indicate which of these elements can, and cannot, also be found in ancient Chinese legal thought.

The first idea is one we have already explored in earlier sections, namely, that the written law can be seen as defective when it tries to cover more cases than it should. For some Chinese thinkers, written law, at least in the form of statutes, is always defective or at least incomplete when compared to customs and rites. We can see this in many ancient writings but perhaps no place clearer than in Confucius.

> If the people be led by laws, and uniformity sought to be given to them by punishments, they will try to avoid the punishments, but have no sense of shame. If they be led by virtue, and uniformity sought to be given them by the rules of propriety, they will have the sense of shame, and moreover will become good.[30]

A second important sense of equity is that it calls for mercy and forgiveness. This idea is perhaps best captured by Confucius' disciple, Mencius, whose main ethical concept was humaneness. First, here is another quotation from Confucius:

> If a man be without the virtues proper to humanity, what has he to do with the rites of propriety.[31]

[29] Aristotle, *Rhetoric*, 1374a18–1374b22, translated by W. Rhys Roberts, in *Basic Works of Aristotle*, edited by Richard McKeon, NY: Random House, 1941, pp. 1371–1372. I have slightly altered the translation at the beginning of the quotation.

[30] Confucius, *Analects*, Bk II, Ch. III, in *The Confucian Analects, The Great Learning, and the Doctrine of the Mean*, translated by James Legge, NY: Cosmo Classics, 2009, p. 146.

[31] Ibid., Bk. III, Ch. III, ibid, p. 155.

Mencius then went into much more detail about the value of humaneness.

> If the king were to institute a government that dispensed humaneness, he would make all the officers in the world wish to stand in his court, all the tillers wish to till his fields, all the merchants wish to entrust their goods to his marketplaces.[32]
>
> When one uses force to make people submit, they do not submit in their hearts but only because their strength is insufficient. When one uses Virtue to make people submit, they are pleased to the depths of their hearts, and they sincerely submit.[33]
>
> One who is humane will be distinguished; one who is inhumane will be disgraced.[34]

Mencius stands as one of the most profound believers in equity understood as humane treatment.

A third sense of equity is that arbitration is preferred to litigation. Here we can look to Confucius who said that it would be best when there were no law suits, and people settled disputes by reference to customs and rites. Indeed, Han Feizi attributes to the Confucians the idea that "Good behavior means to destroy the legal institutions."[35] And Confucius believed that there was no need for law and that the state of "no litigation" is the ultimate end.[36] Confucius did not expressly endorse arbitration over litigation, but this idea can be found in some of his work and in that of his followers.

A fourth sense of equity is perhaps the most difficult to reconcile with the rule of law since it calls for declaring someone innocent who acted in clear violation of the criminal laws. There are two reasons given by Aristotle for such a ruling. One reason is that the intention of the person is not to break the law, even if in fact the person did break the law. Another reason is that we should focus on a person's whole life, not just on what he did at the moment. The Confucians also espoused the idea that humane law would take into account the whole person.

Finally, there is the sense of equity that remembers benefits rather than injuries. This seems most appropriately directed at sentencing rather than conviction. We can remember the dispute between legalists and Confucians about the need for severe punishment. In some respects, the legalists seem to have won this battle for even when there had been a Confucianization of law after the time of the legalists severe punishment remained the norm. The acceptance of severity in Chinese punishments, even with some modification on a case-by-case basis seems to be one of the clear differences between ancient Greek and Chinese legal thought. Mencius, though, was opposed to severe punishment, as we can see here:

[32] *Mencius*, 1A7, translated by Irene Bloom, NY: Columbia University Press, 2009, p. 11.

[33] *Mencius*, 2A3, ibid., p. 33.

[34] *Mencius*, 2A4, ibid., p. 33.

[35] See Tung-Tsu Chu, *Law and Society in Traditional China*, Paris: Mouton and Co., 1965, p. 246.

[36] See ibid., p. 249.

> There are people who say, "I am good at deploying troops. I am good at waging war." This is a grave crime. If the ruler of a state loves humaneness, he will have no enemy in the world ... To punish is to correct. With everyone wishing to be corrected, what is the need of fighting?[37]

But the legalists favored severe punishment as we saw earlier. Han Feizi said: "If penalties are heavy, men dare not use high position to abuse the humble."[38] And Lord Shang said: "there is no better means of prohibiting wickedness and stopping crime than by making punishments heavy. If punishments are heavy and rigorously applied, then people will not dare to try (how far they can go)."[39]

One last point to note is that in ancient Chinese thought we find reference to the five punishments, which are "tattooing, cutting off the nose, cutting off the leg, castration, and capital punishment."[40] And while the Confucians were strongly supportive of moral education and influence, they did not reject the use of these very severe punishments when they were properly called for.

14.5 DISTINGUISHING JUSTICE AND EQUITY

Aristotle referred to equity as a form of natural justice; and the Confucians saw equity primarily in terms of customary moral traditions. Both of these ideas are importantly connected in the modern conception of equity in law. Equity is not a matter of justice in a strict sense of justice where a judge or jury must apply the statutes exactly as they have been written. Equity appeals to a different sense of justice – a justice rooted in morality or in some kind of natural law. Equity taps into a basic sense of fairness that each person can access in his or her conscience. Indeed, in English common law, the appeal to equity was to the conscience of the king, or the judge. There is thus a sense in which the statute law can be overridden by the jury or judge by appeal to a higher or moral law. We saw this very clearly in the case of Antigone that we discussed in the previous chapter.

Antigone claims that she is placed between two competing laws, the laws set out by the state that prohibited burial of her brother Polinices, and the eternal laws of the gods that dictated that she bury her brother. Antigone tells us that when there is such a conflict she must act on the higher laws of natural justice. And while most people today would side with Antigone, her decision is troubling because it allows for her conscience to veto the laws of the state, when it might be that her conscience

37 *Mencius*, 7B4, p. 157.
38 Han Feizi, *Basic Writings*, edited and translated by Burton Watson, NY: Columbia University Press, 2003, p. 28.
39 *The Book of Lord Shang*, p. 59.
40 See Chu, *Law and Society in Traditional China*, p. 268.

is merely an arbitrary source – perhaps a voice from her upbringing. Chinese legal thinkers would have no trouble with this characterization, since they saw tradition passed down from father to child as an important source of how we should live. The Greeks would worry about the effect on the rule of law if a private citizen could veto the clearly defined statute law. It was Aristotle, as we have seen, who reset the terms of the debate by articulating why equity should sometimes be seen as overriding strict considerations of narrow justice. Today we have a similar debate, where Aristotle's voice can be heard, but also that of the Confucians.

Ronald Dworkin has argued that in hard cases such as *Riggs* v. *Palmer*, judges ought to use principles of equity, such as "no person should be allowed to profit from his or her wrongdoing," to ascertain how best to interpret the statute of wills. Following the law does not merely mean looking at a statute and applying it, but rather trying to ascertain what the writers of a statute would say is the right thing to do in a particular case.[41] The law is discoverable, for Dworkin, but it is a mistake to think that the law has only one source. Principles of equity are sources of law for judges and can be appealed to even if it may seem that a statute or other law is crystal clear, as was seemingly true in *Riggs* v. *Palmer*. This is because equity principles are as much law as legislation.[42]

There is today a continuing controversy about how much discretion judges should have, and even a controversy about what discretion means. It sometimes turns out that the principles of equity conflict with other sources of law. In such situations, it is not necessarily a violation of the rule of law to pick one source of law over another. Equity as a type of morality is not merely a subjective matter. Principles of equity, such as the principle that "no person should be allowed to profit from his or her wrongdoing" as articulated in *Riggs* v. *Palmer* is grounded in longstanding custom and tradition that a society ignores at its peril.

41 Ronald Dworkin, *Law's Empire*, Cambridge, MA: Harvard University Press, 1986, p. 20 and elsewhere.

42 For a fascinating discussion of discretion especially in light of Dworkin's early theoretical work, see George Fletcher, *Basic Concepts of Legal Thought*, NY: Oxford University Press, 1996, Chapter 3.

15

Trials, Juries, and Democratic Assemblies

As in many ancient societies, there were trials in ancient China and Greece. In Greece there were jury trials, but not for the first time historically. Ancient Babylonia had jury trials, where even commoners were eligible for jury duty, as we saw in Chapter 2. But until the Greeks there had not been a linking of juries and popular democratic assemblies. There had been assemblies in ancient Babylonia, but they had not been democratic bodies – instead being largely advisors to the king. Ancient China follows more in line with those ancient societies that had the king, or the king's representative, decide the outcome of trials. Greece is known for being the font of democracy because of the way that, at least for 200 years, kings did not rule politically or legally – popular assemblies and juries ruled and set the stage for modern democracies. I will argue that we can find in both Chinese and Greek legal systems precursors of the two most prominent forms of trial today, the Anglo-American jury and the Continental inquisitorial judge-based systems.

Chinese trials, as we will see in Section 15.1, to a certain extent took a form fairly common among ancient societies where a judge was appointed by a ruler to hear the two parties to a dispute and to try to resolve the dispute justly and equitably. In ancient China, one thing that newly emerges is a sophisticated procedure for investigating legal disputes, especially when violence had occurred, and for questioning witnesses. In Section 15.2 we will present ancient Greek trials as having even more radical new forms of procedure whereby large juries acting very much like assemblies are the ones, rather than judges, that determine a resolution or judgment about a particular case.

The Athenian jury system has a tight fit with the direct form of democracy in Athens at the same time. We will spend Section 15.3 describing the connections between the Athenian political assembly and the Athenian jury trial, as contrasted with the monarchical Chinese political system and the form of trials in ancient China. In Section 15.4 we will look to Aristotle's criticisms of Athenian democratic assemblies and related worries about the idea of jury trials, especially the use of the lot in both contexts. Finally, in Section 15.5, we will look to the two models of trials today that correspond to these two ancient trials: the common law jury trial and the inquisitorial judge-based trial.

15.1 CHINESE TRIALS AND INVESTIGATIONS

In the Ch'in legal and administrative rules of the third century BCE we find detailed guidelines for investigating a legal complaint in ancient China. Here is the first model rule:

> Trying lawsuits – If in trying lawsuits it is possible by means of documents to track down his words, obtaining the facts of the person without using the bastinado is the best; applying the bastinado is inferior, for when there is fear, (everything) is spoiled.[1]

The bastinado, a cane used for inflicting blows, is associated with torture and here we see its use restricted only to those cases where it is the last resort. And even in that case, these model rules point out something we are still learning today: torture can lead to results but ones that are spoiled because fear does not necessarily make a person more truthful or forthcoming.

In addition, we can look to the twenty-first model rule for an indication of the detailed and meticulous way that investigative reports are to be constructed.

> When investigating, it is essential first carefully to examine and consider the traces. One should go alone to the place where the corpse is and consider the knot of the rope. If at the place of the knot there are traces of a noose, then observe whether the tongue protrudes or not, how far the head and the feet are distant from the place of the knot and the ground, and whether he had discharged feces and urine or not. Then untie the rope and observe whether nose and mouth emit a sigh or not. Then observe the condition of the blood congealing along the trace of the rope. Try to free the head from the rope ... completely observe the body, from the inside of the hair on his head down to the perineum. If the tongue does not protrude, if mouth and nose do not emit a sigh, if there is no congealed blood along the trace of the rope, if the knot of the rope is so tight that it cannot be slipped off ... Since he has been dead for a long time, mouth and nose may perhaps not be able to produce a sigh. People who kill themselves must first have had reasons. Question members of his household in order to have them reply concerning the reasons.[2]

1 *Remnants of Ch'in Law*, Rule E1, translated by A. F. P. Hulsewe, Leiden: E. J. Brill, 1985, p. 183.
2 *Remnants of Ch'in Law*, Rule E21, ibid., pp. 200–201.

There seems to be a concern for fairness here and it is in the elaborate investigating that a judge will get a balanced idea of what evidence there is and what inferences can be drawn from that evidence.

The ancient Chinese legal practice of the third century BCE also allows for appeal from the ruling by the initial judge to hear the case.[3] And the evidence reveals that amnesty could be granted across a whole range of offenses, and indeed seems to have been relatively common.[4] We will spend more time on the idea of amnesty in a later chapter (Chapter 23). Here I wish to point out that despite lacking a popular jury, ancient Chinese legal thought was concerned about establishing procedures that would produce a fair result, and recognizing that fairness also could call for relief from the oftentimes severe punishments and penalties of the system of law.

Elaborate procedural rules for investigating a crime and conducting a trial can partially make up for the lack of a jury – indeed, in many contexts today the lack of juries is seen as a positive rather than a negative feature of an adjudicatory system. We will later (in Section IV) discuss some of the criticisms of popular juries and assemblies where expertise is not prized. Before doing that, we turn to the development of juries in ancient Greece, where the popular jury was combined with elaborate procedures to produce what many today think of as a model legal system, despite the strong criticisms of that system voiced at the time.

15.2 ATHENIAN JURY TRIALS

In Aristotle's *Politics* he defines a citizen as a person who "shares in the administration of justice, and in offices."[5] He then says that "our definition is best adapted to the citizen of a democracy."[6] There were many legal bodies in ancient Greece that could try cases, but the one that came to have pride of place in the Athenian democracy was what is often translated as "the people's court" (*dikasterion*).[7] During the Athenian democracy, all male citizens over 30 years of age could be jurors. Since one was paid to be a juror, although not quite as well as being in the assembly, the poor were disproportionately members of juries, which tended to be quite large. A panel of 501 people constituted a jury for public prosecutions, such as the one that condemned Socrates to death in 399 BCE.

3 Ibid., pp. 7 and 152.

4 See Mark Edward Lewis, *The Early Chinese Empires: Qin and Han*, Cambridge, MA: Harvard University Press, 2007, p. 231.

5 Aristotle, *Politics*, 1275a22–24, in *Basic Works of Aristotle*, edited by Richard McKeon, translated by Benjamin Jowett, NY: Random House, 1941, p. 1177.

6 Ibid., 1275b5–6, p. 1177.

7 See Mogens Herman Hansen, *The Athenian Democracy in the Age of Demosthenes*, Oxford: Blackwell, 1991, p. 178.

Aristotle tells us that laws are to have a prime place in the arguments presented during trials, but there are two kinds of law the jurors must appeal to.

> If the written law tells against our case, clearly we must appeal to the universal law, and insist on its greater equity and justice. We must argue that the juror's oath "I will give my verdict according to my honest opinion" means that one will not simply follow the letter of the written law. We must urge that principles of equity are permanent and changeless, and that the universal law does not change either, for it is the law of nature, whereas written laws often change.[8]

The parties to a law suit must present the law in their speeches to the jury in the most persuasive way they can.

The assumption appears to be that when common people, even the poorest of the society, are presented with the law and the facts they can discern what the just and equitable verdict should be. This appears to be a kind of democratic assumption that extends even to the domain of knowledge, not merely to pervade the political and legal institutions of ancient Athens. But this democratic assumption creates one of the central criticisms of popular courts and assemblies as we will see in Section 4. Popular assemblies and courts can be swayed by skilled orators and by demagogues. Indeed, there was a profession of orators that arose in ancient Athens to fill the need for skilled people to present cases to juries and persuade them to decide rightly, although the idea seems rather to be that the orators tried to persuade the common people of the assemblies and juries to support the cause that the orators championed regardless of whether it was the more meritorious.

A particular action that could be brought to the people's court was called a *graphe paranomon* and could be brought in court even against a decision of the people's assembly. This seems to show that the jury was supreme in Athenian democratic constitutional structure.[9] But while political matters were handled by the people's court, some of the most serious crimes are handled by other courts that are not democratically arranged. As Aristotle tell us,

> The King Archon supervises the Mysteries together with assistants elected by the people … Cases of impiety come before him [the King Archon] and disputes over priesthoods. He also decides disputes about religious matters which arise between the clans or the priests; all cases of homicide come before him, and he it is who proclaims the exclusion of an individual from customary ceremonies. Charges of murder or wounding where a man either deliberately kills or injures someone are heard before the Areopagus, as are cases of poisoning which result in death, and cases of arson, these are the only cases decided by that body. Charges

8 Aristotle, *Rhetoric*, 1374b26–34, translated by W. Rhys Roberts, in *The Basic Works of Aristotle*, p. 1374.

9 See Hansen, *The Athenian Democracy*, pp. 205–208.

of unintentional homicide, conspiracy to kill, and the killing of a slave, metic or foreigner are heard by the Court of the Palladeum.[10]

These other Athenian courts were not organized as direct democratic institutions in the way that the people's court was.

In the people's court most cases were tried in one day, with two speeches each by prosecutor and defendant. The jury members did not ask questions or consult with each other, although as we see in Plato's *Apology*, describing the trial of Socrates, the jurors did cheer or boo based on what they thought of the speeches during the trial. In this sense the people's court trials were similar to the functioning of the assembly in that the main form of participation by the people was the casting of votes. The popular juries in Athens were not deliberative bodies as they are today in the Anglo-American system of jurisprudence.

The jurors were selected by lot and the determination of who would serve on which panel on a given day was also determined by an elaborate process that was aimed at reducing the likelihood of the rigging of juries by one party or another. Selection by lot is indeed a way to attempt to minimize corruption but it comes with one significant disadvantage, competence is now not prized and it is only by luck that the jury will indeed have people who are competent and care about the proceedings. Selection by lot also allows the possibility that jurors will be biased since there is no screening mechanism as there is today in *voir dire* proceedings. We will address this issue in more detail in the next section.

15.3 POLITICAL AND LEGAL INSTITUTIONS IN GREECE AND CHINA

The people's court and people's assembly are two of the defining institutions of ancient Athenian society, marking Athens as having created the first democratic state. Ancient China lacks such institutions, but as we have seen there were important legal institutions and practices in China aimed at minimizing corruption and increasing the fairness of the administration of law. Indeed, there is some reason to think that ancient Chinese legal practices were fairer than those in Athens. We will explore this possibility in this section of the chapter.

In ancient Athens there were two reasons for employing the lot in selecting jurors. First, it was thought that in selecting by chance it was really the gods that chose the jurors, providing a kind of divine veneer for the jury so selected. Second, it was thought that selecting by lot eliminated human interference in the selection

[10] Aristotle, *The Constitution of Athens*, translated by F. G. Kenyon, in Aristotle, *The Politics and the Constitution of Athens*, edited by Stephen Everson, Cambridge: Cambridge University Press, 1996, p. 255.

process, thus preventing jury tampering and fraud. In either case, it was thought that selecting by lot insulated the legal process, at least in the people's court, from undue factors and hence making a fair outcome of the trial more likely.

Random selection is always no better than a second-best selection. The best method of selection is selecting the most knowledgeable or most fair. Choosing by lot only can claim legitimacy if the best method is ruled out because of epistemic problems. By this I mean that it may be difficult or impossible to know who the best deciders of legal disputes are. We may lack knowledge of the criteria of what makes someone a good decision-maker or we may lack sufficient knowledge of people to be able to tell who manifests the criteria of good decision-making.

Ancient Chinese legal thought sought to solve the problem of corruption and unfairness in trials by creating quite elaborate rules and model codes of behavior for officials. To a certain extent, Chinese legal practices seem to be premised on the idea that the epistemic problems are not insurmountable – it is already known what practices will produce the fairest results. We might think again of the emphasis that Confucius placed on customs. Customs are at least in one sense time-tested methods for achieving certain results. We don't need to know in advance what are the best criteria or the best way to achieve these criteria but instead we just try something and see if it seems to work – selecting only those procedures that have indeed worked. Over time this method will eventually lead to a set of good practices. It is thought that there is no better way to proceed. Even if the customary approach does not produce the best practices, it is likely to produce better ones than sheer random selection, unless we have good reason to think the gods will only intervene when chance is used.

Another important issue to be addressed is the relationship between trial procedures and the form of government in a particular state. Many Athenians, including Aristotle, saw popular participation in trials as a significant part of the popular participation that good forms of democratic government foster and promote. Similarly, those Chinese thinkers who supported customary procedures also supported government forms that were largely non-democratic and not particularly participatory.

There are many well-known problems with direct democracy – indeed there has arguably been only one pure direct democracy governing over a significant state, and that would be ancient Athens from 508/7–322/1 BCE.[11] Before the reforms of Cleisthenes, Athens was ruled by various kings and oligarchs, as it was also after this period. Yet the ancient Greeks developed a wonderful model of democracy at its purest. But many aspects of the Athenian democracy are difficult to rationalize. It is one thing to think that every person is deserving of equal treatment before the law,

[11] See Hansen, *The Athenian Democracy*, pp. 1–3.

and quite another matter to think that every citizen equally deserves to lead the state and its legal institutions.

Ancient Chinese legal thinkers debated whether custom or written law was the best, and also whether strong leaders who meted out strict punishments were better than leaders who ruled with humaneness and compassion. But there does not seem to have been a debate in ancient China about democracy in either legislative or judicial matters. Given that the ancient Chinese texts we have been examining are from roughly the same time period that ancient Athens experimented with democracy, we might ask why other states at the time did not similarly try direct democracy or even indirect democracy.

The ancient Chinese and Athenians did debate the best way to achieve virtue and came to many of the same conclusions, including that habit, custom, and ritual were significant in attaining virtue. The Athenians saw participation in assemblies and trials as a means to display and also to acquire various virtues. The Chinese also saw a value in participation in civic life, although there were certain theorists who thought that staying out of the public domain was perhaps the most virtuous – this was also a position taken by some Greek philosophers. It is notable though that while Socrates and Confucius both expressed disdain for the public sphere they also took full advantage of appearing in public arenas to teach and discuss their views. And Confucius was a government minister at one point in his life.

As we saw earlier, Confucius saw law trials as important for solving certain kinds of problems, but he had mixed feelings about them. "In hearing litigations, I am like any other body. What is necessary however is to cause the people to have no litigation."[12] Joel Kupperman summarizes this point well when he says that Confucius "may very well have believed also that there will be some criminals even in the best governed society. So, we need the protection of law. All the same, in his view frequent and heavy-handed legal compulsion is a sign that the ruling group is either ineffective or full of corrupt desires."[13] Both Aristotle and Confucius are normally said to be paradigm examples of virtue theorists. But Confucius, unlike Aristotle, is highly skeptical of law.[14]

Confucius extolled the "superior man" who was noble in birth and has the manners of a gentleman.[15] Following customs and the example of superior men is better than following the law out of fear. Such discussion supports the view that Confucius favored an aristocratic or kingship model of government. But this view

[12] Confucius, *Analects* Bk XII, Ch. XIII, in *The Confucian Analects, The Great Learning, and the Doctrine of the Mean*, translated by James Legge, NY: Cosmo Classics, 2009, p. 257.

[13] Joel Kupperman, *Classical Asian Philosophy*, NY: Oxford University Press, 2007, p. 91.

[14] See ibid., p. 86.

[15] See Karl Jaspers, *Confucius*, in *Socrates, Buddha, Confucius, and Jesus*, translated by Ralph Manheim, NY: Harcourt Brace and Company, p. 48.

did not support a participatory model of legal trials. For Aristotle, despite having misgivings about the radical democracy of his day, he supported the kind of mixed constitutional government that was at least indirectly democratic. And he supported a participatory form of legal trial as well.

15.4 ARISTOTLE'S CRITICISMS OF DEMOCRACY

Aristotle worried about certain forms of democracy which transform themselves into something else – tyranny or no government at all. In the former case, Aristotle worries that democracy will inspire a demagogue who will, with the people's support, disregard the laws. In the latter case, Aristotle worries that the demagogue will place himself over the laws, obliterating the laws, and thereby destroying the Constitution. And if there is no Constitution, then people are back in a state of anarchy. The rule by decree of the demagogue is the antithesis of the rule of law. And for Aristotle, there needs to be at least a minimal rule of law for there to be a constitutional form of government at all.

In his *Rhetoric*,[16] Aristotle quotes from Sophocles' *Antigone*, where Creon issues a decree, preventing anyone from burying Antigone's brother. More than 2,000 years later, Hegel thought that decrees are a paradigmatic form of public law. But sometimes a decree actually is extra-legal – it nullifies a law in a particular case but is not itself legitimate law-making. To rule by certain highly specific decrees can sometimes be to rule on the basis of particulars not to make general laws.

When rule by the people is taken over by a demagogue, any law can be subject to be overturned in a particular case by a decree being issued that exempts a given person or class of persons from the law's domain. It is possible to rule exclusively by decree, but it would be incredibly time-consuming and subject to tremendous abuse. When the rules are not settled, and only occasionally changed, abuse is less frequent. But if each person can engage in special pleading to get out of a legal obligation, there will be a willingness to engage in bribes or other devices to influence the assembly into issuing a decree to exempt a given person from a general rule.

A demagogue is literally just a leader of the people. But already at Aristotle's time the term had a strongly negative connotation. Demagogues were typically members of the assembly who used the power of rhetoric to move the members of the assembly to adopt decrees that solved particular problems quickly but also operated outside the normal constraints of law. In ancient Athens, demagogues typically appealed to the emotions, rather than the reason, of the members of the assembly. The demagogue used flattery for those who support him or her and ridicule for those who oppose. And once demagogues gained the support of the people, uniting them in ways the people were not united before, it is as if there is rule by a single

[16] Aristotle, *Rhetoric*, 1375b1–4, in *Basic Works of Aristotle*, p. 1374, quoting Sophocles, *Antigone*, 456.

person. The mass of individual people is transformed into a single ruler who is now embodied by the demagogue. And then this type of single-rule can easily slip into tyranny since the demagogue will not have the interest of the whole at heart.

We might though note that Aristotle does not think that all demagogues act against the interests of the commonwealth. The fear though is that since the demagogue is largely unchecked, especially not checked by the rule of law, the demagogue has no incentive to act in the interests of the whole of the people. And this also means that demagogues will be inherently unstable since they can lose the support of the people just as easily as they gained it.

Aristotle seems to have a group of objections to direct democracy that are not necessarily related to each other:

(a) democracy is the rule by the poor masses yet the members of the masses do not have expertise in ruling;
(b) democracies typically (in Ancient Greece) employ the lot, but this method does not determine that the best will rule;
(c) democracies are too easily taken over by demagogues who are themselves likely to become tyrants.

So Aristotle expresses strong support for a mixed polity and representative forms of government instead of the rule by the masses.

Yet, there is also a positive side of democracy for Aristotle. Aristotle has good things to say about the deliberative capacity of assemblies and other groupings of the masses. In his *Politics*, Aristotle says that when the many come together and decide collectively they can do better than "the few good."[17] He goes on to say: "for some understand one part, and some another, and among them they understand the whole."[18] But in the same passage Aristotle warns that there "is still a danger in allowing them to share the great offices of the state, for their folly will lead them into error, and their dishonesty into crime."[19] So, the objections continue to worry him.

In addition, Aristotle says: "the multitude is not only just but likewise expedient among equals. Hence, if the governing class are numerous, many democratic institutions are useful."[20] Yet, again in the same passage, Aristotle says that ordinary people cannot "discern the beginning of evil, but only the true statesman" can.[21] Here Aristotle is probably worried about demagogues, who are clearly not true statesmen. Demagogues exploit the fact that the masses cannot tell what is evil and what is good. So, the worry about direct democracy continues to dominate Aristotle's thinking.

[17] Aristotle, *Politics* 1281b2, p. 1190.
[18] Ibid., 1281b9, p. 1190.
[19] Ibid., 1281b26, pp. 1190–1191.
[20] Ibid., 1308a12, p. 1247.
[21] Ibid., 1308a33, p. 1247.

And his preferred form of government, what Aristotle calls polity, has many of the features of democracy that we would think democracy today has. The lot is regarded as a peculiarly ineffective method of deciding who should hold office. Notice though, that voting, which we today think is characteristic of democracies, is assigned to the oligarchic form of government, and then comes back into one of the preferred forms of government when polity takes the best of oligarchy and democracy. So the kind of democracy Aristotle is opposed to is somewhat peculiar to ancient Greece.

Aristotle also says that he differs from Plato in that he does not regard democracy as the worst of governments. Indeed, Aristotle says that democracy, except in its extreme form, is a "good enough constitution." And Aristotle tells us that various forms of democracy, or ways of ruling democratically, serve the good function of curbing the excesses of other forms of government. And it seems that "ruling democratically" is valued by Aristotle in all forms of government or Constitution. But it is unclear what "ruling democratically" means. It does not seem to be the casting of lots. Perhaps it is the group decision process – deciding collectively – that Aristotle values.

15.5 TRIAL PROCEDURES IN ANCIENT LEGAL THOUGHT

There is a sense that the two models of ancient trials, the Athenian and the Chinese, parallel the two most important forms of legal trial today, the Anglo-American accusatory system and the Continental European inquisitorial system. In this final section we will explore these parallels and also say how these different models are rooted in different understandings of jurisprudence as well. In this final section we will also ask the question what the form of trial procedure has to do, if anything, with the form of government of the state where trials occur.

John Langbein provides us with a good place to start when he summarizes some of the elements of the Anglo-American trial today and what makes it distinctive.

> The striking peculiarity of the Anglo-American trial is that we remit to the lawyer-partisans the responsibility for gathering, selecting, presenting, and probing the evidence. Our trial court, traditionally a jury sitting under the supervision of the judge, conducts no investigation of its own. The court renders a verdict of guilt or innocence by picking between and among the evidence that the contesting lawyers have presented to it. In the European systems, by contrast, evidence is gathered by the judge or judge-like investigators, public officers who operate under a duty to seek the truth. Criminal investigation is understood to be a public rather than a private function. At trial, the presiding judge examines the witnesses.[22]

[22] John Langbein, *The Origins of the Adversary Criminal Trial*, Oxford: Oxford University Press, 2003, p. 1.

In both the adversarial and inquisitorial systems of today, lawyers play various roles, with the adversarial system granting to lawyers a much larger role than the inquisitorial. Lawyers did not play a role in either the ancient Athenian or Chinese legal trials, but there are other similarities that we will explore in what follows.

One thing to note is that the ancient Athenians did not have a judge or a jury conduct investigations – rather it was assumed that the respective parties would do the initial investigation of the facts and bring relevant matters to the attention of the jurors. In this sense the ancient Athenian model was similar to that of the contemporary adversarial method. In ancient China the judge and his underlings did the investigating, as we saw from the record of the Ch'in model rules.

As far as we can tell, there were no professional lawyers in either ancient Athens or China. So, there is already a major difference between ancient times and now. But the task of doing the investigation, in both fact and law, was assigned to different parties – the disputants had that role in Athenian trials while the judge had the role in ancient China. In addition, there were juries in Athens but not in China, although the Athenian juries were so large that they did not initially resemble the 12 or 9 person juries of today. While some inquisitorial systems have juries, this is not the rule, whereas there are normally juries in criminal cases in the Anglo-American adversarial system.

It is not apparent that having juries present is better than not, just as it is not apparent that having judges investigate is better than having investigation done by the disputing parties. Both systems have plusses and minuses. What interests me are other issues: the interesting origins of the two contemporary systems and how if at all the types of government might have influenced the types of trial.

It is sometimes argued that there is a close connection between the Athenian people's assembly and the people's trial court. In a number of respects it is hard to deny this connection. In both cases there were large numbers of citizens who were participating, but their participation was relatively small – witnessing what was said, not deliberating, and then casting votes in favor or against a given proposed edict or judgment. Conceptually, it also appears that the democratic idea – that the people should rule not a king or a small group of elites – also supports the idea that the people should decide the verdicts at trial rather than a judge or group of elites.

The ancient Athenians were certainly exploring the idea of what it might mean for the people to have the political power. From Solon to Cleisthenes the various rulers explored bestowing more power with the people and with expanding who counts as the people. Aristotle is famous for suggesting that the decision to move from a land army to a sea fleet created the situation where Athens then had to bestow rights on the rowers of the triremes and other vessels who were drawn from the lowest strata of the society. But there was probably more than just this set of events. Josiah Ober suggests that there was a true revolutionary moment where the mass of the people united and were able to act without the benefit of an elite leader.[23] Perhaps ancient China lacked this revolutionary moment, or perhaps China lacked an especially sympathetic democratic ruler like Solon or Cleisthenes. One can speculate about such matters and not reach a determinative conclusion. I certainly do not have a view here that I feel comfortable arguing for.

What is more significant for our purposes is to ascertain why ancient Greece developed the popular jury and ancient China did not, at the end of the period before the Common Era. Is it that the revolutionary spirit in Athenian politics then swept into the legal domain as well? One proposal is that the Greek idea of *nomos* as an order that people impose on themselves rather than the older notion of law, *thesmos*, as an order issued from the authority of an agent to the people who were under him, set the stage for the democratization of both politics and law.[24] It is difficult to adjudicate whether it is more plausible to say that there was a revolutionary moment and then the idea of democracy or that there was the idea of democracy and then democratic institution building. Probably it was a bit of both. Politics and law are certainly close enough that once the idea of democracy inspired change in one domain it could similarly affect another domain.

We have been proceeding with the idea that it is somehow a mark of progress that Athens developed democratically and China did not. But in the legal domain, as opposed to the political, it is less clear why this is an advance. As we saw from Aristotle's criticisms of democracy in the assembly, there were serious problems in institutionalizing democracy in ancient Greece. Like assemblies, juries, especially large ones, were open to manipulation in a host of ways that could work to the detriment of justice. Today in Europe, many societies that are democratic politically have not adopted jury trials. And some of the reasons for opposing juries today mirror Aristotle's reasons to oppose pure democracy in the Athenian Assembly. But the point is that we should not be too quick to dismiss the lack of jury trials in ancient China without also dismissing the lack of jury trials in Europe as well as in international law today.

Pure or direct democracy has various problems when applied to the legal or political domains. One important worry is that those who are the best speakers will have undue sway on the rest. This problem is made worse when one side in a trial has more resources at its disposal than the other – income differentials are not eliminated

23 See Josiah Ober, "'I besieged that Man': Democracy's Revolutionary Start," in *Origins of Democracy in Ancient Greece*, edited by Kurt A. Raaflaub, Josiah Ober, and Robert W. Wallace, Berkeley: University of California Press, 2007, pp. 83–104.

24 See Martin Ostwald, *Nomos and the Beginnings of the Athenian Democracy*, Oxford: Oxford University Press, 1969, p. 55.

by democratic procedures. And in trials, we may find that the pursuit of justice is blocked by the parties who act primarily for their own gain and advantage.[25] Many of the problems identified by Aristotle and others concerning the system of direct democracy in the assembly turn out, in a slightly different form, to be problems with the system of trial by jury and we are beginning to see how this may also be true today.

25 John Langbein details these problems concerning the adversarial as opposed to the inquisitorial model in his book *The Origins of the Adversary Criminal Trial*, Oxford: Oxford University Press, 2003.

SECTION VI

Legal Status

16

Citizens and Aliens

In all legal systems, even those that are radically democratic, the administration of the law is differentiated by social status. In ancient Athens, even though all citizens are seemingly treated the same, this is only true of male citizens. And those who are not citizens, including slaves but also those who have been freed from slavery as well as resident aliens (*metics*), are treated very differently from male citizens at law as well as in politics. In a non-democratic society such as ancient China, punishments and penalties were differentiated based on a person's social status, with commoners generally treated much more harshly than members of the various elite groups including officials and those who had been granted various honorary statuses.

In many ancient societies, including ancient Athens and China, aliens are treated worse than those who are regular members of the society who attained their status mainly as a matter of being born into it. In this chapter, I will set out some of the theoretical considerations that underlie the differences between citizens and aliens. And in the two chapters that follow the current one I will then examine the status of women and slaves respectively. I will argue that the differences between democratic Athens and non-democratic China are not as great as is commonly believed and that in significant respects ancient China is more humane.

There is a dilemma facing societies, both ancient and modern, about how to regard aliens. On the one hand, there is a reason to admit aliens and treat them as others in the society are treated at law. Aliens are not significantly different from members of one's society who have been born into that society insofar as they are all humans and have linguistic and cultural practices that are not very different from each other. Indeed, in ancient societies, aliens are often fellow Greeks in Athens and fellow Chinese in various Chinese regions accepting aliens. But on the other hand, there is also a reason to think that a society has the right to treat its own in a favorable way by comparison with those who are not. The argument is that just as parents can rightly treat their own children better than the children of strangers, so political leaders can treat their own subjects or citizens better than aliens.

In Section 16.1 we will examine how citizens and aliens are understood in ancient Chinese legal thought as a way to set a kind of normal line from ancient times. Then in Section 16.2 we look at some of the stark differences, but also many similarities, between the Chinese and Athenian ideas of citizenship. In Section 16.3 I turn explicitly to the idea of a metic, an Athenian conception of resident aliens that is relatively unique to ancient times. In Section 16.4 I look at how the idea of a metic influenced and was influenced by Athenian ideas of democracy. And in Section 16.5 I turn to how refugees and other aliens are treated today to see how they compare to the treatment of aliens in ancient times.

16.1 LAW, ALIENS, AND SOCIAL STATUS IN ANCIENT CHINA

Derk Bodde and Clarence Morris make an interesting point about democratic regimes and how Chinese law is administered:

> The concern of the Confucians was moral development of the individual man, for which reason they have been termed democratic. Yet, in their insistence that for a graded society there has to be a graded law, they were undemocratic. Throughout history the failing of democracy has been a tendency to accept a double standard: equal rights for those who are full-fledged members but discrimination or outright exploitation of those who are not.[1]

As we will see in other sections of this chapter, a similar criticism could also be made of ancient Athenian legal thought as well.

Cho-yun Hsu draws a fascinating comparison between ancient China and Athens concerning the treatment of aliens:

> the native people in these states, some of whom may have been members of old eastern states while others were probably tribal peoples, referred to in Chinese sources as Man, Rong, and Di, the barbarians, were ruled as subjects, but without membership in the state of a type that could be compared to citizenship in the Greek city-states … they were regarded as aliens probably because they held distinctive cultural identities.[2]

And Li Feng argues that these indigenous peoples were nonetheless considered alien and subject to widespread cultural prejudice.[3]

1 Derk Bodde and Clarence Morris, *Law in Imperial China*, Cambridge, MA: Harvard University Press, 1967, pp. 50–51.

2 Chu-yun Hsu, "The Spring and Autumn Period," in *The Cambridge History of Ancient China: From the Origins of Civilization to 221 BC*, edited by Michael Lowe and Edward Shaughnessy, Cambridge: Cambridge University Press, 1999, pp. 548–549.

3 Li Feng, *Early China: A Social and Cultural History*, Cambridge: Cambridge University Press, 2013, p. 180.

For most of its very long history, China had a steeply graded class structure and a legal system that differentiated along the same lines in terms of legal treatment, especially punishments and penalties. Ancient China did not have a clear sense of who or what were citizens – but this could also be said of ancient Athens often thought to be the first state to set out the rights of citizens against the state. Here is an example from China:

> Somebody leading a person who had been unpleasant in his village, to a superior, lets him go; how is he to be sentenced? He is warranted to be detained and to be put to work like the person whom he let go, pending the latter's arrest; in case he possesses aristocratic rank, he is to work in a government storeroom.[4]

Here is how aristocrats are given lesser punishments than commoners for the same offense.

It is also the case that in ancient Chinese law those of higher rank could buy their way out of certain punishments, even very severe ones, by relinquishing their honorary statuses.

> Persons who desire to return to degrees of aristocratic rank in order to liberate one person – their own father or mother – who is a bond-servant or a bond-woman, as well as bond-servants who have been made *kung shi* [the lowest aristocratic rank] for having cut off the head (of an enemy), and who request to return the rank of *kung shi* in order to liberate their wife who is a bond-woman (viz.) one person, this is to be permitted; they are liberated and made commoners.[5]

Tung-Tsu Chu comments:

> The Ch'in law held that those who qualified under the "eight conditions for consideration" were permitted to redeem themselves. They were neither to be shaved nor compelled to wear the iron collar, nor to be beaten. In addition, the giving up of an official post could cancel out a punishment of three years' imprisonment. Such also was the practice in later dynasties. In Northern Wei times nobles who held any of the five peerage titles were permitted to cancel out their punishment by giving up their title.[6]

Law was applied equally within the same status group but often very unequally between different status groups. The lowest caste group often faced very severe punishments while the upper classes could get out of punishment altogether.

It is a mark of democratic rule that citizens are treated equally and allowed to participate in legislative and judicial affairs. But democratic thinking goes deeper

4 D51 of "Answers to Questions Concerning Ch'In Statutes," in *Remnants of Ch'In Law*, translated and edited by A. F. P. Hulwese, Leiden: E. J. Brill, 1985, p. 137.

5 A91 of "Eighteen Ch'In Statutes," in *Remnants of Ch'In Law*, ibid., p. 83.

6 Tung-Tsu Ch'U, *Law and Society in Traditional China*, Paris: Mouton & Co., 1965, p. 181.

than that – it also encompasses how non-citizens are treated. As is true today, questions of how aliens are treated are especially problematic when those aliens have been strongly encouraged to leave their home countries and assimilate in a new country. In both ancient China and Greece, aliens were encouraged to come to make the states more diverse and encompassing a wide array of talents and skills. Yet, in both ancient societies the law did not create an equal status for aliens to that of citizens. As we will see, ancient Athens did create a special protected status for aliens, as metics, but aliens may only have been treated somewhat better than in ancient China which did not have such a special legal status for its aliens.

16.2 CITIZENSHIP IN ANCIENT ATHENS

Ideas about citizenship in Athenian society are often said to first emerge in the laws and poems of Solon in the seventh century BCE. Solon instituted constitutional changes in Athens dividing the society into four classes, as we learn in the *Aristotelian Constitution of Athens*. Plutarch then says that the *thetes* were not allowed "to hold any office, but they participated in the Constitution only by joining in the assembly and serving as jurors."[7]

Yet, it must be pointed out that while women could in some sense be citizens of ancient Athens, they could not participate even as the *thetes* did. We take up the legal status of women in the next chapter. Here I just wish to point out that female citizens were definitely not the equal of even the lowest of male citizens in Athens. And within the group of male citizens, the rights of citizenship were graded based largely on property ownership.

> [Solon] divided them by assessment into four classes, as they had been divided previously also: *pentakosiomedimnos*, *hippeus*, *zeugites*, and *thes*. The great offices he assigned to be held by the *pentakosiomedimnoi*, *hippeis*, and *zeugitai*: the nine archons, the treasurers, the poletai, and the kolakretai, giving each an office corresponding to the size of his assessment. To those in the thetic class he gave only a share in the assembly and law courts. A man was to belong to the class of *pentakosiomedimnoi* who from his own estate produced five hundred measures wet and dry together; to the class of *hippeis* three hundred, or as some say those able to maintain a horse … Those were to belong to the class of *zeugitai* who produced two hundred measures of the two kinds; the others to the class of *thetes*, who had no share in office holding.[8]

7 Plutarch, *Lives*, Solon 18. i-ii. Quoted and translated by Delfim F. Leao and P. J. Rhodes, *The Laws of Solon*, London: I. B. Tauris, 2015, p. 128.

8 Aristotle, *Athenian Constitution* 7. iii–iv, translated and cited in *The Laws of Solon*, ibid., p. 127.

So, in Solon's time, while the members of each class of citizens were treated equally, there was no equality of treatment among all citizen classes in ancient Athens.

It remains interesting though that in determining who should hold a given office, the Greeks used a random method, the lot. Here is an account from the *Aristotelian Constitution of Athens*: "The treasurers of Athena are ten in number, one appointed by lot from each tribe, from the *pentakosiomedimnoi*, according to the law of Solon (for the law is still in force)." By the time of Aristotle, though, the property qualifications were eliminated so that "the man to whom the lot falls holds office even if he is very poor."[9]

Another inequality in who was granted citizenship is found in Plutarch's account of another of Solon's laws:

> Problematic also is the law about men granted citizenship, because it does not give the right to become citizens except to those in permanent exile from their own land or to those who migrate to Athens with their whole household to ply a craft. They say that he [Solon] did this not so much to drive the others away as to invite those to come to Athens for a secure share of citizenship, and at the same time that he thought these would be reliable, in the one case because they had forsaken their own land out of necessity, in the other because they had left it by choice.[10]

Here we see now that attaining citizenship was restricted at the time of Solon.

By the time of Pericles, a century and a half after Solon, citizenship was curtailed in another important way. Previously a person was a citizen if his father was a citizen, but Pericles changed the rule so that in 451/0 a person was considered a citizen only if both of his parents were citizens.[11] It is not clear why this change was made, although Aristotle comments that it might have been because the group of citizens was getting too large, and probably unwieldy, for a purported direct democracy.

Another consideration is that even among those Athenians who had two parents who were citizens, the rights of citizenship were not equal for all. Age turns out to be a major obstacle to full citizenship rights in Athens. One could not become a citizen until one was 18 years of age, and in addition one could not hold most offices, including membership in juries, or in assemblies, until the age of 30. One scholar has been led to claim that because of these age requirements "every third Athenian citizen had only limited citizenship rights."[12]

9 Ibid., p. 130. Also see P. J. Rhodes, *A Commentary on the Aristotelian Athenaion Politeia*, Oxford: Oxford University Press, 1981, 1992, p. 148.

10 Plutarch, *Lives*, Solon, 24.iv, in *The Laws of Solon*, ibid., p. 133.

11 See Douglas M. MacDowell, *The Law in Classical Greece*, Ithaca, NY: Cornell University Press, 1978, p. 67.

12 Mogens Herman Hansen, *The Athenian Democracy in the Age of Demosthenes*, Oxford: Blackwell Publishers, 1991, p. 89.

It is clear that at various times, mainly in the fourth century BCE, Athens encouraged people to come to the city for purposes of trade, or to join the ranks of the rowers in the navy, by offering citizenship as an added incentive. And the effect of these additions was that many people who did not own property were brought into the democracy thereby making the citizenry less elite and much more diverse. There were also specific policies aimed at getting a more diverse group of citizens to participate in the democratic institutions, principally this was done by paying citizens to sit in the assembly, the council, or on juries. As we will next see there was one legal class of non-citizen Athenians who were rather unique in ancient times in the way they were given special rights as well as liabilities.

16.3 METICS AND ALIENS IN ATHENS

One of the most fascinating legal statuses in ancient Athens was that of a metic, a resident alien. Here is how Hansen describes the status of a metic:

> Whatever the etymology of the word *metoikos*, it was used to signify in principle a freeborn person who had left his own city and lived in another city-state without having citizen rights in that state: metics were thus the most important element amongst the general body of *xenoi*, foreigners. But in Athens not only domiciled foreigners were metics, for every foreigner had to have himself registered as a metic if he stayed in Athens even for a very short period – of days rather than months or years. It was not a privilege to be a metic but a duty; and when the Athenians wanted to do foreigners a special favor they released them from the status of metics.[13]

But not all scholars agree with Hansen. Harrison for instance says that it is clear that being a metic was a privilege: "in relation to other *xenoi* the metic enjoyed a privileged position."[14] We will investigate this status in the current section to find out why there are such divergent ideas about these metics.

There seem to be two very different groups of metics: first, those who were freeborn foreigners who settled in Athens, primarily as traders and craftsmen, and second, manumitted slaves.[15] I will mainly address the first of these categories in this section and reserve discussion of the latter category for the chapter where slavery is discussed. Metics could not own property or vote in the assemblies or on juries, yet they were obligated to pay taxes and to perform military service. This seems to be the basis of thinking that being a metic was not a privilege. But metics could trade with citizens on an equal footing, and even Hansen who makes the strongest case for thinking that metics lived under a liability rather than a privilege acknowledges

13 Ibid., pp. 116–117.

14 A. R. W. Harrison, *The Law of Athens*, Oxford: Oxford University Press, 1968, Vol. 1, p. 189.

15 See Hansen, *The Athenian Democracy in the Age of Demosthenes*, p. 119.

that: "In spite of the disadvantages of metic status, foreigners streamed into Athens from all parts of Greece, and the reason no doubt is that citizen and metic were on equal footing as traders and artisans in the largest city in Greece."[16]

Xenophon describes why it was important for Athens to pursue metics by encouraging them to come.

> In metics, we have one of the very best sources of revenue ... inasmuch as they are all self-supporting and, so far from receiving payment for the many services they render to states, they contribute by paying the *metoikion*. I think we should study their interests sufficiently, if we relieved them of the duties that seem to impose a certain measure of disability on the metic without conferring any benefit on the state, and also of the obligation to serve in the infantry along with the citizens ... The state itself too would gain if the citizens served in the ranks together, and no longer found themselves in the same company with Lydians, Phrygians, Syrians, and barbarians of all sorts, of whom a large part of our metics consists ... Then again there are many vacant sites for houses within the walls; if the state approved applicants to erect houses on these and granted them the freehold of the land, I think we should find a larger and better class of persons desiring to live in Athens. And if we appointed guardians of metics, like the guardians of orphans and some kind of distinction were earmarked for guardians whose list of resident aliens was the longest, that too would add to the loyalty of the metics, and probably all without the city would covet the right of settling in Athens, and would increase our revenues.[17]

In the middle of the fourth century BCE, the legal vulnerabilities of the metics was well known and there was a strong motivation to relieve the metics of some of these liabilities to make it more attractive for metics to increase their contributions to Athenian life.

I would note three additional features of being a metic that could nonetheless support the view that being a metic was not a privilege. First, in addition to paying taxes like citizens, the metic had to pay a special fee in order to trade in the *agora* – the Athenian market. Second, metics generally were not allowed to use the normal courts; even as defendants they had to be tried in a special non-citizen court, the court of the polemarch who sat in the Palladion. Third, metics had to have a patron who had various ways of making sure that the metic remained a deserving person.

I would single out the second of these liabilities of the metic that could be quite significant in the metic's day-to-day life. Since Athenians were apparently very litigious, at least from the written record that has come down to us, not being able to participate in the normal Athenian courts could have been a major social and legal

[16] Ibid., p. 119.

[17] Xenophon, *Poroi*, 2.1–7, translated in Elizabeth Meyer, *Metics and the Athenian Phialai-Inscriptions*, Stutgart: Franz Steiner Verlag, 2010, pp. 48–49.

hardship. Yet, it is also true that the metic, like a child, could appear in a normal court if he were represented by a citizen, often the metic's patron or sponsor. And similarly metics could be represented in various other aspects of democratic life in ancient Athens. Indeed it now is clear that metics could prosecute cases before the polemarch even if they were not represented by a patron. We must note that this was not true of cases before the normal courts that Athenian citizens could avail themselves of. As Meyer has argued:

> our view of metics' legal capacities and activities has changed considerably. It has become clear that metics can prosecute and defend without *prostatain* stepping in for them … that they can farm taxes for the Athenian polis, and that they can prosecute in *graphai*.[18]

Meyer bases this claim on her own analysis of court records from the middle of the fourth century BCE.

Metics could attain a life in Athens that was very much honored. Perhaps the best known of the metics in Athens was Aristotle. He was born in the city-state of Stagira, Macedonia and indeed was the tutor of the young Alexander the Great from Macedonia who conquered the Athenians and most of the rest of the known world. But it is as an Athenian philosopher that Aristotle is best known – for he was educated at Plato's Academy in Athens and after Plato's death Aristotle set up his own school, the Lyceum, also in Athens even though he was not an Athenian citizen but only a metic. If one were to think of Aristotle's life, one would be hard pressed to see how he was disadvantaged by being a metic rather than a citizen of Athens.

Yet, the desire to be a citizen – to be on equal footing with citizens of Athens in terms of their democratic participation – seems to have been strong. Metics petitioned to be granted citizenship through the Athenian naturalization process. In part this was so they could become property owners and also avoid the extra taxes that the metic had to pay. But it also seems that the metic understood that he was only half-way between a citizen and a slave. Indeed, freed slaves were given the same legal status as metics.

Despite all of these problems with the status of the metic, it is nonetheless true that the metic had a legally protected status in ancient Athens and this was relatively unique for aliens in ancient times, as well as in our own times. Because resident aliens, metics, had their own legal status with its own rights and liabilities, the metic knew his place in that society and was secure enough to be able to lead a relatively normal life as a trader or artisan in a society that was a very prosperous and desirable place to settle. The metic was not a shadowy character as resident aliens were in other ancient societies – the metic could not be expelled without very good

18 Meyer, *Metics and the Athenian Phialai-Inscriptions*, pp. 72–73.

reasons and this was written into the laws of Athens. So, while the metic was not a citizen and could not own property or participate in the political process, being a tradesman, or a philosopher for that matter, was open to the metic and many came to Athens for these opportunities.

16.4 METICS AND GREEK DEMOCRACY

It is my view that even as the Athenian democracy was one of the most direct and radical in all time there was also a deliberate effort to keep the democratic institutions from being overtaken by people who did not share the cultural history of the Athenians that had set the stage for their deeply democratic society. Metics were treated as fellow Greek citizens in so many ways, yet they were not allowed to participate in the central political and legal institutions of Athens, especially the Boule (the council), the ekklesia (the assembly), and the various courts, except for the court run by the polemarch. Indeed, it was a very serious matter, a crime subject to stiff penalties, for a metic to pretend to be a citizen so as to participate in these institutions. Some have seen this as a contradiction in the Greek democratic spirit. In this section I will explain why I think it made sense to exclude metics from political participation, according to the perspective of the Athenians.

Even with the reforms of the late fourth century BCE described by Xenophon, metics did not get to participate in the main political institutions in Athens. This was also true of women and slaves and generally everyone under 30 for most of these institutions. As there were increasing opportunities for becoming a naturalized citizen, there was still a strong sentiment of exclusion even in this most democratic of states.

The idea of democracy was not just something the Athenians fell into, but it seems to be very consciously adopted by Athenians, as Thucydides declares in the funeral oration he attributes to Pericles:

> We live under a form of government which does not emulate the institutions of our neighbors; on the contrary, we are ourselves a model which some follow, rather than the imitators of other peoples. It is true that our government is called a democracy, because its administration is in the hands, not of the few, but of the many; yet while as regards the law all men are on an equality for the settlement of their private disputes, as regards the value set on them, it is as each man is in any way distinguished that he is preferred to public honors, not only because he belongs to a particular class, but because of personal merits; nor again on the ground of poverty is man barred from a public career by obscurity of rank if he but has it in him to do the state a service. And not only in our public life are we liberal, but also as regards our freedom from suspicion of one another in the pursuits of everyday life; for we do not feel resentment at our neighbor if he does as he likes, nor yet do we

> put on sour looks which though harmless, are painful to behold. But while we thus avoid giving offence in our private intercourse, in our public life we are restrained from lawlessness, chiefly through reverent fear, for we render obedience to those in authority and to the laws, and especially to those laws which are ordained for succor of the oppressed and those which, though unwritten, bring upon the transgressor a disgrace which all men recognize.[19]

This could have been an account of the very best of modern democracies as well.

Yet we should note that even in the words that Thucydides puts into the mouth of Pericles, it is a government "of the many," not necessarily "of all." In Aristotle's account, democracy is described as the rule of all, as opposed to the rule of one or the rule of some. But Aristotle is frankly critical of that way of characterizing the goal of democracy. Indeed, Aristotle is most critical of governments that strive for full equality.[20] Yet Aristotle forthrightly says that the true spirit of democracy is absolute equality: "for they suppose that because they are all alike free they are equal absolutely."[21]

Athenian democracy of the fourth century BCE was based in equality of participation in law and government but only for all citizens, or only for all male citizens. And the idea is that citizens are mainly those who have been born in Athens where the customs of democracy were taught early on. The Greek term *paideia* is perhaps the key to understanding why Athenian democracy was restricted to those who had been born as Athenians. Here is Werner Jaeger on the idea of *paideia* for the Greeks:

> To begin with, education is not a practice which concerns the individual alone: it is essentially a function of the community. The character of the community is expressed in the individuals who compose it; and for man the *zoon politicon*, far more than for any animal species, the community is the source of all behavior. The formative influence of the community on its members is most constantly active in its deliberative endeavor to educate each new generation of individuals, so as to make them in its own image.[22]

Athenians expected that their democracy would work when the citizens had already been acculturated into a certain way of thinking of themselves and their relations to their fellow citizens. Those who had not been so educated into Athenian culture, from a young age, were not trusted to participate in the institutions of the democracy.

[19] Thucydides, *History of the Peloponnesian War*, Book II, Chapter 37, 1–3, translated by Charles Forster Smith, Loeb Library, Cambridge, MA: Harvard University Press, 1919, Vol. 1, pp. 323–325.

[20] Aristotle, *Politics*, Book V, Chapter 1, 6–7, 1301b25–35, translated by H. Rackham, Loeb Library, Cambridge, MA: Harvard University Press, 1932, p. 375.

[21] Ibid., 1301a33, p. 371.

[22] Werner Jaeger, *Paideia: The Ideals of Greek Culture*, translated by Gilbert Highet, Oxford: Oxford University Press, 1945, Vol. I, pp. xiii–xiv.

Yet, the Athenians in the 5th and 4th centuries BCE also knew that their own citizens had often been born on the land and best understood farming rather than trading. And the Athenian land was not especially rich in those things needed for a diverse and self-sustaining economy. So, there was a strong incentive to open the borders for foreigners who could provide what Athens naturally lacked. And some incentives had to be found to entice these foreigners to Athens rather than to some other state.

The resident alien status of metic is devised to offer much that was advantageous about a robust city life to attract foreigners without risking that democratic institutions would be undermined by those that would not understand the value of those institutions. Xenophon is surely right that some metics resented their second-class status, but over time various things were changed to placate the metics, yet without giving them full citizenship unless they were thought to be especially deserving of this honor based on having performed an especially important service to Athens. As the democracy waned, so did the distinction between citizen and metic until eventually at the end of the fourth century BCE the Athenian Constitution was changed and the experiment with radical democracy, and also the idea of the metic, came to an end.

16.5 LEARNING FROM THE ATHENIAN METICS

Today in American and European democracies, there are various attempts to limit who can participate in the political institutions – indeed there is an effort to greatly diminish the number of refugees and migrants coming into these democracies especially from societies that are not democratic. There is a serious conflict between the expression of support especially for refugees who are fleeing civil war and other oppressive conditions and the desire not to dilute the pool of a population that from birth learned to do what was necessary to support democratic institutions.

Lycurgus provides us with an extreme version of the worries that beset Athenians about the fate of their state due to the new citizens.

> When many terrible things were happening against the city, and all the citizens had suffered the greatest misfortunes, one would have especially grieved and shed tears at the misfortunes of the city upon seeing the demos decreeing that slaves become free, that foreigners become Athenians, and that the disenfranchised become enfranchised – a demos that previously boasted of being autochthonous and free.[23]

[23] Lycurgus, I. 41–42, translated and cited in Deborah Kamen, *Status in Classical Athens*, Princeton: Princeton University Press, 2013, p. 111.

The ideology, and perhaps also the myth, that all Athenians descended from the original inhabitants, was very strong. Nonetheless, it is also clear that various classes in Athens who were not full citizens had participated in the affairs of Athens long before Lycurgus had sounded the alarm in 330 BCE.

In one respect, the worry about allowing people into democratic institutions who were not raised to appreciate those institutions can be made more vivid by considering the contemporary case of Algeria. Free elections were held in 1991 CE with all people participating, even those people who strongly supported a version of Islam that opposed democracy, the Islamic Salvation Front. The result was the election of enough members of this Islamic group so that there were now two-thirds of the members of parliament who would support the formation of an Islamic state that was non-democratic. The military staged a coup to save the democracy from the people and a civil war ensued. This case is often mentioned as an example of why democratic states are not in favor of extending the franchise to those with no history of support for democratic institutions.

What the Athenian ideas of democracy and metics might tell us is that it is indeed an important worry to bring people into participation in democratic institutions when those people have not been acculturated into the ideals of those institutions. But the Athenian experience also speaks to how it may be possible to allow foreigners into these institutions after they have received such acculturation. *Paideia* is achieved through time and habituation, but foreigners can attain it, or so at least some of the Greeks thought.

Athens, like various democratic states today, faced a dilemma, which is well articulated by Deborah Kamen:

> Athens, then, was faced with competing motivations, which were in tension but nonetheless coexisted. On the one hand, there was a desire to preserve an ideology of rigidly defined statuses; on the other hand, the city wanted to get the most out of its diverse lot of inhabitants, without necessarily setting up a ladder of incremental steps by which one could rise (or sink) in status. Rather than canceling each other out, however, these two apparently contradictory desires were both satisfied.[24]

Metics in Athens did not have an official "path to citizenship" but there were nonetheless exceptional circumstances that warranted giving metics just that citizenship.

Today there is a similar set of contradictory goals concerning refugees, immigrants, and other resident aliens. Many agricultural businesses rely on immigrant labor, even illegal immigrants. The job of picking fruit and vegetables is one that few citizens are interested in, especially at the low pay that is offered by these agribusinesses. And it is also undeniable that some immigrants have provided a very rich culture

[24] Ibid., p. 115.

especially in the United States, which truly is the land of immigrants. Yet, there is also anxiety about defending the democratic ideology from those foreigners who come without an appreciation of or background beliefs in democracy.

The Athenian experience with metics seems to indicate that these two seemingly conflicting strains can be at least partially reconciled. One part of the Athenian response to this problem is the creation of a specific protected legal status, the metic, that combines rights and duties for the resident alien. The United States has something partially like such a legal status but it is not well recognized and these American metics have not been well integrated into the larger culture. Indeed, if anything there is growing skepticism about foreigners coming into our society from especially Islamic countries that have no history of democratic participation.

Having a patron or sponsor is not part of the American or European tradition concerning aliens. While this practice could be ripe for abuse, as was sometimes true in ancient Athens, the idea of having some citizen take a special interest in helping each alien to integrate into the society seems worth serious consideration. Yet, even then resident aliens today are likely to face some of the same problems as those metics of ancient times unless their sporadic contributions to the life of the society are not merely recognized but extolled and there is a serious attempt to inculcate the democratic principles into the worldview of these aliens.

17

Women

There are conflicting accounts of women's role in ancient Greece, especially in Athens in the 5th and 4th centuries BCE. Some scholars put great weight on what Demosthenes and Xenophon say about women. They claimed that women were consigned to the periphery of life in Athens, by being sequestered in their homes and legally unable to participate in the great democratic institutions of Athens: the assembly, the council, and the courts. But other scholars look to the many strong images of women in Greek literature: Antigone, Clytemnestra, Electra, Medea, Lysistrata, and many others, as well as the strong Greek goddesses of Homer and other poets: Athena, Artemis, Hestia, Hera, and Aphrodite. I will argue that these two images of women sit uncomfortably with each other, especially concerning marriage.

On the first account we find an image of women as unable to own property, participate in politics or war, and consigned to the house unless they are either veiled or accompanied by a male or both. Women cannot pursue legal affairs except by being represented by a male or by presenting a statement under oath which is read at court by someone else and only if both disputing parties agree to allow the statement into evidence. On the second account women were strong leaders who attempted to stop wars, or to get their favored candidate elected into desirable posts. Women are often violent and feared by their husbands. They are seen as sexually "wild" and unrestrained in their ability to choose male or female lovers as they wish. How can these two images of women in ancient Athens be reconciled? Or is it possible that both accounts are true despite appearing to conflict? It is the task of this chapter to attempt an answer to this question which scholars such as David Cohen have posed so well.[1]

1 David Cohen, *Law, Sexuality, and Society: The Enforcement of Morals in Classical Athens*, Cambridge: Cambridge University Press, 1991.

17.1 WOMEN AND CITIZENSHIP IN ANCIENT ATHENS

It is striking how difficult it is to answer the seemingly simple question of whether or not women were citizens in ancient Athens. Sue Blundell explains some of the problems in understanding women's political status in Athens when she says:

> Athenian women were not considered to be *politai* – a word which is normally translated as "citizens," but which specifically signifies citizens with full political rights, who were always male. Instead, the word *astai* was applied to women, and this can be taken as referring to their possession of civil rights. We are often forced, for lack of a corresponding term in our own language, to translate *astai* as "citizens"; but it must be borne in mind that for Athenian women "citizenship" meant only that they had a share in the religious, legal, and economic order of the Athenian community.[2]

When women were married to male citizens they were sometimes treated as somewhat similar to a male citizen, but they never were able to cast votes. Of course this was true of most every society until the twentieth century CE.

What is crucial for us is to figure out what were the civil rights that women had and to what extent these rights allowed women to participate in the legal system even if they could not vote on juries or in the assembly. And here one of the most significant questions, also much debated, is whether women could appear in courts as either plaintiffs or defendants. If Athenian women did have this civil right then there is a strong sense that they were able to participate in one of the most significant Athenian public institutions and hence to be "citizens" of a sort. In what follows I will treat citizenship as a bundle of rights, not a single right, as a way to make sense of why free Athenian women were talked about as *astai*, as having a kind of status in the Athenian society that was like being a citizen – but not as having all of the rights in the bundle of full citizenship. And such a view might also help explain why strong women characters appeared so often in Greek literature.

It is undisputed that women could "appear" in court in two ways: first, as represented by a male guardian or representative, and second, by submitting a statement for which she swore an oath. What is in dispute is whether there was a third avenue open to women as well to personally appear in the courts. But the two uncontroversial ways are already indicative of rights that women had in ancient Athenian legal systems that could be seen as part of the bundle of the rights of citizenship.

Those who could be full citizens changed over time in ancient Athens, and there remained considerable variation of what was required for this full citizenship. There were even for free males qualifications in terms of property ownership.

[2] Sue Blundell, *Women in Ancient Greece*, Cambridge, MA: Harvard University Press, 1995, p. 128.

And as we have seen in an earlier chapter, metics were given various ways to attain citizenship which changed over time as well. So, it would not be surprising if the civil rights of women changed over time as well so that at some times women were granted a status closer to full citizenship and at other times farther way from full citizenship.

It is also interesting that women's status in marriage and as defendants accused of adultery seemed at times to be better than the status of their male partners. Such considerations lead to the question of how the political and legal status of women in Athens was related to the social status of these women. In literature, women were often portrayed as socially equal partners to their male mates. The playwright Aristophanes and the orator Demosthenes provide evidence of the wide social roles of women in Athenian society, as Cohen illustrates:

> Athenian women participated in a wide range of activities which regularly took them out of their houses. These included working the fields (Aristophanes, *Peace* 535; Demosthenes 57.45), or as vendors, midwives, innkeepers, or bakers (Demosthenes, 57.30–1, 34; Aristophanes, *Acharnians* 478, *Wasps* 497, 1380–92, *Frogs* 1346, *Lysistrata* 445, 456ff., *Thesmophoriazusae* 346ff., 447ff.). In an oration of Demosthenes a man testifies that his mother worked as a nurse, and then goes on to say that many Athenian women do the same, or work in the vineyards or at the loom (57.35, 45; see also Plato, *Theaetetus* 149). Finally, a woman in Aristophanes' *Thesmophoriazusae* (445) works to support her five children.[3]

As Cohen and others have pointed out, Athenian women in the middle class or poor women could simply not afford to be secluded in the home and had to participate actively in the economy in order to survive. Cohen argues: "Aristotle makes the same point with considerable force in the *Politics*, when he says that in a democracy it is impossible to prevent women of the poor from going to work (1300a4–9). Athenian law, moreover, made it a delict to rebuke any citizen, male *or female*, from selling in the marketplace (Demosthenes 57.30–1)."[4] Men and women did not freely mix socially, but there was significant freedom within the separate spheres, as many vase paintings make abundantly clear.

17.2 MARRIAGE AND ADULTERY LAWS IN ANCIENT GREECE

Early written laws in Crete, which may predate written laws in Athens, give us a picture of how women were regarded in ancient legal thought in Greece. Here is a part of the Gortyn Code:

[3] David Cohen, *Law, Sexuality, and Society*, pp. 150–151.

[4] Ibid., p. 151.

> If anyone is caught committing adultery with a free woman in the house of her father or her brother or her husband, he shall pay a hundred staters; and if anywhere else, fifty staters; whoever commits adultery with the wife of an *apetairos* (alien), he shall pay ten staters; and if a slave commits adultery with a free woman, he shall pay double this amount …[5]

As Ilias Arnaoutoglou points out, there were no legal consequences for the adulterous woman. And while social sanctions undoubtedly applied, it is significant that only the adulterous man was penalized in early Cretan law.

In ancient Athens, while there is a penalty for the adulterous woman, the likely penalty for the adulterous man seems to have been greater. Here is part of a speech by Demosthenes:

> And he who catches the adulterer, shall not be allowed to continue living with his wife; if he does, he shall be deprived of his civic rights. And the woman who committed adultery shall not be allowed to attend public sacrifices; if she does, she may suffer any penalty, except death, with impunity.[6]

The husband is entitled to kill the adulterous man if he catches him, but can only divorce his wife.

As early as Draco's code in Athens, a husband could kill an adulterer if he was caught in the act of having sex with his wife.[7] And a similar law is attributed to Solon as well: "In fact he gave to the captor [the right] to kill the adulterer caught [in the act]."[8] Of course, that the husband got to choose what to do with the adulterer seems to indicate that the offense of adultery was seen as an offense against the husband. This is at least partially supported by the fact that Solon's laws made an exception to the rule about killing the adulterer if the woman was a professional prostitute or was seized in a brothel: "In addition to this he presented the law that does not allow taking as an adulterer the man who has affairs with women who sit in a brothel or promenade manifestly …"[9]

We can infer from the various laws on adultery in ancient Athens that adultery was an affront to marriage, and specifically an affront to the male marriage partner. Marriage is to be preserved in various ways, protected from outside influence, by

5 *Ancient Greek Laws: A Sourcebook*, edited by Ilias Arnaoutoglou, NY: Routledge, 1998, p. 23.
6 Ibid., pp. 22–23.
7 See A. R. W. Harrison, *The Law of Athens, Vol. 1: The Family and Property*, Oxford: Oxford University Press, 1968, pp. 32–33.
8 *The Laws of Solon*, translated and edited by Delfim F. Leao and P. J. Rhodes, London: I. B. Tauris, Fr. 28a: Plut. Sol. 23 1, p. 42.
9 Ibid., Fr. 29a: [Dem.] LIX. Against Neaera 67, p. 44.

such laws concerning the penalization of the adulterer. Yet, it also remained true that, short of killing, the husband could penalize his wife chiefly by divorcing her.

The idea that a wife is a sexual possession is seen in Xenophon and Demosthenes. The most telling of Xenophon's comments is that women should be educated "in order that she might see and hear as little as possible, and ask the fewest questions."[10] And we learn from Demosthenes about how men should regard women in the following short and pithy statement: "We have courtesans (*hetaerae*) for pleasure, concubines to take care of our day-to-day bodily needs, and wives to bear us legitimate children, and to be the loyal guardians of our households."[11]

Yet, some Greek writers spoke of love among married couples. Even Xenophon talks at one point of the sexual division of labor in his account of the best way for the home to be run. And as we will see there are very interesting changes over time in how the Greeks viewed the acts necessary for the formation of a proper legal marriage where women had fairly important protections. So, even with the claims by Aristophanes and others that women's place in marriage was to be relatively silent in the home, the law recognized the role that money brought into the home would help establish the wife on a strong, even if not equal, footing with her husband.

There is a very curious change in ancient Greek customs concerning the formation of a marriage. The earliest sources speak of a bride-price that the prospective groom must pay to the father of the bride. But by the time of the Odyssey we find a change in that it is the bride's father who provides a dowry that his daughter brings to the groom. It is worth speculating what such a change might tell us about how women were valued in marriage – and it seems to me there are reasons to think that things might be better with the dowry rather than the bride-price despite initial appearances.

It might be thought that if the groom must pay a price in order to entice the father of the bride to part with his daughter, this would show that having the woman enter into the household of the groom is thought to be highly valuable. It could be simply that the groom buys the woman from her father. But the relationship seems to be different from this as J. W. Jones has argued. Marriage was not a simple monetary transaction. Instead, the bride-price seems to signify that there is something needed to compensate the father for the loss of his daughter and that the groom finds the addition of the woman into his household to be of such value that he will part with something valuable to be given to the father of the bride.

If this is right, then over time when the bride-price is eliminated in favor of a dowry-like system, it would seem that the father now wants to be rid of his daughter enough so that he pays the groom to take her off his hands. This change would

[10] Xenophon, *Oeconomicus*, 7.5, quoted in Blundell, *Women in Ancient Greece*, p. 133.

[11] Demosthenes, 59.122, cited and translated by Blundell, *Women in Ancient Greece*, pp. 121–122.

seem to signify a loss of value on the part of the woman. Before considering a very different interpretation, we could think of the bride-price and dowry as similar in that they act as assurance that the parties will not cavalierly back out of the marriage arrangement. For the case of the bride-price, the groom will not wish to dissolve the marriage in favor of a new wife if he realizes that he will have to pay a new bride-price. In the case of the dowry, the father will not undermine the marriage in favor of another suitor because the father will then have to pay a second dowry. Both systems have the effect of assuring the stability of the marriage.

But there is yet another way of thinking of the difference between bride-price and dowry payment, namely in terms of protection of the woman. The dowry protects the wife because it is really her money that is brought into the marriage and the money stays with her in case the marriage is dissolved.[12] The husband would thus lose considerably if he were to divorce his wife – dissuading him from dissolving the marriage for trivial considerations even though divorce itself was easily obtained in ancient Greece. Indeed, there is much more disincentive to dissolution of the marriage when there is a dowry than where there is bride-price. Once the bride-price is paid, there is actually sometimes an incentive to dissolve the marriage with the hopes of getting the bride-price back.

More importantly, the dowry, which is really attached to the wife not bestowed on the husband, gives leverage to the wife in that if she is abused she can walk away from the marriage with her dowry available for another marriage if she decides to remarry. Indeed, the dowry gives the woman not only protection from abuse but also a bit of independence from her husband.

Another change in Greek law in the democratic regimes in Athens concerned the qualifications for citizenship. The change was that in prior times one only needed one parent to be a citizen for the child eventually to claim citizenship, but after the change one needed to have both parents who were citizens. There are several important things here that affected the status of women in Athens. First, since both parents had to be citizens, then there was increased status for women in that a male citizen could not produce a potential citizen offspring without mating with a female citizen – children produced with concubines and prostitutes could not become citizens. Of course, this did not do much for the status of women who were concubines and prostitutes. But for married women who were citizens their status was now more secure since the only path to citizenship of the next generation depended on these women.

The other thing that is rarely mentioned is that a question raised earlier is now partially answered. Women were citizens on equal footing with men in this very

[12] See J. W. Jones, *The Law and Legal Theory of the Greeks,* Chapter IX, Oxford: Oxford University Press, 1956.

important respect: both were necessary and neither was sufficient for the perpetuation of citizenship into the next generation. Men had a greater number of citizenship's rights and privileges than women, but here in terms of perpetuating the next generation of citizens women were treated as citizens equal to men.

17.3 THE STATUS OF WOMEN IN PLATO'S *LAWS*

Famously, Plato often talked as if he were a modern-day feminist. In the *Republic*, Plato said that women could attain the highest political office, the Guardians, and could attain any political offices of lower order as well. And in Plato's *Laws* we have a passage often cited for the equality of women:

> my law would say all the very same things about females that it says about males, including that females should be trained on an equal basis … I assert that if it is possible for these things to turn out this way, then the way they're now arranged in our lands – where it's not the case that all the men with their entire strength, and united in spirit, practice the same things as the women – is the most mindless of all. For this way, almost every city is just about half of what it might be, when with the same expenditures and efforts it could double itself. And this would be an amazing mistake on the part of the lawgiver.[13]

Plato recognized that failing to treat women equally to men means that the potential contributions of one half of the population are neglected. Here there is a strong appeal to prudence intertwined with the beginning of a moral argument. The moral argument turns on the claim that women are equally capable of attaining virtue as well as doing the work of men.

The point of the laws, for Plato, is to educate the citizenry to be virtuous and productive. If men and women are capable of achieving virtue and being productive then the lawmaker would be remiss if the laws aimed only to educate men and not also women. Plato makes this point when he says: "In brief, this was the substance of the agreement: on whatever way a member of the community, whether his nature be male or female, young or old, might ever become a good man, possessing the virtue of a soul that befits a human being."[14] Both men and women have human souls that admit of education to become virtuous, and the community should do what it can to promote this virtue.

In the *Laws*, Plato's last work, there are certainly disparities in treatment based on gender but these are said by Plato primarily to track the physical differences between the sexes. Men can enter political office ten years earlier than women to make up for the fact that women of child-bearing age should concentrate on

[13] Plato, *The Laws*, 804d-805b, translated by Thomas L. Pangle, NY: Basic Books, 1980, pp. 194–195.

[14] Ibid., 770c-770d, p. 158.

that important part of the life of the community and only enter politics after they are no longer bearing and raising children.[15] This difference has practical effects and is also symbolic. Symbolically, women are told that they are the child-raisers as well as the child-bearers, while men are told that they need not interrupt their lives to take care of their children. Practically, women have 10 years' less time to participate in the most important institutions. In both of these ways the equality of men and women is seriously undermined. This was a departure from the position Plato took in the *Republic* where the woman who bore the child was not the same one who had to raise it. In addition, in the *Republic* Plato is clear that the biological differences between men and women should not affect their role in politics:

> if it appears that the male and the female sex have distinct qualifications for any arts or pursuits, we shall affirm that they ought to be assigned respectively to each. But if it appears that they differ only in just this respect that the female bears and the male begets, we shall say that no proof has yet been produced that the woman differs from the man for our purposes, but we shall continue to think that the guardians and their wives ought to follow the same pursuits.[16]

In this respect, Plato's *Republic* is a more radical text than Plato's *Laws*, but in other respects both dialogues support women's right to participate in the political realm equally with men, which was quite different than what one would find in the Athens of Plato's day.

17.4 PRIVATE PROPERTY AND THE FAMILY

Susan Muller Okin and Christopher Bobonich, along with other commentators on Plato's thought, point out that the reintroduction of the institutions of private property and traditional families in Plato's later work makes it hard for him to support the political rights of women. Something similar could be said about ancient Greece in general – without reforming traditional ideas of property and family, women would be unlikely to attain political equality with men. In this section we will look briefly at how property and family were understood in Crete as well as in Athens to see how women could or could not attain political and legal equality. In respect to the latter concept, legal equality, we will be especially concerned with how women's property and family rights at law affected women's participation in politics, also as a matter of law.

15 Ibid., 785b, p. 174.

16 Plato, *Republic*, 454d–454e, translated by Paul Shorey, in *Plato's Collected Dialogues*, edited by Edith Hamilton and Huntington Cairns, Princeton, NJ: Princeton University Press, 1961, p. 693.

It is odd that Plato speaks of "citizens and citizenesses" (*politai kai politides*), even as Plato also denies that women can "succeed to the ownership of land."[17] Something similar can be said about Athens at Plato's time but let us first look at ancient Crete that seems to be a better model than Athens for Plato's "feminist" treatment of the legal status of women.

Here is a passage from the Gortyn Code of Crete that is quite revealing about property ownership of women.

> If her father while he is alive wishes to give to (his daughter) who is getting married, let him give according to what is written, but not more. And any (daughter) to whom he gave or promised before is to have these things, but from the paternal estate she is not to receive (as inheritance) any other property. Any woman who does not have property, either as a gift from her father or brother, or as a promise, as her share (of the inheritance), as (was written?) when the *startos* Aithaleus, Kyllos and his colleagues, were *kosmoi*, they are to have their share; but for those before this time it is not a matter for trial.[18]

Notice, first and most importantly, that women could own property and that it can come from multiple sources. And also note, second, that when women have an inheritance it can accompany them into a marriage but remain the property of the wife. These are very important differences between ancient Crete and Athens at roughly the same time period, the seventh century BCE.

Concerning divorce we also find a much more egalitarian position taken in the laws of Crete than those of Athens.

> If a husband and wife are divorced, she is to have her own things, whatever she had when she came to her husband, and half of the produce, if there is any from her own property, and half of what she has woven, whatever it is, and five staters if the husband is responsible for the separation, but if the husband affirms that he is not responsible, the judge is to swear an oath and decide.[19]

Here we find that in ancient Cretan law the parties divorce relatively equally, where the woman keeps all that she came to the marriage with and roughly half of everything that has been accumulated during the marriage – somewhat like the so-called community property states in the US today where the proceeds accumulated during marriage are simply split between spouses at the time of divorce.

One last provision of the Gortyn Code for us to consider is the legal status of a so-called heiress. The Gortyn Code defines an heiress as a woman or girl who "does

[17] Ibid., 814c, p. 205, and see Glenn R. Morrow, *Plato's Cretan City*, Princeton: Princeton University Press, 1960, p. 113 where he comments on this singular passage.

[18] The Gortyn Code, in *The Laws of Ancient Crete c. 650–400* BCE, edited by Michael Gagarin and Paula Perlman, Oxford: Oxford University Press, 2016, p. 367.

[19] The Gortyn Code, ibid., pp. 350–351.

not have a father or a brother from the same father."[20] As a matter of Cretan law, an heiress can inherit the entire estate of her father. She must marry within the family, starting with the oldest brother of her father and then proceeding through the father's tribe until a match is made.[21] If she does not wish to marry in the tribe and instead wants to choose her own suitor, she can do so but must give up half of her father's estate to a member of that tribe. All of this suggests that women were treated reasonably fairly in ancient Crete, as compared to other ancient societies, concerning property and family matters.

It is a fairly stark contrast then to consider ancient Athenian law concerning the same property and family matters as we just saw in ancient Cretan law. Athenian women were often restricted to acting in public through a male guardian, a *kyrios*, who was normally her father or brother. According to Jones:

> A woman could not strictly inherit property in the same way as a man though she could be the means of transmitting an inheritance, but she could earn money by engaging in trade; for the value of a medimnus of barley, to which all transactions were restricted by law, was not so small as to prevent her from entering into most of the bargains which a tradeswoman would need to conclude in the ordinary way of small business. Outside Athens her legal status was more favorable. In Crete for example, she could act without a kyrios and could acquire property freely by inheritance or *inter vivos*.[22]

There is some controversy about how much control the *kyrios* (guardian) actually exercised over the public decision-making of a woman in Athens. Jones claims that the consent of a *kyrios* "was a matter of course, of merely traditional notarial routine, in all but the most serious transactions."[23] But we should note that the women of Crete did not have this restraint on their public participation in the political and economic domains of their city.

Concerning the role of Athenian women in the family, again there is much dispute. Blundell says:

> In law, an Athenian woman had no independent existence. She was always assumed to be incorporated into the *oikos* which was headed by her *kyrios*, or male guardian. Until she was married, a woman came under the guardianship of her father, or male next-of-kin. On her marriage, her husband took over the role of *kyrios*; if she was widowed or divorced, and she had no sons, she returned to her original guardian. But if she was widowed and had sons she could choose to stay in her late husband's *oikos* … under the guardianship of her sons.[24]

20 Ibid., p. 397.
21 Ibid., p. 390.
22 Jones, *The Law and Legal Theory of the Greeks*, p. 286.
23 Ibid., pp. 286–287.
24 Blundell, *Women in Ancient Greece*, p. 114.

What is disputed, as I said, is how much control the *kyrios* actually exercised over the Athenian woman. But in actual Athenian society, as opposed to that in Plato's dialogues, her status in the family seems always to have been inferior to the adult males in the family.

17.5 THE STATUS OF WOMEN IN DEMOCRACIES

Since the democracy in Athens was much stronger and egalitarian than that in Crete, one lesson seems to be that stronger democracies are not necessarily better concerning the legal status of women than weaker democracies. But of more help is the idea that, as for Plato, even having egalitarian treatment of women in some legal respects will often be overshadowed by what happens in the inegalitarian family and the economy. Plato tried, in the *Republic*, to eliminate such longstanding biases in traditional families by proposing a communal family structure instead. But by the end of his life, Plato came to see that the ideas in his *Republic* were impractical and too far removed from actual institutions of society at his time. So, when he wrote his last work, the *Laws*, he brought back a more traditional family structure, but also brought back inegalitarian relations between men and women. One question to ask then is whether democratic institutions can be egalitarian when the traditional family structure remains in place.

Susan Moller Okin raised this issue about Plato's changed views of women in an especially fresh and original way. At the end of her set of chapters on Plato she says:

> In the *Republic*, in spite of revolutionary proposals regarding the female guardians, he fails to bring into play his beliefs in the power of socialization and education, thereby making his unique argument about women's potential less forceful than it might have been. In the *Laws*, on the other hand, having come to the radical conclusions about women's undeveloped capacities that he expresses in the form of the ambidexterity metaphor, he fails to follow through on these conclusions. The reason is clearly the reinstatement of the family and therefore of the role of the wife – the transformation of women back into appendages and the private property of men … When woman is once again perceived as the privately owned appendage of man, when the family and its needs define her function, the socialization and regulation prescribed for her must ensure that her "nature" is formed and preserved in accordance with this role.[25]

The talk of women as having appendage status and of being man's property is crucial for Okin's claim that in the end Plato could not support a radical egalitarian view of women.

[25] Susan Moller Okin, *Women in Western Political Thought*, Princeton: Princeton University Press, 1979.

The further question is: whether women could be seen as equal to men in the legal and political sphere and yet remain subordinate in the sphere of the family. Could there be separate spheres of equality in the family and yet not separate spheres of equality in the political and legal institutions? Okin does not address this second question and the examination of the Greek legal thought about women we have provided makes it imperative that this more complex question be answered.

Another issue to consider is whether the same considerations bear on the restriction on political participation as those restrictions that bear on legal (jury) participation by women. Could women have a more restricted role in legal participation, say in terms of their testimony, than men and yet this be minimized because of full participation in the political process? Part of the answer turns on whether such matters as jury participation can be changed through the political process. If so, then it may not be as bad that women are currently excluded from the legal process since they could act to change this through that political process. It is more disconcerting if women are granted full participation in juries and other legal processes and yet restricted in political participation in assemblies where the law is made or changed.

Over the centuries since the radical democratic experiment of ancient Athens there have been no societies that gave to citizens the full political and legal participation that they enjoyed at Athens. It is deeply regrettable that the Greeks did not include women fully in such institutions but again most societies since the time of the ancient Greeks have also not included women on equal footing with men in both political and legal institutions. It is especially hard for legal institutions to change toward more gender equality when the political process is also not open to women on equal terms with men.

A third issue concerns the dowry. Today, dowries are quite rare in democratic societies. But we might wonder whether the protection offered by dowries is today secured by any comparable institutions. Given existing physical and power imbalances between men and women, perhaps there should be some kind of institution that protects women who go into relationships where they may be mistreated or abused.

In many discussions about dowries today, there is little attention paid to the way they can protect women, especially when relations between the sexes are not egalitarian in the family. In societies where there is not gender equality in the family, as is true for many societies today, it might indeed be a mistake to criticize the dowry system until the rest of the family structure is rendered more egalitarian. This, at least, is one lesson we could learn from our discussion of the role of women in ancient Athens.

18

Slavery and Democracy

Nearly every ancient society had slavery in some form or other. In ancient China, the society was stratified in rigid classes, with slaves constituting not the lowest class and in any event not numbering more than one percent of the population. The law, mainly customary, regulated slavery somewhat although records are scarce. In ancient Greece, slaves constituted a much greater percentage of the population, especially in ancient Athens. There were many mentions of slavery in the various ancient Greek codes that have survived – and slavery was both regulated and restricted as a matter of law. The oddity of slaves in Athens is that the society was committed to radical democratic values with "respect for persons" high on the list of those values. In this chapter I will pursue the causes and rationales for slavery in ancient Greek society, primarily in Athens, as a test for the democratic values that the Greeks claimed to live by, and that supposedly differentiated Greece from China and other ancient authoritarian societies. I will argue that in many ways slaves were better off in undemocratic China than in democratic Athens.

In the Section 18.1 I will set out some of the most prominent legal texts that regulate slaves. In Section 18.2 I will begin the search for rationales for the lack of freedom in the legal status of slaves, drawing most prominently on Aristotle's analysis and defense of slavery in the first book of his *Politics*. In Section 18.3 I will seek out other rationales for slavery laws in ancient Athens, looking especially to Demosthenes, Xenophon, and Plato. In Section 18.4 I will discuss various ideas of how law and freedom were intertwined in the legal thought of the ancient Greeks. And in Section 18.5 I will attempt to draw some lessons from these ancient sources.

18.1 EARLY GREEK LAWS ON SLAVERY

The laws of the Cretan city-state of Groton (from the seventh century BCE) are among the oldest Greek laws about slavery and that is where we will start. Here is a law that makes it clear that slavery is sanctioned by the legal system in ancient Crete:

> If someone has bought a slave from the *agora* and has not terminated (the purchase) within sixty days, if (the slave) has done wrong to anyone before or after (the purchase), litigation is to be conducted against the one who has acquired him.[1]

This law presents slaves as chattel who can be bought and sold and where the owner is legally responsible for the wrongs of the slave. The clear implication of this law is that slavery is legally sanctioned and regulated by the legal system. It is not merely that the society recognizes slavery but that the relationship of master and slave is recognized at law.

We get a clearer sense of the role of the legal system in the institution of slavery in a second law of the Groton code.

> No one is to buy an indentured person until the one who indentured him obtains his release, nor one who is the subject of litigation, nor is anyone to accept him (as payment) nor accept a promise (to deliver him) nor take him in indentureship. And if anyone should do any of these things, it is to be invalid, if two witnesses should testify.[2]

It is especially telling here that slavery sales must not disrupt litigation putting the concerns of the law above that of the slave holders' interests. The Cretan law is thus thoroughly involved in the regulation of slavery, and the relationship of the slave and master is essentially a legal relationship, which also can be disrupted by legal proceedings.

Another later Cretan law from Samos in 245/4 BCE is of interest for it provides a legally recognized sanctuary for slaves who are fleeing their masters. We have only this brief reference to "slaves who take refuge in the sanctuary."[3] This law shows that the regulation of slavery was not merely for the benefit of the slave owner but could be protection for the slave himself. The legal systems of ancient Greece are thoroughly immersed in the regulation of slaves both for the interests of the slave owners but also sometimes for the protection of the slaves.

One of the best known ancient Athenian laws protecting slaves is found in the laws of Solon (from the seventh century BCE). Here are three fragments concerning Solon's law:

> Fr. 69a: These seem to be the most democratic features of Solon's constitution: first and greatest, that there should be no loans on the security of the person.
>
> Fr. 69b: Having gained control of affairs Solon liberated the people both in the present and for the future, by forbidding loans on the security of the person; and he enacted laws; and he made a cancellation of debts both public and private.

1 *The Laws of Ancient Crete – c. 650–400 BCE*, edited and translated by Michael Gagarin and Paula Perlman, Oxford: Oxford University Press, 2016, p. 389.

2 Ibid., p. 412.

3 *Greek Sacred Law*, second edition, edited and translated by Eran Lupu, Leiden: Brill, 2009, p. 289.

> Fr. 69c: He wrote that existing debts should be annulled, and for the future that nobody should lend on the security of the person.[4]

In these fragments about Solon from Aristotle and Plutarch there is an explicit connection made between Solon's institution of democracy and the freeing of debt slaves. These slaves were largely Athenians who had fallen into debt and were forced to give up their freedom to their creditors.

N. R. E. Fisher summarizes the paradox of the laws on slavery in ancient Athens as follows:

> the laws were framed to serve at least three purposes, which were in part contradictory: first, to maintain and reinforce the fundamental distinction between slave and free people; second, to preserve the institution above all by allowing masters a great deal of control over their slaves and deterring the slave from committing "offenses"; and third, to offer the slaves some legal protection by setting some limits to the powers of masters over their slaves.[5]

In what follows in this section we will see more examples of the legal regulation of slavery with special attention to what we would today call the criminal law.

Concerning homicide cases in Athens, Antiphon, in *On the Murder of Herodes*, provides the following account:

> Even slaves who kill their masters and are caught in the act are not put to death by the victim's relatives but are delivered to the officials according to your ancestral laws. If a slave is allowed to testify against a free man in a murder case, and a master who wishes can bring a case on behalf of the slave, and a verdict can be rendered equally for the murder of a slave and a free man, then surely it was reasonable that he should be given a trial and not be killed by you without trial.[6]

We see that slaves could not be summarily executed even if caught in the act of killing their masters. And masters could bring legal actions in case their slaves were killed and the verdict could be one of murder. In both of these cases of homicide, Antiphon tells us, slaves and free men are treated the same.

Slaves were subjected to corporal punishment in the form of whipping for offenses when freemen are often merely fined for the same offense. According to Demosthenes:

4 *The Laws of Solon*, edited and translated by Delfim F. Leao and P. J. Rhodes, London: I. B. Tauris, 2015, pp. 113–114.

5 N. R. E. Fisher, *Slavery in Classical Greece*, second edition, London: Gerald Duckworth and Co., 2001, p. 58.

6 Antiphon, *On the Murder of Herodes*, 48, in *Antiphon and Andocides*, translated by Michael Gagarin, Austin: University of Texas Press, 1998, pp. 61–62.

> Indeed, if you wanted to contrast the slave and the freeman, you would find the most important distinction in the fact that slaves are responsible in person [with their bodies] for all offenses, while freemen, even in the most unfortunate circumstances, can protect their persons [their bodies]. For it is in the shape of money that in the majority of cases the law must obtain satisfaction from them; but Androtion on the contrary exacted vengeance from their persons, as if they had been bond slaves.[7]

Demosthenes says that for many offenses the slave must pay a price in terms of his body whereas in most of these cases of offense a freeman pays only a monetary fee.

In Crete, rape and sexual assaults were treated differently, and more severely, if the perpetrator was a slave, and more leniently if the victim was a slave than a free man. In Crete, unlike Athens, the penalties are all monetary not corporal. Here is a selection from the Groton code:

> If someone rapes a free man or woman, he will pay a hundred staters. If (someone rapes) an *apetairos*[8] (he will pay) ten. If a slave (rapes) a free man or woman, he will pay double. If a free man (rapes) a male or female serf (he will pay) five drachmas. And if a serf (rapes) a male or female, five staters ... And if (he is caught committing adultery) with the woman of an *apetairos*, (he will pay) ten. And if a slave with a free woman, (he will pay) double. And if a slave with a slave's (woman), five staters.[9]

These penalties are heavily weighted against the slave: having the slave pay twice as much as a free person for rape and sexual assault; and when the slave is a victim, the penalty for the attacker is half of what it would be if the victim was a low class free person.

Even as the penalties for offenses were heavily weighted against the slave, either monetarily or corporally, there were also significant legal protections as well. As we have seen, one of the most significant protections was that if a slave was being mistreated or falsely accused of an offense, the slave could seek sanctuary from his oppressor.[10] The slave could effectively force his master to sell him to another, or in some cases be protected until a court could consider the slave's case, although the slave was not permitted to testify or to appear in court.[11]

Finally, let me mention some of the provisions concerning manumission. Slaves could not attain the status of citizen when freed, but were granted roughly the same

7 Demosthenes, *Against Androtion*, 55, in *Demosthenes III*, translated by J. H. Vince, Cambridge MA: Harvard University Press' Loeb Classical Library, 1935, p. 191.

8 Probably a low status free person. See *The Laws of Ancient Crete – c. 650–400 BCE*, p. 79.

9 Ibid., pp. 345–346.

10 See Fisher, *Slavery in Classical Greece*, p. 64.

11 See ibid., p. 59.

status as metics.[12] Slaves could be freed at the end of a war in which they had served. Sometimes slaves could be freed by their masters as a reward for good service. So, even though the slave could not become a free citizen, the slave could become free – although this appears not to have happened very often.

18.2 ARISTOTLE'S DEFENSE OF SLAVERY IN ATHENS

Aristotle has the best known defense of slavery in ancient Greece, although today his defense is notorious at best. His defense of slavery is indeed very curious, as we will see. Aristotle begins his defense very early in Book I of his *Politics*, with the observation that "the ox is the poor man's slave."[13] This lets us know that Aristotle saw the slave as less than fully human, as more like a beast of burden than a fellow human. Indeed, this sets the tone for the rest of Aristotle's discussion of slavery. He follows his earlier remark by postulating that "a complete household consists of slaves and freemen."[14] It becomes clear that Aristotle found slavery to be a natural phenomenon that had as its *telos*, or end, the good of other human beings.

Aristotle admits that other thinkers "affirm that the role of master over slaves is contrary to nature, and that the distinction between slave and freeman exists by law only, and not by nature and being an interference with nature is therefore unjust."[15] This is the position that Aristotle sets out to refute. And it becomes clear that his own position is that "what is the nature and office of a slave; he who is by nature not his own but another's man ... and he may be said to be another's man who, being a human being, is also a possession. And a possession may be defined as an instrument of action, separable from the possessor."[16]

Aristotle makes a startling claim in response to the idea that slaves are truly human beings. It turns out, he says, that it is grounded in a fact: "For that some should rule and others be ruled is a thing not only necessary, but expedient; from the hour of their birth, some are marked out for subjection, others for rule."[17] Yet, such a position has many evident problems from the outset. Many slaves in ancient Athens were not born slaves but rather fell into slavery because of debt or capture during battle. And it was also a fact that some slaves achieved manumission and assumed

[12] See ibid., pp. 67–70.

[13] Aristotle, *Politics*, 1252b12, in *The Basic Works of Aristotle*, edited by Richard McKeon, translated by Benjamin Jowett, NY: Random House, 1941, p. 1128.

[14] Aristotle, *Politics*, 1253b4, p. 1130.

[15] Aristotle, *Politics*, 1253b20–23, pp. 1130–1131.

[16] Aristotle, *Politics*, 1254a14–17,pp. 1131–1132.

[17] Aristotle, *Politics*, 1254a21–23, p. 1132.

important roles in Athenian society despite being born a slave. These various facts make it hard for Aristotle to maintain his view based on the facts alone. As we will see, Aristotle does provide an argument beyond what he perceives as the facts.

His argument proceeds in the following way by reference to what he calls the principle of necessity, that is, what is naturally necessary.

> this principle of necessity extends to all mankind … the lower sort are by nature slaves, and it is better for them as for all inferiors that they should be under the rule of a master … and he who participates in a rational principle enough to apprehend, but not to have such a principle, is a slave by nature.[18]

There are two arguments intermingled here. The first argument is an attempt to show that it is necessary that those who are inferior should be ruled by those who are superior. The second argument is a normative argument that it is better that those who are inferior be ruled by those who are superior. It should be evident that there is no straightforward way to get from the metaphysical argument to the normative one.

We should note that Aristotle defines humans as political animals (*zoon politikon*), and thus differentiates humans from all other animals. When Aristotle then says that some humans are inferior to others and can be treated as beasts of burden, he seems to go back on his claim that all humans are equal as political or social beings. This is a common problem for those who have tried over the centuries to provide a defense of slavery. But here is the first such attempt, and the attempt is by one of the most respected philosophers of all time, not merely of ancient Greece.

Aristotle does recognize that slaves are humans, only that they are inferior humans in that they have understanding but not the kind of reason that allows them to rule themselves. But if this is true, then there seems to be no good reason to support manumission of slaves, as Aristotle apparently did when he freed his own slaves at his death.[19] If it is better for slaves to be ruled then it seems that freeing slaves would harm them, not be a benefit to them. Despite Aristotle's claim that "slavery is both expedient and right"[20] he does not appear to have provided a defense of such a claim.

Aristotle appears to understand this predicament when he acknowledges that there are two kinds of slavery: "a slave or slavery by law as well as by nature."[21] While it is customary for those defeated in battle to be enslaved by those who have shown their superior force, Aristotle does not view these slaves as naturally slaves. For he points out that the war itself that brought about the enslavement may itself be unjust and

18 Aristotle, *Politics*, 1254b15–20, pp. 1132–1133.

19 See Fisher, *Slavery in Classical Greece*, p. 98.

20 Aristotle, *Politics*, 1255a3, p. 1133.

21 Aristotle, *Politics*, 1255a5, p. 1133.

hence the victors of such a war are not more virtuous than those who are defeated and then enslaved.[22]

Aristotle ends his defense of slavery by acknowledging that the critics of slavery have some legitimate reasons on their side.

> We see then that there is some foundation for this difference of opinion, and that all are not either slaves by nature or freemen by nature, and also that there is in some cases a marked distinction between the two classes, rendering it expedient and right for the one to be slaves and the others to be masters … when the relation of master and slave between them is natural they are friends and have common interest, but where it rests merely on law and force the reverse is true.[23]

In this view, it is only right and expedient that people are slaves when those people are naturally inferior to the point where they cannot rule themselves. Yet Aristotle does not give us a good test for when slaves are naturally inferior and when slaves have been created by what he calls "abuse of authority."[24]

18.3 OTHER ATHENIAN VIEWS OF SLAVERY

In Plato's early dialogue, the *Euthyphro*, we find Socrates meeting Euthyphro on their way to the law courts. Euthyphro explains why he is headed to court.

> In this case, the man who was killed was a hired workman of mine, and when we were farming at Naxos, he was working there on our land. Now, he got drunk, got angry with one of our house slaves, and butchered him. So my father bound him hand and foot, threw him into a ditch, and sent a man here to Athens to ask the religious advisor what he ought to do. In the meantime he paid no attention to the man as he lay there bound, and neglected him, thinking that he was a murderer and it did not matter if he were to die … [and so] I am prosecuting my father for murder.[25]

Plato here recounts this story at least in part to show that the killing of slaves and of servants is contrary to law and justice.

In Plato's last work, *The Laws*, slavery is discussed in the context of the second-best city that the dialogue's participants are planning. One of the most telling accounts concerns the differentiation of free and slave doctors, and here Plato presents an argument from nature to explain why the free doctor is better than the slave doctor.

[22] Aristotle, *Politics*, 1255a24, p. 1134.

[23] Aristotle, *Politics*, 1255b5–9, p. 1134 and 1255b12–15, pp. 1134–1135.

[24] Aristotle, *Politics*, 1255b8, p. 1134.

[25] Plato, *Euthyphro* 4C, in *Plato 1*, translated by Harold North Fowler, Cambridge, MA: Harvard University Press' Loeb Classical Library, 1914, p. 15.

> Presumably we assert that there are persons who are doctors; and then, that there are in addition doctor's servants, whom we also, I suppose, call "doctors" ... Whether they be free men or slaves, they acquire the art by following their masters' commands, by observing, and by experience, but not by following nature, as the free doctors do, who have themselves learned in this way and who teach their disciples in this way.[26]

Here Plato discusses slavery in terms of nature but in a somewhat different way than Aristotle. Plato is not here justifying slavery but indicating why free people are superior to slaves in the medical sciences. Plato's presumptions though are not that different from Aristotle; the free men decide what the best treatment is by consulting nature, whereas the slave must be commanded or told what to do by the free persons. As Plato continues, the free doctor "communes" with the patient whereas the slave doctor only can give commands since he does not have the kind of understanding that allows for consideration of the context and the specific input of the patient.

Plato, in *The Laws*, also indicates that there are better and worse ways to train slaves, being not too lenient or too severe.

> he who in his disposition and actions toward slaves remains undefiled by what is impious or unjust would be a man who is fully capable of sowing the natural seed of virtue ... Of course it is necessary to punish slaves, in a just way, and not spoil them by mere chiding, as if they were free men. And in speaking to a domestic servant one should almost always use a straightforward command, one should never joke with domestic servants in any way ... thereby making life more difficult both for those who are ruled and for themselves who do the ruling.[27]

Plato seems here to regard slaves as similar to young children.

Xenophon in his *Oeconomicus* sometimes offers advice about training slaves as well and recommends treating slaves like they were other human beings: "I guide my slaves onto the path of right behavior with the aid of maxims drawn in part from the laws of Draco, in part from the laws of Solon."[28] But at other times, Xenophon recommends very harsh treatment of slaves especially if they have proven themselves to be incorrigible.[29]

It is curious that in ancient Athens the laws of *hybris* were extended to slaves. These laws make sense if slaves are treated either like freemen or as the property of freemen,

[26] Plato, *The Laws*, 720a-b, in *The Laws of Plato*, translated by Thomas L. Pangle, NY: Basic Books, 1980, p. 107.

[27] Ibid., 777e–778a, p. 166.

[28] Xenophon, *Oeconomicus* 14, in *Xenophon's Memorabilia and Oeconomicus*, translated by O. J. Todd and revised by Jeffrey Henderson, Cambridge, MA: Harvard University Press' Loeb Classical Library, 2013, p. 507.

[29] Ibid.

or both as we have seen in some authors. And earlier we found Demosthenes candidly saying that: "if you wanted to contrast the slave and the freeman, you would find the most important distinction in the fact that slaves are responsible in person [with their bodies] for all offenses, while freemen, even in the most unfortunate circumstances, can protect their persons [their bodies]." One rationale based on this statement is that slaves simply did not own anything other than their bodies and when they got into trouble they had no security to provide or compensation to pay in monetary terms. So, they were then forced to pay with their bodies.

This final rationale though flies in the face of the Athenian attempt, from Solon onward, to abolish debt slavery. Debt slavery is the form of slavery best suited to the rationale of seeing slaves as having only their bodies to offer after they had no other resources. But with the abolishment of debt slavery, the other forms of slavery seem not to be well suited to the rationale implied by Demosthenes since it is not only by their own doing that these slaves lack monetary resources.

18.4 LAW AND FREEDOM IN ANCIENT ATHENS AND CHINA

In Pericles' funeral oration, as reconstructed by Thucydides, we find an inspiring defense of the place of freedom in ancient Greek society, especially in Athenian democracy. Here again is part of that famous speech:

> It is true that our government is called a democracy, because its administration is in the hands, not of the few, but of the many; yet while as regards the law all men are on an equality for the settlement of their private disputes, as regards the value set on them it is as each man in any way distinguished that he is preferred to public honors, not because he belongs to a particular class but because of personal merits; nor again on the ground of poverty is a man barred from a public career by obscurity of rank if he but has it in him to do the state a service … we are restrained from lawlessness chiefly through reverent fear, for we render obedience to those in authority and to the laws, especially to those laws which are ordained for the succor of the oppressed and those which, though unwritten, bring upon the transgressor a disgrace which all men recognize.[30]

Notice again that Pericles speaks of democracy as a form of government that involves the rule by the many. When we consider the status of women and slaves it becomes clear that the many is not everyone. Indeed, Pericles is clear on this point when he speaks of women living up to "the standard which nature has set for your sex" and that they are better off neither being praised nor blamed by men.[31]

[30] Thucydides, *History of the Peloponnesian War*, Bk. II, Ch. 37, in *Thucydides I*, translated by Charles Forster Smith, Cambridge, MA: Harvard University Press' Loeb Classical Library, 1919, pp. 323–325.

[31] Ibid., Bk. II, Ch. 45, p. 341 of Loeb edition.

The idea of freedom is the centerpiece of the Athenian defense of their form of government and especially of their laws. This freedom has both a private and a public component. In private affairs, people do not harbor resentments or suspicions of each other. And in public affairs, "all men are on an equality" Pericles tells us. Most importantly, there is obedience to the authority of the law, "especially to those laws which are ordained for the succor of the oppressed." Yet how does this conception of civic freedom square with slavery in ancient Athens?

In ancient Athens there were basically three classes: freemen, metics, and slaves. Deborah Kamen has helpfully shown that there are realistically ten or more groups, and these groups are made up of subdivisions of the three basic classes.[32] Ancient China had a much larger number of classes that were clearly identified and regulated as a matter of customary law. The Athenians claimed that there was liberty for all; whereas the Chinese never made such a claim and indeed did not seem to think in terms of equality. And yet slavery in China was a fairly minor matter, but a major matter in Athens.

Because slavery was such an integral part of Athenian society the task of justifying it was important especially since slavery seems inconsistent with the self-image of Athenians as portrayed by Pericles' funeral oration. One can surmise that Aristotle felt the need to discuss the justification for slavery at the very beginning of his account of the political and legal state of Athens because the prevalence of slavery would stand in need of a rationale in a state where democratic values were so intertwined with the superior virtuousness of Athens as compared with its non-democratic neighbors and the authoritarian regimes in Persia and Egypt.

So, the temptation to look for a natural explanation, indeed an explanation drawn in terms of natural necessity might have been quite strong. If humans came in clear-cut natural kinds corresponding to free and slave members of society, then the task of showing why there was no inconsistency between democracy and slavery would have been much easier. The premise of democracy is that government should be rule by equals. This premise is not at odds with having many but not all ruling, especially if some are by nature incapable of ruling and are naturally better off when being ruled. Indeed, given the assumption of the natural inequalities of some humans, the goal of universal equality is actually counterproductive and to a certain extent unjust from the ancient Athenian perspective.

The Aristotelian defense of slavery proceeds both in terms of prudence or efficiency on one hand, and justice and right on the other hand. If some are not capable of ruling, then it would make little sense to have them in the group of people who are the rulers. This idea though somewhat flies in the face of the fact that the Athenian democracy at its most radical selected rulers by lots. Lots only

[32] Kamen, *Status in Classical Athens*.

make sense if everyone is not only equal in terms of legal rights but in terms of abilities concerning rulership. Yet, surely this idea is simply wrongheaded – even the Greeks acknowledged that lots made little sense for selecting generals. If abilities to rule citizens, like abilities to rule soldiers, is graded throughout the population then political rulers should not be selected by lots any more than generals should.

From the standpoint of justice and right, there is a better case to be made that democracy should include not just many but all the human members of a society. And it is here that Aristotle is at his most ingenious. He argues that slaves are inferior not only in reasoning and understanding but also in virtue, and are hence not deserving to be rulers instead of ruled. And this would indeed be a reasonable position if Aristotle could explain why having less understanding means that one also has less virtue. It is beyond the scope of this chapter to investigate this point further. Suffice it to say that if slaves really were *naturally* deficient in virtue to the point where they should not be allowed to rule, then why would slaves be considered fit to teach children or, once freed, to participate in business and commercial affairs of the city? So, even in the case of the right to rule as opposed to the ability to rule, one of the most rational of all philosophers seems to present arguments that run aground on the shoals of actual practice in Athens, including his own practices of dealing with his slaves.

18.5 THINKING ABOUT LAW AND FREEDOM

Law can be used as a means of oppression and as a means of ending or mitigating oppression. In this respect, the rule of law has no positive or negative value in and of itself. The legal institutions of slavery, and the laws against slavery, stand as prime examples of how differently law can be used in terms of justice. Democratic rule does not mean that oppression is extinguished or even limited compared with non-democratic societies. So, then, what is the relation between democracy and freedom?

Today, in Western societies, it is nearly an article of faith that a society will be better off if it moves toward a more democratic constitution. Aristotle, who had made a careful and systematic study of many of the constitutions in the Greek city-states of his time, did not think that the more democratic a society's constitution was, the better its society was. As in nearly all things, Aristotle argued for a mixed or moderate position – the mean between extremes – a blend of aristocracy and democracy (perhaps like a Roman Republic). He was well aware that radical democracy, as the Athens of his day was experiencing it, was not the best of constitutions. It is nonetheless true that he failed to see that slavery as conceived in the Greek *polis* of his day was also a flawed and ultimately a theoretically indefensible institution.

Today the central theoretical and practical question is not about slavery but about diversity in societies. Diversity is thought to promote the greatest range of freedom, and democracy is thought to afford that range of diversity better than other constitutional orders. Slavery is not a problem of the scope that it was in ancient Athens, but discrimination against peoples of various races, ethnicities, genders, and religions is rampant. It is not clear that democracy is the best system of government and law to deal with such problems, just as it was not clear that democracy in ancient Athens was the best political and legal system for dealing with slavery.

Freedom can be institutionally supported by democratic legal and political systems, as Pericles claimed. But if democracy is promoted by a social system that consigns large sections of the population to "second-class" status, democracy's promoters may have a vested interest in maintaining the class structure. Indeed, it is easy to see in Pericles' funeral oration the promotion of freedom for only one class – with the literal disappearance of the other classes, except for the singular mention of women being best when not talked about.

We often hear discussions today of American democracy's promotion of freedom that also ignores groups that are marginalized in America. Of course, marginalization and discrimination occur today in non-democratic societies as well. But the one modern society that had as many slaves as ancient Athens was nineteenth century CE America – and the question is whether it is merely a coincidence that both of these societies are often praised as models of democracy. In the final bit of this chapter I will speculate on why it might be that democracy and slavery might fit together.

In ancient Athens, much attention was paid to making sure that all full citizens were treated equally before the law as well as politically, as we also saw in Chapter 16. Perhaps, having provided ingenious ways of guaranteeing equal freedom for citizens, the task of including non-citizens was too large. More likely, the plight of non-citizens was not considered important – for if Aristotle is representative, the best way to provide for them is not to include them in political and legal participation but rather to rule over them.

I do not think it is in the nature of democracy that slavery and other forms of discrimination occur. The idea that people are to rule themselves and not be ruled by only a segment of the population does not necessarily promote slavery. But when put into practice democracy does not break down all class divisions, despite the ideology espoused by promoters of democracy. Within a given segment of the population, democratic political and legal thought does call for the kind of equal freedom that is anathema to slavery. Yet, as long as society is segmented, then the part that has democratic institutions need not feel moved to extend those institutions to other segments of the population, especially if there is no recognition of equality between classes.

We come back to the question of why ancient Chinese society that was far from democratic had so many fewer slaves than democratic Athens. As Aristotle says so clearly, having slaves was an integral component of the Athenian household. And as some have suggested over the years, perhaps having slaves work in the household and in the fields allowed for citizens to have the time to participate in politics and law. Similar things could be said about plantation societies in eighteenth and nineteenth century America. Perhaps slavery was an integral component of the very heavy time-demands that participating in ancient Athenian assemblies and juries demanded. These are all speculations and it is unlikely that we can do more than speculate about why the greatest democratic society also had one of the largest slave populations.

SECTION VII

Responsibility and Punishment

19

Causation and Responsibility

Plutarch – a certain athlete had hit Epitimus, the Pharasalian, with a javelin, accidentally, and killed him, and Pericles … squandered an entire day discussing with Protagoras whether it was the javelin, or rather the one who hurled it, or the judges of the contests, that "in the strictest sense" ought to be held responsible for the disaster. *Lives*, Vol. III, "Pericles" 36 (Loeb edition, p. 105)

One of the most metaphysically fraught concepts in legal thought is causation. Yet, despite being published in ancient Athens, the *Tetralogies* (attributed to Antiphon) provide a fascinating account of causation that even legal theorists today can appreciate. This chapter will take up the hypothetical case from the *Second Tetralogy* that seems to mirror the real case reported by Plutarch above. Along the way we will also examine some of the ideas on causation most applicable to the law that we can find in Plato and Aristotle. But the focus will be the *Second Tetralogy*, to see what ideas of proximate and "but-for" causation existed in ancient Greek times and how such ideas affected the conceptualization of legal responsibility, including contributory negligence for Greek legal thought. I will argue that the idea of negligence presented in the *Tetralogies* grounded a remarkably sophisticated idea of causation in the law.

The case in the *Second Tetralogy* displays very sophisticated arguments about causation in the case of a boy who is struck and killed by a javelin when the boy darted across a practice field. There is not just a question of responsibility, as indicated in the quote from Plutarch above, but a question of whether the javelin thrower was indeed the cause of the boy's death. The question is properly one of causal responsibility and what is said about it makes it highly relevant to discussions today.

19.1 THE JAVELIN THROWER IN THE *SECOND TETRALOGY* OF ANTIPHON

The presentation of this hypothetical case begins with the first speech of the father of the boy victim, who is prosecuting the case, and contains a short statement of the offense that is charged:

> In this case I think that even the defendant will not disagree with me; for my boy, struck in the side on the training field by a javelin thrown by this young man, died on the spot. I therefore charge him not with intentional but with unintentional homicide. For me of course the misfortune he unintentionally caused is just as great as if he had acted intentionally; he has not burdened the spirit of the dead man but of those still living.[1]

Here is the most straightforward, and seemingly commonsensical, causal account: the young man threw the javelin, striking the boy in his side and killing him. Whether the young man's act was intentional or not, the young javelin thrower is responsible for the boy's death.

And the first response speech in behalf of the accused, seemingly presented by the young man's father, stresses that the death was accidental, and that in fact the young man did not cause the death.

> the young man, not through any insolence (*hybris*) or lack of self-control (*akolasia*) but simply practicing with his friends on the playing field threw his javelin but did not kill anyone, according to the truth of what he did; however he is now unwillingly blamed for someone else's accidental self-injury.[2]

We see here a two-part defense: there was no intent to kill and in any event the boy inflicted the deadly injury upon himself.

> Now, if the javelin had hit and wounded the boy because it carried outside the boundaries of its proper course, then we would have no argument against the charge of homicide. But because the boy ran under the trajectory of the javelin and placed his body in its path, one of them was prevented from hitting the target, whereas the other was hit because he ran under the javelin.[3]

Here is the clearest indication of the alternative causal account: the boy ran under the javelin, placing his body in front of it and hence caused his own death. And while this seems initially far-fetched there is much more argumentation in support

1 Antiphon, *Second Tetralogy*, 3.1.1, translated by Michael Gagarin, in *Antiphon and Andocides*, edited by Michael Gagarin and Douglas M. MacDowell, Austin: University of Texas Press, 2006, p. 31.

2 Antiphon, *Second Tetralogy*, 3.2.3, ibid., p. 32.

3 Ibid., 3.2.4, p. 32.

of this account that is quite illuminating of how causation was conceived in ancient Greece.

There is a straightforward appeal to the idea of what today is called "but-for" causation.

> If it is clear to you that the boy was not hit while standing still but while intentionally running under the trajectory of the javelin, then this shows even more clearly that he died on account of his own mistake for he would not have been hit if he had stood still and hadn't run.[4]

"But-for" the boy running onto the practice field, the injury would not have occurred. Indeed, it was the boy's running that was the act "but-for" its occurrence that the injury would not have occurred. And in this view, it is important to note that the boy was not passive but was active.

Today we would also point out that by running the boy inserted himself into the causal chain and was the last human actor in the chain, perhaps negating the previous human act of the young man. Indeed, this idea is present, if not identified specifically, in the account in the *Second Tetralogy*. The defense refers to a principle often adopted that the person is responsible who performed the last act before the injury. Unless the previous act was necessary and sufficient by itself, the last act by a human that is necessary for the injury is the one designated "the cause."

Before we get to the full defense of the account of proximate causation there comes an argument about comparative negligence that is also conceptually sophisticated.

> Since, as you know, both sides agree that the killing was unintentional, the killer can be determined even more clearly to establish which of the two made the mistake. Those who because of a mistake fail to accomplish what they have in mind to do are the agents of unintentional acts, and those who do or experience anything unintentional are responsible for their sufferings.[5]

So, if we believe that an accident caused the boy's death then we must look for the party whose mistake was most clearly the agent of the accident. Indeed, for there to be an accident it appears that some mistake must have been made, yet the javelin thrower did not make a mistake as the father of the young man says:

> the young man made no mistake affecting anyone, for he was practicing what was assigned; he was throwing his javelin on the throwing field, not where others were exercising; and he did not hit the boy because he missed his target and threw toward

4 Ibid., 3.2.5, p. 33.

5 Ibid., 3.2.7–8, p. 33.

> the bystanders; rather, he did everything he intended to do correctly, did nothing unintentional, and suffered by being prevented from hitting the target. The boy on the other hand, wished to run out but mistook the right moment.[6]

The conclusion is that the accident should be attributed to the boy much more than to the young man. Comparatively, the boy made the mistake and should suffer the consequences of his negligence; whereas the young man made no mistake.

The prosecutor's second speech indicates how strange sounding it was to say that the boy was the cause of his own injury, calling the defendant's speech "a wicked subtlety of words."[7] And the prosecutor accuses the defense of bad faith:

> He has the audacity and the insolence to claim that his son, who both threw and killed, did not wound or kill; and he asserts that my son, who did not touch the javelin and never even thought of throwing it, missed the whole earth and everyone else on it and thrust the javelin through his own ribs.[8]

Of course, this is not what the defense claimed, but it does illustrate how weird it must have sounded to Athenians, as to us, to hear that the victim is responsible for his injuries not the assailant.

One of the main arguments of the prosecutor is that the boy did not neglect danger in running onto the practice field.

> For the boy was summoned at the right moment by the trainer who was in charge of picking up the javelins for the throwers, but because of the thrower's lack of self-control, he encountered this young man's hostile missile and died miserably, though he had made no mistake affecting anyone. But the young man made a mistake about the right moment for picking up the javelins.[9]

Here the counter-claim is made that the boy did not make a mistake but followed the directions of the trainer. Instead, it is alleged that the young man made the mistake of throwing when he should not have done so.

Once again, the prosecutor then reminds the jury of who it was that threw the javelin, despite what the defense tries to argue.

> But who threw the javelin? Who is to be credited with the killing? The spectators or the attendants, whom no one accuses of anything? There is nothing obscure about this death; for me it is all too clear. I say the law is correct to prescribe punishment for those who kill.[10]

6 Ibid., 3.27, p. 33.
7 Ibid., 3.3.3, p. 35.
8 Ibid., 3.3.5, p. 35.
9 Ibid., 3.3.6, p. 35.
10 Ibid., 3.3.7, p. 36.

The straightforward causal claim is that those who kill and hence cause suffering are the ones who should be held responsible. But there is nonetheless the defense's claim that the young man was not the one who killed. And here is the nub of the causation question: is the killer the one who threw the javelin or the one who got into the path of the javelin? And as has only recently become clear to modern legal theorists, it is very difficult to answer the causal question without thinking first about who is morally or legally responsible.

The prosecutor also tries to rebut the claims about contributory negligence. Indeed, it is clear that the issue is one of negligence when the talk is of mistake and what failures were made that constituted the mistake.

> If it is right to consider the boy his own killer because he ran into the path of the javelin and didn't stand still, then the young man is not free from blame either, but only if he was standing still and not throwing his javelin when the boy died. But since both contributed to the killing, and the boy has already punished himself more severely than warranted by a mistake that affected only himself – for he's dead – then surely it is not right that his accomplice and partner in a mistake affecting only those who didn't deserve it at all should escape without penalty.[11]

So, if we are to think in terms of contributory negligence and distributive responsibility then there is surely reason to hold the young man responsible since the boy has already paid dearly and disproportionately for his part.

The defense then concludes this exercise in its second speech by making it clearer what exactly is the causal claim that is being made.

> I'm not saying the boy threw a javelin or hit himself with it but that by going under the javelin's blow he was killed not by the young man but by himself; for he did not die standing still. And since his running is to blame, then, if he ran out because he was called by the trainer, the trainer would be the one who killed him, but if he ran on his own impulse, then he was killed by himself.[12]

Here it seems that the issue is one of causal impulse – what initiated the injury? The fact that is the key is that something intruded into a normally occurring set of events, and it was either the trainer calling the boy to come onto the field or the boy in effect calling himself to come onto the field.

At this point in the *Second Tetralogy* we have a different issue introduced than previously: what was the impetus or impulse for the acts that caused the injury. This idea is highly subtle, for it looks to be a notion of causation that is different from the efficient causation that had been previously discussed. There is a sense of normal causal connection in that we look back to a point before anyone acted to see why

11 Ibid., 3.3.10, p. 36.
12 Ibid., 3.4.4, p. 38.

they acted. But there is also the sense that we are now also in the domain of what Aristotle would call the final or the teleological cause: what the goal of the activities was that somehow induced the acts to occur. We will explore this point in more detail in the next section of this chapter.

Last, we get another statement of how the but-for causal analysis is understood by the defense. "The thrower would not have missed his target if no one had run under his javelin, and the boy would not have been hit if he had stayed with the spectators."[13] And the argument turns on what the young man did that was different from any of the other javelin throwers on that practice field that day.

> If the boy died because the young man threw his javelin, then all his fellow practicers would share responsibility for the act, since the reason they didn't hit him is not because they didn't throw their javelins but because he did not run under any of their javelins. The young man did not make a mistake any more than they did.[14]

Here, obliquely we get a sense of how luck is being treated – if the only reason the young man's javelin struck the boy was bad luck, and the only reason the other practicers' javelins did not strike the boy was good luck, then either all are responsible or none of them is, since luck is irrelevant to responsibility.

In this section we have seen indications of a highly sophisticated understanding of causation in Greek legal thought. The ideas of but-for causation and proximate causation were clearly understood by Antiphon, as well as the important considerations of luck in establishing what counts as negligence. In the next section we will look to some explicitly philosophical writing about causation in ancient Greek times.

19.2 PLATO AND ARISTOTLE ON CAUSATION

Aristotle, who lived after the time of the *Tetralogies*, famously wrote about causation in his *Physics*. Plato also wrote about causation, but certainly less systematically. In this section, we will examine some of Plato and Aristotle's writing on causation. I will be especially interested in how these philosophical ideas of causation seemed to affect or could have affected legal thought at their time. We will then be able to add some theoretical meat to the bones supplied by Antiphon in order to get a sense of how causation was understood in Greek legal thought.

In Plato's *Statesman*, we are introduced to a distinction that is crucial for understanding causation in the law.

> there are two arts involved in all production ... The one is a contingent cause and the other is the actual cause ... Those arts which do not produce the actual thing in

[13] Ibid., 3.4.5, p. 38.
[14] Ibid., 3.4.6, p. 38.

> question, but which supply to the arts which do produce it the tools without which no art could ever perform its prescribed work, may be called contingent causes, and those which produce the actual thing are [actual] causes.[15]

Contingent causes do not produce the actual thing, which could in the context of this chapter be the boy's killing, where the contingent cause operates merely to supply what is needed for the actual causing of the killing. There are actual causes that do directly produce the death. The javelin strikes the boy, killing him, and the javelin thrower propels the javelin. But there are other factors involved that contingently cause the boy's death, such as the trainer's calling that the field was clear, and the boy himself running onto the practice field.

In the *Phaedo*, Plato elaborates on his understanding of causation and why the Sophists had it wrong when he has Socrates say:

> I fancy these bones and sinews of mine would have been in Megara or Boetia long ago, carried thither by opinion of what was best, if I did not think it was better and nobler to endure any penalty the city may inflict rather than to escape and run away. But it is most absurd to call things that are of that sort causes. If anyone were to say that I could not have done what I thought was proper if I had not bones and sinews and other things that I have he would be right. But to say that those things are the cause of my doing what I do, and that I act with intelligence but not from the choice of what is best, would be an extremely careless way of talking. Whoever talks in that way is unable to make a distinction and to see that in reality a cause is one thing, and the thing without which the cause could never be cause is quite another thing. And so it seems to me that most people when they give the name of cause to the latter, are groping in the dark.[16]

Here Plato is distinguishing between contingent and actual causes.

For Plato, there is what we might call background conditions that are often crucial for a cause to operate, but those conditions are not themselves properly called causes. Such a distinction allows us to analyze the case from the *Second Tetralogy*. Antiphon suggests several conditions that could be considered causal: the javelin striking the boy, the young man hurling the javelin, the trainer signaling to the boy that it would be safe to cross the practice field, the boy running onto the practice field, as well as the sheer facts that both the boy and the young man were not standing still. Some of these conditions would be considered by Plato to be mere contingencies and others could be called actual causes. And the task of the jury would be to figure out which of the conditions is the actual cause of the boy's death.

15 Plato, *Statesman*, 281D-E, Loeb edition, *Plato* VIII, translated by Harold Fowler, Cambridge, MA: Harvard University Press, 1925, p. 91.

16 Plato, *Phaedo*, 99A-B, in *Plato* I, translated by Harold North Fowler, Loeb edition, Cambridge, MA: Harvard University Press, 1914, p. 341.

We find a somewhat similar set of ideas about causation in Aristotle's more developed work on causation.

In the *Physics*, Aristotle says that "motion is thought to be a sort of actuality, but incomplete, the reason for this view being that the potential whose actuality it is is incomplete."[17] In W. D. Ross' commentary on Aristotle's *Physics*, the idea is rendered as follows: "change seems to be a sort of incomplete actualization. The 'completeness' of change is due to the fact that the potential of which it is the actualization is itself necessarily incomplete."[18]

Aristotle also provides us with his famous account of the four types of cause, again conveniently summarized by Ross:

> Cause means (1) constituent material,
> (2) the form, pattern, or definition, and the generic and other elements of the definition,
> (3) the proximate originator of the change or rest, [or]
> (4) the end or final cause (of means to an end some are actions, others instruments),
> A thing has causes of more than one of these kinds … the one may be final and the other efficient cause.[19]

And the fourth or efficient cause is called "the primary source of the change and the coming to rest."[20]

In the *Eudemian Ethics*, Aristotle says that "States of character are the states that cause the emotions to be present either rationally or the opposite."[21] This is relevant to our earlier discussion of who is responsible and why when injury is caused. Here Aristotle traces the cause of human acts such as throwing a javelin to the emotions of the actor and ultimately back to the actor's character. If the javelin thrower was careless in his acts we should be still able to hold the javelin thrower responsible, since it is one's character that is ultimately who one is. The same could be said about the boy who ran into the arc of the javelin. If he acted carelessly this carelessness would be caused by his character and that might also make him responsible for his own demise.

17 Aristotle, *Physics*, 201b32, translated by R. P. Hardie and R. K. Gaye, in *The Basic Works of Aristotle*, edited by Richard McKeon, p. 255.

18 W. D. Ross, *Aristotle's Physics: A Revised Text with Introduction and Commentary*, Oxford: Oxford University Press, 1936, p. 360.

19 Ross, *Aristotle's Physics*, pp. 351–352.

20 Aristotle, *Physics*, 194b29, Hardie and Gaye, *The Basic Works of Aristotle*, p. 241.

21 Aristotle, *Eudemian Ethics*, 1220b18, translated by R. Hackman, Loeb edition, Cambridge, MA: Harvard University Press, 1935, p. 249.

What is most interesting is the way that Aristotle would trace causes back to a person by finding the roots of the motivation for a person's action in his or her states of character. Of course one could then try to trace the causes back further – to the parents who raised the person in question, for example. But Aristotle, like contemporary legal theorists, seems to stop the causal chain where we can find a person whose character is implicated in that causal chain. In part this is for practical considerations, but it is also based on the idea that in looking for what is itself uncaused, we have to go back to god, but that it is pointless to try to hold god responsible for human affairs.

19.3 CONTEMPORARY PHILOSOPHICAL DISCUSSIONS OF THE *SECOND TETRALOGY*

Bernard Williams has discussed the javelin case of the *Second Tetralogy* in ways important for figuring out how causation could have been understood in ancient Greek times.

> If the question were simply, What brought about his death? it could be said to have been answered in the narration. But what is at issue is a "whole person" social response, so the question has to be, Who brought about his death? That, as the speeches show, is a much more arguable matter … The case that is the subject of the *Second Tetralogy* … is a misadventure … No one denies it was an accident; but the question has to be answered, Who caused his death? The speaker for the young man who threw the javelin concedes that he hit the victim, but not that he caused his death.[22]

Williams provides us with a succinct statement of the relevant question and what the question assumes, namely that we should be looking not just for the physical causes but for a "whole person" who is causally responsible for the death.

Williams then goes on to argue that the defense raised just the right issue in saying that the young man who threw the javelin is not the one who caused the boy's death.

> But, as it was, the victim brought about his own death by his mistake: it is not our doing (*ergon*), the speaker argues, but that of the boy who did not look where he was running (2.5, 8). There is no paradox (the speaker continues) in saying that the victim caused his own death. It does not imply, for instance, as the other side claimed, that the victim must have thrown the javelin at himself. To claim this is to misunderstand the crucial issue – which is that it was not an action of javelin-throwing that killed him.[23]

[22] Bernard Williams, *Shame and Necessity*, Berkeley: University of California Press, 1993, p. 61.
[23] Ibid., p. 62.

In Williams' view, this analysis is not, as some commentators have argued, a manifestation of a primitive form of legal reasoning.

Williams calls our attention to the contemporary US case of *Palsgraff* v. *Long Island Railroad*, where similar causal complications are addressed. Here a Rube-Goldberg scenario unfolded where multiple parties contributed to a package exploding and injuring a passenger.

> Two men run for a departing train. A guard pushes them into it; in the course of this, one of them drops an ordinary-looking package, which, as it turns out, contains fireworks. It explodes, throwing down some scales at the end of the platform. The scales strike and injure a woman, who sues the railroad.[24]

As in the *Second Tetralogy* case, no one intentionally brought about the harm but in the end the central question is what Williams calls the "whole person" response: "someone has to be killed or banished," or in the Palsgraff case someone has to be held liable for the injuries to the woman on the platform quite a way from where the package exploded.

It is unfortunate that Williams does not say more about the "whole person" response and how it relates to causation issues, but we can glean from his text what he might have had in mind. The causal question at issue is for us to pick from among the people who contributed causally to harm that person who should be held responsible. The idea is based in the belief that one specific person has to be singled out on the basis of his or her causal role. Yet Williams himself admits, as does Antiphon, that we could be faced with contributory negligence, where the punishment or penalty is to be split among those who are causally responsible.

We are again in the domain that Plato called to our attention, not where we merely seek the physical condition without which a certain event would not have occurred, but where we seek the best cause for a given purpose that we, the people, or the state, wish to pursue. And in some cases what we seek is not the intentional actor but merely the causal actor who the state has a special interest in (for deterrence purposes, for instance). And in this respect luck may be as important as intent.

Another commentator on the *Second Tetralogy* in our own times is the legal theorist John Walter Jones, who has written one of the very best books on the legal thought of the Greeks. Commenting specifically on the javelin case in the *Second Tetralogy*, Jones says:

> Here in the fifth century we find a clear statement of the doctrine of the break in the chain of causation, or the interruption produced by what has been called a

[24] Williams, *Shame and Necessity*, p. 63.

> *novus actus interveniens*. If anyone is to blame as well as the boy, it was the adult who was, or should have been, in charge of him. On the other side it is urged that an "unwilling" killer is still a killer.[25]

The question was whether there was a human act that intervened in the causal chain – if so, then that person is to be considered responsible if his act was the last human act. In terms of the arguments of the *Second Tetralogy*, we need to know whether the last human act that made a causal difference was that taken by the trainer in advising the boy that it was safe to run onto the practice field.

As we will see, the analysis provided by Antiphon helps us illuminate contemporary problems dealing with proximate causation and contributory negligence. Before turning to the contemporary discussions in legal theory, let us pursue another thread. The *Third Tetralogy* also gives us good evidence that the Greeks took seriously the idea of the causal chain and how in some cases we need to look back further than the act of striking, just as we looked later than the act of the striker (the throwing of the javelin) to see what other significant causal factors occurred before the boy's death. In the *Third Tetralogy*, we have a brawl where an older man insults a younger one and in the ensuing fight the younger man kills the older man, and the younger man then claims something like self-defense.

In fact, what the case illustrates is the idea of provocation as a cause that is more significant than the later causal act of a human agent in fatally striking the older man. As Jones says of this case:

> Again, when the death resulted from a sudden altercation, it might be argued that the dead man's act of striking the first blow amounted to provocation which availed not merely to mitigate the responsibility of the accused but to transfer it altogether to the dead man. There would thus be no killing by the accused at all; once more the killed was also the killer.[26]

The faulty party was the one who provoked his own killing, not the one who struck the fatal blow. And at this point, says Jones, we see that fault rather than intention was the key to responsibility ascriptions.[27] But also notice that the last human act before the injury is not "the cause" – it is rather the act that initiated the fatal blow that is "the cause" of the injury.

[25] J. W. Jones, *The Law and Legal Theory of the Greeks*, Oxford: Oxford University Press, 1956, pp. 262–263.

[26] Ibid., p. 283.

[27] Ibid., p. 264.

19.4 PROXIMATE CAUSATION AND CONTRIBUTORY CAUSATION

The best contemporary book on causation in legal thought is Hart and Honore's *Causation in the Law*.[28] Early in the preliminaries, they provide a summary of a doctrine in contemporary law that they take aim at:

> They have often insisted that, apart from legal rules, or the special requirements of legal "policy," or conceptions of justice, every factor necessary for the occurrence of an event is equally entitled to be called "the cause." Yet this is not the case: neither the plain man nor the historian uses the expression "cause," or any related expression, in this way. For the contrast of cause with mere condition is an inseparable feature of all causal thinking … If a man has been shot, it would usually be stupid or inappropriate, though not false, to give as the cause of his death the fact that his blood-cells were deprived of oxygen, and equally inappropriate to give the manufacturer's action in selling the gun to his father from whom he had inherited it.[29]

We can see the *Second Tetralogy* as exploring the conditions necessary for the boy's death and then trying to defend one condition or another as the most appropriate one of the causes to be used to pin responsibility on one person for the death of another. The conditions are surely not considered to be "equally entitled" to be called "the cause" in Antiphon's view.

Hart and Honore urge that we distinguish "causes from mere conditions."[30] And the way to do this is not merely to make a policy judgment. There is an issue of fact even though shifting contexts for which an explanation is sought may shift our emphasis on which facts are the most significant for establishing "the cause."[31] Here we encounter what is often called the "proximate cause" of a given occurrence. The proximate cause is the cause that is produced by a human act and is closest in time to the occurrence of the harm. Referring to that last human cause cuts off the causal factors initiated by other human agents from being called the cause. Lawyers, and law professors, today often say that proximate cause is simply a matter of policy not metaphysics, but Hart and Honore uphold a counter tradition, going back at least to the *Tetralogies*, of resisting this oversimplified approach.

We can gain further insight into the possible legal thought of the *Second Tetralogy* when Hart and Honore argue that:

> Common experience teaches us that, left to themselves, the things we manipulate, since they have a "nature" or characteristic way of behaving, would persist in

[28] H. L. A. Hart and A. M. Honore, *Causation in the Law*, Oxford: Oxford University Press, 1959.

[29] Ibid., p. 11.

[30] Ibid., p. 23.

[31] Ibid., p. 12.

> states or exhibit changes different from those which we have learnt to bring about in them by our manipulations. The notion, that a cause is essentially something which interferes with or intervenes in a course of events which would normally take place, is central to the common-sense concept of cause.[32]

We could think of the attention paid to which of the parties stood still in the *Second Tetralogy* as in the same spirit of common-sense inquiry as that outlined by Hart and Honore.

If one party stood still and the second party moved then it would seem that the second party is the one who has interfered with or intervened in a course of events that involved the boy being struck with the javelin. One claim that is made in behalf of the young man who threw the javelin is that his activity would normally have resulted in hitting the target not the boy – it was only that the boy moved into the trajectory of the javelin, interfering with the javelin's movement toward the target, which caused the boy's death. This is not as difficult to defend in light of Hart and Honore's analysis as it might have seemed before. And the analysis that Antiphon provided is not aimed at the extreme relativist's position that all causes are of equal value, but at showing how one condition could be plausibly claimed to be called the cause for purposes of attributing responsibility.

We can also look to the contemporary treatment of contributory negligence, especially how negligence is seen as a cause. Hart and Honore say:

> A deviation from such man-made norms will very often be an omission, i.e. a failure to act in some way expected or required by the norm … One source is confusion about negative statements: we easily think of omissions as "negative events" and these in turn as "simply nothing." The corrective here is to realize that negative statements like "he did not pull the signal" are ways of describing the world, just as affirmative statements are, but they describe it by contrast not by comparison as affirmative statements do.[33]

In this light we can regard claims of how the boy did not pay attention to where he was running or that the young man did not pay attention to his surroundings when he threw the javelin as fitting neatly into the common-sense ways of understanding conditions that could turn out to be the cause of the death.

Hart and Honore also distinguish between concurrent and contributory causes in discussing contributory negligence. They say:

> In dealing with contributory causes we take cases of contributory negligence as typical and consider joint and concurrent torts only incidentally. Plaintiff's negligence is of legal significance only if causally connected with the harm, but this

[32] Ibid., p. 27.
[33] Ibid., p. 35.

> is sometimes obscured by the ambiguity of the phrase "contributory negligence" which may mean merely the failure of plaintiff to take reasonable care for his own safety, or may mean such a failure which contributes to the plaintiff's injury. We adopt the second sense and use negligence for the first.[34]

This seems to be the way that Antiphon discussed the failure of the boy to pay attention to where he was running. In one of the speeches in the *Second Tetralogy* it is pointed out that the boy's negligence was the cause of his death to occur since he would not have been killed if he had stood still and simply watched where the javelin throwers were practicing.

It is not merely that the boy did not take reasonable care for his safety but that he actively participated in the event that included his being killed. His running into the playing field where javelins were being thrown was risky and his being struck with a javelin was "within the risk."[35] In this sense, as was argued in the *Second Tetralogy*, there is a sense in which his negligence caused his own death. Once again, the consideration of the boy's contributory negligence by Antiphon is not merely a debating point for those who are "squandering of a day."[36] Indeed the example of the boy being killed by a javelin seems to me to illustrate well the central insights that Hart and Honore have made some 2,500 years after Antiphon.

19.5 THE *SECOND TETRALOGY'S* LESSONS

I have just attempted to show that there is similarity between Antiphon's analysis of causal factors in the *Second Tetralogy* and the analyses of Hart and Honore writing the most respected book on causation in the law today. But beyond such similarly, what can we learn from Antiphon? I will attempt to answer this question and also draw some conclusions in this final section of the chapter.

First, Antiphon illustrates how two things can both be true and significant despite looking like they must conflict. Searching for "the cause" in legal proceedings is largely a factual matter not merely a matter of "policy"; yet at the same time the context matters and may change what is considered "the cause" from one situation to another. Taking account of changing context does not necessarily lead to relativism. Indeed, to talk of causes at all requires one to be specific about what the context is of the situation. Hart and Honore make this clear when they ask about the causal status of oxygen – in most cases it is always present and so it plays a role in every causal chain. But only in some very unusual cases would citing lack of oxygen be considered relevant for legal causation.

[34] Ibid., p. 190.

[35] See ibid., p. 191.

[36] See remarks by Plutarch at the beginning of this chapter.

Here is the central point one can glean from Antiphon's *Tetralogies* and other writings – the legal context is different from all others in that liability is at stake. And in this sense we must focus on human agents, since those are the principal causal actors that concern the law. Aristotle seemed to think that he could give an account of causation across all contexts – and to some extent he succeeded. But the judge and jury-member have to focus on just one kind of causation. And even within that narrow sense of causation, or perhaps because we are within this narrow conception, what other events are going on around what is occurring can be more important than it would normally be outside of the legal domain of inquiry.

Second, Antiphon's examples of people standing still, or not standing still, make it crystal clear what it means to say that someone is intervening or interfering with a causal chain or process. Today we would look for a principle. But the idea that if you are standing still you cannot be thought to have intervened in a causal chain is the intuitively compelling insight needed to begin with. Starting with this example makes it harder to see what it will require to say that inaction, or properly omission, can be an intervention in a causal chain. And Antiphon is clearly aware of the need to account for inaction as well as action in causal terms if the inactive person is to be considered responsible for what results from a causal chain of events.

In a sense inaction must be conceptualized so that it is like the movement of a person who is not just standing still. Indeed, the difference between omissions and merely standing still is the key to understanding, among other things, negligence. Standing still can represent a kind of baseline used to evaluate whether or not a person has intervened into a causal chain. If he or she is literally standing still, and not violating duties he or she had, then there is no relevant connection between this human person and the causal chain. If the human person becomes an agent, either by action or inaction, then he or she intervenes in the causal chain and can be held responsible or liable for things that result.

Third, Antiphon also makes it clearer than it often is today how the ideas of causal responsibility and legal liability are related to each other. As the status of whose action is considered "the cause" changes, so does the legal status of the people in question, especially concerning who is legally liable. These different statuses encompass such things as being labeled "the cause" of a harm or injury, as well as being complicit although not the main perpetrator. We take up this issue in greater detail in another place. But the idea for us here is that it is possible also to share responsibility or liability as well – something that seems clearly to be recognized by the Greek orators like Antiphon.

Cases of joint and contributory liability are recognized as especially likely to occur in cases of negligence. Negligence is mainly understood by Antiphon as failing to take care or to pay attention, and is understood as a full-fledged causal factor. Those who share responsibility due to their negligence must be punished or penalized just as if they were direct perpetrators. If a person is causally responsible then it is highly likely that because of this status the person is legally liable, even if only as a matter of joint liability.

Finally, and on a more modest scale, Antiphon provides the kind of example that can capture not only the imagination of lawyers but also ordinary people, again in ways that legal theorists today often can only aspire to. The imagery of the boy being struck by the javelin while running across a practice field is vivid. And what are even more vivid are the reconstructed arguments made in behalf of the javelin thrower and the boy who is killed. Legal theorists over the ages have been enthralled with this case, and that is true today as well. There are many famous legal speeches written by the Greek orators in the fifth and fourth centuries BCE, but in my view the speeches by Antiphon in the *Tetralogies* are in a special category.

20

Homicide and Pollution

Athenian – "In regards to crimes against the public ... the majority have a share in the decision ... everyone suffers the injustice." Plato, *The Laws*, 768a1

This chapter is about the origins of criminal law in ancient times. It is often claimed that ancient societies lack a conception of crime – treating all harms as civil wrongs (what we call "torts" today). In an earlier part of this work I suggested that already in Hammurabi's Code, with its use of *lex talionis*, we could see the beginnings of the idea of criminality since the "eye for an eye" does not seem to be aimed at compensating the victim but is aimed at aiding the larger society.[1] I will now argue that several aspects of ancient Greek legal thought and practice mark a turn toward recognizing most of the features of criminality – thus much earlier than many scholars would claim. Some of the relevant aspects of Greek criminal law include: having separate courts and procedures for cases of homicide and other crimes; having specially trained judges for criminal courts; allowing individuals to prosecute who were not related to the victim; and having sanctions that were aimed at the harm to the society caused by the crime.

I will mainly focus on this last item. It will be my contention that the ancient Greeks already understood that once a wrongdoer had been punished, as a matter of retribution, there was still something owed to the community. The mark of a crime is that it adversely affects not just the victim but the larger community which has had its peace disrupted and for which there is a fear of similar wrongdoing in the future from this wrongdoer. The wrongdoer needed to be reintegrated into the society as no longer a threat to that society. Purification rituals were to be held for this purpose – merely extending punishment through increased incarceration would not address the problem.[2]

[1] See Chapter 9.

[2] Purification was thought to be required for other acts than homicide as well, as will become clear later in this chapter.

The conceptual point of the chapter is that the ancient Greek ideas of pollution and purification signal an important turn toward approaching homicide as something that is a danger to the community. Beyond retributive punishment, the perpetrator of a crime is required to do more for the society, because of his or her crime, than merely compensating the victim or serving a prison sentence. The perpetrator has to relieve the society of the danger that his or her acts brought upon the society so that he or she can be reintegrated back into that society.[3] I will address this point with reference to both ancient Greek times as well as our own, where I will critically assess the contemporary idea of extending incarceration for the protection of the society after the proportionate punishment has been inflicted. The Greek ideas of pollution and purification will be employed as a critical feature for understanding what is right and also wrong with extended punishment schemes today.

In Section 20.1 I provide some general background considerations on how I understand ancient Greek legal thought. In Section 20.2 I will discuss the earliest of the Greek homicide laws by Draco. In Section 20.3 I discuss several of the orators, especially Antiphon, as well as Plato who wrote about the connection between homicide and pollution in ancient Greek law. In Section 20.4 I take up a series of problems concerning pollution in early Athenian homicide law. Then in Section 20.5 I begin to build the case for thinking that ancient Greek legal thought had a distinct conception of criminality that was not merely a matter of delicts or torts because of the emerging idea of "legal" pollution. And in the final two sections, I argue that the ancient idea of legal pollution helps us today to understand the debate about how to deal with offenders who have served their sentences but who still seem to be a threat to their societies.

20.1 ANCIENT GREEK LEGAL THOUGHT AND CRIMINAL LAW

Ancient Greek legal thought can be characterized as an attempt to deal with the individual in the community. Here we have an emerging understanding of a public harm that is the law's exclusive jurisdiction. And even more basically we have the idea that individuals are members of that public, and that the membership in a public institution, the city-state, is the defining relationship for the legal individual. The law serves the purposes of the public – identifying individuals by their public roles and by the harms or benefits that the individual performs for their public institutions. These institutions are often not defined religiously – it was not membership in the temple or in one's relationship to the gods. Instead, it was one's

[3] In Greek mythology, Heracles' 12 labors were part of his punishment, exceeding a proportionate penalty.

relationship to one's fellow community members that was the key legal idea – and where the community was not seen merely as an extension of family, tribe, or clan.

Private law, concerning contracts, property, marriage, and family, was not much different for the Greeks than for earlier civilizations. But with the Greeks there was now a public law – and the idea of public law pretty much seems to have originated with the Greeks. And so the very idea of what law is, and even what law is for, changes significantly with the rise of the Greeks. It is too strong a claim that the Greeks invented the *public* sphere – yet there are good reasons to think that the idea of *public* law arose in a sophisticated form in ancient Greece.

For the Greeks, retribution and deterrence were not enough for punishing the convicted wrongdoer. Retribution was for the offense itself, and was to be proportionate to the harm that had been done to the victim. Deterrence was for the future, to make an example of the wrongdoer so that others would be less likely to consider committing the same type of wrong against other victims. But something else was required to be done concerning the dangerousness that the wrongdoer exemplified. The public harm was that all other citizens were placed at risk that the wrongdoer would commit a wrong that could make any citizen the next victim. It was in this sense that the wrongdoer was polluted and risked polluting the city with this dangerousness. Here the third form of punishment was that the wrongdoer had to submit to a purification ritual. Only after such purification could the wrongdoer return to the city and take on his or her role as citizen again. This is the most public aspect of punishment.

In some respects, the Greeks understood criminal law better than we do today: where a separate punishment was needed not for the sake of the victim but for the society. Consider Plato's view of crime and punishment in his last work, *The Laws*. Plato's "official theory" (as Stalley puts it) is that punishment is justified to cure the wrongdoer of a corrupt soul.

> The foundation of Plato's penology … is the claim that injustice is bad for us and may therefore be likened to a disease. The primary aim of the penal system must be to cure this disease.[4]

Some people are to be punished to cure their souls, that is, for the future, not as a response to the past. And some other people are to be executed or exiled[5] if it looks like curing them will either take a long time or is impossible. But some of the other things Plato says about punishing homicide and wounding cannot easily fit into this scheme, unless stability also needs to be restored. Again quoting Stalley: "in practice [Plato's] Athenian seeks, not only to make the citizens virtuous, but also to make the

4 R. F. Stalley, *An Introduction to Plato's Laws*, Indianapolis, IN: Hackett Publishing, 1983, p. 143.

5 I will later take up the problems with seeing exile as a way to remove the pollution.

state unified and orderly."[6] And it will be my contention that for Plato as well as for other Greek legal theorists, criminal law functions also to protect the city-state from wrongdoers. I will return to Plato later in the chapter, but I want now to start at the beginning of Greek legal thought about homicide and other crimes.

20.2 DRACO'S HOMICIDE LAW

Here is the beginning of the fragments that have survived from the earliest ancient Greek homicide laws, Draco's 621/620 BCE law:

> Even if someone kills someone without premeditation, he shall be exiled. The Basileis are to adjudge responsible for homicide ... the one who instigated the killing. The Ephetai are to give the verdict. Pardon is to be granted, if there is a father or brother or sons, by all or one who opposes it shall prevail. And if these do not exist, pardon is to be granted by those as far as the degree of cousin's son and cousin, if all are willing to grant it; the one who opposes it shall prevail ... A proclamation is made against the killer in the agora by relatives as far as the degree of cousin's son and cousin. The prosecution is to be shared by cousins, sons of cousins, sons-in-law, fathers-in-law, and members of the phratry.[7]

Here there are several things initially to note. First, it seems that all forms of killing are subject to exile. Second, pardon is possible but only if all of the relatives of the victim agree. And third, the family of the victim is to prosecute, indeed is required to prosecute, the person who has killed a family member.

In very early Greek legal thought anyone who kills another is treated as deserving of exile or death, even if the killing was accidental. And while it is true that pardon was possible, various things had to occur before pardon could occur even in cases of accidental killing. Indeed, for the Greeks killing was special. At least in part this is because, as becomes clear in later Greek times, the killer is seen as someone who is polluted and who risks polluting the whole city by his act of killing. I will now focus on the three aspects of the quotation from Draco's laws that I just highlighted.

First, then, while Draco's law does not draw a distinction between unintentional and intentional homicide in terms of punishment, there is a distinction in terms of the conditions that must be satisfied for obtaining a pardon. Carawan says:

> Because pollution of bloodguilt indiscriminately endangered the community, even in unintentional killings, Draco supposedly created a court to address this threat. And to ensure that the unintentional killer should not purchase his redemption at

[6] Stalley, *An Introduction to Plato's Laws*, p. 149.

[7] Stalley, *An Introduction to Plato's Laws*, p. 149. Stroud, *Drakon's Law on Homicide*, Berkeley, CA: University of California Press, 1968, p. 6.

the community's peril, financial compensation, *poine*, was eliminated even in these less grievous homicides.[8]

The earliest Greek law of homicide, Draco's code, calls for a killer to be subject to more than the payment of compensation to the victim's family. In addition there must be execution or exile as a mark of the seriousness of having killed. Draco does not mention pollution, nor does Homer in this context, but a bit later the idea of pollution is introduced, in my view, to mark the harm to the community that is done by a killer, beyond merely the harm to the victim and his or her family.

Second, for Draco's code the killer could be pardoned in certain contexts – primarily if the victim's family was unanimous in agreeing that the killer could be pardoned. The family of the victim rather than the city-state was the determiner of whether or not pardon could be issued. But it is also important to note that the state was the issuer of the pardon, so the family's judgment was replaced by that of the larger society through a formal pardon mechanism.

Third, public prosecution of the killer must occur. This was especially important as it inserted a layer between the killer and the victim's family. The family of the victim could not on its own kill the killer or decide on the killer's exile, as seemingly would have been true before Draco's code in ancient Greece. The killer could not be exiled, or killed, until there had been a prosecution, and there was a formal judgment of guilt. Indeed, the family not only had to wait for the outcome of a trial, but the family had to secure a prosecution by taking up the role of prosecutor as its duty to the state.

In Draco's code there is already an indication of one of the cornerstones of criminal law: the state has a role to play because of its interest in cases such as killing that harm the society. While the prosecution before a public court may be assigned to the family of the victim, letting the family exact a penalty or even a punishment is now mediated by the society. This sets the stage for the only somewhat later treatment of homicide by some ancient Greek orators, playwrights, and philosophers.

20.3 POLLUTION IN ANTIPHON, AESCHYLUS, AND PLATO

In ancient Greek plays and legal texts, moral pollution plays a fairly prominent role in the context of killing. Consider a passage from the *First Tetralogy*, attributed to Antiphon:

8 Edwin Carawan, *Rhetoric and the Law of Draco*, Oxford: Clarendon Press, 1998, p. 17. Also see Hubert J. Treston, *Poine: A Study in Ancient Greek Blood-Vengeance*, London: Longmans, Green and Co., 1923.

> We know that the whole city is polluted by the killer until he is prosecuted and that if we prosecute the wrong man, we will all be guilty of impiety, and punishment for any mistake you make (in convicting him) will fall on us. Since the entire pollution thus falls on us, we will try to show you as clearly as possible from the facts at our disposal that he killed the man.[9]

The *Tetralogies* seem to have been training guides for lawyers, not verbatim statements of court opinions. Nonetheless, the ideas here seem to be consistent with legal practice in ancient Greece. And the idea is that a killer is polluted and thereby pollutes the city by what he or she has done. This pollution is in need of expiation, of cleansing, since if it is not removed other members of the society may become infected with it. On the other hand, care must be taken in dealing with those believed to be polluted, for in condemning the wrong person the condemners will certainly themselves become polluted.

We also have an example of how purification from pollution was to be attained in ancient Greece. We turn again to the *Tetralogies* attributed to Antiphon:

> You know quite certainly how he died, you know that the tracks of suspicion lead to this man, and you have the attendant's reliable testimony; how in all justice can you acquit him. With this in mind, assist the victim, punish the killer, and purify the city. You will achieve three good results: fewer men will plot crimes, more men will observe their religious duties, and you will free yourself from this man's pollution.[10]

It is very important to notice here that the three good results of punishment are roughly: deterrence, retribution, and purification, and that they are different from one another. Even if the killer is to be allowed to live there are several means by which the city can be purified nonetheless. There can be a ritual purification sometimes followed by banishment from the city, or banishment without the purification ritual, as a means to purify the killer without taking his or her life.

Getting rid of the one who is polluted is the key to purification in most of these early Greek texts. Killing the person is the most straightforward way, but one runs the risk that the wrong person is executed, thus in a sense intensifying the pollution that will be spread throughout the city. Banishment has the advantage that if a mistake has been made, there is still room for correction. Ritual purification is the safest in some respects, but it also may be such that it does not fully remove the stain given the nature of the crime committed. So, while there were various ways of achieving purification or expiation in ancient Greece, and while there seemed to be clear routes open to achieve such purification, there were hazards at each turn – making

[9] Antiphon, *First Tetralogy* 2.1, in *Speeches from Athenian Law*, edited by Michael Gagarin, Austin, TX: University of Texas Press, 2011, p. 18.

[10] Antiphon, *First Tetralogy* 2.3, ibid., p. 25.

the practice of purification fraught with peril because of worries about whether the specific form chosen will indeed remove, or instead intensify, the pollution.

Antiphon also talks about pollution in terms of dirty hands. Here is a long quotation from his speech for the defense in "On the Murder of Herodes":

> You have now heard everything that can be demonstrated by human evidence and witnesses; but before casting your vote, you should also look just as much to the evidence of signs from the gods. You rely on these especially when managing the public affairs of the city safely, in times of danger and other times too; you should also consider these signs important and reliable in private affairs. I think you know that before now, many who have embarked on a ship with unclean hands or some other pollution have themselves perished together with others who led devout lives and fulfilled all their obligations to the gods. Others who did not perish were subjected to life-threatening dangers because of such people. And many others attending sacrifices were shown to be unholy and were prevented from completing the proper rites. With me, however, it's just the opposite in every case. Those I sailed with have enjoyed the finest voyage, and at the sacrificial rites I have attended, the sacrifice has never been anything but the finest. I think this is important evidence that the prosecution's accusations against me are untrue.[11]

Here it is a sign that a person is unpolluted if that person has not suffered for what he or she has done.

For Homeric societies, pollution (*miasma*) is probably best seen as something very much like physical dirt. In these societies, one is unclean right after one gives birth or has sex, and until one literally cleanses oneself one cannot pray to the gods because one is dirty in their eyes. Arthur Adkins proposes this definition of pollution in Homeric societies – "the presence (or supposed presence) of any substance, of whatever kind, which is believed to hamper men's relations with the supernatural."[12] But by the fifth century BCE, pollution for Aeschylus comes to be associated with moral responsibility. If one acts in a way that pollutes oneself then that person has been tainted in some way. And those who come into contact with the polluted person are also tainted (by the gods or even by the state). Committing homicide is the most common cause of pollution in Greek literature, as well as in ordinary Greek life, as we see in the work of Aeschylus, especially the *Eumenides*.

It appears that Greek trials can deal with both criminal guilt and moral pollution, although it is the moral pollution that others could incur by associating with the perpetrator of murder. As I will suggest later, perhaps we should think of some moral

11 Antiphon, *On the Murder of Herodes*, 81–83, ibid., pp. 71–72.

12 Arthur Adkins, *Merit and Responsibility: A Study in Greek Values*, Oxford: Oxford University Press, 1960.

pollution as legal pollution. Indeed, in Aeschylus' play, *Eumenides*, pollution and criminal guilt are linked as they appear to have been in Athenian court proceedings.

Consider these selected passages from the play:

ATHENA: "This is too grave a cause for any man to judge … I will choose out Jurors of homicide, for a perpetual court"

APOLLO: "I cleansed him from this murder; I am here to be His advocate, since I am answerable for the stroke that killed his mother"

ORESTES: "That I struck the blow is true … But was murder justified?"

ATHENA: "As you now try this first case of Bloodshed, hear the constitution of your court … Areopagus … So do not taint pure laws with new expediency"[13]

Beyond the guilt there is also something that needs to be purified, the "taint," and there is evidence that in some trials purification occurred as well as punishment.[14]

In the dialogue, the *Laws*, Plato talks about pollution as related to punishment and both seem to have a strongly institutional, not a religious, dimension. Consider the following passages:

> the evil that now moves you … is neither human nor divine, but a certain gadfly that grows naturally in human beings[15]
>
> The judicial penalty for this is to be death … by which he'll present an example that will benefit the others[16]
>
> The laws … come into being for the sake of the worthy human being, in order to teach them the way in which they might mingle with one another … partly for the sake of those who have shunned education[17]

In Plato's *The Laws*, courts can both expiate guilt and cleanse pollution.

Some forms of punishment seem to be related to pollution for Plato. Consider the case of involuntary homicide where it is by your act that a child dies. You are thereby polluted and the parents of the child seek vengeance against you.[18] And there is a kind of divine response inevitably brought on by the victim's death that pollutes the perpetrator. As the Plato scholar, Saunders, suggests, all the state can do is ensure by its laws "that the situation is managed in an orderly and expeditious manner."[19] There are two forms of response to homicide that need to be managed by the state,

[13] Aeschylus, *Eumenides*, 450–695, in Aeschylus, *The Orestaian Trilogy*, translated by Philip Vellacott, NY: Penguin Books, 1956, pp. 164–176.

[14] It seems that homicide trials were often held outdoors so that the pollution of the wrongdoer was open to the breezes and somewhat more diluted than if the trial were held indoors.

[15] Plato, *The Laws*, 854b1, translated by Thomas Pangle, NY: Basic Books, 1980, p. 246.

[16] Ibid., 855a1, ibid., p. 247.

[17] Ibid., 880e, ibid., p. 277.

[18] In Greek mythology perhaps think of Daedelus fleeing Athens after murdering his nephew.

[19] Trevor Saunders, *Plato's Penal Code*, Oxford: Clarendon Press, 1991, p. 224.

through its laws: what the gods demand and what the victim's family demands. Both are significant for peace and stability in the city-state.

20.4 POLLUTION PROBLEMS

Why would exile be considered a form of purification?[20] Exile seemingly cannot "wipe the stain" from the polluted actor, or eliminate the pollution that could affect members of a city. There seems to be a disconnect between the idea of pollution as something that infects or stains those who kill and the idea that the infection or stain can be removed by exile, which was the most common form of punishment for a killer in ancient Athens. If the idea of pollution is a metaphor, then it might be easier to make sense of it. The institution of pollution might be explainable similar to some religious taboos as serving some other purpose than what is literally suggested.

But we have the remaining problem: why a killer who is polluted and dangerous to his or her countrymen is not likewise polluted and dangerous to the foreign citizens when he arrives in his place of exile. It is of interest that Plato, in the *Laws*, "imposes restrictions on the killer after his return from exile."[21] So it seems that for Plato, pollution is not removed by exile – a position that could help resolve the first of our pollution problems in this section.

Another problem emerges as early as Draco: intention or premeditation does not matter except insofar as its lack might make it easier to secure a pardon – all killing is subject to exile. Yet, it would seem that in terms of dangerousness, the intentional killer is much more of a danger than one who only accidentally and unknowingly killed. So why would all forms of killing indiscriminately bring pollution upon the killer? Perhaps all killers have blood on their hands and pollution is to be understood quite literally as being tainted by the blood of killing, as it was perhaps in Homeric times. But this literal meaning of pollution seems peculiar – since it would be very hard to explain pardoning in these terms (would the victim's family literally have to wash the blood off of the killer's hands?).

So, it makes sense to wonder if there is a sense of pollution that is neither purely metaphorical nor purely literal. It is clear that pollution had its origins as a religious notion – embedded in the sacral law. And it is also clear that pollution had strong resonance as a moral concept as well. But in the legal proceedings for homicide that we have been examining, it is at least worth considering if pollution had a legal sense – a kind of danger that the city-state concerned itself with in the punishment

[20] See Robert Parker, *Miasma: Pollution and Purification in Early Greek Religion*, Oxford: Oxford University Press, 1983, p. 114.

[21] Ibid., p. 122.

of killers. Robert Parker says: "it is reasonable to suppose that, in a fourth-century [BCE] prosecution, murder would have been presented as a threat to society on a secular far more than on a religious level."[22] And Parker also points out that "Ritual and legal status are assimilated to the extent that in contexts of homicide 'pure' and 'not subject to legal sanctions' are often synonymous."[23] While the texts attributed to Antiphon in the *Tetralogies* discuss pollution in religiously ritualistic terms, in other texts by Antiphon and elsewhere these ideas are expressed in more secular, and even legal, terms as we will see in the next section of this chapter.

Yet another problem, having to do with the killer's presence, is expressed by MacDowell:

> When an Athenian was killed outside Attica, steps were taken, in the shape of *androlepsiai*, to get the killer extradited to Athens for trial … A killer polluted the state by his presence, not by his absence. If the legislator was concerned about pollution, one would expect to find that the killer was forbidden to enter Attica. In fact the law mandated that he should enter Attica.[24]

Exiling a killer makes sense if the pollution of the killer goes with him into exile, thus removing the source of pollution from Athens. But then why would Athens want someone who has killed abroad, and who is still abroad, extradited to Athens where it would be risked that the killer would bring pollution back into the city?

If pollution is here a legal category then it makes sense to expiate the pollution whether it is of a citizen or not a citizen, or whether it is a citizen residing inside or outside of Athens. Indeed, as we saw in the previous section, several trials are described as including punishment as retribution and also as pollution. So, even if pollution has a religious and moral sense, it seems that pollution also came to be seen as warranting some sort of legal response as well. And thus it is not out of the question to talk of legal pollution as a category that is becoming recognized in ancient Athenian society by the time of Plato, and perhaps as early as Aeschylus and the Orators. In the next sections I will discuss what evidence there is for an Athenian notion of legal pollution and what value such a notion would serve.

20.5 LEGAL POLLUTION IN ATHENS

Even though the pollution is something the gods instill it is treated in Plato's *Laws* as something that the city-state can change. The city-state can make the doctor who kills by accident while performing his or her normal functions not polluted,

[22] Ibid., p. 128.
[23] Ibid., p. 114.
[24] Douglas M. MacDowell, *Athenian Homicide Law in the Age of the Orators*, Manchester: Manchester University Press, 1963, p. 149.

says Plato. "In the case of all doctors, if the person being cared for should die against their intention, they are to be held unpolluted according to law."[25] Also Plato says: "If someone should kill somebody while defending his father from death … let him be entirely unpolluted."[26] In both of these examples, Plato does not say that the killer is unpolluted but that the law should declare the killer to be unpolluted.

From these passages and others it becomes clear that Plato has a conception of secular legal pollution that differs from the earlier idea of sacral pollution as a religious idea. Indeed, it is hard to make sense of these passages if the kind of pollution that Plato refers to is seen as a religious idea, as a kind of punishment that the gods demand. This seems very different from the way that pollution was treated by the tragic poets – pollution is unavoidable and can only be removed in two ways: exile or death of the polluter. Yet, Plato does not give either of these remedies for the pollution.

MacDowell says it is clear that the concept of pollution played a role in the legal proceedings in ancient Greece.

> Demosthenes says that when an unintentional killer was pardoned and allowed to return from exile, the law ordained "sacrifice, cleansing, and certain other actions" (D.23.72). This proves that the doctrine of pollution was recognized in the law … this passage is, as far as I can discover, the only one which proves it.[27]

Despite such little evidence, commentators claim that pollution played a large role in Athenian law. MacDowell also says that there were three purposes of Athenian homicide law, "'vengeance,' 'cleansing,' and 'deterrence' … and we then have no way of telling which purpose or purposes were in the minds of the men who introduced them."[28]

Here is what some other commentators also have said about our topic. Parker says that "such evidence as is available suggests that intense anxiety was not the norm. If we consider the different sets of people involved, it is the killer himself whose peril is most frequently mentioned."[29] Nonetheless, Calhoun says: "when the idea of pollution became attached to the shedding of blood, the state intervened in the punishment of homicide in order to protect the community … and this is the decisive stage in the evolution of criminal law."[30] I partially follow Calhoun in this

25 Plato, *The Laws*, 865b, p. 259.
26 Ibid., 874d, p. 270.
27 MacDowell, *Athenian Homicide Law*, p. 148.
28 Ibid., p. 141.
29 Ibid., p. 128.
30 George Miller Calhoun, *The Growth of Criminal Law in Ancient Greece*, Berkeley, CA: University of California Press, 1927, p. 9.

approach, but I give a greater place to the concept of pollution than he does in the development of criminal law in ancient Greece.

The concept of pollution (*miasma*) adds a different component from the retributive component of punishment in homicide cases. It is not just that the victim must be satisfied by compensation or retaliatory retribution. Adding the concept of pollution means that, as Garawan says:

> the trial is fundamentally concerned with the threat to the polis, and the judge's verdict should be directed against this urgent danger, [which] implies an immediate understanding of homicide as a public wrong, not merely a private offense … In the *Tetralogies* … we find an emphatic declaration that homicide must be judged as a public wrong.[31]

Carawan did recognize that the religious idea of pollution mattered to Draco as well: "Because pollution of bloodguilt indiscriminately endangered the community, even in unintentional killings, Draco supposedly created a court to address that threat."[32]

In an important comment on the legal status of pollution, Bonner and Smith point out that:

> The whole matter of pollution in homicide looks like a sort of *legalized pollution* which was foisted upon homicide procedure by religion for various reasons. It had considerably to do with the forms of the procedure, but very little to do with the punishment.[33]

Even after a killer had been punished, a ritual of purification was also required so the killer could be "reinstated into the society."[34] And the society is then freed of pollution as well.

J. W. Jones has discussed a famous case from Antiphon usually cited on causation (and which we discussed in the previous chapter) that I think can shed light also on the question of how best to categorize pollution in legal proceedings in ancient Athenian legal thought. Here is Jones' description of the case:

> A youth practicing [javelin throwing] in the gymnasium accidentally hits a boy who runs from among the spectators. Nothing is said expressly by either side on the point of the killing being accidental. The defense is that the boy, by the act of running into the course of the javelin had caused his own death. Aiming

[31] Edwin Carawan, *Rhetoric and the Law of Draco*, Oxford: Oxford University Press, 1998, p. 197.

[32] Ibid., p. 117.

[33] Robert J. Bonner and Gertrude Smith, *The Administration of Justice from Homer to Aristotle*, Chicago: University of Chicago Press, 1938, Vol. II, pp. 200–201, my italics.

[34] Ibid., p. 206.

> at the target was not killing the boy; otherwise the others practicing would be equally responsible; it is not because they did not throw that they are not liable but because the boy did not run into their javelins, and he by his own fault had, unfortunately, brought his own punishment upon himself and thereby absolved the thrower.[35]

There is no guilt in this case that would warrant punishment of the javelin thrower, but seemingly there is no pollution either despite the fact that the javelin thrower was a killer who has the boy's blood on his hands. Yet, if the boy actually killed himself by running into the javelin, then the only pollution is on the boy's head – and since he is dead, the pollution died with him. Or to put it another way, the boy would no longer be a danger to the city.

My claim is that legal pollution in Athenian legal thought concerns the need to curtail dangerousness. Initially, homicide law, as seen in Homer and Draco, did not talk of pollution in legal terms. But then pollution seems to have been introduced as a matter of sacral law and then added into the homicide law. The idea is that the killer risked polluting the city because of the wrath of the gods in not seeing a killer punished. Then later yet the idea arose that a procedure should be added to the homicide law requiring both punishment and purification. So, my claim is that the dangerousness, requiring purification, came to be seen as a non-religious worry about the killer, but a worry for the city nonetheless.

Of course, pollution does not need to be only a legal category, since in modern times the moral idea of guilt merges with the legal idea of liability in criminal law, as was already true since the Middle Ages. The idea of pollution in Athenian law may have continued to be used both in a sacral and secular sense. In both contexts pollution is best understood, I believe, as linked to dangerousness. It seems to me that the idea of secular dangerousness expressed by the idea of legal pollution can be seen as one of several important ideas that showed a developing idea of public criminal law – in the case of legal pollution we have the idea of the dangerousness to the city of letting killers remain in a condition where they are still a danger to others in the city. And we find importantly that the victim is not the primary person that needs to be addressed by the law – rather it is the community that is placed in danger. The law seeks redress for the new danger to the community and this is the epitome of the idea of public law. The idea of criminality arises when acts which are committed by one person against another come to be seen as affecting the whole community as well – making the community the victim that also needs to be redressed.

35 Jones, *The Law and Legal Theory of the Greeks*, p. 262.

20.6 DANGEROUSNESS AND POLLUTION

Today the danger to the community is not thought to be that the killer will spread pollution to others in the community but that the killer, or rapist, etc., will act likewise again. This is a different danger, seemingly, than the danger recognized by Aeschylus, Antiphon, and Plato. But it is similar in that more harm will occur unless some kind of change in the offender occurs. We see this today in the concern about releasing certain persistent offenders back into the community if they are unchanged – often understood as being unremorseful, despite serving their proportionate sentences.

The change or expiation needed is for the danger perpetrated on the community and this is not merely a matter of deterrence only, despite certain similarities. It is the perpetrator who is to be deterred, but reestablishing the safety of the community is a broader goal than that normally associated with special, or even general, deterrence. Deterrence does not include the idea of desert – identifying and demanding expiation is for the Greeks something that is due by the offender to the city. But it is clear that these ideas are related. Yet, even today it is not normally thought to be a matter of deterrence to keep the perpetrator in prison longer than his or her proportionate sentence.

There is also a kind of public retribution that is assuaged when remorse is displayed as well as a need to deter the perpetrator in the future. Indeed, there is a continuing danger to the community that must be addressed that takes killing out of the realm of private compensation by the killer to the victim's family. This is what makes the area of law here public as opposed to private. And as we will see, there are both positive and negative side-effects of this change in legal models.

Parker is opposed to my interpretation of ancient Athenian homicide institutions saying that the basis of these institutions "seems not to be the fear of pollution but the urge to exact retribution."[36] In this section I will advance the view that there is no necessary incompatibility between these two, and that some of the legal institutions concerning murder in contemporary society reflect how these two ideas can be brought into the same framework. Marking someone as polluted calls attention to his dangerousness so others can be warned to avoid him, yet as we will see, it is also ripe for abuse.

Mary Douglas addresses directly the connection between things that are said to be polluted and things that cause or are associated with danger in Greek times and later. Indeed, Douglas claims that "pollution is a type of danger … A polluting person is always in the wrong."[37] For Douglas, the polluted person is in the wrong

[36] Parker, *Miasma*, p. 117.

[37] Mary Douglas, *Purity and Power: An Analysis of the Concept of Pollution and Taboo*, NY: Routledge, 1966, 2002, p. 140.

because he or she has violated the society's rules that are aimed at protecting the society. If one leads a good life then there is no danger to the society. Here we can see how to connect pollution to the idea of breaking the rules of the society – especially those rules that are meant to protect the society from harm.

The connection between pollution and danger, and the connection between avoiding pollution and achieving a good life, give us a different, although related, dimension of pollution than what we have previously explored. Here pollution is not primarily about what one's group has done, or about getting one's hands dirty, or about having blood on one's hands. Here pollution is about violating rules that the society has determined are important, perhaps necessary, for promoting the avoidance of danger. And this lends itself well to a legal analysis rather than a religious or moral one.

Consider that certain kinds of crime today are treated in more than retributive or deterrent terms. If a crime is thought to be sufficiently egregious and if there is sufficient danger that it be repeated, additional incarceration may be called for. Cases involving rapists, murderers, and especially sex offenders and child predators have been thought to warrant lengthened sentences due to the danger to the public of having these offenders put back into the general population. Indeed, the idea of "persistent offender" or an offender who is facing "three strikes and you're out" seems to have an affinity with the idea of legal pollution we have been exploring. But again, retribution is not the same as purification. Instead, purification is more like rehabilitation than retribution.

Notice that today the extended incarceration is not even mainly retributive, although it can also be that, but a form of incapacitation or protective detention – where the community is being protected from the danger that the exposure to the perpetrator brings on – perhaps similar to the ancient Greek idea of exiling the killer. Indeed, the crime is often discussed as a kind of contamination, especially in the case of persistent pedophiles and rapists. And these offenders are sometimes kept in prison until they are determined to be no longer a danger to society because of some kind of reform to the offender.

Perhaps today we can make sense of the movement toward increasing incarceration in terms of seeing such offenders as polluted where there is needed a legal process that cleanses the perpetrator after he has already served his duly authorized and proportionate sentence. The additional incarceration does not have to be proportionate since it is in response to future dangerousness not past offense. In some respects one may never prove that one will not be a danger to the community in the future since we cannot know what the future will bring.

The worries with protective detention and other forms of extended incarceration now come to the fore and the worries are two among others: there may be no clear way for the perpetrator to convince the community that he or she is no longer a danger to that community; and the perpetrator may be scarred indefinitely even after he or she is released from incarceration. These are well-known problems with all forms of incarceration, but are more pronounced when the incarceration is disconnected from the original offense. How does one prove that one will not sexually molest children again? In some cases, the only proof is that a child molester has been castrated, physically or chemically. Here there is the equivalent of purification, with its attendant worries about abuse of this form of punishment. For it is the community that has been victimized and seeks assurance that it will be safe again – but how much can be expected of one offender concerning that larger goal?

Yet short of this extreme punishment, it does not seem to be worth the risk to let a serial killer or sex offender back into the community given the nature of the harm he or she could continue to perpetrate. This all seems true unless we think of punishment in a different way – perhaps in terms of rehabilitation, as was true for Plato as well. If there was a way to rehabilitate the killer so that he or she is no longer now a danger to the community, then he or she could be seen as "purified" and ready to be welcomed back into the community. But of course this does not answer the question of what should be done in the meantime before we have such reliable knowledge.

So, the image of the polluted perpetrator in need of purification is still with us – the offender must pay for what he or she has done, but must also show that the community, the true victim of the offender, will not continue to suffer.[38] This suffering concerns the danger to the community of the harms continuing, along with ancillary harms attendant to them. That danger is what makes the matter a criminal rather than a civil one – we move beyond compensating the individual victim to seeing the community as a potential victim as well because of the increased danger posed by the offender and the community then must figure out how to expiate the danger.

The larger question at issue is this: what is the appropriate response to a public crime that is said to harm the community by increasing dangerousness to the members of the community? And it is my view that just such a question was already posed and partially answered in ancient Greek legal thought with the transformation of the idea of religious pollution into one of legal pollution, where the state made the determination of when the offender was now cleansed.

Here is a revealing comment by J. W. Jones concerning the importance of some of Plato's relevant innovations in legal thought:

> It was a distinct advance when, as is shown in Plato's *Protagoras*, punishment was discussed in terms of the future rather than the past, as a means of preventing crime by deterrence or cure. Moreover in the *Laws*, Plato had come to the conclusion

[38] At least in principle, purification or reform could take place in public or not.

> that the movement and change which were to be found everywhere in nature must be traced back finally to what he called psyche or soul.[39]

Plato's innovation was to see that some kind of change in the psyche of the wrongdoer was needed to show that there was a kind of "cure" that meant that this wrongdoer was no longer a threat to the society. Incarceration does not necessarily bring about such a cure.

Interestingly, for the ancient Greeks incarceration was often not a realistic means of punishment in any event. Resources were often not available for jails and jailers. And most imprisonment was for debt rather than as a punishment. This is why punishment by death and banishment were more common forms of punishment than incarceration. As I said, death serves the dual goals of retribution and purification. Banishment is harder to understand as satisfying the goal of purification, as I have indicated earlier. But as punishment came to include imprisonment, as was already true by the time of Socrates, it was as much a holding place while the death penalty was awaited as it was the site of the punishment itself.[40] Already with the ancient Greeks, the shortcomings of incarceration were understood.

Today, imprisonment is used for retributive purposes and also sometimes as a holding place for wrongdoers who have served their sentences but who are deemed too dangerous to be readmitted into society, sometimes because they are repeat offenders. It is interesting to note that there was something like a three-strikes rule in ancient Greece. A. R. W. Harrison points out that "a man who was convicted three times in certain cases became *atimos* [an outlaw] in addition to whatever penalty had been imposed by the court on the third occasion."[41] Subjecting someone to more imprisonment, to cure the dangerousness of the wrongdoer when the earlier imprisonment did not seem to affect this dangerousness, seems misguided.

20.7 REDRESSING HARM TO SOCIETY

The problem of crime and punishment that we have been pursuing is one that arises with the idea of a crime as primarily a harm to the society rather than to the victim. If we think of harm in terms of setback to interests,[42] we must then ascertain which interests of the society are set back when a crime has occurred. Of course, one setback concerns the interest the society has in having its rules followed rather than disregarded. There is some value in merely having a rule-governed society, but the

[39] Jones, *The Law and Legal Theory of the Greeks*, p. 41.

[40] See Danielle Allen, *The World of Prometheus: The Politics of Punishing in Democratic Athens*, Princeton, NJ: Princeton University Press, 2000, pp. 224–232.

[41] A. R. W. Harrison, *The Law of Athens*, Oxford: Oxford University Press, 1971, Vol. II, p. 172.

[42] See Joel Feinberg, *Harm to Others*, Oxford: Oxford University Press, 1984.

main interest of society is that these rules are aimed at the well-being of the citizens, or some other equally important social good. Yet, even such an important interest has to be weighed against the loss of liberty of the person imprisoned.

One of the difficulties is that once the wrongdoer has served his or her sentence, the person has no longer forfeited his or her rights and is now best seen as a regular citizen, who is deserving of equal respect by the society. So, merely extending imprisonment as a means to prevent future harm looks like it will require an added rationale because of the abridgement of rights of the person imprisoned even though that person's rights forfeiture has ended.

The ancient Greek models we have been examining can be cast as providing at least two related ideas. First, there is the idea of pollution espoused by the orators and poets. The wrongdoer has not only harmed the victim but has polluted the society insofar as the gods have been offended since the peace has been disrupted, calling for some form of public purification. Second, there is Plato's idea of punishment as curative. This is more secular, although Plato also uses the language of pollution. But unlike the offense to the gods' peace, Plato focuses on the inner illness of the wrongdoer that needs to be cured of its anti-social tendencies. Both ideas see the need for additional redress, beyond the retributive punishment, which would focus on the interests of the society rather than those of the victim.

In my view, the ancient Greeks had a clear early conception of crime as different from the "private" harm to victims that calls for redress in terms of compensation. And the Greeks also had a developing sense that retribution was not sufficient to redress the societal harm. Most importantly, the Greeks did not support further imprisonment for the redress of the societal harm, but rather saw the need for what they called purification. As for the Greeks, there is no easy answer about what else to do to deal with the remainder of dangerousness after a wrongdoer has served a proportionate sentence. And yet if criminal law is supposed to provide redress for the society, we fail if we continue merely to add more prison time to those who are judged to be still a danger to society.

21

Justification, Excuse, and Mitigation

Just as in the case of causation, ancient Greek legal thought displayed quite a subtle understanding of justification and excuse, especially self-defense. One issue that has recently received attention is how to characterize the reasonable or proportionate response on the part of the person who has been attacked and is now defending himself or herself. It is perhaps surprising that this question vexed ancient Greek thinkers and somewhat mirrors the discussion today. So, I will spend time on how the ancient Greeks saw the ideas of justification and excuse and then single out the issue of proportionality, as well as necessity in this chapter. I will also explore some related notion in ancient Chinese legal thought related to lack of virtue.

I will begin with several passages from Sophocles, from his plays the *Ajax*, *Oedipus Tyrannus*, and *Oedipus at Colonus* that discuss the ideas that ignorance and compulsion remove or diminish responsibility. In Section 21.2 I then turn to an extended discussion of the *Third Tetralogy* attributed to Antiphon concerning a case of self-defense, where proportionality and necessity considerations are broached. In Section 21.3, I then proceed to Aristotle's important contribution to the development of the ideas of excuse and defense, as well as what he says about proportion and necessity that are relevant to our legal inquiries. In Section 21.4 I explore the idea of a perpetrator's lack of virtue as an excuse or perhaps as a mitigation factor in ancient Chinese thought. In Section 21.5 I look at some contemporary views of these issues. In general, I see the ancient Greek discussion of justification and excuse, especially concerning the restraining influences of proportionality and necessity, as marking significant advances which mirror some of the debate today.

21.1 AJAX AND OEDIPUS

In his play *Ajax*, Sophocles provides an interesting take on those who commit acts under ignorance of what they are doing. This topic today is normally addressed concerning cases where one believed what one was doing was legal but it turned out to be illegal. The case of Ajax is the reverse: he slaughtered and tortured sheep and cattle (not a crime) believing that he was actually slaughtering people (which would have been criminal acts). We also encounter the origins of the contemporary insanity defense since it is claimed that Ajax tried to kill the soldiers while under a sickness that had taken over him. I will explore the play here in the first half of this section and then turn to Sophocles' Oedipus plays for another example of ignorance and its effect on liability in ancient Greek legal thought.

Tecmessa, a character in Sophocles' play *Ajax*, describes what Ajax did in the following terms: "Alas! It was from here that he came bringing the captive flock. Some of them he slaughtered indoors, on the ground, and the rest he tore apart, hacking at their sides."[1] The Chorus had just explained why Ajax probably acted in this way: "Never were you in your right mind when you went so far astray and fell upon the flocks! No, a godsent sickness must have come upon you."[2] And here is a longer account of what transpired:

ODYSSEUS And why did [Ajax] lash out so foolishly?
ATHENA He was stung by anger on account of [not getting] the arms of Achilles.
ODYSSEUS Why did he launch this onslaught on the flocks?
ATHENA He thought he was staining his hands with your blood.
ODYSSEUS Was his plan aimed against the Argives?
ATHENA Yes, he would have accomplished it, had I been negligent …
ODYSSEUS And how did he come to hold back his eager arm from murder?
ATHENA It was I that held him back from his intolerable delight casting upon his eyes mistaken notions, and I diverted him against the herds and the various beasts guarded by the herdsmen and not yet distributed. Here he fell upon them and hacked the horned beasts to death, cleaving their spines all around him, and at one time he thought it was the two Atreidae whom he held and was killing with his own hand, at another that he was attacking now this chief, now that. And as the man wandered in the madness that afflicted him, I urged him on and drove him into a cruel trap.[3]

Here we have reference to mistake as a possible excuse as well as madness as a justification, the two types of defense that Aristotle marks off in his famous account of responsibility, as we will see in the next section.

But we also run into the question of proportionate response if we believe that Ajax thought he was attacking humans rather than the sheep he did attack. His explanation is that he was upset that he had not been rewarded when he thought he should have been, and that he was justifiably angry with the person who was rewarded. And

1 Sophocles, *Ajax* 233–235, translated by Hugh Lloyd-Jones, *Sophocles 1*, Loeb edition, Cambridge, MA: Harvard University Press, 1994, p. 53.
2 Sophocles, *Ajax* 175–178, ibid., p. 49.
3 Sophocles, *Ajax* 40–60, ibid., pp. 33–37.

here we see why Ajax's actions are so abhorrent to us as well as to the Greeks – his actions were completely out of proportion to what he has suffered. And this is even true if we look at his slaughter and torture of the sheep. Ajax says that he deserves to die, and when he falls on his sword there is a sense that justice has been done.

In *Oedipus Tyrannus*, Sophocles also gives us the classic case of mistake in reference to Oedipus' killing his father and committing incest with his mother. Oedipus says:

> Without the knowledge of my mother and my father I went to Pytho, and Phoebus sent me away cheated of what I had come for, but came out with other things terrible and sad for my unhappy self, and to show to mortals a brood they could not bear to look on, and I should be the murderer of the father who had begat me … who now could be more miserable, and who more hateful to the gods? … And am I polluting the bed of the dead man with the hands by which he perished. Am I a criminal? Am I not altogether unholy … may I vanish among men before I see the stain of such a disaster come upon me![4]

Here Oedipus seemingly accepts that he is guilty of patricide and incest, even though he did these acts unknowingly.

But in *Oedipus at Colonus*, set near the end of his life, Oedipus rejects the guilt he had felt and cites an excuse as relieving him of responsibility.

CHORUS. You killed …
OEDIPUS. I killed, but I have …
CHORUS. What is this?
OEDIPUS. … a plea in my defense
CHORUS. What plea?
OEDIPUS. I will explain! I murdered and slaughtered as the victim of the power that sent me mad, but according to the law I am clean! It was in ignorance that I came to this.[5]

A bit later Oedipus declares: "I have suffered, Theseus, cruel wrong upon wrong."[6] Here he uses the term *kakos*, wrong, to describe what has happened to him, not what he is, when in *Oedipus Tyrannus* he had called himself *kakos*.

So, by the end of his life, Oedipus seemingly comes to the realization that he had not done wrong by killing his father and marrying his mother since he did not do these things knowingly or intentionally. Notice, he does not deny that he did these things, but he only denies that it was wrong for him to have acted in this way, to

4 Sophocles, *Oedipus Tyrannus* 785–805, translated by Hugh Lloyd-Jones, Loeb edition, *Sophocles* I, Cambridge, MA: Harvard University Press, 1994, pp. 405–409.

5 Sophocles, *Oedipus at Colonus* 545–549, translated by Hugh Lloyd-Jones, Loeb edition, *Sophocles* II, Cambridge, MA: Harvard University Press, 1994, p. 477.

6 Sophocles, *Oedipus at Colonus* 596, ibid., p. 483.

have broken the taboos, at least as would be recognized by the criminal courts. And Oedipus asserts that rather it is he who has been wronged by being unjustly exiled. Since he was fated to do what he did, he was the victim rather than the perpetrator or someone who is complicit. He has been wronged; and he is not the one who has done wrong. He is innocent of guilt even as he is properly said to have been stained by his acts.

It is interesting to wonder about the homicide charge stripped of the parricide charge. Was it necessary and proportionate for Oedipus to kill Laius, not knowing who he was? Here we have an early reference to self-defense. Oedipus claims that four men attacked him and the only way he could save his life was to kill some of his assailants. Both questions, of necessity and proportionality, are seemingly easy to answer given these facts. He thought he had only one option in order to save his life, namely, killing his attackers. And the lethal violence he unleashed on them seems to be proportionate given the lethal violence his attackers unleashed on Oedipus. Things get more complicated, and more interesting, in the case of self-defense that Antiphon discussed in the *Third Tetralogy*.

21.2 ANTIPHON'S *THIRD TETRALOGY*

In the *Third Tetralogy*, we get a case of self-defense overlaid with considerations of incitement, as well as an important although brief discussion of proportionality. Initially, we find a recitation of the relevant facts and a beginning of a claim about who is responsible:

> If he had killed the man unintentionally, he would deserve some leniency, but since he killed the old man in drunken arrogance (*hybris*) and without self-control (*akolasia*), hitting and choking him till he could no longer breathe, he is liable for punishment for murder … You have heard the witnesses who were with him when he was drunk. You must stem the lawlessness of this injury, punish his arrogance for the suffering he caused, and take away his life as he took away another's by this deed he planned.[7]

The principle behind the prosecution's case, we are told, is "a high value on our life."[8] When life is taken illegally, then punishment must ensue. And the prosecutor tries to diminish the defendant's drunkenness and instead focus on the arrogance of the defendant, arrogance itself being illegal in ancient Greek law. (I take up arrogance – *hybris* – in Chapter 22.)

7 Antiphon, *Third Tetralogy*, 4.1.6, translated by Michael Gagarin in *Antiphon and Andocides*, Austin: University of Texas Press, 2006, pp. 41–42.

8 Antiphon, *Third Tetralogy* 4.1.2, ibid., p. 41.

The defense begins its case with a fairly common claim of justified assault, in terms of who struck first.

> I don't think their claim is either just or righteous. He hit me first, and even if I had defended myself with a sword or a rock or a stick, I still wouldn't be wrong since those who start a fight should rightly be repaid, not in the same degree but more severely. He hit me with his hands and I returned the blows with my own hands … I say that I did not kill him. If the man had died from the blows on the spot, though his death would be attributable to me, it would still be just.[9]

The defendant denies that he initiated the fight and thereby claims his right to retaliate in self-defense.

Curiously, the defendant claims that he did not kill the victim, initially for the reason that the victim did not die on the spot from the blows that the defendant admits he meted out. Two others are claimed to be the true killers: the doctor who let the victim die under his care, and the victim himself for having brought on his own death by his attack on the defendant.

> But as it was, he was entrusted to the care of a bad doctor and died many days later, not from the blows, but from the doctor's incompetence … The victim is the killer, and if it was unfortunate that he died, he was the victim of his own misfortune since he had the misfortune to start the fight. But if he died through thoughtlessness, then it was his own thoughtlessness, for he wasn't thinking well when he struck me.[10]

In this analysis, either the doctor is to blame or the victim himself.

The prosecutor responds to these claims by saying that "they should be rejected out of hand." Nonetheless the prosecutor tries to respond point by point:

> His first argument is that although the man died from his blows, he didn't kill him because by law the initiator of a fight is to blame for what happened and should be convicted, and the victim started the fight. But first of all you know that young men are more likely to get drunk and start a fight than old men; for they are proud of their birth, at the peak of their physicality and not used to drinking … but he did not use the same means to defend himself but just the opposite, for he killed the man then at the peak of strength.[11]

There are several argument threads here, the first of which is that the two fighters were not in equivalent positions, since the older one, the victim, was not at the peak of strength as was the younger one, the defendant. This not only implies an

9 Antiphon, *Third Tetralogy* 4.2.2–3, ibid., p. 42.
10 Antiphon, *Third Tetralogy* 4.2.4 and 4.2.6, ibid., pp. 42–43.
11 Antiphon, *Third Tetralogy*, 4.3.2–3, ibid., p. 44.

inequality of the blows that were delivered but also that the older man was less likely to start a fight given the asymmetrical strengths involved.

Here proportionality of response arises again as it did in the defendant's first speech. In the defendant's speech he asserts that when one is attacked it is appropriate to strike back with greater force, seemingly so as to deter this attacker as well as future ones. Now the prosecutor makes the point that if one's attacker is considerably weaker it makes no sense even to apply as much force as did the assailant since the attacker will bear these blows worse than the defendant bore the blows of the old man.

Importantly for us is the claim that comes next: "the one who hit but didn't kill only planned the blow, but the one who struck the fatal blow planned the death."[12] This issue is one of intentionality and was already being considered as important in ancient Greek legal thought, especially by the time of Plato and Aristotle. For Draco, intentionality did not seem to matter, but for the orators starting with Antiphon and carrying over into the Greek philosophers, the person who intended to kill was more to blame than the one who did not. In our case, we are asked here to compare the one who intended to injure with the one who intended to kill.

In the final speech, delivered after the defendant had fled the city, we find a response to the point about intentions made by the prosecutor.

> if the striker, by striking a blow and forcing you to seek care of a doctor, is the murderer rather than the one who killed him, then the initiator of the fight is in fact the murderer, for he compelled the other to strike back in self-defense and who was then struck to go to the doctor ... The defendant did not plot the death any more than the plaintiff. For if the initiator of the fight had intended to strike but not kill and the defendant had intended to kill, then the latter would be the plotter, but he too intended to strike, not kill; he just made a mistake, and his blow had unintentional results.[13]

Here we have one of the first discussions of premeditation, a topic we will not be able to address here but which bears scrutiny in its own right.

Finally, we get to the main issue concerning self-defense in the final speech for the defendant.

> The other man acted entirely out of drunken arrogance, with no thought of self-defense, but the defendant only wanted to avoid suffering and ward off the blows; what he suffered was involuntary, and in trying to avoid suffering he did less than the initiator of the fight deserved. It was self-defense, not aggression. Even if his own greater strength made his blows stronger than those he suffered, it is not right

[12] Antiphon, *Third Tetralogy* 4.3.4, ibid., pp. 44–45.

[13] Antiphon, *Third Tetralogy* 4.4.3–4, ibid., p. 46.

> to convict him; for large penalties are everywhere prescribed for the initiator of a fight, but nowhere is any penalty written for someone who defends himself.[14]

This involves a classic self-defense claim along with more novel claims, at least to contemporary ears, about what an initiator is due.

As this chapter proceeds we will examine two issues: what are the grounds of a justification or excuse, and at least as important, how are we to regard the ideas of proportionality and necessity in understanding the limits on justifications and excuses, especially in the case of self-defense? To deal with the first of these issues we will turn to Aristotle's account of justification in his discussion of responsibility.[15] To deal with the second issue, we will look to Aristotle's account of necessity and proportionality in attempting to set out the limits of justified homicide. Here we will have to do some inferring since Aristotle does not address this issue directly by reference to self-defense claims.

21.3 ARISTOTLE ON JUSTIFICATION AND PROPORTIONALITY

Aristotle begins Book III of the *Nicomachean Ethics* by setting out briefly when acts are involuntary, that is, when acts are not blamed but "condoned, and sometimes pitied."[16]

> It is then generally held that actions are involuntary when done (*a*) under compulsion, or (*b*) through ignorance; and that (*a*) an act is compulsory when its origin is from without, being of such a nature that the agent, who is really passive, contributes nothing to it, for example when he is carried somewhere by stress of weather, or by people who have him in their power. But there is some doubt about actions done through fear ... (b) an act done through ignorance is in every case not voluntary, but it is involuntary only when it causes the agent pain and regret.[17]

Compulsion and ignorance make acts not voluntary and create excuses or justifications for the agents involved, at least in some cases.

Aristotle makes a subtle distinction that has great significance for both moral and legal responsibility. Acting by reason of ignorance is not the same as acting in ignorance. A person who is drunk acts in ignorance but not by reason of ignorance since his drunken actions are due to prior choices he or she made concerning how much to drink. Related to the case Antiphon discusses, we should note that Aristotle is of two minds about compulsion supposedly caused by fear. In one respect, fear seems

14 Antiphon, *Third Tetralogy* 4.4.6–7, ibid., pp. 46–47.

15 We examined Aristotle's doctrine of responsibility more broadly conceived in Chapter 19.

16 Aristotle, *Nicomachean Ethics* 1109b32, in *Aristotle* XIX, translated by H. Rackham, Loeb edition, Cambridge, MA: Harvard University Press, 1926, p. 117.

17 Aristotle, *Nicomachean Ethics* 1109b35–1110a5 and 1110b7–19, ibid., p. 123.

to be like a compulsion and we can see that in the way that Athena describes how she acted on Ajax – she put into him a force that then compelled him away from his true target and toward the non-humans who he then attacked. In another respect, fear is an internal not an external force and seems to be consistent with calling the fear-driven actor one who acts voluntarily since no outside force has moved him or her.

Aristotle provides what is now seen as the classic account of proportionality in relation to justice in his *Nicomachean Ethics*.

> The just, then, is a species of the proportionate (proportion being not a property only of the kind of number which consists of abstract units, but of number in general). For proportion is equality in ratios ... rectificatory [justice] ... being an inequality, the judge tries to equalize things by means of the penalty, taking away from the gain of the assailant.[18]

On first sight, it seems that Aristotle would think that a proportionate response must be in some sense equal to the character of the assault. But in connection to rectificatory justice, it may be that there is need to do more to the assailant than what he or she did in order to make sure that the assailant suffers in such a way that a balance is returned.

It may be that the assailant profits from the assault beyond the initial infliction of inequality between himself and the one he assaults. In the case of robbery, merely giving back what was stolen does not return things to the previous equilibrium. It may be that the robber has profited from having the stolen object and so must pay additionally to merely returning the stolen object. And insofar as the person robbed did not have the occasion to profit from the use of the object, he or she is owed more than merely the return of the object.

Proportionate response is especially interesting in the case of self-defense. In the *Third Tetralogy* we find that one who responds to an attack is warranted in responding with greater force than was used in the original attack. And Richard Sorabji adds another consideration to the Aristotelian position, that when a person kills, even involuntarily, he "might have to pay a heavy penalty, apparently to rid the state of pollution,"[19] a topic we considered in a previous chapter.

Concerning necessity, Aristotle has much to say from which we can draw, although he is not directly addressing self-defense. Aristotle gives us a good example to contemplate in connection to necessity in human affairs. He says: "if you take my hand and strike someone else with it, I do not act voluntarily, for the act was not in

[18] Aristotle, *Nicomachean Ethics* 1131a29–31 and 1132a9–11, translated by W. D. Ross, *The Basic Works of Aristotle*, edited by Richard McKeon, NY: Random House, 1941, pp. 1006–1007.

[19] Richard Sorabji, *Necessity, Cause, and Blame: Perspectives on Aristotle's Theory*, London: Duckworth, 1983, p. 296.

my power."[20] It was necessary for you to act because your actions in this case were not under your power but under the power of someone else. And there is an obvious connection to self-defense, as we already encountered in Antiphon. If one is in fear for his or her life due to being attacked, there may be a sense in which the self-defensive, and fearful, strike was not in your power but in that of the attacker who incited your assault. We may though have a mixed case here, where our response is not fully up to us because our attacker has preempted some of our options and perhaps has also added an emotional element, fear of death, which we would not have wanted to be influenced by.

If we take this more subtle idea from Aristotle then it is not fully clear that the justification of self-defense is limited to those cases where all deliberation is taken away.[21] And there is another way to understand the relevance of necessity that does not seem to have been directly dealt with in Greek legal thought, namely, whether all options have been exhausted leaving only lethal violence as the only means left to save one's life. Antiphon comes close to addressing this issue when he talks of the role of the initiator and the way the initiator compels the response as when he says: "he compelled the other to strike back in self-defense."[22]

21.4 LACK OF VIRTUE AND MITIGATION OF PUNISHMENT IN ANCIENT CHINA

Another factor like compulsion or ignorance is lack of virtue on the part of a perpetrator of a crime. In ancient Chinese legal thought, the idea that a burglar or assailant lacked a good moral upbringing, or was not a virtuous person due to some other factors, was considered in deciding how to treat the perpetrator. I propose to examine this idea in light of the ancient Greek sources we have just been examining in previous sections of this chapter.

Here are two extraordinary examples reported by Tung-Tsu Ch'u about how some legal officials took punishment upon themselves when it was clear that a perpetrator acted due to poor moral education:

> Lu Kung was a magistrate who depended entirely upon moral influence. Once a chief of a canton borrowed an ox and refused to return it. The owner sued. Lu Kung urged the man to return the ox, but he could not be persuaded to do so. Lu Kung sighed and said, "This is because education has not been in operation." He

[20] Aristotle, *Nicomachean Ethics* 1135a27; Sorabji, *Necessity, Cause, and Blame*, p. 233.

[21] See Sorabji's discussion of some of these issues, ibid., pp. 233–234.

[22] Antiphon, *Third Tetralogy*, 4.4.3, translated by Michael Gagarin in *Antiphon and Andocides*, Austin: University of Texas Press, 2006, p. 46.

> intended to resign. All his subordinates wept and asked him to stay. The borrower was ashamed of himself and return the ox.
>
> There were two brothers who accused each other because of property. Hsu Ching, the governor of the province sighed and said, "The failure of education is the fault of the governor." He then ordered his subordinates to present a memorial and asked to be sent to the Ministry of Justice for punishment. The two brothers were sorry and apologized.

Commenting on these cases, Tung-Tsu Ch'u says: "the Confucian School firmly believed that the good or bad intentions of the people depended on education, and that this education resulted from the moral influence exerted by some one or two individuals at the top."[23]

If taken literally, the idea is that only with proper moral education are people not likely to commit crime. So, it is the ruling class that should be properly subject to punishment, not those commoners who have committed crimes and delicts. In fact, what seems to have happened is that demonstrable lack of virtue became a mitigating factor, not an excuse, in the decision on whether and how much to punish.

In some respects this Confucian doctrine of mitigation of punishment can be seen in some of the ancient Greek plays. In Aeschylus' *Eumenides*, Orestes is on trial for killing his mother (who had killed his father). At the trial, Apollo arrives to speak in Orestes' defense:

> CHORUS: Divine Apollo, handle what belongs to you. Tell us what right you have to meddle in this case.
>
> APOLLO: I came to answer that in evidence. This man has my protection by the law of suppliants. I cleansed him from this murder; I am here to be his advocate, since I am answerable for the stroke that killed his mother.[24]

Apollo here, like some early Confucian judges, claims that he should be punished if anyone should since it was Apollo who influenced Orestes to kill his mother.

The Confucian doctrine that it is the ruler who is responsible for bad behavior among the common people was changed as it was later confronted with the legalists who believed that crime could only be stopped by very severe punishments inflicted on the perpetrators. Over time there was something like a blending of these doctrines so that the rulers were not punished for the misbehavior of the common people, but where lack of education toward virtue became something that was closer to a factor to consider in assigning proportionate punishment.

23 Ch'u, *Law and Society in Traditional China*, p. 254.

24 Aeschylus, *The Eumenides*, 576, in *Aeschylus's Oresteian Trilogy*, translated by Philip Vellacott, NY: Penguin Books, 1956, p. 167.

Put in other terms, at least part of the blame for some criminal acts should be assigned to the rulers who failed to stop or educate properly the perpetrators. As I have said, this is best seen as a doctrine of mitigation of punishment for the perpetrator. It is also possible to see this issue in terms of proportionality – a sentence is disproportionate if it assigns a severe penalty to a commoner for something that was really the joint endeavor of the ruler and the perpetrator.

We see here emerging a proportionality doctrine that is later summarized as: let the punishment *fit* the crime. Confucius and Aeschylus seem to think that at least part of the punishment should be mitigated in order to achieve proportionality if the perpetrator was influenced by those who were his superiors or rulers. As we will see there has been a recent debate about such considerations in terms of the Just War doctrine, which we will examine next.

21.5 JUSTIFICATION AND EXCUSE IN LEGAL THOUGHT

Many contemporary theorists have drawn on Aristotle's treatment of compulsion and ignorance. In one of the most accessible and illuminating, J. L. Mackie draws on Aristotle to posit the following principle:

> the straight rule of responsibility: an agent is responsible for all and only his intentional actions ... What is unintended because it is brought about by physical compulsion is not really anything that the agent does: it is done by some outside force which acts, perhaps, through his body ... And in general in so far as I am ignorant of what I am doing or bringing about, the actions which are for this reason unintentional can be seen not as belonging to me as a conscious agent, but to have been foisted upon or obtruded into my course of action by the facts or circumstances of which I am unaware.[25]

Mackie and others regard Aristotle's account of compulsion and excuse as the canonical view that is still widely accepted today in morality and law.[26] Aristotle's analysis of compulsion and ignorance can be seen as relevant to the analysis of many instances of justification and excuse.

Concerning self-defense, there has been an enormous amount written in the last decade. It is seen as obvious in moral and legal theory that when a person is unjustifiably attacked, the person attacked has a right to defend himself even by lethal means. LaFave and Scott summarize the state of contemporary Anglo-American legal thought as follows:

25 J. L. Mackie, *Ethics: Inventing Right and Wrong*, NY: Penguin Books, 1977, pp. 208–209.

26 One of the best accounts that follow Mackie's analysis of Aristotle's straight rule of responsibility is Carl Eliot, *The Rules of Moral Insanity: Moral Responsibility and the Mentally Ill Offender*, Albany: State University of New York Press, 1996, Chapter 2.

> One who is not the aggressor in an encounter is justified in using a reasonable amount of force against an adversary when he reasonably believes (a) that he is in immediate danger of unlawful bodily harm from his adversary and (b) that the use of such force is necessary to avoid this danger.[27]

These legal conditions somewhat mirror the moral conditions that are often put forth to justify self-defense.

Suzanne Uniacke points out that the legal conditions for self-defense are more and more diverging from the traditional moral conditions. There has been an especially important divergence between these two domains on the subjects of proportionality and necessity.[28] And the divide between law and morality on these topics has only grown over the last 20 years – most especially in the way self-defense is understood in Just War theory.

There has been an explosion of writing about self-defense in the context of Just War theory. In a famous essay, Elizabeth Anscombe said:

> what is required for the people attacked to be non-innocent in the relevant sense is that they should themselves be engaged in an objectively unjust proceeding which the attacker has the right to make his concern; or – in the commonest case – should be unjustly attacking him.[29]

Commenting on this passage, Jeff McMahan says that if the view is correct then there are implications for wartime killing as well as two-person cases – "all unjust combatants are morally liable to attack in war, since they are engaged in a form of objective wrongdoing,"[30] insofar as they are the aggressors. Or as he elsewhere claims concerning the principle of self-defense as a justification for killing: "The relevance of the principle for our purposes is that if it applies to killing in self-defense, then it also applies to killing in war" since the difference between these two domains is one of degree and not one of kind.[31]

Yet, even if killing in war and killing in two-person cases are similarly analyzed, self-defense is understood differently in law and morality, concerning the proportionality and necessity conditions. In traditional Just War theory and international law, proportionality only comes into effect when we are considering collateral damage, namely, to see whether the unintended killings of a military operation can be justified by comparing these costs with what is hoped to be gained by the

27 LaFave and Scott, *Criminal Law*, second edition, St. Paul, MN: West Publishing Co., 1986, p. 454.

28 Suzanne Uniacke, *Permissible Killing: The Self-Defense Justification of Homicide*, Cambridge: Cambridge University Press, 1994, pp. 32–34.

29 G. E. M. Anscombe, "War and Murder," in her *Ethics, Religion, and Politics, Collected Philosophical Papers*, Vol. III, Minneapolis: University of Minnesota Press, 1981, p. 53.

30 Jeff McMahan, *Killing in War*, Oxford: Oxford University Press, 2009, p. 155.

31 Ibid., p. 156.

military operation. But Jeff McMahan and other so-called "revisionist" Just War theorists think that proportionality has greater scope than merely concerning collateral damages.

Necessity considerations hardly ever are thought to be overriding unless it is impossible that a given tactic would achieve a certain result. Necessity, as in military necessity, is nearly synonymous with merely having a given military goal. But for the Greeks, as for our common-sense ways of talking, necessity is interpreted more strictly – as a "no other way" requirement. In contemporary legal thought one of the questions that arises is whether one has to have exhausted such options as retreating or surrendering.[32] We will explore such considerations by briefly turning back to Antiphon and Aristotle.

One of the questions raised by Antiphon is whether a much larger and younger man could say that his only option to stymie an attack by a smaller and older man was to kill this attacker. Does the younger man have anything like what we might today call "a stand your ground" defense? In the *Third Tetralogy*, the prosecutor effectively denies this, and the defendant offers a claim to something like this when he says that an old man can still kill a young man. In the case of lethal threats, the defense seems to believe something like the "stand your ground" defense in that the mere initiator of the fight is said to deserve what he gets in return, and there is no consideration given to whether the blows inflicted by the deceased could have been fended off in a non-lethal way.

Today the one who strikes first is indeed given a certain privilege but the question for us is whether such a view is consistent with the restraints on self-defense of necessity and proportionality. But Aristotle seems to take a different path from that of Antiphon and the majority position today. Aristotle sees proportionality as requiring a strict equality in most respects. And Aristotle also seems to see necessity in a more commonsensical way as well – necessity is different from contingency in that when something is necessary it must occur, it is not merely one of several ways that an event can be brought about.

[32] On necessity see Jens Ohlin and Larry May, *Necessity in International Law*, NY: Oxford University Press, 2016; and on proportionality see Michael Newton and Larry May, *Proportionality in International Law*, NY: Oxford University Press, 2014.

22

Hubris and Impiety

For excess (*koros*) breeds insolence (*hubris*), whenever great
prosperity comes to men who are not of sound mind. Solon, *Fragment* 6[1]

The duke of Sheh informed Confucius, saying, "Among us here there
are those who may be styled upright in their conduct. If their
father has stolen a sheep, they will bear witness to the fact."
Confucius said, "Among us, in our part of the country, those who are
upright are different from this. The father conceals the misconduct
of the son, and the son conceals the misconduct of the father."

Confucian Analects, Bk. XIII, Chap. XVIII

Euthyphro. It is ridiculous, Socrates, that you think it matters whether
the man who was killed was a stranger or a relative, and do not see
that the only thing to consider is whether the action of the slayer was
justified or not … and if not, one ought to proceed against him,
even if he share one's hearth and eat at one's table.

Plato, *Euthyphro*, 4B-C

As *hubris* is understood today, primarily as a form of arrogance, it seems bizarre that it would be criminalized, and especially odd that *hubris* was seen as one of the prime crimes to be prosecuted. And yet I will argue that this is true of ancient Greek law

[1] Solon, Fragment 6, in *Greek Elegiac Poetry*, translated by Douglas E. Gerber, Loeb Classical Texts, Cambridge, MA: Harvard University Press, 1999, p. 123.

and legal thought. In ancient Greece, *hubris* is more than arrogance; indeed some scholars think it does not have to involve arrogance at all. Rather *hubris* is gratuitous insult or injury aimed at dishonoring or shaming another person, with no motivation other than to gain pleasure by exercising power over another person. Even with this description, it is not clear why the ancient Greeks thought it should be seen as one of the most serious of crimes to be prosecuted and punished. In trying to make sense of this rather unique crime it will be important to understand how ancient Greeks understood their democracy and what was seen as most to be confronted in protecting that democracy.

It is also odd today to think that impiety, either toward the gods or toward one's elders would be similarly criminalized in ancient Greece and ancient China. Socrates was condemned to death in the most democratic of societies for his impiety and in China one of the worst things a person could do was to dishonor one's parents or elders. It is perhaps not so surprising that impiety would be seen as immoral, but why would it be criminalized, and punished as severely as it was in the case of Socrates? We will find a similar answer to the puzzle of the crime of impiety as was also true of *hubris*. I will argue that the sophistication of Greek and Chinese legal thought can be seen in the criminalization of *hubris* and impiety contrary to what might be expected.

22.1 ANCIENT GREEK CONCEPTIONS OF *HUBRIS*

Here is one of the earliest laws concerning *hubris*, probably similar to the law from Solon's time, but notice that it does not provide a definition of the term:

> If anyone commits *hubris* against another, whether child or woman or man, whether free or slave, or if he does anything *paranomon* [illegal] against any of these, let anyone who wishes of the Athenians to whom this is permitted bring a *graphe* before the Thesmothetai; let the Thesmothetai bring the case before the court (*heliaia*) within thirty days of the bringing of the *graphe*, unless any public business prevents this and if it does, as soon as possible. Where the court convicts, let it immediately determine the penalty, what it decides the defendant deserves to suffer or pay. Those who bring *graphai* under the law, if anyone does not carry through the case, or carrying through with it does not receive one fifth of the votes, let him pay one thousand drachmae to the treasury. If someone convicted of *hubris* is assessed to pay a fine, let him be imprisoned, if he committed *hubris* against a free man, until he has paid a fine.[2]

[2] Demosthenes, *Against Meidias* 47, translated by N. R. E. Fisher in his *Hybris: A Study in the Values of Honor and Shame in Ancient Greece*, Warminster: Aris & Phillips, 1992, p. 36.

This is the law as it existed in fourth century BCE Athens, as recorded by Demosthenes in his speech, *Against Meidias*. There is good evidence for thinking that a law very similar to this one was first promulgated by Solon.[3]

In Solon's poems, *hubris* is mentioned often. As we saw in the poetry fragment at the beginning of the chapter, Solon saw hubris as resulting from those who came into positions of power but were not of a mature enough mind. In fragment 4, Plutarch says of Solon: "But Solon himself says that at first he undertook public life reluctantly, and in fear of one side's love of money and the other side's *hubris*."[4] Solon felt that hubris was a threat to democratic politics. And in the early sixth century BCE it is thought that Solon introduced the first law against *hubris*.[5]

It is highly significant that the law against *hubris*, which Aristotle tells us concerns gratuitous insults or injuries, could be violated even in the case of a free person assaulting a slave. Here is Aristotle's account of the features of hubris:

> The man committing *hubris* also slights: for hubris is doing and saying things at which the victim incurs shame, not in order that one may achieve anything other than what is done but simply to get pleasure from it. For those who act in return for something do not commit *hubris*, they avenge themselves. The cause of the pleasure for those committing *hubris* is that by harming people, they think themselves to be superior … Dishonor is characteristic of *hubris*, and he who dishonors someone slights him, since what has no worth has no honor, either for good or for bad.[6]

There is here normally a kind of arrogance – seeing oneself as superior to another and hence entitled to act a certain way toward the other person. But for Aristotle, the key is the intentional dishonoring of another person, normally an inferior, by insulting or injuring him. Fisher comments that on this Aristotelian account, *hubris* "is revealed by the evidence of sneers and mockery, or by other indications of sheer enjoyment in the act of insulting."[7]

We can begin to see already why the ancient Greeks were so concerned about *hubris* that it was severely penalized. Things get clearer yet when we see how the Greeks understood the effects of *hubris* on their democracy. In the *Politics*, Aristotle says:

3 Fisher, *Hybris*, p. 81.

4 *Greek Elegiac Poetry*, p. 121.

5 For a discussion of whether this exact law was promulgated by Solon or by Pericles at a later time, see *The Laws of Solon*, edited and translated by Delfin F. Leao and P. J. Rhodes, London: I. B. Tauris, 2016, pp. 47–48.

6 Aristotle, *Rhetoric*, 1378b23–35, translated by Fisher, *Hybris*, p. 8.

7 Fisher, ibid., p. 11.

> Of these, what force *hubris* and *kerdos* (gain or profit) have, and how they are causes of changes, is pretty evident; when those in office commit *hubris* and *pleionexia* (demanding more than is one's due), men engage in *stasis* (political strife) both against each other and against the constitutions that grant such power.[8]

The idea is that *hubris* is dangerous for a democratic system of government – since there is supposed to be an equal share of honor that is recognized and respected for each citizen. Yet *hubris* is characterized by one citizen, normally in a position of superiority, dishonoring another, normally of inferior status. The attempts to dishonor certain people, or class of people, undermine the democratic spirit and are dangerous in a way similar to treason – calling for similarly severe punishments.

It would make sense that the first law against *hubris* would have been promulgated by Solon who also is often considered to have first promulgated democracy in ancient Athens. The laws of Draco were thought to be fear inspiring because of their severity, although we have seen evidence to doubt this common characterization. Solon overturned Draco's laws, except for Draco's homicide law, which is the only one of his laws to survive. We do not have a complete set of the laws of Solon either, but quite a number of these laws have survived in the writings of the Greek orators and historians. The idea behind Solon's laws seems to be to overcome the entrenched power situation in Athens where a small group of wealthy and powerful individuals could oppress the vast majority of citizens. Criminalizing the use of power to insult or injure those of inferior status is a key component in this transformation from oligarchy to democracy.

22.2 TWO CASES OF *HUBRIS* FROM DEMOSTHENES

Most of the best examples we have of *hubris* in ancient Greece are in the court speeches of Demosthenes. I will rehearse two cases here that illustrate well how *hubris* was conceived in practice in ancient Greece. The first case is *Against Conon*. Here is a statement of the facts:

> the defendant Conon together with his son and the son of Andromenes threw themselves upon me. They first, stripped me of my cloak, and then, tripping me up, thrust me into the mud and leapt upon me and beat me with such violence that my lip was split open and my eyes closed; and they left me in such a state that I could neither get up nor utter a sound. As I lay there I heard them utter much language, a great deal of which was such foul abuse that I should shrink from repeating some of it in your presence. One thing, however, which is an indication of this fellow's *hubris*, and a proof that the whole affair has been of his doing, I will tell you. He

[8] Aristotle, *Politics* 1302b5–9,translated by Fisher, *Hybris*, p. 27.

> began to crow, mimicking fighting cocks that have won a battle and his fellows bade him flap his elbows against his sides like wings.[9]

This was not just a matter of assault; there was also an attempt to dishonor and then even to gloat over the victim's suffering.

Demosthenes focuses not only on the terrific assault perpetrated by Conon and his two sons, but on the way that Conon reacted to the suffering that he had meted out. Indeed, the crowing like a cock is a paradigmatic way of seeing what *hubris* looks like. Here are the "sneers and mockery" that Aristotle discussed as clear signs of the intention to dishonor and shame the victim, not merely physically to assault him or her. In addition, Conon seems to display contempt for democratic values that is also one of the hallmarks of *hubris*.[10] We do not here have a case of one person of much higher standing abusing his power over an inferior since the parties seem to be of equal standing. But the other elements of *hubris* are very clearly on display.

A second case is taken from the most famous of Demosthenes' speeches, *Against Meidias*.

> Thereupon I came forward and volunteered to act as chorus-master, and at the drawing of lots I was fortunate enough … You, Athenians, all of you, welcomed [me] with utmost cordiality … But there seems to have been one solitary exception, Meidias, who in his chagrin kept up a constant fire of insults, trifling or serious, during the whole period of my service … The sacred apparel provided for use at a festival … he plotted to destroy … And he did destroy them … But not content with this, men of Athens, he actually corrupted the trainer of my chorus … he bribed the crown Archon himself; he banded the choristers against me; he bawled and threatened … he blocked the gangways from the wings nailing up those public thoroughfares without public authority; he never ceased to cause me untold damage and annoyance … [then two more acts of] *hubris*: he assaulted my person, and he was chiefly responsible for preventing my tribe, which was winning, from gaining the prize.[11]

This case in *Against Meidias* is more complex than the one in *Against Colon*. The *hubris* is seen in a cascading series of insults and indignities that eventually lead to assault. And in the lengthy analysis that follows, we get a quite clear legal principle upon which the charge of *hubris* is said to depend: "under a democracy each man has his share of just and equal rights."[12]

9 Demosthenes, *Against Conon*, [LIV] 1259.8–9, in *Demosthenes* VI: *Orations*, translated by A. T. Murray, Loeb Classical Library, Cambridge, MA: Harvard University Press, 1939, pp. 133–135.

10 See Fisher, *Hybris*, p. 81.

11 Demosthenes, *Against Meidias*, [XXI] 519.13–520.18, in *Demosthenes III*, translated by J. H. Vance, Loeb Classical Library, Cambridge, MA: Harvard University Press, 1935, pp. 15–18.

12 Ibid., 536.67, p. 51.

Meidias is presented as a paradigmatic abuser of status and power. He bribes officials, including one of the highest of the rulers, and uses his position to interfere with the workings of a chorus-master, prohibiting him from making the kind of impression that would lead to gaining a prize. We also find Meidias threatening people who were trying to use public thoroughfares. This is an assault on a person of inferior status from acting as he has a right to do. And then there is also the assault itself. But as in the other cases, the assault is presented as almost as an afterthought. The *hubris* is the abuse of power to gain advantage and to dishonor a fellow citizen, in an arrogant display of disrespect, which cannot be tolerated in a democracy.

22.3 IMPIETY IN ANCIENT GREECE AND CHINA

It is my contention that we can see similar considerations to those involving *hubris* occurring in cases of impiety. Here there is a dishonoring of elders or gods – a kind of putting oneself above them for one's own aggrandizement. But there is more than arrogance and aggrandizement involved in impiety – there is a challenge to the order of the society. It is not immediately evident if the crime of impiety is more a problem in a democracy than in other societies, but the challenge to the social order seems to be similar to that in the crime of *hubris*.

The laws of Solon deal in various ways with impiety displayed by disrespect for one's parents, especially elderly parents. Fragment 55b of these laws attests to a written law, where there had been none before, "in order to protect parents, thus through threat of punishment forcing even those who are not worthy by nature to give their parents what is needed."[13] Solon made exceptions for those parents who did not teach their sons a craft, or who prostituted their sons, or for sons who were illegitimate. These sons did not have the legal obligation to support their parents, especially in old age, but all other sons did have this obligation.

In the *Euthyphro* we first encounter two examples of impiety in Plato's corpus. In the first example, Socrates says that he is being prosecuted for having corrupted the youth by making up new gods and not believing in the old gods (3b).[14] This is a kind of impiety. But we also find that Euthyphro is prosecuting his father for having killed a slave and Socrates suggests that it is impious of Euthyphro to prosecute his father because by doing so he is dishonoring his father. In both cases, piety is said to be doing that which the gods expect of us.

In the *Apology*, where Socrates' trial is recounted by Plato, Socrates defends himself as follows:

[13] *The Laws of Solon*, edited and translated by Delfin F. Leao and P. J. Rhodes, p. 93 with commentary on pp. 96–97.

[14] Quotations from Plato's early dialogues are taken from *Plato 1*, translated by Harold North Fowler, Loeb Classical Library, Cambridge, MA: Harvard University Press, 1914.

> you will find through all my life, both in public, if I engaged in any public activity, and in private, I have always been the same as now, and have never yielded to any one wrongly, whether it were any other person or any of those who are said by my traducers to be my pupils ... I ask questions and whoever wishes may answer and hear what I say ... But why then do some people love to spend much of their time with me? You have heard the reason, men of Athens; for I have told you the whole truth; it is because they like to listen when those are examined who think they are wise and are not so; for it is amusing. (33A-C)[15]

Here we get a glimpse of why Socrates might have been seen as impious. He admits that he made fun of the leading wise people in Athens. And Socrates never denies that he did challenge his listeners to be critical of the gods as well.

So, the characterization of Socrates as impious is perhaps not completely unreasonable. What to us may seem odd is that Socrates would be *legally prosecuted*, and convicted of the capital crime of impiety. We should remember though that in the 1940s the United States Supreme Court ruled that laws making it illegal to be a communist sympathizer were held to be constitutional. And today, there are laws in the US and elsewhere that make it illegal and subject to severe punishment to be merely "supporting terrorists."

In the quotation from the *Confucian Analects* at the start of this chapter, we see that piety and fidelity are prized very highly by Confucius. We are also told that the "son was later executed on the grounds that the loyalty showed to his ruler in reporting his father's crime was outweighed by the resulting disloyalty to his father."[16] As far as I can tell, execution was sometimes the punishment for impiety as far back in ancient China as the time of Confucius, which is roughly the same time that Socrates lived. So, Socrates' death sentence for impiety is something that would also have been seen as potentially justifiable in ancient Chinese as well as ancient Greek legal thought.

At the beginning of Confucius' *Analects*, we find filial piety praised:

> 1. The philosopher Yu said, "They are few who being filial and fraternal, are fond of offending against their superiors. There have been none, who, not liking to offend against their superiors, have been fond of stirring up confusion.
> 2. "The superior man bends his attention to what is radical. That being established, all practical courses naturally grow up. Filial piety and fraternal submission! – are they not the root of all benevolent actions?"[17] ...

[15] Ibid., p. 119.

[16] Chin Kim and Theodore R. LeBlang, "The Death Penalty in Traditional China," *Georgia Journal of International and Comparative Law*, Vol. 5, 1975, pp. 92–93.

[17] Confucius, *Analects*, Bk I, Ch. II, in *The Confucian Analects, The Great Learning, and the Doctrine of the Mean*, translated by James Legge, NY: Cosimo Books, 2009, pp. 138–139.

And then we also learn this:

> The Master said, "A youth, when at home, should be filial, and abroad, respectful of his elders. He should overflow in love to all, and cultivate the friendship of the good. When he has time and opportunity, after the performance of these things, he should employ them in polite studies."[18] …

And then we have a strong statement supporting filial piety:

> The philosopher Tsang said, "Let there be a careful attention to perform the funeral rites of parents and let them be followed when long gone with the ceremonies of sacrifice – then the virtue of the people will resume its proper excellences."[19]

The legal thought of Confucius concerning piety derives from these seminal ideas at the beginning of Confucius' most important work.

According to a noted expert in Chinese legal thought, Derk Bodde, impiety was incorporated into the legal system as a crime:

> the more extreme provision, also known from Han times onward, [is] that a son who brings an accusation of parental wrongdoing before the authorities is thereby unfilial and hence subject to heavy punishment … Probably China is the world's only country where the true reporting of a crime to the authorities could entail legal punishment for the reporter … Another remarkable instance of filial piety in law is the provision that a criminal sentenced to death or long-term servitude, should he be the sole support of aged or infirm parents, might have the sentence commuted in various ways.[20]

Impiety was not only condemned morally but it had strong influence over the Chinese legal codes that developed after Confucius.

As in other ancient societies, punishments seem to have gotten more severe in China than they were earlier. So, while impiety was condemned as far back as we have writings about ancient China, the severity of punishment was not a constant in ancient China. The ancient Chinese seem to be focused on filial impiety and not also on impiety toward the gods – indeed it is unclear whether Confucianism acknowledged a role for gods in any event. But the concern seems to be the same, namely a concern for the order of the society, and an order that provided for the peaceful maintenance of society in a way that recognized obligations of citizens to do their parts.

18 Ibid., Ch. VI, p. 140.

19 Ibid., Ch. IX, p. 141.

20 Derk Bodde and Clarence Morris, *Law in Imperial China*, Cambridge, MA: Harvard University Press, 1967, pp. 40–41.

22.4 IMPIETY AND *HUBRIS* AS ANCIENT HONOR-BASED CRIMES

What the acts of *hubris* and impiety have in common is that they violate strong norms against dishonoring other people. There is also a religious dimension in some of these norms that needs to be explored. But it is interesting that both ancient Greek and Chinese moral systems are often said to be, and indeed seem to me to be, conceptually able to be disconnected from the religious dimensions. In this respect the special case of impiety shown toward the gods needs to be examined better to understand how honor is conceptualized in these ancient societies, and translated into legal norms in those societies.

Greek society is infused with talk of the gods; whereas Chinese society barely mentions gods at all. So, this would seem to be a huge difference that needs to be accounted for in considering such matters as the common crime of impiety in both of these ancient societies. But many scholars do not think that Greek law was heavily influenced by religion, at least not after the time of Pericles. Athenian democracy spawned a legal system that focused on maintaining order – indeed, as we have seen there is good evidence to think that even such notions as pollution that were indebted to Greek religious ideas came to be a secular matter of legality.

In China, there is a sense that Confucianism became a kind of state-religion, but a religion without mention of anything like a deity. As Herbert Fingarette has put it, Confucianism embodied "The Secular as Sacred."[21] It seems to me that one could say something similar about democratic Athenian society as well, even though Fingarette thinks we misunderstand Chinese thought if we do not recognize the importance of religion. Nonetheless, the majority view among scholars is articulated by Bodde who thinks the issue is simply unquestionable when addressed to Chinese legal thought: "in China, no one at any time has ever hinted that any kind of written law – even the best written law – could have had a divine origin."[22] He also says: "law in China was from the beginning viewed in purely secular terms."[23]

In Confucian thought, *li* is the key element, and is often translated as ritual or custom. This idea can denote a religious ritual. But it seems that in respect to law, *li* does not refer to religious but to secular rituals, such as "ceremonial politeness, etiquette, or certain rules of proper conduct" as often manifested in various institutional practices.[24] In this respect, Confucian legal thought, which dominated Chinese legal thought from approximately 400 BCE until the nineteenth century CE, seems to stand opposed to *hubris*, as was ancient Greek legal thought. Here is a quotation from a second century BCE Confucian legal philosopher, Ssu-ma T'an:

[21] Herbert Fingarette, *Confucius: The Secular as Sacred*, NY: HarperCollins, 1972.
[22] Bodde and Morris, *Law in Imperial China*, Cambridge, p. 10.
[23] Ibid., p. 49.
[24] Ibid., p. 19.

> The legalists make no distinction between kindred and strangers, nor do they differentiate the noble from the humble. All such are judged by them as one before the law (*fa*), thereby sundering the kindliness expressed in affection toward kindred and respect toward the honorable ... they are stern and deficient in kindliness.[25]

The rules of polite behavior differ for different classes in ancient Chinese legal thought, but it is very hard to see how impiety could be consistent with *li* for any group in Chinese society.

The same principles that undergird the prohibition on impiety seem to undergird a prohibition on *hubris* here, even if not written into law. "Respect toward the honorable" is a principle of Confucianism that undergirds prohibitions on impiety and emotional expressions like *hubris*. Despite such strong support for respect for others, Chinese legal thought did not support democratic institutions, as was true of Greek legal thought of roughly the same time period.

The ancient Chinese "legalists" favored a rule of law that did not have a graded law, but they were not successful in their struggles against Confucians. Honoring one's fellow people was a key consideration, and rites and customs allowed for differential treatment based on social status. In any event, there were strong penalties, although different ones, for all who engaged in impiety in ancient Chinese law. And despite the graded punishments, the idea was that everyone owed respect to each other person and that one was prohibited from dishonoring another person. Similar things, at least to this extent, can be said about why ancient Greek law severely punished *hubris* and impiety as well, when dishonor was the result.

Honor and respect are legally enforced norms that are seen as significantly important for maintaining ancient societies, whether they are democratic or not. *Hubris*, as understood by the Greeks as gratuitous insults or injuries primarily by those in positions of power over their subordinates, was a clear affront to the democratic aspirations of Solon and those who followed in his footsteps in ancient Greece. *Hubris* reinforced a graded society that Solon and other legal reformers tried to diminish if not eliminate. Interestingly, in ancient Confucian China, the prohibitions on impiety were aimed at maintaining a graded society. Impiety for the Greeks probably had aspects of both of these considerations. Impiety toward the gods was a threat to the harmony of the state which relied on Greek religion to legitimize it.

Impiety toward elders and parents in Greece was seemingly not about maintaining strict gradations in society but about respecting the positions that people actually held where those positions were important for stability. This was especially important in a society that was increasingly, in many other respects, moving toward equality. Full equality was never achieved and instead there was a double standard

[25] Translation by Burton Watson, modified by Bodde and Morris, *Law in Imperial China*, p. 22.

that allowed for more and more people to be in the category of citizens, but always excluded women and slaves and many resident aliens. We investigated the dynamics of how law worked specifically to maintain and also begin to break up such class distinctions in Chapter 16.

22.5 DISHONOR AND *HUBRIS* IN LEGAL THOUGHT

One of the current examples of dishonor in law today occurs in those societies that hold strongly to the idea that family dishonor is linked to violations of certain norms, especially concerning sexual relations. Honor-killing is recognized in countries such as Afghanistan, India, and Pakistan today – where women, and sometimes men as well, can be killed for having sexual relations that were not approved by the male heads of family, or even for marrying a person not approved by the family. Shari'a law is often associated with such strict honor-codes. Honor is also a matter of at least quasi-legal sanction in the societies today of Sicily – where dishonor is met with condemnation to death. These laws are in some respects even more "Draconian" than the ancient Greek and Chinese laws we have been examining.

Honor may be seen as playing an important and less controversial role today in laws that aim at promoting integrity in various professions. Lawyers and politicians are held to a higher standard of behavior than average citizens. And there is something like the charge of *hubris* or impiety that is made when the members of these professions abuse their authority – indeed, a prime example is the increasingly prevalent prosecutions for sexual harassment of those in positions of power who exploit that power to harass those who are their subordinates. The honor in question is that of the profession, or sometimes of the professional, which is seen as in need of protection lest the profession slip into dishonor and disrespect.

There are no laws today that criminalize *hubris*, but we can look at other ways that *hubris* has been dealt with today in terms of moral or political criticism and perhaps find Greek legal thought helpful here as well as in the case of impiety. Arrogance, which is not the same as ancient Greek *hubris* but surely related, is sometimes prized today but only up to a point in political contexts. Diplomacy is thought to be endangered by extreme arrogance as is the ability to rule effectively domestically. But by and large these norms have not been instilled in law.

It is tempting to think of the current President of the United States, Donald Trump in terms of ancient Greek *hubris*. Trump seems to revel in insulting people, especially those who are members of minority groups – Hispanics, Blacks, Jews, etc. He also has admitted that he has groped women, and defended himself by making reference to his celebrity status. Indeed, he has incited his supporters to violence in various contexts. And the only point of the insults and injuries is self-aggrandizement. Many have condemned Trump for these acts, but few have seen them as criminal or quasi-criminal acts. To make out this case, it is important to understand in more depth why *hubris* and impiety were seen as threats to political order, especially democratic order.

Remember one of the key points that Aristotle made: "The cause of the pleasure for those committing *hubris* is that by harming people, they think themselves to be superior."[26] For Solon, democracy required that citizens see themselves as roughly equal to one another, not as superior or inferior. Even in ancient China, where Confucian principles of appropriate behavior were applied differently based on social class, impious behavior that dishonored was condemned and punished legally, even if the punishment differed somewhat based on which class one was a member of.

Stability required harmony and both impiety and hubris were condemned for their destabilizing effects on the state. But there is much more to be said about the threat posed by *hubris* and impiety to democratic states than to other types of state. For Aristotle, *hubris* not only led to disrespect for certain people and groups, but it also could lead to the rise of a demagogue. In his *Politics* Aristotle worries about certain forms of democracy which transform themselves into something else – tyranny or no government at all. In the former case, Aristotle worries that democracy will inspire a demagogue who will, with the people's support, disregard the laws. In the latter case, Aristotle worries that the demagogue will place himself over the laws, obliterating the laws, and thereby destroying the Constitution. And if there is no Constitution, then people are back in a state of anarchy. The rule by decree of the demagogue is the antithesis of the rule of law. And for Aristotle, there needs to be at least a minimal rule of law for there to be a constitutional form of government at all.

A demagogue is literally just a leader of the people. But already at Aristotle's time the term had a strongly negative connotation. Demagogues were typically members of the assembly who used the power of rhetoric to move the members of the assembly to adopt decrees that solved particular problems quickly but also operated outside the normal constraints of law. Demagogues typically appealed to the emotions, rather than the reason, of the members of the assembly. The demagogue used flattery for those who support him or her and ridicule for those who oppose. And once demagogues gained the support of the people, uniting them in ways the people were not united before, it is as if there is rule by a single person. The mass of individual people is transformed into a single ruler who is now embodied by the demagogue. And then this type of monarchy can easily slip into tyranny since the demagogue will not have the interest of the whole at heart.

We might realize that Aristotle does not think that all demagogues act against the interests of the commonwealth. The fear though is that since the demagogue

[26] Aristotle, *Rhetoric*, 1378b25, translated by Fisher, *Hybris*, p. 8.

is largely unchecked, especially not checked by the rule of law, the demagogue has no incentive to act in the interests of the whole of the people. And this also means that demagogues will be inherently unstable since they can lose the support of the people just as easily as they gained it.

In the case of a democratic ruler who displays *hubris*, the risks are two-fold. First, there is the risk that the leader could become a demagogue. A ruler who is consumed by *hubris* will try to find ways to rule that benefit him or her and this will often involve issuing decrees (or executive orders) that overturn or work around the legislature. From an Aristotelian perspective, there was a link between *hubris* and the risk of demagoguery. Demagoguery was especially likely when it was a democratic leader who has acted hubristically.

Second, there is the risk that the people, especially those who have been insulted by the ruler, will rise up and attempt to overthrow that ruler. Aristotle and most political philosophers saw anarchy as the chief danger to be countered. A society of laws, rather than decrees by strong rulers turned into demagogues, was one way to lessen the risk of anarchy. Leaders who were driven by *hubris* were less likely to observe institutional and procedural restraints and to act unilaterally to mollify the populace. But over time the populace will realize that the demagogue has his own rather than their interests at heart and this will unsettle the populace, making it more likely that they will not only overthrow the demagogue but the whole of the polis.

SECTION VIII

War and Amnesty

23

Amnesty, Sanctuary, and Exile

In discussing ancient Chinese legal thought in a previous chapter we saw that the granting of amnesty (or pardon) could be an exercise in the administration of equity. This is also true of ancient Greek thought as I will argue. And the discussion in this section will move us toward a better understanding of ancient equity, and hopefully lead us to some conclusions, in the final section of this chapter, about problems for the idea of equity in ancient legal thought or legal thought in general. I will also argue that the ancient practices of amnesty, sanctuary, and exile are best understood as equitable remedies for deficiencies in a legal system.

When it becomes clear that Oedipus has killed his father and had sexual relations with his mother, he is condemned to walk the earth – never to set foot back in Athens. This is a form of exile that was a substitute for corporal or capital punishment in ancient Athens. And in 403 BCE, a famous amnesty was issued after a war involving Athens. Cicero later describes it as an act of forgetting (hence *amnestia*), but Edwin Carawan argues that at the time it was understood as a contract of reconciliation rather than a blanket act of forgetting (and forgiving).[1]

Amnesty and exile were alternative ways to deal with people who had done wrong, even very serious wrong. In addition, there is evidence that people could seek sanctuary in certain religious shrines – not permanently but until there could be a trial or until the trial was likely to be "fair." Here is one additional place where equity enters into the discussion of ancient legal thought. As we will see in this chapter, some responses to wrongdoing called not for standard forms of justice but the creative expression of equity and fairness. The rule of law could be maintained in some cases not by following strict justice but by acts that reached the fairest result for the society.

1 Edwin Carawan, *The Athenian Amnesty and Reconstructing the Law*, Oxford: Oxford University Press, 2013.

In the Section 23.1 we will encounter the famous Athenian amnesty of 403 BCE as it was discussed by philosophers and historians. In Section 23.2 we will examine the evidence, somewhat scanty as it is, for the idea of sanctuary, a place to hide from the retributive arm of the law. In Section 23.3 we will look at the ideas of exile and ostracism as alternatives to standard forms of punishment. In Section 23.4 we return to the Greek understanding of equity and link it to these extraordinary practices in ancient Athens as well as in ancient China. And in Section 23.5 we will discuss some of the debates today about amnesty and sanctuary in light of the ancient ideas encountered in the earlier sections of the chapter.

23.1 THE ATHENIAN AMNESTY OF 403 BCE

We begin by examining, taken in parts, a long passage from the Aristotelian *Constitution of Athens*[2] that sets out the terms of the amnesty of 403 BCE. Here is the first part:

> The group which held the Piraeus and Munichia gradually gained the upper hand in the war as the whole people went over to their side, and so the men of the city deposed the Ten who had first been elected, and chose another ten men with the reputation of being outstanding citizens; it was under them that the reconciliation was arranged and the democracy returned ... The peace and the end of hostilities was brought about by Pausania, the Spartan king.

Here we learn that there had been a civil war in Athens between those favoring oligarchy and those favoring democracy. The democrats won and were aided by the king of Sparta.

We next learn that a reconciliation agreement was signed between the two previously warring parties.

> The reconciliation was brought about in the Archonship of Eucleides on the following terms. Those of the Athenians who had remained in the city and wished to leave should live in Eleusis, where they should retain full citizenship rights, have complete self-government and enjoy their incomes. The temple was to be common to both sides, under the traditional control of Eumolpidae. Those living in Eleusis were not allowed to visit the city of Athens, nor were those living in Athens allowed to visit Eleusis, with the exception for both sides of celebration of the Mysteries. The people at Eleusis were to contribute to a defense fund from their revenues like the other Athenians. If any of those leaving the city took over a house in Eleusis,

[2] *The Aristotelian Constitution of Athens*, sections 37–39, translated by J. M. Moore and edited by Stephen Everson, Cambridge: Cambridge University Press, 1996, 2013, pp. 239–240. The quotations on the next few pages are from this translation of the Aristotelian Constitution.

> they were to do it with the agreement of the owner; if agreement proved impossible, each was to select three assessors, and the owner was to accept the price they fixed.

The main terms of the reconciliation concerned allowing Athenians to return to the city where they were to regain full citizenship and their previous incomes. The people who wished to leave Athens (and its reconstituted democratic government) would be accepted in the city of Eleusis which was to be secured against even visiting Athenians. And the houses that were abandoned and then occupied by new residents were to be paid for according to a fair price acceptable to both previous and current residents.

Next came a system for registering inhabitants of the reconstituted cities of Athens and Eleusis.

> Any inhabitants of Eleusis acceptable to the new settlers were to live with them there. Those wishing to move out to Eleusis had to register within ten days of the swearing of the reconciliation oaths if they were in the city at the time, and move out within twenty; those abroad at the time had the same periods from the moment when they returned to Athens. Nobody living in Eleusis could hold any office in the city of Athens until he had been registered as having moved his residence back to the city.

The procedures for marking who had a right to be in which of these two cities was set out in detail as we see. This feature of the reconciliation was important for making sure that people did not continue to engage in war with each other by clearly separating the sides into different cities.

In the previous passage we find a reference to "the reconciliation oaths" but Aristotle gave no specification of what was involved. In other sources we find the actual wording of the mutual oaths. Here is what Andocides reports:

> And it seemed best "not to recall wrong" against one another for past events … The common oath that affects the whole city, which you all swore after the reconciliation, [is this]: "And I will not recall past wrongs against any citizen, except for the Thirty [and the Ten] and the Eleven; and not against these if any is willing to submit to accounting for his office."[3]

We will take this up in greater detail soon but now only note that there seemed to be a mutual pledge of forgetting the offenses of the civil war.

The final piece of the amnesty agreement is in many ways the most important for it called for immunity from prosecution for wrongs committed during the war. The *Aristotelian Constitution of Athens* says that:

3 Andocides, *On the Mysteries*, paragraphs 81 and 90, translated in Carawan, *The Athenian Amnesty and Reconstructing the Law*, p. 24.

> Homicide trials in cases where someone had killed or wounded a person with his own hands were to be conducted in accordance with the traditional practice. There was to be total amnesty covering everyone except the Thirty, the Eleven and the ten governors of the Piraeus; even they were to be immune from prosecution once they had submitted to the *euthuna*.

Amnesty is here linked to immunity from prosecution for killing or wounding. Indeed, the immunity was to stretch even to the leaders of the oligarchy that had overthrown the democracy, assuming that they submitted to the *euthuna*, a kind of accounting of what wrongs they had committed.

There are two schools of thought about why the amnesty was agreed to – one interpretation is that the amnesty was simply a contract reached in an effort to stop the bloodletting of the war. Another interpretation is that the amnesty was a genuine attempt at proper reconciliation, where the two sides wanted to be able henceforth to live amicably with one another. The second interpretation would see the amnesty as a forerunner of the reconciliation connected to the ending of the South African apartheid, where a very serious effort was made for both sides to "forget" the wrongs done to each other so that the society could move on.[4] Over the millennia many have seen the 403 BCE amnesty as the most significant and original amnesty to be emulated as a means of ending civil strife by forging an agreement whereby perpetual recriminations would not continue to destabilize the society.

23.2 SANCTUARY IN ANCIENT GREECE

Sanctuaries in ancient Greece were places of worship that typically contained a statue of one of the gods. Within the sanctuary was a separate locale that was sacred ground. The people who entered the sacred ground of the sanctuary were granted a kind of immunity from being seized and taken away by civil authorities. These people were seeking refuge and it was a sacrilege to remove them from the sanctuary because it was seen as an affront to the god whose statute was in the sanctuary.

There were rights of asylum connected to those who sought refuge in sanctuaries that were well recognized in ancient Greece and into the Roman era.[5] Indeed, the Greek word for "to steal" is *sylan*, from which the Greeks derived the word asylum, the right not to be stolen. Hence we get the idea that any person who is seeking refuge was not to be stolen or taken from the sanctuary. One of the documents of

4 Edwin Carawan argues forcefully against this interpretation in his book, *The Athenian Amnesty and Reconstructing the Law*.

5 See Simon Price, *Religions of the Ancient Greeks*, Cambridge: Cambridge University Press, 1999, p. 156.

sacral law from Samos around 245 BCE, makes it clear that runaway slaves and other freemen seeking refuge were to be accommodated and protected at the sanctuary.[6]

There are two significant problems of asylum in sanctuaries in ancient Greece. First, for a person to be able to enter a sanctuary to begin with, that person had to be unpolluted. And the very reasons that might cause someone to seek asylum, such as having killed or stolen, even with justification or excuse, would also make them polluted and not eligible to enter the sanctuary. Of course one could engage in ritual purification and then seek sanctuary from civil authorities, but the act of seeking purification would expose the person to the possible seizing by the authorities before one could then seek refuge.

Second, as the sacral law from Samos indicates there were often very strong conditions placed on the person who sought asylum which made it very difficult for anyone to stay in a sanctuary for very long. Most significantly, people in sanctuaries were not allowed to engage in commercial trade and perhaps even to engage in exchanges with shopkeepers. Here is the comment from one scholar, Eran Lupu:

> The inscription [at Samos] seems to distinguish two types of supplicants: (1) runaway slaves (line 21) and (2) all other suppliants, obviously free persons. Both appear to be unwelcome, but the treatment of runaway slaves seems more strict. The shopkeepers are to offer them neither employment nor food. As for other suppliants, taking their residence at the sanctuary as a given, the authorities appear to attempt to make their living conditions harder: they are not allowed to engage in retail trade (8–9) and the shopkeepers are not allowed to hand their shop over to them (12–13) or to receive anything from them (16–17). These restrictions make it clear that living at the sanctuary will be very difficult if not impossible, for prospective suppliants, and it is conceivable that they were listed, at least in part, in the hope that suppliants, like other unwelcome visitors would avoid the Heraion in the first place. In other words, the authorities of the sanctuary appear to try to eliminate the problem before it arises.[7]

Yet, it is nonetheless true that those same religious authorities were supposed to intervene with the legal authorities in behalf of the suppliants.

We can turn to another source for how sanctuary and asylum were regarded in ancient Athens by considering Euripides' play, *Children of Heracles*. Heracles' children had sought asylum for protection from foreigners who sought them out. Here is an excerpt:

DEMOPHON Three paths of conscience compel me, Iolaus, not to reject your words.
Most importantly is Zeus, at whose altar you sit with the assembly of fledglings;
second, is kinship, and the obligations longstanding that these children should

[6] See Document 18 in *Greek Sacred Law*, edited by Eran Lupu, Leiden: Brill, 2009, pp. 285–297.
[7] Ibid., pp. 293–294.

for their father's sake be well treated at our hands; and last, fear of disgrace, the thing I must be most concerned about. For if I am to allow this altar to be forcibly plundered by a foreigner, it will be thought that it is no sovereign land I govern but that I have betrayed suppliants for fear of the Argives ... But you shall never take these children away ...

HERALD Put them beyond your border, and we will take them from there.
DEMOPHON You are a fool to think you can outwit the god.
HERALD This is the place, it seems, for criminals to take refuge.
DEMOPHON The gods' sanctuaries are a common defense for all.[8]

In this passage it is clear that sanctuary and its right of asylum was very much an accepted, even if a problematic, idea in the fourth century BCE in Athens.

Euripides presents three rationales in support of the idea of sanctuary: all grounded in conscience: religious, moral, and political or legal. Religiously, the sanctuaries are the shrines for a god and the gods protect especially children from harm. Morally, it is an obligation on all of us to defend children who have been orphaned or who in other ways cannot defend themselves. And politically or legally the defense of citizens from foreigners is crucial for demonstrating that sovereignty has not been abrogated.

For accused criminals seeking sanctuary, those who maintain the sanctuary were supposed to aid the criminals in their legal cases. So, in such cases it does not appear that the accused criminal could evade the law completely but only slow the process down sufficiently so that the accused criminal could get legal counsel. For those who were not accused of crimes, but who were still in need of protection, it seems that sanctuary was of unlimited duration, although as we have seen the sacral laws of sanctuary seem to make it difficult for a person to stay in sanctuary for very long.

23.3 EXILE AND OSTRACISM

A third institution in ancient Greece, exile or ostracism, also somewhat interfered with the process of punishment, although there were some statutes that integrated exile into the system of justice. We have legal records of exile as early as Draco's code. Here is an excerpt from that earliest legal code: "Even if without malice aforethought [one man kill another], let him be exiled."[9] In this early fifth century BCE text it seems that exile is a form of state-sanctioned punishment.

In Antiphon's fourth century BCE writings we find that it is common that a defendant who is about to lose his case will voluntarily go into exile. In this sense exile is

8 Euripides, *Children of Heracles*, 236–260, in *Euripides III*, translated by David Kovacs, Cambridge, MA: Harvard University Press' Loeb Classical Library, 1995, pp. 33–37.

9 Draco's Code, translated by Edward Carawan in *Rhetoric and the Law of Draco*, Oxford: Oxford University Press, 1998, p. 33.

not a state-sanctioned form of punishment but a socially acceptable attempt to evade the state's punishment. In the *Third Tetralogy*, the second speech of the defense says:

> The defendant, not because he has judged himself guilty, but because he was alarmed by the vehemence of the prosecution, has withdrawn. As to us, his friends, we were discharging our sacred duty to him more fitly by aiding him while he is alive than by aiding him after he is dead.[10]

The translator adds a note saying: "It is recognized that the defendant in a *dike phonou* had the right of withdrawing into exile half-way through the trial, if he saw no hope of an acquittal."[11] And in this case the prosecutor had just argued for the death penalty, giving the defendant even more incentive to flee into exile. Notice that while exile is extra-judicial, it was in some sense the defendant's legal right to seek exile.

So, we have seen that exile could be mandated by the court, or it could more informally be allowed by the court, and in neither case does it seem that going into exile was at odds with the rule of law that would normally have required a punishment of death or compensation. Perhaps going into exile was thought to be a kind of "death" since the exiled person no longer could participate in the institutions and customs of both state and home that he or she had grown up with. To borrow a phrase from Orlando Patterson, perhaps exile was seen as "social death,"[12] but unlike slavery there were often plenty of opportunities while in exile to live an otherwise normal life of an alien.

Another source of the legal idea of exile is related to the idea of *atimia*, outlawry. In the *Aristotelian Constitution of Athens* we find an example of a law that called for tyrants and their supporters to be subjected during the rein of Peisistratus to *atimia*.

> Athenian laws about tyranny were mild at the time, and in particular the law about the establishment of a tyrant, which ran as follows: "This is the law and traditional practice of the Athenians; any man who attempts to establish, or aids in the establishment of, a tyranny shall lose his citizenship [atimia] along with his family."[13]

Sara Fordyke explains that "Outlawry, *atimia*, meant 'loss of honor,' and a person so sanctioned – at least in the archaic period – could be killed without penalty. In most cases, the outlaw fled into exile to avoid death."[14] Here in early Athenian times the

[10] Antiphon, *Third Tetralogy* 4.1, in *Minor Attic Orators*, translated by K. J. Maidment, Cambridge, MA: Harvard University Press' Loeb Classical Library, 1941, p. 137.

[11] Ibid.

[12] See Orlando Patterson, *Slavery and Social Death*, Cambridge, MA: Harvard University Press, 1982.

[13] *The Aristotelian Constitution of Athens*, section 16, p. 222.

[14] Sara Fordyke, *Exile, Ostracism, and Democracy*, Princeton, NJ: Princeton University Press, 2005, p. 83.

exile flees the jurisdiction of the court, seemingly without having a right to do so and without the court's permission.

Yet another form of exile was called ostracism, where the assembly voted annually on whether or not to exile a particular person, normally an official or well-known figure in Athens, by vote of the whole. *The Aristotelian Constitution of Athens* gives this account: "In the sixth prytany, in addition to the business already discussed, they put to the vote the question of whether an ostracism should be held."[15] Here is Fordyke's account:

> An Athenian citizen wishing to participate in the ostracism took his potsherd to the entrance that corresponded to his tribe. The members of the council and the nine archons presided over the ostracism, presumably to ensure that each citizen voted only once, and that only citizens voted. When all had voted, the ballots were collected and counted. If at least six thousand votes had been cast, then the individual with the most votes was required to leave the city for ten years. During the time of the exile, the property of the ostracized person was left unharmed, and he could continue to draw revenues from it. After ten years the ostracized person could return to Athens and take up full citizenship rights again.[16]

Here exile was based on a political not a legal institution and was for only a fixed period of time.

We thus have seen several ways that exile was used both extra-judicially and judicially in ancient Greece. Even when exile was extra-judicial it did not seem to disrupt but to enhance justice in Greece. In the next section of this chapter I will explore some of the differences and similarities among exile, sanctuary, and amnesty in ancient Greece as well as in ancient China.

23.4 EQUITY AND EXTRAORDINARY PRACTICES IN CHINA AND GREECE

Aristotle's famous account of equity that we examined in Chapter 14 sees equity as a form of fairness that corrects for the overly severe decisions of strict justice. In many ancient societies, the death penalty was called for even in cases where it was not fully clear that the defendant was guilty of a crime that warranted death given the circumstances of his or her case. In this respect, the three extraordinary practices surveyed in the first sections of this chapter could be seen as equitable remedies in at least some respects.

Amnesty, sanctuary, and certain forms of exile or ostracism all allowed the defendant to escape the death penalty by leaving the city or swearing a certain type of oath. In many cases, there was a judicial proceeding that was found wanting by

[15] *The Aristotelian Constitution of Athens*, section 43.

[16] Fordyke, *Exile, Ostracism, and Democracy*, p. 149.

the defendant and his friends or family members. Consider the case of Socrates in Plato's dialogue the *Crito*. Socrates seems to have been wrongfully convicted and sentenced to death, at least according to Socrates' associates such as Crito. An escape into exile is planned and the system of justice in Athens is exploited to allow it to happen (by bribes and perhaps by appeals to the sense of fairness of the jailers). Socrates chooses not to take the option to go into exile, despite what has seemed to generations of philosophy students to be a clearly justified basis for doing so – given that the charges were almost certainly "trumped-up."

Amnesty is the easiest to reconcile with the rule of law. The Athenians seem to have understood that the rule of law could not be restored without peace and stability returning among the Athenians – those who supported the oligarchs and those who supported the democracy. "Forgetting," (amnestia), the wrongs on both sides seemed to be the obvious way to bring about lasting peace at the end of the civil war. As it was, the Athenian amnesty reinstated the democracy, but there was no reason an amnesty could not have restored the oligarchy instead. Amnesty favors stability, but it does not necessarily favor justice – for the wrongs on both sides are unpunished. Instead, amnesty is a practice of equity, of fairness for all concerned.

Sanctuary can be reconciled with the rule of law especially when miscarriages of justice are stopped. This occurs when a person takes sanctuary when he is fleeing vigilante justice. But what of a person who is fleeing the authorities who are duly authorized to seize her for her wrongdoing? In this case, sanctuary may not be consistent with strict justice. But, insofar as the keepers of the temple or shrine see their role as aiding the person fleeing to present his or her case to the court, perhaps by counting on the furor to pass and cooler heads to prevail. In this sense, it is again equity that is better served than strict justice. Sanctuary, for instance, gives runaway slaves a place to go where they will not evade justice in the long run but will evade the unfairness of dealing with angry slave owners at the moment.

Exile provides the most difficulty on one level and the least difficulty on another level in reconciling it with the rule of law. If the exile is court-ordered or at least court-sanctioned, it can serve to remedy the problem of not having prisons for wrongdoers to serve their sentences.[17] Exile also provides an alternative to capital punishment and thus can also contribute to stability. And as long as exile is not truly "social death" then it seems to be the kind of remedy that could be seen as equitable.

When exile is chosen to evade a legitimate judgment and sentence, there appear to be problems for the rule of law. Socrates makes just this case to Crito when he decides not to take Crito's offer of help in escaping into exile. But if that sentence, although conforming to strict justice, nonetheless violates equity, there is reason to

17 On the problems in Athens of penal imprisonment see Danielle S. Allen, *The World of Prometheus: The Politics of Punishing in Democratic Athens*, Princeton: Princeton University Press, 2000, pp. 224–230.

see exile as consistent with the rule of law. Indeed, to block an unfair sentence from being administered could be seen as supporting rather than harming the rule of law. When a legal decision is seen as inequitable there is a risk of a negative effect on fidelity to law, the cornerstone of motivation to obey and more importantly respect the law.

Equitable remedies can include amnesty, sanctuary, and various forms of exile. In all three cases we have practices that provide for cases where strict justice should not in the end be enforced. Justice and equity differ in several ways, most notably in that equity takes account of the distinct plight of persons in a particular situation that may not be of their own making. Indeed, as we will see some thinkers in the Chinese tradition eschew justice altogether in favor of what is called humaneness, a concept closely related to equity.

Contemporary to the ancient Athenian discussions we have been examining are discussions in ancient China about how best to understand Confucianism. Pardoning and amnesty were discussed favorably as ways for the ruler to display humaneness, on Mencius' understanding of Confucianism. Here is a passage from Mencius that also seems to convey the sentiments underlying the ancient Greek ideas of amnesty, sanctuary, and exile.

> Mencius saw King Xiang of Liang. On emerging he said to someone, "Seeing him from a distance, he does not appear to be a ruler of men; approaching him, one sees nothing imposing about him. He abruptly asked, 'How can the empire be settled?'
>
> "I replied, 'It can be settled through unity.'
>
> "'Who is able to unite it?'
>
> "I replied: 'One who is not fond of killing people can unite it.'"[18]
>
> Mencius thought that capital punishment is both inhumane and a practice that makes the people not respect the ruler.
>
> Instead, Mencius argued for a government based in humaneness rather than strict justice with its harsh penalties.
>
> If the king bestows humane government on the people, reduces punishments, and lightens taxes, causing the plow to be deep and the weeding thorough, the strong will be able to use their leisure time to cultivate filiality and brotherliness.[19]

Mencius advises that the main duty of the ruler is to "protect the people" where this will mean that "no one is able to stop him."[20] On the basis of such ideas as humaneness Chinese thinkers argued that pardon and amnesty can be easily justified insofar as they lead to greater peace and stability.

[18] *Mencius*, 1A6, translated by Irene Bloom, NY: Columbia University Press, 2009, p. 6.
[19] *Mencius*, 1A5, ibid., p. 5.
[20] *Mencius*, 1A7, ibid., p. 7.

23.5 WHY AMNESTY AND SANCTUARY ARE IMPORTANT

Today, the ideas of amnesty and sanctuary are under assault by "conservatives" who think that these ideas simply coddle criminals and make the rest of society less safe. The ancient Greeks, as well as the ancient Chinese, could be cited to the contrary. In this last section I will employ the ideas of the Greeks and Chinese in support of the contemporary ideas and practices of amnesty and sanctuary. I just began to present the defense in terms of equity, so before going further I wish to say more about this key legal idea.

One contemporary legal scholar says that equity "may mean flexibility rather than rigidity." Equity Courts of Chancery in England were understood "in the sense of higher justice, and also committed to doing equity in the sense of providing flexible approaches where the law had become too rigid … The Chancellors of England developed an enormous body of equity doctrine, much of which survives in some form."[21] In the Middle Ages equity was supported by a set of moral principles having to do with fair dealing and the need to take account of special circumstances that could not be addressed as a matter of strict justice.

Today, equity can call for extraordinary remedies, such as the writ of habeas corpus forcing a jailer to produce the body of the defendant and to provide reasons for why he should remain incarcerated.[22] This equitable writ is not extra-judicial but it is contrary to strict justice and legality. The writ of habeas corpus today is often used in death penalty cases in the United States, where an attempt is made to stop an execution or to replace a death sentence with a sentence for life imprisonment. In this sense, the equitable writ of habeas corpus is like a practice of recognizing the right of a runaway slave or accused criminal to seek refuge from those who sought to kill him. Indeed, in both the contemporary and the ancient case, the remedy sought could be against the attempt by the state to kill the accused. And yet it was not thought then that such practices upset the proper deterrence of the law by coddling criminals.

Amnesties have been employed in modern times even by conservative politicians and legislatures, and it is worth exploring why this is. In part, the ancient explanations are similar to those today – there is a need for the society to move on, and if not to forget completely, at least to allow people who are likely to live peacefully with their neighbors the ability to do so free of the threat of governmental action to remove them from the society. In this sense, amnesties are most frequently discussed in two contexts: at the end of war, as in ancient Greece, and for groups of people who have

[21] Dan B. Dobbs, *Handbook on the Law of Remedies: Damages, Equity and Restitution*, St. Paul, MN: West Publishing Co., 1973, p. 24.

[22] Ibid., p. 112.

illegally entered the society but are now integrating and benefitting that society. This latter group does not have an ancient correlate but as I will next explain there is certainly an ancient rationale readily available.

The Athenian amnesty of 403 BCE, as we have seen, involved a mutual oath swearing that was crucial for its working. Here is the wording of that oath:

> And I will not recall past wrongs against any citizen, except for the Thirty [and the Ten] and the Eleven; and not against these if any is willing to submit to accounting for his office.[23]

These mutual oaths are known as the reconciliation agreement – reconciliation is needed where there have been wrongs and offenses on both sides and the perpetrators now seek to end their conflict. This is the essence of amnesty – which was most famously used in contemporary times at the end of the apartheid regime in South Africa.

Sanctuary is currently one of the most hotly disputed ideas in contemporary America. There are more than 11 million undocumented aliens in the United States as I write this chapter. Most of these people work hard, pay taxes, and raise families in their communities. In addition, many of these families have some members that are undocumented and others who are citizens or who possess "green cards" as resident aliens. To deport all 11 million would mean to rip these people from their communities as well as from their families. Sanctuary is a contemporary movement to try to provide temporary protection for undocumented aliens who are sought by the government for deportation. Churches and even whole cities have declared themselves sanctuaries for the people who are being pursued by US immigration and customs agents.

As with the sanctuaries in ancient Greek temples and shrines, sanctuaries today provide a place of refuge for those who are fleeing legal authorities. The idea in both cases is not to provide permanent refuge – even if this is the idea in some cases the logistics of supporting a person and family indefinitely would be overwhelmingly complicated and prohibitively expensive. Instead, the idea was to provide temporary refuge until various legal complications could be overcome or various inequities could be remedied.

The rationale for sanctuaries in ancient times was moral, religious, and practical. Morally, those seeking refuge were fellow citizens or slaves to whom other citizens had obligations of respect and friendship. From a religious perspective the gods looked out especially for those who could not protect themselves, and for those who asked for aid from the gods. From a practical perspective, the law could not take

[23] Andocides, *On the Mysteries*, paragraphs 81 and 90, translated in Carawan, *The Athenian Amnesty and Reconstructing the Law*, p. 24.

account of all complexities and for this reason should not be interpreted so strictly that people could not escape when it seemed only fair that they could.

Today, these same rationales apply especially in immigration and refugee cases. But more importantly, the considerations of equity discussed earlier speak directly to the issue of whether contemporary sanctuaries and amnesties are contrary to the rule of law. For more than two millennia sanctuary and amnesty have been adopted by democratic and non-democratic governments without obvious loss of the ability to deter criminals from committing wrongful acts.

I have argued that the ancient practices of amnesty, sanctuary, and exile are best understood as equitable remedies for deficiencies in the legal system. And when these ancient practices are adopted for today, it seems natural to think of them as equitable remedies as well, if we somewhat broaden the meaning of equity. As in the Middle Ages, the idea is that the conscience of the society is offended when the operation of a strict notion of justice does not take account of special circumstances. People must be allowed to seek temporary reprieve from the coercive force of the law while the argument for the unfairness of incarceration or execution is debated in the public arena. And again as in ancient times, it is imperative that there be no rush to judgment when the lives and livelihoods of the members of society are at stake.

24

Justified War and the Law of Nations

The idea that those who are guilty can have wars waged against them is ancient in origin, although it is not always as straightforward as it has seemed to some commentators. Nearly all ancient discussions of war have a place for justified use of concerted violence in response to aggression. The question posed in this chapter is whether there was any sense in which the prohibition on aggressive war, and on the violation of treaties, was seen as a *legal* requirement in ancient societies. In this respect, and in how treaty obligations were understood, was there anything like an emerging international law in ancient societies? I argue that significant early advances are made in what comes to be seen as the Just War tradition in ancient Greek and Chinese legal thought.

International legal thought is characterized by the discussion of several significant ideas: the prohibition of aggressive war, the idea that there can be a just war, the humane treatment of civilians (on both sides during war), the maintenance of rules of restraint for warriors (on both sides), the protection of ministers when sent abroad, and the keeping of treaty obligations. Ancient Greek and Chinese thought, I will argue, can be interpreted as encompassing all of these ideas, at least in rudimentary form, and of providing sustained arguments in their behalf in most cases. There are also variations on the modern ideas of international law that are highly intriguing and potentially useful. Two ancient Chinese ideas, for example, that I will explore are the Confucian idea that rituals rather than explicit rules are to be preferred in guiding soldiers to be virtuous, and the Moist idea that most even defensive wars are unnecessary if a proper regard is made to non-lethal defensive actions well in advance of any possible acts of aggression.

In Section 24.1 I will briefly explore key thinkers in the Confucian tradition, including Confucius, Mencius, Xunzi, and a prominent Daoist (Taoist) Mosi, as well as Sima Rangju a military theorist. In Section 24.2 we look at ancient Greek views of justified war, starting with the pacifist views of Isocrates, and as then discussed by Xenophon and Aristotle. In Section 24.3 I examine texts from ancient Greece that support a view of the law of nations and possibly of international law. In Section 24.4 I look at how Chinese and Greek thinkers saw the obligation to keep treaties. And in Section 24.5 I try to summarize these ancient sources examined earlier in the chapter concerning the legal status of treaties and prohibitions on aggressive war.

24.1 ANCIENT CHINESE IDEAS OF THE JUSTIFICATION FOR WAR

The fifth century BCE writings of Confucius, who lived at roughly the same time as Buddha, Pythagoras, and Socrates, are rarely seen as related to international legal thought. In part this is no doubt because Confucius' texts are so fragmentary and difficult to interpret, but also because they do not fit neatly into any particular system of legal thought at all. Confucius will be seen as providing an argument for the moral development of leaders, including military leaders, where virtuous leadership is crucial for justice, as well as the idea that all rulers are bound by the same duties since morality is universal. Mencius will be seen as a very early defender of the idea of humaneness, a concept central to today's international legal thought. Xunzi will be seen as a defender of the idea that military affairs must be subject to ritual, on both sides, presaging today's ideas of the rules of war.

The ancient Chinese argument was often couched in terms of what is the righteous path. Mencius, second only to Confucius among ancient Chinese sages, says the following:

> there are no just wars. It does happen that some are better than others. "Punishment" involves superiors attacking inferiors. Opposing armies do not "punish" each other …
>
> If the ruler of a state loves humaneness, he will have no enemy in the world … To punish is to correct. With everyone wishing to be corrected, what is the need of fighting?[1]

Mencius argues that killing people is not truly a kind of punishment since they will not be alive to be corrected.

Mencius who lived in China at roughly 350 BCE during the period where there were many wars occurring also has this to say:

> From this it can be seen that one who enriched a ruler who was not given to the practice of humane government was cast off by Confucius. How much more would this be true in the case of one bent on making war? Wars that arise from territorial

[1] *Mencius*, 7B2 and 7B4, translated by Irene Bloom, NY: Columbia University Press, 2009, pp. 156–157.

> contests kill so many people that the fields are packed with corpses; wars that arise from contests over cities kill so many people that cities will be packed with corpses.[2]

Mencius, like some ancient Mesopotamian rulers, thought that considerations of humanity and humaneness were crucial moral concepts in assessing war.

Confucius already set the stage for the views of Mencius when in the *Analects* he said this about perfect virtue: "It is when you go abroad, to behave to everyone as if you were receiving a great guest; to employ the people as if you were assisting at a great sacrifice; not to do unto others as you would not wish done to yourself ..."[3] Confucius also said in the *Analects*: "Let a good man teach the people seven years, and they may then likewise be employed in war";[4] and, "To lead an uninstructed people to war is to throw them away."[5]

Here is another long passage from Mencius that is especially important for understanding early Chinese ideas about war.

> SONG KENG: "I have heard that Qin and Chu are at war, and I am going to see the King of Chu to persuade him to stop it ... I shall explain the unprofitability of war."
>
> MENCIUS: "Your intentions, sir, are great but your argument is faulty. If you, sir, use profit to persuade the kings of Qin and Chu, and if the kings of Qin and Chu, being amenable to the idea of profit, stop their armies, the personnel of those armies will be delighted with the cessation hostilities and amenable to profit ... rulers, ministers, parents, children, and older and younger brothers will abandon humaneness and rightness and encounter one another based on a preoccupation with profit ... If, sir, you rely on humaneness and rightness to persuade the kings of Qin and Chu ... [to] stop their armies, then the personnel of their armies will be delighted with the cessation of war and amenable to humaneness and rightness ... Whenever this has happened, the ruler has become a true king. Why must you speak of 'profit'?"[6]

Again, humaneness was, and is still, crucial for supporting rules of war.

Another ancient Chinese sage, Mozi, was a strong believer that only defensive war could be justified but that it was better still to build defensive fortifications. In a section titled "Against Offensive Warfare" Mozi says:

> Now all the gentlemen in the world know enough to condemn such crimes and brand them as unrighteous. And yet when it comes to the even greater unrighteousness of offensive warfare against other states they do not know enough to condemn it.[7]

2 *Mencius*, 4A14, ibid., p. 81.

3 Confucius, *Analects*, Bk XII, Ch. II, in *The Confucian Analects, The Great Learning, and the Doctrine of the Mean*, translated by James Legge, NY: Cosimo Books, 2009, p. 251.

4 Ibid., Bk XIII, Ch. XXIX, p. 275.

5 Ibid., Bk XIII, Ch. XXX, p. 275.

6 *Mencius*, 6B4, pp. 134–135.

7 *Xunzi: Basic Writings*, translated by Burton Watson, NY: Columbia University Press, 2003, p. 54.

> When the wise men of ancient times planned for the welfare of the world, they were careful to consider and accord with what is right, and only then did they act.[8]
>
> But even if all these conditions are met before one sets out to war, the state will still lose its fighting men and the common people will be forced to abandon their occupations.[9]
>
> Such is the injury which warfare inflicts upon men, the harm it brings to the world. And yet the rulers and officials delight in carrying out such expeditions. In effect they are taking delight in the injury and extermination of the people of the world. Are they not perverse?[10]
>
> The world has for a long time been plagued by warfare and is as weary as a little boy who has spent the day playing horse.[11]
>
> If one conducts one's affairs in accordance with what is correct, acts in the name of righteousness, strives for lenience in ruling one's subjects and good faith in dealing with one's army, and this sets an example for the armies of the other feudal lords, then one will have no enemy under heaven and will bring incalculable benefit to the world ... offensive war is in fact a great harm to the world.[12]

Mozi is often seen as a practical pacifist who saw that aggressive wars did not have to be engaged in as long as a state had properly fortified itself.

Xunzi set out a set of conditions that any justified war must satisfy, including these:

> Be cautious with regard to the enemy, and never neglectful ... The king's army does not kill the enemy's old men and boys; it does not destroy crops. It does not seize those who retire without a fight, but it does not forgive those who resist. It does not make prisoners of those who surrender and seek asylum. In carrying out punitive expedition, it does not punish the common people; it punishes those who lead the common people astray. But if any of the common people fight with the enemy, they become enemies as well. Thus those who flee from the enemy forces and come in surrender shall be left to go free.[13]
>
> A true king ... takes up arms in order to put an end to violence and to do away with harm, not in order to contend with others for spoil.[14]
>
> There are three methods by which you may annex a neighboring state: you may win them over by virtue, by force, or by wealth. If the people of a neighboring state respect your reputation, admire your virtuous actions, and desire to become your

[8] Ibid., p. 55.
[9] Ibid., p. 57.
[10] Ibid., p. 58.
[11] Ibid., p. 62.
[12] Ibid., p. 63.
[13] Ibid., p. 70.
[14] Ibid., pp. 71–72.

> subjects, they will throw open their gates, clear the roads, and welcome you to their cities.[15]
>
> Therefore I say, he who annexes a state by virtue is a true king; he who annexes it by force will be weakened; and he who annexes it by wealth will be impoverished. From ancient times until the present, it has always been the same.[16]

Xunxi takes a pragmatic approach to war in contrast to Mencius who was explicitly providing a moral approach.

Finally, I would cite one of the military strategy classics of this period of ancient Chinese thought, c. 430 BCE, by Sima Rangju:

> In antiquity, taking benevolence as the foundation and employing righteousness constituted the Way of governance. However when governance failed to attain the desired moral and political objectives, we have to resort to authority. Authority comes from waging warfare, not from harmony among men. For this reason, if one must kill men to give peace to the people, then killing is permissible. If one must attack a state out of love for their people, then attacking is permissible. If one must stop war with war, although it is war, it is permissible. Thus, if a ruler shows benevolence, he will be loved; if a ruler shows righteousness, he shall willingly be submitted to; if a ruler shows wisdom, he will be relied upon; if a ruler shows courage, he will be embraced; if a ruler shows integrity, he will be trusted.[17]

War was justified only in certain circumstances, largely for defensive, not offensive reasons. And for Sima Rangju and other Chinese thinkers, war needed a kind of authority that we can see as at least quasi-legal as epitomized by "the Way of governance."

Concerning tactics during war, Sima Rangju was also guided by moral and legal ideas drawn from Confucian thinkers. The general principle is that the ruler must have "sympathy for the wounded and sick; thereby showing what is benevolence" acting only from righteousness and not from gain or profit.[18] And rules and laws should be formed to instill this principle in the minds of those who engage in warfare: "in warfare, laws can regulate men."[19] It is not accidentally that this discussion is framed in terms of the *laws* of warfare.

[15] Ibid., pp. 78–79.

[16] Ibid., p. 80.

[17] Sima Rangju, *Methods of War*, in *Military Strategy Classics of Ancient China*, translated by Chen Song, NY: Special Editions Books, 2013, p. 143.

[18] Ibid., p. 144.

[19] Ibid., p. 166.

24.2 ANCIENT GREEK IDEAS ABOUT AGGRESSIVE WAR

Isocrates held views that were basically pacifist in character, but there were also many Greek authors who condemned the idea of aggressive war without condemning all war. Let us begin with Isocrates, who wrote a discourse, "On the Peace." In the translator's preface to this work, George Norlin says Isocrates "is seeking a permanent cure for the troubles into which Athens has fallen, and he finds it only in a radical reversal of her policies of aggression."[20]

At the beginning of his discourse "On the Peace" Isocrates says "those who lightly espouse war have already plunged us into many great disasters."[21] And in discussing a non-aggression pact that Athens contemplated abrogating, Isocrates says: "For we shall not find terms of peace more just than these nor more expedient for our city."[22] For Isocrates, it was not enough that peace agreements would be signed but that there is an expressed will to follow them. "But I think we should not go forth from this assembly, having merely adopted a resolution in favor of the peace, without also taking counsel how we shall keep it."[23] And as I said, Isocrates railed against the misfortunes and injustices that are associated with "a policy of aggression."[24] States have greater need to cultivate the virtues than individual persons do since states are "deathless" so "sooner or later must submit to punishment at the hands of men and gods."[25]

Many other thinkers including Thucydides, Herodotus, and Aristotle found some wars to be justified, and for a variety of reasons, as we will see. Like their Chinese counterparts, the ancient Greeks tried to avoid pitched battles where they were likely to lose many soldiers, and instead advocated building defense structures.

> By the late fifth century, the Athenians, in the hopes of spreading their untraditional ideas about the avoidance of hoplite battle on the plains, sent out corps of "long wall builders" to other cities, such as Argos or Patros, to advocate the construction of similar systems of defense.[26]

Avoiding war except in the case of countering aggression was the general idea from the fifth century BCE in Greece.

[20] Isocrates, *On the Peace*, in *Isocrates II*, translated by George Norlin, Cambridge, MA: Harvard University Press' Loeb Classical Library, 1929, p. 3.

[21] Ibid., p. 13.

[22] Ibid., p. 17.

[23] Ibid., p. 23.

[24] Ibid., p. 59.

[25] Ibid., p. 83.

[26] Victor Davis Hanson, *The Western Way of War: Infantry Battle in Classical Greece*, Berkeley, CA: University of California Press, 1994, p. 39.

During the fourth century BCE there arose in Greece the idea of a common peace (*koine eirene*).[27] Standing over and above the peaceful and peacemaking efforts of ancient Greek states is the idea from Homer that revenge and retaliation were necessary to restore the honor of a state. One can see the push and pull of the idea of revenge as interacting with the desire for peace and not for pursuit of war.

24.3 ANCIENT GREECE AND THE LAW OF NATIONS

Arthur Nussbaum states the standard position on ancient Greek views about interstate relations: "the rules observed in the relations among the ancient Greek states were largely religious and, despite the independence of the states, in reality rather intermunicipal," not international in any recognizably modern sense.[28] Coleman Phillipson argues for another interpretation that gets to the same result, when he says:

> Greece consisted of a large number of independent and sovereign cities, jealous of each other's advancement in power and dominion, and constantly astir with dissention. But sovereignty and independence seemed at times ready to sacrifice themselves in greater or lesser measure by the formation of leagues and combinations to repel non-Hellenic invaders … [but] Whatever efforts were made to effect a real union were invariably defeated.[29]

Yet Phillipson nonetheless argues for an incipient sense of international law in ancient Greece, in the sense of that idea that derives from religion and morality.

Specifically, Phillipson argues that there were recognized rules for how states were to interact and that each state had an obligation to adhere to these legal rules and customs.[30] We can look to Aristotle for the underlying moral ideas supporting a rudimentary law of nations in ancient Greece. In the *Rhetoric*, Aristotle says:

> By the two kinds of law I mean particular law and universal law. Particular law is that which each community lays down and applies to its own members: this is partly written and partly unwritten. Universal law is the law of nature. For there really is, as everyone to some extent divines, a natural justice and injustice that is binding on all men, even on those who have no association or covenant with each other.[31]

27 See Lawrence A. Tritle, "'Laughing for Joy': War and Peace among the Greeks," in *War and Peace in the Ancient World*, edited by Kurt A. Raaflaub, Oxford: Blackwell Publishing, 2007, pp. 180–181.

28 Arthur Nussbaum, *A Concise History of the Law of Nations*, NY: The Macmillan Company, 1953, p. 9.

29 Coleman Phillipson, *The International Law and Custom of Ancient Greece and Rome*, Vol. 1, London: Macmillan and Company, 1911, p. 29.

30 Ibid., pp. 50–51.

31 Aristotle, *Rhetoric*, 1373b3–10, in *The Basic Works of Aristotle*, edited by Richard McKeon and translated by W. Rhys Roberts, NY: Random House, 1941, p. 1370.

The recognition of a law that applies to all people and states is a lynchpin for the later conception of the law of nations or of international law.

One of the most important components of the universal law that Aristotle and others discuss is the idea of hospitality to the stranger or alien. In Sophocles' *Oedipus at Colonus* we find the following speech by Theseus, king of Colonus addressing Oedipus:

> now that I see you after this journey I am even more certain; for your clothing and your stricken face make it clear to me who you are; and in pity for you, Oedipus, I wish to ask you what request of the city and of me you have come to make, you and your unfortunate companion. Tell me! For you would need to speak of a terrible misfortune indeed for me to turn you away! I have not forgotten that I myself was brought up in exile, as you were, and that in my exile I struggled against such dangers to my life as no man has met with; so I would never turn aside from helping to rescue any exile such as you, since I know that I am a man, and that I have no greater share in tomorrow than you have.[32]

And Andocides also recognizes a right of hospitality that undergirds various legal conventions that the Greek states have entered into, saying: "In our treaties with other states we make it a condition that no free man shall be imprisoned or placed in durance, and a heavy fine is prescribed as the penalty for doing so."[33] And with this writing of universal law into treaties the ancient Greeks come to a sense of international law that is, in several respects, very close to our own today.

We could also note that over time the ancient Athenian state "gradually developed into a decisive political preponderance, and the confederacy was after time virtually transformed into an Athenian empire."[34] Within this empire and the ones that followed up to the Roman Empire, we certainly have more than merely intermunicipal law. And when we add the numerous mentions of how diplomats and ambassadors had strongly protected rights we can get a sense of how the relations of states that allowed for the formation of leagues, alliances, and ultimately empires to be established on the law and custom of the rights of all peoples across national borders.

24.4 THE OBLIGATION TO KEEP TREATIES

One of the best known treaties in ancient Greece was that establishing the peace of Nicias in 422 BCE ending the Peloponnesian War between Athens and Sparta. Here is part of the treaty as recorded by Thucydides:

[32] Sophocles, *Oedipus at Colonus* 555–568, in *Sophocles II*, translated by Hugh Lloyd-Jones, Cambridge, MA: Harvard University Press' Loeb Classical Library, 1994, p. 479.

[33] Andocides, *Against Alcibiades*, 18–19, in *Minor Attic Orators I*, translated by K. J. Maidment, Cambridge, MA: Harvard University Press' Loeb Classical Library, 1941, p. 557.

[34] Coleman Phillipson, *The International Law and Custom of Ancient Greece and Rome*, Vol. II, London: Macmillan and Company, 1911, p. 15. Also see David Bederman, *International Law in Antiquity*, NY: Cambridge University Press, 2001, pp. 35–36.

> The treaty is to be in force between the Athenians, with their allies, and the Spartans, with their allies, for fifty years without fraud or damage by land or sea.
>
> It shall not be lawful to take up arms with the intent to do injury either for the Spartans and their allies against the Athenians and their allies, or for the Athenians and their allies against the Spartans and their allies, in any way or by any means whatever. If any dispute should arise between them, they are to deal with it by law and by oath as may be agreed between them.
>
> The Spartans and their allies are to give back Amphipolis to the Athenians. In the case of all cities given back by the Spartans to the Athenians, the inhabitants shall have the right to go where they please taking their property with them …
>
> The Athenians shall take an oath to the Spartans and their allies, city by city. The oath shall be the most binding one that exists in each city, and seventeen representatives on each side are to swear it. The words of the oath shall be these: "I shall abide by the terms of this treaty honestly and sincerely." In the same way the Spartans and their allies shall take an oath to the Athenians. This oath shall be renewed annually by both sides. Pillars are to be set up at Olympia, Pythia, the Isthmus, in the Acropolis at Athens and in the temple at Amyclae in Lacedaemon.[35]

This treaty is a model of many others formed in ancient Greece.

There are five things to note about the Treaty of Nicias. First, the treaty was also a truce that ended a ten-year war between the Athenians and Spartans. Since neither side clearly won that war, the parties approached the treaty as roughly equal, not as a vassal state and a lord state. Second, the treaty was multilateral, not merely bilateral as most ancient treaties had been. Thucydides tells us that some of the allies of Sparta rejected the terms of the treaty but that Sparta and the rest of her allies signed the treaty in any event.[36] Third, the terms were the same on each side, including the length of time of the treaty as well as the rights and duties created by the treaty. Fourth, the treaty's duties were memorialized and enforced by mutual oaths with witnesses present. Fifth, and most importantly for this chapter, the states were bound "by law" and the breaking of the treaty will "not be lawful." In the next few paragraphs I will say more about the fourth and fifth points.

The mutual swearing of oaths is a means of enforcing the terms of treaties that goes back to the very first recorded treaties in Mesopotamia and Egypt. The same can be said about the memorialization of the treaty by setting up monuments in both states. The oaths were linked to the common religion that both parties shared. And these oaths by Athens and Sparta and their allies were the strongest available, giving the most deterrent effects. Yet, the peace did not in fact last for 50 years – Thucydides

[35] Thucydides, *History of the Peloponnesian War,* Book v, section 18, translated by Rex Warner, Harmondsworth: Penguin Books, 1954, pp. 359–360.

[36] Ibid., section 22, p. 361.

says it lasted less than seven years[37] – leaving us to wonder why the treaty did not succeed with the use of the Greek religion's strongest oaths behind it.

Aristotle raises the perennial problem with treaties among independent states despite the deterrent effects of mutual oaths.

> Nor does a state exist for the sake of exchange and mutual intercourse; for then the Tyrrhenians and the Carthaginians, and all who have commercial treaties with one another, would be the citizens of one state. True, they have agreements about imports, and their engagements that they will do no wrong to one another, and written articles of alliance. But there are no magistracies to the common contracting parties who will enforce their engagements; different states have each their own magistracies. Nor does one state take care that the citizens of the other are such as they ought to be, nor see that those who come under the terms of the treaty do no wrong or wickedness at all, but only that they do no injustice to one another. Whereas those who care for good government take into consideration virtue and vice in states.[38]

For Aristotle, oaths are seemingly not enough to create a bond among states that would be equivalent to the bond among citizens within a state. One missing element is the common enforcer of the laws and rules. Another missing element is the concern on the part of one state for the welfare of the other, which exists among citizens within a state. In this account, there may be justice among states, but not virtue.

Here Aristotle is almost surely using "justice" in the narrow, strict, sense he discussed when contrasting justice with equity in his *Nicomachean Ethics*. Narrow or strict justice involves an adherence to the letter of the law. Yet, given Aristotle's scepticism, it is hard to understand why even narrow justice would be secured merely by oaths if there is no other institution backing up the provisions of the treaty. Despite what Aristotle says, there is no reason to think that enforcementless treaties will even guarantee "the prevention of mutual crime."[39] As we will see, such concerns remain today, especially in the field of international criminal law, although there are perhaps a few answers to blunt some of Aristotle's scepticism.

But there is reason to think that even Aristotle recognized some kind of law or rule of nations – and it seems that this law extended beyond narrow justice. The universal law that Aristotle discussed in his *Rhetoric* looks like it would be the sort of law that the obligation of states to keep their agreements could be grounded in. Yet, such a universal law would seemingly have the problem that Aristotle identifies with the

37 Ibid., Book V, section 25.

38 Aristotle, *Politics*, 1280a35–1280b6 in *Basic Works of Aristotle*, edited by Richard McKeon, translated by Benjamin Jowett, NY: Random House, 1941, p. 1188.

39 Ibid., 1280b33, pp. 1188–1189.

problematic nature of treaties. The question is how a universal law that transcended any particular state's borders, and hence any enforcement mechanism, could be motivation for these states. It is to this topic to which we finally turn.

24.5 TREATY ENFORCEMENT IN INTERNATIONAL LAW

In contemporary times, much of international law is a matter of multilateral treaties, including even the establishment of the United Nations itself. And among the many multilateral treaties are the Hague and Geneva Conventions that have set the rules of war that nearly all nations follow. But one question that keeps arising is what the basis of the obligation is of states to keep to these agreements. We have a system of international laws as well as a series of courts that interpret and apply these laws. But there is no consistent enforcement since there is no global sovereign that can require compliance. Aristotle raised just the right question nearly 2,500 years ago. And now, as then, various attempts to answer Aristotle's challenge have been made, all starting from the fact that international laws are widely adhered to despite the lack of a strong enforcer of those laws.

One of the contemporary issues in international legal theory is how best to ground the principle of *pacta sunt servanda* (the principle that agreements must be kept). It is at this point in the debate that some theorists will then talk of universal norms such as those that Aristotle discussed in ancient Athens, although most of the participants in this debate do not often cite Aristotle by name. Sometimes the idea is expressed in natural law terms, as controversial as these laws are for today's secular society. In what follows in this final section I will sketch an Aristotelian sense of universal laws that are not necessarily grounded in religion.

Aristotle talks about universal laws in the following terms, quoting him from his *Rhetoric* but also from his *Politics* and *Nicomachean Ethics*. I quoted from the *Rhetoric* earlier but it is worthwhile to quote a key passage again. "Universal law is the law of nature. For there really is, as everyone to some extent divines, a natural justice and injustice that is binding on all men, even on those who have no association or covenant with each other."[40]

In Aristotle's *Nicomachean Ethics* Book V, political justice, a form of particular justice, has two components. One part, "natural justice," is universal ("which everywhere has the same force"),[41] and does not depend on what people think is politically just. The other, "legal justice," was "originally indifferent" until it was "laid down." This distinction tracks to a certain extent the criminal law distinction today

[40] Aristotle, *Rhetoric*, 1373b3–10, translated by Roberts, in *The Basic Works of Aristotle*, p. 1370.

[41] Aristotle, *Nicomachean Ethics*, 1134b18, translated by W. D. Ross in *The Basic Works of Aristotle*, p. 1014.

between *mala in se* crimes and *mala prohibita* crimes. It also is important for various philosophical debates about justice today, where liberal theorists talk of certain "natural duties" that could be seen to be grounded in natural justice. The idea of natural justice also had a powerful impact on the idea of natural law, in the way Aquinas extended Aristotle's ideas in the Middle Ages. There is a debate about whether Aristotle had something fairly narrow in mind, as is true of the criminal law distinction, or something much broader, such as the natural lawyers would have it.

In his *Politics*, Aristotle argues that politics can be understood in terms of universal categories and that one can make normative assessments of the benefits of those types of government. The Greek term for nature is *physis*; and the Greek term for law is *nomos*. But neither of these Greek terms is captured by these English terms. To see some of this, consider a passage from the orator, Demosthenes:

> The whole life of men, Athenians, whether they dwell in a large state or a small one, is governed by nature and by the laws. Of these, nature is something irregular and incalculable, and peculiar to each individual; but the laws are something universal, definite, and the same for all. Now nature, if it be evil, often chooses wrong, and that is why you will find men of an evil nature committing errors. But the laws desire what is honorable and salutary; they seek for it and when they find it they set it forth as a general commandment, equal and identical for all ... every law is an invention and gift of the gods ...[42]

Law (*nomos*) is an invention that is imposed, it is contingent for the Greeks; while nature (*physis*) is a matter of necessity. But for the natural world to have a law it must be imposed by someone or something.

To speak of a law of nature is to speak of a necessary order of the universe. In this sense the law of gravitation is a law of nature. What is interesting is that for Demosthenes, and perhaps for Aristotle, nature is generally law-like but because of chance it is not always so. To a certain extent, law must be imposed on nature, either by humans or by gods. For Aristotle, the gods impose an order on nature. And when a state is formed – an order is created out of what was without order. But in what sense is the state natural? It is natural at least in one sense in that it has a necessary end, some human good. The puzzle is that what was conventional in origin takes on a necessity – and yet at the beginning of the *Politics* we are not told how this happens.

Plato and Aristotle talked in terms of a universal morality (the form of the good, etc). There is an interesting question about how a cosmopolitan ethic would differ from a universalistic ethic. Aristotle often appeals to "what all hold," perhaps implying that he derives his universal moral truths from what all humans think – thus mixing universal with cosmopolitan categories. And when Aristotle then talks

[42] Demosthenes, *Against Aristogeiton*, I.15–16, in *Demosthenes III*, translated by J. H. Vance, Cambridge, MA: Harvard University Press' Loeb Classical Library, 1935, p. 525.

of universal law he may still be talking of universal morality or trying to see if there is a kind of universal law that corresponds to universal morality but is binding in a different way.

So why do states feel obligated to keep their treaties, especially the multilateral treaties that today make up a regime of international law and the laws of war? One reason that would be supported by Thucydides is that states only adhere to treaties when the terms of these treaties are in the self-interest of the states. In the famous (or infamous) Melian dialogue, Thucydides has the Athenians say:

> ATHENIANS: "you know as well as we do that right, as the world goes, is only in question between equals in power, while the strong do what they can and the weak suffer what they must" …
>
> MELIANS: "And how, pray, could it turn out as good for us to serve you as for you to rule?"
>
> ATHENIANS: "Because you would have the advantage of submitting before suffering the worst, and we would gain by not destroying you" …
>
> ATHENIANS: "you have the choice given you between war and security" …
>
> Then "the Athenians put to death all the grown men whom they took, and sold the women and children for slaves."[43]

Such a view is clearly at odds with Aristotle's view as well as most supporters of international law today.[44]

The most plausible view is that states feel something like a moral obligation, but a heightened obligation since it is a clearly universal moral obligation, which can be seen in the way that states indeed talk about their international obligations, and contrary to how Thucydides characterized such discussions. But Aristotle is right that while such an obligation can be said to be a kind of legal obligation, it is not supported by the kind of punishment institutions that exist for intra-state illegalities. The law of nations, or international law, is a form of law but not the same as the law of a municipal state. From an ancient perspective, though, it should not be surprising that the law of nations is indeed adhered to in most situations by most states.

[43] Thucydides, *History of the Peloponnesian War*, Book V, section 17, translated by Crawley, NY: The Modern Library, 1951, pp. 331–337.

[44] See Larry May and Shannon Fyfe, *International Criminal Tribunals: A Normative Defense*, NY: Cambridge University Press, 2017.

CONCLUDING THOUGHTS FOR PART B

Ancient Greek legal thought can be characterized as an attempt to deal with the individual in the community. One striking way to see this is in Greek laws concerning homicide. The focus of homicide law was on the individual perpetrator, seen primarily as a citizen or other member of a city-state, not as a member of a tribe or clan. And the harm of homicide was identified as a harm to the city-state, to all of the members of a community. This ancient Greek idea was more elaborately set out and institutionalized than a similar idea in ancient Babylonian and Egyptian societies. For the Greeks, the most common penalty for homicide is exile – the perpetrator was banished from the community that he had harmed. The ancient Chinese also focus on the individual and have a clear sense of criminal liability, especially concerning those who kill intentionally.

For the Greeks, the idea of legal pollution plays an important role here as does the legal institution of the Areopagus court, both inventions of the Greeks. The killer has become polluted and risks polluting the city-state. Pollution is here a kind of danger to the community that must be expiated not merely by punishment in the sense of retribution or even deterrence. There must also be purification – but not primarily in a religious or moral sense. The danger to the community must be averted by either the removal of the killer from the community or by a ritual that demonstrates that the killer resolves not to kill again. And the perpetrator is to be tried primarily in a court that is specifically and exclusively dedicated to dealing with killers. In both Greece and China the idea of "self-help," where the victim's family killed either a member of the killer's family or the killer himself, is being replaced by a new institution. Certain procedures and protocols must be followed – not by the victim's family but by the state, which is seen as the true victim of the killing.

Here we have an emerging understanding of a public harm that is the law's exclusive jurisdiction. And even more basically we have the idea that individuals are members of that public, and that the membership in a public institution, the state, is the defining relationship for the legal individual. The law serves the purposes of the public – identifying individuals by their public roles and by the harms or benefits that the individual deserves from their public institutions. For both ancient Greeks and Chinese, these institutions are not defined religiously – it was not membership in the temple or in one's relationship to the gods, and it was not about one's relationship to the palace, which was important. Instead, it was one's relationship to one's fellow community members that was the key – and where the community was not seen merely as an extension of family, tribe, or clan.

In terms of thinking about war and law, some of the earliest pacifists were Isocrates in Greece and Mencius in China. But there are also on display a whole range of views about war that match those today. And the trouble in thinking about law as applying to the interactions of states turns out to be similar to our own worries today about the binding power of international law. Of special interest is that in ancient Greece and China the idea of amnesty and sanctuary for those who commit harm is fairly well established and in many ways not nearly as controversial then as today. This is at least in part because both Chinese and Greek legal thought put a heavy emphasis on humaneness, and this is, in some ways, more pronounced than in the supposedly more civilized political and legal systems of the Romans.

PART C

India and the Roman Republic

INTRODUCTION FOR PART C

Ancient India's *Code of Manu* tells us that a king who "is lustful, partial, and vile" will be slain by the law.[1] The Roman *Twelve Tables* asserts that laws concerning capital punishment can only be enacted by the assembly not by the rulers, and that "For anyone whosoever to be put to death without a trial and unconvicted ... is forbidden."[2] In both of these ancient texts we can see a very strong sense of the rule of law being imposed even over very strong rulers. These ancient laws that call for the punishment of rulers who overstep their authority are in many ways stronger than legal restraints on sovereign authority today. Law has gone from the dictate of the sovereign to place a restraining limit on that very sovereign – indeed in Rome it is clear already in the *Twelve Tables* that it is the people that are ultimately sovereign.

With ancient Indian legal thought and that of the Roman Republic, principally of the last several centuries BCE and the first century CE, we find elaborate codes of law that while not especially systematic are nonetheless quite encompassing of many areas of common life. We have here two of the best known ancient codes of law, at least as important as Hammurabi's Code: The Roman *Twelve Tables* and the Indian *Code of Manu*. These codes set the agenda for legal thinking for hundreds of years in ancient India and Rome, as well as the rest of the world.

In this period we find the first great commentator on law and legal theory, the Roman lawyer and politician, Cicero. Indeed, much of the early Roman law is today available only as imbedded in the speeches that Cicero delivered in defense or in prosecution in high profile cases in the last century BCE. As Roman law broke from its strongly religious roots, Indian legal thought remained admixed with religious

1 *Manu's Code of Law*, 7.27–28, translated by Patrick Olivelle, Oxford: Oxford University Press, 2005, p. 155.

2 *The Twelve Tables*, IX.1–2, in *Ancient Roman Statutes*, translated by Allan Chester Johnson, Paul Robinson Coleman-Norton, and Frank Card Bourne, Austin: University of Texas Press, 1961, 2012, p. 12.

thought, although we have an Indian code of law, *The Naradasmrti*,[3] which is highly secular and often compared in style to Roman statutes.

For both Indian and Roman law, criminality was tied to acts that in some manner undermined or threatened the social or political order. Indeed, political and legal abuse is punished severely, as are various acts that were seen as undermining the moral order. Law was also used to maintain class differences where this became characteristic of India, and in the Roman use of law to repress slave revolts. Yet, there was concern for the lowest classes also expressed in law. Indeed prisoners of war were given special treatment in the laws of India and the Roman Republic.

Statutes and codes of law became more important than custom in the legal thought we will here examine. And it is the concern for, indeed the respect for, formal institutions of law that were also characteristic of India and Rome in the last few centuries BCE and the first few centuries CE, as we will see in detail in what follows in this third part of my work on ancient legal thought.

[3] *The Naradasmrti*, translated by Richard W. Lariviere, Delhi: Motilal Banarsidass Publishers, 2003.

SECTION IX

Law, Justice, and Equity

25

Law and Its Sources in Ancient Roman and Indian Law

One of the terms for law, *ius* in Roman legal thought, and *dharma* in Indian legal thought, also can mean "right." *Dharma* and *ius* can also mean justice or custom. We see in these linguistic facts that the idea of law is not well separated from morality in ancient times in Rome and India, as was also true in other ancient societies. Yet, even before the Roman Republic, the term *lex* came to stand for a more strict understanding of the law as cut off from other normative considerations. Indian legal thought had the concept of *sutra*, meaning science or knowledge of specific parts of human life, and *sutra* when linked to *dharma* as in *Dharmasutra* – hence the science of right or justice – seems to have some of the connotations of the Roman *lex*.

In this chapter we will look at various texts from the Roman Republic and ancient India from roughly the same time period – the several centuries leading up to the beginning of Common Era CE (also known as *anno domine* – the years AD). It is commonly said that Indian law is derivative of Indian religion, whereas Roman law is thoroughly secular. While there is some truth in such a bold dichotomy, I will argue that there are many commonalities between especially the Roman law of the *Twelve Tables* and also of Cicero as compared to the India law of the Dharmasutras as well as especially the *Code of Manu*. Ancient religion and law were rarely clearly separated, just as is also true of the comingling of morality with ancient law, especially in the various ideas of criminal law.

As we will see in this chapter, there is also considerable overlap between ancient Roman and Indian legal thought concerning the origin of the binding character of law in something like laws of nature. Indeed, the idea of a law of nature seems to emerge in the early Roman legal thinkers who were influenced by the Greek Stoics and who may also have played a role in the beginnings of Indian legal thinking. In any event, in this chapter we will explore the ideas about the origins of law and the sources of law in two of the best examples of developing legal systems in Roman and Indian legal thought.

In Section 25.1 we look at the Institutes of Gaius especially concerning what he says about the earliest of the codes and we contrast Gaius' account of the sources of Roman law with the early Ḍharmasutras of India and the incipient ideas of the nature of law that they contain. In Section 25.2 we turn to the *Twelve Tables*, the oldest of Roman statutes, as well as to Cicero, the greatest of the Roman philosophers, especially concerning his understanding of the relationship between the civil law and the law of nature. In Section 25.3 we look at the laws of the Dharmasutras and also the *Code of Manu* to see how Indian legal thought addressed our main questions at about the same time as Cicero. In Section 25.4 we attempt to explain why these ideas from Rome and India have had such a profound influence today.

25.1 SOURCES OF ANCIENT ROMAN AND INDIAN LAW

Gaius, one of the most significant Roman commentators on law, writing in the first century CE, right at the end of the period of our current study, gives a definitive statement of the sources of Roman law.

> All people who are ruled by laws and customs partly make use of their own laws, and partly have recourse to those which are common to all men; for what every people establishes as law for itself is peculiar to itself, and is called the Civil Law, as being that peculiar to the State; and what natural reason establishes among all men and is observed by all peoples alike, is called the Law of Nations …
>
> The Civil Law of the Roman people consists of statutes, plebiscites, Decrees of the Senate, Constitutions of the Emperors, the Edicts of those who have the right to promulgate them, and the opinions of jurists.[1]

Gaius is especially known for his ability to distill the elements of law into concise and understandable sentences. And his bifurcation of law into two types, the civil law and the law of nations, and then his exhaustive list of sources of the civil law of Rome were nearly canonical.

Cicero, the most significant Roman philosopher, had his own division of law, which included another category that he called the law of nature. In his treatise on *Law* (*De Legibus*) he says the following:

> I find that it has been the opinion of the wisest men that Law is not a product of human thought, nor is it any enactment of peoples, but something eternal which rules the whole universe by its wisdom in command and prohibition. Thus they have been accustomed to say that Law is the primal and ultimate mind of God, whose reason directs all things either by compulsion or restraint. Wherefore that

[1] Gaius, *The Institutes of the Civil Law*, First Commentary, I. (1) and (2), in *The Civil Law*, translated by S. P. Scott, Clark, NJ: The Law Book Exchange [1932] 2001, p. 81.

Law which the Gods have given to the human race has been justly praised; for it is the reason and mind of a wise lawgiver applied to command and prohibition.[2]

Here Cicero claims that law properly understood is from God not from human hands and gives a sense of what it would mean to say that law is both divinely inspired and also supremely rational, at least that law that is universal in its prohibitions.

As important as the division of sources of law was Gaius' division of the laws themselves into three types: "All the law which we make use of has reference either to persons, to things, or to actions."[3] Persons are either free or slaves.[4] Things are divided into those which are subject to divine right and those which are subject to human right.[5] Actions are either real or personal.[6] This is a division of the kinds of suits that can be brought. Even though law is either divine or civil, the Roman lawyers by and large stuck to the civil law, with only occasional references to divine law.

Concerning sources of law, some of the oldest Indian texts, dating from the first centuries before the Common Era, are the treatises of the religious experts in Vedic interpretation, which are contained in the four surviving *Dharmasutras*. At the beginning of the *Baudhayana*, the third of the *Dharmasutras*, we find:

The law is taught in each Veda, in accordance with which we explain it. What is given in the tradition is the second, and the conventions of the cultured people are the third. Now cultured people are those who are free from envy and pride, possess just a jarful of grain, and are free from covetousness, hypocrisy, arrogance, greed, folly, and anger. As it is said:

Cultured people are those who have studied the Veda together with its supplements in accordance with the Law, know how to draw inferences from them, and are able to adduce as proofs express Vedic texts.[7]

The *Baudhayana* gives a perhaps surprisingly similar list of sources of law to that of the Roman jurist Gaius. Indeed, a prominent place is given to scholars and cultured people as themselves being sources of law. But notice that all three sources of law are in some sense religious.

In the *Code of Manu*, from a somewhat later period in Indian history, but probably only a few hundred years after the *Baudhayana*, we find a more elaborate account of the sources of law:

2 Cicero, *De Legibus*, in *Cicero XVI*, translated by Clinton Walker Keyes, Cambridge, MA: Harvard University Press' Loeb Classical Library, 1928, pp. 379–381.

3 Gaius, *The Institutes of the Civil Law*, First Commentary, II (8), in *The Civil Law*, p. 83.

4 Ibid., First Commentary, II (9), p. 83.

5 Ibid., Second Commentary, (2), p. 111.

6 Ibid., Fourth Commentary, (1), p. 184.

7 *The Law Code of Baudhayana*, Book 1, 1. 1–6, in *Dharmasutras: The Law Codes of Apastamba, Gautama, Baudhayana, and Vasistha*, translated by Patrick Olivelle, Delhi: Motilal Banarsidass, 2000, p. 197.

> The root of the Law is the entire Veda; the tradition and practice of those who know the Veda; the conduct of good people; and what is pleasing to oneself. Whatever Law Manu has proclaimed with respect to anyone, all that has been taught in the Veda, for it contains all knowledge. After subjecting all this to close scrutiny with the eye of knowledge, a learned man should apply himself to the Law proper to him on the authority of the scriptures; for by following the Law proclaimed in scripture and tradition, a man achieves fame in this world and unsurpassed happiness after death. "Scripture" should be recognized as "Veda," and "tradition" as "Law Treatise." These two should never be called into question in any matter for it is from them that the Law has shined forth.[8]

As in the *Baudhayana*, the *Code of Manu* places the Vedas as the primary source of law in ancient India. There are four Vedas, each attributed to the direct divine knowledge passed down to humans from the gods. They date from approximately the fourteenth century BCE and form the most basic writings of the Hindu religion as well as the ground for law in Hindu Indian society.[9]

Perhaps the most important difference between ancient Indian law and ancient Roman law is that the codes of Indian law, such as the *Baudhayana*, intertwine rules for sacral practices with the civil and criminal rules that govern the affairs of people. For the Romans, especially for Cicero, while law properly is a kind of divinely inspired law, there is a separation of texts dealing with religious practice from the law dealing with civil and criminal affairs of humans. For ancient Indian legal thought the touchstone was a largely religious text, the Veda, while for ancient Roman legal thought the touchstone was the *Twelve Tables*, a much more secular grounding document. But it is also true that especially for Cicero, the most important of the legal theorists of the Roman Republic, law also refers, perhaps most basically to the eternal law of god, as we will see in the next section.

25.2 THE *TWELVE TABLES* AND CICERO ON THE NATURE OF LAW

Long before Cicero's time, the *Twelve Tables* set out basic rights of citizens in respect to the law:

> Table IX, Law I: No privileges or statutes shall be enacted in favor of private persons, to the injury of others contrary to the law common to all citizens, and which individuals, no matter of what rank, have a right to make use of.
>
> Table IX, Law II: The same rights shall be conferred upon, and the same laws shall be considered to be enacted for all the people residing in and beyond Latium, that have been enacted for good and steadfast Roman citizens.

8 *Manu's Code of Law*, 2.6–10, p. 94.

9 See the introduction to *The Vedas*, translated by Ralph T. H. Griffith, Delhi: Kshetra Books, 1914, 2017.

> Table IX, Law IV: No decision with reference to the life or liberty of a Roman citizen shall be rendered except by the vote of the Greater *Comitia*.[10]

Here we find law understood primarily as a matter of statutes or customs, which distribute rights and liabilities. And law is generally understood as made by the people or at least appealable to the people. Law is also seen as guaranteeing equality of rights, and not just to citizens.

At the end of the *Twelve Tables* we learn more about how to understand the sources of law and also what to do if conflicts arise:

> Table XI Law I: Affairs of great importance shall not be transacted without the vote of the people, with whom rests the power to appoint magistrates, to condemn citizens, and to enact laws. Laws subsequently passed always take precedence over former ones.[11]

We have a strong statement here that statutes are to be enacted only with the vote of the people that also establishes the magistrates who decide legal cases. If one statute conflicts with another, the most recent takes priority. Thus the *Twelve Tables* provided Roman legal thinkers, from the earliest of times, with seemingly a firm secular grounding and a democratic dimension.

The greatest philosopher of the Roman Republic was undoubtedly Cicero. Concerning his writings about law, he was influenced by Stoic philosophers from Greece, especially Chrysippus. Here is a passage from Philo that provides one of the main ideas on law that Stoics like Chrysippus espoused:

> For this world is a great city, has one constitution and one law, and this is the reason of nature, commanding what should be done and forbidding what should not be done. Now states which we know about have … various constitutions and laws which are by no means identical, for different people have different customs and rules of behavior which are … extra constructions and additions … states which are by nature constitutional are rather an addition to the universal constitution of nature, and the laws of these several states are additions to the right reason of nature … for a house is a state compressed into small dimensions, and its management may be called a kind of state management, just as a state is also a great house and statesmanship is the household management.[12]

The Stoics saw law as largely a product of nature, and law's domestic domain of the state was no different than the domestic domain of the house. Indeed, Chrysippus

10 *The Twelve Tables*, in *The Civil Law*, translated by S. P. Scott, Clark, NJ: The Law Book Exchange [1932] 2001, p. 73.

11 Ibid., p. 76.

12 Chrysippus, *De Jure et Lege*, from *Stoicorum Veterum Fragmenta* [SVF] III, 323, edited by Hans von Arnim, translated by Jason L. Saunders, in *Greek and Roman Philosophy after Aristotle*, NY: Free Press, 1966.

also said "it is not possible to discover any principle or beginning of justice other than from that of the gods and common nature."[13]

Cicero draws heavily from the Stoics like Chrysippus, but he also diverges from them, especially in thinking that the common nature of all men can provide what Cicero often calls the law of nations, which he does not always distinguish clearly from the law of nature. Here is a passage from Cicero's *On Duties* (*De Officiis*):

> I see that because custom is so corrupted such behavior [deception and pretense] is neither thought dishonorable nor forbidden by statute and civil law [of the Praetor]. It is, however, forbidden by the law of nature. For there is a fellowship that is extremely widespread, shared by all with all (even if this has often been said, it ought to be said still more often); a closer one exists among those of the same nation, and one more intimate still among those of the same city. For this reason our ancestors wanted the law of nations and the civil law to be different: everything in the civil law need not be in the law of nations, but everything in the law of nations ought to be a part of civil law We however do not have the firm and lifelike figure of true law and genuine justice: we make use of shadows and sketches. I wish we would follow even those! For they are drawn from the best examples of nature and truth.[14]

Later authors distinguished between the law of nature and the law of nations. The former is the domain of universal laws somehow connected to human nature; the latter is simply what all or most nations have thought to be morally binding. Both of these domains were distinct from the specific provisions of law or morality in a given society. Cicero seems to equate the laws of nations with the law of nature. By the seventeenth century CE, philosophers saw these two as separable, such that the law of nature could be used to criticize the law of nations, even if all nations had the same view.

Cicero tells us that law is crucial for realizing justice and for protecting the rights of the citizens:

> Therefore since law (*lex*) is the bond which unites the civic association, and the justice enforced by law is the same for all, by what justice can an association of citizens be held together when there is no equality of citizens? For if we cannot agree to equalize men's wealth, and equality of innate ability is impossible, the legal rights at least of those who are citizens of the same commonwealth ought to be equal. For what is a State except an association or partnership in justice (*iuris*)?[15]

[13] Ibid., 326.

[14] Cicero, *On Duties* (*De Oficiis*), Book III, para. 69, edited and translated by M. T. Griffin and E. M. Atkins, NY: Cambridge University Press, 1991, pp. 125–126.

[15] Cicero, *De Re Publica*, in *Cicero XVI*, pp. 75–77.

This is an explicit statement of the equal legal rights of all citizens, something only implied in the Greek democratic models.

The idea of equality before the law is a hallmark of the Roman Republic at Cicero's time. And this idea links justice and law in that justice can only be attained with the legal rights of all respected. Justice then comes to be seen as giving to each his or her due, where in most cases their due is that they be treated equally as citizens. In a sense procedural rights then are the ground for substantive rights, but if the different abilities and wealth do not afford each person to be the equal of each other, there is still sufficient equality for justice if each person is treated equally before the law concerning such things as the right to appeal and the opportunity to attain political office.[16]

In Cicero's *Laws* (*De Legibus*) we find what he takes as most important in the Stoic philosophers that he has avidly read:

> out of all the material of philosophers' discussions, surely there comes nothing more valuable than the full realization that we are born for justice, and that right (*ius*) is based, not upon men's opinions, but upon Nature. This fact will be immediately plain if you once get a clear conception of man's fellowship and union with his fellow-men. For no single thing is so like another, so exactly its counterpart, as all of us are to one another.[17]

The equality of legal rights for citizens is grounded in the natural affinity of all people for each other – although one might wonder why this applies only to citizens and not also to the rest of the humans who reside in the Roman Republic.

Cicero was not a believer in Greek-style democracy – instead he, like Aristotle, supported a mixed constitution. Cicero was himself a consul and senator in Rome, as well as a successful lawyer. He did not think that all people had the same abilities and hence he did not believe that political leaders should be selected by lot. Yet, Cicero was a strong defender of liberty, and especially equal legal rights for citizens, regardless of their abilities. This position led him to support a whole host of rule of law ideas, as we will see in subsequent chapters, which were so characteristic of legal thought in the Roman Republic.

25.3 ANCIENT INDIAN CONCEPTIONS OF LAW IN THE SUTRAS AND CODE OF MANU

For ancient Indian legal thought, law had at least two characteristics that were sometimes in tension. First, law was issued from a king who, according to the *Code*

[16] See Dean Hammer, *Roman Political Thought: From Cicero to Augustine*, NY: Cambridge University Press, 2014, p. 55.
[17] Cicero, *De Legibus*, in *Cicero XVI*, p. 329.

of Manu, "is a great deity who stands here in human form."[18] The law is divinely inspired. But, second, law is also highly specific concerning the proper order of the person subject to the law, "the Laws of all the social classes," where there was a rigid system of four classes.[19] The term for law is also the same term for righteousness (*dharma*) and law is thus seen as part of a wider moral order established by the gods.

> For the protection of the whole creation, that One of dazzling brilliance assigned separate activities for those born from the mouth, arms, thighs, and feet. To Brahmins, he assigned reciting and teaching the Veda, offering and officiating at sacrifices, and receiving and giving gifts. To the Ksatriya, he allotted protecting the subjects, giving gifts, offering sacrifices, reciting the Veda, and avoiding attachment to sensory objects; and to the Vaisya, looking after animals, giving gifts, offering sacrifices, reciting the Veda, trade, moneylending, and agriculture. A single activity did the Lord allot to the Sudra, however: the ungrudging service of those very special classes.[20]

These four classes, in descending order – Brahmins, Ksatriya, Vaisya, and Sudra – are classes that people are born into and that are legally differentiated in terms of rights and duties. This is often thought to be a major difference with Roman legal thought at the same time period in India. But in fact, as we will see in a later chapter, Roman society was also highly class differentiated and enforced at law. In addition to laws differentiated by social class, laws are differentiated based on temporal age of the civilization. Manu says that "There is one set of Laws for men in … each Age."[21]

So, we have the potential conflict between law seen, on the one hand, as divinely inspired and to a certain extent universal – not a product of human hands; but on the other hand we have law that is very different for each class as well as for each age. One way to reconcile these views is to see that the divine ruler of the world is lenient if a person is of the priestly class, and is much stricter on the lowest class, the Sudra. And while the scriptures (Vedas) are the ultimate source of all law, its interpretation will differ based on the class and temporal age of the person in question.[22]

The two main sources of law are actually both related to the Vedic scriptures – the actual words of the Vedas and the traditions that have grown up by how the Vedas have been interpreted by wise and good people. Manu recognizes that there could be conflicts between these sources and even conflicts between two traditional readings of the Vedic scriptures. Manu does not give especially helpful advice about what to do when there are these inevitable conflicts, but the earlier Dharmasutras

18 *Manu's Code of Law*, 7, p. 154.
19 Ibid., 1.2, p. 87.
20 Ibid., 1.87–91, p. 91.
21 Ibid., 1.85, p. 91.
22 Ibid., 2.8–10, p. 94.

have more to say about this issue, and in one case the answer might be seen as surprising by readers today.

Manu does say at the very end of his code of laws that the word of even a single Brahmin

> who knows the Veda determines something as the Law, it should be recognized as the highest Law, and not something uttered by the myriad of ignorant men. Even if thousands of men who fail to follow the observances, who are unacquainted with the Veda, and who merely use their caste to earn a living, come together, they do not constitute a legal assembly.

These groups of ignorant people are called "fools enveloped by darkness" who have no authority to declare what the law is.[23]

In the Dharmasutras, we find somewhat more helpful answers to the question of how to ascertain the law when the sources of law conflict. The first of these, the Code of Apastamba, says:

> It is difficult to gain mastery of the Law by means of scriptures alone, but by acting according to the markers one can master it. And the markers in this case are as follows: he should model his conduct after that which is unanimously approved in all regions by Aryas who have been properly trained, who are elderly and self-possessed, and who are neither greedy nor deceitful. In this way he will win both worlds.[24]

Other Dharmasutras say that less than unanimity among the experts may be sufficient to establish what the law is in a particular case.

What is especially interesting about the Law Code of Apastamba is the ending:

> The knowledge found among women and Sudras forms the conclusion, and they point out that it is a subsidiary component of the Atharva Veda … According to some, one should learn the remaining Law from women and people of all classes.[25]

The whole tone of the Dharmasutras is that knowledge of the law can come only from the experts. So it is surprising to see the Code of Apastamba ends by saying that women and all classes, not merely the top classes, can gain knowledge and teach others about the law.

In the other Dharmasutras we do not find the openness of the Apastamba. Here is the end of the Law Code of Gautama:

> In matters that are unclear, one should follow what is endorsed by a minimum of ten persons who are cultured, skilled and free from greed. A legal assembly is said

[23] Ibid., 12.113–115, p. 236.
[24] *The Law Code of Apastamba*, Chapter XXIX, 13–14, in *Dharmasutras*, p. 115.
[25] Ibid., 11 and 15, p. 115.

to consist of a minimum of ten members – four who have mastered the four Vedas; three belonging to the three orders enumerated first; and three who know three different Legal Treatises. When such persons are unavailable, one should follow in doubtful cases what is recommended by a learned and cultured Brahmin who knows the Veda, because that man is incapable of hurting or favoring creatures.[26]

Here it is clear that unanimity of experts is not necessary for establishing the true source of the law.

Sometimes it will be difficult to determine what the law is and its true source in a particular case, as the Law Code of the Baudhayana says:

When these fail to address an issue, it falls to a legal assembly with a minimum of ten members. Now they also quote these verses:

Four men, each proficient in one of the four Vedas; one exegete; one man who knows the Vedic Supplements; one legal scholar; and three learned Brahmins belonging to three different orders of life – these constitute a legal assembly with a minimum of ten members.

Or they could be five, or three; or even a single man, if he is of unimpeachable conduct, may explain the Law, but not others, be they in their thousands.[27]

Here, in the third of the Dharmasutras, we find a wide assortment of possibilities for finding who can interpret the law when the sources of law conflict. Indeed, it is unclear why so many are listed when one learned man is sufficient.

And in the Law Code of Vasistha, the final Dharmasutra, we get even less helpful guidance.

The Law is set forth in the Vedas and the Traditional Texts. When these do not address an issue, the practice of cultured people becomes authoritative. Now, a cultured man is free from desires. For something to be the Law, it must not have a tangible motive … When there are no specific rules in Vedic texts, Manu has said that one may follow the Laws of one's region, caste, or family.[28]

As we can see, this Dharmasutra directs us to the *Code of Manu* where there is some guidance about what to do in conflict of laws situations. We saw that the *Code of Manu* affirms that even one learned man can be sufficient for resolving conflicts of the law sources.[29]

The various discussions of resolving conflicts among sources of law are difficult to parse. But what seems clear is that the two main sources of law, the Vedas and

[26] *The Law Code of Guatama*, Chapter XXVIII, 48–51, in *Dharmasutras*, p. 189.
[27] *The Law Code of Baudhayana*, Book I, 1. 7–8, in *Dharmasutras*, p. 197.
[28] *The Law Code of Vasistha*, Chapter I. 4–7, in *Dharmasutras*, p. 351.
[29] *Manu's Code of Law*, 2.6–10, p. 94.

the traditions that arose around the Vedas, are sometimes at odds with each other. This is quite a recognition by ancient Indian legal thinkers, especially since both of these sources are largely religious. And while there was not a consensus on how to resolve such conflicts, it is nonetheless of great interest that in a highly stratified society women and members of all classes would be seen as possible authorities for resolving such conflicts. Indeed, it seems to be that ancient Indian legal thought, which is both largely religious and highly stratified, has such a pluralistic dimension, putting it much closer to ancient Roman thought than one might expect.

25.4 THE NATURE AND SOURCES OF LAW

In the US we have a somewhat similar issue as concerned the ancient Indian legal thinkers, where we have both a Constitution and a series of cases that have interpreted the Constitution – what constitutes the common law of the US. And it is easy to see how conflicts between the Constitution and the common law have arisen when one realizes that the tradition of interpretation of the Constitution often takes on a life of its own that over time no longer much resembles the original text of the Constitution. We can think about the right to privacy as well as the right to bear arms, as each epitomizing the way that court decisions have moved far away from the meaning of the document, like the Vedas for the ancient Indians, that is supposed to ground the legal system of the US. At least part of the explanation for such divergence is that the times change and the type of situations changes as well.

Roman law was grounded in the *Twelve Tables* and Indian law was grounded in the Vedas, the first secular and the second religious. But as Cicero pointed out, the *Twelve Tables* were themselves grounded in the divine eternal and universal law. So, there is commonality between these ancient grounding sources of law. Similarly, the US Constitution is a secular human-made document, but the Founding Fathers said that the Constitution was grounded in God's divine law as well. Conflicts in all three systems of law are bound to arise since the religious law is not always clear in how it forms the secular law that in all societies the people look to for determining the restraints over their own conduct. Such conflicts can be managed, although never eliminated. And it is interesting that in all three societies it is mainly experts that have the task of reconciling the sources of law. And "the people" also are seen as the ultimate adjudicator.

Roman legal thought also well illustrates that having a strong respect for equality before the law does not necessarily mean that equality of social classes will also be strongly supported. Indeed, in many respects that we will see in later chapters, the Roman Republic was nearly as strongly class differentiated as was the class system of ancient India. It is sometimes said that one of the salient differences was that the ancient Indian class system was supported by the legal system – in fact the class structure is described in several of the legal documents from ancient India that we have already examined – as we will see later in more detail. But in the Roman Republic class differentiation was embedded in law as well, although a person could move among classes much more easily in Rome than in India.

One lesson here is especially relevant today for the US – respect for equality before the law can sit quite comfortably with a social class structure with major differences among classes in terms of social position, wealth, and opportunity. This is clearly recognized by Cicero, as we have seen. The law can follow and only sometimes lead the society but legal rights are certainly not the same as social standing. The Roman Republic's legal thinkers were mainly convinced on, and gave convincing arguments for, equality of legal rights, even as they were themselves slave holders and patriarchal autocrats of their families. We can think of Thomas Jefferson in a similar light, as owner of slaves and yet advocating equality before the law. And it is not too hard to see the class structure of today's society standing side by side with well-entrenched legal rights for all in the US and elsewhere.

We need also to consider what counted as sources of law for the ancient Roman and Indian thinkers we are examining in this part of my work. Here is possibly the greatest difference between ancient India and the Roman Republic. The Indian sources of law are primarily religious, whereas the Roman sources of law are mainly secular. Roman legal thinkers like Cicero certainly refer to the gods quite a bit, and this is especially true in the discussion of the universal law of nature or of nations that stands apart from and undergirds the civil law for the Romans. Indeed, most of the legal thinkers of the Roman Republic also speak of the gods and the universal or eternal law.

There is a good question raised here about what would be the sources of a natural law – quite independently of whether statutes and edicts are also sources of law. The Stoics, as we will see in Chapter 27, largely discussed natural law in secular terms, as is sometimes also done today in international law, especially as natural rights connect to human rights. People in Western countries are today suspicious of religious grounding of natural law since they assume that the religion will be sectarian. But what both the Roman and Indian texts we have examined, and will examine, do for us is to talk of a *universal* religious basis of law. This is clearer for the Romans than it is for Indian legal thought, since the Vedas are largely Hindu texts of rites and hymns. Perhaps the Judeo-Christian Bible is like that today in Western societies, especially the US.

And it is here that the Roman ideas of natural law might be most relevant to contemporary legal theorists and practitioners who struggle to find a basis for human rights, as something like natural rights, that is not tied to any one canonical religious text. This debate continues today in a legal culture that claims to be indebted to the Romans, but where contemporary lawyers and law scholars do not often have a good sense of the resources of Roman law for dealing with such questions. As this part of my work on ancient legal thought continues I hope somewhat to fill that gap.

26

Legal Procedures and Trials

Both ancient Roman and Indian texts are rich in accounts of legal procedure and trials. The Romans are justly known for developing the most elaborate and in many ways the most modern-looking system of procedures. And while Indian law is not known for this, I will argue that Indian law did make important advances over earlier legal systems and matched that of Rome in several key areas. The Roman Republic was a representative democracy and ancient India was largely a monarchy, but I will argue that there are similar restraints on the lawmakers and law-enforcers in both societies.

Legal procedure is often regarded today, especially by many law students, as dry as toast. But it has been recognized for quite a long time that some of the most important legal ideas are contained in what Henry Sumner Maine called "the interstices of procedure." We will find this to be true as well in our study of ancient India and the Roman Republic – indeed, sometimes the procedural issues are more significant and interesting than the substantive law in telling us how law was conceptualized in these ancient times.

In Section 26.1 we look at the legal procedures set out in two very early Roman texts, the *Laws of the Kings* and the *Twelve Tables*. In Section 26.2 we explore ancient Indian texts that give us some idea of the very early legal procedures from the Dharmasutras and the *Code of Manu*. In Section 26.3 we look at the composition of trials in Rome and India. In Section 26.4 we examine the ways that witness testimony was tested in both ancient Rome and India. And in Section 26.5 I set out how understanding especially the idea of proof is concerned with similar issues as those of today.

26.1 PROCEDURE IN THE *LAW OF THE KINGS* AND THE *TWELVE TABLES*

The earliest known legal code of Rome is the so-called the *Laws of the Kings*. In the earliest part of that law, known as the *Laws of Romulus* (736–716 BCE) there is some discussion of procedural matters. Here are a few sections of this legal text:

> Romulus 1. After Romulus had distinguished the persons of higher rank from those of inferior condition, then he passed laws and apportioned the duties for each to do: the patricians to be priests and magistrates and judges; the plebeians to be farmers ... permitting each plebeian ... to choose for his patron the patrician whom he wished ... and by calling this protection patronage.
>
> Romulus 2. The following regulations in regard to patronage were determined then by him: the patricians were required to interpret the law for their clients ... to bring suit on behalf of clients when wronged ...
>
> Romulus 3. ... When he had determined these regulations, he then distinguished the ... powers which each class was to have.
>
> For the king he chose the following prerogatives: first, to have the chief authority in rites and sacrifices ... then, to maintain the guardianship of the laws and the national customs ... to judge in person the greatest crimes, but to leave the lesser crimes to the senators ... to have absolute command in war.
>
> To the council of the Senate he assigned the following authority: to decide and vote on whatever matter the king introduced.
>
> To the common people he granted three things: to elect the magistrates and to ratify the laws and to decide on war whenever the king permitted ... The people did not vote all together, but they were convoked by curias.[1]

These procedural rules and considerations amount to a mini-constitution for the Roman monarchy, the early stage of Rome before the Republic.

Two things can at first be seen here. First, in early Rome there is a clear class structure that is enforced at law, very much like the class system in ancient Indian law. The plebeian, or lower, class had to be represented by a patrician patron, and even to have the law explained to them as if this is something they were not thought to be capable of themselves. But second, there is already introduced the idea that the people get to vote on who should make laws and even on matters that were properly under the king's purview. The Senate plays a relatively small role as compared to the king and also as compared to the people.

Nearly 300 years after the *Laws of the Kings*, we find the most famous of the early laws of Rome, the *Twelve Tables* (451–449 BCE). Table I concerns Proceedings Preliminary to Trial and here we find some of the most famous early procedural stipulations of the Roman Republic:

> 1. If the plaintiff summons the defendant to court the defendant shall go. If the defendant does not go the plaintiff shall call a witness thereto. Only then the plaintiff shall seize the defendant.

[1] *Ancient Roman Statutes*, translated and edited by Allan Johnson, Paul Coleman-Norton, Frank Bourne, and Clyde Pharr, Austin: University of Texas Press, 1961, 2012, p. 3.

2. If the defendant attempts evasion or takes flight the plaintiff shall lay hands on him …
6. When the parties agree on the matter the magistrate shall announce it.
7. If they agree not on the terms, the parties shall state their case before the assembly in the meeting place or before the magistrate in the market place before noon. Both parties being present shall plead the case through together.
8. If one of the parties does not appear the magistrate shall adjudge the case, after noon, in favor of the one present.
9. If both parties are present sunset shall be the time limit of the proceedings.[2]

These procedural rules give us the earliest sense of how Roman trials were to proceed, with various practical problems at the forefront, such as how to make sure that the defendant appears at the proceedings. There is also a close attention to the idea of speedy justice, an idea still very much alive today.

There is also here expressed the idea that arbitration could replace the need for a trial. Arbitration seems to be written into the law, as an alternative that must be tried and its success or failure announced to the magistrate before trial can commence. Indeed, the role of an arbiter is discussed in Table II and elsewhere. And in the case of debt, if the arbiter or magistrate calls for the debtors to pay to their creditors an amount they are liable for, the debtor must seek an acceptable settlement on his own; if not there will be penalties for delay or refusal to compromise as we see in Table III:

> Meanwhile they have the right to compromise, and unless they make a compromise the debtors shall be held in bonds for sixty days. During these days they shall be brought to the praetor into the meeting place on three successive market days, and the amount for which they have been judged liable shall be declared publicly. Moreover on the third market day they shall suffer capital punishment or be delivered for sale across the Tiber River.[3]

While arbitration and compromise are called for in these ancient laws, it is also clear that there will be very severe punishments inflicted if one of the parties is unwilling to cooperate with the judgment of the court. Nonetheless, it is very interesting that there is "right to compromise" which in some cases might favor the debtors.

One of the most important ideas expressed in the *Twelve Tables* concerns capital punishment. The idea is that capital punishment can only be administered after a trial and that capital punishment statutes can only be legitimate if the assembly of citizens has authorized it, not merely that the king has passed an edict. Here is the provision in Table IX:

[2] Ibid., p. 9.
[3] Ibid., p. 10.

> Laws of personal exception shall not be proposed. Laws concerning capital punishment of a citizen shall not be passed … except by the Greatest Assembly.
>
> A judix or an arbiter legally appointed who has been legally convicted of receiving money for declaring a decision shall be punished capitally …
>
> For anyone whomsoever to be put to death without a trial and convicted … is forbidden.[4]

This stipulation that capital punishment cannot be administered except after conviction in a trial remains one of the hallmarks of the rule of law. And the idea that judges must be beyond reproach, or else subject themselves to the death penalty, is also still very influential. While capital punishment has been banned in the vast majority of countries today, the idea that corrupt judges should be penalized severely is definitely still with us.

26.2 ANCIENT INDIAN PROCEDURAL LAW

In the Dharmasutra text, *Gautama* (third century BCE), the judicial process is described as follows:

> His (the king's) administration of justice shall be based on the Veda, the Legal Treatises, the Vedic Supplements, Subsidiary Vedas, and the Purana. The laws of regions, castes and families are also authoritative if they are not in conflict with sacred scriptures. Farmers, merchants, herdsmen, moneylenders, and artisans exercise authority over their respective groups. He should dispense the Law after he has ascertained the facts from authoritative persons of each group. Reasoning is the means of reaching a correct judgment. Having reached a conclusion in this manner, he should decide the case equitably.[5]

We shall discuss this reference to equity in the next chapter. Note now that it is the king who is to decide cases, just as in the earliest of the Roman texts, the laws of Romulus. But here we see a characteristic difference between early Indian and Roman law: the Indian reliance on sacred scripture that is all but missing from Roman law.

As in early Roman law, ancient Indian law is a law based on the legal classes of that society. Indeed the very first of the Dharmasutras, *Apastamba*, already lists the legal classes: "There are four classes: Brahmin, Ksatriya, Vaisya, and Sudra. Among these, each preceding class is superior by birth to each subsequent … Sudras are to serve the other classes; the higher the class they serve, the greater

4 Ibid., p. 12.

5 *Gautama* 11.19–23, in *Dharmasutras*, translated and edited by Patrick Olivelle, Delhi: Motilal Banarsidass Publisher, 2000, p. 147.

their prosperity."[6] And the laws are graded in terms of these classes – more severely punishing members of the lowest, Sudra, class.

We next turn to the *Code of Manu* (second century BCE) where we find some of the procedural law more fully explained.

> When the king is going to try a case … he should look into the cases of the plaintiffs every day in accordance with the standards of the region and those specified in the legal texts, lawsuits that fall individually under the eighteen avenues of litigation …
>
> When the king does not try a case personally, however, he should appoint a learned Brahmin to do so …
>
> When Justice (*dharma*), pierced by Injustice (*adharma*), comes to the court for redress, and the court officials do not pluck out that dart from him, then they are pierced by it. A man must either not enter the court or speak candidly; by refusing to speak or by speaking deceitfully, he commits a sin …
>
> He who knows the Law should examine the law of castes, regions, guilds, and families, and only then settle the Law specific to each …[7]

In Manu's Code we have a specification of the various categories of litigation and a reaffirmation of the importance of class to the way the judge is to determine justice for each party.

Manu stresses that judicial decision-making is to be largely based on regional and class-specific, as well as profession-specific, customs. This way of understanding the way to make legal decisions is in some ways at odds with looking to the sacred texts that are clearly the source of law in the earlier Dharmasutra texts. Yet, at another place Manu also says that judges should adhere to these sacred texts somewhat muddling the advice about how best to make judicial decisions.

In the *Naradasmrti* (approximately a century or two after the *Code of Manu*) we have a more elaborate discussion of legal procedure. In the Prolegomena of Narada's laws, we find the following texts that are especially important for legal procedure:

> When men had dharma as their sole purpose and were speakers of the truth, then there was no legal procedure, no enmity, and no selfishness. Legal procedure came into being at the time when dharma was lost among men. The overseer of the legal procedures is the king; he has been made the rod-bearer.
>
> There are two methods for clarifying a matter in dispute between two people: a document and witnesses …
>
> The four feet of legal procedure are dharma, legal procedure, custom, and the king's decree: each latter one overrules the former.

6 Apastamba, 1.1.4–7, in *Dharmasutras*, p. 25.

7 *Manu's Code of Law*, 8.9–41, translated and edited by Patrick Olivelle, Oxford: Oxford University Press, 2005, pp. 167–169.

> Dharma is based on truth: legal procedure on witnesses; custom on what is recorded; the decrees on the edicts of the king.[8]

We will examine the idea of witnesses and how the truth of their statements can be tested in the next section.

Notice that the secular sources of law can "overrule" *dharma*, which is the truth found in the scriptures. This is why many commentators see ancient Indian law proceeding closer to Roman law by the beginning of the Common Era. It is also of note that the word of the king is most associated with the law of the land and that this has resulted because *dharma* "was lost among men." There is a recognition that the society was becoming more secular and that the knowledge of the traditional texts was receding at this time in ancient Indian legal thought.

Next let us consider some of the other procedures described in the law of Narada. At one point, we find the following: "when the king takes the judgment seat, he should abandon selfishness, be neutral to all beings."[9] Here is one of the fundamental cornerstones of the rule of law – that the decision-maker will be neutral. Indeed, neutrality is of such prime importance today that judges should not even have the appearance of bias in their rulings.

Narada somewhat clarifies the muddle that can result from reading the *Code of Manu* by indicating that *dharma*, understood here as ancient religious custom, is one of several sources, but that the king's decrees take precedence over *dharma* as well as other customs when there is a conflict. This makes the law very much a matter of what the king says it is, similar to how some modern legal theorists understood the nature of law, as we will discuss at the end of this chapter.

In ancient Indian law, as in early Roman law, there seems to be a movement toward a set of procedures that secular jurists can use to determine the law and how a particular case fits under the law. In the next section of this chapter we will try to discern some of the main features of the trials in both ancient Indian and Roman systems of law. We will begin with some of the later material – texts from the end of the BCE era for both systems of law. In both societies, there is emerging the idea that law is different from religious dogma and that a need has arisen for law to be interpreted for the populace so that it can be understood and obeyed.

26.3 TRIALS IN ANCIENT INDIA AND THE ROMAN REPUBLIC

Continuing with the laws of Narada, we find some of the most explicit treatments of the mechanics of an ancient Indian trial and the status of the parties.

[8] *The Naradasmrti*, translated by Richard W. Lariviere, Delhi: Motilal Banarsidass Publishers, 2003, pp. 254–257.

[9] Ibid., p. 260.

> The hearing should be fourfold: first, the appearance should be made, then the title of the legal doctrine, the inquiry, and the decision.
>
> In cases about debt and the like, because of the complexity of disputes, and because of the limited capacity of memory, he may, if he chooses, grant a delay in order to ascertain the truth.
>
> He should hear the dispute at once in cases dealing with cattle, land, gold, women, theft, abuse, urgent matters, assault, and accusations of grave sins.[10]

Here we have a very straightforward exposition of the elements of a trial and whether or not the trial should begin and end quickly.

The four stages of the trial correspond to what many societies today would also recognize. The first stage, the appearance, is often the most difficult in ancient societies that lack a police force. Here is where a form of "self-help" is often referred to – where the plaintiff is allowed or even required to bring the defendant before the judge or tribunal. The second stage is where the facts of the case must fit into one of 18 categories that are the only ones that are subject to litigation. This is highly reminiscent of the "forms of action" in early English common law which itself is indebted to the actions that are recognized in Roman law as permissible subjects of litigation. Here arises the idea of the form of law as being as important as its substance – certain matters cannot be prosecuted because they do not fit into recognizable legal types and are hence beyond the scope of judges to address. We take up this topic again in the next chapter when discussing how equity enters into the formalities of law that define strict adherence to justice. We can already have a premonition of why there is a need for equity – the formal law leaves many matters out for which unfairness would result if not addressed by judicial proceedings.

In other laws, Narada tells us how to regard the parties to a suit and at what point it is reasonable to allow for an appeal if one of the parties is unsatisfied by the results of the trial.

> Once one lodges a plaint, he should not introduce any changes to it, nor should he adopt another position altogether. If he does so, he loses his first claim.
>
> One must not make false accusations. A false accuser incurs sin and the punishment prescribed for it.
>
> One who feels that a case has been adjudged and settled in a manner inconsistent with dharma may have the case tried again after agreeing to pay twice the penalty if he loses.
>
> If the legal proceeding is improperly heard, the judges should incur that penalty, for no one keeps to the straight and narrow without the threat of punishment[11]

[10] Ibid., pp. 262–263.

[11] Ibid., pp. 264–266.

It appears that there were not separate appellate courts in ancient India, so appeals were made for the case to be retried altogether, not in the limited way that appellate courts tend to function today.

It is also of significance that the laws of Narada lay great stress on the idea that parties to a suit and the judge should be above reproach in the way they conduct themselves, seeing that the trial process can easily be hijacked by unscrupulous parties or judges. We will see this even more explicitly in the next section on how truthfulness was ascertained and how untruthfulness was punished. Before taking on that task, let us look at some of the ancient Roman writings about trial procedure prior to the time of the great legal commentators such as Gaius and Ulpian.

The *Twelve Tables* give a rather brief statement of how trials are to begin as follows:

> Table II. The penal sum in an action by solemn deposit shall be either 500 asses or 50 asses … it shall be argued by solemn deposit with 500 asses, when the property is valued at less than 1,000 asses. But if the controversy is about the freedom of a person, although the person may be very valuable, yet the case shall be argued by a solemn deposit of 50 asses.
>
> Whoever needs evidence shall go every third day to shout before the doorway.[12]

There is here an assurance given that the plaintiff is not proceeding with a deceitful or frivolous suit. And there is some attention given to alternative acceptable ways to procure evidence, but little about how the trial should then proceed.

There is an unplaced fragment that concerns appeals, namely: "*The Twelve Tables* indicates in several laws that it is allowed to appeal from any judgment and penalty."[13] But to get more on the actual trial practice of the Roman Republic we will have to go to the accounts of trials by those who practiced before the courts. And here the best known source is Cicero. Cicero was a practicing lawyer as well as a politician of some repute. His writings tell us quite a bit about the legal procedure of his time (the last century BCE). Drawing on Cicero, Greenidge summarized the steps in a court proceeding:

> The contest itself was opened by the plaintiff as *vindicant*; grasping the thing with one hand he touched it with the staff (*festuca*), the symbol of power, held in the other, asserting at the same moment his legal right to the object. The *vidicatio rei* thus completed, the defendant appeared on the scene. His role was not fulfilled by a mere denial of the plaintiff's right; he too grasps the thing and wields the staff and repeats the same solemn claim of right. When the *contra-vindicatio* had been completed both parties had their hands on the object of dispute and were touching the clod with their feet. Then the praetor intervened in the interests of peace.

[12] *Ancient Roman Statutes*, ibid., *The Twelve Tables*, pp. 9–10.

[13] Ibid., p. 13.

> At the words "both of you release that man" or "both of you quit that field," the parties separated and the symbolic strife was at an end. Then began the peaceful assertion of the grounds of the claim. "Why have you vindicated?" asks the plaintiff. "Because it is my right" replies the defendant. "Your vindication is unjust" is the retort; "I challenge you by a sacrament of 50 (or 500) asses"; "And I repeat the challenge to you."[14]

Here is a graphic account of how the meager rules in the *Twelve Tables* got filled out in a way that created a ceremonial beginning of the trial, and allowed the Praetor, the chief judge at this time, to begin to try to ascertain if settlement was possible and at what terms. It is now a question of the interplay of justice in terms of the relevant statutes and equity in terms of the fairness seemingly required by the particular circumstance of the case at issue.

26.4 WITNESSES AND PROOF

For both ancient Indian and Roman trials witnesses were a key component of proof of whether the plaintiff or defendant is to be believed. And the question that arises for these societies, as well as other ancient societies, is how to ascertain if the parties or witnesses are telling the truth. This remains a major problem for trials today as well. In this section we will look at how the parties and witnesses were regarded in ancient India and in the Roman Republic as well as focusing on how the truth of what the witnesses say was adjudged. We will start with the most developed position on this topic in the laws of Narada in ancient India.

Chapter 20 of the Naradasmrti is devoted to the subject of ordeals used to test the truth of statements by the accused.

> The king should administer ordeals in matters involving serious offenses; in minor matters, that best of men should make the accused swear an oath. These oaths have been prescribed as effective in minor disputes, but when violent crimes are involved, the rules for ordeals apply.
>
> Lord Manu has said there are five ordeals for those accused in doubtful matters especially if the events took place in secret: the balance, fire, water, poison, and, finally, holy water. These are the ordeals prescribed for the exoneration of the falsely accused.
>
> Narada, the great-souled one, has prescribed ordeals, which reveal what is true and false, for the exoneration of those accused in doubtful matters. A wise man should administer an ordeal with the consent of the plaintiff, not otherwise.[15]

[14] A. H. J. Greenidge, *The Legal Procedure of Cicero's Time*, Oxford: Oxford University Press, 1901, pp. 56–57.

[15] *The Naradasmrti*, pp. 447–448.

What follows then is an elaborate description of how each of the ordeals functions. The "balance" is the least violent and is described, in part, as follows:

> The accused should be weighed a first time and the balance marked against the counterweight; the man should be taken off it. After he has given his sworn testimony the accused should again be made to get onto the balance and be weighed in the same manner until the balance comes to a stop.
>
> If the accused weighs more when he is weighed, he is definitely innocent; but if he weighs the same or less, he is guilty.[16]

We have no indication of whether anyone is actually exonerated by this method.

There are also discussions of how to treat documents and witnesses to ascertain the truth of what is asserted. There are norms for witnesses, including the following general description: "There are many types: some who lie may seem to be truthful, and some who are honest may seem to be untruthful. Therefore scrutiny is in order."[17]

One rule that is seen in other ancient Indian sources as well is this: "Witnesses must come from good families, be upright, pure of birth, deed and purpose, no less than three in number, unimpeachable, unsullied, and intelligent."[18] And then we find that: "The wise have also indicated in the texts five ways in which witnesses are disqualified: because of explicit rules to that effect, because of faults, because of contradictions, because of voluntary testimony, and because of intervening death."[19]

In order to assure that a witness is telling the truth, the judge "should instill great fear in the witness by means of ancient *dharma* texts extolling the truth and reviling untruth."[20] And one of the ways to instill such fear is to threaten the witness with the ordeals previously mentioned: "he shall press him by means of ordeals such as the fire, water" etc.[21] In many ways the use of the oath and ordeal in ancient India is not significantly different than what we find in ancient Mesopotamian law from a period over a thousand years earlier. In Rome, though, we can begin to see less emphasis on the ordeal and more on oaths in pursuing the truth of the parties and witnesses.

In the laws of the Roman Republic we can start to understand how the truth of witnesses and the accused can be tested by referring to the *Twelve Tables* as we have before. Concerning the parties to the suit, the money wagered is one way that the truthfulness of the parties is encouraged.[22] This is a very different way to encourage truth-telling than was true for the ancient Indian legal texts we just examined. There

16 Ibid., p. 448.
17 Ibid., p. 267.
18 Ibid., p. 316.
19 Ibid., p. 317.
20 Ibid., p. 325.
21 Ibid., p. 330.
22 See Table II of *The Twelve Tables* in *Ancient Roman Statutes*, pp. 9–10.

are other respects in which the Roman legal texts are just as brutal, or more so, than the Indian texts, but it is curious that coercion or threats of violence do not seem to be part of early trial practice in Rome. Indeed, we find this rather clearly expressed in a law from around the same time as the *Twelve Tables*, the *Junian Law concerning the Plebeian Tribunes*, lower-class Romans who had been given political status: "No person shall compel a plebeian tribune, as if one of the ordinary citizens, to do anything unwillingly, or to scourge him …"[23]

It is nonetheless true that the oath is employed freely in Roman law at Cicero's time. And the main way that administering an oath was thought to work was by the threat that the gods to whom the oath was taken would punish the witness who presented false testimony. Here is where the Roman legal system was not fully secular. But it is also fair to say that our own systems of law today, which also rely heavily on oath swearing, bring a religious dimension into otherwise secular legal processes.

26.5 WHY LEGAL PROCEDURE MATTERS

So far we have identified at least four areas where the ancient law of procedure matters. The first is the way that legal procedures form, influence, and preserve the rule of law. The second procedural area that matters is the way procedures play a role in encouraging truth-telling by participants in a trial. The third area of procedural importance is the way that procedures frame what the law can solve, and what it cannot, so that all judges are on the same page when looking at cases that come before them even in disparate parts of a territorial regime. This last point proved especially important for the expanding Roman Empire in the early centuries CE. And the fourth area concerns how trials became matters that were further distanced from the simple rulings of a king and encompassed something less subjective and arguably because of this, also fairer. We will end this chapter by saying more about each of these matters of importance for procedures in ancient times as well as today.

The first area of importance for legal procedures concerns the rule of law. The rule of law is the doctrine that a good society is ruled primarily by laws consistently applied, and not by the arbitrary decision of "men" – a rule by law not men, as it is often put (see Chapter 2). This aspect of legal procedure can be seen as having several dimensions. Above we have canvassed various ways in which ancient law, and the legal thinking that interpreted it, tries to minimize the abuse of bias and favoritism from entering into the deliberations about the innocence or guilt of defendants. Of course, nothing will be foolproof here as long as people continue to act at least in part in terms of self-interest rather than in terms of the societal good.

[23] The Junian Law on the Sacrosanctity of the Plebeian Tribune, in *Ancient Roman Statutes*, p. 8.

But procedures can minimize the effects of bias, especially by heavily penalizing those legal officials who act against the common interest.

The rule of law also often is said to involve the principle that the harshest penalty, the death sentence, should not be administered unless a conviction has occurred at the end of a trial of the accused. One of the most prevalent abuses throughout history has been the elimination of one's political opponents by making them disappear – and in many cases simply to have them killed. For the abuse by such persons to be curtailed it is vital that capital punishment only be inflicted after a fair trial.

Another aspect of the rule of law is that the law should be applied the same to each person who is under the law's jurisdiction. In certain ways, both early Rome and India fail this test, since these legal systems are graded based on the class that a person occupies rather than matters that are relevant to guilt or innocence. Yet, we can see that in the later Roman Republic the class differential, especially between plebeians and patricians, is eliminated. Yet, it is still true, as we will see in later chapters, that slaves and women, as well as other non-citizens continue to be treated disparately in ancient Rome. Until the twentieth century CE India continued to have a differential treatment of members of different classes.

The third area of importance for legal procedure in ancient times concerns the establishment of clearly articulated forms or frames into which cases must fit in order to be subject to judicial decision-making. In both ancient India and the Roman Republic, the forms of action were settled clearly marking which suits fell under the purview of the law and which suits did not. Having said this, it should also be pointed out though that these forms or frames were not especially comprehensive or even forming a coherent system of actions that could be the basis of litigation.

In Rome the *actiones* were being developed already before Cicero's time and quickly became so complex a matter that it gave rise to the need for professional legal experts to figure out how to fit the facts of a given case into the form of law that could be the subject of adjudication. In India, since the forms recognizing suits were only 18 the matter did not require a new class of lawyers but it did encourage a group of experts to advise plaintiffs about how best to bring their suits, if indeed those suits were justiciable.

The fourth area where procedures were of importance for the ancients and also for us today comes in the idea that trials were not to be merely the judgment of the king but were to be at least somewhat more objective than that. Ancient India remained very much a traditional monarchy throughout the ancient period whereas Rome moved quite far away from the monarchy of its most ancient times. Yet in both societies, legal thought was characterized by respect for an objective form of adjudication that was removed from the personal decision-making of a ruler.

The rise of procedural law is often accompanied by a move to make of law something objective, or quasi-objective, so that it is possible for people to make plans with a clear understanding of what is expected of them legally, and this required rules that will not change in unpredictable ways in the future. Commerce and the general well-being of those subject to the law depend on such predictability – especially that decisions will not be radically altered when one ruler is replaced by another. What makes a legal system out of a set of decisions by a ruler is just this constancy of application over time. Even when the subjects do not have a say in what the law is, having stable procedures in place is one of the first signs that there is a legal system that has what H. L. A. Hart would call not only primary rules, which tell the people what they are obligated to do, but also secondary rules of procedure that tell people how the law will be applied, interpreted, and changed in predictable ways.[24]

[24] See H. L. A. Hart. *The Concept of Law*, Oxford: Oxford University Press, 1961.

27

Equity and Justice

Legal thought in the Roman Republic and ancient India share in common an understanding that law is not merely about strict justice but encompasses considerations of fairness and equity. While the idea of equity is developed in most detail by Roman legal thinkers like Cicero, I will argue that the Indian Dharmasutras also employ the idea of equity in several important ways that will be explored in this chapter.

The classic work on equity is traced back to Aristotle, in Book V of his *Nicomachean Ethics* as well as in his *Rhetoric*, but in earlier parts of my work in ancient legal thought we saw that already in Babylonian times equity is referred to as a significant idea in debt relief edicts, for instance, even if it is not set out in any sophisticated form. Indeed, it seems that many societies that move from an oral system of custom and tradition to a written system of law are faced with the problem of the written law being too rigid to deal fairly with new types of cases that were not contemplated by the lawmaker.[1]

In Section 27.1 we look to Cicero who develops Aristotle's idea of equity in its relation to justice. Next, in Section 27.2 we look to ancient India for examples of how equity played a role in legal codes and laws. In Section 27.3 we turn to examples from legal practice in the Roman Republic that also illustrate the way that equity and justice interacted in legal judgments, especially by the Praetors, the chief legal officials in the Republic. In Section 27.4 we turn to commentators like Henry Sumner Maine on ancient Rome and Robert Lingat on ancient India. And in Section 27.5 and Section 27.6 we consider especially vexing problems about equity, such as when it is appealed to overturn otherwise fair judgments, a problem that is still of importance today.

1 See Henry Sumner Maine, *Ancient Law*, London: John Murray, 1871, Chapter 3.

27.1 CICERO ON EQUITY AND JUSTICE

Cicero's book, *De Inventione*, is especially helpful for beginning to understand the nature of justice and equity in the ancient Roman Republic. Here is Cicero's now-famous account of justice:

> Justice is a habit of the mind which gives every man his desert while preserving the common advantage. Its first principles proceed from nature, then certain rules of conduct become customary by reason of their advantage; later still both the principles that proceed from nature and those that had been approved by custom, received the support of religion and the fear of the law. The law of nature is that which is not born of opinion, but implanted in us by a kind of innate instinct.[2]

In this very broad sense of justice, Cicero includes concepts such as equity.[3] But there is then a narrow sense of justice that is opposed to equity, as was also true for Aristotle. Here Cicero says that equity must be understood as "what is just and fair to all," not what is merely stipulated in the statute law as strict justice.[4]

Justice, the habit of giving to each person what he or she deserves, is altered in the written law of the statutes. We are faced with the problem of how to interpret the written law's stipulation of strict justice when that interpretation is at odds with what was the intention of the lawmaker.

> A controversy over the letter and the intent occurs when one party follows the exact words that are written, and the other directs his whole pleading to what he says the writer meant ... But there is another kind of argument brought forward by advocates of the intent in which the wish of the writer is shown not to be absolute, i.e. having the same weight for every occasion and for every action but it is argued that his wishes ought to be interpreted to fit the occasion in the light of some act or some event. This argument will be supported largely by topics under the assumptive branch of the issue of equity.[5]

Here there is a conflict between a strict interpretation of a law and the equitable result that the circumstances seem to call for.

Cicero gives an especially appealing example of why equity is needed to correct the strict interpretation of the law in some cases:

> the case of the man who, though the law forbade opening the gates at night, opened them in a certain war and let certain auxiliary forces into the town in order that they

[2] Cicero, *De Inventione* II, LIII, 160–161, in *Cicero II*, translated by H. M. Hubbell, Cambridge, MA: Harvard University Press' Loeb Classical Library, 1949, p. 329.

[3] Ibid., LIV, 162, p. 329.

[4] Ibid.,p. 331.

[5] Ibid., XLII, 123, p. 291.

> might not be wiped out by the enemy if left outside, for the enemy was encamped near the walls.[6]

Even in such cases, though, the appeal to equity should be made by reference to some specific principle.

> One who is speaking against the letter of the law ought always to adduce some principle of equity. For it would be the height of impudence for one who wishes to gain approval for some act contrary to the letter of the law, not to attempt to gain his point with the help of equity.[7]

For Cicero, appeals to equity, to basic fairness, were honorable appeals to principle.[8]

The Ciceronian idea about equity is that it countenances an exception to the normal bindingness of the law, specifically an "excuse" for not following the law. Here is a concise statement of Cicero's position on the honorableness of appeals to equity:

> He will point out that there is no law which requires the performance of any inexpedient or unjust act; that all penalties provided by law were established to punish wickedness or vice … After all, he will ask his opponents: "Suppose that I had so and so; suppose that so and so had happened – mentioning any of those acts for which there is a most honorable excuse or a certain plea of necessity – would you still accuse me?" But the law makes no exception. Therefore all cases are not covered by exceptions, expressed in writing, but some that are self-evident are covered by exceptions understood but not expressed.[9]

The law makes no exceptions and should in that sense be interpreted strictly, and yet it is counter-intuitive to ignore self-evident exceptions that must be allowed for the law to be considered itself to be just, now understood in the broad sense that encompasses equity.

The Ciceronian account of equity makes it a very common-sense based doctrine. Think again of the case of the guard at the city-gate who has to follow the law that says that the gates must not be opened after dark. There is probably quite a good reason for this law. Yet, the exception of opening the gates so as to save the life of one's own troops is surely a self-evident exception to the law. In this view, equity complements justice, and as Cicero says: "how unfair it is that justice and equity, which it is the intention of the legislator to protect, should be hindered by words."[10]

6 Ibid., p. 293.
7 Ibid., XLVI, 136, p. 305.
8 Ibid., XLVII, 138, p. 307.
9 Ibid., XLVII, 139–140, pp. 307–309.
10 Ibid., XLVIII, 143, p. 313.

27.2 EQUITY IN ANCIENT INDIAN LEGAL THOUGHT

The *Code of Manu* has a trenchant comment about how kings should adjudicate lawsuits: "After he has tried a lawsuit, the king should be both harsh and gentle."[11] Here is probably a reference to the need for considerations of strict justice as well as equity. The equity aspect of deciding is seen in another comment about how lawsuits are to be decided: "the king should decide their cases based on the eternal Law."[12] And in addition: "one should never trample justice."[13] In this section we will seek to develop these ideas to understand how judgments were made in lawsuits in ancient India.

In several of the codes of law, the term *nyaya* is used in discussing how to resolve conflicts between legal texts. Some commentators translate *nyaya* as equity, because it calls for a consideration of circumstances. Robert Lingat says that this is a mistake since equity normally means that a subjective element is added into the decision-making process, and yet *nyaya* does not involve anything subjective.[14] Yet, we do have Brahmins who could intervene in a lawsuit to represent the conscience of the king and this seems so much like the role of the Praetor in Rome as to make it possible that there was a subjective dimension in at least some early decision-making at the time of the Dharmasutras.[15] And in any event it is not quite right to think of equity as "subjective" since for the Stoics as well as for the Roman Republic theorists equity can be associated with natural law which is not subjective at all. As we will see in the next section, when equity is connected to natural law we find an objective sense of basic fairness that is employed to criticize the strict application of statutory justice.

The idea of justice is perhaps easier to see than equity in ancient Indian texts. *Dharma* is the ancient Indian term closest to our term justice. And yet *dharma* has so many different meanings that it is unclear how to assess what justice means in India. Upendra Nash Ghoshal puts the point this way:

> the authors [of the Dharmasutras] seem to imply that justice administered by the king is human reason in its application to the sources of the State law. Criminal justice in particular involves an elaborate examination of all the relevant factors of the suit along with the application of the twofold source of the law, namely, the Sacred Canon and judicial precedent.[16]

[11] *Manu's Code of Law*, 7.140p. 161.

[12] Ibid., 8.8, p. 167.

[13] Ibid., 8.16, p. 168.

[14] Robert Lingat, *The Classical Law of India*, translated by J. Duncan and M. Derrett, Oxford: Oxford University Press, 1973, p. 161, note 40, and p. 168, note 55.

[15] See ibid., p. 12.

[16] Upendra Nath Ghoshal, *A History of Indian Political Ideas*, Oxford: Oxford University Press, 1959, pp. 48–49.

Here we have a suggestion that human reason of the king acting as judge could be based in what is sacred; once again this source would not be subjective but an objective basis for judicial decision-making that may be interpreted as similar to the way that natural law was understood in ancient Rome.

Examining all of the relevant facts seems to be a reference to the idea that the correct application of the law needs to be highly sensitive to changes in circumstance from case to case, where fine discriminations will have to be made by the use of human reason. The question then becomes what should guide the judicial decision-maker in such matters. And at least one plausible answer is that the decision-maker looks inside himself. Next we have the question of whether this looking inside oneself is best understood as an appeal to subjective or objective factors. What is inside the judge's mind need not be subjective if it is common to all rational people. And with this idea we can begin to understand how the idea of conscience (as in the judge as representing the conscience of the king) connects to a natural order understandable by any rational person but not subjective in the sense of being unique to the desires of the decision-maker in question – since reason is the same for each person.

27.3 EQUITY IN ROMAN LEGAL THOUGHT AND PRACTICE

Some Ciceronian conceptions of equity are clearly different from the idea of mere subjective appeal to the desires or interests of the decision-maker. Here we must confront the difference between *jus gentium*, the law of peoples or common customs, and the idea of *jus naturale*, the law of nature, which is the law that is the same throughout the natural world. It is not clear that Roman legal thinkers understood fully the distinction, but it is clear that some of Cicero's texts, as well as those of Ulpian, did recognize a truly objective and universal law of nature that was different from merely what peoples had held as laws in common.

In Cicero's *Laws*, there is an extended discussion of how civil laws relate to the natural order:

> we are so constituted by Nature as to share the sense of Justice with one another and to pass it on to all men. And in this whole discussion I want it understood that what I shall call Nature is [that which is implanted in us by Nature]; that, however the corruption caused by bad habits is so great that the sparks of fire, so to speak, which Nature has kindled in us are extinguished by this corruption, and the vices which are their opposites spring up and are established … For those creatures who have received the gift of reason from Nature have also received the gift of Law, which is right reason applied to command and prohibition.[17]

[17] Cicero, *De Legibus*, I. XII. 33, in *Cicero XVI*, translated by Clinton Walker Keyes, Cambridge, MA: Harvard University Press' Loeb Classical Library, 1928, p. 333.

Cicero here links an inborn sense of justice to nature which then grounds his ideas about natural law.

Cicero argues that "the most foolish notion of all is the belief that everything is just which is found in the customs or laws of nations."[18] Unlike most Roman legal theorists, Cicero seems to draw a distinction between the laws of nature and the laws common to all nations. He then links equity with the laws of nature, as providing a basis for correcting the written law.[19] So, at least one form of equity for Cicero, that having to do with what is common law for all creatures of nature not merely all members of nations, is not grounded in subjective but in objective considerations.

In this respect let us consider the role of the Praetor, the most significant judicial official in the Roman Republic. One of the greatest of the Roman legal theorists, Ulpian, tells us that there was a strong obligation "to protect the weak against the strong" and that this is best captured by speaking of the Praetor's obligations of equity. Yet, says Ulpian's interpreter, Buckland, this is only one of the functions of the Praetor and as the Roman Republic moved more to an empire this aspect of the Praetor's role was diminished.[20] The law was to be administered in such a way so that its severity was tempered. The expression '*ex bono et aequo*' expressed the idea that law was to be administered for the good and also for the fairness (equity) of the people. In pursuing this goal, Buckland tells us that "the Praetor gave a remedy in many cases that was clearly outside the Statute."[21]

27.4 FROM *JUS GENTIUM* TO *JUS NATURALE*

In seeking to determine what these "outside the statute" rulings were grounded in, we should remember that at the same time that the office of the Praetor arose, Roman law was still paying homage to the religious roots of the law. And the Praetor was able to issue edicts covering various matters including deficiencies in the statute law. Yet it is not clear what the Praetor felt he could use as a source for his edicts. Cicero and others have contended that the Praetor appealed to the laws of nature, but the evidence for this claim is hard to assess.

The edicts of the Praetor were only valid for the length of the term of the Praetor, which was only one year. But the successive Praetors took it upon themselves to accept all of what the earlier Praetors had decried, thereby creating a growing body of rules and principles that became as important as the statute law in deciding cases. In this sense, Buckland is right to say that the edicts of the Praetors came to take on the character of legislation and did not much resemble the individual edict that was

[18] Cicero, *De Legibus*, I. XV. 42,p. 343.
[19] Cicero, *De Legibus*, I. XVIII. 48, ibid., p. 351.
[20] See W. W. Buckland, *Equity in Roman Law*, London: University of London Press, 1911, Chapter 1.
[21] Ibid., p. 7.

set out for a particular kind of case. Yet, this does not deny that the Praetor had the good of the people and the fair treatment of the people as the guiding motivation for the issuing of edicts.[22]

Henry Sumner Maine devoted a chapter of his study, *Ancient Law*, to the relationship between equity and natural law, especially in ancient Roman law. Here is his influential account of how the Roman Praetors, and other Roman lawyers, understood equity:

> The Latin word "aequus" carries with it more distinctly than the Greek "isos" the sense of *leveling*. Now its leveling tendency was exactly the characteristic of the Jus Gentium which would be striking to a primitive Roman. The pure Quiritarian law recognized a multitude of arbitrary distinctions between classes of men and kinds of property; the Jus Gentium, generalized from a comparison of various customs, neglected the Quiritarian divisions ... The neglect of demarcations and boundaries seems to me therefore, the feature of the Jus Gentium which was depicted in Aequitas.[23]

Maine is attempting to explain how the *jus gentium* eventually became the *jus naturale*, a topic we need to pursue in order to understand how the Romans understood the role of the Praetors in ruling according to equity.

The Praetor needed to fashion his decisions from sources of law that would be relatively uncontroversial. He then was able to construct a rule that could be employed just as if it had been affirmed by a legislature. As Maine puts it, the Praetor:

> no doubt used the Edict as the means of giving a wider application to those fundamental principles which he and the other jurisconsults, his contemporaries, believed themselves to have detected underlying the law ... as soon as the Edict had evolved an equitable rule the Praetor's court began to apply it in place of the old rule of the Civil Law, which was thus directly or indirectly repealed without any express enactment of the legislature.[24]

The source of the Praetor's Edict was in an important sense moral – the moral foundations of the system of law in Rome. And it is here that the *jus gentium* becomes a true *jus naturale*.

If we follow Maine's reconstruction of the development of equity, we can see how the jurists needed to look back to what was the grounding of the laws in Rome and also to what the laws of Rome had in common with other systems of law of the peoples that Rome conquered and incorporated into its emerging empire. There

[22] There are very interesting discussions of these issues in the most comprehensive study of the Praetors in the Roman Republic, T. Corey Brennan's *The Praetorship in the Roman Republic*, 2 volumes, Oxford: Oxford University Press, 2000.

[23] Maine, *Ancient Law*, pp. 59–60.

[24] Ibid., pp. 66–67.

was a tendency to look for what was common and to disregard what was not. By this process an idea of law that could extend to all peoples was formed – a law of nature not merely a law of current or past nations.

In ancient Indian law it is also clear that the judge is to look at not only statutes, and not even primarily at them. The Vajnavalkya, similar to many law codes of ancient India, says:

> The King should dispose of the issues under consultation with the learned Brahmins. While doing this he should be free from anger and greed ...
>
> The King should appoint as courtiers the persons who are well conversant with the laws of morality, have learnt the Vedas, are conversant with the scriptures and are true persons, i.e. free from bias even toward an enemy or friend in behavior.[25]

Here we find that the king is to appoint judges who are well versed in the laws of morality. And while it is controversial what precisely these laws are, it seems that the religious texts, especially the Vedas, are to be supplemented with the ideas of morality of the judge. And such ideas are not meant to be subjective but objective.

Such an account fits with what Cicero says about the law of nature. And this account fits with what we know about the institution of the Praetor in the Roman Republic. This understanding of the laws of nature makes them not at all spooky metaphysically – rather the laws of nature are merely the moral principles that undergird any reasonable system of law. The universality and objectivity of these laws are modest yet as we will see this does not mean that it is without problems.

27.5 EQUITY'S PROMISE AND PROBLEMS

The idea behind equity is that judges can appeal to some more basic legal principles when the strict application of statutes seems to provide unfair results. And the appeal that judges can make is not merely to what seems to them to be fair or reasonable. Instead the judges can appeal to something fundamental yet still circumscribed by the system of law that they are duty bound to work within.

The promise of equity is that it will even-out a system of law, making it more responsive to the actual situations that parties to law suits face. It will not be possible to hide behind the "words" of the statute. Indeed, Cicero says: "how unfair it is that justice and equity, which it is the intention of the legislator to protect, should be hindered by words."[26] Equity provides the judge with the leeway to act according to his discretion rather than to be handcuffed by the words of a statute. And in many cases

[25] *The Vajnavalkya Smrti*, II. 1.A., translated by B. S. Best, Delhi: Chaukhamba Sanskrit Pratishthan, p. 117.

[26] Cicero, *De Inventione*, II. XLVIII, 143, translated in *Cicero XVI*, p. 313.

this is a very good thing for overall respect for the law that each of us is supposed to display.

Yet, one of the most significant problems with appeals to equity is also articulated by Cicero in his book *De Inventione*. When judges substitute equity for the clear rule of the statutes it is as if they are acting to veto the legislature, a criticism hinted at by Maine when he said it was as if the Praetor was repealing the law passed by the legislature without having gotten consent from that legislature. Here is a passage from Cicero that lucidly states this problem:

> the author of the law did not lack the intelligence, diligence, or opportunity to write plainly what he intended; it was not hard or difficult to make an exception of the excuse which the opposing advocates offer, if he had thought that any exception ought to be made. The lawmakers are accustomed to make exceptions ... he would have made an exception if he had thought one ought to be made. Furthermore ... accepting an excuse is nothing more than repealing the law, because when once an excuse is taken into consideration there is no point in weighing it with reference to the law, seeing that it is not written into the law. And if this principle is set up, all men will be given a reason and opportunity for violating the law, when they know that you are deciding the case by the character of the man who broke the law rather than by the law which you are sworn to uphold.[27]

This argument is remarkably similar to that made in the famous nineteenth century CE case of *Riggs* v. *Palmer*, and elaborated by Ronald Dworkin in the late twentieth century CE. Indeed, Cicero's reasoning here, which he will come to reject, is so carefully drawn that it can serve as a model for how to argue against equity defenses today as well as in ancient times.

Indeed, the equitable principle cited in *Riggs* v. *Palmer* – that no person should be allowed to profit from his own wrongdoing – is already cited by Cicero and other Roman orators as a principle of equity 2,000 years before *Riggs* v. *Palmer* was argued. These principles are said to undergird the ideas of the sanctity of contract and wills, and can be used to nullify the terms of the contract or will. It is in this way that the employment of equity seems to go against the very idea that the people should make the law not the judiciary.

The appeal to equity allows the judge to disregard the statute law and may lead to the complete erosion of the respect for statutes that is a cornerstone of the idea that the people should make the law through their representatives, and that law should not be made by those elites who are not responsive to the people. If equity is narrowly drawn then this result may be avoided but it is not clear that Roman legal thought allowed for such a restriction or drew it especially clearly.

[27] Ibid., II.XLV.130–131, p. 299.

Another significant challenge to the idea of equity is that there is nothing about equity that favors mercy or the protection of the weak – equity favors the party who can make out a case for being an exception to the law, and that party can be strong or weak, and the decision can show mercy or not. Indeed there were cases in earlier times, such as a wife whose silence facilitated her husband's murder, where it was argued that strict justice should not be followed so that this poor woman would get what she truly deserved, rather than that mercy should be displayed toward her. Equity has the sense of fairness that does not necessarily favor the weak against the strong. Exceptions to the law have been urged for many different kinds of cases and parties to a suit. In this respect, equity is most like "even-handedness" rather than mercy.

A third problem with equity has also been well known since Roman times – once the principles of equity have themselves been collected into a canon they can then fall prey to some of the same problems of statutes that equity was supposed to solve. Of especial significance today is that the principles of equity now have a kind of pedigree that makes it hard for them to be disregarded. We find ourselves in need of another kind of equity – meta-equity perhaps – that can help us deal with stultifying equity principles that are as rigidly enforced as statutes are.

Ulpian, the Roman jurist writing in the second century CE, argued that equity was best understood as closely connected to the principle of humanity.[28] If equity is so understood then it is easier to see that equity would tend to favor those who are poor or less powerful,[29] although all people should be able to benefit from principles of humanity since all people are humans and should be treated equally. Yet, at least for the texts from the Roman Republic we have been examining, the connection between equity and humanity does not seem to be of central importance.

If equity is connected to divine law or natural law understood broadly as the law of god for those of us on earth, as was true already for the early Christians who lived under the Roman Empire, then perhaps some of these problems can be overcome. Yet, then the problem will arise of how to justify having the law of the people in effect overturned by the law of a god that not everyone accepts as authoritative.

Similar problems developed in ancient India as the law moved away from explicitly religious texts and yet still was thought to encompass moral ideas from which the judge could draw ideas about the proper judgment in the case at hand. In India, there was never as stark a separation of legal sources and extra-legal sources for the judge to draw on. Yet, when we consider the place of equity in Roman law we find

[28] See D. H. van Zyl, *Justice and Equity in Greek and Roman Legal Thought*, Pretoria: Academica Press, 1991, pp. 134–135.

[29] See Martha Nussbaum, "Equity and Mercy," *Philosophy & Public Affairs*, Vol. 22, no. 2 (Spring 1993), pp. 83–125.

that there is also not a clear separation between strictly legal sources such as statutes and extra-legal sources of judicial decision-making.

27.6 LAW AND ITS RELATION TO MORALITY

In the final paragraphs of this chapter it is important to reflect on the ancient ideas of the relation between law and morality that is still of central concern today. Indian legal thought addresses most directly the idea that judges must take into account moral and religious custom. But the references to the Vedas are not merely to religious custom but to the divine teaching that is to hold good for all time. Indeed, the Vedas literally are the divine knowledge, and all of the early law codes say that the king and anyone he appoints as judge must know the Vedas.[30] In addition, judges are supposed to know the moral customs as well. One question that arises is why judges should know and refer to these extra-legal sources in making their decisions.

Indian legal thought is infused with religious and moral ideas, making some commentators say that it is not properly legal thought at all, unlike Roman legal thought that is said to be purely and properly secular. But both of these claims are problematic. In both of these ancient societies law only emerges out of the customs of the society, which are themselves largely moral and religious. As we will see in the set of chapters that we will pursue next, statute law was merely a formalization of what was already well entrenched in these customs. This is especially evident in the laws concerning the status of women and of the various classes.

The best cases for seeing the overlap of morality and law come in the way that the Romans understood equity and the similar way that Indians saw the wide discretion of judges to disregard statute law if it was warranted by religious and moral ideas of ancient origin. Let me provide just a few more examples of each of these ideas before attempting to give a more generalized account of the place of extra-legal sources in ancient law, as well as today.

The *Code of Manu* is regarded as the main code of ancient India. Here is a passage from that text:

> The root of the Law is the entire Veda; the tradition and practice of those who know the Veda, the conduct of good people, and what is pleasing to oneself. Whatever Law Manu has proclaimed with respect to anyone, all that has been taught in the Veda, for it contains all knowledge. After subjecting all this to close scrutiny with the eye of knowledge, a learned man should apply himself to the Law proper to him on the authority of the scriptures.[31]

[30] See the foreword to *The Vedas*, translated by Ralph T. H. Griffith, Delhi: Kshetra Books, 1914, 2007.

[31] *Manu's Code of Law*, 2.6–9, p. 94.

It is here quite clear that judges are to be schooled in religious and moral traditions and to apply the scriptures when deciding particular cases that come before the judge.

In the most "secular" of all the ancient Indian law codes, The Narada, *dharma*, understood as the ancient truth, is said to be one of the four feet of legal procedure, and while the king's edicts can "overrule" *dharma* it must be taken into account just as is true of custom. "The four feet of legal procedure are *dharma*, legal procedure, custom, and the king's decree: each latter one overrules the former."[32] Divine knowledge remains a significant source of law even in the most secular of the ancient law codes of India. This is at least in part because there is no clear distinction between divine law and secular law.

In the legal thought of the Roman Republic, extra-legal sources of law come into play in judicial decision-making in terms of principles of equity, especially by the edicts of the Praetors, as we have seen. In addition we can cite Seneca's famous essay *De Clementia*:

> Mercy (*clementia*) has freedom in decision; it sentences not by the letter of the law, but in accordance with what is fair and good (*ex aequo et bono*); it may acquit and it may assess the damages at any value it pleases. It does none of these things as if it were doing less than justice, but as if the justest thing were that which it has resolved upon. But to pardon is to fail to punish one whom you judge worthy of punishment; pardon is the remission of punishment that is due. Mercy is superior primarily in this, that it declares that those who are let off did not deserve any other treatment; if is more complete than pardon, more creditable.[33]

Seneca seems to have the Praetor in mind in defending the discretion to omit punishment in certain cases. But this is only when it is thought that a larger justice is served by failing to follow strict justice. Equity is the attempt to correct for strict justice not to overcome justice altogether.

We can see in Seneca's defense of equity in omitting punishment, the moral idea of what is deserved having precedence over what is strictly called for by statutes. The discretion of the Praetor and some other judges is grounded in the moral idea of giving to each what that person deserves. What is here argued is that justice, defined as getting what one deserves, does not always come simply by following the strictures of the law, but by appealing to extra-judicial ideas. In this sense, the judge can call on what is extra-legal in order to make a more just judgment, not a judgment which is contrary to justice in the larger sense of this term.

32 *The Naradasmrti*, Prolegomena, paragraph 10, translated by Richard W. Lariviere, Delhi: Motilal Banarsidass Publishers, 2003, p. 256.

33 Seneca, *De Clementia*, II. VII. 3, in *Seneca I: Moral Essays I*, translated by John W. Basore, Cambridge, MA: Harvard University Press' Loeb Classical Library, 1928, p. 445.

Equity involves a kind of discretion where the judge is at liberty in some cases to disregard what the law strictly requires of him. In this sense the judge answers to a "higher" authority than the law of statutes. And yet, insofar as the law is itself grounded in justice, one could say that the extra-legal and moral sources appealed to are still legal in the sense that they are themselves the grounding of law. Such a view only makes sense if discretion is not unfettered.[34]

It is in this way that judges, especially the Praetor, were able to act in accordance with Aristotle's idea of equity that Seneca and Cicero, as well as other Roman jurists like Ulpian, had adopted. There is for Seneca and Ulpian a link between the principle of humanity and that of equity that allows them to avoid some of the problems that seem to have afflicted Cicero's account that we encountered earlier.[35] But for all three Roman legal theorists morality is an extra-legal source of judicial decision-making that complements the broad interests of justice.

In ancient India, there is a less explicit reference to equity in the discretion that judges have to serve the demands of *dharma*. Indeed, *dharma* is even broader than the broad idea of justice employed by Aristotle and the Roman jurists. Here we have even a better example of what Henry Sumner Maine characterized as the vision of "a type of perfect law,"[36] which in his view only emerges in the seventeenth and eighteenth centuries CE. What we have found is that the ancient legal thought of India and the Roman Republic does already manifest the idea of a perfection of justice that unites morality and the law. The good judge serves a larger justice or *dharma* that is the manifestation of the desire to return to the foundations of the law.

[34] van Zyl, *Justice and Equity in Greek and Roman Legal Thought*, pp. 127–128, for a gloss on the passage by Seneca quoted above.

[35] See Tony Honore, *Ulpian: Pioneer of Human Rights*, second edition, Oxford: Oxford University Press, 2002.

[36] Maine, *Ancient Law*, p. 77.

SECTION X

Legal Status and Social Class

28

Legal Status of Women

The legal status of women in the Roman Republic and ancient India, during the last centuries BCE and the first centuries CE, seems quite similar, at least on first sight. Women were under the legal control of various men: their fathers, their husbands, their sons, or their guardians and tutors. In this chapter I will set out the evidence in support of this commonly accepted view. Then we will also consider the evidence, from both of these ancient societies, that complicates the way women are viewed legally. In the end I will argue for a more nuanced position and this will then lead us to ask questions about the legal status of women in other societies.

The Roman term "*pater familias*," or male head of the family, encapsulates the idea that legally the oldest male was the head of a family and ruled the family's members as if they were all children. We also find that the male head of household was also recognized as the authoritarian ruler over the members of the Indian household as well. The underlying idea in both of these societies was that women were by nature incapable of making decisions for themselves.

And yet, there are plenty of examples of successful women in these societies who excelled in decision-making in business, in politics, and in religion. So, as was true of the ancient Greeks, there is an anomaly in the law and rhetoric on the one hand, and the actual situation of women on the ground on the other hand. There remained an attempt to protect or shield women from the harsh realities of life even as women moved readily in that world to support the family when men were not available or even in some cases when they were available. And the model of marriage also epitomized this conflict in that women were said to be always under the rule of their husbands even as sometimes the best marriage was said to be a partnership.

28.1 THE EARLY ROMAN LAWS ON WOMEN

In the Roman laws attributed to Romulus we find one of the most commonly cited sources of the idea that the Roman man was legally the head of household but also the idea that women were to share in the family property.

> By the enactment of a single ... law ... Romulus brought women to great prudence and orderly conduct ... The law was as follows: A woman united with her husband by a sacred marriage shall share in his possessions and in sacred rites ...
>
> The lawgiver of the Romans gave the father absolute ... power over his son throughout his whole lifetime, whether for imprisonment, for flogging, for keeping in bonds for labor in the fields, or for putting to death ... He also allowed the father to sell his son ...[1]

It appears that the father was absolutely in control of his son but not of his wife. And yet we also find that the husband had the "legal power (along with the cognates) to pass sentence in cases of adultery," to divorce his wife but no right of women to divorce their husbands, and to sacrifice his daughter-in-law to the deities if she strikes her father-in-law.

These laws of Romulus, the earliest known laws in Rome dating from 753–716 BCE, do not admit of a straightforward interpretation of the male head of household's authority over the wife. The father has absolute right over the son, but it is not clear what the limits are of the rule of the husband over his wife. The wife seems to have some legal rights to property and to divorce in the earliest of Roman laws but in just a few centuries things seem to have changed considerably.

The legal status of women in Rome changes significantly in just a few centuries by the time of the *Twelve Tables* in 451–449 BCE. Here the absolute right of the father over his son is affirmed, and there is now a strong right of the male head of household over women in the household.

> Table V, 1. ... Women, even though they are of full age, because of their levity of mind shall be under guardianship ... except vestal virgins, who ... shall be free from guardianship.
>
> 2. The conveyable possessions of a woman who is under guardianship of male agnates shall not be acquired by prescriptive right unless they are transferred by the woman herself with the authorization of her guardian.[2]

[1] *The Laws of the Kings: Romulus*, in *Ancient Roman Statutes*, edited and translated by Allan Chester Johnson, Paul Robinson Coleman-Norton., and Frank Card Bourne, Austin: University of Texas Press, 1961, 2012, p. 3.

[2] *The Twelve Tables*, V.1–2, in *Ancient Roman Statutes*, p. 10.

Here we have a reference to a guardian that made legal decisions, or at least had to approve legal decisions, for women in the Roman Republic.

There is in the *Twelve Tables* an ambiguous reference that seems to qualify the claim that wives were subject to the absolute control of the husband concerning property of the household: "If a woman is unwilling to be subjected in this manner to her husband's marital control she shall absent herself for three successive nights in every year and by this means shall interrupt his prescriptive right of each year."[3] In this set of laws, we do find the idea of the *pater familias* idea, at least concerning the role of men over the women in the family, but the extent of this rule became clearer in the next few centuries.

The full idea of the *pater familias* was articulated by the time of Cicero in the last century BCE and was then also attested by Gaius in the second century CE. Here the idea was expressed thus: a daughter is in the legal control of her father; when she is married she is under the legal control of her husband; and when her husband dies, she is under the control of her sons or the brothers of her husband.

In each situation, the woman (or girl) is under the control (literally in the hand) of the man who assumes the head of household – she cannot attain independence except in very special circumstances.

> Males were released from guardianship when they reached puberty, since they were then capable of having children of their own … Women were never released … [but] this lifelong guardianship was whittled away by legal devices, though as a formality it hung on grimly.[4]

This is the source of the idea that Roman law was paternalistic in that it epitomized the idea of *pater familias*. Women were always under the authority of some man, and even after her husband and father died, the court would appoint a guardian whose consent was needed for her to acquire property in her own name, for example. We shall see later in this chapter though that there were so many "exceptional" cases to make us doubt the doctrine that Roman law epitomized what we today know as *pater familias*.

28.2 THE EARLY INDIAN LAWS ON WOMEN

The earliest of the Dharmasutras, *Apastamba*, has an early reference to women when it is held that "To his mother and father he should show the same obedience as to his teacher."[5] There is also a reference to when sex is appropriate and the

3 *The Twelve Tables*, VI.5, in *Ancient Roman Statutes*, p. 10.

4 J. A. Crook, *Law and Life of Rome, 90 B.C.–A.D. 212*, Ithaca, NY: Cornell University Press, 1967, p. 114.

5 *Apastamba*, 1.14.6, in *Dharmasutras*, edited and translated by Patrick Olivelle, Delhi: Motilal Banarsidass Publishers, 2000, p. 49.

dictum is that a man should only have sex with his wife "between seasons" "if his wife wants it."[6] Both of these rules seem to show respect for women. And the rule about marriage also shows this: "So long as his wife participates in religious rites and bears children, a man may not take another wife."[7] A husband should show respect for his wife and generally yield to women on the road.[8] And we also find that: "The husband and wife have joint control over their property."[9] This legal text ends with the acknowledgment that reference to "knowledge found among women" is important for understanding the law.[10] The legal status of women is relatively high in this very early text, but not as we will see, in later Indian texts.

Things seem very different in the most important of the ancient Indian legal codes, and one that is dated later than the *Apastamba*, the *Code of Manu*. Here is one famous statement of the role of women:

> Even in their own homes, a female – whether she is a child, a young woman, or an old lady – should never carry out any task independently. As a child she must remain under her father's control; as a young woman, under her husband's; and when her husband is dead, under her sons. She must never seek to live independently ... She should be always cheerful, clever at housework, careful in keeping the utensils clean, and frugal in her expenditures ... Though he may be bereft of virtue, given to lust, and totally devoid of good qualities, a good woman must always worship her husband like a god.[11]

Manu also dictates that a widow should "remain patient, controlled, and celibate until her death."[12] But widowers "should marry a wife again and establish anew his sacred fires."[13] In addition we are told that the proper age of men to marry is in their late 20s or early 30s, but that a girl should marry just before puberty.

Also in the *Code of Manu*, women are said to be untrustworthy and to lead their husbands astray.

> It is the very nature of women here to corrupt men. On that account, prudent men are never off guard in the presence of alluring young women. For an alluring young woman is capable of leading astray not only the ignorant but even learned men under the sway of anger and lust. He must not sit alone with his mother,

6 Ibid., 2.1.19, pp. 75–77.
7 Ibid., 2.11.12, p. 91.
8 Ibid., 2.11.7, p. 89.
9 Ibid., 2.29.3, p. 115.
10 Ibid., 2.29.11, p. 115.
11 *Manu's Code of Law*, 5.147–154, edited and translated by Patrick Olivelle, Oxford: Oxford University Press, 2005, p. 146.
12 Ibid., 5.158, p. 146.
13 Ibid., 5.168, p. 147.

> sister, or daughter; the array of sensory organs is powerful and overpowers even a learned man.[14]

This discussion is in the context of setting rules for a student when he is dealing with the family of his teacher. The worry seems to be that the student may be much closer to the age of the teacher's wife and more prone to feel attracted to her. Yet, it is also undeniable that Manu is also discussing women in general and in this respect women are seen as naturally corrupt and corrupting.

We can also look to how adultery was treated in the early texts of the Dharmasutras as compared to the way these matters seem to be addressed in the later text of Manu.

The *Apastamba* deals with rape, adultery, and other sexual crimes in the following manner.

> If a young man all primped up barges accidentally into the presence of another man's wife or young woman, he should be verbally reprimanded; but if he does so deliberately, and with malicious intent, he should be punished. If intercourse took place, his penis should be cut off along with his testicles. If it was a young woman, he should be banished and his property confiscated ... An Arya who has sex with a Sudra woman should be banished, while a Sudra who has sex with an Arya woman should be executed, and that wife of his should be emaciated. If a man has sex once with a married woman of his own class, they say, the punishment is one-quarter of what is prescribed for one fallen from his caste.[15]

These penalties are relatively severe, but not nearly as severe as those penalties in the *Code of Manu*, as we will see. Pranati Ghoshal approvingly quotes the following assessment: "Indian civilization is unique because here we find a surprising exception to the general rule. The further back we go, the more satisfactory is found to be the position of women."[16] We have seen though that the same can be said of ancient Rome as well.

The *Code of Manu* assigns the death penalty for males who commit adultery, except for Brahmins.[17] In addition, the death penalty is assigned for certain acts of sexual assault.

> A man who defiles a virgin against her will merits immediate execution. When a man of equal status defiles a willing virgin, however, he is not subject to execution. No fine should be imposed on a virgin who falls in love with a man superior to herself; but if she makes love to a man inferior to herself, she should be put under

[14] Ibid., 2. 213–215, pp. 105–106.

[15] *Apastamba*, 2.26.18–2.27.11, in *Dharmasutras*, pp. 111–113.

[16] Pranati Ghoshal, "Women's Education in Vedic India," in *Women in Dharmasastras*, edited by Chandrakala Padia, New Delhi: Rawat Publications, 2009, p. 26, quoting A. S. Altakar, *Education in India*, IX, p. 207.

[17] *Manu's Code of Law*, 8.359, p. 186.

> restraint and confined to her house. When a man of inferior status makes love to a superior woman, however, he merits execution; if he makes love to a woman of equal status, he should pay a bride-price if her father so desires.[18]

Here we see that by the time of Manu, between the second century BCE and the second century CE, most forms of sexual assault warrant the death penalty for the man. And the woman in adultery is also treated relatively strictly compared to the earlier codes such as the *Apastamba*.

28.3 ALTERNATIVE ACCOUNTS OF THE LEGAL STATUS OF WOMEN IN ROME AND INDIA

In the scholarship on the Roman Republic, there have been voices that challenged the traditional understanding of patriarchal Rome and the subordination of women. Here is an account by J. A. Crook that is quoted earlier but only in part:

> lifelong guardianship was whittled away by legal devices, though as a formality it hung grimly on. In the Herculaneum Tablets, for example, when Catatoria Themis went bail to Patronia Iusta for appearance in court she promised "with authorization of her guardian" (who was a freedman of her deceased husband). Pudentilla, the wealthy wife of Apuleius, bought a farm; even as a married woman she did so with her guardian's authorization, and he was brought into court to testify that she had bought it for herself and not for Apileius.[19]

Here in this last case, even though a guardian's approval was needed, the woman in question could buy property in her own name and exclude her husband from it. This significantly enriches our understanding of how guardianship of women limited, or did not limit, their actual legal capacity.

We can then look to see how women actually fared in the society of the Roman Republic. Here is Marcus Terentius Varro in his work entitled "On Agriculture":

> Those however who pasture their herds in mountain valleys and woodlands and keep out of the rain not in the villa but in temporary shelters, for them there are many who think it useful to bring along women who follow the herds and bring out food for the herdsmen and make them more attentive to their work. But these women should be strong and not bad-looking. In many places they are not inferior to men in the work, such as one can see here and there in Illyricum, since they can pasture the herd or carry wood for the fire … you had seen mothers carrying at the same time logs and children who were nursing.[20]

[18] Ibid., 8.364, p. 186.

[19] J. A. Cook, *Law and Life of Rome, 90 B.C.–A.D. 212*, Ithaca, NY: Cornell University Press, 1967, p. 114.

[20] Marcus Terentius Varro, *On Agriculture*, 2.10.6–9, in *Women in Ancient Rome: A Sourcebook*, translated by Bonnie MacLachlan, NY: Bloomsbury Academic, 2013, p. 120.

This account speaks not only to the public role that some Roman women assumed but also to the way they managed to take on traditionally masculine jobs and excel in those jobs despite also needing to continue with their traditionally female jobs.

Throughout the Roman Republic, women played a vital role in Roman religion, and this is best illustrated by the role of vestal virgins. Here is Livy's account of the first vestal virgins supposedly installed before the time of the Republic by King Numa:

> He chose the virgins for Vesta, a priesthood originating in Alba and by no means unsuitable to the race of the founder. So that they might be constant overseers of the temple he established for them a stipend from the public treasury. He saw to it that they were treated with reverence and sanctity because of their virginity and because of their other ritual observances.[21]

We also learn that Numa's laws conferred a special legal status on women who became vestal virgins: "On the vestal virgins he conferred high honors, among which was the right of making a will while their fathers lived and of doing other juristic acts without a guardian."[22]

Cicero writes often of his respect for his wife and his daughter, even though he supported the reigning idea of *pater familias*. Here is part of a letter Cicero wrote to his wife Terentia as he was going into exile:

> From the letters of many people and from everyone's report I am made aware of your incredible courage and strength, and that you are never worn down by your efforts of mind and body. How miserable I am with the thought that you, with that courage of yours, your loyalty, your generosity, have fallen into such hardship because of me![23]

Even though Cicero spoke in public against many women whom he often called prostitutes, his respect for his wife and daughter show a more complicated conception of women in his legal thought.

Turning now to India, in the beginning section of the *Code of Manu*, there is a cosmogony that is difficult to interpret but that has given rise to an alternative understanding of the status of women in ancient India. Here is one of the relevant parts of this cosmogony:

> There was this world – pitch dark, without distinguishing marks, unthinkable, incomprehensible, in a kind of deep sleep all over. Then the Self-existent Lord

[21] Livy, *History of Rome*, 1.20.3–4, translated by B. O. Foster, Cambridge: Harvard University Press, Loeb Classical Library, 1926, p. 39.

[22] *Laws of Numa Pompilius*, in *Ancient Roman Statutes*, p. 4.

[23] Cicero, *Letters to his Friends*, 14.1.1, in *Women in Ancient Rome: A Sourcebook*, translated by Bonnie MacLachlan, p. 95.

> appeared … As he focused his thought with the desire to bring forth diverse creatures from his own body, it was the waters that he first brought forth; and into them he poured forth his semen. That became a golden egg, as bright as the sun; and in it he himself took birth as Brahma, the grandfather of all worlds … Dividing his body into two, he became a man with one half and a woman with the other.[24]

Scholars have proposed that this is "the fundamental pivot" for interpreting Manu's Code. In particular these scholars argue that there is an equality between men and women in the image of the body divided into half – "both man and woman are equal partners in the ideal sexual union."[25]

Another source of the alternative reading of early Indian legal texts concerns the distinction between men's public sphere and women's private sphere. Some scholars have pointed out that the seeming consignment of women to the home coincided with the various foreign attacks on India and the need to protect women from marauding troops. Here is one such account:

> public (men) and private (women) are regarded as supplementary to each other. Dharmasastra's ideal is gentleman and gentle woman each fulfilling a distinct place in the domestic and the social scheme, never entering into conflict with each other but ever supplementing the qualities of each other and ever making life's ways smoother for each other … the private realm of life is regarded as where all the public responsibilities get fulfilled.[26]

Here there is a rethinking of how public and private can be seen – as complementary or supplementary rather than opposed to each other in ancient Indian legal thought.

It is also important to point out that despite women being formally consigned to the private sphere, in practice women are known to have held various jobs and professions. Women are acknowledged as having earned their livings from spinning and weaving, and lower-class women earned their income from "agricultural and industrial pursuits."[27] Women also became accomplished musicians and even bodyguards to the king. And prostitution was a highly regarded profession as well. According to some interpretations, the acceptance of women in a great variety of

[24] *Manu's Code of Law*, 1.5–6, 8–9, 32, pp. 87–88.

[25] Devapriya Roy, "My Hours with Manu and Some Unlikely Answers," in *Women in Dharmasastras*, p. 101. Also see Pushpa Tiwari, "Social Dimensions of the Discourse on Women and Sex as Reflected in Manusmrti – The Earliest Known Indian Code of Law," in *Women in Dharmasastras*, pp. 62–72.

[26] Preeti Singh, "Re-reading Dharmasastras through Indian Eyes: A Feminist Perspective," in *Women in Dharmasastras*, pp. 87–89.

[27] Annapurna Chattopadhyaya, "Studying the Economic Position of *Women in the Dharmasastras*: Perspectives in Occupation, *Stridhana*, Property, and Inheritance," in *Women in Dharmasastras*, pp. 198–199.

fields and professions showed that the supposedly patriarchal character of Roman and Indian law was more complicated than it seems.

28.4 THE LEGAL STATUS OF WOMEN IN THEORY AND PRACTICE

In ancient India, by the time of the *Narada* (written after the *Code of Manu*), women's legal status became even more complicated. Narada recognizes the legal form of marriage where "the girl and the suitor mutually seek out one another."[28] Although we also find the idea behind the discriminatory treatment of women: "Women are created for the sake of offspring. The woman is the field, the offspring belong to the possessor of the seed."[29] This latter position reduces the woman to a container for the child growing in utero – giving the woman no rights over her own child once it is born. This does not at all line up with the idea that women are free to consent to marry whomever they choose.

So, we do not have a clean progression in the way women are regarded in ancient Indian law, but instead there are many different ideas that at times tug against each other. It is also true that there is no clean progression in one direction or another in the legal thought about women in the Roman Republic. One thing that is clear is that the formal legal provisions which often seemed highly discriminatory toward women as compared to men did not always match with the way that women seem to have been treated in these ancient societies.

Formally, women were seen as not capable of representing themselves or their interests; and hence women were seen as in need of men to be their representatives and guardians – and this is true for the ancient law in India and the Roman Republic. Since the laws are written by men and men have an interest in protecting or restricting the activities of the women in their lives, the idea of guardianship makes sense. But as a practical matter, there are many situations where it is better for all concerned if women can conduct their affairs without the need for a guardian, or where the consent of the guardian was a mere formality. We see this again in the Narada. The law comes to recognize marriages that were not consented to by the woman's male guardian, even as this form of marriage is not the favored form. What would have been the alternative? If the marriage between consenting man and woman is not legally recognized at all then the state ceases to exert influence over one of the most important aspects of societal life – the repopulation of the society in the next generation.

[28] *The Naradasmrti*, 12.40–43, translated by Richard W. Lariviere, Delhi: Motilal Banarsidass Publishers, 2003, p. 387.

[29] Ibid., 12.19, p. 382.

The legal status of women is also deeply entwined with the way that classes were understood and controlled through the law – and this was true for both ancient India and the Roman Republic. There were severe penalties in India for women who attempted to marry a man of a lower class than she was. Here is one such law:

> A Sudra may take only a Sudra woman as wife; a Vaisya, the latter and a woman of his own class; a Ksatriya, the latter two and a woman of his own class; and a Brahmin, the latter three and a woman of his own class. Not a single story mentions a Brahmin or a Ksatriya taking a Sudra wife … According to Atri and the son of Utathya, a man falls from his caste by marrying a Sudra woman … a Brahmin … he will not go to heaven.[30]

In all of the ancient Indian legal texts it is strongly recommended that a man and woman marry in their own class. We will explore in the next chapter why class was so important for ancient Indian legal thought. Suffice it here to say that the legal regulation of marriage served a very important function in the legal regulation, and separation, of the classes so as to achieve a desired form of social stability.

In the legal thought of the Roman Republic, many of the laws governing marriage and the relations of the sexes were also seemingly designed to enforce class separation, especially in the relations between free and slave classes. It is also important to note that the control of property, especially through inheritance, was also deeply entwined with the control of marriage in the Roman Republic. In this respect, consider a few of the laws of the *Twelve Tables*:

> Table IV. 3. To repudiate his wife her husband shall order her to have her own property for herself, shall take the keys, shall expel her.
>
> 4. A child born within ten months of the father's death shall enter into the inheritance.
>
> Table V. 1. Women, even though they are of full age, because of their levity of mind, shall be under guardianship …
>
> 4. If anyone has no direct heir dies intestate the nearest male agnate shall have the estate.
>
> 5. If there is not a male agnate, the male clansman shall have the estate.
>
> 6. Persons for whom by will … a guardian is not given, for them … their male agnates shall be guardians.[31]

We see here that male guardians assumed control of property when there is no will or where the heirs are in question. Since women could not own property without

[30] *Manu's Code of Law*, 3.13–18, pp. 108–109.

[31] *The Twelve Tables*, in *Ancient Roman Statutes*, p. 10.

a guardian's consent, and all guardians were male, we see how the legal control of women also worked to keep control of property within the Roman Republic.

28.5 LEGAL STATUS OF WOMEN AND THE SOCIAL CONTROL OF MARRIAGE

The idea that women were not able to make decisions in their own behalf and were in need of men to make these decisions for them was not born out by actual practices in ancient India or the Roman Republic. The centerpiece of the idea of women as in need of protection was the Roman idea of guardianship and the Indian idea that at all stages of life a woman was never to be independent of the men in her life. Yet, women were left in charge of the education of children and of the maintenance of the household. While these were "inside jobs" of the private rather than the public sector, they were crucial for the family and it would not make sense to entrust women with these jobs if they really were incapable of making good decisions on their own.

Such considerations have led many theorists over the millennia to look for other explanations for why women were legally controlled. There are many examples that women were educated in a similar manner to men in these societies. In ancient India, some women are educated in the Vedic texts just as was true for some men.[32] In Rome there are many examples of women who were not only highly educated, such as Cicero's daughter, Tullia, but who became successful in various business enterprises.[33] Women were not incapable or uneducated in practical affairs. In this final section of the chapter I will take up two possible reasons for the diminished and restricted legal status of women that do not turn on the easily refutable charge of women's incompetence.

First, is the idea that women in these ancient societies needed to be controlled legally in order to maintain a system of property distribution which was thought to be necessary for the economic survival of these societies at a certain high level. Tying property transfer to marriage regulations keeps property in the hands of the people who currently hold it and provides a stability hard to achieve through any other social institutions.

Second, is the idea that the legal control of women was important for the maintenance of a rigid class structure which was thought to be necessary for a certain sort of political stability. We can see this at work especially in the early Roman Republic where the attempt was to undermine the rise of the plebeians over the patricians.

32 See Pranati Ghoshal, "Women's Education in Vedic India," in *Women in Dharmasastras*,.

33 See Bonnie MacLachlan, *Women in Ancient Rome: A Sourcebook*, NY: Bloomsbury Academic, 2013.

This effort failed over time but the idea was connected to the attempt to prevent or at least restrict intermarriage among these two classes.

The lynchpin of the legal control of women was the regulation of marriage. The ancient Indian texts are very clear that a girl who leaves her father's control is in danger of being overwhelmed by the society. The way to overcome this problem was in effect to transfer the control of the father to the control of the husband. And if the husband should predecease the wife, there was another crisis point. Here the solution in ancient India, where the widow is under the control of her sons, in many ways makes even less sense to us today than the passing of the girl from the control of the father to that of the husband.

And yet it is in understanding the concern for the widow that perhaps we can get a glimmer of what might have worried the legal theorists at the time. Since the very beginning of legal thought in ancient Mesopotamia those who were unmoored have been of chief concern: principally the orphan, the widow, and the impoverished. In ancient societies where a proper welfare state is lacking it is the extended family or the kin who are left to take care of those who are cut off from the support of their immediate families. The orphan has lost both of his or her parents; the widow has lost her husband; and the poor have by misfortune lost the thread that connected them to their communities of support.

Marriage laws that provide protection for women when either death or divorce dissolves the marriage are a form of minimal safety net for the women who are disconnected from their support network. Normally, we think of that safety net in terms of the children who literally cannot support themselves outside of the family. So, the idea that marriage is mainly about protecting women is not the best one for defending the legal institution of marriage. But there is an argument to mount that the legal restriction of women could be justified, at least in part, because of the protection that these women received from such restrictions. But there were other ways to protect women without also greatly restricting their actions.

And of course, it is not inevitable that a society develops the legal institution of marriage. People have been forming dyads (and triads, etc.) for the purpose of sex, procreation, and child-raising long before there was the legal institution of marriage. And it was already well-known, at least in Rome, that Plato had proposed doing away with marriage and raising children communally. Indeed, Cicero spent time commenting on just such a proposal.

It is fascinating that ancient India and the Roman Republic developed legal and social institutions that were similarly focused on protecting and also greatly restricting the actions of women. By the time of the Roman Empire, there was cross-fertilization between Rome and India. But the similarities in marriage institutions go back much further than then and cannot really be accounted for in terms of cross-fertilization. The similarities seem to have arisen due to similar concerns about protecting women from rapid social changes occurring in these societies.

The rise of patriarchal marriage and family law in ancient India and the Roman Republic is defended in the legal thought of those societies in different ways to be sure. Ancient Indian legal thought is very heavily influenced by religious thought at the time; whereas Roman legal thought was much less influenced by explicit religious views. I will take up this issue in more detail in another chapter. Here I just wish to end by discussing one of the salient differences in marriage and family law between ancient India and the Roman Republic, having spent a disproportionate amount of time discussing the similarities.

In the Roman Republic, the idea of guardianship of women could be legally challenged in various ways that were not true for ancient India. Indeed, there was no corresponding formal legal institution of guardianship in ancient India to begin with. Ancient Indian law was much more customary than was the law of the Roman Republic, despite the fact that there were many legal texts setting out the law in India from quite an early point in time. Yet, the "codes" of ancient India were at least as much religious as they were secular law collections. It was not until the *Narada* code that India had anything like the *Roman Twelve Tables* or the other more systematic legal codes of Rome. What this meant was that it was harder to challenge the laws of family and marriage in India than in Rome since to challenge the law in India meant that one was also challenging the religious customs at the same time and thereby risking the wrath of the religious leaders. Yet, it remains true that the system of family and marriage control in these two ancient societies was quite similar, despite these differences in origin and enforcement as we will begin to see more clearly in the chapters that follow.

29

Social Class and Slavery

The legal enforcement of differential duties and rights based on class is most closely associated with India. Indeed, the idea of a legally enforced rigid class – what would later be called a caste – comes from the earliest of legal documents in ancient India. But it is also true that ancient Rome had a rigid class structure that was very much enforced by law. Here the class of slaves was the most regulated, and one of the most oppressed, in the ancient world. In this chapter I will argue that lowest classes in India were in at least some ways better off than the slaves in the ancient Roman Republic.

In both ancient India and Rome, law was tied to class status in ways not seen previously in ancient societies. In India, it was very difficult to move from one class to another since the classes were largely determined by birth, and the legal system graded all penalties in terms of one's class. In Rome, while it was somewhat easier to move from one class to another, the law distinguished among the duties and rights of these classes in a highly rigid manner.

In Section 29.1 we will look at the earliest legal sources for the Indian system of classes. In Section 29.2 we will examine the class structure in the earliest recorded times of Rome. Then in Section 29.3 we will examine the Sudra, the lowest class in India. And in Section 29.4 we compare the Sudra class to that of the slave in Rome. In the final section we explore why law has been so often in the service of class structure in ancient societies.

29.1 CLASS AND LAW IN ANCIENT INDIA AND ROME

The Indian word for class is *Varna*, which literally means color. Indeed the lowest class in ancient India was the class that was the darkest skin color. The four classes of Indian society are set out in the earliest religious texts and then also in the oldest of the legal texts as well. As for the Vedas it is clear already in the earliest of them that the four classes are recognized and the social hierarchy is established and the priestly class at the top has very few duties except ones relating to the ritual sacrifices and some teaching to those of the lower classes, although not to the Sudras.[1]

Here is how the Code of Manu, the most authoritative of all the Dharmasatras, explains the origin of the class system:

> For the protection of this whole creation, that One of the dazzling brilliance assigned separate activities for those born from the mouth, arms, thighs, and feet. To Brahmins, he assigned reciting and teaching the Veda, offering and officiating at sacrifices, and receiving and giving gifts. To the Ksatriya, he allotted protecting the subjects, giving gifts, offering sacrifices, reciting the Veda, and avoiding attachment to sensory objects; and to the Vaisya, looking after animals, giving gifts, offering sacrifices, reciting the Veda, trade, money-lending, and agriculture. A single activity did the Lord allot to the Sudra, however; the ungrudging service of those very social classes.[2]

These four classes are also described as follows: the Brahmin are the priests; the Ksatriya are the political and military leaders; the Vaisya are the herders, farmers, and merchants; while the Sudra are simply to be the servants of the other three classes. In some early Indian texts the Sudra have such a low position in the society that they are not seen as being a class of the same sort as the other three classes.

The Dharmasutras likewise discuss the Indian class system. In the oldest of these codes of law, the *Apastamba*, begins with this statement:

> There are four classes: Brahmin, Ksatriya, Vaisya, and Sudra. Among these, each preceding class is superior by birth to each subsequent. Those who are not Sudras and are not guilty of evil deeds may undergo initiation, undertake Vedic study, and set up the sacred fires; and their rites bear fruit. Sudras are to serve the other classes, the higher the class they serve, the greater their prosperity.[3]

And the Gautama similarly begins by differentiating among classes in terms of when initiation into "second birth" can occur: Brahmin in the eighth year, Ksatriya in the eleventh, and Vaisya in the twelfth.[4] The Sudras are not eligible for initiation, and this is one of the reasons the Sudras are sometimes not even counted as one of the classes.

1 See Brian K. Smith, *Classifying the Universe: The Ancient Indian Varna System and the Origins of Caste*, Oxford: Oxford University Press, 1994.

2 *Manu's Code of Law*, 1. 87–91, translated by Patrick Olivelle, Oxford: Oxford University Press, 2005, p. 91.

3 *Apastamba Dharmasutra*, Book I. 4–7, in *Dharmasutras*, translated by Patrick Olivelle, Delhi: Motilal Banarsidass Publishers, 2000, p. 25.

4 *Gautama Dharmasutra*, 1.5–11, in *Dharmasutras*, ibid., p. 121.

The *Vasistha*, the latest of the Dharmasutras, specifies the social classes as: Brahmin, Ksatriya, Vaisya, and Sudra and then indicates what the proper occupations for each are:

> A Brahmin has six occupations: studying the Veda and teaching, offering sacrifices and officiating at sacrifices, giving and receiving gifts. A Ksatriya has three occupations: studying, offering sacrifices, and giving gifts. The Law specific to him is the protection of his subjects by the use of weapons; he should obtain his livelihood by this means. The same three are the occupations of the Vaisya, and in addition agriculture, trade, animal husbandry, and lending money on interest. To serve these classes is the unrestricted means of livelihood of the Sudras.[5]

These class differentiations are written into the earliest of the law codes as we have seen and they also frame the differential penalties for various wrongs and crimes as well.

We will examine many differentials of punishment according to class in subsequent chapters. Here let us only mention the penalties for assault in the various law codes. The *Code of Manu* tells us this about the penalties for verbal assault:

> For assailing a Brahmin, a Ksatriya ought to be fined 100, and a Vaisya 150 or 200; but a Sudra ought to suffer corporal punishment. A Brahmin should be fined 50 for abusing a Ksatriya, 25 for abusing a Vaisya, and 12 for abusing a Sudra ...[6]

Here we see that if the victim is of a higher class, the perpetrator must pay more than if the victim is of a lower class. Similarly, if the perpetrator is of a lower class he must pay more than if the perpetrator is of a higher class.

Concerning the earliest Roman law to survive, that supposedly made by Romulus in 753–716 BCE, we find this account:

> After Romulus had distinguished the persons of higher rank from those of inferior condition, then he passed laws and apportioned duties for each to do: the patricians to be priests and magistrates and judges; the plebeians to be farmers ... cattle breeders, and artisans of gainful trades ... He entrusted and gave the plebeians to the patricians by permitting each plebeian ... to choose for his patron the patrician whom he wished ... and by calling this protection patronage.[7]

This distinguishing among classes for purposes of legal treatment is of a similar type to that which we just saw in ancient India at about the same time period. The lower-class plebeians are not treated as badly as the Sudras, but when Rome sets out the duties and rights of slaves we see that they are the ones closest to the Sudras.

5 *Vasistha Dharmasutra*, 2.13–20, *Dharmasutras*, ibid., pp. 357–359.

6 *Manu's Code of Law*, 8.267–268, p. 181.

7 *Manu's Code of Law*, 8.267–268p. 181..

In the *Twelve Tables* (451–449 BCE), the legal status of slaves is already discussed – indeed slaves have a passing mention already more than a hundred years earlier in time in the laws of Servius Tullius.[8] In the *Twelve Tables* we find: "Anointing of slaves is abolished and every kind of drinking bout ...;"[9] but the Roman law was very soon thereafter to describe penalties for slaves that were much worse than for non-slaves.

Ancient India and Rome were highly structured class societies and the law played an important role in enforcing the class structure. This was more the case in India where a class system was fully integrated into the law's enforcement structure. In Rome class was most strongly enforced concerning slaves – indeed every aspect of Roman law took account of the difference in treatment based on whether one was free or a slave. Let us look more closely at the two worst off classes: slaves in Rome and the Sudra in India.

29.2 THE SUDRA IN ANCIENT INDIAN LAW

In the *Code of Manu* we find especially harsh penalties for members of the Sudra, once-born men, who insult higher class members, twice-born men:

> If a once-born man hurls grossly abusive words at a twice-born man, his tongue shall be cut off for he originated from the lowest part. If he invokes their names and castes with disdain, a red-hot iron nail ten fingers long should be driven into his mouth. If he arrogantly gives instruction on the Law to a Brahmin, the king should pour hot oil into his mouth and ears.[10]

These penalties seem to be designed greatly to frighten the Sudra into keeping to their place in society and not saying anything that would show disrespect for those higher in the social hierarchy.

The most striking difference in how the classes were treated comes in the way that the Sudra, the lowest class member, is treated for mere verbal assault. Corporal punishment seems to be the preferred method of penalizing the Sudra even for relatively small verbal slights. And then for hurling abusive words or daring to give legal instruction to a Brahmin, terrifying tortures are the required penalties. These penalties are especially significant in light of the relatively light monetary penalties assigned for similar behavior by members of the three other classes. And such remedies are similar as we will see to the disproportionate way that slaves were penalized in ancient Rome.

[8] *Law of the Kings: Servius Tullius*, in *Ancient Roman Statutes*, translated by Allan Chester Johnson, Paul Robinson Coleman-Norton, and Frank Card Bourne, Austin: University of Texas Press, 1961, 2012, p. 5.

[9] *The Twelve Tables*, X.6a, in *Ancient Roman Statutes*, p. 12.

[10] *Manu's Code of Law*, 8.270–272, p. 182.

Various laws addressed injuries caused by Sudras as well as how they were to be treated in relations with the sexes.

> When a lowest-born man uses a particular limb to injure a superior person, that very limb should be cut off – that is Manu's decree. If he charges with a hand or a stick, his hand ought to be cut off; if he strikes with his foot in anger, his foot ought to be cut off. If a low-born man attempts to occupy the same seat as the man of high rank, the king should brand him on the hip and send him into exile or have his buttocks slashed. If he arrogantly spits at such a person, the king should cut off both of his lips; if he urinates at him, his penis; if he breaks wind at him, his anus.[11]

Once again, these are extremely harsh penalties not matched if the assailant is of a higher class.

In matters of adultery and rape the ancient Indian laws are also very harsh toward the lowest class members of the society.

> When a Sudra has sex with a guarded or unguarded woman of a twice-born class – he loses a limb and all his possessions, if she was unguarded. If she was guarded a Sudra loses everything; a Vaisya is imprisoned for one year and his property is confiscated; and a Ksatriya is fined 1000 and his head is shaved using urine … Shaving the head is prescribed as the death penalty for Brahmins; but other social classes are actually subject to the death penalty.[12]

The penalty for the Sudra is always worse than for other classes convicted of the same crime. And if the Sudra is successfully prosecuted for homicide or theft, he will be executed, underlining how "most of the regulations are dominated by caste-feeling" as Hopkins has claimed.[13]

There is a grading of punishments for all classes, leading to the Brahmin class receiving the lightest punishments. And it is forbidden to administer the death penalty for the Brahmin regardless of how awful the act in question is. And we are told that the Brahmin may enslave the Sudra in certain cases.

> A Brahmin should support a Ksatriya or a Vaisya who is starved for a livelihood out of compassion and employ them in activities proper to them. If a Brahmin makes twice-born men who have undergone vedic initiation do slave labor against their will through greed and to show off his power, the king should fine him 600. He may, however, make a Sudra, whether he is bought or not, do slave labor; for the Sudra was created by the Self-existent One solely to do slave labor for the Brahmin.

[11] Ibid., 8.279–282, p. 182.

[12] Ibid., 8.374–379, p. 187.

[13] E. Washburn Hopkins, Chapter x:"Family Life and Social Customs as They Appear in the Sutras," in *The Cambridge History of India*, Vol. 1, edited by E. J. Rapson, Cambridge: Cambridge University Press, 1922, p. 248.

> Even when he is released by his master, a Sudra is not freed from his slave status; for this is innate to him.[14]

Here is the fascinating identification of a Sudra as a slave of the upper classes, especially the Brahmins.

It is also interesting that the categorization of the Sudra is said to be grounded in innate characteristics of the Sudra. This is what distinguishes the Sudra from slaves in some other ancient societies, where slaves are capable of moving into other classes through manumission. From the sources in these ancient Indian texts it does not seem that the Sudra can rise to another class. But as we next see there are other ways that a person becomes a slave, and this parallels quite closely what the Roman texts also say about categories of slaves. We discuss this point in more detail in Section 29.4 of this chapter, but only after we look at how slaves were regarded in the Roman Republic.

In the *Code of Manu* we learn that there are seven kinds of slaves, but the Sudra is not listed, even though the list comes immediately after the discussion I quoted above concerning how the Sudra is to do slave labor and have slave status. The seven kinds are: "a man captured in war, a man who makes himself a slave to receive food; a slave born in the house; a purchased slave; a gifted slave; a hereditary slave; and a man enslaved for punishment." It might be that the Sudra is thought to fit into the class of hereditary slaves but this is not stated directly in Manu's Code.

29.3 SLAVERY IN THE ROMAN REPUBLIC

In a definitive study of slavery in Roman law, W. W. Buckland starts by refuting the idea that slaves are defined by "subjection to a *dominus*." Buckland points out that there are several types of slave in Rome who have no owner:

(a) the slave abandoned by his owner,
(b) convicts,
(c) slaves manumitted by their owner while some other person had a right to them,
(d) a freeman who allowed a usufruct of himself to be given by a fraudulent vendor to an innocent buyer.

Instead, Buckland proposes that Roman slaves are defined by their "rightlessness": "A slave is a man without rights, i.e. without the power of setting the law in motion for his own protection."[15]

[14] *Manu's Code of Law*, 8.411–414, p. 189.

[15] W. W. Buckland, *The Roman Law of Slavery*, Cambridge: Cambridge University Press, 1908, p. 2.

In ancient Rome, a slave is a thing, *res*, which can be owned, bought, or sold, like any other commodity. Any rights the slave has are those that are given to him or her by dint of having a protector. In this sense, the slave in the earliest of ancient Rome is not different from a child, a woman, or even a man's son. Again quoting Buckland, "From the fact that a slave is a *Res*, it is inferred, apparently as a necessary deduction, that he cannot be a person." Yet, Buckland then points out that there are two meanings of person in Roman law: the strictly legal sense of person is a "man capable of rights," but another sense of person is simply someone "who is a 'man.'"[16]

Unlike at least some slaves in India, a slave could become a citizen of Rome and a citizen could become a slave, as in the case of a citizen who had to sell himself into slavery for a debt. Slavery was a legally enforced status in all of Roman law and it had just the same problems for Roman legal thought as was true in ancient Greek legal thought. The slave was rightless and yet was a human person. This is seen most clearly in the laws concerning manumission. There is a debate about how many slaves there were in the Roman Republic as compared to the Roman Empire. Most authors tend to agree though that the sheer number of slaves and their importance was much less in the Republic than in the Empire.[17] But there is no doubt that slaves could attain the status of some form of citizen by becoming freedmen.

Cicero and other theorists of the Roman Republic had the same problem that plagued Aristotle, slavery was accepted by the *jus gentium* and yet it was clearly contrary to the *jus naturale*. Many societies at this time saw slavery as a legal institution where the slave was a mere *res*; yet the law of nature dictated that all humans were to be treated as free and equal by dint of being persons. Indeed, in his *De Legibus*, Cicero says that law and justice both originate in nature and as such all human persons are equal, and should be treated as equals, in the sense that they can attain virtue.[18] And this is why slaves, despite their rightless status, must have the legal basis to attain a status of rights in order to achieve virtue.

In this view, slaves were not innately inferior since they were innately human persons. There is a sense in which Roman slaves were only temporarily rightless. Yet, there was no denying that the law allowed the slave to be bought and sold as chattel. We find the paradox understood when it is recognized that the slave's master may take the slave's life and yet the recognition that doing so would be murder.[19] If the slave was a mere *res* then there was a sense in which the slave owner could

[16] Ibid., p. 4.

[17] See Sandra R. Joshel, *Slavery in the Roman World*, Cambridge: Cambridge University Press, 2010, especially pp. 53–56.

[18] Cicero, *De Legibus* I.vi., in *Cicero* XVI, translated by Clinton Walker Keyes, Cambridge, MA: Harvard University Press' Loeb Classical Library, 1928, pp. 317–319.

[19] See J. A. Crook, *Law and Life of Rome*, 90 B.C.–A.D. 212, Ithaca, NY: Cornell University Press, 1967. pp. 56–57.

do anything he wished to a slave. And yet, since the slave was a human person, the deliberate taking of his life was murder just as it was for any other human person. As a matter of the law of nations, *jus gentium*, the slave owner could do whatever he wanted to the slave; but as a matter of the law of nature, *jus naturale*, the deliberate killing of a slave was murder. As a matter of the civil law, though, the slave could not appear in court and press his claims. Yet, concerning the deliberate taking of the slave's life, an intermediary could go to court and press a charge of murder in the slave's behalf.

Perhaps even more interesting is that the corruption of slaves is also an actionable matter before the courts. The Permanent Edict of the Urban Praetor (c. 129 CE) says:

> Action on corruption of slaves. Whosoever is said to have harbored another's male or female slave or to have persuaded with malicious deception the same slave to anything whereby he makes him or her worse in character, against him I shall grant an action of double of what that matter is worth.[20]

Notice that there is recognition that the character of slaves could be good or bad and that it was actionable to contribute to the corruption of a slave's good character.

This Permanent Edict once again recognizes the humanity of the slave. Of course it is possible to argue that the value of a good slave is understood in terms of the value to the slave's owner. But from what we have seen, there is this conundrum where the slave is the property of his or her owner but where the humanity of the slave is an important consideration in how the slave is to be treated. If the Roman slave is merely a piece of property the humanity should not matter.

29.4 COMPARING THE LOWEST CLASSES IN ANCIENT ROME AND INDIA

One of the salient differences between the Sudra in ancient India and the slave in ancient Rome is that the Sudra was said to be born to his or her status and there were thus no clear ways for the Sudra to change his or her status. In Rome only some slaves were born as slaves and even then they could through manumission become free. If the Sudra served the upper classes appropriately, then there was the possibility that the Sudra could be rewarded in the next life. But in this life, the Sudra was consigned to a servile life.

In Rome, most slaves could be manumitted in this life and even become citizens (although second-class citizens) in this life. The freed slave in fact occupied a distinct place in Roman society and, while not equivalent to the status of a free citizen, had many privileges and rights. One of the most important was that the freed person

[20] *The Permanent Edict of the Urban Praetor*, *Ancient Roman Statutes*, Document 244, p. 186.

could sue in his or her own behalf. In addition, of nearly equal importance, was that the children of freed persons could become full Roman citizens. So, in these respects the Roman slave was better off than the Indian Sudra. But in other respects this was not true.

The status of the Sudra was not as bad as that of the Roman slave in that while the Sudra was the lowest of the classes in ancient India, the Sudra was not the property of a higher class person as was true of the Roman slave. In a sense this is true because there was not as fully a worked out idea of private property in India as there was in Rome. But this would be insufficient to explain the difference. Indian law could have regarded the Sudra as a thing to be bought and sold, like cattle, but that also does not seem to be true. Yet we should also recognize that the Sudra was not allowed to own property and if he did acquire property it "becomes the property of the man to whom they belong," although in this respect the Sudra is no different from wives or sons.[21]

It is true that the Sudra was a defiled class, where even the shadow of the Sudra was to be avoided by the other classes. And in some treatments of class in India, the Sudra is placed so low as not even to count as one of the classes. In Rome, while there was a broad sense in which slaves were persons, as a matter of strict legal status the Roman slave was not a legal person at all. Indeed, there were "slave markets" in Rome which were not substantially different from markets for other animals.[22] There is no sense that the Sudra was similarly treated so badly.

There is another sense in which the Sudra was better off than the Roman slave. Neither in Rome nor in India did compassion or mercy extend to the slave or Sudra class. Yet, because of the religious nature of much of the Indian laws, there is some accommodation especially for the Sudra who is suffering from hunger. Farmers are supposed to leave a part of their crops available for those who are in need, and this seems to include the Sudra.[23] Indeed, one of the few differentials in punishment that favors the Sudra is theft – "With respect to theft, the liability of the Sudra is eight times; for a Vaisya, sixteen times; for a Ksatriya, thirty-two times; for a Brahmin, sixty-four times."[24] One reason is that the Sudra is not supposed to know right from wrong. But another reason could be that there is a recognition that the Sudra would be most in need of stealing to provide for the necessities of life.

Yet, in most other respects the sheer brutality of the laws concerning offense and assault by Sudra marks this ancient legal system as abhorrent to us. It seems that the

[21] *Manu's Code of Law*, 8. 416, p. 189.

[22] See the *Edict of the Curule Aediles* (129 CE) where the rules governing the sale of slaves are followed by similar rules governing the sale of beasts of burden, in *Ancient Roman Statutes*, Document 245, p. 204.

[23] See E. Washburn Hopkins, "Family Life and Social Customs as They Appear in the Sutras," in *The Cambridge History of India*, Vol. 1, edited by E. J. Rapson, Cambridge: Cambridge University Press, 1922, p. 242.

[24] *Manu's Code of Law*, 8.337, p. 185.

Indian treatment of the Sudra is a bit worse than that of the slave in Rome. The idea of pouring boiling oil into a person's mouth or cutting out his tongue is simply cruel in the extreme. And while capital punishment of slaves was common this form of punishment was not necessarily cruel, although it certainly could be.

Since it was common for both slaves and Sudra to be in the household of the upper classes, the punishments may have been moderated, but from the early law codes the severity of treatment of the Sudra seems to have exceeded even that of a Roman society that was also known for its cruelty – one can think here of Roman slaves being torn apart by wild animals in the Roman Coliseum, seemingly just for the sheer pleasure of the Roman audience, to see that Rome was not much less of a brutal and cruel society than ancient India.

Perhaps one of the best ways to judge between them is by looking at how mixed-class children are regarded and here Rome is slightly less terrible than India. In the *Code of Manu*, we find this general provision:

> When men violate the wives of others, the King should disfigure their bodies with punishments that inspire terror, and then execute them for such violations which give rise to the mixing of social classes among the people, creating deviation from the Law that tears out the very root and leads to the destruction of everything.[25]

And the punishment for having sex with a Sudra for someone of an upper class is the highest of the penalties.[26]

Concerning the children born from such class mixing, ancient Indian law is also very severe. Any upper class man who takes a Sudra wife reduces his family to that of the Sudra.

> a man falls from his caste by marrying a Sudra woman … [and] by producing offspring by her. By taking a Sudra woman to bed, a Brahmin will descend along the downward course; and by begetting a son through her, he falls from the very rank of Brahmin. When such a woman plays the leading role in his divine, ancestral, and hospitality rites, gods and ancestors do not partake of them, and he will not go to heaven. No expiation is prescribed for a man who drinks the saliva from the lips of a Sudra woman, who is tainted by her breath, and who begets himself in her.[27]

Notice that even the Brahmin will lose his status by begetting a child with a Sudra woman and there is no recourse. Also note the use of the term "tainted" here to refer even to the breath of a Sudra woman.

Roman law was not as severe as India in treating those who had children with partners from a different class, and even with a slave. Gaius gives us a good idea of

[25] Ibid., 8. 352, p. 186.
[26] Ibid., 8.383, p. 187.
[27] Ibid., 3. 16–19, p. 109.

how the children born from partners, one of whom was a slave and one of whom was not, are to be treated at law (probably considerably before his time in the second century CE as well). The rule of the *jus gentium* was that the status of the mother determined the status of her child. Here is how Gaius put it:

> the child of a slave-woman and a free man is born a slave by the rule of the *jus gentium*, while on the other hand the child born of a free woman and a slave is born free. But we must be careful to observe whether the rule of the *jus gentium* has not in any particular case, been varied by some *lex* or by some equivalent of a *lex*. Thus under the *SC. Claudianum* it was possible for a Roman woman who cohabited with another person's slave with that person's consent, while remaining herself free in virtue of the agreement, to give birth to a slave; for the senatusconsult ordains that what has been agreed between the woman and the slave's owner shall hold good. But subsequently the late emperor Hadrian was moved by the hardship of the case and the legal anomaly to restore the rule of the *jus gentium*, so that the woman, where she remains free herself, gives birth to a free child.[28]

The offspring of slaves and free partners are not penalized and are treated according to the same common law principle as for other offspring who do not have a slave parent. And also note that there is some indication that mixed birth children are regarded as a kind of hardship that the emperor treats humanely.

Thus, while both Roman law and Indian law treat slaves and Sudra rather severely, it seems on balance that ancient Indian legal thought was probably worse on this account than was ancient Roman law. We should keep in mind though that the laws in question are, as we shall next see, much less humane and compassionate than was true for other earlier ancient systems of law such as in Mesopotamia and the ancient Israelites for instance.

29.5 LAW AND THE WORST OFF

Today one of the most important indicators of the humaneness of a society is how the worst off members of the society are treated, especially as a matter of law. John Rawls says that the way to think of fairness is how we treat the least well off – indeed any society that claims to be just must pass the test of "the veil of ignorance" – how would you regard the societal practice in question if you were the one made worst off by such a practice?

In ancient legal systems older than the Roman and Indian, there was considerable compassion for the least well off – often referred to as "widows, orphans, and the

[28] *The Institutes of Gaius*, Book 1, 82–82, translated by Francis De Zulueta, Part 1, Oxford: Oxford University Press, 1946, pp. 27–29.

poor." The kings and other political leaders were supposed to have these worst off as those they specially protected. If one were to posit a progressive evolutionary view of ancient legal thought, one would be hard pressed to explain why Indian and Roman legal texts seem to have been so much less supportive of the least well off members of their societies compared to earlier legal texts.

What we do find in ancient Indian and Roman legal texts is a near obsession with status. Of course the laws here were also a reflection of these ancient societies – the law did not create these rigid classes out of whole cloth. And while the more democratic spirit of the Roman Republic seems to have treated slaves better than the Roman Empire, the worst off members of the society did not get special relief. The "middle class" in the Roman Republic, the plebeians, did receive special consideration that eventually allowed them to attain nearly the same status as that of the upper-class patricians. But the Roman law was not especially attuned to those who were in the lowest class, the slaves.

In ancient India, the law codes clearly reflected the religious views expressed in the earlier texts of the Vedas and Upanishads, and these religious texts were very rigid in not being compassionate in the treatment of the worst off members of the society. But in previous eras, it was often the religious influence on the lawmaker that brought compassion for the worst off into the laws.

So we have two ancient societies which were very different from one another yet where both seemingly broke with older societies and manifested a lack of compassion and care for the worst off members of the society. And in India the worst off class was institutionalized and enforced by the law, as was also true of slavery in Rome. The law made mobility out of the lowest class more difficult than it would have been otherwise. The measure of a fair society in ancient Rome and India was not how it treated the worst off – and this was a significant break with ancient legal thought.

Yet it is surprising that two societies that seemed especially attuned to the idea of equity as a way for judges to soften the harshness of strict justice were nonetheless not attuned to equity in the treatment of the worst off. Indeed, in Rome we also find tolerance for foreigners as they were incorporated into Rome – there seems more compassion for peregrines, as the Romans called foreigners, than for members of their own society. Perhaps the Romans realized that their society, like the Greek society the Romans so much admired, could not function without a slave class to do the work that then freed the upper classes to pursue the higher intellectual and practical pursuits.

In India, the rigid class structure, enforced by law, lasted for several millennia, never seemingly faltering in its contempt rather than compassion for the Sudra. And the law remained deeply influenced by the Hindu religion all of this time as well. In Rome, the ultimate rise of Christianity did not end slavery but it did die out nonetheless, leaving the Roman Empire as a socially stratified society but not one that worked on the backs of a slave class. Why Rome and India developed the way they did is a story I will have to leave for another occasion in a different work.

Today, how the worst off are treated is often a measure employed in political and legal thought. Class is no longer institutionalized as part of the legal system and those who attempt to move up in class are not generally subject to legal penalties for doing so. Indeed, we do not often discuss class in legal terms – instead focusing on specific circumstances of individuals. Yet it might make for better discussions about the law's fairness if we were to discuss the way that class is still enforced at law, even if it is not as blatant as was true for ancient India and Rome.

SECTION XI

Responsibility and Punishment

30

Political and Moral Crimes

In early Roman and Indian law, certain wrongful acts were treated as distinctly contrary to the public interest and subject to judicial procedures different from other wrongs that were treated as disputes between two private parties. In this chapter we will examine criminal laws from the Roman Republic and ancient Indian law for a sense of how criminal law emerged as a matter that concerned the state – where the state was not merely an arbitrator between parties but itself an aggrieved party. I will argue that for both of these ancient societies there is a sense of urgency in the state's attempt to root out certain wrongdoers and deal with them severely for the sake of the public peace, and that these crimes included both affronts to political as well as moral authority.

In Section 30.1 we will examine the wrong of poisoning in the Roman Republic, a wrong that seems to be one of the first to be prosecuted as a distinctly criminal matter. In Section 30.2 we will look at treason in the various ancient Indian texts. In Section 30.3 we contrast Roman Republican views about crimes with those of ancient India. In Section 30.4 we look at specific procedural differences between the ways that crimes as opposed to civil matters are handled in these ancient societies. And then in Section 30.5 we will assess what "developments" there are in these ancient societies as compared to earlier ancient societies that were also beginning to distinguish crimes from private disputes, looking most especially at the way that public and moral crimes were differentiated. I will argue that ancient crime in India and Rome concerned both disruptions of the political peace but also assaults on the morals of the country.

30.1 POISONING IN THE ROMAN REPUBLIC

Poisoning, especially the use of "drugs or magic on account of children," as a wrong is first mentioned in the oldest of the Laws of the Kings, the laws attributed to Romulus.[1] And again we find a broader reference to "the administering of drugs"

[1] *The Law of the Kings I: Romulus*, 9, in *Ancient Roman Statutes*, translated by Allan Chester Johnson, Paul Robinson Coleman-Norton, and Frank Card Bourne, Austin: University of Texas Press, 1961, 2012, p. 3.

in the *Twelve Tables*, which seems to be one of the wrongs for which capital punishment is the prescribed punishment.[2] Poisoning is here associated with the use of drugs and magic which are thought to be especially dangerous for the people at this time. But in these very early texts it is not clear that crime and delict (or tort) are distinguished.

The first full-scale treatment of the crime of poisoning is a law of Sulla from 81 BCE, which Cicero quotes from in a trial from 66 BCE:

> Whoever makes, sells, buys, has, gives poison … and he shall investigate judicially concerning the capital crime of the person … whatever military tribune of the first four legions or whatever quaestor, plebeian tribune … or whoever in the Senate has expressed, expresses an opinion … whoever of these has conspired, conspires, has combined, combines, plots, has plotted, has given, gives, false evidence, whereby anyone is convicted by a public court … whoever has made, makes baneful poison … and he shall investigate judicially about the capital crime of the person who holds a magistracy or expresses an opinion in the Senate: whoever of these has conspired, conspires …[3]

Indeed, this law also creates a special court to examine murders and poisoners or magicians.[4] So poisoning is treated as a distinct crime as early as 81 BCE in Roman law.

O. F. Robinson has attempted to provide an understanding of why murder by poisoning, or even just the possession of poisons, was singled out for criminal prosecution.

> Self-evidently the statute covered murder by poisoning. Making, selling or even possessing a murderous drug or potion brought liability under chapter five of the statute. Drugs compounded for this purpose were distinguished from those which might have a medicinal use, but love potions and fertility drugs were, like abortifacients, considered dangerous, and if their use brought about a death, however inadvertently, such use was made punishable under a resolution of the Senate.[5]

Chief among the reasons for the special treatment of wrongs like poisoning was the dangerousness of the wrong.

It is not surprising that from the earliest of times, codes of conduct during war have singled out poisoning as banned in all situations. Along with assassination, poisoning is a stealth or secret method that gives the victim little or no chance to save himself or herself by fighting back. There is also evidence that poisoning is

2 *The Twelve Tables*, VIII, 25, in *Ancient Roman Statutes*, p. 12.

3 *Cornelian Law on Murderers and Poisoners or Magicians*, in *Ancient Roman Statutes*, p. 65.

4 See note 2 accompanying text on *Cornelian Law*, in *Ancient Roman Statutes*, p. 65.

5 O. F. Robinson, *The Criminal Law of Ancient Rome*, Baltimore, MD: Johns Hopkins University Press, 1995, pp. 43–44.

considered a domestic crime as it can be used to kill a close relative without detection. Even to possess poison is to risk that it can be used in a lethal way and in a way that might not be detected. This was not mere deviance, although it surely is that. The moral side of this wrong is seen in the sense that there are no good reasons to use poisons on a fellow human and it is primarily people of bad dispositions who would employ the poisons.[6]

Roman legislators took a special interest in prohibiting poisoning for the common good: the use of poison almost always resulted in there not being a live victim who could proceed against the perpetrators as a matter of private wrong. In addition, it will often take concerted effort and resources to determine who it was who employed the poison, putting the investigation outside the realm of the abilities of most private citizens of Rome.

30.2 POISON AND TREASON IN ANCIENT INDIA

The idea of crimes is treated in most of the ancient Indian texts in terms of the "removal of thorns." The thorns in question are the wrongs that adversely affect the king and the society at large. Here is how Kautilya treats poisoning in the *Arthashastra* (a famous book on management):

> Whoever is suspected of administering poison (*rasa* = mercury) to others by reason of his talking of it or selling or purchasing, or using it in preparing medicines, may be approached with the tale that a certain enemy of the spy may be killed and that a certain amount of money may be received as a reward. If he does so, he shall be proclaimed a poisoner (*rasada*), and banished … There are thirteen kinds of criminals who, secretly attempting to live by foul means, destroy the peace of the country. They shall either be banished or made to pay an adequate compensation according as their guilt is light or serious.[7]

Notice that the crimes are identified by what destroys the peace of the country. In the case of poisoning, one of the chief problems seems to be the way in which poison allows for the secret assault on a person. It is also of note that this rationale is similar to that offered in the Roman Republic, and yet the punishment is not death but only banishment in India as opposed to the Roman Republic.

In the *Arthashastra* there is considerable discussion of the importance of using spies to ferret out the crimes that could disrupt the peace of the country. The use of spies is not limited to the attempt to find the secret wrongs of the general populace

6 See Jill Harries, *Law and Crime in the Roman World*, Cambridge: Cambridge University Press, 2007, pp. 123–131.

7 *Kautilya's Arthashastra*, Book IV, Ch. IV, translated by R. Shamasastry, 1915, reprinted by Bottom of the Hill Publishing, 2010, p. 221.

but of even greater concern are the wrongs of the officials who are entrusted to maintain the peace.[8] Here we might note that those responsible for the financial well-being of the society are singled out, especially those who manufacture coins or who "lower the quality of gold by mixing it with an alloy."[9] These wrongs are equivalent to engaging in treason against the state and are the sorts of "thorns" that must be removed for the country not to be seriously harmed.

The idea of the "eradication of thorns" is most closely associated with the Code of Manu, where a separate category of wrongs is added after discussing the grounds for litigation between private individuals. We find the supporting idea expressed by Manu in terms of "protection of their subjects." Here is a segment of Chapter 9's treatment of the "removal of thorns."

> He should promptly execute anyone who breaches the rampart, fills the moat, or breaks the gates.
>
> For all types of black magic, a fine of 200 should be imposed, as also for root-witchcraft when done by an unrelated person, and for various types of sorcery. Anyone who sells infertile seed corn or jacks up the price of seed corn, or who destroys boundary marks, shall be executed by mutilation.
>
> A goldsmith who operates dishonestly, however, is the most wicked of all thorns, and the king should have him cut to pieces with razor knives.[10]

Here are mixed together wrongs that directly weaken the defensive structures of the country with wrongs that harm individuals by dishonesty or the use of magic. In this respect we can see a mixing of political and moral crimes.

Moral crimes are wrongs that undermine the integrity or virtue of the populace; political crimes are wrongs that undermine the integrity of the king or otherwise adversely affect the state. Manu lists the seven political constituents of a kingdom as: "Lord, official, capital, realm, treasury, army, and ally." A wrong done to any of these "seven limbs" of the state must be considered to be a "serious" harm to the kingdom.[11] Then, Manu also discusses what are better seen as moral wrongs – especially concerning the diminishment of one or another of the classes.

> Even in the face of the deepest adversity, he must never anger Brahmins ... When angered they could create other worlds, and other guardians of the world, they could convert gods to non-gods ... Whether he is learned or not, a Brahmin is a great deity ... When a Ksatriya becomes haughty in any way in his behavior towards

[8] *Arthashastra*, ibid., p. 220.

[9] *Arthashastra*, ibid., pp. 220–221.

[10] *Manu's Code of Law*, 9.289–292, translated by Patrick Olivelle, Oxford: Oxford University Press, 2005, p. 205.

[11] Ibid., 9.294–295, p. 205.

> Brahmins, the Brahmin himself must be their controller, for the Ksatriya sprang from the Brahmin.[12]

Angering or in other respects harming Brahmins is a moral crime as I construe it because of its adverse effect on the social and religious order upon which the moral integrity of the country depends.

Ancient Indian law does not clearly distinguish moral from political crimes, but in most other ancient societies the same is true although often to a lesser extent. These crimes are clearly distinguished procedurally, though, from private wrongs. As Robert Lingat cogently argues:

> Matters falling within *prakirnaka* [public litigation] are characterized by the fact that the king can take them up *ex officio*. By contrast, the king must abstain from taking up a case appertaining to private disputes when no one has addressed a plaint to him.[13]

As in other ancient societies, ancient India separates private from public wrongs procedurally and seems to be moving toward different ways of dealing with crimes, as opposed to civil wrongs, in terms of how trials should proceed.

30.3 HIERARCHY AND CRIME

One type of what I have been calling moral crime concerns the maintenance of hierarchy in a society, as can be seen in the ancient Indian laws concerning violations of class. The criminal laws of the Roman Republic also were sometimes employed to maintain class hierarchies. In this section we will examine the contrasting ideas of hierarchy as it relates to the criminal law in ancient societies in Rome and India. This will help us to see if there is indeed a distinction between political and moral crimes in these ancient societies.

In early Roman times there was a fairly strict hierarchy between patrician and plebeian classes, with the latter definitely lower than the former. In the Laws of the Kings from the earliest period of Romulus (753–716 BCE) we find the following account:

> After Romulus had distinguished the persons of higher rank from those of inferior condition, then he passed laws and apportioned duties for each to do: the patricians to be priests and magistrates and judges; the plebeians to be farmers … cattle breeders, and artisans of gainful trades … He entrusted and gave the plebeians to the patricians by permitting each plebeian … to choose for his patron the patrician

12 Ibid., 9.313–320, p. 206.

13 Robert Lingat, *The Classical Law of India*, translated by J. Duncan and M. Derrett, Oxford: Oxford University Press, 1973, p. 237.

> whom he wished … and by calling this protection patronage … it was neither holy nor lawful to bring suit, to testify, or to cast a vote the one against the other … He who was convicted of doing any of these matters was held by the law of treason, which Romulus enacted, so that it was lawful for anyone to slay the person convicted of this crime, as a sacrifice to the god of the underworld.[14]

It is especially interesting that those who violated the laws that established class differences would be tried for treason in the earliest of Roman statutes.

It is also highly relevant that at least some of the class differences that were protected by criminal laws were overturned also fairly early in the early history of Rome. We can here examine two laws from the early fifth century, from 494 and 492 BCE:

> *Junian Law on the Sacrosanctity of the Plebeian Tribunes* – No person shall compel a plebeian tribune, as if one of the ordinary citizens, to do anything unwillingly or to scourge him, or to order another person to scourge him, or to kill him, or to order another person to kill him …
>
> *Icilian Law on the Noninterruption of the Plebeian Tribune's Speech* – When a plebeian tribune is declaring an opinion among the people, no person shall say anything in opposition or interrupt the speech. If anyone acts contrary to these rules, he, when required, shall give to the plebeian tribunes sureties for the full payment of whatever fine they may impose on him. But if he does not give surety he shall be punished by death …[15]

Here we find the criminal law being used to protect the lower class in the Roman Republic. So, while class hierarchy continued to be a focus of the criminal law, it was not always true that the criminal law promoted rather than disrupted hierarchy.

In ancient India, the class system was much more resilient and long-lasting than the class hierarchy in Rome. The laws concerning the Sudra or lowest class are established from the earliest Dharmasutras, the *Apastamba*. At the very beginning of this code we find a clear demarcation of the society by class. And then as the text proceeds we find passages such as the following: "Social interaction with outcastes is not permitted as also with degraded people" and "sex with Sudras on the part of Arya women" … "make people sordid."[16]

The *Gautama*, also a very old Indian legal code, specifies the occupations that the various classes can occupy. Yet, we are also told that "The King … should be impartial toward his subjects and work for their welfare."[17] Yet, we continue to find such legal provisions as: "Punishment should be meted out after taking into account the

[14] *The Laws of the Kings*, I. *Romulus*, in *Ancient Roman Statutes*, p. 1.

[15] *Ancient Roman Statutes*, pp. 8–9.

[16] *The Apastamba*, 1.21.5–13, in *Dharmasutras*, translated by Patrick Olivelle, Delhi: Motilal Banarsidass Publishers, 2000, p. 59.

[17] *The Gautama*, 11.5, in *Dharmasutras*, p. 147.

type of man he is ..."[18] The strongly religious and moral pronouncements within the early Dharmasutras, where invocations of sin and crime are mixed with this-worldly and other-worldly punishments, marks a significant difference between ancient Indian and Roman law.

We find that the distinction between political and moral crime is consistently blurred in these ancient Indian texts in ways that we do not find, at least to the same extent, in the ancient Roman codes. In another chapter I discussed the extent of religious influence on ancient law in Rome and India. Here I wish just to say a bit more about morality and criminal law. In Rome, morality and criminality were linked but not through religion. The connection between crime and moral wrong remains with us today in nearly all codes of criminal law.

30.4 ANCIENT ROMAN AND INDIAN CRIMINAL PROCEDURE

I have already remarked, in passing, that in ancient Indian criminal law the king did not need to wait for a complaint to be made by a private party who had been wronged. Procedurally, when a crime had been committed the king initiated the trial and was effectively the complaining party himself. As we will see, in the Roman Republic special courts dealt with criminal matters, first in people's courts and then in courts of the Praetor or other high officials. It is to these Roman criminal procedures that we first turn.

O. F. Robinson gives us a good sense of some of these procedural issues in his book on early Roman criminal law.

> Criminal procedures of the [earliest] period comprised the domestic jurisdiction of the paterfamilias, private criminal actions, the exercise of their powers by the *tresviri capitales* (minor magistrates with police functions), and the jurisdictions of the assemblies of the people; i.e. trials before one of the comitia. In 207 BCE the Senate ordered a special commission, a *quaestio*, to investigate the conduct of certain allies arising from the Second Punic War ... Thereafter, both the senatorial commissions and also the jurisdiction of the assemblies began in their turn to be superseded by the *quaestiones perpetuae*, permanent jury courts ... Some of Sulla's reforms produced courts dealing with forgery of documents and coining, with murder and banditry and poisoning, with assault, and also with treason, extortion, and embezzlement of public funds.[19]

The *quaestio* courts were ad hoc tribunals "set up to 'investigate' offenses against public interest."[20]

[18] *The Gautama*, 13.12, in *Dharmasutras*, ibid., p. 151.

[19] Robinson, *The Criminal Law of Ancient Rome*, pp. 1–3.

[20] Harries, *Law and Crime in the Roman World*, pp. 16–17.

It is worth distinguishing two kinds of Roman criminal courts that were not ad hoc. The people's courts (*publica iudicia*) were quaestio courts that became permanent (*quaestiones perpetuae*). These courts replaced the popular courts of the assembly (*iudicia populi*), where suits were initiated by a magistrate before being presented to the assembly for confirmation. These popular courts were replaced by courts that had juries deciding the cases – seemingly a positive development in the history of legal thought concerning trial procedures.

Yet, it is interesting that Cicero preferred the older criminal courts because he thought that the magistrate and assembly were less likely to be corrupted than a smaller jury.[21] The Roman jury trials in a sense grew out of the procedure of having the assembly confirm the magistrate's judgment, but Roman juries seem to be less involved in ascertaining the truth of the criminal matter. Here is the cumbersome yet perhaps fairer way that popular magistrate-run trials (as opposed to jury trials) occurred:

> First came a notice of trial. Then three sessions at intervals of (at least) one day, at which the magistrate investigated the case, then after an interval of (at least) a *trinum nundinum* the formal judgment of the magistrate and the vote of the people [in assembly].[22]

This procedure is contrasted with the later *quaestio* proceedings of jury trials, also summarized by Robinson: they were "presided over by a praetor or *iudex quaestiones* and presented to a large jury, who gave the verdict by majority vote."[23]

The procedures for criminal trials in ancient India more closely resembled the older popular magistrate trials than the *quaestio* jury trials, although as we will see there is scarce evidence for how criminal trials were supposed to proceed. The various Indian codes make it clear that the king is the one to investigate and decide cases, although he can delegate some of his ministers to perform these tasks for him. Indeed, Kautilya speaks of criminal proceedings where the king entrusts "three functionaries called *pradestr*, agents of the executive" who are supposed to be versed in knowledge of the various Dharmasutras and other codes.[24]

The Indian king has wide discretion in investigating and deciding criminal cases, much like the magistrates in the Roman Republic. And when the king delegates to the *pradestr* the two systems of criminal law look quite similar, although we certainly lack the details about the Indian as compared to the Roman criminal law's procedures. In ancient India, it is clear that various ordeals were used as a method

[21] See A. H. M. Jones, *The Criminal Courts of the Roman Republic and Principate*, Oxford: Basil Blackwell, 1972, pp. 3–4.

[22] Ibid., p. 6.

[23] Ibid., p. 45.

[24] Lingat, *The Classical Law of India*, p. 241.

for testing the truth of the witnesses and parties to a criminal law suit. And there is a somewhat similar use of oaths of calumny in the Roman Republic, although the penalty was social rather than religious.

Let us look more closely at the oaths of calumny and the Indian ordeals to see what we can learn about the differences between Indian and Roman criminal procedures. We begin with the ancient Indian ordeals that we already touched on in an earlier chapter. Manu discusses both oaths and ordeals as seemingly alternatives to one another in the following part of his code:

> When two persons are litigating matters for which there are no witnesses and the judge is unable to discern the truth, he should discover it even by means of an oath … A wise man must not take an oath falsely even with regard to a trifling matter; for by taking an oath falsely, he comes to ruin here and in the hereafter … Alternatively, he may make the person carry fire, stay submerged in water, or touch separately the heads of sons and wife. When the blazing fire does not burn a man, the water does not push him up to the surface, and no misfortune quickly strikes him, he should be judged innocent by reason of his oath.[25]

Here it appears that ordeals are actually conceived as a type of oath, where the person swears he or she is telling the truth and lets the gods determine by ordeal if what is said is true.

Other codes give us more detail on how ordeals were understood in ancient Indian legal thought. Here is how oaths and ordeals are distinguished in the Code of Narada:

> The king should administer ordeals in matters involving serious offenses; in minor matters, that best of men should make the accused swear an oath. These oaths indeed have been prescribed as effective in minor disputes, when violent crimes are involved, the rules for ordeals apply.[26]

This account in the late Code of Narada sets the ordeal as the means of proof of truth for violent criminal matters.

It is clear that the ordeals are thought to operate through some kind of religious intervention. Here is how the Code of Narada explains the working of the poison ordeal:

> If a king wishes to know the truth, he should administer to those accused of a major crime the *srnga* poison from the Himalayas, which has the proper aroma, color, and flavor, but not to children, the sick, or the elderly, nor to those accused of minor offenses …

[25] Ibid., 8.109–115, p. 173.

[26] *The Naradasmrti*, 20, 3–4, translated by Richard W. Lariviere, Delhi: Motilal Banarsidass Publishers, 2003, p. 447.

> An accused who has been approved in accordance with the preceding rule should touch brahmanas, fast, and then swallow the poison in the presence of the gods and brahmanas.
>
> If the poison is peacefully digested without paroxysms or languor, the king realizing that the accused is innocent, should treat him with respect and release him.
>
> "You O Poison, are the son of Brahman, grounded in the joy of the truth and righteousness, clear this man of sin and through truth become like ambrosia to him."[27]

Here the appeal to the poison ordeal seems literally to be an appeal to a god, the god of poison, to intercede and show the accused to be innocent. If the accused succeeds in the poison ordeal he is then to be regarded as innocent of the crime for which he had been charged.

In the ancient law of the Roman Republic the taking of an oath provides a disincentive to lying as we next see. It is somewhat unique that the way that the oath was understood in ancient Rome had an especially strong incentive associated with it. A. H. M. Jones describes the procedure as follows:

> Under the *lex Acilia* the first stage in an action was *nominis delatio* before the praetor, who forthwith exacted an oath against *calumnia* (that is that the accuser was not bringing a false charge) and assigned him advocates and made arrangements for empanelling a jury.[28]

Here is the actual text of that law which originally concerned private not public disputes:

The Denunciation of the Name of the Defendant and the Selection of Judices:

> Whoever in accordance with this law claims money from his adversary … subsequent to the selection of a panel of 450 judices for said year in accordance with this law, shall summon the defendant to court before the praetor who is created for said year in accordance with this law, and shall denounce him; and if he has taken solemn oath that he does not sue for malice (*calumnia*), the said praetor shall accept the denunciation …[29]

This oath against *calumnia* in effect authorized a counter-suit if the original suit had been brought with malice that meant that the one complaining in the original suit could then be sued for the same wrong.[30]

If *calumnia* was proven, showing that the original suit was brought with malice or as a matter of slander, the penalty could be what he who was convicted of calumny

27 *The Naradasmrti*, 20, 35–40, ibid., pp. 451–452.

28 Jones, *The Criminal Courts of the Roman Republic and Principate*, p. 63.

29 *Acilian Law on the Right to Recovery of Property Officially Extorted* (122 BCE), 10, in *Ancient Roman Statutes*, p. 40.

30 See Harries, *Law and Crime in the Roman World*, p. 41.

sought against the opposing party in the suit, or it could result in a public branding or loss of social status. The procedure was that if a party lost his suit, the court then had the obligation to investigate the intentions of this losing party. If the intentions were found to be wrongful then punishment or penalties were assessed against the calumnious party. Here we have a mixing of moral considerations in criminal procedure – if the initiator of a suit was judged to have acted badly in bringing suit, then that person's bad action could then be prosecuted.[31]

In ancient India, the sanction for untruthfulness was that one risked the wrath of the gods, whereas in ancient Rome the sanction was largely moral and social. In both cases the penalties seem to have been largely effective in preventing or minimizing parties from abusing the criminal justice system by lying or seeking revenge or advantage against one's perceived enemies.

30.5 THE MORAL AND POLITICAL AIMS OF ANCIENT CRIMINAL LAW

Ancient law in India and Rome singled out certain wrongs for special prosecution because those wrongs were seen as threats to the political or moral order. And the parties were restrained by what were often seen as a mixing of moral (or religious) motivations. In this last section I will explore more broadly the idea of ancient crime as growing out of political, moral, and religious concerns. The idea of requiring an examination of the intention of the parties seems to mark one of the most important links of criminal guilt with the character of the parties.

In many ancient societies, the idea of crime arose because certain wrongs were seen as threats to the security or stability of the state. The state was in effect the victim and that consideration preempted the claims of the individual person who was often also wronged and harmed. One can think of these wrongs to the state as either political or moral. Treason is an example of a crime that is understood as jeopardizing the political stability of the state. Adultery is an example of a crime that jeopardizes an essential moral institution, the family.

Once a domain of criminal law has been established there is then the question of penalties. In civil law, the state enters as arbiter and basically coerces restitution or reconciliation so as to return to a peaceful state. But in criminal law, something more seems to be needed as a response to the wrong. Yet in the absence of prisons and jails, and even of a police force, other remedies than incarceration were needed. In ancient India and the Roman Republic there was much use of capital punishment, but also and perhaps just as often corporal punishment, sometimes in the extreme as we will see in the next chapter.

[31] See Robinson, *The Criminal Law of Ancient Rome*, pp. 99–101.

In criminal procedure, the problem plaguing ancient societies is how to encourage cooperation and compliance with the justice system as well as how to discourage abuses of the criminal justice system of those who would lie or seek to manipulate that system for their own ends and to the detriment of their enemies or competitors. In addition there was the thought that the state should take a role in the remedial education of the members of the state whose bad character was working to the society's detriment. Here the problem is how to incentivize good character, especially aimed at getting people to act on good rather than bad motives.

Wrongs such as poisoning, and other secret harms, cause an especially difficult and pressing problem for ancient legal systems. With no formal investigative staffs or institutionalized detection mechanisms, the incentives against such behavior have to be very strong. Sometimes the state can rely on self-help remedies where the secret adulterer, for instance, is punished or killed by those who are most acquainted with the parties. But self-help is notoriously subject to abuse as we find today with vigilante justice.

Painting with a broad brush we can say that the ancient law of the Roman Republic seems more interested in political crimes and the ancient law of India seems more concerned with moral crimes. Perhaps this is due to the fact that ancient Indian law is deeply indebted to religious customs that are often moral as well, whereas ancient Roman law is increasingly secular in orientation. In addition, crimes such as treason had proved of great concern to various Roman political leaders and seemed of less concern to Indian political leaders.

What was of pressing concern for the stability of the state seems to have been what was designated as a crime in ancient societies. And the procedures that were developed to deal with crime seem to have been influenced by what were considered paradigmatic wrongs seen as crimes. In particular, we have seen that the idea of oaths is understood quite differently in more secular as opposed to more religious societies, perhaps reflecting the connection between secular wrong and crime versus religious wrong and crime. And yet, the ancient legal systems of India and the Roman Republic nonetheless resembled each other to a very great extent as well even though, in the most ancient times of these societies in any event, there is little evidence of cross cultural influence.

Because of these similarities of criminal procedure and remedy, even among otherwise very different societies, it is tempting to see some kind of wider or universal norm at play. Indeed, one can see similarities to the earliest Roman and Indian criminal law also in ancient China and Greece, and even in far earlier times in ancient Mesopotamia, as we saw in earlier parts of this work. I will not here hazard a strong claim about why these similarities exist except to point out that there is a common-sense central idea that the king or the state could be harmed in ways that are different from the way that one private party harms another private party.

Without evidence of direct influence from one ancient society to another, it may be that the rise of criminal law was due to a somewhat obvious recognition that the state could be harmed just as individual human persons could be harmed by the wrongful actions of other human persons. Perhaps there can be a link to something like human nature at this point in the explanation – and H. L. A. Hart's contemporary view about such a link in his seminal work *The Concept of Law*[32] can be cited to this effect, even from a theorist today who does not countenance much more than the thinnest of natural law components in his otherwise positivistic legal theory. Some moral rules provide a kind of common grounding for the legal rules of a society.

32 H. L. A. Hart, *The Concept of Law*, Oxford: Oxford University Press, 1961.

31

Punishment, Cruelty, and Humaneness

In the legal thought of the Roman Republic, especially in the works of Cicero and Seneca, punishment was criticized when it was cruel but praised when it was humane. In ancient India, punishment was often as cruel as in Rome but the debate was not about that but about what was appropriate punishment for the various classes. Roman legal theorists also debated the appropriate punishment for the various classes, especially between the *honestiores* as opposed to the *humiliores* (and slaves). In some respects this debate about class-differentiated punishment was about morality, but only some of the time. Members of the Senate in Rome, and members of the Brahmin class in India, were favored and harsh punishment for them was seen as wrong on several levels. But the need for deterrence seemed to override such considerations when discussing the non-privileged classes.

What is surprising, I will argue, is that there are several commonalities between ancient Rome and India, despite how different these societies were. In some respects the punishments seem to be less severe in the earliest recorded times than in later times in both societies. And in part this is because while the death penalty was often the punishment for many crimes, there was also the possibility of voluntarily going into exile instead of the death penalty in both ancient India and the Roman Republic. In both societies there is some condemnation of cruelty that one does not find as often in later times in these societies. In this chapter we will explore the rationales for various punishments and how cruelty was understood and condemned.

In Section 31.1 we will discuss the varieties of punishment in the law of the Roman Republic, especially considering the use of capital punishment. In Section 31.2 we will examine punishments in the law of ancient India, again focusing on capital punishment. In Section 31.3 we will discuss the sanctions of exile, banishment, and being an outcaste, employed in ancient Rome and India as alternatives to capital punishment. In Section 31.4 we pause to consider the most developed text on punishment in these ancient societies, the work of Seneca entitled *De Clementia* (*On*

Mercy). Finally, in Section 31.5, we will discuss the various ways that punishment can be seen as humane even as it may also be severe.

31.1 PUNISHMENT IN THE *TWELVE TABLES*

Several delicts and crimes listed in the *Twelve Tables* (451–449 BCE) set capital punishment as the penalty for various harms. Here are some examples:

> Table VIII. 1b ... If anyone sings or composes an incantation that can cause dishonor or disgrace to another ... shall suffer a capital penalty.
>
> (9) If anyone pastures on or cuts by night another's crops obtained by cultivation, the penalty for an adult shall be capital punishment.
>
> (10) Whoever destroys by burning a building or a stack of grain placed beside a house... shall be bound, scourged, and burned to death, provided that knowingly and consciously he has committed this crime.
>
> Table IX. 3. A judex or an arbiter legally appointed who has been convicted of receiving money for declaring a decision shall be punished capitally.
>
> (5) ... Whoever incites a public enemy or whoever betrays a citizen to a public enemy shall be punished capitally.[1]

Here we see a wide variety of capital offenses ranging from treason to causing disgrace by singing.

Another crime that was severely punished involved "whoever walked around with a weapon for the purpose of killing someone" but who did not in fact kill anyone. This law was part of Sulla's *Lex Cornelia de Sicariis*. Here as Cicero pointed out, the intention to kill was sufficient for the conviction and punishment.[2] But there was also a fair amount of arbitrariness, despite the emphasis on humaneness. Theodor Mommsen reports that a person was spared execution if on the way to be executed the felon accidentally met one of the sacred virgins of Vesta.[3] All of this is in keeping with what seems to be the fact that in the Roman Republic despite the declaration of many execution sentences, there were very few actual executions.

There is also evidence that despite retaining the death penalty in the late Roman Republic the principle of humanity was employed by Cicero and Sallust to argue for less extreme methods of execution than "being decapitated, beaten to death, drowned in a sack, hurled from the Tarpeian Rock, burnt alive, or thrown to wild animals."[4] By

1 *Ancient Roman Statutes*, translated by Allan Chester Johnson, Paul Robinson Coleman-Norton, and Frank Card Bourne, Austin: University of Texas Press, 1961, 2012, pp. 11–12.

2 See Richard A. Bauman, *Crime and Punishment in Ancient Rome*, NY: Routledge, 1996, p. 39.

3 Theodor Mommsen, *The History of Rome*, Oxford: Benediction Classics, 2001, p. 80.

4 Bauman, *Crime and Punishment in Ancient Rome*, p. 18.

the late Roman Republic, these means of execution were disappearing as was the use of capital punishment in general. The most common execution, simple strangulation, was by no means the most severe punishment in the ancient Roman Republic, at least in terms of suffering physical and mental pain. One of the most dreaded was being "whipped with scourges" (Table VIII.14). Another kind of punishment that was much feared that did not always result in death was the sack, which involved being sewn up in a sack while still alive and in the company of a snake or a monkey. The sack was then thrown into the river. The use of torture does not seem to be much used in the Roman Republic at least not as compared to the later Roman Empire period.

An unplaced fragment of the *Twelve Tables* provides this summary: "Eight kinds of penalties are in the laws: fines, shackles, flogging, retaliation in kind, ignominy, exile, death, slavery."[5] In the Roman Republic, capital punishment could not be assigned unless there was a trial – as the *Twelve Tables* declared in Table IX: "For anyone whomsoever to be put to death without a trial and unconvicted … is forbidden."[6] And it seems that the death penalty was not often carried out even if it had been assigned at trial. As we will see, there were alternatives to death such as exile that could be chosen in the Roman Republic – but this option seems to have been phased out in the period of the Roman Empire.

There are various rulers who made attempts to make the laws more humane than those in the *Twelve Tables*, such as the reforms of Sulla during the first century BCE. Specifically, the penalty for adultery was changed so that both partners were held to be liable and punished. Although there were such reforms, there was also a mass execution of hundreds of people, male and female, convicted in the Bacchanalian rite scandal. And there was a Senate Decree of 186 BCE making association with the Bacchanalian cult "a capital offense."[7] Yet, by the middle of the Roman Republic period, scourging and execution of Roman citizens was by and large put to an end.[8]

31.2 PUNISHMENT IN THE *CODE OF MANU* IN ANCIENT INDIA

In Chapter 8 of the *Code of Manu*, we are told of the way that corporal punishment is to be inflicted:

> Manu, the son of the Self-existent One, has proclaimed ten places upon which punishment may be inflicted. They are applicable to the three classes; a Brahmin

5 *Ancient Roman Statutes*, p. 13.

6 Ibid., p. 12.

7 *Decree of the Senate on the Bacchanalia* (186 BCE), in *Ancient Roman Statutes*, pp. 26–27.

8 See Wilfried Nippel, *Public Order in Ancient Rome*, Cambridge: Cambridge University Press, 1995, p. 6.

> shall depart unscathed. They are: genitals, stomach, tongue, and hands; feet are the fifth; and then, eyes, nose, ears, wealth, and body. He should inflict punishment on those deserving punishment only after he has fully ascertained the proclivity, as also the time and place, accurately, and considered carefully the ability of the criminal and the severity of the crime. Unjust punishment shatters his fame and destroys his reputation in this world, and it is also an obstacle to heaven in the next; therefore, he should avoid it completely. When a king punishes those who do not deserve to be punished and neglects to punish those who deserve, he brings great infamy upon himself and he will also go to hell. He should employ first the punishment of verbal reprimand; next a public denunciation; third a fine; and finally corporal punishment, then he shall impose on them all these four.[9]

Manu's Code is relatively fair and proportionate in its punishments. And as we will see in the next chapter even some of the harsher penalties of capital punishment are moderated by the possibility of banishment instead.

Yet, there are many crimes that are said to deserve the death penalty. Here is some of what is said in Chapter 9 of Manu's Code:

> A righteous king must never execute a thief unless he is caught with the stolen goods; if he is caught with the stolen goods and the tools of his trade, the king should execute him without hesitation. He should also execute every individual in the village who gives food, implements, or shelter to thieves … Those who rob the king's treasury, those who act contrary to his interests, and those who conspire with his enemies – he should inflict diverse kinds of capital punishment on them.[10]

In general though, the actual punishments or penalties inflicted will vary based on the class of the perpetrator. The lower the class is, the greater the punishment or penalty. But there are some exceptions such as when the king himself has violated the law. Here is a particularly interesting law from Manu's Code:

> A king should never fail to punish even his father, teacher, friend, mother, wife, son, or personal priest when they deviate from the Law proper to them. In a case where an ordinary person is fined 1 Karsapana, the king should be fined 1,000 – this is the fixed rule. With respect to theft, the liability of the Sudra is eight times, for a Vaisya, sixteen times; for a Ksatriya, thirty-two times; and for a Brahmin, sixty-four times, or fully 100 times, or twice sixty-four times; for he knows whether it is good or bad.[11]

Normal the penalties are harsher for the lower classes than the upper classes – but here that is reversed. At least one explanation, offered by Washburn is this:

9 *Manu's Code of Law*, 8.124–130, translated by Patrick Olivelle, Oxford: Oxford University Press, 2005, pp. 173–174.

10 Ibid., 9.270–275, p. 204.

11 Ibid., 8.335–338, p. 185.

> In one particular, however, the rule of increased fines is reversed, for in any case where a common man would be fined one penny (karshapana) the king is fined one thousand (Manu, VIII, 336) probably on the principle that he who knows more should suffer more.[12]

Yet one would think that this principle should apply to many other types of crime, but it does not.

There is another reference in Manu's Code that is stark by comparison with other passages we will examine where alternatives to strict punishment are countenanced. Here is the troubling passage: "A king incurs as great a sin in releasing someone who ought to be executed as by executing someone who ought not to be executed."[13] It seems that what is called for is strict adherence to the terms of the law, yet we will also see that mercy is also prized in other contexts.

It is interesting that some punishments in ancient India result in loss of class status – the perpetrator becomes an "outcaste" due to engaging in grievous wrongs. Here is the relevant passage in the Code of Manu:

> A murderer of a Brahmin, a man who drinks liquor, a thief, and a man who has sex with an elder's wife – all these men should be considered individually as guilty of a grievous sin causing loss of caste ... These wretched men – with whom one is not permitted to eat, to participate at a sacrifice, to recite the Veda, or to contract marriages – shall roam the earth, excluded from all activities relating to the law. Branded with marks, they shall be forsaken by their paternal and maternal relations; they should be shown no compassion and paid no reverence ... If they do perform the required penance, on the other hand, the king should not brand the higher classes on the forehead, but make them pay the highest fine ... When others commit these sins, however, they deserve to have all their property confiscated, if they did them thoughtlessly, or to be executed, if they did them willfully.[14]

This passage is hard to interpret. It seems to say that loss of class status is a kind of substitute for paying fines and even for execution. And loss of one's class status is described as having lost all status with respect to law and having to roam the earth without familial support. We will next examine banishment and outcasting in more detail in relation to the Roman practice of exiling as a substitute for capital punishment.

12 E. Washburn Hopkins, "The Growth of Law and Legal Institutions," in *The Cambridge History of India, Vol. I: Ancient India*, edited by E. J. Rapson, Cambridge: Cambridge University Press, 1922, p. 285.

13 *Manu's Code of Law*, 9. 249, p. 203.

14 Ibid., 9.235–242, p. 202.

31.3 EXILE, BANISHMENT, AND OUTCASTING AS ALTERNATIVES TO CAPITAL PUNISHMENT

It is striking that in two ancient societies normally thought to be so different they would both have supported the idea of exile (whether voluntary or not) as an alternative to the death penalty. Here are two Roman authors on exile:

> Polybius (2nd century BCE): Only the people have the right to confer office or to inflict punishment, the two bonds that hold society together. The people have a notable custom. When those who are tried capitally are found guilty they are given the opportunity to depart openly, thus sentencing themselves to voluntary exile.[15]
>
> Cicero (1st century BCE): Exile is not a capital punishment; it is an escape from punishment. In no *lex* of ours is exile a punishment for a crime. Those who would avoid imprisonment, death or disgrace (*ignomia*) seek refuge in exile as if at a sanctuary ... when they go into exile they do not lose their citizenship by law; they are stripped of it by their own act of abandonment.[16]

There were no laws that stipulated this right of exile until the time of Sulla; rather the right was customary but probably extended back quite far into the early history of Rome.[17]

O. F. Robinson tells us how the idea of exile came to be understood in the later Roman period:

> One significant difference between the Republic and the Empire was the disappearance of the practice of "voluntary" exile and the interdiction from fire and water. It was replaced by the more formal penalty of deportation, always permanent, with loss of citizenship and civil rights. Provincial governors did not have the power to deport. A milder form of exile was relegation, with retention of civil rights, even if the sentence was in perpetuity.[18]

There is evidence that exile was understood as making oneself an outlaw. In some respects becoming an outlaw shares features in common with the ancient Indian practice of making someone an outcaste.

In ancient India, certain people could save themselves from the death penalty by becoming outcastes, that is by losing their class status (and corresponding rights) and being banned from society. Hopkins summarizes the point nicely:

[15] Polybius, 6.14.4–8 adapted. Translations of this passage and the next one are by Bauman, *Crime and Punishment in Ancient Rome*, p. 14.

[16] Cicero, *Pro Caecino*, 100, translated in ibid.,.p. 14.

[17] See ibid., p. 16.

[18] O. F. Robinson, *Penal Practice and Penal Policy in Ancient Rome*, NY: Routledge, 2007, p. 81.

> Treason of all kinds is punishable by death, whether it consists in attacking the king or falsifying an edict or bribing the ministers of the king or helping his foes. Instead of other penalties, the guilty man, especially a priest, may be outcasted, that is, formally thrown or banned from society, for in losing his caste he loses all his social rights.[19]

Being removed from one's class was less severe than other penalties such as death.

Here is how the Code of Manu addresses crimes committed by Brahmins, who were not to be subjected to capital punishment:

> Shaving the head is prescribed as the death penalty for Brahmins; but the other social classes are actually subject to the death penalty. The king should never put a Brahmin to death, even if he has committed every sort of crime; he should banish such a Brahmin from his kingdom along with all his property, without causing him hurt.[20]

And there is evidence that even though conviction for adultery carries the death penalty, the normal penalty was monetary.

Banishment or outcasting functions somewhat differently in ancient India than exile does in ancient Rome. There were classes and sometimes strong class differences as we can see from the war of the orders in Rome as the plebeians clashed with the patricians. But soon thereafter there was not so firm a class division as there was before, and in some respects still is, in India concerning the class system. The class system defined the privileges, rights, and duties of the members of ancient Indian society based on which class one was born into. Being outcaste from ancient India was in many ways different, and also worse, than being exiled from Rome.

In Rome, it seems that a person sentenced to death could choose to go into exile and such a choice would be recognized as valid. In this respect the comparison of death with exile is made subjectively and there are no special worries about whether one of these punishments is worse than the other. The humaneness comes from the option rather than from the exiling itself. In India, since apparently the person sentenced did not have a choice between death and banishment or outcasting, we are still left with the question of whether or not it was humane to choose for the convicted person which of these punishments he should suffer.

In India, perhaps the humaneness of law, insofar as the laws were humane, comes from the fact that despite there being many crimes that were subject to the death penalty, in the end death sentences were not often meted out. Again, though, banishment or outcasting are only humane if we think that these alternatives are somehow more humane than the death sentence. And it seems to me not always clear-cut that

19 Washburn Hopkins, "The Growth of Law and Legal Institutions," p. 284.

20 *Manu's Code of Law*, 8.379–380, p. 187.

banishment or outcasting is indeed more humane than capital punishment, especially in the deeply and morally stratified ancient Indian society.

There are alternative explanations for why in ancient India and Rome there were alternatives to capital punishment. One possibility is that having too many people subject to the death penalty destabilized the control over the society by the king. Indeed, Seneca, whose work we examine more fully in the next section, suggests that just as it is not good for physicians to have too many deaths associated with them, so this is also true of rulers: "Numerous executions are not less discreditable to a prince than are numerous funerals to a physician."[21]

Another possible explanation, also somewhat suggested by Seneca, is that the exercise of severe and even cruel punishments can inflate the ego of the ruler, playing on the basest instincts of those who crave adulation and power. Yet, the ruler who acts in this way will not be long remembered beyond the possible immediate gratification of striking a blow at one's opponents, for instance. The ruler who is cruel is no better than a tyrant.

Even if there are no good explanations for why ancient India and Rome allowed alternatives to the death penalty that involved people being excluded from society, it is nonetheless fascinating that these two societies would have come to this same result. There is a possible common influence here, namely ancient Greece, which certainly had literature on the idea of exile or banishment – we can think of the Oedipus saga in this respect. After Oedipus learns that he is both the murderer of his father and the husband of his mother, he subjects himself to ostracism in that he wanders the earth thereafter. The Romans are well known for mimicking the Greeks in many respects; and India was likewise influenced but not until the conquest of Alexander the Great. In all three societies ideas of pollution also are often related to the idea that exile can be less problematic than execution of a criminal. This is all highly speculative, but may possibly explain some of these common ideas.

31.4 A FEW WORDS FROM SENECA

The most significant writing on punishment just after the end of the Roman Republic was by the Roman Stoic philosopher and politician, Seneca. In many ways, I believe Seneca's views reflect the earlier Roman Republican attitudes toward punishment and so examining some of his writings, especially his *De Clementia* (*On Mercy*), will give us some of the flavor of at least one of the most important thinkers in Rome. We should also note that Seneca also had a strong influence on one of the early Roman emperors, Nero.

[21] Seneca, *De Clementia*, Book I. xxiv. 2, in *Seneca: Moral Essays I*, translated by John W. Basore, Cambridge, MA: Harvard University Press' Loeb Classical Library, 1928, p. 423.

Cicero begins his discourse on mercy by explaining what his method is and how he thinks Nero should similarly approach the subject of punishment:

> I have undertaken, Nero Caesar, to write on the subject of mercy, in order to serve in a way the purpose of a mirror, and thus to reveal you to yourself as one destined to attain the greatest of all pleasures … it is a pleasure to subject a good conscience to a round of inspection … and finally to commune with oneself.[22]

Seneca then explains what he thinks conscience should tell a ruler about the proper attitude toward punishment:

> I have been moved neither by anger nor youthful impulse to unjust punishment … With me the sword is hidden, nay, sheathed; I am sparing to the utmost of even the meanest blood; no man fails to find favor at my hands though he lack all else but the name of man. Sternness I keep hidden, but mercy ever ready at hand. I so hold guard over myself as though I were about to render an account to those laws which I have summoned from decay and darkness into the light of day.[23]

Here we have the Stoic position on punishment eloquently displayed – the ruler should be slow to be moved by emotions to inflict severe punishment. The laws should be applied not with sternness but with an outlook ready to extend mercy to a fellow human who has happened to run afoul of the law.

Seneca goes on to explain to Emperor Nero that he has taken upon himself a "mighty burden" in that he should not let himself be moved by the emotions that would affect normal citizens of Rome: "For great power confers grace and glory only when it is potent for benefit."[24] And in the end since the ruler is the "soul of the state" the ruler is merciful to himself when he is "merciful to another."[25]

Seneca then makes an argument for what should be the character of the virtuous ruler that surely resonates today as well:

> no one will venture to gainsay, nay, even to entreat – that this man should lay a restraining hand upon himself, and use his power to better and more peaceful ends when he reflects, "Any one can violate the law to kill, none but I to save"? A lofty spirit befits a lofty station … Cruel and inexorable anger is not seemly for a king, for thus he does not rise much above the other man, toward whose own level he descends by being angry with him. But if he grants life, if he grants position to those who have imperiled and deserve to lose them, he does what none but a sovereign may.[26]

[22] Seneca, *De Clementia*, Book I.i.1, ibid., p. 357.
[23] Seneca *De Clementia*, Book I.i.3–4, ibid., p. 359.
[24] Seneca, *De Clementia*, Book I.ii.3, ibid., p. 365.
[25] Seneca, *De Clementia*, Book I.v.1, ibid., p. 371.
[26] Seneca, *De Clementia*, Book I.v.5–6, ibid., p. 373.

Here is Seneca at his most morally persuasive as he extols Nero to act as only a ruler can act in sparing the lives of those who break the law.

And Seneca also has an argument that bolsters the moral argument now by reference to prudence.

> Consider, too, that whereas private citizens, by enduring the wrongs already received, lie more open to receiving others, yet kings by clemency gain a security more assured, because repeated punishment, while it crushes the hatred of a few, stirs the hatred of all. The inclination to vent one's rage should be less strong than the provocation for it.[27]

Seneca follows these arguments with the conclusion that "Mercy makes rulers not only more honored, but safer, and is at the same time the glory of sovereign power and its surest protection."[28] Indeed, "it is mercy that makes the distinction between a king and a tyrant as great as it is."[29] Seneca then postulates the rule for kings: "No one resorts to the exaction of punishment until he has exhausted all other means of correction. This is the duty of a father, and it is also the duty of a prince."[30]

Finally, let us note that Seneca links mercy and lack of cruelty in punishing to the idea of equity, which we explored already in Chapter 27 and with slavery that we explored in Chapter 28.

> It is praiseworthy to use authority over slaves with moderation. Even in the case of human chattel you should consider not how much he can be made to suffer without retaliating, but how much you are permitted to inflict by the principles of equity and right, which require that mercy must be shown even to captives and purchased slaves. With how much more justice do they require that free, free-born, and reputable men should not be treated as mere chattel ... Even slaves have the right to refuge at the statue of a god, and although the law allows anything in dealing with a slave, yet in dealing with a human being there is an extreme which the right common to all living creatures refuses to allow.[31]

This passage, and others like it, have led to the interpretation that Seneca's position against cruelty in punishment is linked to a notion not only of equity but also of human rights. And Seneca also links mercy to what he calls humanity.[32]

27 Seneca, *De Clementia*, Book I, viii, 6–7, ibid., p. 381.
28 Seneca, *De Clementia*, Book I, xi, 4, ibid., p. 391.
29 Seneca, *De Clementia*, Book I, xii. 3, ibid., p. 393.
30 Seneca, *De Clementia*, Book I, xiii. 1–2, ibid., p. 399.
31 Seneca, *De Clementia*, Book I, xviii. 1–2, ibid., pp. 407–409.
32 Seneca, *De Clementia*, Book II, iv. 3, ibid., p. 439.

31.5 THINKING ABOUT PUNISHMENT HUMANELY

Due to the influence of utilitarians writing in the late eighteenth and early nineteenth centuries CE, it is now widely accepted that the death penalty can be administered more and also less humanely – and that some forms of the death penalty can be seen as a form of humane punishment at least as compared to the alternatives. What is fascinating about the ancient legal texts we have just examined is that apparently such things as exile and outcasting were seen as better, and perhaps more humane, than the death penalty.

It does not appear, for ancient Roman and Indian legal thought, that physical suffering is the key consideration in determining which form of penalty or punishment is more humane. Death itself is what seems to be the punishment to be avoided – indeed Brahmins are never to be executed in ancient India because of their high status. Yet, it is surprising that exile or banishment would be seen to be preferable to death, since in these ancient societies being cut off from one's relatives and from the rights and privileges of social position would be a kind of "social death," to use a term that Orlando Patterson has used to describe the status of slaves especially in the nineteenth century CE in the US. Losing one's rights made a person not any longer citizen or subject or even a bearer of respect. It seems that that would be worse than being physically dead, or at least not as much better than being dead in these ancient times.

Cruelty in punishment is on display in various ancient societies including ancient India and the Roman Republic. Indeed, some commentators think that cruelty is the best way to describe ancient punishment schemes in general. And there are no shortage of laws such as those of India that call for severing of the penis of men who commit adultery or the cutting out of tongues of those who insult their rulers or even just their social betters. And as we have seen, in the Roman Republic the sack was one of the most horrible and most feared of punishments as was the prospect of being thrown off a high peak into a river. And we have Manu explaining that cruel punishments can be warranted:

> He should locate all prisons along the royal highway where people will see the criminal, grieving and mutilated …
>
> A goldsmith who operates dishonestly, however, is the most wicked of all thorns, and the king should have him cut to pieces with razor knives.[33]

And the rationale for such severe punishment is that "the king should hold his subjects in his grip."[34] Here deterrence is the rationale for even the cruelest of punishments.

[33] *Manu's Code of Law*, 9.288–292, p. 205.

[34] Ibid., 9.307, p. 205.

And yet in these ancient societies, there is also the clear call for proportionality and fairness in the way that punishment is meted out. We have both moral and pragmatic reasons mixed together as rationales against cruelty or overly-cruel punishments, just as we saw in Seneca's *De Clementia*. Indeed it is a misunderstanding of cruelty if it is merely portrayed in terms of severity. Cruelty is better understood as severity that has no rationale for its use except perhaps the pleasure that the one inflicting the punishment feels. In approaching this subject it is also important to think more about the deterrence rationale often mentioned in ancient legal texts such as the ones we have seen.

One rationale for severe punishment that deters is that it is for the overall good of the society, since the population at large is made less fearful of the deterred criminal conduct. Here again is Manu:

> By protecting those who follow the Arya way of life and by clearing the thorns [criminal harms], kings devoted to the protection of their subjects reach the highest heaven ... After publicizing accurately the crimes they have committed in their respective activities, the king should duly punish them, each in proportion to his capacity and his crime. For without punishment, it is impossible to suppress the crimes of evil minded thieves who prowl the land in secret.[35]

Protection and security are two of the chief goals of any ruler and the proper use of punishment, even severe punishment, can be seen as consistent with such goals.

Humane punishment must be understood in terms both of the person punished and the society that has been disrupted and rendered insecure by the actions of the one who is now to be subjected to punishment. Humane punishment, understood in ancient legal thought, takes into account the type of act committed, the character of the one who commits the act, the respect due to all members of the society, and the importance of protecting the community. Truly cruel punishment does not satisfy these conditions because it exceeds what is needed for such protection – the punishment is excessive in terms of what deterrence or retribution calls for.

Seneca is not opposed to severe punishment for deterrence sake. Here we could mention two of his arguments. First, and perhaps most importantly (and reflecting the sentiment at the time) Seneca distinguishes mercy from pity. Mercy is related to equity and fairness but does not go beyond what equity would call for. Pity calls for being swayed by emotions not to do what should be done – such as use severe punishment when deterrence warrants it. Second, Seneca advises Nero that he should not appear to be so sympathetic to the plight of criminals that he is perceived as not taking seriously that rulers should protect their population. So, for both of these reasons Seneca's view of mercy is not inconsistent with some severe

[35] Ibid., 9.252–263, p. 203.

punishments, and indeed such punishments would also be consistent with his principle of humanity along with the idea of humaneness and human rights.

Cruelty is inconsistent with the principle of humanity because it treats human beings as not deserving of respect since there are no morally or pragmatically good reasons to engage in excessive severity of punishment. We saw this in the ancient discussion of the methods used in capital punishment. Extreme fear and pain could be employed in the way a person was executed. But humaneness called for the use of methods that, while still killing the convicted criminal, did not cause excessive suffering.

Nonetheless there was apparently a consensus in the Roman Republic that even extreme forms of punishment could be justified if it seemed necessary as a deterrent. In ancient India, restraint in punishment was also prized, except in those cases where the stability or social order of the state was threatened. Even without a well-articulated principle of humanity, ancient Indian legal thought seems to have come to much the same conclusion as that of the Roman Republic. Rulers were wise not to use excessive punishment methods, because these methods could cause a backlash among the populace and speak to the weakness of character of the ruler. But if the ruler could make a case for the need to use such methods for countering various threats to the state then the people would not only accept but also often demand extreme methods of punishment. In some respects this position mirrors that today.

32

Crimes Concerning Political and Legal Abuse

In both ancient Rome and India, various crimes were established to protect the political and legal processes from abuse. This was not unique, since Hammurabi's Code began with this law:

> LH 1. If a man accuses another man and charges him with homicide but cannot bring poof against him, his accuser shall be killed.[1]

And we have already seen there is a very similar law in the ancient Roman Republic where calumnia could be charged if a lawsuit was deemed frivolous or deceitful. In this chapter we will examine particular laws of the Roman Republic and ancient India that seem to be similarly directed at protecting the political process. Indeed, I will argue that protecting the political and legal processes was probably as important as protecting the citizenry from one another.

We will begin with an examination of various sections of Manu's Code that are best understood as using the criminal law to protect political and legal processes. Then in Section 32.2 we will look at the laws concerning *majestas* and *ambitus* in ancient Rome, crimes that protected Rome from unscrupulous attacks. In Section 32.3 we then examine particular Roman penalties that are connected to the protection of process such as *infamia* as well as *calumnia*, now seen in a somewhat different light from earlier in our work. In Section 32.4 we return to some considerations about laws that sanctioned the killing or removal of political leaders in both ancient India and Rome. And then in Section 32.5 we will try to explain what the impetus was in ancient legal thought for these laws protecting political and legal processes.

[1] *Law Collections from Mesopotamia and Asia Minor*, second edition, translated by Martha Roth, Atlanta, GA: Scholars' Press, 1997, p. 81.

32.1 ANCIENT INDIA'S PROTECTIONS OF POLITICAL AND LEGAL PROCESS

Several key provisions in Manu's Code of Law can be cited to show that abuse of legal and political process was seen as requiring a response in terms of punishment. Here are two examples:

> Manu. 9.273. When a man who gains his livelihood by the Law deviates from the conventions of the Law, the king should make him also suffer a punishment, for he has deviated from the Law specific to him.
>
> Manu. 9. 275. Those who rob the king's treasury, those who act contrary to his interests, and those who conspire with his enemies – he should inflict diverse kinds of capital punishment on him.[2]

Here we have laws directed at those who have been entrusted to serve the public interest or who try to act contrary to that interest, who are dealt with according to the criminal law of ancient India.

Manu's Code also has specific crimes connected to abuse of the political process, such as this one:

> Manu. 9.258. Bribe-takers, frauds, cheats, gamblers, those who live by adjuring good luck, fortune-tellers, high officials and physicians who act crookedly, those engaged in exhibiting their artistic skills, skilled prostitutes – people such as these should be recognized as open thorns on his people's side … After publicizing accurately the crimes they have committed in their respective activities, the king should duly punish them, each in proportion to his capacity and his crime.[3]

Manu followed earlier codes in regarding certain crimes as thorns in need of eradication. And the kind of acts here mentioned are ones that can be committed by high officials and are in need of specific punishments.

We also have sections of Manu's Code that concern the misdeeds of the ruler himself, which are punishable as well – sometimes quite harshly. Here are two more of Manu's laws:

> Manu. 7.26. The proper administration of Punishment, they say, is a king who speaks the truth, acts after careful examination, is wise, and has a masterly grasp of Law, Wealth, and Pleasure. When a king administers Punishment properly, he flourishes with respect to the triple set; but the king who is lustful, partial, and vile is slain by that very Punishment. For Punishment is immense energy, and it cannot

[2] *Manu's Code of Law*, 9.273–275, translated by Patrick Olivelle, Oxford: Oxford University Press, 2005, p. 204.

[3] Ibid., 9.258–262, p. 203.

> be wielded by those with uncultivated selves. It assuredly slays a king who deviates from the Law, along with his relatives ...[4]

Here we find that even the king is subject to the law and to its harshest punishments if he abuses his power, especially the power to punish. Indeed, the king's ministers are also subject to severe punishment as we see here:

> Manu. 8.12. When Justice (dharma), pierced by Injustice (adharma), comes to the court for redress and the court officials do not pluck out that dart from him, then they are themselves pierced by it ... When Justice is struck by Injustice, and Truth by Untruth, while the court officials remain idle onlookers, then they are themselves struck down.[5]

We have here a series of laws and corresponding punishments aimed at those who jeopardize the political or legal process, extending even to the king himself. And this is true even though the king is also "a great deity who stands here in human form."[6]

In the later text, the *Narada*, we find an elaborate set of rules for court proceedings. Among these rules are the following in the introductory section called Matrka:

> 1.57. If a legal proceeding is improperly heard, the judges should incur the penalty, for no one keeps to the straight and narrow without the threat of punishment.
>
> 1.58. A judge who would give an incorrect verdict out of passion, ignorance, or greed, is not worthy of the office, and the king should punish him harshly.[7]
>
> 3.2. If a judge speaks appropriately, he incurs neither hatred nor sin; but if he speaks otherwise he incurs both.
>
> 3.8. When righteousness is wounded by unrighteousness in the court, then the members of the court are also wounded unless they remove those thorns.[8]

These laws are aimed at protecting the integrity of the judicial process by holding judges to account if the legal proceeding is tainted in some fashion or other.

We also find in the *Narada* various laws that assign punishments to the king himself if he has not followed the proper procedures or is in some way complicit in crime.

> 14.26. If the thieves are not caught, the king should compensate for it out of his own treasury; for a king who fails in this is a sinner whose righteousness and fortunes are lost.[9]

4 Ibid., 7.26–28, p. 155.

5 Ibid., 8.12–14, p. 167.

6 Ibid., 7.8, p. 154.

7 *The Naradasmrti*, translated by Richard W. Lariviere, Delhi: Motilal Banarsidass Publishers, 2003, pp. 266–267.

8 Ibid., pp. 269–270.

9 Ibid., p. 416.

19.47. A king incurs as much unrighteousness in releasing a guilty man as in injuring an innocent one. There is righteousness in exacting punishment.[10]

We see here that the defense of political and legal process is very well established and it seems that the integrity of those processes is put above the respect for the king – which is itself a rule of law statement from ancient India.

32.2 THE ROMAN CRIMES OF *MAJESTAS* AND *AMBITUS*

In the ancient Roman Republic there are also various criminal penalties for those who jeopardize the political or legal processes. And while these are described in greater detail than in ancient India, the underlying ideas seem very similar indeed. In this section we will examine two crimes that are aimed at protecting processes. One of the earliest Roman laws concerning process is the following law attributed to Numa Pompilius (716–673 BCE):

5. Legislation about the boundaries of landed property: Having ordered each one to draw a line around his own landed property and to set stones on the boundaries, he consecrated the stones to Jupiter Terminus … but he ordained by law that if anyone destroyed or displaced the boundaries the person who had done this should be dedicated as a sacrifice to the god.[11]

Destroying or displacing boundary stones could be seen as a kind of theft but it is better seen as a process violation since the moving of the boundary stones could adversely affect the process of determining ownership.

Like the ancient Indian *Code of Manu*, the *Twelve Tables* also have several laws aimed at punishing those who abuse the political or legal process. Here are three:

VIII. 21. If a patron defrauds a client he shall be accursed.

22. Unless he speaks his testimony, whoever allows himself to be called as a witness or is a scales-bearer, shall be dishonored and incompetent to give or obtain testimony.

23. … Whoever is convicted of speaking false witness shall be flung from the Tarpeian Rocks.[12]

These early Roman laws provide the beginnings of the idea that no one in an official capacity should engage in deception that undermines a legal process, and that if one does then strong punishment is assigned, similar to ancient Indian codes.

10 Ibid., p. 441.

11 *Ancient Roman Statutes*, translated by Allan Chester Johnson, Paul Robinson Coleman-Norton, and Frank Card Bourne, Austin: University of Texas Press, 1961, 2012, p. 4.

12 Ibid., p. 12.

Concerning *ambitus*, the illegal interference with the electoral process, Richard Bauman tells us:

> When the lawgiver was free to choose between civil disabilities (*infamia*), fines (*multae*) and temporary expulsions (*relegatio*), the scope for experimentation was very wide. The potential is illustrated by the legislation on electoral corruption (*ambitus*) in the first century BCE. Enactments from 67–52 BCE covered a whole range of penalties. Sulla created a *quaestio perpetua* for *ambitus*; the penalty was that offenders were disqualified from again standing for office for ten years. In 67 the tribune C. Cornelius proposed an *ambitus* law with severe penalties.

And Cicero in 63 BCE "made exile the definitive penalty for *ambitus*."[13] *Ambitus* is the quintessential process crime and it is no wonder that over time the penalties for this crime increased substantially.

Another crime of the Roman Republic that had often to do with process, when it was not being abused, was the crime of *majestas* – diminishing or dishonoring the greatness of the Roman people. This crime became synonymous with treason of various forms, but initially this crime was applied against those who demeaned Roman crowds as "rabble." Yet the most often application was for those who instigated the myriad conspiracies that engulfed the end of the Roman Republic. The conspiracies were aimed at overturning the legitimate political and legal authority, and in that sense aimed at process.

The Roman Republican period lacked kings or other autocratic rulers of this sort and this was because of concerns about abuse of political and legal processes. And in addition, the rulers of the Roman Republic were held to very high standards. We can see this in many ways, especially in the fact that the ruler was allowed only to hold office for one year and had to share that office with another person. Also, we find laws aimed at possible abuse of office that was often assimilated to the crime of *majestas*. The rulers as well as normal citizens could be accused and convicted of majestas if their acts threatened the Republic. In some cases this meant that the rulers were said to diminish the greatness of the Roman Republic when they sought to hold too much power thus usurping the right of the people to be the ones ultimately that ruled Rome. Julius Caesar was accused of just such a usurpation and he was killed as a result. And Cicero was similarly thought to gain too much power causing him to be killed as well.

32.3 *INFAMIA* AND *CALUMNIA*

In an earlier chapter we discussed *calumnia* as a way to diminish the likelihood of frivolous lawsuits. But there is also a sense that *calumnia* and *infamia* were used as

[13] Richard A. Bauman, *Crime and Punishment in Ancient Rome*, NY: Routledge, 1996, pp. 29 and 48.

punishments for those who abused the political or legal process of Rome. *Ambitus* and *majestas* were crimes that were perpetrated through the abuse of the judicial system. One way to deter such abuse was through *calumnia* – the fraudulent accusers were themselves subject to the same charge that they fraudulently brought against others. In fact there was a sense that *calumnia* was really a crime rather than a punishment – *calumnia* was the crime of malicious or frivolous prosecution, and the punishment was a form of *infamia*, whereby the malicious prosecutor lost his right to bring prosecutions or to appear in court for either a fixed period of time or for the rest of his life.[14]

Calumnia can be considered as a crime, the crime of malicious prosecution, or as a punishment, where the prosecutor was subject to be tried for the crime he had maliciously been prosecuting. In either case, *calumnia* was aimed at abuse of legal process. Losing one's right to prosecute or to appear in court does not sound like a serious penalty but it surely was if the person subject to the penalty made his living by bringing legal actions. There is often a close connection between *calumnia* and *infamia* as we next see.

Infamia was a punishment or penalty that involved the loss of one's reputation or status affecting one's legal or political rights. There was a wide variety of uses of *infamia*, similar to the wide scope of the crime of *majestas* in the Roman Republic. We will sketch some of these uses of *infamia* before turning to what were some similar although less complicated ideas in ancient India.

Infamia is first mentioned conceptually in the *Twelve Tables* concerning when dishonor attaches:

> Table VIII.22. Unless he speaks his testimony whoever allows himself to be called as a witness or as a scales-bearer shall be dishonored (*infamia*) and incompetent to give or obtain testimony.[15]

Here the law is that certain people are dishonored because of their wrongful conduct, in this case as a procedural matter, and lose their right to give or obtain testimony in a court of law. Another early reference to *infamia* comes in the *Ancilian Law on the Right of Recovery of Property Officially Extorted* from 122 BCE:

> 4. Whoever seeks restitution in accordance with this law … the praetor … shall grant to said plaintiff … provided that he … no person … who has been condemned by the judicial process and a public trial whereby he cannot be enrolled in the Senate.

[14] See A. H. J. Greenidge, *The Legal Procedure of Cicero's Time*, Oxford: Oxford University Press, 1901, pp. 468–470.

[15] *Ancient Roman Statutes*, p. 12.

> 5. If the person granted as patron in accordance with this law is suspect because of his character, the person to whom he is granted in accordance with this law shall reject him.
>
> 8. The praetor ... shall provide for the selection of the 450 persons as specified ... provided he selects no one who ... has been condemned by the judicial process or by a public trial whereby he cannot be enrolled in the Senate.[16]

We see that *infamia* is a bridging concept spanning moral and legal domains – the moral character of an individual is shown to be flawed and from this it follows that one's civil rights are adversely affected.

Infamia was a remedy that could be employed by the Roman Censor as a mechanism to shame those who violated the moral norms of Roman society. *Infamia* was literally a disqualification from the ability to hold various offices in Rome. And the main reason for this disqualification is that a person has dishonored the political or legal process by one's wrongful acts. In effect the punishment that was called *infamia* was a moral punishment that carried with it various political and legal consequences. Greenidge says:

> *infamia* is used of the ill report which accompanies moral turpitude of almost every kind ... it is used as synonymous with words, which we know from direct evidence, bore a quasi-legal by the side of their ordinary signification. It is thus found conjoined with *probrum*, which ... was regularly employed to denote the offense which led the censors to "mark" (*notare*) an individual: and with *ignominia*, which we know was the name usually given to the dishonor attaching to an individual in consequence of the censorian *notatio*.[17]

Infamia was a form of civil dishonoring especially in cases where a person had been convicted of *ambitus* or *majestas*.

In ancient India, people who were adjudged to have bad character were also subject to various moral and legal liabilities. Indeed, the idea of becoming an outcaste, as we saw in an earlier chapter, was a very severe penalty for those who were seen as not of good character. And in some cases this penalty was applied to those who engaged in crimes against political or legal process. In Manu's Code it is clear that character was at the forefront of prosecutions:

> 8. 25. He should discover the internal disposition of men by external signs – voice, color, expression, bearing, eyes, and gestures. Inner thoughts are discerned by the

[16] Ibid., pp. 39–40.

[17] A. H. J. Greenidge, *Infamia: Its Place in Roman Public and Private Law*, Oxford: Oxford University Press, 1894, p. 18.

> bearing, expression, gait, gestures, and manner of speaking, and by changes in the eyes and face.[18]

We then find such laws as: "Neither the king nor any official of his shall initiate a lawsuit independently; nor shall he in any way suppress an action brought before him by someone else."[19]

There is also a similar idea to the Roman concept of *calumnia* in Manu's Code of law:

> 8. 58. If the plaintiff fails to present his case, he is subject to corporal punishment and a fine in accordance with the Law; and if the defendant fails to respond within three fortnights, he loses the case in the eyes of the Law. The amount that one man falsely denies and the amount that the other falsely claims – the king should impose a fine equal to double those amounts on those two men ignorant of the Law.[20]

False accusations are here seen as deserving of penalization as was true in the Roman Republic because of the adverse effect on the legal process. There is also a sense that ancient Indian law also had penalties aimed at dishonoring the wrongdoer.

32.4 ANCIENT LAWS CONCERNING PUNISHMENT OF LEGAL OR POLITICAL OFFICIALS

In both ancient India and the Roman Republic, there were laws that seemingly authorized regicide or removal of officials, ministers, and perhaps even rulers from office if their conduct was a grievous threat to the state. We have already seen that Manu calls for divine retribution of kings who act unjustly: 8.128 "When a king punishes those who do not deserve to be punished and neglects to punish those who deserve, he brings great infamy upon himself and he will go to hell."[21] Notice that the translator of Manu's Code uses the term infamy, which is the English translation of the Latin term, *infamia*, also used in the Roman Republic for such punishment connected to abuse of office.

In the Roman Republic, officials who betray their office, especially when it is clearly to the detriment of the state, are subject to capital punishment. We have already seen a law of the Twelve Tables, Table IX.5, which states: "Whoever incites a public enemy or whoever betrays a citizen to a public enemy shall be punished capitally."[22] And we find in the *Ancilian Law on the Right of Recovery* (122 BCE) this provision:

[18] *Manu's Code of Law*, 8.25, p. 168.
[19] Ibid., 8.43, p. 169.
[20] Ibid., 8.58–59, p. 170.
[21] Ibid., p. 174.
[22] *Ancient Roman Statutes*, p. 12.

> (44) No one shall hinder a trial. In regard to a trial which should be held properly in accordance with this law: when it should be held properly in accordance with this law, no magistrate or promagistrate or person by virtue of any imperium or authority shall act in such manner that a trial cannot be held or a verdict given; nor shall anyone call from or cause to be called from this trial the person presiding over the trial in accordance with this law, nor a judex in accordance with this law, nor a plaintiff in accordance with this law, nor a defendant ... nor shall he abduct said person, or cause him to be abducted ...[23]

This wide-ranging law fixed stiff penalties for judicial officials who undermined the integrity of a trial. In the Roman Republic there were no kings – indeed there was a law against anyone seeking to become a king. But there were various types of rulers nonetheless and they were held strictly accountable to the Roman people.

In ancient India, the officers of the king are held to a high standard and the criminal law is used to punish their transgressions especially those that would undermine the legal or political order. Here are two laws of the *Law Code of Visnu*:

> 3.74. He should appoint as court officials learned men of good pedigree consecrated by rites, men who are the same toward friend and foe, men who cannot be influenced by litigants through lust wrath, fear, greed, and the like.
>
> 5.196. When a judge rescinds a punishment from an accused who deserves to be punished, or inflicts punishment on an accused who does not deserve to be punished, that vile man should be assessed twice the punishment of the accused.[24]

These laws are similar to those in other codes but it is of special importance to see how the penalties for misbehaving officials is greater than what those officials should have assigned to those who they judge.

In Kautilya's *Arthashastra*, we find one of the clearest statements that even the king is not above the law and will have his misbehavior punished if not in this life then in the next:

> A wise king can make even the poor and miserable elements of his sovereignty happy and prosperous; but a wicked king will surely destroy the most prosperous and loyal elements of his kingdom.
>
> Hence a king of unrighteous character and of vicious habits will, though he is an emperor, fall a prey either to his own subjects or to that of his enemies.[25]

[23] *Ancient Roman Statutes*, p. 43.

[24] *The Law Code of Visnu*, translated by Patrick Olivelle, Cambridge: Harvard University Press, 2009, pp. 54 and 62.

[25] *Kautilya's Arthushastra*, Book VI, Chapter I, translated by Shamasastry, 1915, reprinted by Bottom of the Hill Publishing, 2010, p. 264.

The *Arthashastra* is more secular and pragmatic than the other ancient Indian codes. And we see here the worry that a king who corrupts the political or legal process opens himself to enemies within or without the kingdom.

One last consideration here is found in the *Vajnavalkya* where there is the suggestion that the king might even be punished or penalized:

> II. 307. If the king under greed, passions, etc., has once fined any party innocent in a given matter, he should (when his consciousness awakens) offer an amount thirty times more that the amount of the fine, given to Varuna, and make a gift of that amount to the Brahmans. (Further, he should refund the amount charged as a fine to the party innocent of the matter).[26]

This law shows that considerations of process were so important that the king could be in effect sentenced to pay a fine for his crime. We next try to draw some general lessons from the material we have considered in the previous sections.

32.5 THE IMPORTANCE OF PROTECTING LEGAL AND POLITICAL PROCESSES

Criminal law is often characterized as distinct from civil or private law in that the victim is the whole society. It is often difficult to see how one murder or rape could adversely affect the whole society. But in the case of acts that threaten the legal or political process it is much easier to see why such acts would be best dealt with as crimes rather than as delicts or torts since the society is so clearly harmed. Indeed, such acts do not often have a particular person that is directly harmed in any event. So, the acts would not be well handled through delict or tort proceedings.

We have here in ancient India and Rome a recognition of what the criminal law is best adapted to handle. Bribery of officials, theft of tax revenue, or failing properly to apply the law are cases that need to be deterred if a society is to proceed according to the rule of law. In the Roman Republic we have a very clear recognition of this fact in that there were special courts set up to handle just such cases, marking such acts off from wrongful acts that more directly harmed an individual person. In earlier societies we found that kings spoke of a desire for something like the rule of law, but in the ancient Roman Republic we also find specific institutional support for this idea.

In addition, ancient Indian codes of law, especially Manu and Narada, have extensive lists of procedural crimes that should be prosecuted. Here is one list from Manu's Code of Law:

> 8.120. For giving false testimony through greed, he should be fined 1,000; through delusion, the lowest fine; through fear, double the middle fine; through friendship,

[26] *Vajnavalkya Smrti*, translated by B. S. Best, Delhi: Chauhamba Sanskrit Pratishthan, 2004, p. 212.

> four times the fine; through lust, ten times the lowest fine; through anger, three times the highest fine; through ignorance, a full 200; and through immaturity, just 100. These are said to be the punishments for false testimony prescribed by the wise in order to prevent the miscarriage of justice and to arrest injustice. When individuals of the three classes give false testimony, a righteous king should first fine them and then execute them; a Brahmin, on the other hand, should be sent into exile.[27]

These penalties are fairly severe, and the punishment for repeated violation, execution, is of course of the utmost penalty.

Legal processes are utterly dependent on witnesses' giving truthful testimony. In various ancient and modern societies there are strong disincentives for lying in court proceedings. Condemnation by the gods is a common theme as punishment for lying in court. What we find in ancient India and the Roman Republic is an attempt to use a quasi-religious, and in many ways a secular, mechanism to protect the legal system from lying or cheating in court – namely, dishonoring the offender either through stripping him or her of various honors or by various penalties or punishments that make it clear how seriously the society disrespects the offender.

Political processes, especially electoral processes, are also dependent on maintenance of the integrity of these processes. So, we find that in the Roman Republic much attention is paid in criminal law to prohibiting and punishing wrongful acts that jeopardize the electoral process. The Roman Senate was a political institution that could, and regularly was, manipulated adversely. As discussed earlier, the crime of *ambitus* was originally designed to name and deter acts of bribery and lying that disrupted the electoral process. Unfortunately, there were already orators who were well schooled in rhetoric who were manipulating that system without having to bribe or lie to do it.

In partial recognition of the way that rhetoricians and philosophers could corrupt the electoral process, laws were passed in the Roman Republic against them. Here is a description of one of those laws from 161 BCE:

> In the consulship of Gaius Fannius Strabo and Marcus Valerius Messala, the praetor Marcus Pomponius consulted the Senate.
>
> Whereas a report was made concerning philosophers and rhetoricians, the senators proposed as follows in regard to this matter:
>
> Marcus Pomponius, the praetor, shall take measures and shall provide that no philosophers or rhetoricians shall dwell in Rome, if it appears to him to be in the public interest and in accordance with good faith.[28]

[27] *Manu's Code of Law*, 8.120–123, p. 173.

[28] *Decree of the Senate on Philosophers and Rhetoricians*, 161 BCE, in *Ancient Roman Statutes*, p. 31.

This was a reaction to the influence of Greek orators and philosophers who were seen as dangerous to the Republic – and of course we should remember that Socrates was executed by a jury in Athens for corrupting the youth, teaching false gods, and thereby weakening the Athenian democracy.[29]

In many respects the criminal law was perfectly suited for addressing these crimes of process – but unfortunately the criminal law in these matters was ripe for abuse as well. We learn from Cicero just how easy it was to manipulate juries in high profile cases where it was alleged that the fate of the Republic was at stake. In fact, reading Cicero's most famous speeches at trials makes one aware of how Cicero was himself quite willing to use whatever rhetorical means he could think of for his client. In these cases, one could say that the Roman Republic's jury trials were almost a caricature of what we today call the adversary method. And yet Cicero is also a good example of how the unscrupulous tactics of lawyers could land these lawyers in very difficult straits. Like Socrates, Cicero was executed in part because of his philosophizing, or at least his rhetorical skill.

In ancient India, there was not a republic or democracy and yet there was also a serious concern about protecting political and legal processes, especially those legal processes having to do with trials. Indeed lying as a witness was one of the most serious offenses. It is true that the offense was described as being a violation of a duty to the king or to a god. But within the religious and moral parameters of the legal system, lying to and bribing officials was seemingly as serious an offense in ancient India as it was in the Roman Republic.

In part this is probably because court proceedings are important in nearly every form of government – and in ancient times it is exceedingly difficult to tell when a person is taking advantage of the legal system since there is no police force, although in ancient India the Code of Manu calls for a cadre of spies to ferret out those who would disrupt or distort the legal system for their own ends and in contravention of justice. Here is one of the provisions of this code that details the role of spies:

> 9.256. The king, using spies as his eyes, should identify the two kinds of thieves who steal the property of others, those who operate overtly and those who operate covertly ... Bribe-takers, frauds, cheats, gamblers, and those who live by abjuring good luck, fortunetellers, high officials and physicians who act crookedly ... After identifying these through honest undercover agents practicing those same occupations and instigating them through mobile agents posted in various establishments, he should lure them into his power ... the king should duly punish them.[30]

[29] See Plato's *Apology* and *Crito* for the defense of Socrates.

[30] *Manu's Code of Law*, 9.256–262, p. 203.

Spies were a partial replacement for a police force but more was needed to guarantee the integrity of the political and legal processes in ancient India.

In discussing the eradication of thorns, Manu lists some of the crimes of process we have been discussing in this chapter, and they are listed along with other more mundane crimes such as stealing. In the Roman Republic we also find the mixing of various kinds of crime. In Rome we do find special courts set up for some of these crimes of process, but these are seemingly run in such a similar fashion to ordinary courts that it is unclear that having special courts made much of a difference. Criminal jurisprudence was certainly more elaborate and involved in ancient Rome than in ancient India, but we find very similar processes and concerns, nonetheless. It was well recognized that some of the chief thorns or wrongs to be dealt with in these ancient courts were crimes that did not have a specific victim – rather the society at large was the victim when the crucial political and legal processes were undermined. And in this respect, both ancient India and the Roman Republic recognized the most salient form of distinctly criminal law.

The Roman Republic had more institutional safeguards against abuse of process in that no one was allowed to assume the role of king and was constantly under the purview of the Senate and ultimately of the people. In ancient India, even with a strong monarch, there were nonetheless customs and practices designed to rein in a king who abused his considerable power. In both ancient Indian and Roman legal thought, that existed at roughly the same time, there was a similar concern for abuse of power by whoever was most likely to act abusively. And it remains especially interesting that these very different societies chose criminal law sanctions to be used to deter abusive behavior of the most powerful legal and political parties in the state. Officials were the ones who were most often singled out for being subject to special criminal laws and sanctions if they engaged in wrongdoing. Yet we have also seen that the most powerful, including the rulers, could also be subject to criminal sanctions for their wrongdoing if the political or legal processes were undermined or threatened.

SECTION XII

War and Treaties

33

Treaties, Hostages, and Keeping Faith

In the history of legal thought the central problem for treaties, as also with promises in general, is securing or maintaining compliance. Throughout ancient times, the wrath of the gods was called upon if one party violated the terms of a treaty. By the time of the Roman Republic, other means were being employed in addition to recourse to the gods – perhaps most commonly the exchange of hostages was meant to add an incentive for the parties not to violate a given treaty. And one Indian emperor stressed mutual respect as the key consideration, surely not even a position that many would embrace today. I will argue that the methods devised to secure compliance with treaties are considerably more subtle in ancient Rome and India than at first appears.

In Section 33.1 we will look at ideas from ancient India and the Roman Republic about how treaties and other agreements were understood. In Section 33.2 we will examine again the crucial idea of keeping faith that is of importance in ancient legal systems. In Section 33.3 we turn to the somewhat unusual way that hostages were employed in the late Roman Republic as a vehicle of compliance. Then in Section 33.4 we examine the views of the ancient Indian ruler Asoka on a non-coercive way to maintain compliance with peace treaties. And then finally, in Section 33.5, we seek a better appreciation of how ancient Indian and Roman conceptions of faithfulness differed from earlier accounts of the incentives needed to assure compliance especially when we see the emerging idea of empires – amalgamations of many previously autonomous states into a single political and juridical entity.

33.1 TREATIES IN ANCIENT INDIA AND THE ROMAN REPUBLIC

In ancient India, various law codes discuss the bindingness of treaties and the importance of keeping faith. We find the following in the *Code of Manu*:

> He should constantly think about the sixfold strategy: forging alliances, waging war, marching into battle, remaining stationary, pursuing a double stratagem, and seeking asylum. After forming an alliance or waging war, he should carefully examine the state of affairs and adopt the tactic of remaining stationary, marching into battle, pursuing a double stratagem, or seeking asylum. The king should … know that there are two kinds of alliance: the one is when both parties march together into battle with the same objective – it is of immediate significance; the other is its opposite – and it looks to the future … After ascertaining the collective wishes of them all, he should install there a relation of the enemy king, and draw up a treaty; make the Laws commonly held among them authoritative; and honor the new ruler, together with his chief officials, with precious gifts.[1]

Ancient Indian legal thought seems to regard treaties mainly in terms of peace treaties. And in the context of peace and war, treaties are only to be pursued if it is advantageous. The caveat is that advantageousness can be viewed either in terms of immediate gain or in terms of future gain.

Attaining compliance to the terms of a treaty seems to be seen as a matter of always keeping resort to war as the option to employ against a treaty breaker. The *Arthashastra* elaborates on the doctrine from Manu as we see in the following:

> Of two powerful kings who are on amicable terms with each other, a king shall make alliance with one of them who likes him and whom he likes; this is the best way of making an alliance. A king desirous of expanding his own power shall make use of the sixfold policy. Agreements of peace shall be made with equal and superior kings; and an inferior king shall be attacked.[2]

Here vassal treaties are not recommended if the state contemplating them is the superior state. Yet, it seems that attaining and maintaining peace is of major concern so these treaties are not ruled out altogether, but it is only the second choice since waging war and conquering the inferior state seem to be preferred.

We have quite a bit more discussion of treaties in the legal literature of the Roman Republic than in ancient India. The earliest recorded Roman treaty dates from approximately 509 BCE and is struck with Carthage:

> There shall be friendship between the Romans with their allies and the Carthaginians with their allies on the following conditions:

1 *Manu's Code of Law*, 7.160–7.203, translated by Patrick Olivelle, Oxford: Oxford University Press, 2005, pp. 162–165.

2 *Katilya's Arthashastra*, Book VI, Chapters II–III, translated by R. Shamasastry, 1915, reprinted by Bottom of the Hill Publishing, 2010, pp. 272–273.

> The Romans and their allies shall not sail beyond the Fair Promontory, except if driven by storm or by their enemies. If anyone is compelled to land he shall not be permitted to buy anything or to take anything except such as is necessary for ship's supplies; and within five days he shall depart.
>
> For those persons who come for trade, no transaction shall be valid unless it is executed in the presence of a herald or notary. Whatever is sold in their presence in Libya or Sardinia, the price shall be secured to the vendor on the credit of the State.
>
> If any Roman comes to the Carthaginian dominion in Sicily, all his rights shall be the same.
>
> The Carthaginians shall do no harm to the people of Ardea, Antium, Laurentum, Cirdeii, Terracina, or to any other people of the Latins that may be subject to Rome. But if any Latin cities are not subject to Rome, the Carthaginians shall not molest them. But if they capture any city they shall deliver it undamaged to the Romans.
>
> They shall not build a fortress in the Latin territory. If they enter the land under arms, they shall not spend a night there.[3]

This very early Roman treaty does not discuss sanctions for noncompliance, but like the ancient Indian account seems to presume that war will be the result if one party violates the agreement.

There were as many as four other major treaties between Rome and Carthage before Rome was able to conquer and subjugate Carthage. In each of these treaties Rome and Carthage approach each other as equals and attempt to create spheres of influence that the other was not to transgress. Here is a portion of the third treaty between Rome and Carthage from 279 BCE:

> If they enter into an alliance against Pyrrhus both parties shall make a formal covenant that they will go to the assistance of each other, whichever is attacked.
>
> Whichever party has need of assistance, the Carthaginians shall provide ships for transport and for attack, but each shall furnish provision for its own forces. If necessary, the Carthaginians indeed shall give assistance to the Romans by sea, but no one shall compel the crews to disembark against their will.[4]

This and other early Roman treaties look very much like even earlier treaties in the ancient Near East. But we will next see that there were other components of treaties entered into by Rome and by India that are strikingly different from earlier treaties.

3 *Treaty between Rome and Carthage* 509 BCE, in *Ancient Roman Statutes*, translated by Allan Chester Johnson, Paul Robinson Coleman-Norton, and Frank Card Bourne, Austin: University of Texas Press, 1961, 2012, p. 7.

4 *Ancient Roman Statutes*, p. 7.

33.2 KEEPING FAITH

In the late fifth century BCE, Rome entered into an alliance with many of its Latin neighbors that formed a kind of league of states. The centerpiece of this treaty was that all parties swore to keep to the terms of the treaty as a matter of faith. Here is that treaty:

> That there shall be peace among the Romans and all the Latin cities so long as the heavens and the earth shall remain in the same position.
>
> That they shall not make war nor cause war to be made against each other, nor permit each other's enemies to pass through their respective territories.
>
> That in case of attack they shall aid each other with all their might, and all plunder and booty captured by their allied forces shall be shared equally between them.
>
> That disputes arising out of private contracts between their respective citizens shall be determined within ten days by the tribunal of the city where the contracts in question were entered into.
>
> That nothing shall be added to this compact, and nothing taken away without the mutual consent of the contracting parties …
>
> That the command of the allied armies shall be exercised by Roman and Latin generals alternately.[5]

It does not appear that this multi-state compact had any more incentives added than merely that the members of the "league" trusted one another to keep to their word.

We can see similar considerations in ancient Indian codes of law that stress the importance of keeping faith. In Manu's Code we find these qualities sought in a king:

> The proper administrator of Punishment, they say, is a king who speaks the truth, acts after careful examination, is wise, and has masterly grasp of Law, Wealth, and Pleasure. When a king administers Punishment properly, he flourishes with respect to the triple set; but the king who is lustful, partial, and vile is slain by that very Punishment … Punishment can only be administered by someone who is honest and true to his word …[6]

We here see that one of the most important virtues of a king is to be "honest and true to his word." This virtue is just as crucial for international relations as for internal relations. We also find this idea expressed in the following pithy statement: "A king does not prosper as much by getting gold and land as by securing a firm ally."[7]

5 Translated in Coleman Phillipson, *The International Law and Custom of Ancient Greece and Rome*, Vol. II, London: Macmillan and Co., 1911, pp. 34–35.

6 *Manu's Code of Law*, 7.26–31, p. 155.

7 Ibid., 7.208, p. 165.

The general virtue that must be displayed by a king who follows the Code of Manu recognizes no higher law than that of "proper conduct."[8] In ancient Rome, it was similarly recognized that in international relations, *foedus* and *fides*, the characteristics associated with "a pledge of good faith" institutionalized through "on the one hand, the offerings and other rites used at the making of a solemn oath, and on the other, the solemn compact itself."[9]

Throughout the ancient world the problem of compliance was of central concern. In normal promise-making, swearing an oath to a god was a common way to signify that the promiser was serious about keeping the promise. In the case of treaties, gods of each party were appealed to, as in the famous treaty struck between Egypt and the Hittite Kingdom (see Chapter 11). There is also ample evidence that one party that was stronger than the other tried to use coercion, often brutally administered, to keep the weaker party from violating the terms of the agreement.

For oaths to succeed at providing an incentive for compliance there needs to be acceptance of the power of the gods to enforce breaches of the treaty, or there has to be a common acceptance of the necessity to keep one's word for all parties to benefit from mutual self-help. It sometimes seems as though there is a common law among ancient states that calls for treaties to be kept, especially when alliances are held together over long stretches of time with little coercion. As in the case of the institution of personal promise-making, treaty-making serves the goal of mutual benefit for the parties.

Yet, sometimes it appears that breaking a treaty is more beneficial than keeping it. And it is in such cases that something additional is needed to deter such treaty-breaking. We will next see examples from ancient Rome and India that depart from the older ways of procuring compliance. In the first case, the mutual exchange of hostages, the deterrence of noncompliance is a straightforward institution that appeals to self-interest. In the other case, in India the appeal is to an altruism that comes from the instilling of mutual respect among the parties. We will devote Section 33.3 to the role of hostages in ancient Roman legal thought and Section 33.4 to the instilling of mutual respect in ancient Indian legal thought.

33.3 THE ROLE OF HOSTAGES

The ancient Romans and their contemporaries seem to have settled on a truly secular means of self-help enforcement of treaties that is different from earlier treaty compliance in the Near East. In bilateral parity treaties, there was the mutual exchange of hostages; and in vassal treaties, the weaker party was forced to provide

[8] Ibid., 1.108, p. 92.

[9] Phillipson, *The International Law and Custom of Ancient Greece and Rome*, Vol. 1, pp. 391–392.

hostages. Here is an example where the Aetolians were forced to sue for peace after several battles they lost to the Romans in 189 BCE:

(1) The people of the Aetolians shall in good faith maintain the empire and the majesty of the people of Rome.
(2) They shall not allow hostile forces to pass through their territory or cities against the Romans, their allies or friends; nor grant them any supplies from the public fund.
(3) They shall have the same enemies as the people of Rome; and if the Roman people go to war with any, the Aetolian people shall do so also.
(4) The Aetolians shall surrender to the praefectus in Corcyra within a hundred days of the treaty, runaway slaves and prisoners of the Romans and their allies … And such persons, after the completion of the treaty, shall not be allowed to return to Aetolia.
(5) The Aetolians shall pay to the consul in Greece at once two hundred Eubonic talents of silver … They shall pay the money in the six years next following the completion of the treaty in yearly installments of fifty talents; and shall deliver the money in Rome.
(6) The Aetolians shall give the consul forty hostages, not less than ten or more than forty years old, to remain for the six years; they shall be selected by the Romans freely, excepting only the strategus, hipparch, public secretary, and such as have already been hostages at Rome. The Aetolians shall deliver such hostages in Rome; and if any of them die, they shall give another in his place.[10]

Hostages are a kind of surety of compliance. On the assumption that no state wants to have 40 of its most prominent citizens killed, the terms of the treaty will be kept.

Rome sometimes found itself forced to sue for peace also as in the 321 BCE Caudine Forks treaty. Here is Phillipson's account:

> Thus in connection with the notable capitulation at the Caudine Forks, the subsequent ratification of the peace entered into between the Roman Consuls and Pontius, the leader of the Samnites, was to be guaranteed by the delivery to the latter of six hundred Roman knights; and in default by the Roman authorities, the hostages were to suffer death.[11]

And when Rome was the victor, we have a similar arrangement required by Caesar who "insisted on six hundred" hostages from his defeated foe. And later yet, at the beginning of the Roman Empire, it was not uncommon for Rome to demand that hostages included women from their defeated adversaries.[12]

10 Phillipson, *The International Law and Custom of Ancient Greece and Rome*, Vol. II, pp. 79–80.
11 Phillipson, *The International Law and Custom of Ancient Greece and Rome*, Vol. I, p. 400.
12 See ibid., p. 401.

It appears that ancient Rome and those states with whom treaties were made sought a more secure guarantee of compliance than relying on the retribution of gods or the oaths of the rulers. Exchanging hostages, especially if they were valued members of the community, was a highly practical form of self-help in the enforcement of treaties. As in many aspects of Roman legal thought, practicalities were always foremost. Rome initiated so many treaties in Italy and beyond that there was a need to have very concrete assurances that the peace would be kept – what the Romans called the *Pax Romana*.[13]

There is also a very different kind of situation that occurred in ancient Rome and states in its sphere of influence. Rome retained a very large army even in times of peace so as to deter states with which Rome made treaties from not keeping to the terms of the treaties. One could say, somewhat metaphorically, that the Roman legions held the people hostage of the states with whom Rome entered into treaties. And especially at the end of the Roman Republic and beginning of the Roman Empire, Rome made it known that it would use its mighty military to enforce the laws of the empire and also to punish states that failed to comply with the treaties Rome had signed.

We should note that the two uses of hostages provide quite different incentives from one another. When a stronger state extracts hostages from a weaker state that sues for peace, this is still a vassal treaty where the terms are one-sided. But when both parties exchange hostages, each party has strong incentives to keep to the treaty and to regard the other party as an equal participant. Even perceived breaches or breaking of trust could result in serious loss of lives of the hostages.

Rome was amassing a very large area over which it ruled and keeping the peace in that empire was of prime consideration. It is of interest that Rome sought treaties with those states within its empire and treated these states as at least semi-autonomous, letting the other state's laws remain the law of the land even as Rome was owed allegiance in terms of paying tax money and providing soldiers for its armies. Rome saw the relations among itself and these states in legal terms and the problem of compliance of treaties was of pressing concern. And similar things can be said about the ancient Indian use of treaties in the way that its empire was built gradually from incorporating many smaller states. The development of an empire in ancient India is also an occasion for new approaches to providing incentives for compliance.

33.4 CONQUEST BY MORALITY

The Edicts of Asoka from the third century BCE in India provide a fascinating commentary on the practice of settling disputes by truces and peace treaties. The idea

[13] See Adrian Goldsworthy, *Pax Romana*, New Haven, CT: Yale University Press, 2016.

that Asoka presents is that trust can be achieved due to mutual respect with only minimal coercion. Here is a crucial part of Asoka's edict:

> Unconquered peoples along the borders of my dominions may wonder what my disposition is toward them. My only wish with respect to them is that they should not fear me, but trust me; that they should expect only happiness from me, not misery; that they should understand further that I will forgive them for offenses which can be forgiven; that they should be induced by my example to practice Dharma; and that they should attain happiness in this world and the next.[14]

One of the ideas here is that fear is not the best source of compliance with agreements.

Asoka was an emperor in India who lived approximately from 274–232 BCE. According to legend, he was a warlike king who had a conversion experience to Buddhism, and as a result came to see the way that Indian conquerors acted in a new light.[15] The conversion coincides with Asoka's repugnance at seeing the slaughter of war that commonly occurred during and immediately after a conquest. Asoka argues that:

> Immediately after the Kalingas had been conquered, King Priyadarsi became intensely devoted to the study of Dharma, to the love of Dharma, and to the inculcation of Dharma. The Beloved of the Gods, conqueror of the Kalingas, is moved to remorse now. For he has felt sorrow and regret because the conquest of a people previously unconquered involves slaughter, death, and deportation.[16]

Asoka came to see that the killing involved in conquest is morally wrong.

> No living creature should be slaughtered here ... Many hundreds of thousands of living creatures were formerly slaughtered every day for curries in the kitchens of His Majesty ... During the twenty-six years since my coronation, I have ordered the release of prisoners twenty-five times.[17]

Asoka also came to see the killing of all creatures as morally wrong from his newly acquired Buddhist perspective.

In terms of the securing of peace, Asoka calls for a radical change in how rulers view their tasks.

> King Priyadarsi now thinks that even a person who wrongs him must be forgiven for wrongs that can be forgiven.

[14] *The Edicts of Asoka*, edited and translated by N. A. Nikam and Richard McKeon, Chicago: University of Chicago Press, 1959, p. 53.

[15] See ibid., p. 4.

[16] Ibid., p. 27.

[17] Ibid., pp. 55–57.

> King Priyadarsi seeks to induce even the forest people who have come under his dominion [that is, primitive peoples in the remote sections of the conquered territory] to adopt this way of life and this ideal. He reminds them, however, that he exercises the power to punish, despite his repentance, in order to induce them to desist in their crimes and escape execution.
>
> For King Priyadarsi desires security, self-control, impartiality, and cheerfulness for all living creatures.
>
> King Priyadarsi considers moral conquest [that is, conquest by Dharma, *Dharma-vijaya*] the most important conquest. He has achieved this moral conquest repeatedly both here and among the peoples living beyond the borders of his kingdom, even as far away as six hundred *yojamas* [about three thousand miles].[18]

Here we see that agreements between even very far flung peoples can be achieved when mutual respect has been instilled, along with only a bit of the threat of punishment.

Moral conquest involves relying primarily on moral suasion to keep the peace and hold parties to their agreements.

> Where conquest is achieved by Dharma, it produces satisfaction. Satisfaction is firmly established by conquest by Dharma [since it generates no opposition of conquered and conqueror]. Even satisfaction, however, is of little importance. King Priyadarsi attaches value ultimately only to consequences of action in the other world.
>
> This edict on Dharma has been inscribed so that my sons and great-grandsons who may come after me should not think conquests worth achieving. If they do conquer, let them take pleasure in moderation and mild punishments. Let them consider moral conquest the only true conquest.[19]

It seems that it is the mutual satisfaction that comes from mutual respect that is considered the best motivation for peoples to comply with their agreements.

We have in the Edicts of Asoka a radical break with the past understanding of relations among states. Here is how N. A. Nikam and Richard McKeon see it:

> Asoka used the idea of Dharma to reorganize his administration of the empire … Indian rulers were absolute sovereigns limited by social disorder, political intrigue, and military rivalry. Asoka inherited a system of administration from his grandfather and father. The Edicts were one means by which he laid down fundamental policies interpreting the laws. Subordinate officials were given discretion in their own districts within a system which provided for constant inspection and supervision. A special class of officers was specifically charged with morality or Dharma,

[18] Ibid., pp. 28–29.

[19] Ibid., p. 30.

> and provision was made against unjust imprisonment and undue torture and for appeal before the execution of sentence. The functions of officials were extended to include provision of medical aid, roads, watering sheds for man and beast, shade trees, and rest houses. The whole political organization was made subsidiary to moral law in a concrete translation of the law into specific forms of human and social relations.[20]

As we will see, this particular Indian ruler's ideas of how best to establish and run an empire have parallels with some similar ideas in Rome.

It is unclear though how influential Asoka's Edicts were for future Indian rulers. Nikam and McKeon conclude that the edicts did not "serve as a guide to Asoka's descendants."[21] Indeed there is some reason to think that Asoka was simply an outlier in the legal thought of ancient India. Yet, as we will next see, and despite many critics, there is evidence that Indian legal thought favored the idea of peaceful alliances rather than violent conquest.

33.5 TREATIES IN EMERGING ANCIENT EMPIRES

In both ancient India and the late Roman Republic there was becoming a preferred way to attain compliance for treaties that involved respecting the autonomy of the weaker or vassal state, even as that state was incorporated into the larger state by means of treaties. When previously hostile states are conquered and a peace treaty is signed, the compliance problem is often exasperated by the bitterness of defeat. Being invited to join an emerging empire is a way to offset the bitterness of having been defeated. The Romans were famous for such a strategy but we can also see reference to this model in some of the ancient Indian texts as well.

S. I. Viswanatha speaks of a set of powerful states of ancient India that formed an alliance:

> The political cohesion of the tribes which originally should have been loose is a remarkable feature of this age. The sixteen great Powers of India were truly national states, whether monarchical or republican, and the nature of the relations among them in peace and war is in evidence in the literature of the time. These may be said to have had in them all the elements of a nation … International law in India was accepted by all Indian states, for it was based on Dharma … [yet] there was no single sovereign person.[22]

[20] Ibid., p. 21.

[21] Ibid., p. 2. Also see Richard Solomon, "Ancient India: Peace Within and War Without," in *War and Peace in the Ancient World*, edited by Kurt A. Raaflaub, Oxford: Blackwell Publishing, 2007, especially pp. 55–56.

[22] S. I. Viswanatha, *International Law in Ancient India*, Bombay: Longmans, Green & Co., 1925, pp. 7–10.

The idea of forming large alliances was becoming common in ancient Indian legal thought.

In ancient times, the autonomous states of India recognized the same rules and also formed alliances of various types:

> Alliances are in evidence even in the earliest age of the history of India. In the Rig Veda some of the Aryan tribal communities are seen to enter into leagues with one another and with some non-Aryan tribes to form a "confederacy" against the most powerful Aryan political organization of the Titsus under the leader Sudas ... in the Mahabharata ... the "alliance" was for offensive and defensive purposes.[23]

In this respect ancient Indian legal thought resembles the legal thought at the end of the Roman Republic.

Phillipson considers the standard account of how Rome dealt with the peoples that were conquered or with whom treaties were reached.

> Did Rome recognize the territorial sovereignty of the law? It cannot be claimed that the Romans systematically emphasized this principle and invariably acted in conformity with it. As they usually permitted aliens to have recourse to their own particular legal systems and customs, the solution of real conflicts of legislation was ipso facto avoided.[24]

Phillipson recognizes that as early as the first treaty between Rome and Carthage, the principle of territorial sovereignty was accepted. In these treaties, Rome already set forth a doctrine that would be the centerpiece of its treatment of states in the emerging empire.

It is evident that Rome built its empire, at least in the early years, by forming treaties with those Latin states in Italy that it conquered. And the treatment of these states as at least semi-autonomous was crucial for keeping the peace. We have also seen evidence of a similar strategy for the formation and maintenance of empire in ancient India. The discretion afforded to local rulers is the great hallmark of these ideas of conquest and treaty-making. Indeed, the keeping of faith that is so crucial for successful and long-lasting peace is premised on the idea of mutual respect among the various peoples that make up these empires.

It should be admitted, though, that for both of these emerging empires there was an iron fist within the velvet glove. In the case of India, despite the Code of Manu preaching restraint and the Edict of Asoka stressing mutual respect, there were also strongly violent measures taken when a state breached a peace agreement. Richard Solomon cites an ancient Indian inscription that is quite different from Asoka's Edicts:

[23] Ibid., pp. 92–93.

[24] Phillipson, *The International Law and Custom of Ancient Greece and Rome*, Vol. 1, p. 295.

> Skillfully, by means of his strategic counsels [which served] the ritual prayers [mantra], he tirelessly sacrificed his enemies like cattle in the special rite of battle, in which his fearful whirling sword was the oblation ladle, the streaming blood [of his enemies] served as clarified butter, the buzzing of his bowstring was the ritual cry "*vasat*," the soldiers marching in order were the priests, and his burning hatred was the fire, fanned by the winds of his unquenchable rage.[25]

This is the fate that awaited those states that broke the peace and challenged the ancient Indian emperor.

Clearly it matters which ruler or period of ancient history one is examining in answering the question of how brutal the Indian rulers were to those who broke their treaties. We have seen examples of two extremes, but it is surely the case that there were many positions taken in between brutality and mutual respect. The idea though is that ancient Indian legal thought did not follow older regimes in stressing only the brutality side of this continuum.

We can also cite evidence for the brutality that Rome was willing to inflict upon those states that did not accept incorporation into the early Roman Empire. Here is an account given by Nathan Rosenstein:

> The Romans could be quite brutal toward those they defeated: they were not above the kind of atrocities that the Athenians visited upon the Melians, and we have some truly horrific descriptions of the atrocities Roman soldiers inflicted in such cases: "one may often see in towns captured by the Romans not only human beings who have been put to the sword, but even dogs cloven down the middle, and the limbs of other animals hewn off," as Polybius, an eye-witness observed … Survivors were enslaved, a fate that befell tens of thousands of the Republic's opponents … Brutality could be an extremely effective diplomatic tool.[26]

The *Pax Romana* was maintained on the basis of fear as well as respect. Like ancient Indian legal thought, ancient Roman legal thought fluctuated between the two extremes of brutality and respect for autonomous partners.

Cicero portrays Rome as being enlightened in how it dealt with the different peoples that it incorporated into its emerging empire.

> Wars, then, ought to be undertaken for this purpose, that we may live in peace, without injustice; and once victory has been secured, those who were not cruel or savage in warfare should be spared … In my opinion, our concern should always be for a peace that will have nothing to do with treachery. If I had been followed in this we would still have some republican government (if perhaps not the very best); whereas now we have none. And while you must have concern for those whom

[25] Solomon, "Ancient India," especially p. 55.

[26] Nathan Rosenstein, "War and Peace, Fear and Reconciliation at Rome," in *War and Peace in the Ancient World*, edited by Kurt A. Raaflaub, Oxford: Blackwell Publishing, 2007, pp. 234–235.

> you have conquered by force; you must also take in those who have laid down their arms and seek refuge in the faith of generals, although a battering ram may have crashed against their wall. In this matter, justice was respected so greatly among our countrymen that the very men who had received into their good faith cities or peoples conquered in war would, by the custom of our forefathers, become their patrons.[27]

Cicero here speaks of a tradition in Rome of treating conquered peoples the way patrons treat their students.

As we have seen, Cicero holds up the idea of "good faith" as the centerpiece of the just wars of conquerors. This is also hailed as the hallmark of ancient Indian thought by thinkers like Asoka and by other Indian legal theorists as well. The idea of keeping faith is crucial here, at least in the ideal. And we will next see that there is a code of law for war that was similarly recognized, at least in the ideal, as the way to pursue a just war.

[27] Cicero, *On Duties* (*De Officiis*), 1.34–35, translated by Margaret Atkins and edited by M. T. Griffin and E. M. Adams, Cambridge: Cambridge University Press, 1991, pp. 14–15.

34

The Rules of War and the Law of Peoples

It was common for the theorists and historians of the Roman Republic to refer to the rules or laws of war. Rome was said to be more civilized than many of its neighbors because it exercised restraint even in war, for instance by giving other states ample warning that war was imminent and giving these states a period of time to sue for peace before they were attacked by the Roman legions. Such restraining considerations were part of the wider law of peoples, the *jus gentium*, which Cicero and Caesar, among many others, discussed. Yet Caesar and Cicero also justified war when it benefitted Rome not for moral considerations but for pragmatic ones. We do find, though, that Cicero provides the first full account of what constitutes a "just war" as an ideal to which he believes Rome can and should aspire.[1]

Ancient Indian law also made reference to broader or universal law, most especially in the greatest of the legal texts of ancient India, the *Code of Manu*. We discussed this issue in Chapter 27 dealing with the relation between equity and justice. Equity is linked to objective considerations of natural law. In this chapter I argue that there was an emerging idea of international justice that was also linked to natural law considerations in ancient Indian and Roman legal thought. In Section 34.1 I discuss the texts from ancient India and Rome that concern the law of nature. In Section 34.2 we will then take up the idea of rules of war that were seen as manifest and binding on states in ancient times, especially in the legal thought of the Roman Republic. In Section 34.3 we look closely at the *Code of Manu* concerning the laws or rules of war and contrast this idea to that of the more pragmatic text, the *Arthashastra*. Then in Section 34.4 we look at the particular case of the treatment of prisoners of war to see whether the rules of war were consistent with this practice. And finally, in Section 34.5, we discuss how the emerging ideas of international law are connected to the ideas of natural justice espoused in ancient times.

[1] Cicero, *On Duties* (*De Officiis*), 1.34–35, translated by Margaret Atkins and edited by M. T. Griffin and E. M. Adams, Cambridge: Cambridge University Press, 1991, pp. 14–15.

34.1 THE LAW OF NATURE AND THE LAW OF PEOPLES

The law of peoples, *jus gentium*, concerns the laws that are commonly recognized by all people; whereas the law of nature, *jus naturale*, concerns the laws that are objectively true for all times and all peoples. Obviously, there is an overlap between these two ideas since some law can be both common to all peoples and so recognized because it is also the universal law of nature. But the two are quite different in the sense that the *jus gentium* has laws that are laws only because states recognize them as such; whereas the laws of nature are laws regardless of whether states recognize these laws since the authority of the laws of nature exists in the normative force of the natural order itself.

Cicero recognizes the laws of nature in an important set of passages from his book, *De Officiis* (On Duties):

> Perhaps we should examine more thoroughly what are the natural principles of human fellowship and community. First is something that is seen in the fellowship of the entire human race. For its bonding consists of reason and speech, which reconcile men to one another, through teaching, learning, communicating, debating, and making judgments, and unite them in a kind of natural fellowship. It is this that distances us from the nature of other animals.[2]

The laws of nature for Cicero are laws grounded in human nature, as this passage makes clear. The laws are dictated by our rational nature, or to put the point only slightly differently, the laws of nature are the laws found out by reason concerning what leads to human fellowship and community.

Here is how Cicero saw that reason relates to the laws of nations and the laws of nature:

> Reason demands that nothing is done insidiously, deceptively, or with pretense … [but] because custom is so corrupted such behavior is neither thought dishonorable nor forbidden by statute and civil law … however forbidden by the law of nature.[3]
>
> Everything in the civil law need not be in the law of nations, but everything in the law of nations ought also to be a part of civil law.[4]
>
> Many things that seem honorable by nature become dishonorable through circumstances … to keep promises … if what is beneficial changes.[5]

In this account, reason allows humans to discern the law of nature from which derives the law of nations and the civil law.

2 Cicero, *De Officiis*, I.50, p. 21.
3 Ibid., III.68–69, pp. 125–126.
4 Ibid., III.69, p. 126.
5 Ibid., III.96, p. 137.

Later authors distinguished more carefully between the law of nature and the law of nations. The former is the domain of universal laws somehow connected to human nature; the latter is simply what all or most nations have thought to be required by morality. Both of these domains were distinct from the specific provisions of law or morality in a given society. Cicero seems to distinguish these domains but does not see how one could be used to criticize the other. By the seventeenth century CE, philosophers saw these two as separable, such that the law of nature could be used to criticize the law of nations, even if all nations had the same view.[6]

For the Romans, the *jus naturale* was a universal law that governed human affairs and extended to all of humanity. In terms of nations, the *jus naturale* contained rules that all nations should adhere to, and this gave the framework for a kind of international law. The same can be said about the *jus gentium* – what all states agreed to was what then governed the dealing of these states. But the customs and agreements of states can change over time so if international law is grounded in the *jus gentium* it will not be as secure as if it is grounded in the *jus naturale*. It remains unclear if the ancient legal thinkers of the Roman Republic understood this difference between *jus naturale* and *jus gentium*, or if they did, which of these laws were thought to ground something like an international law.

Ancient Indian legal texts also address the relation between universal laws of nature and the civil law. The *Code of Manu* begins with an account of how law arose in different ages eventually reaching humans:

> In the Krta Age, the Law is whole, possessing four feet; and so is truth. People never acquire any property through unlawful means. By acquiring such property, however, the Law is stripped of one foot in each of the subsequent Ages; through theft, falsehood, and fraud, the Law disappears a foot at a time.
>
> In the Krta Age, people are free from sickness, succeed in all their pursuits, and have a life span of 400 years. In the Treta and each of the subsequent Ages, however, their life span is shortened by a quarter. The life span of mortals given in the Veda, the benefit of rites, the power of embodied beings – they all come to fruition in the world in conformity with each Age.
>
> There is one set of Laws for men in the Krta Age, another in the Treta, still another in the Dvapara, and a different set in the Kali, in keeping with the progressive shortening taking place in each Age.[7]

These different laws for different ages culminate in the law for humans at the moment. This law seems to be closer to the Roman ideas of *jus naturale* than *jus gentium*.

6 See Hugo Grotius, *The Laws of War and Peace (De Jure Belli ac Pacis)*, 1625, especially the Prolegomena.

7 *Manu's Code of Law*, translated by Patrick Olivelle, Oxford: Oxford University Press, 2005, p. 91.

In the *Code of Manu*, the higher law of each age governs the people of that age. At the end of the first chapter of his code, Manu says:

> Proper conduct is the highest Law, as well as what is declared the Veda and given in traditional texts. Applying himself always to this treatise, therefore, let a twice born man remain constantly self-possessed … Seeing thus that the Law proceeds from proper conduct, the sages understood proper conduct to be the ultimate root of all ascetic toil.[8]

The civil law of the current age is based in the Veda and scriptures: "The root of the Law is the entire Veda … Whatever Law Manu has proclaimed with respect to anyone, all that has been taught in the Veda for it contains all knowledge."[9]

For ancient Indian legal thought, the law governing the relations among states is grounded in dharma, the law of justice. As we will see later in this chapter, ancient Indian legal thought grounds all human law, whether for individuals or for nations, in universal moral law. And there is a kind of Law of Nature here that seems to be the proper basis for international law, independently of what the customs of nations have been over time.

34.2 ROMAN IDEAS OF THE LAW OF WAR

Cicero is the best known Roman philosopher to espouse what will come to be known as the Just War theory.

> In my opinion, our concern should always be for a peace that will have nothing to do with treachery … Indeed, a fair code of warfare has been drawn up, in full accordance with religious scruple, in the fetial laws of the Roman people. From this we can grasp that no war is just unless it is waged after a formal demand for restoration, or unless it has been formally announced and declared beforehand.[10]

Cicero goes on to say:

> There are laws of warfare … if an agreement is made with pirates in return for your life, and you do not pay the price, there is no deceit … For a pirate is not an enemy proper, but is the common foe of all.[11]

Cicero is generally thought to be one of the very first Just War theorists (perhaps Plato is earlier, but Augustine, often thought to be the founder of this theoretical perspective, is definitely later).

[8] Ibid., p. 92.
[9] Ibid., p. 94.
[10] Cicero, *De Officiis*, I.36, pp. 15–16.
[11] Ibid., III.107.

Cicero addresses *jus ad bellum* (justice in initiating war), *jus in bello* (justice in the conduct of war), and *jus post bellum* (justice at the end of war). Concerning *jus ad bellum*, he argues that war must only be initiated as a last resort;[12] it must be conducted for a just aim; and there must be a formal declaration of war.[13] Concerning the *jus in bello*, he says that only soldiers are permitted to fight during war;[14] and that cruelty should not be employed. Unlike many early Just War theorists, Cicero also considers the *jus post bellum*, specifically that at the end of war those who were not cruel should be spared;[15] and that those who have laid down their arms must also be spared.[16]

There are two interesting wrinkles in Cicero's Just War theory. First, in discussing those who have laid down their arms, Cicero breaks with previous authors in claiming that even if people do not lay down their arms until a battering ram has crashed through their walls, they should still be spared. Before the battering ram was used on a given fortress, it had been thought that this was the last point at which people could surrender and not be killed. Soldiers were given the chance to surrender before the wall was crashed. But after this event, they could be killed even if they then surrendered. Cicero sets the stage for contemporary moral and legal treatment of this issue, where surrender is always seen as a change in status, making the surrendering person no longer liable to be killed, even if one is facing imminent defeat.

The second interesting twist is that Cicero says that an enemy should be properly called a stranger (*hostis*).[17] Cicero thinks the term stranger applied to one's enemies is a gentle reminder that these soldiers are people. But in later discussions, *hostis humani generis* (almost always translated as "enemy of humanity" rather than "stranger to humanity") is used in quite a strongly negative sense in the discussion of pirates, and today in the discussion of terrorists. Cicero is aware that the term *hostis* is already changing its meaning, but he sees it still as a reminder to us not to demonize our enemies, as unfortunately happens today when the enemies are called terrorists or pirates.

There is also though considerable evidence that the Romans did not always exercise restraint once they entered into battle. When certain people were captured during war they could then be enslaved and either given as prizes of war or sold in the marketplace. And when Romans were attacked, the response was often very

12 Ibid., 1.34.
13 Ibid., 1.36.
14 Ibid., 1.37.
15 Ibid., 1.35.
16 Ibid., 1.35.
17 Ibid., 1.37.

severe and verging on the level of massacre. We see some of this evidence in subsequent sections of this chapter.

34.3 ANCIENT INDIAN IDEAS ON THE LAW OF WAR

In the *Vajnavalkya*, there is a clear articulation of the principle of necessity, a cornerstone of the idea of a just war. "A king should resort to punishment [through war] only when no other option is left for establishment of peace."[18] Only as a last resort should war be initiated. The *Code of Manu* also calls for first employing other methods short of war:

> He should strive for triumph over his enemies through conciliation, gifts, and fomenting dissention, employed collectively or separately, but never through war. Victory and defeat in battle are uncertain for the two combatants; he should therefore avoid war. When the aforementioned three strategies fail, then let him, always on his guard, pursue war in such a manner that he will triumph over his enemies.[19]

These passages from two important legal codes of ancient India speak most clearly to the prudential reasons for adhering to the principle of necessity, not necessarily to the moral ideas behind that principle.

In the *Code of Manu* we do find some calls for restraint that indicate a strong sense of *jus in bello* rules of war.

> When he is engaged in battle, he must never slay his enemies with weapons that are treacherous, barbed, or laced with poison, or whose tips are ablaze with fire. He must never slay a man standing on the ground, an effeminate man, a man with joined palms, a man with loose hair, a seated man, a man declaring "I am yours," a sleeping man, a man without his armor, a naked man, a man without his weapons, a non-fighting spectator, a man engaging someone else, a man with damaged weapons, a man in distress, a badly wounded man, a frightened man, or a man who has turned tail.[20]

This is a list that could easily be given today for identifying those who should not be targeted during war.

Yet, in the *Code of Manu* we also find passages that are antithetical to the Just War ideals. This is especially true in that when war was seen as necessary, and the enemy was fighting with normal soldiers, there were then very few limitations on the conduct of war.

[18] *Vajnavalkya*, 1.346, translated by B. S. Bist, Delhi: Chaukhamba Sanskrit Pratishthan, 2004, p. 106. On this point see S. V. Viswanatha, *International Law in Ancient India*, Bombay: Longmans, Green & Co., 1925, p. 118.

[19] *Manu's Code of Law*, 7.198–199, p. 164.

[20] Ibid., 7.90–93, p. 159.

> After laying siege to the enemy, he shall remain stationary – he should plunder his realm; constantly ruin his supplies of fodder, food, water, and fuel; demolish reservoirs, ramparts, and moats; launch surprise assaults against him; frighten him at night; foment sedition among the seditious; keep close watch over enemy activity; and when omens are propitious, fearlessly launch the attack with the determination to win.[21]

One commentator says: "But once on reasonable grounds belligerency was declared, victory was to be achieved at all costs."[22]

Ancient Indian law seems to recognize *jus ad bellum* principles and for soldiers it did recognize *jus in bello* restraints. But the reasons for adhering to such rules were sometimes pragmatic rather than moral. And this is not merely true of the *Arthashastra*, which was thoroughly pragmatic in its approach, but also sometimes of the more moral texts such as the *Code of Manu*. Even in the case of the justice of initiating war, the desire for conquest was recognized as a legitimate rationale to go to war. Yet, there is an underlying moral rationale for how one state should treat another state's threat that we will explore in the final section of this chapter.

34.4 PRISONERS OF WAR

Cicero can again be cited for his views about the justice of treating prisoners after war ends:

> once victory has been secured, those who were not cruel or savage in warfare should be spared.
>
> you must also take in those who have laid down their arms and seek refuge.[23]

Here we have Cicero's unambiguous stance on the humane treatment of prisoners of war.

Coleman Phillipson argues that, for legal thought of the Roman Republic, it mattered whether the prisoners had voluntarily surrendered or not.

> It is important to distinguish the case of voluntary surrender of the enemy, and that where the adversary was entirely vanquished, his fate depending on the will of the conqueror. In the latter case, prisoners if not put to death for the previous commission of an offense against the majesty of Rome, or for treacherous acts against her ambassadors or generals, were often enslaved ... In the case of voluntary

[21] Ibid., 7.195–197, p. 164.
[22] Viswanatha, *International Law in Ancient India*, p. 120.
[23] Cicero, *De Officiis*, 1.35, p. 15.

> surrender a different policy was usually adopted ... [they were] assimilated to the class of freedmen.[24]

So, in ancient Roman legal thought prisoners of war were treated humanely if they had surrendered but not necessarily if they had been forcibly captured.

In the *Code of Manu* we find several references to the proper treatment of prisoners of war. Here is one set of passages:

> After the victory, he should pay homage to the gods and righteous Brahmins; grant exceptions; and issue proclamations of amnesty.
>
> After ascertaining the collective wishes of them all, he should install there a relation of the enemy king and draw up a treaty ...
>
> All activities here depend on divine and human dispensations. Of these however, the divine is inscrutable; action is possible only with respect to the human.[25]

Ancient Indian legal thought is forthright in calling for amnesties after the end of a war and this normally means that prisoners would be released, not enslaved.

Yet we also find that for both ancient Indian legal thought and that of the Roman Republic, prisoners of war could be treated as slaves in certain circumstances, especially if they were considered to be still *hostis*, hostile enemies who could be treated like pirates for whom the laws of war did not apply. Pirates were considered to be enemies of humanity, not merely enemies of Rome. And because pirates did not recognize normal restraints they did not deserve to be treated with restraint either in this view.

Cicero makes it clear that pirates are not to be treated according to the laws of warfare.

> Moreover, there are laws of warfare, and it often happens that faith given to an enemy must be kept. For if an oath has been sworn in such a way that the mind grasps that this ought to be done, it should be kept; if not then there is no perjury if the thing is not done. For example, if an agreement is made with pirates in return for your life, and you do not pay the price, there is no deceit, not even if you swore to do so and did not. For a pirate is not counted as an enemy proper, but is the common foe of all.[26]

Here Cicero again asserts that there are laws of war, but that they do not apply to all enemies, only to those that are "proper" enemies. Pirates are not proper enemies because they are foe to everyone. And it appears that some prisoners of war are also

[24] Coleman Phillipson, *The International Law and Custom of Ancient Greece and Rome*, Vol. II, London: Macmillan and Co., 1911, pp. 254–256.

[25] *Manu's Code of Law*, 7.201–205, pp. 164–165.

[26] Cicero, *De Officiis*, III.107, p. 141.

not seen as proper enemies, because they have not acted with restraint, and the laws of war do not apply to them either.

Toward the end of Cicero's *De Officiis* (On Duties), we run across the idea of how pirates are not proper enemies, but are *hostis*, strangers. Pirates do not conform to the laws of nations and are not owed reciprocal treatment, perhaps not even reciprocal respect. It is not clear why Cicero now thinks they are not deserving of such respect when he had earlier said that we should use the more gentle term *hostis*, rather than *ex perduelliuma*. Nonetheless, one translator translates "*communis hostis omnium*" as "common foe of all." Here it will matter how to translate this term especially since Cicero is clearly in favor of the idea of cosmopolitan morality, where all people are seen as citizens of the cosmos.

For most ancient societies, the idea was that defeated soldiers owed their lives to the ones who captured them and hence they could be enslaved since this was better than the alternative – death on the battlefield. The Greeks held this view, as did other societies in the ancient Near East. The ancient Romans and Indians seem to have this same view but only concerning some prisoners, namely those prisoners who had not fought as moral soldiers should fight.

The Code of Manu is striking in its mandate of restraint against a large class of individuals that could be found on the battlefield. It is a sign of humanitarianism that restraint be practiced against those who just a short while ago were ready to kill you. Cicero is, as we saw above, also often pointed to as the founder of the Just War tradition, yet he is not as humane toward prisoners of war as Manu is. Another Roman philosopher is closer to Manu – namely, Seneca.

In Seneca's book *De Clementia* (*On Mercy*), which is dedicated to the young Emperor Nero, we find many passages that call for restraint. At the beginning of this book, Seneca offers this statement that rulers should say to themselves:

> Have I, of all mortals, found favor with the gods and been chosen to act on earth in their stead? I am the judge with power of life and death over nations. I have the fate of everyone in my hands … Such is the extent of my power. Yet I have not been driven to unjust punishment by anger or youthful impulse, nor by the rashness and obstinacy of men … My sword has been sheathed, indeed hung away altogether. I have spared to the utmost even the meanest blood … My sternness I conceal, my mercy I hold at the ready. I watch over myself as though the laws, which I have summoned from decay and darkness into the light, will call me into account …[27]

Seneca called for restraint in treating slaves even though the slave owner has the right to do anything to the slave the owner wishes. Similar things can be said about prisoners of war.

[27] Seneca, *On Mercy*, 1.2–4, in *Seneca: Moral and Political Essays*, translated by John M. Cooper and J. F. Procope, Cambridge: Cambridge University Press, 1995, pp. 128–129.

Mercy, closely related to equity, called for captured soldiers to be spared and Seneca is perhaps the best example in Roman legal thought of an advocate of this position. In Indian legal thought, as we saw in the previous chapter, Asoka is the best example of an advocate of the idea that prisoners of war should be spared. Here again is a short passage to this effect from Asoka's Edicts:

> The edict of Dhrama has been inscribed so that my sons and great-grandsons who may come after me, should not think new conquests worth achieving. If they do conquer, let them take pleasure in moderation and mild punishments. Let them consider moral conquest the only true conquest. This is good, here and hereafter. Let their pleasure be pleasure in morality [*Dharma-rati*]. For this alone is good here and hereafter.[28]

Asoka is perhaps even more straightforwardly motivated by universal morality than is Seneca.

34.5 INTERNATIONAL LAW IN ANCIENT INDIA AND ROME

As was pointed out briefly in the last chapter, there were leagues of states in ancient India and Rome, where there were common customs governing the formation and compliance with treaties. Indeed, it seems that the empires of ancient India and Rome were already models for international law in these ancient societies. Here is Thomas Walker's assessment of Roman international law:

> the praetor administered for all foreign sojourners resident at Rome a regular system of equity. This system was *Jus Gentium*. The history of *Jus Gentium* will, perhaps, continue to furnish matter for controversy amongst modern jurists, but whatever may have been the origin of *Jus Gentium*, whether as a conscious abstract of the laws common to the nations of the Roman world made by Roman magistrates for, and applied to the disputes of, the foreign visitor, or whether it was at the outset a purely Roman Equity, a place in international legal history belongs to a conception which marks the recognition by the Romans of the necessity of the application in certain cases by Roman Courts of legal maxims other than those of *Jus Civile*. The Roman possessed, in fact, in his *Jus Gentium* a system of Private International Law.[29]

Walker goes on to say that from the earliest of times the Roman idea of *jus gentium* as a higher law, "trenched upon the field now occupied by Public International Law" as well.[30]

[28] *The Edicts of Asoka*, translated by N. A. Nikam and Richard McKeon, Chicago, IL: University of Chicago Press, 1959, p. 30.

[29] Thomas A. Walker, *A History of the Law of Nations*, Cambridge: Cambridge University Press, 1899, Vol. 1, p. 45.

[30] Ibid., p. 46,

Among the components of the higher law of peoples are the laws of war which correspond to the laws of peace. The Roman ruler Camillus declared that these laws of war should be enforced "not less justly than bravely" which set a limit to the savagery perpetrated by soldiers.[31] We can also find an account of the Roman practice of war in the contemporaneous writings of the historian Polybius condemning the Aetolian commander Scopas:

> He imagined that he was doing nothing wrong in giving rein to his anger, and retaliating upon impious acts of the Aetolians by similar impieties and "curing ill by ill" ... But the fact is, that whereas the taking and demolishing an enemy's forts, harbors, cities, men, ships, and crops, and other such things by which our enemy is weakened, and our own interests and tactics supported, are necessary acts according to the laws and rights of war; to deface temples, statutes, and such like erections in pure wantonness, and without any prospect of strengthening oneself or weakening the enemy, must be regarded as an act of blind passion and insanity. For the purpose with which good men wage war is not the destruction and annihilation of wrongdoers, but the reformation and alteration of wrongful acts.[32]

Polybius sets out the common law of mankind concerning war in a way which is supposed to match the contemporary view of war that Roman political leaders held.

Concerning ancient India, it has also been claimed that the rules of war were more humane than in other ancient societies primarily because of a recognition of an eternal law concerning battle. S. V. Viswanatha says:

> The warrior is not to swerve from the eternal law when he strikes in battle. A Ksatriya who renounces righteousness and transgresses all wholesome barriers does not deserve to be reckoned as such, and society should drive him out. The incidents of warfare in ancient India were not so inhuman as in other countries of the world at the time, as is clear from the accounts of foreign travelers. Megasthenes bears testimony to the fact that the [Indian] laws of war were humane and that wholesale destruction and devastation was forbidden. And we read in the *Mahabharata*:
>
> They must win who are strong in virtue
>
> Fight for virtue's stainless laws;
>
> Doubly armed the stalwart warrior
>
> Who is armed in righteous cause.[33]

The ancient Indian idea that eternal law dictated that wars be fought virtuously presents us with a strong parallel to the ancient Roman ideas of the laws of war as emanating from the *jus naturale*.

31 Ibid., pp. 48–49.

32 Translated in ibid., pp. 53–54.

33 Viswanatha, *International Law in Ancient India*, p. 126.

One question that arises is whether the emerging empires in ancient India and Rome played any role in inspiring the legal thought about the *jus gentium* of ancient Rome, and the eternal law concerning battle of the ancient Indians. Is there a kind of similarity from thinking of the laws of one's own country made up of the laws of the various regions of that country, to thinking about the laws of the empire made up of the laws of the nations that constitute the empire? And is it only a small step from the idea of the common laws of existing nations to the eternal law or *jus naturale*? Writers at the end of the nineteenth century and the beginning of the twentieth century CE attempted to make this case and then to extend their reasoning to support the idea of a true international law of ancient times.

It should be admitted though that for all of the claims that Rome was different from its neighbors by being less cruel, there were also instances where Rome felt it had to respond in kind to mass atrocities by those neighbors. Here is an account of one such incident which was described as "the largest and most famous massacre of Roman civilians." The massacre was ordered by King Mithridates VI of Puntus in 88 BCE: "They should set upon all the Romans and Italians in their towns, and upon their wives and children and the freedmen of Italian birth, kill them and throw their bodies out unburied ..." And it "was claimed that 80,000 died in the ensuing bloodbath."[34] Rome felt it had to respond to such a massacre and to respond in kind.

Yet, in most cases the nations conquered by Rome did not seek vengeance against Romans – rather the *Pax Romano*, the peace that Rome offered to those nations that peacefully were incorporated into the Roman Empire, was sought after. Goldsworthy argues that as governor of Cilicia:

> Cicero simply did not have the resources to carry out the day-to-day administration of all the communities within his province, nor was he expected to do this. The Roman way was to let each city or other grouping – tribes were common in some regions, especially in the west – govern itself. The governor was there to protect the province against internal and external threats, to oversee administration and taxation from a distance, and to act as the supreme judicial authority.[35]

The *Pax Romano* depended on allowing self-government and respect for the nations in the empire and leaving the people alone unless they did not pay taxes.

There are similarities between the way the Roman Empire was constructed and the way the Indian Empire was also created. E. Washburn Hopkins tells us that:

> It is interesting that both Manu and Vishnu state that when a king has conquered a foreign foe he shall make a prince of that country (not of his own) the king there, and (Vishnu adds, III.49) he shall not destroy the royal race of his foe unless that

[34] Adrian Goldsworthy, *Pax Romano*, New Haven, CT: Yale University Press, 2016, pp. 100–101.

[35] Ibid., p. 115.

> royal race be of ignoble birth. He is to honor the gods and the customs of the conquered country and grant exemptions from taxation (for a time) (Manu, VII.201).[36]

It seems that the idea of leaving the conquered people to govern themselves was practiced among ancient Indian rulers just as among ancient Roman rulers.

While controversial, various writers on ancient Indian legal thought make a straightforward case for international law in ancient India.

> International law in India, was accepted by all Indian states, for it was based on *Dharma*, which regulated also the conduct of the individual in society. The *Dharma*, we are told, was to prevail all over India ... there was common subjection to the unifying force of *Dharma* due to the fear that violation of the rules would entail the wrath of the Almighty. Thus, in India the general rules of conduct were already in existence and the nations had only to act up to them unquestioningly.[37]

Viswanatha goes on to say that Indian international law was based on a "superior ethical sense" embodied in *dharma*.[38] And in this respect ancient Indian and ancient Roman legal thought were similar in seeing their empires governed by universal moral norms.

CONCLUDING THOUGHTS FOR PART C

The idea that there was an eternal law or law of nature that governed over the whole world and from which civil laws of various societies drew authority was given strong theoretical support by the end of the first century CE. And alongside this universal law there was an emerging law of peoples that governed the relations of states in certain regions of the ancient world.

The emerging empires of India and Rome created the space for a broader and more encompassing legal regime than previously. But we also found that the idea of autonomy of the various conquered states was recognized as a matter of law. Some scholars have seen models for international law developing in these emerging empires of Rome and India. The practical problems of extending a legal system over vast territory forced these ancient societies to conceive of the same law having quite different applications from one part of the empire to another. Problems of conflict of laws were also addressed in ways that had not been seen previously.

One of the central legal concepts in Roman legal thought (which we have seen previewed in Hammurabi's Code as well as in the works of Aristotle) is the idea

[36] E. Washburn Hopkins, "The Growth of Law and Legal Institutions," in *The Cambridge History of India*, Vol. 1, Cambridge: Cambridge University Press, 1922, pp. 289–290.

[37] Viswanatha, *International Law in Ancient India*, pp. 9–10.

[38] Ibid., p. 11.

of equity. The idea that justice can be understood too strictly so that unfairness is produced was the basis of the later debates about how much discretion judges should have. In Roman times, an institution grew up, the Praetorship, which could overrule other courts on grounds of equity and fairness so that law could not be used for oppression of those who were vulnerable. In India, judges were expected to rule on matters of both justice and equity, where equity was thought to be the key to the overall fairness of the system of law.

Despite the fact that ancient Roman and Indian criminal law is often characterized as brutal – and there certainly are many examples of this – we also found that as in other ancient legal systems there was a striking concern for humaneness nonetheless. That a system of law could be characterized as both cruel and humane is somewhat paradoxical. But that a system of law could be both respectful of differences in class and yet rigid in seeing law as differently applied based on those class differentiations is not necessarily problematic. Our exploration of the legal thought of ancient India and the Roman Republic has yielded a picture of what law could have been for even ancient times that is highly meaningful for the way law must bend to the contours of an ever changing world.

We saw that some of the worst crimes that a person could commit were those that, as the Romans put it, undermined the majesty of the people of Rome. It was also considered a crime to prosecute a frivolous or false case – resulting in very severe punishment in both Rome and India. The law was to be used for the good of the society and not merely to enhance one's own position in that society. Of course, in practice the law was used for the purpose of personal aggrandizement, but the task of the overseers of the legal system was to minimize those occasions when law was misused. We have here the critical self-examination of the law that was soon to be one of the hallmarks of legal scholarship and writing, as we will see in the final part of this work.

PART D

Rabbinic Law and the Roman Empire

INTRODUCTION FOR PART D

We will next examine legal thought at the end of the ancient period – roughly from the second until the fifth century CE. During this period law became a subject of study and writing at a high level of sophistication and abstraction. Various schools of law scholars competed and clashed with each other. Arguments about how to interpret the law were a matter of public record with the greatest minds of the time engaged in writing commentaries on the law, which are still regarded today as masterpieces, such as the work of the Roman theorists Gaius and Ulpian as well as the Rabbis who wrote the Mishnah and the Talmud. This is the richest legal literature of the ancient period but also the hardest to survey because of the sheer extent of the writings – the Babylonian Talmud ran to over 30 volumes as did Justinian's *Institute*, *Code*, and *Digest*. And these texts concerned some of the most difficult of legal questions, such as how to understand the relationship between a person's state of mind and his or her guiltiness.

At the end of the ancient period, law became increasingly concerned with many aspects of social and even personal life. The law was propounded in enormous detail in very long legal texts: the Hebrew Bible, along with the Mishnah, as well as the *Code*, *Digests* and *Institutes* of the Roman Emperor Justinian. But there were also other large legal texts of great importance in the first half-millennium of the Common Era. For example, the Codes of Theodosia and Constantine played a larger role for Romans at the time, than did the Justinian Code. And the Babylonian Talmud played a very large role in the daily life of the Jews, almost as much as the Bible itself.

The increasingly legal regulation of daily life in the first few centuries CE was matched by ever-lengthening commentaries on the law by some of the most significant legal theorists at the time. In Rome, we find the writings of Gaius and Ulpian to surpass even the writings of Cicero in importance. And among the Jews we find the writings of Josephus and Philo to match the Roman thinkers in scale and importance. We find here commentators on the Biblical and Roman law becoming a full-blown profession – where jurists and lawyers became serious students of the law in ways not seen previously.

Unlike earlier periods of ancient legal thought that we have examined, we find a unique occurrence in the fact that Roman and Rabbinic Law developed largely within the same political territory, giving rise to questions concerning the conflict of laws not seen in such widespread scale previously. Indeed, the Romans provided a set of laws just to deal with the governance of the Jews, who were in their midst, which we will examine in this last part of my work. And we continue to find also a clash between Roman laws that are increasingly seen as fully secular in contrast to Jewish law that remained firmly grounded in deep religious commitments. Despite this major difference we will also see many similarities between the legal thoughts of the Romans and the Jews that had a profound impact on the entire Medieval period and up to and including our own day.

SECTION XIII

Justice, Equity, and Conflict of Laws

35

Law, Morality, and Religion

Jewish law was always understood as the law of God, literally handed down to Moses in the form of inscribed stone tablets. Roman law of the Republican period also involved inscribed stone tables of law, but even as early as the fifth century BCE Romans understood these laws as human creations. This appears to be a very great difference and it is commonly said that the Jewish law was really a religious law while the Roman law was thoroughly secular. In this first chapter I will argue that the difference between these two legal systems was not as profound as it might appear since both the Jewish and Roman law were deeply influenced by morality – so the difference is best understood as that between a legal system based on religious morality and one based on secular morality. The common link to morality is much more significant than the differences between religiously and secularly grounded systems of law, as I will argue.

It is clear that the earliest of Roman law is religiously inspired and it is only in the later periods, especially in the time of the Roman Empire, that religious considerations are submerged in favor of explicitly moral ones. It is also clear that the Biblical Code of the Covenant while portrayed as arising *ab initio* from God's hand was actually heavily influenced by earlier Babylonian law, especially Hammurabi's Code that we explored extensively in Part A of this work in ancient legal thought.[1] Throughout this chapter I will highlight the common concern for justice and equity in Jewish and Roman law of the first five centuries of the Common Era.

In Section 35.1 I will explore the ideas of justice that underpinned the Jewish and Roman law at the end of the ancient period. In Section 35.2 I will summarize the way the Jewish civil and religious law was intertwined. In Section 35.3 I will similarly

[1] See David P. Wright, *Inventing God's Law: How the Covenant Code of the Bible Used and Revised the Laws of Hammurabi*, Oxford: Oxford University Press, 2009. Also see Stanley Cook, *The Laws of Moses and the Code of Hammurabi*, London: Adam and Charles Black, 1903. Note that these two books were written over a century apart but came to roughly the same conclusions about the strong influence on the Hebrew Bible of the Code of Hammurabi.

summarize how Roman civil and moral law was intertwined in our period. In Section 35.4 I will set out the differences between these Jewish and Roman conceptions of law. And in the final Section 35.5 I will argue that the common source of morality is more important than the differences between these systems of law.

35.1 JUSTICE AND EQUITY IN RABBINIC AND LATE ROMAN LEGAL THOUGHT

As I have argued throughout the previous parts of this work, justice and equity are the key concepts in ancient legal thought. While it is true that stability and even class oppression are also important considerations in most ancient legal systems, the legal thought of the ancient period is thoroughly infused with discussions of how law can be used so that justice, especially for the least fortunate, can be achieved. We can begin with the start of Justinian's *Institutes*, a text meant to be used in the teaching of law students, which also surveyed the legal developments in the four centuries prior to its publication in the middle of the sixth century CE. Here is part of the very beginning of Justinian's *Institutes*:

> The imperial majesty should be not only made glorious by arms but also strengthened by laws, that, alike in time of peace and in time of war, the state may be well governed, and that the emperor may not only be victorious in the field of battle, but also by every legal means repel the iniquities of men who abuse the laws, and may at once religiously uphold justice and triumph over his conquered enemies …
>
> Justice is the constant and perpetual wish to render every one his due.
>
> Jurisprudence is the knowledge of things divine and human; the science of the just and the unjust.[2]

These famous lines are meant to summarize the task of the law in the times of the Roman Empire.

Here is the commentary by Thomas Collett Sanders on the first part of Justinian's *Institutes*:

> The term *jus*, in its most extended sense, was taken by the Roman jurists to include all the commands laid upon men that they are bound to fulfill, both the commands of morality and of law. The distinction between commands which are only enforced by the sanction of public or private opinion, and those enforced by positive legal sanctions, may seem clear to us; but the Roman jurists in speaking of the elementary principles and divisions of jurisprudence, did not keep law and morality distinct. Celsus defines *jus* as *ars boni et aequi* [the art of the good and equitable] …

[2] *The Institutes of Justinian*, translated by Thomas Collett Sandars, London: Longmans, Green and Co., 1917, pp. 1 and 5.

> This extension of the term would sink positive law in morality; that would only be supposed to be commanded which ought to be commanded.[3]

We can see this clearly in the very next paragraphs of the Institutes where it is declared that "The maxims of law are these: to live honestly, to hurt no one, and to give everyone his due."[4] These maxims are moral just as much as legal.

There is a remarkable similarity between the beginning of Justinian's *Institutes* and the beginning of Hammurabi's Code over two thousand years earlier. Hammurabi says:

> the gods Anu and Enlil, for the enhancement of the well-being of the people, named me by name Hammurabi, the pious prince, who venerates the gods, to make justice prevail in the land, to abolish the wicked and the evil, to prevent the strong from oppressing the weak, to rise like the sun-god Shamash over all humankind to illuminate the land.[5]

There is also a well-documented connection between Hammurabi's Code and the Covenant Code of the Hebrew Bible. Indeed, as we saw earlier, the *lex talionis* provisions thought to be unique to the Bible were already included in Hammurabi's Code from a considerably earlier period.

In Biblical times, law is considered the command of God. Justice is basically understood as following God's law. In the time of the Talmud, the Hebrew term *halakhah* refers to the law which governs daily life for Jews. The Mishnah set out rules to govern most aspects of Jewish life that were not explicitly enunciated in the Hebrew Bible. The early Biblical codes of law are enhanced many times over in the Mishnah, Tosefta, and the Talmud. And it is the rabbis who create these interpretive texts and present them as the law which must be obeyed.

As one scholar of the Talmud has said, the rabbis who wrote the Talmud were as much lawyers as religious leaders.

> The Rabbis were not only theologians; they were principally ecclesiastical lawyers. This was necessarily so, because Rabbinic Judaism aimed at controlling the whole life of its adherents. Even the Pentateuchal code touches upon many matters which are usually excluded from the sphere of religion; and Judaism, in its later developed form, drew no sharp line of demarcation between the secular and the religious. If God is omnipresent, every phase of human existence must be influenced by that idea.[6]

3 Ibid., p. 5.

4 Ibid., p. 6.

5 *Laws of Hammurabi*, in *Law Collections From Mesopotamia and Asia Minor*, second edition, translated by Martha T. Roth, Atlanta, GA: Scholars' Press, 1997, pp. 76–77.

6 Reverend A. Cohen, *The Babylonian Talmud: Tractate Berakhot*, Introduction, Cambridge: Cambridge University Press, 1921, p. xxix.

As with the lawyers of the Roman Empire, some of the rabbis became scholars of the law, not merely those who applied the law.

The ideas of justice and equity were central to late Roman and Jewish legal thought, as they were in other ancient societies. As we saw in Part C, Roman ideas of equity were strongly influenced by Aristotle. On one construal, equity was a correction of justice so that law could be applied in ways that were more in keeping with the intent of the lawmakers than would be true according to strict justice. This is the view that Cicero takes over from Aristotle. According to Boaz Cohen, Biblical law understood equity in terms of the idea "to make straight, to rectify" and stood opposed to the strict application of the law.[7]

As this chapter develops we will say much more about justice and equity in Roman and Jewish legal thought. This section has been meant to introduce some of the main themes that will be developed, not just in the remaining sections of this chapter but also in subsequent chapters. One key similarity that will be noted is that providing for the poor was a key legal theme in both systems of law. One significant difference is that the protection of the alien is much more pronounced in Jewish law than in Roman law, probably due to the fact that the Jews were aliens in several countries over their history and continued to be aliens in the Roman Empire as well.

35.2 RELIGION AND LAW IN ANCIENT RABBINIC THOUGHT

The rabbinic text called the Mishnah sets out the law for Jews at the time who were living in Rome during the first few centuries CE. The Talmud is a somewhat later (sixth century CE) interpretation of the Mishnah. Both the Mishnah and the Talmud are written law that attempts to interpret the Oral Law conveyed by God. Here is a bit of the Mishnah's book "Aboth":

> Moses received the Law from Sinai and committed it to Joshua, and Joshua to the elders, and the elders to the Prophets, and the Prophets committed it to the men of the Great Synagogue. They said three things: Be deliberate in judgment, raise up many disciples, and make a fence around the Law.[8]

And this part of the Mishnah ends with the following:

> Rabbi Hanniah ben Aksahya said: The Holy One, blessed is he, was minded to grant merit to Israel; therefore hath he multiplied for them the Law and commandments, as it is written, *It pleased the Lord for his righteousness sake to magnify the Law and make it honorable*.[9]

7 Boaz Cohen, *Jewish and Roman Law: A Comparative Study*, Vol. 1, New York: Jewish Theological Seminary, 1966, p. 49.

8 *The Mishnah*, translated by Herbert Danby, Oxford: Oxford University Press, 1933, p. 446.

9 *The Mishnah*, ibid., p. 461. The passage from the Bible quoted in italics is from Isaiah 42.

The Mishnah and then also the Talmud trace their lineage back to the Law that Moses received directly from God. So, these legal texts are derived from a divine source and yet they do more than just set religious law – for the law of property and even criminal law provisions are contained in these ancient texts.

Rabbi Samuel ben Meir, writing in the eleventh century CE, explains the ancient ideas of legal interpretation as follows:

> I will explain the laws and rules [of the Torah] in a manner that conforms to the [natural] way of the world. Nevertheless, it is the halahic level of interpretation that is the most essential one, as the rabbis said (b. Sotah 16a) "Halakhah uproots [the plain meaning of] the biblical text."[10]

Samuel Greengus comments:

> in Judaism in particular we see an extraordinarily strong focus upon the written laws and a deeply felt need to bring older texts in line with evolving postbiblical life and practice. To achieve conceptual harmony, the rabbis presented their interpretations in a seamless interface with the ancient biblical texts. For them, law was religiously definitive, the basis of their covenant with God.[11]

Halahic law is the law of the rabbis, which reached its golden age in the same period as the law of the Roman Empire.

Unlike the Roman law, the halahic law remained rooted in the Bible, a divine ancient religious source, and the halahic law was meant to be an adaptation of the Biblical law. The halahic law was like the Roman law in that it governed nearly every aspect of Jewish life. But unlike Roman law, the Jewish halahic law remained intimately connected to religious law. Yet it is interesting that Jewish law is deeply connected to a religious law that is intertwined with ideas of the natural way of the world. In this respect Jewish law and Roman law are actually very close, as we will see.

The ancient rabbis were commentators on the law of the Bible and they were scholars of the law as well as religious scholars. As scholars, the rabbis created an immense body of work that interpreted the Bible – the largest of these works was the Babylonian Talmud which was created at roughly the same time as the Roman legal scholars were creating the codes of Theodosia and the Digest and Code of Justinian. Indeed as we will see later in this chapter we have perhaps for the first time the idea that the word of the legal scholars was itself a source of law.

Even when the writings of the rabbis seemed to conflict with the law of the Bible the rabbinical writings had the force of law. But this was only true if the rabbis could

10 Quoted in Samuel Greengus, *Laws in the Bible and in Early Rabbinic Collections*, Eugene, OR: Cascade Books, 2011, p. 3.

11 Ibid., p. 3.

make a convincing case for linking their views to those Biblical sources. And in this respect the Talmud offers often very creative hermeneutical exposition, as we will see during the various chapters of this fourth part of my study of ancient legal thought. Here is just one passage from the Talmud which I will spend much more time on in a later chapter:

> Since the frame of the passages [from Exodus in the bible] makes reference to generative causes it is to be inferred that there are derivative causes as well … So then what is the difference between an act that falls into the generative category and one that falls into the derivative category? The upshot is that if one simultaneously carried out two actions that fall into the generative acts of labor, or two actions that fall into the derivative category, he is liable for each such action, while if he performed simultaneously both a generative act of labor and a derivative of that same generative act he is liable on only one count.[12]

In this part of the Talmud, the rabbis create an account of causation in the law that is generated out of the consideration of just a few lines from the Biblical book of Exodus. But it is important that the rabbinic writing is indeed plausibly connected to the word of God. The Jewish secular law is deeply intertwined with Jewish religious law.

A cursory look at the Mishnah and Talmud structure reveals how intertwined law and religion are in ancient Jewish legal thought. The divisions are:

i. laws dealing with agricultural produce and feeding the poor;
ii. laws concerning religious feasts;
iii. laws affecting women;
iv. laws concerning damage and property;
v. laws concerning temple rites and affairs;
vi. laws concerning pollution and uncleanness.

Thus we have standard secular legal matters such as how to assess damage and what rights of property are in various situations, along with standard religious matters such as how people are to act at religious feasts and in their homes when preparing meals.

So, not only does the authority of law have a religious grounding, but the lists of laws for governing Jewish life also mix the secular and religious. At least in part, this is because all aspects of life are thought to be interrelated, where the conduct of a ritual took place in a public place and so there needed to be law for the proper way to order the ritual and also the proper response when one person assaulted another in the public sphere.

[12] *The Babylonian Talmud*, translated by Jacob Neusner, Vol. 13: *Tractate Baba Qamma*, Peabody, MA: Hendrickson Publishers, 2005, pp. 1–2.

35.3 MORALITY AND LAW IN THE ROMAN EMPIRE

Roman law, especially that of the Roman Empire, is often said to be thoroughly secular; it is perhaps the first such secular legal system in the world. And in this respect Roman law is contrasted with the religious law of the Jews. But it is also true that Roman law is intimately connected with morality, not just Roman mores but with a universal morality. And the morality here is one that is in many respects a natural morality or a natural law morality, as we will see, and thus in many ways quite similar to Jewish law of roughly the same time period.

In earlier chapters we discussed the way that Cicero and others of his time in the Roman Republic were influenced by the Stoic philosophical idea of nature and of natural law. This influence continued to be important in the legal writings of Gaius and Ulpian as well as in the way that the Justinian Institutes were begun. Here for instance is how Gaius, one of the most significant jurists of the Roman Empire, understands the various types of law at the beginning of his *Institutes*:

> Every people that is governed by statutes and customs observes partly its own peculiar law and partly the common law of all mankind. That law which a people establishes for itself is peculiar to it, and is called *ius civile* (civil law) as being the special law of that *civitas* (State), while the law that natural reason establishes among all mankind is followed by peoples alike, and is called *ius gentium* (law of nations, or law of the world) as being the law observed by all mankind. Thus the Roman people observes partly its own peculiar law and partly the common law of mankind.[13]

Notice that the common law of all mankind is said to derive from what natural reason can ascertain.

For Gaius, the common law is a kind of custom that is found in most societies. That custom is itself a kind of moral law in that it is not propounded by lawmakers but is what seems to be morally reasonable behavior. The people of Rome are bound by this moral law just as these same people are bound by the explicit and specific laws that have been enacted or otherwise promulgated by lawmakers. In this respect, law has both a moral component and a strictly civil component. Or in other words, law in the Roman Empire is not merely secular rules but also moral rules which derive from many sources perhaps including religious ones.

Another great Roman jurist, Ulpian, also gives us a sense of what law is and how lawyers are to proceed, at the beginning of his *Institutes*, as reported at the beginning of Justinian's *Digest*:

[13] *The Institutes of Gaius*, Book 1.1, translated by Francis De Zulueta, Oxford: Oxford University Press, 1946, Part 1, p. 3.

> Those who apply themselves to the study of law should know, in the first place, from whence the science is derived. The law obtains its name from justice, for (as Celsus elegantly says) law is the art of knowing what is good and just. Anyone may properly call us the priests of this art, for we cultivate justice and profess to know what is good and equitable, dividing right from wrong, and distinguishing what is lawful from what is unlawful, desiring to make men good through fear of punishment but also by the encouragement of reward; aiming (if I am not mistaken) at a true, and not a pretended philosophy.[14]

Law, for Ulpian, has a distinctly moral set of concerns, including not only the identification of what is good but also the instilling of the good in humans. Punishment in law is given a significantly moral justification.

Ulpian has similar although importantly different things to say than what Gaius says about natural law also as reported by Justinian:

> Of this subject there are two divisions, public and private ... Private law is threefold in its nature, for it is derived from either natural precepts, from those of nations, or from those of Civil Law. Natural Law is that which nature teaches to all animals, for the law is not peculiar to the human race, but affects all creatures which deduce their origin from the sea or the land, and it is also common to birds. From it precedes the union of male and female which we designate as marriage ... The Law of Nations is that used by the human race, and it is easy to understand that it differs from natural law, for the reason that the latter is common to all animals, while the former only concerns men in their relations to one another.

Here Ulpian draws a distinction between the law of nature and the law of nations, which Gaius had seemingly confused and run together.

But the distinction that Ulpian attempts to draw is itself not as clear as it could be and as it had been drawn in ancient Greek times. The difference for Ulpian seems to be whether we are addressing all animals (law of nature) or just humans (law of nations). Yet, it would seem that these categories would overlap quite significantly – humans are governed by the law of nature along with all other nonhuman animals. The law of nations, if it is to be truly different than the law of nature, would have to concern the unnatural state of humans interacting with each other. Such a state does not appear to be easily characterized as unnatural, especially since the beings whose relations are the subject of the law of nations are natural human beings.

Nonetheless, for Ulpian and Gaius, there is a kind of moral law that has an influence over the civil law. Marriage for instance is seen as a natural relation among humans and one that is regulated by the civil law. And natural reason is seen as the

[14] *The Digest or the Pandects of Justinian*, Book 1, Title 1, in *The Civil Law*, translated by S. P. Scott, Vol. II, Cincinnati, OH: The Central Trust Co., 1932, p. 209.

key to ascertaining what law should be enacted and whether or not the existing law should be obeyed.

Justinian begins his *Institutes* in a similar fashion to that of Gaius and Ulpian as follows:

> The law of nature is that law which nature teaches to all animals. For this law does not belong exclusively to the human race, but belongs to all animals, whether of the air, the earth, or the sea. Hence, comes that yoking together of male and female, which we term matrimony; hence the procreation and bringing up of children. We see, indeed, that all other animals besides man, are considered as having knowledge of this law.
>
> Civil law is thus distinguished from the law of nations. Every community governed by laws and customs uses partly its own laws, partly laws common to all mankind.[15]

Justinian, like Gaius who he follows, seems to somewhat confuse the law of nations and the law of nature.

If there are laws that are common to all of mankind, not merely all nations at a particular time, then there is a sense that the law of nature and the law of nations would be at least overlapping if not covering the same ground for humans. Nonetheless the ground of these laws would differ significantly. The laws of nature are discovered by natural reason whereas the laws of nations would simply be what all nations did in fact have as their laws in common. Of course, one can then ask why it is that all of the nations of mankind would have some laws in common unless it turned out that these laws, such as laws against homicide, were seen as reasonable laws for any nation to have.

As with the ancient Greeks, the differences between the law of nature and the law of nations come out clearly in how slaves are understood in Roman legal thought. As a matter of the laws of nature, all humans are due equal respect especially concerning their liberty – and this would seemingly rule out slavery. But as a matter of the common laws of the nations of the world, slavery was permitted. As we will see, the idea that civil law could be and should be influenced by moral considerations is seen in these texts, even given their differences.

35.4 THE RELIGIOUS ASPECTS OF LAW

In this section I will attempt to provide a sense of how Jewish and late Roman conceptions of law differed, but also begin to explain how they are nonetheless significantly similar. As we have already seen, Jewish law is said to come directly from

[15] *The Institutes of Justinian*, Book I, Ch. II, translated by Thomas Collett Sandars, London: Longmans, Green and Co., 1917, pp. 7–8.

God's word. Roman law is said to be, at least by the time of the Rome Empire, thoroughly secular. Yet, the law of the early Roman kings is couched in religious terms as we see in the first laws attributed to Numa Pompilius (716–673 BCE):

> Numa ordered that fish that have no scales, except the scar, should not be offered to the gods.
>
> When spoils of the first class are captured by a general with a citizen army under his auspices, he shall sacrifice an ox to Jupiter Feretrius …
>
> Having embraced … all his legislation about religious matters in writing, he divided it into eight parts, as many as were the classes of priests.[16]

We also see a mixing of religious and secular civil law in the most famous early Roman legal text, the *Twelve Tables* (451–449 BCE), where Table X explicitly concerned "Sacred Law" as these examples illustrate:

1. A dead person shall not be buried or burned in the city.
2. … More than this one shall not do; one shall not smooth a funeral pyre with an ax.
3. … Expenses of a funeral shall be limited to three mourners wearing veils and one mourner wearing an inexpensive purple tunic and ten flutists.
4. Women shall not tear their cheeks or shall not make a sorrowful outcry on account of a funeral.[17]

In these earliest Roman codes, religious matters and purely civil matters are mixed. And in the Roman Empire there are also laws that concern religious practice – for instance distinguishing how Jews and Christians can interact concerning matters of religious rite. In a later chapter we will survey this material in much greater detail. I will merely mention here that there were several important Roman laws on who could be circumcised, a religious rite associated with the Jews and condemned by early Christians, such as the law of Constantine of October 21, 335: "The Prohibition of the Circumcision of Non-Jewish Slaves and of Persecution of Jewish Converts to Christianity."[18]

Even as the later Roman laws of the Empire removed many but not all references to Sacred Law, religious conceptions played a role in the discussion of how the laws were normatively grounded. Some of the emperors were considered to be gods, or to be god's representative on earth, giving the lawgiver a quasi-religious status or

[16] *Laws of the Kings II: Numa Pompilius*, in *Ancient Roman Statutes*, translated by Allan Chester Johnson, Paul Robinson Coleman-Norton, and Frank Card Bourne, Austin: University of Texas Press, 1961, 2012, p. 4.

[17] *The Twelve Tables*, in *Ancient Roman Statutes*, p. 12.

[18] This is listed as Law No. 10 in *The Jews in Roman Imperial Legislation*, translated and edited by Amnon Linder, Detroit, MI: Wayne State University Press, 1987, pp. 138–143.

authority. Here is one example that concerns the reception of the Senate of the Theodosian Code:

The assembly shouted:

> "Augustuses of Augustuses, the greatest of Augustuses!
>
> "God gave You to us, God save You for us! ...
>
> These are the prayers of the Senate, these are the prayers of the Roman people!"[19]

We see here that the emperor was treated as god's representative who was empowered by god to promulgate what is largely a secular code of law.

More significantly, the references to the law of nature in the works of Cicero and later in the works of Gaius, Ulpian, and the writers of Justinian's *Institutes* sometimes talk as if the laws of nature are divine laws. In Justinian's *Institutes* we see that:

> The Laws of nature, which all nations observe alike, being established by divine providence, remains ever fixed and immutable. But the laws which every state has enacted, undergo frequent changes, either by the tacit consent of the people, or by a new law being subsequently passed.[20]

Here we have an explicit link between laws of nature, which are legally binding on all people, and divine providence. Gaius also talks of natural reason as tapping into a kind of divine reason.[21]

Ulpian gives us a different understanding of the role of the divine in civil law when he says:

> Justice is the constant and perpetual desire to give every one that to which he is entitled.
>
> The precepts of the law are the following: to live honorably, to injure no one, to give to every one his due.
>
> The science of the law is the acquaintance with Divine and human affairs, the knowledge of what is just and unjust.[22]

Notice here that part of the science of law involves knowledge of divine affairs which seemingly are important for understanding justice in the legal domain. We next take up the similarities in both Roman and Jewish law concerning the place of morality, whether religious or secular morality, in the study of law.

[19] *The Theodosian Code*, translated by Clyde Pharr, Princeton, NJ: Princeton University Press, 1952, p. 5.

[20] *The Institutes of Justinian*, Book I, Ch. II, p. 13.

[21] See *The Institutes of Gaius*, De Vol. II, pp. 12–13.

[22] *The Rules of Ulpian*, Book I, excerpts of which are presented in Justinian's *Digest*, in *The Civil Law*, translated by S. P. Scott, ibid., Vol. II, p. 211.

35.5 MORALITY AND THE DOMAIN OF LAW

Jewish religious law concerns more than is normally a matter of religious belief but also encompasses aspects of the domain of morality, similarly to the way that law is influenced by morality for the legal theorists of the Roman Empire. In both cases, custom is often merely the term for moral norms that have existed from time immemorial – founding the bedrock of the Mishnah and Talmud for the Jews and many of the provisions in Justinian's *Code* and *Digest*.

One might initially think that all of Jewish law is purely religious in the sense that it is all supposed to derive from God's delivering the law to Moses. Yet, the laws of the Mishnah, Tosefta, and the Talmud offer a huge number of laws that are only very remotely related to the religious laws of the Torah. Indeed much of the Talmud concerns moral matters that appear to be secular or only loosely religious. Indeed, it seems that there are various moral norms of the Talmud that ground both religious and secular rules governing Jewish life.

Similarly one might think, as some scholars assert, that the law of the Roman Empire period is purely secular in the sense that it is all propounded by the Senate or the Emperor or by certain high-ranking judges. Yet it is also true that the propounded laws of the Roman Empire often read like moral norms or are seemingly grounded in various moral norms. I will next provide more analysis of the centrality of the moral component of both Jewish and Roman law.

In one respect, as I have already indicated, both Jewish and Roman law encompass certain moral norms insofar as they incorporate customs which have origins so far back in time that there is no religious or political pedigree to these norms in terms of being propounded at Moses' time or by some past Roman legal authority. So, morality comes into both the largely religious law of the Jews and the largely positivist secular law of the Romans of the Empire.

In another respect, we can look to the emerging commentary on the law by theoretically inclined lawyers and rabbis to see the moral dimension of both of these sets of laws. This is the task of the following chapters, perhaps best seen in Chapter 37 where I investigate these professional groups in order to understand both their possible role as "lawmakers" and also as conveyers of the moral customs of the past.

Ulpian is perhaps the best example of a Roman jurist who placed morality at the center of his legal philosophy.[23] The extent to which this is true is a matter of considerable debate. Yet, to me the best account of Ulpian's legal philosophy, insofar as it was strongly moral in its core, comes from Tony Honore who argued that we can find the origins of the contemporary doctrine of human rights and the

[23] See Chapter 3 of Tony Honore, *Ulpian: Pioneer of Human Rights*, Oxford: Oxford University Press, 2002.

dignity of humans throughout Ulpian's writings. As we will see in more detail in later chapters, Ulpian also stands as one of only five legal theorists whose words were considered a "source" of law. In other words, Ulpian's portrayal of the moral foundation of Roman law was itself relied on by judges in their legal opinions and in the codifiers of the law of the Roman Empire – his writings are referred to more than anyone else in Justinian's *Digest*.

The Talmud as well as Justinian's *Code* plus his *Digest* were constructed at about the same time, the sixth century CE, and had roughly the same goal – the fairly minute regulation of daily life. In the next chapter we take up the fascinating question of what happened when these laws conflicted for Jews in Roman Imperial society. At the moment I wish to point out that not only did these bodies of law have roughly the same goal but they were also heavily reliant on moral custom and principle and that it does not seem to have mattered much to the people who were subject to these laws whether the morality had a secular or religious character.

36

Dual Legal Regimes

Jews living under the Roman Empire were faced with two legal systems that governed them – the extensive legal system of the Roman Empire and the equally extensive legal system of Judaism's halakhah. In this chapter I explore the way the conflicts were resolved, or not, as well as specific laws of the Roman Empire that sought to override Jewish law especially in matters of religious conversion. Roman law in the early years of the Empire seems to have been characterized by tolerance of Jews and their laws, or so I shall argue. It also seems that Roman laws of the later Empire, perhaps under the influence of Christianity, were considerably less tolerant toward Jews than earlier in the Empire.

In my study of ancient legal thought we have not previously encountered a clash of mature legal systems claiming to govern people's lives. The topic of the conflict of laws is increasingly important in our interconnected world today. In this sense it is interesting to see the flash points of controversy for Jews living under Roman law but also subject to their own system of law. The conflict might have been easier to resolve if Jewish law was solely about religious matters and Roman law solely about secular matters. But the domain of these legal systems was not so restricted.

In Section 36.1 I will set out in a preliminary way the domains of the two legal systems. In Section 36.2 I will examine an example of the conflict in question: Roman and Jewish laws concerning circumcision. And in Section 36.3 I examine the laws concerning Purim, a Jewish day of mischief where Roman rulers were often skewered. In Section 36.4 I take a step back from these laws to examine the views of various theorists on the way to understand the conflict of the laws for Jews living under Roman rule. In the final section, the idea of autonomy of legal systems is discussed with an eye toward the role of tolerance in ancient legal thought.

36.1 OVERLAPPING LEGAL DOMAINS

The scope of Jewish law of the Mishnah and then later the Talmud encompasses most of the life of a Jew. Jewish law concerned not just religious worship but also ordinary affairs of interactions among people. Even in the otherwise secular life of a Jew, the law of God was supposed to govern, and the religious leaders were supposed to adjudicate so as to maintain the peace of the community.[1] For centuries, Jews had governed themselves according to Jewish law. Once incorporated into the Roman Empire, Jewish law's wide domain sometimes conflicted with Roman law.

The law of the Roman Empire had several features that made conflict with Jewish law more likely. First, in terms of religious beliefs and practices there was an immediate problem since at least some of the emperors were supposed to be gods who were to be worshipped by all of the people in the empire. Yet, Jews believed that they should worship only the one true god. Citizenship required such worship, thus undercutting the ability of Jews to attain citizenship.

Second, and most importantly for our study, the law of the Roman Empire governed nearly all aspects of ordinary life of the people in the empire. So, while the Romans granted to Jews a certain amount of autonomy in their religious practices, there was an inevitable conflict between Jewish law and Roman law concerning the ordinary affairs of Jews when interacting with each other and especially when Jews interacted with non-Jews. When Jews married each other, Romans could leave such matters to be governed by Jewish courts. But when Jewish courts sought to exercise authority over criminal matters, this posed a challenge to the Roman state.

Once again, the problem can be seen in that Jews did not really distinguish between religious and civil law. Romans would probably have allowed autonomy for Jews in the religious domain if Jews recognized Roman law as governing civil or secular matters. Jews were not only to be governed by the Ten Commandments, but also by all of the laws in the Torah as well as the laws that the rabbis saw to be emanating from the Torah. And here the minute regulation of the life of Jews was set out in the texts that were all said to be based in God's word.[2] Many Jews saw obedience to the emperor as an instance of idolatry, which was forbidden by the Ten Commandments.

The early emperors of the Roman Empire favored giving indigenous peoples a wide swath of autonomy, but in the case of the Jews there were severe complications. Tolerance of the customs of the Jews would mean exempting Jews from the purview of Roman law. And yet such exemption would undermine the often fragile relations

[1] See Dora Askowith, *The Tolerance and Persecution of the Jews in the Roman Empire*, Part 1, NY: Columbia University, 1915, p. 182.

[2] See Emil Schurer, *A History of the Jewish People in the Time of Jesus Christ*, Second Division, Vol. 1, translated by Sophia Taylor and Rev. Peter Christie, Edinburgh: T & T Clark, 1890, pp. 306–312.

between Rome and its many subject peoples in the empire. Indeed, the very idea of Jews as citizens of the empire was fraught since many Jews did not recognize the sovereignty of the empire or the emperor's law. As we will see, tolerance was strained especially after the empire recognized Christianity as the religion of the empire. The polytheism of the early empire was easier to reconcile with the Jews worshipping yet one more god. But once the empire was officially monotheist, with the rise of Christianity, and the one god was seemingly not that of the Jewish religion, tolerance of the Jews was sorely tested.

From a theoretical perspective, it is not clear why the Christian monotheism of the later Roman Empire could not tolerate Jewish monotheism. After all, both Christians and Jews seemingly worshipped the same God and their monotheisms were thus very similar. And both Christians and Jews held the Torah to be God's word and the Ten Commandments as governing all people. What separated these monotheisms was the interpretation of God's word. And as often happens, people are most intolerant of those who are seemingly closest to them.

Here is how one scholar characterized the problem we will spend this chapter analyzing:

> Besides the conflict which arose from the inconsistencies of the demands of religion on one hand and those of civil government on the other, the Jews found themselves at variance with the Romans in still another respect. The tension between the two nationalities became all the more strained, the more the conflict involved each other's peculiarities. The claim of the Romans to universal empire rested on their power as a great conquering nation, while the Jews, as the "chosen people," considered themselves superior to all the others.[3]

I would add that deification of the Roman emperor also added to the conflict in ways that a claim to power alone would not. And the idea of being the "chosen people" does not necessarily mean that Jews could not live among those who were not "chosen" although it may create difficulties when the not-chosen people exert the right to rule over the chosen ones.

The conflict of laws comes to the fore when the religious idea of being chosen is extended to the domain of all aspects of life. In such a conception, there is no room for secular or civil law divorced from the one true religion. And such an idea results in a conflict of laws when the Jews as chosen people are subjects in a regime that also comes increasingly to govern most aspects of life. In the next section we will see an illustration of this conflict, the Jewish practice of circumcision.

[3] Askowith, *The Tolerance and Persecution of the Jews in the Roman Empire*, p. 160.

36.2 CIRCUMCISION AND CONVERSION

In Judaism, all males are to be circumcised. In the book of Genesis, we find the following command of God:

> God further said to Abraham, "As for you, you and your offspring to come through the ages shall keep My covenant. Such shall be the covenant between Me and you and your offspring to follow which you shall keep: every male among you shall be circumcised. You shall circumcise the flesh of your foreskin, and that shall be the sign of the covenant between Me and you. And throughout the generations, every male among you shall be circumcised at the age of eight days. As for the homeborn slave and the one bought from an outsider who is not of your offspring, they must be circumcised, homeborn and purchased alike. Thus shall My covenant be marked in your flesh as an everlasting pact. And if any male who is uncircumcised fails to circumcise the flesh of his foreskin, that person shall be cut off from his kin, he has broken My covenant."[4]

Notice that the law is that all male members of a Jewish household must be circumcised, including slaves, regardless of where they were born. It is this provision that came to be problematic for the Jews, given various Roman laws that forbad the circumcising of non-Jews.

The practice of circumcision seems to be a trivial matter, but it came to stand for much more than the simple removing of the foreskin of the penis. Josephus, one of the greatest of the ancient Jewish philosophers and historians, says the following:

> This, therefore, is what Herodotus says, that "Syrians that are in Palestine are circumcised." But there are no inhabitants of Palestine that are circumcised excepting the Jews.[5]

While circumcision seems to have been practiced by other peoples in very ancient times, by the time of the Greeks, Josephus tells us that only the Jews in Palestine were circumcised. And as far as slaves were concerned, circumcising them was tantamount to converting them to Judaism.

One commentary on Genesis sets out some of the background of the law on circumcision and its importance from the earliest of time in Judaism:

> In the days of Jacob, it is so important to the Israelite tribes as to be an essential precondition of marriage with outsiders … and the rite is a precondition for participating in the Passover offering … Not only is circumcision the earliest institution

4 *Tanakh: The Holy Scriptures*, Genesis 17.9–14, Philadelphia, PA: The Jewish Publication Society, 1985, pp. 23–24.

5 Flavius Josephus, *Against Apion*, 1.22.171, in *Josephus: The Complete Works*, translated by William Whiston, Nashville, TN: Thomas Nelson Publishers, 1998, p. 938.

> of Israel, its introduction being assigned by our narrative to the time of Abraham, but the text tacitly implies that it preexisted the patriarch since it is taken for granted that he understands the procedure to be followed even though no specific instructions are forthcoming.[6]

Circumcision is the earliest legal institution in Judaism and yet it is in conflict with certain Roman laws as we will see.

One of the earliest references to circumcision in Roman law concerns a rescript of Antoninus Pius (c. 138–155 CE) on which the legal commentator Modestin, in his work *The Rules*, says:

> Jews are permitted to circumcise only their sons on the authority of the rescript of the Divine Pius; if anyone shall commit it on one who is not of the same religion, he shall suffer the punishment of a castrator.[7]

Notice here that an earlier law that had forbidden all circumcisions is repealed, but that circumcision was not allowed for anyone who was not a Jew, later especially including slaves in Jewish households.

This law was probably directed at the circumcision of slaves upon entering into the employ of Jews, as Linder comments.[8] And the penalty is quite stiff, including banishment or execution. So, in this Roman law there is both a sign of tolerance for Jewish religious practices but also a restriction of those practices. One of the fears was that Jews might circumcise their slaves and others as a first step toward converting them to Judaism.

Another law from the end of the third century CE seeks to punish Roman citizens from becoming circumcised as a step toward conversion to Judaism. The following comes from the Roman jurist Paul:

> Roman citizens who suffer that they themselves or their slaves be circumcised in accordance with Jewish custom, are exiled perpetually to an island and their property confiscated; the doctors suffer capital punishment. If Jews shall circumcise purchased slaves of another nation, they shall be banished or suffer capital punishment.[9]

Non-Jewish Roman citizens are now brought into the domain of being penalized for suffering circumcision for themselves or their slaves. And the penalties are equally

6 *The JPS Commentary on Genesis*, commentary by Nahum M. Sarna, Philadelphia, PA: The Jewish Publication Society, 1989, p. 385.

7 Law No. 1 in *The Jews in Roman Imperial Legislation*, edited and translated by Amnon Linder, Detroit, MI: Wayne State University Press, 1987, p. 100.

8 Ibid., pp. 101–102.

9 Law No. 6, in *The Jews in Roman Imperial Legislation*, p. 118.

strong as those for the doctors as for the Jews who would employ circumcision on non-Jews.

Several laws, from slightly later than the circumcision laws above, penalized those Jews who persecuted other Jews who converted to Christianity. One of these laws was also a law against circumcision on non-Jews. Here is the first of these laws of Constantine the Great from October 18, 329 CE:

> We want the Jews, their principals and their patriarchs informed, that if anyone – once this law has been given – dare attack by stoning or by other kind of fury one escaping from their deadly sect and raising his eyes to God's cult, which as we have learned is being done now, he shall be delivered immediately to the flames and burnt with all his associates ...[10]

Burning at the stake was a particularly extreme form of punishment reserved for the worst offenders. So we see how seriously the Romans viewed the retaliation of Jews against those other Jews who converted to Christianity. As we proceed into the Christian era of the Roman Empire the laws against Jews get harsher, as we will see.

Here is another law of Constantine, from October 21, 335 CE, where we see that Jews who circumcise their slaves in effect free these slaves:

> Indeed, a long time ago we published the most salutary sanction of our law, which we renew by the veneration of our repeated law; it is our wish that if one of the Jews shall not be horrified from buying and circumcising a Christian slave or of any other sect whatsoever, the circumcised slave shall be made, by measure of this statute, participant and in liberty and acquire its privileges; it shall not be lawful for a Jew who has circumcised a slave of the aforementioned kind to retain him in slavery's obedience. This in fact we order in this same sanction, that if one of the Jews shall unlock for himself the door of eternal life, shall bind himself to the holy cults and choose to be a Christian, he shall not suffer ought of harassment or molestation in the hands of the Jews. For if anyone of the Jews shall consider that a Jew who became a Christian should be attacked and injured, we want the instigator of such contumely to be subjected to avenging punishments commensurate with the nature of the crime committed ...[11]

Notice the terminology: the Christians are here described as participating in "eternal life," whereas in the previous law of Constantine, Jews are said to participate in a "deadly cult."

We find the terminology used to describe Jews changing over the course of the Roman Empire in other ways as well. In the early years of the Empire Jews are often referred to as a religion or nation, whereas in later years Jews are most

[10] Law No. 8, ibid., pp. 126–127.
[11] Law No. 10, ibid., p. 140.

often said to subscribe to a superstition. This terminological change corresponds to the change in laws concerning such practices as circumcision. We next look at another set of Roman laws that are aimed at a specific Jewish religious holiday, Purim.

36.3 ROMAN INTERFERENCE WITH JEWISH RELIGIOUS LIFE

The idea that Roman legislators were tolerant of the religious practices of Jews and other groups who did not endorse the Roman religion faces a difficulty when it comes to Roman laws concerning Purim from 408 CE prohibiting the mocking of Christians on Purim.

> The governors of the provinces shall prohibit the Jews from setting fire to Aman in memory of his past punishment, in a certain ceremony of their festival, and from burning with sacrilegious intent a form made to resemble the saint cross in contempt of the Christian faith, lest they mingle the sign of our faith with their jests, and they shall restrain their rites from ridiculing the Christian Law, for they are bound to lose what had been permitted them till now unless they abstain from these matters which are forbidden.[12]

This law from Theodosian II was aimed at protecting "the Christian religion against defamation by Jews."[13]

Of course, there is no Jewish law that mandates that Purim include mockery of the Romans. But here we can see the beginnings of interference into the religious practices of the Jews. Previously, the Roman Empire had been relatively tolerant of religious practices, except for those that concerned conversion. Indeed, there is a famous Roman edict that says that the Jews are free to practice their religion because there are no laws ever passed in Rome to outlaw these practices. Arcadius expressed this view as late as 397 CE:

> The Jews shall be bound by their rites, while we shall imitate the ancients in conserving their privileges, for it was established in their laws and confirmed by our divinity, that those who are subject to the rule of the Illustrious Patriarchs … shall persevere in keeping the same privileges that are reverently bestowed on the first clerics of the venerable Christian Law … Let them therefore be exempt even from the curial liturgy and obey their laws.[14]

Yet, shortly after the time of the law of Arcadius, there were intrusions into the religious life of the Jews by Roman emperors.

[12] Law No. 36, ibid., p. 237.

[13] Amnon Linder's Introduction, in ibid., p. 85.

[14] Law No. 27, in *The Jews in Roman Imperial Legislation*, p. 202.

We also find the quite surprising law of Justinian from 553 CE that regulates which books can be read in Jewish religious services. And while the law seems to be in part tolerant in that it allows all language translations, there is a prohibition on the reading of the Mishnah, the book that set out rules and laws concerning all aspects of Jewish life.

> It is right and proper that the Hebrews, when listening to the Holy Books, should not adhere to the literal writings ... Having therefore studied this matter we decided that the better case is that of those who want to use also Greek in reading the Holy Books, and generally in any language that is more suited and better known to the hearers in each locality ... Furthermore, those who read Greek shall use the Septuagint tradition, which is more accurate than all the others ... What they call Mishnah, on the other hand, we prohibit entirely, for it is not included among the Holy Books, nor was it handed down from above by the prophets, but it is an invention of men in their chatter, exclusively of earthly origin and having in it nothing of the divine.[15]

This law of Justinian is remarkable for its interference into Jewish religious practices. Permission is granted to read the Bible in several different languages, but if in Greek then only one particular version.

The interdiction of the Mishnah is the most astounding. In the Introduction to Herbert Danby's English translation of the Mishnah, we are told of the book's importance:

> From the time of its compilation by Rabbi Judah the Patriarch, the Mishnah has, in Jewish eyes, ranked second only to the Hebrew Scriptures as a national-religious creation and possession. It provided a link between Palestinian and non-Palestinian Judaism strong enough and authoritative enough to endure and to bind together the Jewish people despite their geographical disintegration; it serves as the core of the Babylonian and Palestinian Talmuds, and for orthodox Jewry it is still, what it has been for sixteen centuries, an essential ingredient in the education of youth and an object of devotional study.[16]

The Mishnah provided the application to daily life of the laws of the Torah, and it thus provided the coherent and minute regulation of Jewish life, that was said to represent God's law just as much as the Torah itself. The Torah was a compilation of the written law just as the *Mishnah* was a compilation of the Oral Law which God had delivered to the Jews. And in the *Mishnah* there is an explicit claim that it was handed down from God to the many disciples of Moses with the explicit dictate that its rules should be executed.[17]

[15] Law No. 66, in ibid., pp. 408–409.

[16] *The Mishnah*, translated by Herbert Danby, Oxford: Oxford University Press, 1933, p. xiii.

[17] *The Mishnah*, Aboth 1.1–1.18, ibid., pp. 446–447.

If the Jews were to be allowed to practice their religion at all, then it was crucial that the Mishnah be allowed to be read. Its interdiction sets up a clear conflict for Jews given the important place that the *Mishnah* was afforded in Jewish religious practice. Here it seems that the Jews could not practice their religion in a way that the Roman state approved. Like the restrictions on Purim, Roman law restricted any aspect of Jewish religious life that could be seen as at direct odds with the dominant Christian religion. And such interference, from late in the Roman Empire, could concern seemingly any aspect of Jewish religious life, not merely Jewish secular life as had been true in the early years of the Roman Empire.

One last law from Justinian in 545 CE is also noteworthy since it regulates Jewish synagogues, converting some to Christian churches and prohibiting the building of any new synagogues.

> We order that no heretic shall receive real estate from the holiest church or another venerable place in rent, emphyteusis or purchase or in any other way … If an Orthodox who possesses a property with a church in it shall alienate it forever, or give it to an emphyteusis, or in a lease, or in any other way of management to a Jew … the holiest church of that village shall vindicate the ownership of this property … or if any Jew shall dare build a new synagogue, the holy church of the place shall vindicate the buildings to its ownership.[18]

Here the terminology is significant again – no Jews shall "dare build a new synagogue" is not just a prohibition but a promised confrontation. And there are explicit prohibitions on converting churches to synagogues. Justinian is attempting to restrict the growth of Judaism and actively shrink its outgrowth into new geographical areas within the Roman Empire.

These laws of the Roman Empire show a growing intolerance of Jews by the emerging Christianized state – an intolerance that is markedly different from the much more tolerant stance toward Judaism that was found in the early "pagan" Roman Empire. We next take a step back and look at how the conflict of laws of the Jews in the Roman Empire was understood in legal thought of the time.

36.4 CONFLICT OF LAWS FOR JEWS IN THE ROMAN EMPIRE

Cicero and other legal theorists of the Roman Republic often displayed anti-Semitism in their writings, although this did not necessarily manifest itself in how they understood the laws to apply to the Jews.

> And as for the miserable farmers of the revenue (miserable man that I also am, when I see the miseries and sufferings of those men who have deserved so well at

[18] Law No. 65, in *The Jews in Roman Imperial Legislation*, pp. 400–401.

> my hands), he handed them over as slaves to the Jews and Syrian nations, themselves born for slavery. He laid down as a rule from the very beginning, and he persevered in it, never to decide an action in favour of a farmer of the revenue; he rescinded covenants that had been made without any injustice, he took away all the garrisons established for their protection; he released many people who were subject to pay tributes and taxes from such payments; whatever town he was living in or whatever town he arrived at, there he forbade any farmer of the revenue or any servant of such farmer to remain. Why need I enlarge on this? He would be considered a cruel man if he had shown such a disposition towards our enemies, as he did show towards Roman citizens, especially towards those of that order which has hitherto always been maintained by its own dignity and by the goodwill of the magistrates.[19]

Here is one of the first attempts to describe the Jews as miserable tax collectors and to see the Jews as born to slavery – and this is by one of the greatest thinkers of the Roman Republic, Cicero.

In 59 BCE Cicero delivered a speech on behalf of Flaccus, in which Cicero refers to the Jews as espousing a barbaric superstition.

> Justice demands that that barbaric superstition should be opposed; and it is to the interest of the state not to regard that Jewish mob which at times breaks out in open riots … At one time the Jewish people took up arms against the Romans; but the gods showed how little they cared for this people, suffering it to be conquered and made tributary.[20]

Again, Cicero does not appear to have advocated for laws discriminating against the Jews, even though he expressed strong anti-Semitic sentiments.

Seneca, otherwise known for his compassion, also criticized the Jews for wasting one day's work a week in their ritual of the Sabbath. More significantly for us, Augustine says that Seneca claimed that "the vanquished [Jews] have imposed their laws on the conquerors."[21] These criticisms of Seneca, and also of Cicero, are all the more surprising since we have seen in earlier chapters the cosmopolitan perspective that was so prominent in the philosophies of both of these legal theorists of the Roman Republic. As we next see, though, the great Roman legal theorists of the Empire did not follow Cicero and Seneca in their anti-Semitism.

The great Roman jurist, Ulpian, is reported in Justinian's *Digest* to have said that the early Roman emperors "permitted those who enter the Jewish religion to enter

[19] Cicero, *On the Consular Provinces*, 5.10, translated by C. D. Yonge in *The Orations of Marcus Tullius Cicero*, London: George Bell & Sons, 1891.

[20] Cicero, *Pro Flacco*, section 28, translated in Askowith, *The Tolerance and Persecution of the Jews in the Roman Empire*, pp. 174–175.

[21] Seneca quoted in Augustine, *City of God*, Book 6, Chapter 11, translated by Henry Bettenson, London: Penguin Books, 1972, pp. 251–252.

[political] offices, but also imposed upon them liturgies such as should not transgress their religion."[22] The idea was that since Jews were citizens of the Roman Empire they had obligations that other citizens of Rome also had, including liturgical rites of sacrifice and prayer to the Roman gods. But Ulpian's humaneness comes out clearly when he endorses the idea that this was only true of liturgies that could be practiced by Jews without transgressing their religion. Here is one early attempt to parse the problem of conflicting legal obligations of Jews who were citizens of Rome. In the case of conflict of laws which could cause a Jew to violate his or her religious creed the Jew, says Ulpian, should be exempted from following the Roman law about liturgies.

Modestin, who was Ulpian's student, also says that the Jews should serve the various obligations of the state but puts the exception even more strongly and clearly when he says that "the [Roman] laws command that they [the Jews] should not be vexed" by performing the liturgies of the Roman religion.[23] Here it appears that the standard was not merely that the Jews not be obligated to obey Roman laws that transgress Jewish religion, but that how Jewish citizens reacted to the Roman law was the key. The passage admits of different interpretations but it appears to me that Modestin takes his teacher's view further in support of Jewish sensibilities when following the Roman law was objectionable to their consciences.

This interpretation seems to be supported by various laws as late as the Theodosian Code:

> We particularly enjoin on Christians, genuine as well as false, that they shall not dare to raise their hands, abusing the authority of religion, against peaceful Jews and pagans who are not attempting anything seditious or unlawful. For if they shall act violently against peaceful people, or plunder their property, they shall be convicted and compelled to restitute not only what they had plundered, but twice the value of their plunder.[24]

This law seems to be especially aimed at the increasing persecutions of Jews by Christian mobs.

But later in the Roman Empire period, Jews were required to perform Roman liturgies after all. Justinian mandated that Jews who serve in official capacities in the Roman government shall

> be burdened with the curial liturgies, just as they should be burdened with the liturgies of the Taxeotae, conforming to previous legislation and no superstition shall

22 Law No. 2, in *The Jews in Roman Imperial Legislation*, p. 104.

23 Law No. 4, in ibid., p. 112.

24 Law No. 49, in ibid., p. 300.

> discharge them from this order … and they shall perform personal as well property liturgies, and no law shall free them from these.[25]

This law only singles out those Jews who serve in government, which was a rare thing for Jews to be allowed to do, yet it nonetheless goes against the earlier laws that had manifested tolerance of the consciences of the Jews with regard to participating in Roman liturgies.

36.5 AUTONOMY AND TOLERANCE OF STATES WITHIN STATES

One of the central problems in the conflict between the Jews and the Romans is that the Jews were different from other peoples conquered by Rome. The Jews were, or at least saw themselves, as a people set apart, as "God's chosen people." But even this would not be enough, in my estimation, to explain the reason the Romans spent so much time in their legislation in dealing with the Jews, especially in trying to bring them more fully under the authority of the Roman law. There is a sense that the Jews also were, or saw themselves, as a nation, not merely as members of a religion. In this sense, Jews living in the Roman Empire were a "state within a state."[26] Even with the destruction of the Temple in Jerusalem and the splintering of the Jewish population into many communities within the Roman Empire, the Romans continued to worry about the Jewish nation that existed within the Roman Empire's borders.

Managing the conflict of laws that existed when the Jews were faced with following their own laws or those of the Romans was clearly on the mind of the emperors from the time of Julius Caesar. Initially, especially with Julius Caesar, toleration was at its height and Jews were left largely to govern themselves as long as their interactions were among other Jews. Here the fact that Jews kept to themselves, indeed seemed to prefer to live in what would later be called ghettos, allowed for the legal management of the Jews to be relatively easy. The tribalism of the Jews, painting now in very broad brushstrokes, actually made that task easier. But as Jews moved out from Jerusalem into nearly all parts of the Roman Empire, the cabining of the Jews became more difficult, while still manifesting toleration.

Overlapping legal systems can exist in many forms. In the current United States there is a federal system where both the individual states and the national government issue laws that affect the same people and can overlap and even conflict. In most cases in the US the federal law supercedes, but not in all cases. What is needed is some sort of method for determining when one legal system has priority over another. In the case of the conflict between Jewish law and the law of the Roman Empire, there were no clear rules concerning conflicts.

[25] Law No. 64, in ibid., p. 396.

[26] E. G. Hardy, *Studies in Roman History*, London: S. Schonschein, 1906, p. 23.

There is a sense that the problem was not initially straightforwardly confronted since Jewish law was not based in elaborate statutes such as in Roman law. Indeed, the Mishnah and Talmud did not try to systematize the enormous number of rules in the way that Theodosian or Justinian attempted concerning the law of the Roman Empire. If there had been two codes, one Jewish and one Roman, it would have been easier to see exactly where they conflicted, but this was not to be since there is no rabbinic code of law. The closest is the Mishnah, but it is far from systematic and is as concerned with daily religious rituals as civil matters. But since the Mishnah is the closest the Jews had to a code of law, perhaps this is why Justinian interdicted the reading of the Mishnah in the Roman Empire.

Some commentators suggest that Jews were tolerated when they could be seen as geographically isolated in Jerusalem, but became more potentially dangerous to the Empire when the Jews were dispersed more widely. In some sense, being dispersed would seem to be a dilution of the influence of the Jews. But the difficulty was that even in the Diaspora, Jews maintained their own identities as a people set apart who largely followed their own laws.

The Jews in the Roman Empire were unlike the metics in ancient Athens, which we explored in an earlier chapter. The metics were not full citizens but had a special legal and political status in Athens, nonetheless. Their non-citizen status was a subject of both privilege and also disability. Both metics and Jews are pariahs, to use the preferred term of Max Weber. But by the time of the Roman Empire the Jews became citizens, as was true of nearly all of the people living in the Roman Empire. Unlike the Greek metics, the Jews formed a cohesive group, bound together by strong religious and cultural customs. Yet, this had a disadvantage for Jews in that they were taxed as citizens of Rome and also as members of the Jewish nation. But the taxation disadvantage was not the only or even the most significant disadvantage of the Jews in the Roman Empire in that they were increasingly targeted for oppression during the Christianized Roman Empire. The Jewish nation became a target of the fears and insecurities of the Christianized Romans, especially as we have seen concerning economic matters.

In this respect the Jews were not fully a state within a state but rather a nation within a cosmopolitan state. Let us return to Seneca's criticisms that the Jewish nation imposed their laws on the conqueror, Rome. This comment highlights the problem of overlapping legal systems of two nations or states, especially when one of the nations has conquered the other. If the conqueror seems to be too tolerant of the conquered it can inspire resentment and worry that can cause instability. Indeed, the idea of sovereignty which relies on the idea of rulership that is not ruled over by another is at least partially undermined when there is a system of law that is itself autonomously operating within another legal system.

As we have seen, there are reasons to think that Seneca was simply wrong about the relationship between the Romans and the Jews in the Roman Empire. Jewish law could be used by Jewish litigants. But if one of the litigants was not Jewish, the non-Jewish litigant would have to agree to let the Jewish court arbitrate rather than the Roman court. This was in the most tolerant period of the Roman Empire. As the Empire became Christianized, Seneca's earlier criticism became more inapt. Jews were treated more and more as if they were aliens rather than citizens, with more and more restrictions placed on them, as we will see in subsequent chapters, beginning with the next one where we discuss the emergence of professional lawyers and dedicated legal scholars.

37

The Law and Ancient Legal Scholars

In both Jewish and Roman law of the first centuries of the new millennium, a striking change occurs, where a profession of scholars comes to prominence and even to have their opinions count as law. In Judaism, it is certain prominent rabbis who arise to claim special standing especially in the Mishnah and then just a bit later in the Talmud. In Roman law, five legal scholars dominated the field of legal theory, but also their opinions were collected in the Code of Theodosia and Justinian's *Digests* and given the status of sources of law. Even when they were not named, their ideas permeated legal textbooks, such as Justinian's *Institutes*. This is a major development in legal thought but one which does not necessarily correlate with a more humane law than in previous times, or so I shall argue in this chapter. The law does not develop in a progressive way in every respect.

The canonical legal texts of Judaism and the Roman Empire are filled with the legal opinions of the most respected legal scholars. This was a distinctly different source of law than statutes or edicts of rulers or of assemblies, or of the decreed word of God. It is mirrored today in international law in that one of the sources of law is the opinions of the most distinguished legal scholars, such as the seventeenth century CE philosopher Hugo Grotius. It is not an overstatement to say that this idea of legal scholars being sources of law started in the first few centuries CE in the legal texts of Judaism and the Roman Empire.

In Section 37.1 we will see the influence of certain rabbis on Jewish law. In Section 37.2 we will then see the influence of certain scholars on the law of the Roman Empire. In Section 37.3 we will explore the possible reasons for why this source of law arose in these two systems of law. In Section 37.4 we will consider to what extent there was an emerging field of professional legal scholars at the same time that professional lawyers also arose in ancient Judaism and Rome. And in the final section we will critically assess the influence of professional scholars of law on humane treatment of those who were subject to the law.

37.1 RABBIS AND ANCIENT RABBINIC LAW

The Mishnah is believed to have been compiled by Rabbi Judah the Patriarch. Here is one account of who he was and how he compiled the Mishnah from the Oral Law tradition of the Jews:

> The Mishnah nowhere states that its editor was Rabbi Judah the Patriarch, but in both Talmuds the fact is recognized and never disputed. According to an early tradition, "Rabbi" (as he is variously styled in the Mishnah) was born in 135 CE on the day that Akiba was put to death. He belonged to the sixth generation in direct descent from Hillel the Elder, and he succeeded his father, Simeon ben Gamaliel II, as Patriarch about 165 … As Patriarch he resided first at Beth Shearim in Galilee, and during the last seventeen years of his life he lived in Sepphoris, also in Galilee. Here he compiled his Mishnah and here he died at a great age.[1]

Notice that Rabbi Judah is described as a collator or editor rather than an author. Rabbi Judah was considered a great scholar especially of the Oral Law tradition of Judaism.

The Mishnah is meant to be a compilation of traditional oral law, not a systematic code of law.

> Rabbi did not aim at promulgating the Mishnah as an authoritative, definitive legal code, a final summary of Jewish law It was simply a compilation of the Oral Law as it was taught in the many rabbinical schools at the time; it sought to contain all that was worthy of preservation in older or more recent collections, preserving even divergences of opinion … Many of these opposing views he leaves without any attempt to decide between them.[2]

The legal scholarship of Rabbi Judah does not mainly result in an original written legal text but in an original editing of the legal opinions expressed by those rabbis of the past. So, in this sense, Rabbi Judah is a source of law not for his own opinions about the law, but for his own editorial decisions about what is the most worthy legal opinions of the past. In some respects this is also true of Roman legal scholars of this same time period – the first few centuries CE, as we will see.

Before turning to the Roman legal scholars, let us consider the other major contribution of rabbis to Jewish law and legal thought, the Babylonian Talmud. A group of rabbis probably writing in the fifth century compiled the Talmud. Traditionally it is thought that two rabbis were especially important in compiling this massive work: Rav Ashi and Ravina. And while work was to continue on the Talmud for

[1] *The Mishnah*, translated by Herbert Danby, Oxford: Oxford University Press, pp. xx–xxi.

[2] *The Mishnah*, p. xxii.

many years thereafter, it is likely that the first great scholars completed a version of the Babylonian Talmud in 475 CE.

The Talmud's compilers, like the compilers of the Mishnah, were rabbis who attained fame as legal scholars. These Talmud compilers, also like the Mishnah compilers, had their writings ascribed the status of law for Jews at this time. In this respect, these rabbis were treated similarly to certain legal scholars of the Roman Empire. The legal scholars of the Roman Empire, unlike Cicero in the Roman Republic for instance, did not often also practice law. Yet, as we see some rabbis did become lawyers. Indeed, rabbi scholars became the lawyers of the Jewish legal system.

There were distinct ways that the rabbis of the Mishnah and Talmuds were recognized as not only compiling the law but also in changing the law by their writings. There were at least two ways that rabbis could make law binding on Jews at their time. In both cases rabbis often employed the following form: "at first the law was X," "but now, in the light of circumstance Y, it will be Z."[3] Here either the rabbis first employed the strategy of changing the previous law to make it more equitable in light of circumstances, or, second, employed something like a decree to narrow the scope of the law.

There is much debate about whether the rabbis of the Mishnah and the Talmuds saw themselves as making entirely new law or whether they thought they were merely extending or narrowing what was already imminent in the Torah. But it is clear that the Mishnah and Talmuds greatly increased the sheer amount of law under which Jews were obligated. The Mishnah is not significantly longer than the Torah, but the articulated laws are much longer in the Mishnah than in the Torah. And in the Babylonian Talmud the laws are many volumes more than were found in the Torah.

Perhaps the most interesting case to consider is where a rabbi seems to be contradicting the Torah and claiming that the law is now the opposite of what it was in the Torah, which after all was supposed to be God's law directly conveyed to Moses. The explicit form, "this used to be the law, but it is now something else," certainly seems to indicate that the law of the Torah was being overturned and replaced by the law of the rabbis.

Indeed, the rabbis were increasingly seen as providing a source of law which some described as also a part of divine law. The difficulty with this strategy is that it means that divine law can be conflicted. In the Mishnah this idea is conveyed even more strongly when there are two different and conflicting opinions by rabbis presented without resolution as if the law itself could provide conflicting commands. One way to resolve this difficulty is to see that context matters and so what appear to be

3 See Christine Hayes, *What's Divine About Divine Law?* Princeton, NJ: Princeton University Press, 2015, p. 288.

conflicting commands are only seemingly so; one command of law can be different from another if the contexts being examined are themselves sufficiently different.

Another way that rabbis could make law that differed from the Mosaic law is that times could be seen to be significantly different – perhaps by a thousand years – from the time of the Mosaic law to that of the rabbinic scholars. Some rabbis argued that even the divine law could be seen as changing due to vastly different times and it was the role of the rabbis to ascertain what changes in the law were needed for these changed times. One can think of the story of Isaac where God tells Isaac to kill his son but then at the last minute tells Isaac to spare his son's life. God gave divine commands in both situations without the problem of these commands being contradictory. In these various ways the rabbis tried to explain how they could be "making" law even in those cases where what they declared to be law seemed to be different from God's law handed down to Moses.

37.2 THE LEGAL SCHOLARS OF THE ROMAN EMPIRE

There were many legal scholars in the Roman Empire whose commentary on the laws came to prominence, but five of these scholars were singled out as providing authoritative interpretations of the law. Two of these scholars, Gaius and Ulpian, were especially distinguished. They wrote many works on the Roman law, but their most important works were Gaius' *Institutes* and Ulpian's *Rules*. Both of these works were significant sources for the Theodosian Code as well as Justinian's *Digest*, *Institutes*, and *Code*.

Gaius' *Institutes* provide some of the clearest legal categorization and summary of law of the Roman Empire, or perhaps of any period of time. While Gaius is clearly summarizing the state of law at his time as well as significant past legal developments in the Roman Empire, he is also shaping the law. Here is how Zulueta characterizes Gaius' *Institutes*:

> The threefold division of the work is much more than a great advance on the order of the *Libri Iuris Civilis* of Q. Mucius and Massurius; it is an outstanding and permanent contribution to systematic jurisprudence. Gaius may not have originated it … The work is carefully subdivided; occasionally topics are introduced out of the professed order, but never … so as to put the reader in doubt as to the thread of the discourse. Rightly enough Gaius was ready at times to prefer convenience to rigid system.[4]

The division of his work has had a lasting impact on how law has been conceptualized ever since, seeing law as divided into the law of persons, of things, and of

4 Francis De Zulueta, *The Institutes of Gaius*, Part II: Commentary, Oxford: Oxford University Press, 1952, p. 7.

actions. This division allows for the label a "systematic jurisprudence" to be used in describing Gaius' work. Yet, it is also true that Gaius did not explicitly write new law except in the way he reorganized old and current law of his time.

Ulpian may lay claim to be a legal scholar who did more than summarize and organize the law. Indeed at least one prominent legal scholar of today, Tony Honore, has claimed that Ulpian was the first to lay out a theory of human rights that is grounded in the idea of the equal respect due to each person:

> Following on the extension of citizenship by the Antonine constitution, he expounds Roman law as a law based on the view that all people are born free and equal and that all possess dignity. These three values, freedom, equality, and dignity, are the essential elements of what we now term human rights ... Ulpian is the first lawyer who can, given the scale of his work and its influence, properly count as the pioneer of the human rights movement.[5]

Ulpian not only summarized the Roman law but he interpreted it in such a way that people saw the rights orientation of the law in a sense that they had not seen before. In this sense, Ulpian is presenting a jurisprudence that itself becomes a source of law.

In the beginning of his *Institutes*, as recorded in the first part of the Justinian's *Digest*, Ulpian says:

> Those who apply themselves to the study of law should know, in the first place, from whence the science is derived. The law obtains its name from justice; for (as Celcius elegantly says), law is the art of knowing what is good and just.
>
> Anyone may properly call us the priests of this art, for we cultivate justice and profess to know what is good and equitable, divining right from wrong, and distinguishing what is lawful from what is unlawful, desiring to make men good through fear of punishment, but also be the encouragement of reward; aiming (if I am not mistaken) at a true, and not a pretended philosophy.[6]

If the task for lawyers and jurists is to "cultivate justice" then there is a distinctly moral goal to interpreting law – in a way that serves the interests of the welfare of the people.

It is also well recognized that certain legal scholars of the Roman Empire period were themselves considered sources of law. Indeed, Justinian's *Digest* is essentially a collection of the writings of legal scholars, with Ulpian and Gaius having the most prominence. As Buckland tells us, there were five jurists or legal scholars whose work was considered a source of law.

[5] Tony Honore, *Ulpian: Pioneer of Human Rights*, second edition, Oxford: Oxford University Press, 2002, p. 76.

[6] Justinian, *Digest*, Book 1, Title 1, Chapter 1, Section 1, Vol. 2 of *The Civil Law*, p. 209.

In 426 came the famous *lex de responsis prudentium* – the Law of Citations. Its provisions may be shortly stated as follows:

(a) Any writing of Papinian, Paul, Gaius, Ulpian, and Modestinus are confirmed and may be cited, except the notes of Paul and Ulpian on Papinian. Gaius is to have the same authority as the others.
(b) Any writers cited and approved by any of these may be cited, such as Scaevola, Sabinus, Julian, and Marcellus, provided by reason of the doubt due to their antiquity their books are confirmed by comparison of manuscripts.
(c) If the jurists cited disagree the majority is to be followed: if numbers are equal, Papinian. If he is silent, the iudex may please himself.[7]

These five authorities had already been recognized as sources of law a century or two before the Law of Citations. And so we have probably the first ever recognition of legal scholars as not only summarizing law but as being sources of law in the Roman Empire.

For Ulpian, lawyers are like priests or perhaps like rabbis as both stating the law but also helping to make people morally good and motivating them to do what is equitable and just. As in the case of rabbis making law, and perhaps being an influence on that practice, there were many cases where legal scholars like Gaius and Ulpian made law by correcting the law so that is was more equitable. The Praetors had had the role of deciding cases according to equity in the Roman Republic, as we saw in an earlier chapter. In the Roman Empire, as the role of the Praetor declined, certain law scholars sometimes took over the role of making law by changing old law so that it was more equitable concerning new situations or circumstances. The role played by equity in the way that law was made by lawyers will occupy us in the next section of this chapter.

37.3 WHY DID LEGAL SCHOLARS AND RABBIS COME TO MAKE LAW?

John Crook reminds us that there were two very significant events that played a large role in the development of a legal system in the Roman Empire. A crucial period can be defined as going "from the legislation of 90–89 BCE by which all free persons in Italy south of the River Po became entitled to possess Roman citizenship, to CE 212, the traditional date of the legislation of the Emperor Caracalla, by which almost all free persons in the whole Roman Empire became possessors of Roman citizenship."[8]

7 W. W. Buckland, A *Textbook of Roman Law from Augustus to Justinian*, Cambridge: Cambridge University Press, 1921, p. 34.

8 J. A. Crook, *Law and Life of Rome*, Ithaca, NY: Cornell University Press, 1967, p. 8.

These two events, which greatly expanded the citizen ranks of the Roman Empire, called for a standardization of law throughout large swaths of the world. If Roman law did not treat people roughly the same in the various parts of the Empire then the idea that all were equal citizens of Rome would be undermined. There was thus a need to train lawyers and jurists to interpret and apply Roman law evenly across the Empire.

There is a somewhat similar story to be told about the way that Judaism spread far into the Diaspora after the political turmoil in Jerusalem resulting in the destruction of the great Temple. Because of the existence of the Roman Empire, Jews could move easily into many of the major cities of this time. And with the spread of Judaism across the Roman Empire there were similar issues of fairness in how Jews were treated according to Jewish law. For the Jewish law to treat all Jews the same, there was a need for schools to train rabbis to interpret and apply Jewish law evenly across the Diaspora.

On first sight one might expect that the standardization of law would require that lawyers and jurists faithfully follow the law and not change the law. But this view is mistaken in several crucial ways that can be seen when we again consider the importance of equity in any legal system. Here in Jewish law for instance:

> Just as equity is not so much reform as a realization of the law's true essence, the interpretations and enactments of rabbis that modify and develop the law are regarded as the fulfillment of the true intent of scripture rather than an innovation or modification of it … Jewish law also holds that when strict adherence to the law creates injury or injustice, a corrective is needed. In Jewish law, that corrective is the body of rabbinic interpretations and enactments that are made in the interest of justice.[9]

As in Roman law, when the law is interpreted so as to conform to equity, this was largely conforming the law to morality. And while it is not clear that such equity-based interpretations of law were truly "making new law," it often seemed to be so.

Considerations of equity operate at two levels in any legal system, and in both cases there is an expanded need for jurists to "make new law." First, if the laws of a legal system treat certain groups differently from other groups, despite there being no legitimate legal reasons to do so, those laws need to be reformed in the sense of being changed to laws that properly reflect the equal status of all citizens or subjects. Second, if the equal treatment of all cases fails to take account of legitimate differences between cases, then another kind of unfairness needs to be corrected by "new law" as well, which treats different cases differently rather than the same.

9 Christine Hayes, *What's Divine about Divine Law?* Princeton, NJ: Princeton University Press, 2015, p. 311, in part discussing the views of Aaron Kirschenbaum, *Equity in Jewish Law*, Hoboken, NJ: Ktav, 1991.

It is true that changing the law by legislative act or executive decree might be preferable to judicial law change, but in many cases change will only come in a timely manner if it is done judicially. The legitimacy of law change is enhanced when it is accomplished by an institution that is at least arguably accountable to the people. Yet, when jurists and rabbis make equitable changes in the law, these professionals are not utterly beyond accountability since the legislature or the ruling body can remove them from office. Today we are still in the midst of this debate, which arguably began when lawyers and rabbis first saw themselves as able to change law, in a sense, on their own authority.

In Judaism there is an additional problem when law is changed, namely that the law that is changed has the status of being divine law. Divine law seems to be the sort of law that should not be changed merely by mere humans. God's law handed down directly to his chosen people has a very different status than law that is made by fallible humans. There is no special problem in changing what was fallible – yet this is not true of God's divine law.

Several recent scholars have argued that what the Jews called divine law, especially the Covenant Code, was really constructed largely from such sources as Hammurabi's Code from 1750 BCE.[10] There is an intense debate about who were the original authors of the Biblical codes of law, but the idea that these laws were directly handed to Moses from God is not commonly accepted by many scholars. There were undoubtedly Jews in ancient times who also did not believe in the literal divinity of the Covenant Code, but many Jews did seem to believe in its truth.

For those Jews who thought of their religious law as divine, there was a special problem in making changes to that law by rabbis. One thing to consider in this respect is whether divine law must also be seen as eternally true. It could be that divine law was given directly by God at a certain time, with the understanding that this law would change with changing times. It also could be that divine law was inspired by God in broad brushstrokes but that humans, especially rabbis, were to put specific provisions into effect that filled out that divine law. Or yet again it could be that part of divine law was the provision that certain religious leaders (rabbis primarily) were to interpret and apply that law and make it conform to principles of morality such as equity.

In many respects, then, the ways that God's divine law was reconciled with rabbis who seemingly changed that law, were similar to the reconciliation of jurists and legal scholars who changed Roman law. And most significantly, the main reasons for the making of law by lawyers as for rabbis was similar – namely that the law needed to be corrected for it to become a fair and just law. The fine-grained way that law

[10] See David P. Wright, *Inventing God's Law: How the Covenant Code of the Bible Used and Revised the Laws of Hammurabi*, Oxford: Oxford University Press, 2009.

needs to be adapted to changing times and circumstances is simply much better accomplished by those whose profession it is to consider legal problems casuistically. Rabbis and what Ulpian called the priests of the Roman law were those who were called upon to make judgments on the basis of equity and thereby to correct or to change the old law for current times.

37.4 PROFESSIONAL LEGAL SCHOLARS AND LAWYERS

There were some Jews who became regular lawyers during the Roman Republic and for a while into the Roman Empire. Indeed, there is one Roman law that confirms that Jews could attain the status of lawyers despite being prohibited from other public sector jobs. In the Theodosian Code we find:

> The entrance to the State Service shall be closed from now on to those of the Jewish superstition who attempt to enter it ... Nevertheless, we do not exclude Jews educated in the liberal studies from the freedom of practicing as advocates.[11]

This law from 418 CE was repealed just a few years later when in 425 a new version of the Theodosian Code stipulated that:

> We also deny to the Jews, and to the pagans, the right to practice law and to serve in the State service; we do not wish people of the Christian Law to serve them, lest they substitute, because of this mastery, the venerable religion by a sect. We command, therefore, that all persons holding an unpropitious error be excluded, unless they are succored by a timely amendation.[12]

Jews were able to practice law among their fellow Jews but excluded from practicing law among Roman citizens who were not Jews as the Christian era proceeded.

In Jewish and Roman law, schools of lawyers and rabbis developed where the members were encouraged to think of themselves as a separate group and to develop their own ways of interpreting the law. Andrew Riggsby comments on the transformation of both advocates and legal scholars during the Roman Empire:

> As the justice system came under the control of the emperors, it was professionalized (and "professional" now becomes a more literally accurate term). Leading jurists were hired into government positions. While the Republican posts with influence over the law, most notably the urban Praetorship, were not normally filled with experts, as the corresponding imperial jobs (say, the urban and praetorian prefects) were.[13]

[11] Law # 45, ibid., p. 280.

[12] Law # 51, ibid., p. 308.

[13] Andrew Riggsby, *Roman Law and the Legal World of the Romans*, Cambridge: Cambridge University Press, 2010, p. 53.

Riggsby also says that eventually a "law degree was required to practice law before the higher courts, and this was also in turn a qualification for positions in government."[14]

Similar things could be said about the requirement of rabbis to get legal training as well. Here is Christine Hayes' assessment:

> While the Patriarch claimed descent from the house of David, the rabbis based their authority not on heredity (like that of priests and kings) or divine charisma (like that of the prophets) but on their mastery of the sacred scriptures and ancestral tradition, and on their legal expertise … According to rabbinic tradition … Rav brought the Mishnah to Babylonia where it became the central element in the rabbinic curriculum.[15]

And later rabbinic academies, called yeshivas, were formed with "an elaborate institutional structure."[16]

The authority of rabbis, like that of Roman legal scholars, jurists, and lawyers, came from the expertise they claimed as a result of their studies often in professional schools. The idea behind schools or academies was a characteristic of philosophical training in ancient Greece. There were important academies founded by Plato and also by Socrates. In the Roman period we are now examining, Stoic philosophers had well-known academies that the elite of Roman society often attended. Certainly, Jews were also exposed to these ideas since they were prominent in ancient Greek societies.

But the idea that one could pursue the profession of lawyers or rabbis as scholars of the Roman or Jewish law was relatively unique to the first centuries CE. Rabbis were different from priests in that rabbis were primarily scholars of the Jewish law. Roman lawyers or jurists were different from Greek orators again in that they were primarily scholars of the Roman law. What marked these people off from the rest of the society, and even from other professionals in those societies, was that they claimed an expertise based on their study of the law.

We have seemingly come a long way since Hammurabi could say, nearly 2,000 years earlier, that all people had to do was look at his laws engraved on various stone pillars to be able to seek justice on their own. Now, in the Roman Empire it is thought to require a specialized training in order to understand the multiple volumes of the law. In Jewish law, the homey stories of the Bible are now not considered understandable without elaborate training that required years of study under the tutelage of other scholars.

[14] Ibid., p. 65.

[15] Christine Hayes, "Law in Classical Rabbinic Judaism," in *The Cambridge Companion to Judaism and Law*, edited by Christine Hayes, Cambridge: Cambridge University Press, 2017, pp. 77–78.

[16] Ibid., p. 78.

There are other markers of the professionalization of law that on some accounts indicate the movement from a "primitive" to a proto-modern type of legal thought. Raymond Westbrook has argued that the profession of law can be seen as of a piece with two other developments that mark a change from "primitive" legal thinking, namely categorization and definition, on the one hand, and a system of citation of precedent authorities or cases, on the other hand.[17] Indeed, it seems that having a professional class of lawyers and jurists will often mean that there is training in the law that would involve categorization as well as citing of authorities. In any event, we see both of these phenomena accompanying the professionalization of Roman lawyers and Jewish rabbis.

37.5 DID PROFESSIONAL LEGAL SCHOLARS MAKE THE LAW MORE HUMANE?

Categorization, abstraction, and the citing of authorities constitute a change in the way ancient societies came to think about law. But is such thinking better than more ancient times when abstraction was less subtle and there was little citing of authorities? The law is conceived as a much more complex phenomenon in the times of the professionalized Roman lawyers and Jewish rabbis, but does the law better serve the people at the time? In this last section I will argue that while there is progress in complexity of law, there did not necessarily follow progress in the humaneness of law.

One of the problems with increasing professionalization of law practitioners and scholars, as well as with the ensuing greater complexity of the legal system, is that ordinary people are rendered less able to employ the law on their own. Indeed, if one peruses the Babylonian Talmud's 30-plus volumes or the many volumes of Justinian's *Digest*, one is struck even today at how hard it is to decipher these works, and how much harder still it would have been in these ancient times where literacy and education were nowhere near what they are today. This fact alone does not make the law less humane, but it means that the law will be in the hands of an elite who may not serve the interests of the ordinary people who most need the law's help.

Of course it could be that the greater professionalization of the legal system meant that law practitioners used their expertise and status to help those who are most in need of the law's help. It seems to be that Ulpian is one such professionally trained legal scholar who advocated for the equal dignity of all people before the law. And there are also cases of rabbis who used their status to work for the humane tradition

17 Raymond Westbrook, *Ex Oriente Lex*, Baltimore, MD: Johns Hopkins University Press, 2015, especially pp. 228–230.

espoused in the Torah. But in what follows I will explain some of the constraints on having the professionalization of law and humaneness of law accompany each other.

When careful and lengthy study is seen as a requirement of acquiring expertise then there is a premium placed on understanding the most arcane and obscure parts of the law, debating its fine points, and displaying one's superior knowledge. Simple provisions such as that the widows, orphans, poor, and aliens are in need of the most protection at law seemingly are not of the right sort to count as arcane knowledge not readily understandable by the non-professional.

There is no evidence that I have found for thinking that the professionalization of law in the Roman Empire correlated with an increasing concern for the worst off in the society. But there is also no evidence that the situation of the worst off became worse due to the professionalization of law. This raises though a question about the "progress" of the law. There is certainly progress if becoming more complex and abstract is indeed progress – and I think there is progress at least in this one respect – legal thought is much richer theoretically. Yet progress according to one measure does not necessarily mean progress in other respects.

The progress of the law understood in moral terms is much harder to discern than the progress of the law in terms of conceptual richness and complexity. Morality is itself multidimensional. Some would say, as I just did, that a measure of the moral progress of a legal system is how much it protects the most vulnerable. Others might rightly think that moral progress of the law is measured in the terms of the two most central moral concerns of the law – justice and equity. There certainly can be overlap between justice and aiding the least well off. If justice minimally means giving to each his or her due, then aiding the poor, for instance, who are often poor through no fault of their own, is a requirement of justice.

If equity involves fairness, as nearly everyone would agree, then perhaps making moral progress in terms of equity would also involve aiding the worst off members of the society. But some would say that one meaning of fairness is a kind of formal status where all are treated the same before the law. In the Roman Empire, as we have seen, from the third century CE, nearly all free persons were granted Roman citizenship. In the next two chapters we will see that there were certainly still people who were left out of this arrangement, most notably women and slaves. Perhaps surprisingly, Jewish law also treated all males as roughly equal, but did not extend this status to women or slaves either.[18] And as time progresses, there is not a corresponding progress in how women and slaves are treated in these ancient societies.

As legal complexity brings in formal equality for more of the population, there is no necessity that equity is advanced. Indeed, as we have seen in previous parts of this work, equity can sometimes be opposed to formal equality insofar as treating

[18] See Richard H. Hiers, *Justice and Compassion in Biblical Law*, NY: Continuum, 2009, Chapter 4.

people fairly means treating them unequally because of the different needs and circumstances of the people in question. As Anatole France ironically said: "The law, in its majestic equality, forbids the rich as well as the poor to sleep under bridges, to beg in the streets, and to steal bread."[19]

Formal equality can be a very important moral goal of any legal system, even if it sometimes is at odds with equity as fairness. What I am exploring here at the end of this chapter is the question of whether moral progress in the time of the Roman Empire is correlated with formal progress judged by standards of increased complexity and richness. And the answer seems to be "no." Despite Ulpian's admonition that the law and lawyers are to aim at making people good, he does not seem to have succeeded. Indeed, there is some evidence for thinking that the law was more compassionate toward the worst off in the Roman Republic and the time of Biblical law than in the Roman Empire and the time of the Rabbinic law of the Mishnah and the Talmuds. We will find more evidence on this issue as we move into chapters dealing with women and slaves.

[19] Anatole France, *Le Lys Rouge* 1894 [*The Red Lilly*], Paris: Calman-Levy, 1906.

SECTION XIV

Differential Status

38

Women in Jewish and Roman Thought

The status of women in the rabbinic period of Jewish legal thought and the legal thought of the Roman Empire are in many ways very similar, as we will see in this chapter. In some respects it seems that women gained more liberty and even more rights during this period than was true in earlier times of Biblical Jewish thought and the legal thought of the Roman Republic. But this is only partially true, for as we will see there were significant losses for women over this time as well. Once again we face the fact that there is no clear path of unidirectional progress from older to more recent times, a topic we will address directly at the end of this chapter.

For women of the upper classes, the first few centuries CE seem to have progressed from more ancient times. Women were given citizenship early in this period in Rome. Women were given significant roles in society, including in religious life. Some women achieved very high status indeed. But it is also true that the affairs of government and law remained exclusively the purview of men, perhaps even more than in earlier times. And laws about marriage, divorce, and rape were also not clearly better for women in our period than in earlier periods. Similar things can be said of the status of women in rabbinic legal thought.

We will begin with a section on the general legal status of women in Jewish and Roman thought. In Section 38.2 we look at how religion affected the status of women in the societies at the beginning of the centuries CE. In Section 38.3 we will look specifically at laws concerning marriage and divorce. Then in Section 38.4 we will look at laws concerning rape and other crimes against women. And in the final section we will assess why it might be that progress is not so clearly seen for women in these otherwise more advanced societies than had existed previously among the Jews and Romans.

38.1 THE STATUS OF WOMEN IN RABBINIC AND IMPERIAL ROMAN TIMES

In rabbinical times, "only husbands had the legal authority to issue a divorce document." This stands in stark contrast to earlier times. As Samuel Greengus tells us:

> it is clear that a written document was apparently not seen as always necessary during earlier, biblical times, where one finds that divorce, initiated by either spouse on unspecified grounds, might normally be accomplished by a formal, oral declaration presented before an assembly or congregation. This in fact was the practice of the Jewish community living in Egypt at Elephantine during the fifth century BCE.

Greengus attributes the change in divorce with the increasing influence of Roman practices on Jewish legal thought, where written documents were crucial to divorce and where only men could make these written documents.[1]

So, we can begin with the idea that over time legal relations became more formal in a way that is normally thought to be more protective of the rights of the parties, but where the formalism can work against the status of women in various ways as distinguished from more informal legal relations in marriage and divorce. We will explore this particular topic in a later section of this chapter. I want to note this difference in status of divorce now to give us a sense of how one kind of progress, establishment of formal rights, does not necessarily track progress in the status of the individuals previously governed by less formal legal arrangements.

Similarly, in the Roman Republic "there were no fixed grounds for divorce."[2] Indeed, divorce was seen "as a private act and as such was not subject to limits by law."[3] During the Roman Empire, marriage and divorce became public matters governed by elaborate legal procedures. Yet, it is common to think that formal status is better than private or informal status for women. As we will see in this chapter, the record is much more mixed than is often thought.

Another issue that looms large concerning the status of women in the early centuries CE concerns changes in the way in which religion intersects with marriage and divorce as well as other issues directly relevant for the status of women overall. In this respect, the Christianization of the Roman Empire from the time of Constantine onward seems to have adversely affected the status of women. Indeed, in the most

[1] Samuel Greengus, *Laws in the Bible and in Early Rabbinic Collections*, Eugene, OR: Cascade Books, 2011, pp. 37–39.

[2] Jane F. Gardner, *Women in Roman Law and Society*, Bloomington, IN: Indiana University Press, 1986, p. 84.

[3] Ibid., p. 82.

obvious way this can be seen in that divorce became much more difficult under Christianity than it had been under "pagan" Rome.

In Jewish law, we can see that the increasing assertion of Rabbinic law over marriage and divorce also seems not to have helped improve the status of women. It is perhaps not surprising since rabbis, as well as Christian priests, were all men and the laws became more male-focused as a result. There was no necessity that the status of women would change in this way by having men increasingly in charge of their lives through changes in the law, but nonetheless women's status seems to have been adversely affected.

We should remember that the idea that women were under the direct social control of men, the Roman idea of paterfamilias that we discussed in an earlier chapter, was certainly not one that was libratory. One might hypothesize that a change from having women's lives controlled by their fathers and husbands (and even their sons) was worse than having women's lives controlled by the laws of the society. We will explore this idea a bit more in this section before turning to specific laws in the period of the first few centuries CE.

In theory, one might certainly expect that social control by formal laws and rules would be better than social control by personal influence. The publicity of laws often sheds light on oppressive conditions that are then subject to change because of the inherent equality that systems of law provide – especially in the idea that people are all to be treated the same under law. This would seem to be especially true of societies where the personal control of women by fathers and husbands was largely about the control of property. While laws are also often instituted for the control of property, legal systems like that of the Roman Empire seemed to distinguish laws that controlled property from laws that regulated social institutions such as marriage and divorce. Although we shall also see that inheritance laws were conceived as regulating marriage and divorce in a way that controlled property transfer.

In general, the record is definitely mixed about whether there was progress in the status of women as this status became regulated by Rabbinic law and Roman civil law in the first few centuries CE. Women had, in one sense, greater rights but, in another sense, perhaps less freedom, especially in marriage, as we move from the last centuries BCE to the first few centuries CE.

Before looking at specific texts let us note the conclusions of one contemporary Jewish scholar, Solomon Zucrow:

> There is no direct statement in the Bible confirming the right of the father but the rabbis established and assigned this right by positive legal statements. According to them, the father could coerce his daughter into marrying a repulsive person or one who was inflicted with a loathsome skin disease. The Talmudic law was in that respect even more severe on the daughter than the Roman law which, as a rule,

> gave the father, as paterfamilias, unlimited power over his children but forbade him to coerce his daughter into marrying an unworthy or disgraceful character.[4]

And also consider another of Zucrow's comparative conclusions:

> The husband was not responsible for his wife's prenuptial debts or for debts contracted by her after marriage even though he enjoyed the income of her property. In respect to the wife's property, the Rabbinical law was harsher on the women than the Roman or Greek ... The Greek law permitted the wife to sell her property; the Roman law granted her the right to support her relatives from it, and both codes allowed her to bequeath it to her relatives.[5]

And Zucrow concludes that "Rabbinical law actually degraded the wife to the level of chattel ... The Roman law in this respect raised the wife to equal rank with her husband."[6] Yet even as we will have occasion to challenge the severity of this conclusion, we will also see that some of what Zucrow said will ring true.

38.2 RELIGION AND THE STATUS OF WOMEN IN RABBINIC AND ROMAN LAW

The organized religions of Rabbinic Judaism and the Roman Empire did allow for the participation of women in some offices, even some important ones, and yet, as we will see, the status of women was not much enhanced, if at all, by these religious institutions in the first few centuries CE. Here is one assessment by Mary Beard, John North, and Simon Price:

> In some [Roman] cults ... women are found at the margins ... In other cults there were roles for women. They served, for example, as priestesses of Magna Mater and participated in the cult of Dionysus ... At least outside Palestine, Jewish women held various offices: "elder," "leader of the synagogue," "mother of the synagogue." Christianity also attracted many women who – both rich and poor – had specific roles within the church ... On the other hand there is no evidence to suggest that women were particularly powerful within these cults in general ...[7]

So, while there does seem to be an increased role for women in some of the religions within the Roman Empire, including Judaism, there is little evidence that such a change empowered women or changed the status of women for the better.

4 Solomon Zucrow, *Women. Slaves, and the Ignorant in Rabbinic Literature*, Boston, MA: The Stratford Company, 1932, p. 29.

5 Ibid., p. 56.

6 Ibid., p. 62.

7 Mary Beard, John North, and Simon Price, *Religions of Rome*, Vol. I: A History, Cambridge: Cambridge University Press, 1998, pp. 297–299.

Indeed, there is some evidence for thinking that there were religious cults that did give women a kind of empowerment in the last few centuries BCE. We have already discussed in earlier chapters the important role of vestal virgins in "Pagan" Rome, and to this we can add that the cult of Dionysus seems to have been stronger and provided more important roles for women before the Roman Empire than during it. In Judaism, there are many famous women who achieved the status of prophet or leader in Biblical times and very few such cases in rabbinical times – in part because women could not be rabbis.

Any attempt to deal with the status of women in Jewish and Roman law must take account of the peculiar issue of purity and pollution, especially with the rules governing food preparation and sexual activities, where the regulation of women's bodies was most acute. And in this respect, we need to consider the differences between the Biblical rules laid out in Leviticus as opposed to the way these rules were refined and changed in the Mishnah and Talmud. In addition, purity rituals in Roman times also had a strong impact on the status of women in the Roman Republic as opposed to the Roman Empire.

It is of note that in both Jewish and Roman societies there was a premium placed on procreation and hence also of sexual activity, at least within the rules of marriage. But alongside of this concern was the concern that women (or really girls) enter into marriage as virgins so that the offspring's lineage could be easily traced. In addition, in both societies it was important that there be male heirs for keeping property in the hands of citizens.

Concerns for procreation and legitimacy of offspring is, though, certainly not enough to account for the dramatic rise in the number of regulations concerning women's sexuality and to say nothing yet of food preparation. The dietary laws of Judaism, especially as elaborated in the Mishnah and the Talmud, are not a topic that can be covered in a part of a section of a chapter of my work. I wish here only to mention the enormous variety of such laws and rules that seemed to multiply exponentially during the Rabbinic period. More than one-third of the Mishnah is devoted to regulation concerning women, especially their sexuality, and the cleanness or purity of food preparation.[8]

38.3 MARRIAGE AND DIVORCE

In both Talmudic law and the law of the Roman Empire, marriage and divorce was often handled as a matter of property considerations, just as was true in earlier times.

[8] See the third and sixth divisions (out of six) of the *Mishnah*, translated by Herbert Danby, Oxford: Oxford University Press, 1933.

Questions of inheritance loomed very large in the laws of marriage and divorce, especially since marriage itself involved property transfer of various kinds.

There is some reason to think that divorce laws were made more egalitarian by rabbinic interpretations of Biblical injunctions. Indeed here is how Solomon Zucrow describes the Talmudic law:

> As if to offset the carte blanche regarding divorce given to the husband by them, the Rabbis formulated the following two principles:
>
> (1) The woman has the right to demand, in certain contingencies, a divorce from her husband, and the Beth Din obliged to compel the husband to grant her request …
> (2) The Rabbis have the right to annul any marriage whether directly or retroactively …
>
> These two principles, especially the last one, besides their manifestly progressive nature, opened up numerous avenues for the promotion of the welfare of the women. In post-Talmudic times, however, these principles became sterile and dead letters.[9]

This assessment is by no means uncontroversial as we will see in this section.

The Mishnah sets a standard for divorce that seems only to allow the husband to divorce: "a man may only divorce his wife if he has found in her (some) shameful matter."[10] Greengus comments that "the majority of scholars disagreed … allowing the husband an unlimited right to divorce his wife upon any grounds."[11] In somewhat earlier times, in the Jewish community in Elephantine, there was a recognition of the right of a woman to similarly divorce her husband for any grounds. Here is a part of a document cited by Greengus:

> Tomorrow or a later day, if Anani will stand up in an assembly and say "I hate Tamut my wife," divorce money is on his head …
>
> Tomorrow or a day later, if Mibtahiah will stand up in an assembly and declare: "I hate Eshor my husband" divorce money is on her head …[12]

This humane, egalitarian practice seems to have continued up to the rabbinic period but not clearly during the time of the Talmud.

A very interesting equal treatment of both spouses is found in the Mishnah's rules concerning the case of the rebellious wife or husband.

9 Zucrow, *Women. Slaves, and the Ignorant in Rabbinic Literature*, pp. 71–72.
10 Mishnah, Git. 9: 10, translated in Greengus, *Laws in the Bible*.
11 Greengus, *Laws in the Bible*, p. 37.
12 Greengus, ibid., p. 38.

> (If) a woman "rebels" against her husband (by refusing him sexually), they (the court) may order a deduction from her marriage settlement of seven dinars per week … And similarly, if a husband "rebels" against his wife, they (the court) will add to her marriage settlement three dinars per week.[13]

While these amounts are not equal for men and women, there is nonetheless a recognition that wives have somewhat similar rights to those of husbands during marriages that are on the rocks. And also in the Mishnah we find that if a wife says "he is repulsive to me," the rabbis should not press her to remain married to him.[14] Despite this recognition of bilateral divorce in some situations, Greengus tells us that rabbis remained reluctant to affirm the wife's decision to divorce her husband, "unless such provisions were written into the marriage contract."[15]

Matters were similar in divorce laws of the Roman Empire in that there seems to have been a reluctance to extend to wives the legal right to divorce their husbands on the same grounds that husbands had the right to divorce their wives, even before the principle of equal rights in marriage was eventually undermined by the rise of Christianity. According to one scholar, divorce was easy during the Roman Republic: "As marriage was based on consent, so the will of the consenting parties in free marriage to renounce it sufficed."[16] Husbands divorced their wives for nearly any reason, including that the wife had failed to produce offspring.[17] We will return to Justinian's *Corpus Juris* to learn more about divorce in the Roman Empire. Here is a section of Justinian's *Novel Constitutions*, first concerning the husband's grounds for divorce and then the wife's grounds which are in many ways quite similar to the husband's:

> The following are good causes for repudiation.
>
> (1) Where a woman is aware that certain persons are plotting against the government, and does not inform her husband …
> (2) Where a husband thinks he can convict his wife of adultery; but he must previously file a complaint against her …
> (3) Where a wife has plotted against the life of her husband …
> (4) Where she attends banquets, or bathes with strangers, against the wishes of her husband.
> (5) Where she remains away from her husband's house without his consent, unless she is visiting her own parents.

[13] Mishnah, Ket. 5: 7, translated by Greegus, *Laws in the Bible*.
[14] Greengus, *Laws in the Bible*, p. 45.
[15] Greengus, ibid., p. 46.
[16] Gardner, *Women in Roman Law and Society*, p. 81.
[17] Ibid., p. 84.

(6) Where without the knowledge, or against the prohibition of her husband, she attends circuses, theatres, or other public exhibitions.[18]

And here are the grounds upon which a woman may divorce her husband.

> We decree that the following are the only causes for which a wife can reasonably serve notice of a repudiation upon her husband …
>
> (1) Where the husband was implicated in some plot against the Empire; or where being informed that others were, he did not denounce them to the government either in person or by someone else.
> (2) Where the husband has, in any way whatsoever, attempted to kill his wife, or if being informed that others desired to do so, did not warn her, or take measures to avenge her in conformity with the laws.
> (3) Where the husband has attempted to violate the chastity of his wife by seeking to deliver her to other men for the purpose of committing adultery.
> (4) Where the husband has filed an accusation of adultery against his wife, and was unable to prove it …
> (5) Where a man, having contempt for his wife, is known to have entertained another woman in the house where he lives with her …[19]

And in another chapter Justinian also mentions the case where a husband has not "been able to copulate" as a reason for dissolving a marriage by a wife without any penalty.[20]

The grounds for divorce in this text from the Roman Empire do not provide equivalent reasons for husbands and wives, and in this respect it is a bit of a regression from the equality of the Roman Republic. But unlike the Roman Republic, there are now formal grounds for divorce and hence perhaps more protection for the divorcee than existed in the very informal private domain of divorce in the Roman Republic. In addition, it is interesting that the idea of consent is still of significance for the husband in the Roman Empire, as it was in the Republic. But the same is not true for divorcing wives where there has to be some harm or wrong that the husband has done in order to give the wife grounds for divorce. So, in general we find that the situation of women in terms of divorce is somewhat worse off in the Roman Empire than in the Roman Republic, thus once again calling into question the thesis that progress was achieved the later we are in the ancient period of legal thought.

[18] Justinian, *Novel Constitutions*, Title VIII, Chapter 8, in *The Civil Law*, Vol. 17, pp. 54–55.
[19] Justinian, *Novel Constitutions*, Chapter 9, The Civil Law, Vol. 17, ibid., pp. 54–55.
[20] Justinian, *Novel Constitutions*, Chapter 12, The Civil Law, Vol. 17, ibid., pp. 57–58.

38.4 RAPE AND SEXUAL VIOLENCE

The Biblical law distinguished strictly between rape that occurred in the city and rape occurring in the field. The woman or girl who is raped is subject to punishment if the rape occurred in the city, since it is assumed she should have, but did not, cry out for help. In the field or the country it is assumed that even if she had called out no one would have heard her and so the rape is not considered to be something the woman or girl should be punished for.[21] Things were only somewhat different in the Rabbinic period, as Samuel Greengus says:

> The rabbis in their later exegesis [of Deuteronomy] found reason to criticize the girl for venturing out of her house – evidently alone and unaccompanied. Rashi, paraphrasing *Sifre* D 243.23 on Deut. 22–23, states: "A breach (in the wall) is an invitation to a thief; if she had stayed at home, this would not have happened to her." But other rabbis, in a less condemning fashion, restructure the case in order to ease the burden it placed upon the woman and also to ease the rigid distinction between city and field … Nahmanides, in his commentary, goes even further and argues more sympathetically that one must allow for other ways of female resistance, whether audible or not.[22]

We find here in the Midrash that the girl or woman is still not given the benefit of the doubt, and the continued support of punishment (even by death) for the victim of rape is not much more humane than the earlier treatment of rape in Deuteronomy.

In the Babylonian Talmud we find support for taking the life of the rapist, but only as he is in the midst of the crime:

> A betrothed maiden, whether at home or in the field, one may "save him" (i.e., the man who is attacking her) from committing this transgression even at the cost of (taking) his life … however, after the transgression has been committed, one does not save her by taking his (i.e., the attacker's) life.[23]

Here even bystanders can slay the rapist caught in the act. But after the rape, bystanders cannot slay the rapist. It is unclear whether this is because it is now a matter that should be taken up by the courts, or whether since it is no longer possible to prevent the rape, the rapist is simply not subject to vigilante justice.

If the girl or woman who is raped is not betrothed, there is rabbinic support for the Biblical view that the rapist must marry the girl or woman. The rabbis seemed to countenance the possibility that the girl or woman could refuse to marry her rapist, although this remained only the unstated right of a daughter.[24]

[21] See Deuteronomy 22: 23–27.

[22] Greengus, *Laws in the Bible*, p. 60.

[23] Talmud, Sanh. 73a, translated in ibid., p. 61.

[24] See Greengus, *Laws in the Bible*, p. 67.

As far as prosecution for rape and other sex crimes is concerned, Talmudic jurisprudence put major impediments in the way of conviction, especially in capital cases. Samuel Mendelsohn contends:

> Rabbinic humanity … precluded every possibility of convicting of crimes which, through ignorance of the law, men are liable to commit … Talmudic jurisprudence allows conviction only when the criminal is not ignorant of even the slightest point of law, knowing the law, and being forewarned of the necessary consequences of his intended violation, still sins with a high hand, thus clearly manifesting his presumptuousness or malice prepense, without proving which there can be no legal conviction.[25]

Mendelsohn says that the provision that criminal conviction requires intent to break the law is in agreement with the Roman doctrine of *actus non facit nisi mens sit rea* which he translates as "an act is not guilty unless the intention is guilty."[26] We will have occasion to consider this issue in much more detail when we take up criminal jurisprudence in Chapter 42.

In the Roman Empire it seems that the penalty for rape was set at death at least by the time of Hadrian. Jane Gardner tells us:

> Rape was a capital charge. The emperor Hadrian took a lenient attitude towards people who took the law into their own hands and killed someone attempting rape upon themselves or one of their family; he allowed their discharge … What recourse there was for rape under the Republic is not certain.[27]

Yet, prosecutions for rape were apparently rare. Rape was hard to prove because one had to show lack of consent on the woman's part. Yet, the rapist would not have gotten off "scot-free. He would still be liable to a charge of adultery (if the woman was married) or *stuprum* (if she was not)."[28] But Gardner points out that a successful prosecution of the man for adultery or *stuprum* left the woman open to a similar charge, "and her husband would face prosecution if he did not divorce her. The social and legal consequences of failure may have been a deterrent to bringing prosecutions for rape."[29]

Ulpian provides us with a good commentary on the Lex Julia that concerned various sexual crimes including adultery.

[25] Samuel Mendelsohn, *The Criminal Jurisprudence of the Ancient Hebrews*, Baltimore, MD: M. Curlander, 1891, pp. 32–33.

[26] Ibid., note 57.

[27] Gardner, *Women in Roman Law and Society*, pp. 118–119.

[28] Ibid., p. 121.

[29] Ibid., p. 121.

> The law punishes the pandering of a husband who retains his wife, after she has been surprised in adultery, and permits the adulterer to depart. For the husband should be angry against his wife who has violated her marriage vow, and he ought also to be punished when he cannot excuse his ignorance, or conceal his indifference under the pretext that his information is incredible. Therefore, the law says he "shall permit the adulterer surprised in his house to depart," because it wishes to punish the husband who caught her in such an infamous act … Anyone who has pecuniarily profited by the adultery of his wife shall be punished; for he who acts as his wife's pander does not commit a trivial offense.[30]

Ulpian makes it clear that adultery can be punished quite severely but that there are various reasons for why this did not often happen.

The Roman Empire's treatment of rape is more straightforward, because as Marcianus says, "the crime of rape exceeds in scope the Julian law relating to adultery."[31] Yet we see some of the same issues arising in Roman law about rape as were true of the Jewish law as understood by the rabbis. Despite the difference in the severity of the crime of rape as compared to adultery, there were nonetheless difficulties in prosecuting this crime.

38.5 LACK OF ADVANCES FOR WOMEN AT THE END OF THE ANCIENT PERIOD

We have seen that there were differences in the law from the last few centuries BCE to the first few centuries CE in Jewish and Roman legal systems, but the story of whether there was progress for women has been complicated indeed. The law became more formalized and detailed over time, but it is not clear that women's status improved as a result. I will attempt to offer some possible explanations for this fact in this final section of the chapter.

In the case of rape and other crimes of sexual violence, moving to a more formal system had the clear advantage that "vigilante justice" was diminished in favor of court determined punishments. Of course it mattered if the judges were still operating within the frame of mind of the paterfamilias ideas that dominated in the informal legal domain concerning women. And the idea that women had to have a patron that was also central to the law of the Roman Republic is at best only a mixed blessing – providing a protecting guardian but also requiring the guardian's consent for many things women might seek to do.

30 Ulpian, "On Adultery," Book IV, in Justinian's *Digest*, Book XLVIII, Title V, 30 (29), in *The Civil Law*, translated by S. P. Scott, Cincinnati, OH: The Central Trust Company, 1932, Vol. 11, p. 45.

31 Marcianus, "Institutes," Book XIV, in Justinian's *Digest*, Book XLVIII, Title V, 30 (29), in ibid., p. 52.

It makes sense to have the legal system rather than social system decide what is best for people as well as what are their rights, since fewer biases are endemic. And so one can see why many thinkers over the centuries have seen progress as one gets to the end of the ancient period compared to earlier times in Roman and Jewish societies. But in the case of the status of women, the control remains in the hands of men, and men who are quite likely to have patriarchal views about women at best.

Rape seems to be treated more humanely in the Rabbinic and Roman Empire periods than before. This is because the woman was not automatically assumed to be in need of a defense of the charge of adultery as in earlier times, for which the penalty was death and could be perpetrated without any trial. With the more regulated system of the later ancient period, the focus became more squarely on the perpetrator, not the victim of sexual assault. And so there was certainly progress in this respect. But the legal complexities that were actually contained in such Roman laws as the Lex Julia left the wife in a quandary about whether to avail herself of the legal system since, if successful or unsuccessful, she was open to being prosecuted for various crimes. In the law of the rabbis we don't even find this much of an advance for the status of women since we find a continued emphasis on what the victim did or did not do as well as whether the perpetrator intended to commit a crime by his act of "seduction."

In the case of divorce, there is even less evidence for thinking that women's status got better the later in the ancient period we look. Informal procedures are often less protective than are formal ones, but this is not true if the informal procedures often leave matters to the parties in question to decide what to do. Here, in the case of divorce, letting people decide on their own whether to divorce and how to divide property was somewhat better for women than a formal system where divorce could only occur for very specific reasons and the males in charge of the system made divorce harder for women than for men.

The rabbis increasingly inserted themselves into the regulation of family matters in the first few centuries CE and not necessarily for the betterment of the status of women. The rabbis say that they can annul a marriage on behalf of a woman for any reason, but this puts the matter in the hands of the all-male rabbis. Insofar as the earlier model was one controlled by the paterfamilias, as in the Roman Republic, the rabbinic regulation of marriage might be somewhat better for women or it might be worse depending on the rabbis in question.

One general point we can conclude from the discussions in this chapter is that moving from an informal to a more formal system of regulation of women's lives remains a mixed benefit when men remain in charge of the more formal system, even as these men are different from those of earlier times who had a familial relationship with the women. Having a more public and hence transparent process for resolving disputes about women's rights seems that it should be better than having these decisions made outside the public sphere. But our study has cast some doubt on this general normative principle.

Today, many people find it odd that so many societies continue to have family affairs handled outside the sphere of the rule of law – either by religious officials or as a matter of private family relations. But at least one reason why these customs have continued into the modern age from their ancient roots is that some women surely prefer that the larger society or the state not regulate their family affairs.

Yet it is very unclear that the same reasoning concerning family affairs – marriage, divorce, inheritance, etc. – can be easily applied to sexual violence issues. The regulation of rape by private means, including vigilante justice administered without any due process considerations, is dangerous for women and also for men. It is a fair point that customary law in the last few centuries BCE was at times better for women concerning sexual violence but this seems more like an accidental result than one that is linked to the private resolution of these matters.

Finally, let us return to the issue of whether there is clear progress, evolutionary or otherwise, as we move through the ancient period, concerning the status of women. My view is that one can see progress in certain areas and regress in other areas over the centuries. And perhaps of even more importance, one can see that where there was once progress, there can then be regress in only a slightly later historical point. The rise of Christianity in the Roman Empire provides evidence for thinking that there can be progress in some respects and regress in other respects. In my projected work on Medieval legal thought, this will be one of the main topics that must be considered.

39

Slaves in Jewish and Roman Legal Thought

If the history of legal thought, at least of ancient legal thought, is supposed to be one of moral progress, then the hardest case to account for is that concerning slaves. As in other ancient periods, the legal thought of the Roman Empire and of Jewish thought of the rabbis, slaves were not distinguished by being of different races, religions, or languages than the slave masters. Slaves can become free, and free men can become slaves. Indeed over the course of a lifetime a person can go from slave to free and back again to slave. And yet, a slave is treated as a "thing" in Roman thought and not as different from an ass, or other beast of burden, in Jewish thought.

In the Roman legal thought of Gaius and Ulpian, perhaps the most sophisticated and otherwise humane of any in ancient legal thought, there is a clear recognition that slavery violates the laws of nature as well as moral laws, and yet slavery is not condemned.[1] And since the slave had the status of a mere beast of burden in rabbinic thought, and since the law of the Jews was said to have divine origins, the treatment of slaves as not human was given divine sanction.[2] These views were, if anything, less humane than those of earlier ancient times. It may be said that the more systematic and even more rational that legal thought became, there was no corresponding greater sense of morality of how slaves as fellow humans should be treated. Indeed, the Romans came to see slaves as human persons, even as they had no rights, as was fitting the fact that slaves were mere things. Yet, these matters are both more complex and also sometimes even worse as far as moral progress is concerned as we will see in this chapter.

In Section 39.1 we will explore the odd view in the legal thought of the Roman Empire that slaves were both persons and also things. In Section 39.2 we explore the odd view in the legal thought of the rabbis that slaves were no different than beasts

[1] See the first chapter of W. W. Buckland, *The Roman Law of Slavery*, Cambridge: Cambridge University Press, 1908.

[2] See Solomon Zucrow, *Women, Slaves, and the Ignorant in Rabbinic Literature*, Boston, MA: The Stratford Company, 1932, p. 174.

of burden despite the fact that Jews had been enslaved in Egypt in Biblical times. In Section 39.3 we will consider the problem of seeing all people as deserving of respect and equality of status, and yet seeing nothing wrong with slavery in both Roman and Rabbinic legal thought. In Section 39.4 we will explore the few writers among the Romans and the rabbis who were outliers and did express moral sympathy for slaves. And finally, in Section 39.5, we will once again assess the moral progress, or its lack, in this final period of ancient legal thought concerning the status of slaves.

39.1 SLAVES AS BOTH PERSONS AND THINGS IN LATE ROMAN THOUGHT

In an earlier chapter we began to discuss some of the ideas of Gaius toward slavery. In this section Gaius will be front and center since his views were some of the most significant for the period of the Roman Empire influencing Justinian more than only one other legal scholar. In Book I of Gaius' *Institutes*, we learn the following:

> The whole of law observed by us relates either to persons or to things or to actions. Let us first consider persons.
>
> The primary distinction in the law of persons is this, that all men are either free or slaves. Next, free men are either *ingenui* (freeborn) or *libertini* (freedmen). *Ingenui* are those born free, *libertini* those manumitted from lawful slavery …
>
> Slaves are in the potestas of their masters. The potestas is *iuris gentium*, for it is observable that among all nations alike masters have power of life or death over their slaves … But at the present day neither Roman citizens nor any other person subject to the rule of the Roman people are allowed to treat their slaves with excessive or causeless harshness … And even excessive severity on the part of masters is restrained … For we ought not to abuse are lawful right.[3]

Here slaves are treated as persons, but not as free persons or freed persons.

The slave's master had the power of life or death over the slave; the master had *potestas* (legitimate power) over the slave. In this respect one would expect that the slave has no rights. Yet, we are also told by Gaius that excessive harshness or even killing of a slave is not condoned. The restraint on the master does not come as a result of the slave's rights, at least not civil rights. As we will see, the slave is to be treated with restraint because as a matter of natural law, although not civil law, the slave is recognized as a human person.

The most common claim about Roman slaves was that they mere things. In Book II of the *Institutes* of Gaius we also learn:

[3] *The Institutes of Gaius*, Bk I, Sections 8, 9–11, and 52–53, translated by Francis De Zulueta, Oxford: Oxford University Press, Vol. 1, pp. 5 and 17.

> The leading division of things is into two classes: they are subject either to divine right or to human ... Things subject to human right are either public or private. Public things are regarded as belonging to no individual, but as being the property of the corporate body. Private things are those belonging to individuals. Further, things are divided into corporeal and incorporeal. Corporeal things are tangible things, such as land, a slave, a garment, gold, silver, and countless other things.[4]

Here slaves belong to individuals in the same way as land or clothes or beasts of burden.

The status of slaves as mere things comes as a matter of civil law – indeed the claim is that all societies regard the slave as a mere thing. This explains why the slave can be bought and sold and where the earnings of a slave are actually the earnings of the master. And yet as we have seen, slaves cannot be killed indiscriminately where this would be true of other creatures treated as things, such as beasts of burden. Once again, the slaves are open to such treatment as a matter of civil law in the law of nations, yet the status of the slave in natural law is very different.

Concerning the issue of how to understand slaves as *both* persons and things, a distinction that Justinian takes over from Gaius, Thomas Collett Sandars says:

> Slaves were personae in the sense that they were not merely things, and they could go through some legal forms, and were entitled in later times to a certain amount of legal protection; but although they are thus treated of under the law of persons, it is chiefly their want of legal capacities that attracts attention.[5]

Roman jurists saw the law of slavery as primarily part of the law of peoples or nations, not part of the law of nature or divine law.

Because the slavery laws were merely a matter of civil law, the slavery laws could be changed. So one question to ask is why didn't the various Roman lawyers and jurists advocate for changing the law of slavery to make it more humane? Why didn't the Romans see that such a change would bring the civil law into conformity with the natural law?

One explanation offered for why the lawyers of the Roman Empire did not advocate for rights of slaves, even as the rights of many other people were being championed, such as Italians, foreigners, and even barbarians, is that slaves were too important for the economy of Rome. In the Empire, agriculture was increasingly conducted in very large estates (like later plantations) and there was a very strong need for the cheapest labor for these estates. Slavery seemed to be a reasonable solution to this problem. And those who made the law, or who could change the law,

4 Ibid., Bk II, Sections 2 and 1013, p. 67.

5 *The Institutes of Justinian*, translation and notes by Thomas Collett Sandars, London: Longmans, Green and Co., 1917, p. 13.

were themselves often invested in these agricultural estates – as was certainly true even of otherwise humane thinkers such as Cicero and his later followers.

Buckland sets out a summary of the conceptual and moral problem of slavery for the Roman Empire as follows:

> Work of the most responsible kind was left in the hands of slaves. Among the more important functions may be mentioned those of *negotiator, librasrius, medicus, actor, dispensator, villicus, paedegogus, actuarius*. They managed businesses of all kinds. We find a slave carrying on the trade of a banker without express orders. A slave rents a farm and cultivates it as a tenant, not as a mere steward. Aulus Gellius gives us a list of philosophers who were slaves among the Greeks and Romans. Broadly it must be said that in private life there was scarcely any occupation in which a slave might not be employed; almost any industry in which freemen are now engaged might be carried on in Rome by slaves. It must however be remembered that all of this is not true in the greater part of the Republican period. In that period the evidence shows that slaves were relatively few and unimportant.[6]

We will later investigate whether slavery in the Empire showed moral regress rather than progress.

For all the well-acknowledged precision of the law of the Roman Empire, and especially of the jurist Gaius, we are left with an unsettling situation where a slave straddles the line between person and thing. Persons have social status and even legal standing; things have no special legal status or standing. We will examine the various ways that were proposed to reconcile this divide. But we are still left wondering why the Roman legal theorists did not more forthrightly recognize that they had conceptualized slaves in two nearly irreconcilable ways. We will next see something of the same predicament in Rabbinic law.

39.2 SLAVES IN RABBINIC LAW

Rabbis in the first few centuries CE saw slavery, except of Jews by Jews, as acceptable. Indeed, there is evidence that the Rabbinic law was less humane than earlier Biblical law on the treatment of slaves. Consider this set of passages from the Tractate Berakhot, the first volume of the Babylonian Talmud:

> There was the precedent involving Rabbi Eliezer, who came into the synagogue and did not find a quorum of ten, so he freed his slave and thereby completed the necessary quorum of ten. Thus, if he freed him, he would be [counted], but if he did not free him, he would not be [counted] ... But how could he have acted in this way? For has not Rabbi Judah said, "Whoever frees his slave violates an affirmative

6 Buckland, *The Roman Law of Slavery*, p. 7.

> [obligation], for it is said, 'They shall be your slaves for ever' (Leviticus 25:46)." For carrying out a religious duty [in this case reaching the necessary quorum], the law is different. But is this not the accomplishment of a religious duty through the commission of a transgression? Accomplishing a religious duty for the community at large falls into a separate category [from any other, and that is permitted even under the present circumstances].[7]

Here we find that there is an affirmative obligation not to free slaves, and that such an obligation is grounded in God's law.

The exception to the affirmative obligation not to free slaves is made in terms of some perhaps greater obligation to serve the larger community. Yet, it is still true that the rabbis thought that freeing a slave violated God's eternal law. We might then agree with Zucrow who has said of this passage and others that "It is sad to state, but it is a fact that the Talmud is the only code of laws among the ancient codes, religious or civil, which considered manumission a religious crime."[8]

In Biblical law, a passage from Deuteronomy addresses runaway slaves as follows: "You shall not turn over to his master a slave who seeks refuge with you from his master. He shall live with you in any place he may choose among the settlements in your midst, wherever he pleases; you must not ill-treat him."[9]

The rabbis take a very restricted view of this passage from Deuteronomy in the Babylonian Talmud:

> As to Rabbi Hisda, a slave of his fled to the Samaritans. He sent word to them to return him to him. They sent word to him, "You shall not deliver unto his master a bondsman" (Deut. 23:16). He sent word to them, "But that speaks of a slave who fled from overseas to the land of Israel, as set forth by Rabbi Ahi son of Rabbi Josiah." And how come he cited them the statement of Rabbi Ahi son of Rabbi Josiah [and not Rabbi's]? It is because that sense of the verse would make more sense to them.[10]

Samuel Greengus comments:

> This episode took place in Babylonia; and Rabbi Hisda felt he was justified in seeking recovery of his runaway slave. The point of the story is that even the Samaritans … who adhered to the literal text of Scripture, were persuaded that Rabbi Hisda's narrow interpretation of Deuteronomy 23:16–17 was the correct one.

7 *The Babylonian Talmud*, Berakhot 47b, translated by Jacob Neusner, Vol. 1: *Tractate Berakhot*, Peabody, MA: Hendrickson Publishers, 2005, pp. 317–318.

8 Solomon Zucrow, *Women, Slaves, and the Ignorant in Rabbinic Literature*, Boston, MA: The Stratford Company, 1932, p. 194.

9 Deuteronomy 23:16–17, JPS Translation of the *Tanakh*, p. 310.

10 *The Babylonian Talmud*, Gittin 45a, translated by Jacob Neusner, Vol. 11: *Tractate Gittin*, Peabody, MA: Hendrickson Publishers, 2005, p. 186.

> The law therefore held no currency for slaves and their owners living outside of the land of Israel.[11]

All of this shows that slavery was not challenged by the rabbis even when there were clear Biblical restrictions of slavery.

The Talmud is fairly clear in treating slaves, especially those that are not themselves Jews, as beasts of burden:

> Said Rabbi, "All concur that a slave has no valid genealogy whatsoever: 'Stay here with the ass' (Gen. 22:5) – people who are classified along with the ass [which has no genealogy and is merely chattel]."[12]

Zucrow claims that the rabbis in this Talmudic passage changed the meaning of "Abide ye with the ass" to stand for a statement about slaves: "stay you people who are mere asses." He concludes:

> Thus, the rabbis gave divine sanction to this lamentable opinion, the justice of which was never questioned by a single Talmudical or post-Talmudical Rabbi since it would be questioning the justice of God. Since a slave was considered a mere animal, and animals have no legal power of possession, there was a consensus of opinion among the Rabbis that whatever the slave acquired belonged to his master. This law was common to all nations, but regrettable as it is, the Rabbinical law was the most severe in practicing this principle … Indeed, according to Rabbi Meir, even if some benevolent person did give money to a slave on the express condition that he should buy his freedom, as soon as the money was in the slave's hand, it automatically became the property of the master. The only way a benefactor could redeem a slave was by paying the money directly to the master.[13]

For this opinion Zucrow cites the Talmud where it is said:

> A Canaanite slave is acquired through money, through a writ, or through usucaption. "And he acquires himself through money paid by others or through a writ [of indebtedness] taken on by himself," the words of Rabbi Meir. And sages say, "By money paid by himself or by writ taken on by others, on condition that the money belongs to others." Then what about the case of a slave, for he can't accept his writ of emancipation in his own behalf … It is quite appropriate that a slave may accept a writ of emancipation in behalf of his fellow from the hand of the other's master, but not from his own.[14]

[11] Samuel Greengus, *Laws in the Bible and in Early Rabbinic Collections*, Eugene, OR: Cascade Books, 2011, p. 119.

[12] *The Babylonian Talmud*, Yebamot 45a, translated by Jacob Neusner, Vol. 8: *Tractate Yebamot*, Peabody, MA: Hendrickson Publishers, 2005, p. 321.

[13] Zucrow, *Women, Slaves, and the Ignorant in Rabbinic Literature*, pp. 173–174.

[14] *The Babylonian Talmud*, Qiddushin 23b, 23c, translated by Jacob Neusner, Vol. 12: *Tractate Qiddushin*, Peabody, MA: Hendrickson Publishers, 2005, pp. 101 and 106–107.

And so we see that slaves had no legal status for the rabbis, not even the capacity to buy themselves out of slavery.

39.3 THE QUANDARY OVER SLAVERY REVISITED

The legal thought of the Roman Empire was driven by and also influenced the movement toward universal citizenship among all peoples of the Empire. And the Stoic idea of a natural law that saw all people as equal was a guiding idea in the Empire. Yet, slavery existed and was justified roughly on the grounds that the law of all nations accepted slavery as legitimate and even necessary. The Rabbinic legal thought also stressed the dignity of all people as a principle that came directly from God. Indeed, the Bible had several very strong statements condemning slavery. Yet, slavery was also condoned and even justified by the rabbis, many of whom held slaves and saw no reason to stop this practice that had gone on for many years, despite the Jews celebrating their freedom from slavery at the hands of the Egyptians. This is the quandary we are left with at the end of the ancient period.

The quandary over slavery was not new to the Romans and the rabbis. As we have seen in previous chapters, Aristotle is the best known thinker to accept the principle that all people should be treated as roughly the same and yet to defend slavery on moral grounds. We have also seen that Cicero followed Aristotle in this respect as did other important thinkers of Rome such as Seneca. In Biblical thought, Jewish leaders are seen to rail against their own enslavement. And yet, even the enslavement of Jews by other Jews is sometimes condoned. In Rabbinic thought, as we have seen in the previous section, slaves are seen as beasts of burden, as asses, and treated accordingly.

The explanations, or rationalizations, for slavery fit into a number of similar patterns among the Rabbis and the Roman lawyers. First is the idea that some people deserve their slave status as a punishment. People who have been convicted of various crimes were subject to slavery conditions, especially since jail and prison sentences were often unrealistic in the ancient world. If people convicted of very serious crimes could be put to death, it seemed reasonable that they could be subjected to what seemed to be the lesser penalty of enslavement.

Yet, both Roman and Rabbinic legal thought, as we have seen, put great stock in what today we would call due process considerations. If slavery was to be justified as a punishment then there should have been some sort of clear procedure by which a person was judged guilty of violating a law that had as its assigned punishment that the convicted person would be sentenced to enslavement. Yet, this was not always the case. And such an explanation could not be persuasive for the large number of people who were simply born into slavery – where they could hardly have committed criminal acts that made them deserving of the punishment of slavery.

Second, there is also the very old argument that we saw in the very earliest of discussions about slavery in Mesopotamia that since defeated soldiers could be killed on the battlefield, they could be subject to the lesser status as slaves, and indeed this was to show mercy to the defeated soldiers. There is no doubt that in very ancient times, defeated soldiers were sometimes massacred. But there is also evidence for thinking that their lives were spared, not out of mercy but out of pragmatic considerations – not wanting to rile the enemy peoples who had not been defeated on the battlefield.

There is in addition the comparative issue of why mercy did not dictate even more humane treatment of defeated soldiers, such as was sometimes seen in general grants of amnesty at the end of a battle or war. True mercy would be hard to square with enslavement when amnesty or pardons were an alternative as well. We will discuss this issue in the context of the emerging notion of a just war in the final chapter of this part of my larger project.

Third, the idea that some slaves were no better than beasts of burden, such as asses or oxen, has an important role in another justification of enslavement for those who were born as slaves. Here we return to the idea from the ancient Greeks that some people are by nature in need of protection and direction because of their inferior mental capacity. The natural inferiority of slaves could help explain, and even justify, why so many ancient societies accepted the idea of slavery and practiced even the enslavement of co-ethnic and co-religious people who seem to be otherwise just like the masters. They were like the masters in terms of ethnicity or religious background, for instance, but not in terms of being able to govern themselves.

Yet, as it turned out this idea was especially hard to maintain when the slaves were of the same ethnic and social status as the slaveholders. Jews worried about enslavement much more when the slaves were fellow Jews, and Romans worried more about slavery when it was fellow Romans who were enslaved. And it is also hard to maintain when slaves are trusted with childcare and business supervision that even some non-slaves were not trusted to perform.

The practice of Jews enslaving other Jews seems to die out completely just before or during the early course of the Rabbinic period. In part the idea seems to be that if Jews are God's chosen people then they should not be enslaved by anyone, least of all by fellow Jews. There are similar considerations in how Romans viewed enslavement of fellow Romans. Yet, even as we can see this as a kind of moral progress, the institution of slavery seemed to get an even stronger foothold in these societies than it had in earlier times.

39.4 THE FEW CRITICS OF SLAVERY DURING LATER ANCIENT TIMES

In the Roman Empire two philosophers loom large as critics of slavery; one who is a slave, Epictetus, and the other who is an emperor, Marcus Aurelius. In his *Handbook*, Epictetus expresses his view that external restrictions and impediments like slavery should not be seen as overwhelming considerations:

> Abide by whatever is set before you as if it were a law, and as if you would be committing sacrilege if you went against it. Pay no attention to what anyone says that falls outside what is yours.[15]

This Stoic position on such matters as slavery is not meant to condone it but to explain how one should regard it. In the end the only thing that matters is what you can control and those are all internal matters.

At the beginning of the *Handbook*, Epictetus sets out in more detail why our views of slavery or freedom are generally misdirected and this from the standpoint that Epictetus was himself a slave.

> Some things are up to us and some are not up to us. Our opinions are up to us, and our impulses, desires, aversions – in short, whatever is our own doing. Our bodies are not up to us, nor our possessions, our reputations, or our public offices, or, that is, whatever is not of our own doing. The things that are up to us are by nature free, unhindered, and unimpeded; the things that are not up to us are weak, enslaved, hindered, not our own. So remember, if you think that things naturally enslaved are free or that things not your own are your own, you will be thwarted, miserable, and upset, and will blame gods and men. But if you think that only what is yours is yours, and that what is not your own is, just as it is, not your own, then no one will ever coerce you, no one will hinder you, you will blame no one, you will not accuse anyone, you will not do a single thing unwillingly, you will have no enemies, and no one will harm you, because you will not be harmed at all.[16]

Slavery of the body is not as important since it does not really restrict your freedom, which is all internal and completely under your control.

The other Roman Stoic philosopher to have written importantly on slavery was the Emperor Marcus Aurelius. At several crucial points in his *Meditations*, Marcus Aurelius favorably quotes Epictetus such as at the end of Book 11:

> No man can rob us of our free will.

[15] *Handbook of Epictetus*, sec. 50, translated by Nicholas White, Indianapolis, IN: Hackett Publishing Co., 1983, p. 28.

[16] *Handbook of Epictetus*, sec. 1, ibid., p. 11.

> Epictetus also said, a man must discover an art (or rules) with respect to giving his assent; and in respect to his movements he must be careful that they be made with regard to circumstances, that they be consistent with social interests, that they have regard to the value of the object.[17]

And concerning slavery, Marcus Aurelius says: "He who flies from his master is a runaway; but the law is master, and he who breaks the law is runaway."[18] And we also find this admonition:

> How hast thou behaved hitherto to the gods, thy parents, brethren children, teachers, to those who looked after thy infancy, to thy friends, kinsfolk, to thy slaves? Consider if thou hast hitherto behaved to all in such a way that this may be said of thee:
>
> *Never has wronged a man in deed or word.*[19]

And we get this explicit injunction: "and pass through the rest of life … making thyself neither a tyrant nor the slave of any man."[20] Marcus Aurelius was known as one the most legally learned of all Roman emperors, and also as a strong advocate of manumission of slaves, perhaps influenced by the slave Epictetus.

In the Rabbinic period a philosopher, Philo, also was one of the main opponents of slavery. In his essay, "Every Good Man is Free" (*Quod Omnis Probus Liber Sit*), Philo says:

> Slavery, then, is of two kinds: slavery of the soul and slavery of the body. Now, of our bodies, men are masters; but over our souls, wickedness and the passions. And we may speak of freedom in the same manner. For one kind of freedom gives fearlessness of body in respect of any dangers which can come upon it from men of still more powerful body; while the other produces peace to the mind, by putting a check on the authority of the passions. Now about the former kind, scarcely any one ever raises any question; for the chances of fortune which happen to men are infinite in number, and it often happens that men of highest virtue have fallen into unexpected misfortunes, and so have lost their freedom which belonged to them through their birth … Therefore discarding all mention of those kinds of freedom which are only pretense, and of all those names which are quite unconnected to nature, but which owe their existence only to opinion, such as slaves born in the house, slaves purchased with money, slaves taken in war. Let us now investigate the character of the man who is truly free, who is also possessed of independence, even

[17] *The Meditations of Marcus Aurelius Antoninus*, Book XI, sections 36 and 37, translated by George Long, in *Great Books of the Western World*, edited by Robert Maynard Hutchins, Chicago, IL: University of Chicago Press, 1952, p. 306.

[18] Book X, section 25, in ibid., p. 299.

[19] Book V, section 31, in ibid., p. 273.

[20] Book IV, section 31, in ibid., p. 266.

> if ten thousand men set themselves down, as his masters; for he will quote that line of Sophocles, which differs in no respect from the doctrines of the Pythagoreans – "God is my ruler, and no mortal man."[21]

Philo is one of the very few who breaks with the rabbis who had by and large defended slavery. And it is interesting that Philo, like Epictetus and Marcus Aurelius, was heavily influenced by Stoicism.

Philo does not advocate for the abolition of slavery but rather condemns those who think that it is even possible for one human to enslave another. Enslavement only comes to those who are judged not to be good persons, and this only follows on from an assessment of God. In this view, only those are truly free who are virtuous, not those who are unchained or wealthy in belongings.

Yet it is also true of Philo that he believed that those who were not virtuous deserved to be enslaved. And so in this sense Philo was not opposed to all enslavement but only to that which is unconnected to the character of the person in question. In the end, Philo's condemnation of slavery is a moral or metaphysical doctrine, not one that he thinks leads to conclusions about the legal status of persons. Here Philo is also like Epictetus. It is only Marcus Aurelius, who as emperor tried to increase the likelihood that manumission of slaves would occur, whose negative views of slavery led to legal change.

39.5 RECONSIDERING THE IDEA OF MORAL PROGRESS IN LIGHT OF SLAVERY

As in the case of the status of women during ancient times, it is hard to discern moral progress in the status of slaves as we move from the time of Hammurabi to that of the rabbis and the Roman lawyers. We have seen that humaneness, equity, and justice are characteristic of nearly all periods of ancient legal thought. Of course humaneness can come in various degrees, so it is possible that moral progress was had nonetheless despite early ancient legal thought being much more humane than it is often characterized. Yet it is striking that the defense of law in humane terms runs consistently through this long 2,500-year period from the end of the third millennium BCE to half-way through the first millennium CE.

It is well established that Biblical law, especially in Deuteronomy, provides an especially compassionate and humane way to view human relations and the rules that govern them.[22] Indeed, what is characteristic is that the innocent include the

[21] *The Works of Philo, Complete and Unabridged*, translated by D. D. Yonge, Peabody, MA: Hendrickson Publishers, 1993, p. 683.

[22] See Richard H. Hiers, *Justice and Compassion in the Bible*, NY: Continuum, 2009; and Jeffries M. Hamilton, *Social Justice and Deuteronomy*, Atlanta, GA: Scholars' Press, 1992.

most vulnerable – the widows, orphans, poor, and strangers (aliens). So, one question to ask is why the rabbis did not follow in these Biblical footsteps and expand the humaneness of Jewish law to include slaves? Given the overwhelming support for humaneness in the Biblical law, why did not Rabbinic law progress further yet? And why is there evidence, we cited above, that there was moral regress from Biblical to Rabbinic law in how slavery was viewed?

In Roman law we find strong support for democratic values in the Roman Republic, which then set the stage for the early Empire's doctrine that all those who lived in the emerging Roman Empire had the same status as citizens. Yet, slaves were not granted this status and it was as if the moral progress enshrined in the idea of universal citizenship was thwarted by the case of slaves (as well as women to a certain extent). Again, the question is this: if over time there is moral progress, why did not Rome progress in the most obvious way that it could, in terms of the equal treatment and manumissions of slaves?

Perhaps it is anachronistic to use slavery as a benchmark of moral progress or regress. This would be true if it were not the case that in each ancient period that we have examined, there were some voices that condemned slavery even as it was part of the customary law of nearly every ancient society. It is, though, not anachronistic to judge these ancient societies by how they dealt with the widows, orphans, poor, and aliens of their societies. Indeed, this is the measure that is advocated from Hammurabi to Justinian. Yet, it is rare that the treatment of slaves is added to the list of those most vulnerable and most in need of legal protection.

One could contend that slaves were not treated the same as were widows, orphans, the poor, and aliens because slaves were not seen as human – slaves were even characterized as beasts of burden rather than human. But this cannot be the full explanation since in other domains slaves were recognized as human persons. As we saw in the canonical writings of the Roman legal scholar, Gaius, slaves are categorized as persons. Yes, it is also true that Gaius categorized slaves as things as well. But if slaves were things like beasts of burden then there was no reason also to characterize slaves as persons.

In rabbinic writings, similar problems arise. Yes, it is true, as we have seen that the rabbis of the Talmud see slaves as asses. But notice that when Rabbi Eliezer frees his slave, the slave becomes not just a person but a Jewish person in terms of counting whether there was a minion – a group of at least ten Jewish men in the synagogue. And also note that by the Talmudic period the idea that Jews were slaves is roundly condemned since Jews should not be masters over other Jews – the implicit recognition being that Jewish slaves were slaves who were Jewish humans.

We should also note that at least among prominent philosophers and theorists in these ancient times, slavery was at best treated as morally problematical. As we saw in an earlier part of this work, Aristotle and Cicero are both aware of how odd it is to treat slaves as not deserving of protection of the law when the law of nature dictates that all humans are treated as equals. And we see Jewish philosophers like Philo, and Roman philosophers like Marcus Aurelius, recognizing the common humanity of slaves.

So, it is not truly anachronistic to judge the moral progress or regress of ancient societies and their laws to look to the treatment of slaves. Of course, there is not much moral progress on this issue in Medieval times or even in modern times until the nineteenth century CE. So, again, it may be unfair to judge ancient societies like those of the Roman Empire or the rabbinic period by their lack of progress on the issue of slavery in the law. But what has been more damning is that there is evidence that there was moral regress on the issue of slavery as the ancient period comes to an end. In what next follows we will assess the status of criminal law and the beginnings of international law where we will find a case for some moral progress in Rabbinic law and the law of the Roman Empire.

SECTION XV

Responsibility

40

Intention and Causation in Criminal Law

One of the most significant developments in the several centuries at the beginning of the Common Era concerned criminal law. Two of the most important elements in what constitutes a crime – intention and causation – received significant new formulations that have lasted until today. I will explore these developments, asking how the legal thought of the Roman Empire differed from that of the ancient Rabbis at roughly the same time. It is with the development of a doctrine of intention that criminal law arose as we know it today, although this is not necessarily to say that we would now approve of the way the criminal law was employed, as we will see in subsequent chapters about murder and injury.

Today, at least in the Anglo-American tradition, a crime is characterized as having an *actus reus* (a wrongful act that causes an injury or other harm) and a *mens rea* (a guilty state of mind or intention to do a wrongful act). These Latin terms should already signal that the Roman law's influence is profound over this area of law. Indeed, the idea that crime was significantly different from tort (especially negligence) is here very clearly set out, although we have seen many instances of earlier societies that recognized other aspects of crimes, such as that there are acts that harm the society, not merely the individual victim.

So, in this chapter there will be an argument presented that the legal thought of the Roman Empire and of the ancient Rabbis is very close to that today concerning the elements of a crime. In Section 40.1 we will explore the ideas from the very first book of the Talmud concerning causation. In Section 40.2 we will see similar, although importantly different, ideas about causation and crime in the legal thought of the Roman Empire. Then in Section 40.3 we will look at the very significant ideas that were developed in the rabbinic period of Jewish legal thought about how intention is necessary for criminal responsibility. In the fourth section we will see that an even more detailed construction of intention, now fully distinguished from motive, came into full flourishing in the Roman Empire. And in the final section we will catalog the main similarities and differences of approach taken to the idea of intention in Rabbinic and Roman legal thought.

40.1 CAUSATION AND CRIME IN RABBINIC LEGAL THOUGHT

Let us consider the following text from the Babylonian Talmud's Tractate Baba Qamma:

> Since the frame of the passages [from Exodus in the Torah] makes reference to generative causes it is to be inferred that there are derivative causes as well. Well there is no difference between one's inadvertent carrying out an act of labor that falls into a generative category, in which case he is liable to present a sin-offering, and one's inadvertently carrying out an act of labor that falls into a derivative category of labor, in which case he is also liable to present a sin-offering. [The outcome is the same as to penalty.] There is no difference between one's deliberately carrying out an act of labor that falls into the generative category in which case he is liable to the death penalty through stoning, and one's deliberately carrying out an act of labor that falls into a derivative category of labor, in which case he is also liable to the death penalty through stoning. So then what is the difference between an act that falls into the generative category and one that falls into the derivative category? The upshot is that if one simultaneously carried out two actions that fall into the generative acts of labor, or two actions that fall into the derivative category, he is liable for each such action, while if he performed simultaneously both a generative act of labor and a derivative of that same generative act he is liable on only one count.[1]

Here we encounter the very important idea that it is the state of mind that is crucial for liability. We will return to this idea later in this chapter. At the moment I wish to examine this passage for the light it throws on the idea of causation and guilty acts rather than intentions.

Causation is discussed in the Mishnah and the Talmud in terms of generative and derivative acts of labor (of the body). One example that is used repeatedly is the movement of an ox's horn, which is a generative act, and the butting of the ox which is a derivative act. Acts bring about states of affairs: there is the movement of the horn and then the butting into another ox, for instance. Both acts can be said to cause the goring of the ox, and to a certain extent (for purposes of liability) these causal acts can be treated the same, according to the Babylonian Talmud.

If I incite you to kill someone, my act is a generative act and yours is a derivative act. Both acts can be punished the same if they are deliberate. But in the above passage we are not told how to treat these acts if my act is deliberative and yours is

1 *The Babylonian Talmud*, translated by Jacob Neusner, Vol. 13: *Tractate Baba Qamma*, Peabody, MA: Hendrickson Publishers, 2005, pp. 1–2.

not – given the importance of intention, as we later will see, we would not be entitled to treat both acts as similarly liable. The deliberate inciter will be due a punishment more severe than the one incited who did not deliberate about killing.

Causes are discussed in terms of acts (of labor), that is, causation is an element in liability based on the way that human acts bring about events in the world. In this sense, as we will see in the next section, the Rabbinic and Roman understandings of causation are quite similar. There must be an act (of labor) for liability to arise, but the causal act alone is not sufficient for liability. Rather the act is a necessary, but not sufficient, element in a crime, for instance. Only after each of the elements has been established, does punishment or penalty follow.

One of the crucial ideas here is that a person must indeed perform some act in order to be liable for punishment or penalty. The rabbis are quite clear in expressing this idea when it is said:

> For has it not been taught on Tannaite authority: One is liable only on account of something which is the practical consequence, such as sacrificing, burning incense, pouring out a libation, or prostrating oneself. And in this connection Rabbi Simeon b. Laqish said, "Who is the Tannaite authority who includes the manner of prostration [which is hardly a concrete action in the category of a sacrifice]?" ... But it was from the standpoint of Rabbi Aqiba, that is a self-evident fact. The person at hand falls into the category of a blasphemer.[2]

Here one is liable only if one does something that has a practical consequence. And the doing in question seems to refer to both positive and negative acts.

Next consider Samuel Mendelsohn's assessment of how best to understand the above passage from the Tractate *Sanhedrin* of the Talmud:

> Talmudic jurisprudence inflicts punishment for such [613] transgressions only as they are accompanied by bodily action. Now, as violations of law may be committed in two ways, either by omission or commission: by not doing that which ought to be done, or by doing that which ought not to be done – it is clearly seen that, according to this principle, no punishment can be inflicted for any or all of the two hundred and forty-eight positive commands, and a large number of the prohibitive, where the transgression is not accomplished by means of bodily action.[3]

What remains unclear is whether some violations by means of negative actions can involve something like an action that brings about a consequence. Mendelsohn is seemingly not sure, but it seems to me that the passage from the Talmud does

[2] The Tractate *Sanhedrin*, 63a, Vol. 16 of the *Babylonian Talmud*, translated by Jacob Neusner, Peabody, MA: Hendrickson Publishers, 2005, p. 331.

[3] Samuel Mendelsohn, *The Criminal Jurisprudence of the Ancient Hebrews*, Baltimore, MD: M. Curlander, 1891, pp. 26–27.

countenance such "negative actions," as we may call them, as constituting grounds for liability to punishment.

It might be useful to examine the example of prostration and how this might be seen as an act and how its absence might also be seen as an act of some sort. The passage from the *Sanhedrin* says that someone prostrating, as well perhaps as not prostrating, oneself can be seen as being a blasphemer. To put the point more straightforwardly, the question is whether someone who does not prostrate oneself, when prostration is an obligation, is engaging in the act of blaspheming. It is certainly true that we can "do" things by our inaction as well as our direct action. This comes out especially well in Roman law, as we next see, when actions are discussed in terms of obligations. Once a person is under an obligation, then that person can "do" things either by commission or omission. And here in the case of prostration, we can see that not prostrating oneself when one had a duty to prostrate is a doing in the sense that one has blasphemed.

The question of criminal liability, though, may be harder to answer when one has only engaged in an omission rather than a commission. Mendelsohn seems to interpret the Talmudic texts as only holding people liable to criminal punishment if they engaged in a commission, not an omission. In this view, one could be seen to sin by means of omission, but not to be held criminally liable. It is not clear to me that this is the best interpretation of the Talmudic texts. But it would not be incoherent or normatively problematic if Mendelsohn is right. Yet, it seems to me a better interpretation of the Talmudic texts that the causal action required for criminal liability can include omissions but not bare inaction. This interpretation would then suggest that we cannot tell whether there is a doing of the right sort unless we know something about the obligations a person antecedently has.

40.2 CAUSATION AND CRIME IN THE LEGAL THOUGHT OF THE ROMAN EMPIRE

In Justinian's *Digest*, Ulpian is quoted as saying: "No one suffers a penalty for merely thinking."[4] There has to be an act, normally a physical act, for penalty or punishment to be assigned. Claudius Saturninus sets out some of the considerations that should be examined in order to assess an act:

> Acts such as theft or homicide; verbal statements, such as insults, or betrayal by advocates; written ones, such as forgeries and criminal libels; and advice such as is given in conspiracies and the agreement of thieves are punished, for it is the same as a crime to assist others by persuasion.[5]

4 Justinian's *Digest*, 48, 19, 18, in *The Civil Law*, Vol. 11, translated by S. P. Scott, Cincinnati, OH: The Central Trust Co., 1932, p. 118.

5 Ibid., 48, 19, 16, p. 116.

We see here the wide variety of acts that can trigger penalty or punishment in the Roman Empire. Even advice and agreement, which look like mere verbal acts, could rise to the level of criminal acts in certain cases.

Claudius Saturninus also provides a fascinating catalogue of the seven considerations of an act that can constitute an offense:

> (1) These four kinds of offenses should be considered under seven different heads; namely, the cause, the person, the place, the time, the quality, the quantity, and the result.
> (2) The cause in the case of blows which are unpunished when inflicted by a master or a parent; for the reason that they seem to be given rather for the purpose of correction than injury. They are punishable when anyone is beaten by a stranger in anger.
> (3) The person is considered from two points of view: first, that of him who committed the act; and second, that of him who suffered it …
> (4) The place renders the same act, one either of theft or sacrilege, and determines whether it should be punished with death or with a penalty of less severity.
> (5) The time distinguishes a person temporarily absent from a fugitive, and a house-breaker or a daylight thief from one who commits the crime by night.
> (6) The quality, when the act is either more atrocious or less grave, as manifest thefts are usually distinguished from those that are non-manifest; quarrels from highway robberies; pillage from ordinary theft; impudence from violence …
> (7) The quantity distinguishes a common theft from one who drives away a herd of cattle, for anyone who steals a sow shall be punished merely as a thief; and he who drives away a number of animals shall be punished as a cattle stealer.
> (8) The result should also be considered even when it is brought about by a man of the most amiable character; although the law does not punish with less severity a person who was provided with a weapon for the purpose of killing a man than him who actually killed him …[6]

This catalogue of the considerations or factors of liability is one of the most sophisticated and comprehensive in all of Roman legal thought. In fact it resembles the similar set of considerations that were advanced by Jeremy Bentham in his *Introduction to the Principles of Morals and Legislation* over 1,000 years later.[7]

In the criminal law of the Roman Empire, there must be an act for there to be a crime – mere thoughts are not sufficient. Physical acts were the most common to generate criminal charges, but verbal acts were also recognized as well. Notice that

6 Ibid., 48, 19, 16, pp. 116–117.

7 Jeremy Bentham, *Introduction to the Principles of Morals and Legislation* (1789), edited by J. H. Burns and H. L. A. Hart, Oxford: Oxford University Press, 1970.

the person who injures is not necessarily the one who is punished most severely, compared to those who are various types of accessories. Also of importance is that the character of the person, seemingly including the motivation of the person, is not as significant as what the person's act brings about.

Yet, it is also true that a person's act can trigger criminal liability even though the act does not lead to injury or other harm. Here is where the intention, which we will discuss in greater detail in a later section of this chapter, is perhaps more important even than the act itself. Consider a famous example from Justinian's *Institutes*:

> Whence the following question arises: Titius has urged the slave of Maevius to steal from his master certain things, and to bring them to him; the slave informs his master, who wishing to seize Titius in the act, permits the slave to take certain things to Titius: is Titius liable to an action *furti* (theft), or to one *servi corrupti* (corrupting a slave), or to neither? This doubtful question has been put to us, and we examined the conflicting opinion of the ancient jurists on the subject, some of whom thought Titius was liable to neither of these actions, while others thought he was only liable to the action of theft; and to prevent such subtleties, we have decided that in this case both these actions may be brought. For although the slave has not been corrupted, and the case does not seem therefore within the rules of the action *servi corrupti*, yet the intention to corrupt the slave is indisputable, and he is therefore to be punished as if the slave had been really corrupted, lest his impunity should incite others to act in the same criminal way towards a slave more easy to corrupt.[8]

Here, taking steps to attempt to steal were sufficient to satisfy the *actus reus* even though these acts did not result in an actual theft.

The actual result of an action must be taken into account but it is not definitive for the question of liability. Yet merely thinking about a result is also not sufficient for liability, as we saw Ulpian say above. There must be steps taken toward accomplishing a result, even if the result is not actually achieved. And while there is an emerging doctrine of attempt, it is not fully worked out. The acts taken as part of the attempt remain crucial.

One last point to make before turning to the intention element is to realize that severity of punishment could turn not on the act but sometimes on issues of the need to deter certain people from even beginning to think about certain acts. We find this stated explicitly by Claudius Saturninus as follows:

> (9) It happens that the same crimes are more severely punished in certain provinces; as, for instance, in Africa, those who burn harvests; in Mysia, those who burn vines; and counterfeiters, where mines are situated.

[8] *The Institutes of Justinian*, Book IV, Chapter 1, Section 4, translated by Thomas Collett Sandars, London: Longmans, Green and Co., 1917, pp. 401–402.

(10) It sometimes happens that the punishments of certain malefactors are rendered more severe whenever an example is necessary, as for the suppression of many persons engaged in highway robbery.[9]

In part, this is just a recording of Roman law during the Empire period, but there is also an attempt here to justify the differences in severity of punishment on prudential grounds, surely an important set of normative considerations during the Roman Empire.

40.3 INTENTION IN ANCIENT RABBINIC LEGAL THOUGHT

In *The Mishnah*'s Baba Kamma, the Rabbis give many examples of how important the intention is to the assessment of responsibility. Indeed, we find this very clear statement: "a man is liable only when he acts with intention [of causing injury]."[10] A distinction is made between the actions of an ox and of a man:

> Herein greater stringency applies to a man than to an ox, since the man must pay for injury, healing, loss of time, and indignity, and make restitution for the value of the young; whereas the ox only pays for the injury and is not liable for the value of the young.[11]

The ox is liable for injuries inflicted, as was true also throughout the Middle Ages, but because the ox could not intend to do injury, the five types of liability assigned to humans were not also assigned to oxen.

Let us consider a passage from the *Mishnah's Sanhedrin* which discusses variations on the theme of mistake:

> If he had intended to kill a beast and killed a man, or a gentile and killed an Israelite, or an untimely birth and killed an offspring that was likely to live, he is not culpable. If he intended to strike a man on the loins a blow that on the loins was enough to cause death, but it lighted upon his heart and it was a blow that on the heart was enough to cause death, and he died, he is not culpable. If he intended to strike a man on the heart a blow that on the heart was enough to cause death, but it lighted upon his loins and if it was a blow that on the loins was not enough to cause death, and yet he died, he is not culpable. If he had intended to strike a grown man a blow that was not enough to cause death to a grown man, but it lighted upon a child and it was enough to cause death to a child, and it died, he is not culpable. If he had intended to strike a child a blow that was enough to cause death to a child,

9 Justinian's *Digest*, 48, 19, 16, in *The Civil Law*, Vol. 11, p. 117.

10 *The Mishnah, Baba Kamma*, 7, 8, 1, translated by Herbert Danby, Oxford: Oxford University Press, 1933, p. 342.

11 Ibid., *Baba Kamma*, 7, 8, 2., p. 342.

> but it lighted upon a grown man, and it was a blow that was not enough to cause death to a grown man, and yet he died, he is culpable.[12]

As we progress through these examples of variations of mistake, the controlling factor for determining culpability is what was intended. This position is summarized when Rabbi Simeon is quoted as saying: "Even if he had intended to kill one but killed another, he is not culpable."[13]

We learn that intent has as one of its chief components the free choice of the will, as in a set of passages in *The Mishnah's Makkoth*. Indeed, every act of free choice that causes death will result at least in the charge of unwitting murder.[14] But what we would call first-degree murder requires, in addition to free choice, a proof that what one caused is what one planned to cause.

It is also a matter of luck, or its lack, that becomes an element in the crime. As we saw, mistake can relieve one of culpability even when the mistake seems to be solely a matter of luck, as in the case where one aims to kill one person but kills another and thereby is not culpable of murder. We should note, though, that luck can also enter into the case and make one culpable – such as the case mentioned in the *Makkoth* where a judge "gave him one stripe too many and he died, he must escape into exile because of him" or be subject to capital punishment.[15]

One question to ask at this point is whether the judgment that a person acted intentionally is subject to these luck considerations, or is it being claimed that intention can be overridden by certain kinds of good, or bad, luck? And if it is true that Rabbinic legal thought granted intention a pride of place, why consider luck at all – either one intended to cause harm or one did not. The answer to this question turns on what we have already seen to be the importance of what one has caused by one's actions, and so while intention has pride of place it is not sufficient for criminal liability or culpability – there must be a connection between what one actually did and the injury in question.

So, we can return to the formulation we started with in this section from *The Mishnah's Baba Kamma*: "a man is liable only when he acts with intention [of causing injury]."[16] Here we see that there are two elements: the act and the intention. But we can also see a glimmer of recognition that there might be a third element as well: that the act and the intention must be connected in the right way. If they are, or are not, this could be due merely to luck of the circumstances surrounding the act and intention.

[12] Ibid., *Sanhedrin*, 8. 9.2, pp. 395–396.

[13] Ibid., *Sanhedrin*, 8, 9, 2; p. 396.

[14] Ibid., *Makkoth*, 2, 2; pp. 403–404.

[15] Ibid., *Makkoth*, 3, 14; p. 408.

[16] Ibid., *Baba Kamma*, 7, 8, 1p. 342.

40.4 INTENTION IN THE LEGAL THOUGHT OF THE ROMAN EMPIRE

In Justinian's *Digest*, there are many examples of legal writers who proclaim the centrality of intention to the perpetration of a crime. Callistratus, for instance, is quoted as saying: "In the perpetration of crime, the intention, and not the event, is considered."[17] Ulpian takes this point further, saying that the intention is more important than the actual act itself. "It makes no difference whether one actually kills another, or merely causes the death of another. He who orders another to be killed is considered a homicide."[18] We also find that the lack of an ability to form an intention excuses someone from criminal liability, as Modestinus says: "When an infant or an insane person commits homicide, he is not liable under the Cornelian Law; for absence of intention protects the one, and his unhappy fate excuses the other."[19]

In attempting to explain what all is involved in intention, Modestinus is also quite helpful when he says: "Those who voluntarily or maliciously commit murder are usually deported."[20] Here, intent is understood in terms of what is voluntary or malicious. The reference to voluntariness is indeed helpful, although as Aristotle already pointed out, the voluntary and the intentional are not necessarily the same. What is not as helpful is the idea that intention can be understood as the malicious. The idea is probably related to what came to be considered "malice aforethought," a category that sometimes stood in for intent. But since Modestinus does not say that the maliciousness of the murder connected to the previous thoughts, as opposed to the contemporaneous ones, of the assailant, we don't have a useable stand-in concept for intent. And there are other problems when Roman legal theorists tried to identify what evidence was needed to prove intent.

Consider the case of rape and how it was distinguished from adultery. If the woman consented to have sex with a man who was not her husband, then she and her lover were subject to various penalties and punishments, as had been true since the earliest codes we have examined – typically both of them were executed. If the woman did not consent, then the man could be charged with rape and dealt with very severely. Unlike in some earlier times, the rapist was thought to have done something wrong to the woman rather than to the woman's husband or father.

Yet, as O. F. Robinson points out: "Rape, sexual intercourse against the woman's will, is, however, surprisingly difficult to detect in the sources" – it seems to have been thought by some that it should be classed as adultery except that this did not

[17] Justinian's *Digest*, 48.8.14, in *The Civil Law*, Vol. 11, p. 63.
[18] Ibid., 48.8.15, p. 63.
[19] Ibid., 48.8.12, p. 62.
[20] Ibid., 48.8.16, p. 63.

fit the facts because "she was innocent of *dolus*" (criminal intent).[21] But what sort of proof could be offered was the crucial question. In Justinian's *Code* we find the following:

> The laws punish the detestable wickedness of women who prostitute their chastity to the lusts of others, but does not hold those liable who are compelled to commit fornication through force, and against their will. And, moreover, it has very properly been decided that their reputations are not lost, and that their marriage with others should be prohibited on this account.[22]

Notice here that there is an attempt to set out what would constitute proof of lack of consent on the woman's part: that she acted against her will and that force had been inflicted on her. And in Justinian's *Digest*, Ulpian is quoted as saying that the key is whether or not she has suffered violence.[23] If so, then she cannot be accused of adultery or fornication. Violence or force is crucial as evidence of rape, but it seems it is still required to show something else as evidence of the woman's intent.

It is of course possible that a person could be forced to do something and yet also intend that it be done to them. Rape is unlikely to be one of the things that would fit this odd characterization. But the Roman legal theorists seemed to recognize this possibility and to worry about how it could be proved, beyond the proof of force or violence that the woman did not intend to have sexual relations with her assailant. The Theodosian Code speaks of evidence "beyond doubt" that rape or ravishment has occurred, and then imposes very severe punishment. But we do not find much help in figuring out what that evidence would be, especially since the Theodosian Code, like Ulpian's treatment, seems to countenance the possibility that the woman or girl might collude with her ravisher or rapist in order to gain marriage to him.[24] The difficulty, quoting O. F. Robinson, was that, as today, "women may have kept quiet about rape because they felt ashamed,"[25] and it was then difficult to tell whether their silence was a sign of consent or mere shame.

The development of the criminal law in the Roman Empire did not come up with a clear-cut account of the evidence necessary to prove intent, but rather with the recognition of how hard it was to prove this crucial element of a crime. Let us think about this issue in one other context from Roman Empire times. Jill Harries draws our attention to the problem of determining who was responsible when a harm was perpetrated by a mob or other group of people. It is still today difficult to figure

[21] O. F. Robinson, *The Criminal Law of Ancient Rome*, Baltimore, MD: Johns Hopkins University Press, 1995, p. 72.

[22] *The Code of Justinian*, Book IX, Chapter 9, no. 20, in *The Civil Law*, Vol. 15, p. 13.

[23] Justinian's *Digest*, Book 48, Chapter 5, no. 13, in *The Civil Law*, Vol. 11, p. 37.

[24] *The Theodosian Code*, 9.24.1. 1–2, translated by Clyde Pharr, p. 245.

[25] Robinson, *The Criminal Law of Ancient Rome*, note 266, pp. 141–142.

out who had the criminal intent in such situations since many perpetrators were just following others with no clear idea of what they hoped to accomplish. Harries says: "evidence of conspiracy and intent was sufficient to justify a charge. The statute caught those who gathered a crowd together and incited a riot (but not the crowd itself) ..."[26] Evidence of intent to assault by use of a mob was seen by acts of "gathering" the crowd in the first place, and then in providing the spark, the inciting act that moved the crowd toward a certain act and outcome.

Interestingly, the crowd that actually performs an assault is not held to be guilty instead of the organizers of the group. And it seems to be the case that the reason is that the members of the crowd or mob did not have a criminal intent. Here is the relevant part of the Justinian *Digest*, quoting from Marcianus' *Institutes*:

> Anyone who, by means of an assembly, a crowd, a tumult, or a sedition, causes a conflagration; or who maltreats a man whom he has wrongfully confined; or who prevents a body from being buried, to better enable him to disperse and plunder a funeral procession; or forcibly compels someone to be obligated to him, for the law rescinds an obligation of this kind, is liable.[27]

Here the central idea is that one person can cause another person to do his bidding, and that that person is the one who is criminally liable. Or to put the point another way, if one person causes another person to perpetrate harm, it is the first person not the second who is liable despite the fact that it is the second person who physically does the harming. And hence between the act and the intent, it is the intent that carries the most weight in determining criminal liability in the legal thought of the Roman Empire.

40.5 CONCEPTUALIZING CRIMINAL RESPONSIBILITY

Many of the elements recognized today to constitute a crime were already also recognized at the end of the ancient period, by the time of Justinian's *Digest* and the Babylonian *Talmud*. The central idea is that punishment cannot be inflicted unless the defendant freely chose an act that was aimed at an illegal consequence of grave concern to the society. Indeed, the Roman jurists and the rabbis were even more concerned than we often are today that people should be relieved of culpability if there was some sense in which they were not free or some sense in which they did not aim at the consequence that actually occurred. The scrupulous attention to the

[26] Jill Harries, *Law and Crime in the Roman World*, Cambridge: Cambridge University Press, 2007, p. 111.

[27] Justinian's *Digest*, Book 48, Chapter 6, no. 5, in *The Civil Law*, Vol. 11, pp. 51–52.

state of the act and the mind of the defendant was a hallmark of this period and is one of the central legal ideas to extend from the ancients until today.

Conceptually, we have a mixing of what is morally and legally required in the criminal law. People are not to be legally punished unless there is moral culpability. The idea here is deeply connected to the respect that should be shown to all (or all male) citizens or subjects. As we see in the Mishnah, most people, with few exceptions, are to be treated as if they are free to choose to act as they do, and are held accountable on that basis, not merely on the basis of whether there are untoward events that happen. Or to put the point only somewhat differently, legal punishment was only justified if there was moral responsibility. While somewhat controversial today, this idea is still often stated as the key difference between civil and criminal guilt.

The rabbis were explicit in linking the moral law of God to the way that criminal and other forms of liability were understood. And while the Romans certainly had a more secular view of the law than did the rabbis, criminal law was nonetheless connected to moral responsibility. We can see the effects of certain moral principles on the shape of the Roman criminal law as well as Rabbinic law, a topic we will take up now at the end of this chapter.

Clyde Pharr has made the following point that is relevant to the question we are currently pursuing:

> It is a fundamental principle of most legal systems, including our own, that the attempt or intent to commit a crime is punishable. Thus an assault with intent to commit murder, rape, or robbery is punished more severely than simple assault. In Roman law this principle is stated many times, and, in some cases, the intent or attempt is punished with the same severity as the completed crime.[28]

Intent, as well as attempt, is a moral category first and foremost and it is normally only part of what is legally required to prove liability. But with intent alone, and sometimes attempt, we find that the law takes a moral notion and wholly and simply criminalizes what was a moral matter.

In the ancient Rabbinic tradition, various moral principles were crucial in determining the extent and severity of criminal punishment. Here is Samuel Mendelsohn:

> The philosophic maxim, that it is absurd to apply the same punishment to crimes of different malignity, which the great commentator [Blackstone] so ably and justly advocated only one century ago, was early recognized and acted upon in Talmudic jurisprudence. Not only is there in Rabbinic law a well drawn scale of crimes and punishments – the latter ranging from flagellation to death – but in the mode of

[28] *Ancient Roman Statutes*, translated by Allan Chester Johnson, Paul Robinson Coleman-Norton, and Frank Card Bourne, Austin: University of Texas Press, 1961, 2012, p. 27, note 1a.

> capital punishment itself, as will appear hereafter, there is a gradation commensurate with the magnitude of the crime.[29]

We will examine this and similar doctrines in more detail in Chapter 42. But note here that the gradation of punishments to fit the severity of the crime is largely drawn in the terms of morality according to Mendelsohn.

The point though is that the humaneness and humanity of the emerging criminal law doctrines were inspired by longstanding moral principles among the Romans and the Jews. In the latter case, Boaz Cohen tells us:

> In the Pentateuch and in the Talmud there is no distinct term for ethics because as we shall note presently, the goal of ethics and law coalesce … It has often been noticed that in ancient society in general, and in Hebrew society in particular, religion, law, and morals were undifferentiated, and Leviticus, chapter 19,was cited as a classical example … The lawmaker was laying down rules for the purpose of establishing a sound economy and a great society. It is not the business of the legislator to engage in subtle analysis of the nature or relative value of the precepts that should prevail in society … what the rabbis call the laws between man and his neighbor.[30]

How people should behave toward their neighbors was what ethics was about, and over time ethical principles were incorporated into the criminal law in both Roman and Rabbinic legal thought.

29 Samuel Mendelsohn, *The Criminal Jurisprudence of the Ancient Hebrews Compiled from the Talmud and other Rabbinical Writings*, Baltimore, MD: M. Curlander, 1891, pp. 37–39.

30 Boaz Cohen, *Jewish and Roman Law: A Comparative Study*, NY: The Jewish Theological Seminary of America, 1966, pp. 66–60.

41

Injury and Murder

In the legal thought of the Roman Empire and the rabbis, an idea crystallized that would have a profound impact on later legal thought, namely the concept of injury. Injury is understood in both Roman and Rabbinic legal thought to be criminal when there is some public outrage or where the individual person is denied his or her dignity. In most cases of injury, even those that cause death, civil remedies are allowed, such as the payment of monetary compensation. What seems to call for punishment, including capital punishment, is when there is some sense that the act or the consequences were a matter of grave public concern. In this chapter I will argue that the idea of grave public concern is only beginning to be associated with threats to the community and hence not fully assimilatable to the modern notions. But we will also see that there is a clear attempt to differentiate the civil and criminal in terms of what gives outrage to that community, which is also something that is crucial today for understanding some crimes.

In Section 41.1 we will explore the fascinating case of *injuria* in the Roman law of the Empire, where this idea is linked to outrageousness; either outrage to the victim or to the society. In Section 41.2 we will examine the rabbinic treatment of injury and assault where the rabbis struggled to move beyond the talionic treatment of this topic in the Torah, where one of the features of the harm, the indignity, was hard to capture solely in monetary terms. In Section 41.3 we examine the treatment of murder in the Roman Empire, where the use of violence and weapons were thought to put the killing into a different category than could be handled by civil courts. In Section 41.4 we look at how homicide and murder were understood in the Talmud, where a sharp distinction was made between willful, deliberate killing and killing that is done inadvertently. We will attempt to find why this distinction was important for treating the killing as criminal and deserving of death at the hands of the state. In Section 41.5 we will put the various lessons learned together to construct a view of crime at the end of the ancient period.

41.1 *INJURIA* IN THE ROMAN EMPIRE

We find special mention of a crime (that could also be a delict or tort) in the idea of causing outrage by an act of harming. Here is the classic treatment by Gaius:

> Outrage (*injuria*) is committed not only by striking a man with the fist or a stick or by flogging him, but also by raising a clamor against him, or if, knowing that he owes one nothing, one advertises his property for sale as a debtor's, or by writing defamatory matter in prose or verse against him, or by following about a matron or a youth, and in short in many other ways … Under the Twelve Tables the penalties for outrage used to be: for destroying a limb retaliation; for breaking or bruising a bone 300 asses if the sufferer was a free man, 150 if a slave; for all other outrages 25 asses. These penal sums were considered sufficient in those days of extreme poverty. But the system now in force is different. For the praetor allows us to make our own assessment of the outrage, and the iudex may, at his discretion, condemn in the amount of our assessment or in a lesser sum. But it is customary for the praetor impliedly to assess an aggravated outrage himself.[1]

Injuria was a delict or tort in the early days of the Roman Republic but in some circumstances in the Roman Empire it came to be seen as a crime when aggravating factors were present.

The idea that crimes could be differentiated from delicts or torts by the aggravating conditions of the situation is an important addition to the emerging idea of a distinct realm of criminal jurisprudence. Assaults could be seen as matters of civil law or even of private dispute resolution, but not if there was a sufficient outrage suffered by the person assaulted. Here the penalty was sometimes imprisonment rather than the levying of a monetary fine. O. F. Robinson says: "Injuria was an offense against a person's honor, his reputation, his dignity, or his physical integrity."[2] This idea marks off certain assaults as matters that the society at large is especially concerned with.

We can distinguish another form of crime, *vis*, from *injuria* as well as from those delicts that did not also concern an assault on the public. Public instances of *vis* were "usually grave offenses against public order."[3] Again, as Robinson argues: "*Vis* was something of a catchall crime. It is mentioned here because it could cover physical assault, but such assault seems necessarily to have been either political, or for the sake of lust or gain."[4]

1 *The Institutes of Gaius*, Book III, sections 220–224, translated by Francis De Zulueta, Oxford: Oxford University Press, 1946, Vol. I, pp. 227–229.

2 O. F. Robinson, *The Criminal Law of Ancient Rome*, Baltimore, MD: Johns Hopkins University Press, 1995, p. 50.

3 Ibid., p. 79.

4 Ibid., p. 48.

Today, the idea of crime combines ideas from both of the Roman ideas of *injuria* and *vis*. Simple physical harm was not enough for criminal liability. Instead monetary fines as compensation or other self-help remedies were pursued. Indeed, physical harm was not necessary to establish criminal liability. There had to be some sense in which the community had been assaulted – hence the paradigm case for *vis* appears to have been sedition. *Injuria* and *vis* we might say today were both forms of criminal injury – there was sufficient outrageousness or affront to the community so that punishment was inflicted.

41.2 INJURY AND ASSAULT IN THE TALMUD

The Biblical law set retaliation in kind as the penalty for some injuries – the *lex talionis* of an eye for an eye and a tooth for a tooth. But there is reason to think that the rabbis rejected the literal *lex talionis*. Here is a passage from the Babylonian Talmud:

> Why [should there be monetary compensation]? Scripture states, "An eye for an eye" (Ex. 21: 24), so might I not say that it means an eye literally?
>
> Perish the thought! For it has been taught on Tannaite authority: Might one suppose that if someone blinded a person's eye the court should blind his eye? Or if he cut off his hand, then the court should cut off his hand, or if he broke his leg, the court should break his leg? Scripture states, "He who hits any man … and he who hits any beast" – just as if someone hits a beast, he is assigned to pay monetary compensation, so if he hits a man, he is required to pay monetary compensation …
>
> Rabbi Dosethai b. Judah says, "An eye for an eye" means that monetary reparations are to be paid.
>
> You say that monetary reparations are to be paid. But perhaps it means an eye literally?
>
> Say: Lo, if the eye of this one was big and the eye of that one was little – how am I going to invoke the statement, "an eye for an eye"?[5]

In these passages from the Talmud, injury is treated as a matter of civil law compensation not truly as a criminal matter.

We then face the question of how monetary compensation is to be assessed, especially in the case where there is pain but no loss of limb. The *Mishnah* speaks directly to this question in the following passage:

> If a man wounded his fellow he thereby becomes liable on five counts: for injury, for pain, for healing, for loss of time, and for indignity inflicted. "For injury" – thus,

5 The Tractate *Baba Qamma*, 83b, Vol. 13 of the *Babylonian Talmud*, translated by Jacob Neusner, pp. 352–353.

> if he blinded his fellow's eye, cut off his hand, or broke his foot, [his fellow] is looked upon as if he was a slave to be sold in the market; they assess how much he was worth and how much he is worth now. "For pain" – thus, if he burnt his fellow with a spit or a nail, even though it was on his finger-nail where it leaves no wound, they estimate how much money such a man would be willing to take to suffer so. "For healing" – thus, if he struck him he is liable to pay the cost of his healing …[6]

Here we have a method of assessing compensation for injury rather than literal talon. The rabbis sometimes said that it was the choice of the victim how to mete out punishment and sometimes said that the talionic compensation was too brutal and too difficult to make fair.[7]

Similar to the legal thought of the Roman Empire, the ancient rabbis discussed a kind of injury that adversely affects one's dignity. Greengus cites a passage from the *Tosefta's Baba Qamma* that is especially revealing for our purposes:

> If he [a scribe] struck him [another scribe] with the back of his hand or with a sheet of paper or with an account book (or) with undressed leather skins (or) with a sheaf of documents which (he held) in his hand, (in all of these cases) he must pay him 400 *zuz*; and this (penalty) is (so high) not because (we are dealing with) an injury causing physical pain but because (each one is) an injury causing public shame.[8]

Here it is the public shame that the victim is forced to endure that brings forth the liability to extra severe compensation.

We see the difficulty that the rabbis are struggling with when they try to explain how to determine and then measure the indignity inflicted by a criminal act. In the passage from the *Mishnah* above that I partially quoted, the passage continues with this:

> "For loss of time" – thus he is now looked upon as a watchman of a cucumber-field, since he has already been paid the value of his hand or foot.
>
> "For indignity inflicted" – all is in accord with [the condition of life of] him that inflicts and him that suffers the indignity. If a man inflicted the indignity on a naked man, or a sleeping man, he is [still] liable; but if he that inflicted the indignity was asleep he is not liable … man is liable only when he acts with intention [of causing injury].[9]

6 *The Mishnah, Baba Qamma*, 8, 1, translated by Herbert Danby, Oxford: Oxford University Press, 1933, p. 342.

7 See Samuel Greengus, *Laws in the Bible and in Early Rabbinic Collections*, Eugene, OR: Cascade Books, 2011, pp. 130–132.

8 *The Tosefta*, Baba Qamma, 9: 31, translated by Samuel Greengus, in ibid., p. 137.

9 *The Mishnah, Baba Qamma*, 8, 1, p. 342.

Indignity can be *felt* by any human person, even if that person is not aware of what is happening to him or her, as when asleep. But a person cannot *produce* indignity if he or she is not aware of what he or she is doing, as when asleep. What the criminal law concerns itself with is the conscious infliction of injury, which includes inflicting indignity, on a fellow person. The society seems to care about such acts because the society is outraged by the manifestation of evil – and so they are treated as criminal acts.

41.3 MURDER IN THE ROMAN EMPIRE

Murder is dealt with in the legal thought of the Roman Empire as a form of killing. Ulpian tells us:

> those are understood to be included in the term "killed" who have been put to death by violence, or murdered; for instance, by having their throats cut, by being strangled, or thrown down from some height, or struck with a stone or a club, or deprived of life by the use of any other kind of weapon ... whenever force is employed as usually causes death, it must be held that there is ground for the application of the decree of the Senate.[10]

There was a dispute about whether someone poisoned was murdered by the friend who put the poison into the victim's drink, since it was the poison rather than the friend that caused the death and in any event there was no violence employed.[11]

O. F. Robinson tells us that during the Roman Republic, "most murders were family affairs that would therefore be under the jurisdiction of the relevant *paterfamilias* or owner (or patron)."[12] In the Roman Empire murders were not confined to the family and so a different jurisprudence developed in considering murder. The crime of murder, like the public crime of *injuria*, was mainly concerned with the offense against public order than with the harm to the victim.

Julius Paulus, who is quoted in Justinian's *Digest*, gives a summary of the relevant law concerning killing in his *Opinions*:

> The *Lex Cornelia* imposes a penalty of deportation upon anyone who kills a man, if he does so with a weapon for the purpose of stealing his property; or if he has in his possession, sells, or prepares poison for the purpose of killing another; or if

10 Justinian's *Digest*, Book 29, Chapter 1, nos. 17 and 20, translated in *The Civil Law*, Vol. 6, translated by S. P. Scott, Cincinnati, OH: The Central Trust Co., 1932, p. 320.

11 See Jill Harries, *Law and Crime in the Roman World*, Cambridge: Cambridge University Press, 2007, p. 120.

12 Robinson, *The Criminal Law of Ancient Rome*, p. 41.

> he gives false testimony through which anyone might lose his life, or which might afford occasion for his death. It has been decided that persons of superior rank who commit crimes of this kind shall be capitally punished, and those of inferior rank shall be crucified, or thrown to the wild beasts.[13]

Unlike in the Roman Republic, capital punishment was meted out in the Roman Empire against those who intentionally kill; in this case voluntary exile was not an acceptable alternative even for those who are of superior rank.

We also find this interpretation of the Lex Cornelia by the jurist Marcianus in his *Institutes*:

> Under the Cornelian Law relating to Assassins and Poisoners, anyone who kills a man; or through whose malice a fire has originated; or who has gone about armed for the purpose of killing someone or committing theft; or who, being a magistrate, or presiding in a criminal case, enables false testimony to be given by which an innocent man may be prosecuted, or convicted, is liable … Anyone who has committed homicide is punished without taking into account the legal condition of the person who was killed.[14]

Notice that the person who merely carries weapons with a criminal purpose, but who has not done anything harmful, is subject to criminal liability and punishment.

Assassins and poisoners are considered especially outrageous killers. Marcianus provides us with many details of these crimes:

> Anyone who has prepared poison, or sells it, or keeps it for the purpose of killing human beings is punished by the Fifth section of the same Cornelian Law relating to Assassins and Poisoners.
>
> The penalty of this law is imposed upon anyone who publicly sells injurious poisons or keeps them for the purpose of homicide.
>
> The expression "injurious poisons" show that there are certain poisons that are not injurious. Therefore the term is an ambiguous one, and includes what can be used for curing disease as well as for causing death. There are also preparations called love philters. These however are only forbidden by this law where they are designed to kill people …
>
> It is provided by another Decree of the Senate that dealers in ointments who rashly sell hemlock, salamander, aconite, pine-cones, buprestis, mandragora, and give cantharides as purgative, are liable to the penalty of this law.[15]

[13] *The Opinions of Julius Paulus*, Book V, Chapter 22, section 1, translated by S. P. Scott, in *The Civil Law*, Vol. 1, p. 325.

[14] Justinian's *Digest*, Book 48, Chapter 7, no. 1, pr and 2, in *The Civil Law*, Vol. 11, p. 59.

[15] Ibid., pp. 59–60.

These types of homicide that involve stealth or that cannot easily be detected and hence avoided are singled out for special attention and severe penalty – such as "being thrown to wild beasts."[16]

Certain forms of killing are considered so important that even the preparation for such killing is penalized as if the killing had been carried out. What matters is the purpose or intent of the perpetrator, not whether the purpose had indeed been accomplished. And as we have seen, the condition or status of the person killed or attempted to be killed is irrelevant to the penalty. In the legal thought of the Roman Empire we do still see that the penalties are sometimes differentiated based on the status of the perpetrator, but not on the basis of the status of the victim. This idea will also be very important as the idea of "equality before the law" becomes more important in later epochs.

41.4 HOMICIDE IN THE TALMUD

One of the difficulties in assessing the rabbinic treatment of homicide is that it seems that Roman criminal law superceded Jewish courts. Here is a passage from the Palestinian Talmud to this effect: "Forty years before the destruction of the (second) Temple (i.e., c. 30 CE), the power over capital cases was removed (from the local Jewish courts)."[17] There is nonetheless discussion of how to think about homicide in the Babylonian Talmud, for instance in the *Sanhedrin*: "in the case of murder … the law does not treat inadvertent action as equivalent to deliberate action, or action done under constraint as equivalent to action done willfully."[18]

In the *Talmud's Sanhedrin* we find a good attempt to differentiate civil from criminal liability in the context of killings:

> Scripture has said, "He who smote him shall surely be put to death, for he is a murderer" (Num. 35: 21). It is in the case of a murderer that the law has made such a one liable in the consequence of an act of confinement, but in a case of causing civil damage, the law has not made such a one liable in an act of confinement. And said Raba, "If one tied up [another person] and the latter dies of starvation, he is exempt … there is no penalty (for) indirectly causing death."[19]

Willful acts that cause death directly are the concern of the criminal law where severe punishments are handed out; civil law is the domain of inadvertence and negligence according to the rabbis.

[16] Ibid., p. 60.

[17] *The Palestinian Talmud, j. Sanhedrin* 18a, translated in Samuel Greengus, *Laws in the Bible and in Early Rabbinic Collections*, Eugene, OR: Cascade Books, 2011, p. 157.

[18] The Tractate *Sanhedrin*, 77a, Vol. 16 of the *Babylonian Talmud*, translated by Jacob Neusner, p. 406.

[19] Ibid., p. 407.

The question to ask though is why deliberation and willfulness are matters of concern for the society to punish whereas inadvertence and negligence are not. The answer seems to be that the willful and deliberate act is in some sense "evil" and the rabbis then cite the Biblical doctrine that "you shall put away evil in the midst of you (Deut. 13: 6)."[20] Here we have a moral and religious notion, evil, imported into the legal domain and employed to explain what the difference is between criminal and civil liability. One interpretation is that punishing evil acts is the responsibility of the society because such acts are highly dangerous to that society. In this sense, the outrage is that one person should act in contempt of the life of another person, thereby denying that person's dignity as a fellow human being.

We should not overlook the importance of violence in the Talmudic understanding of the crime of murder. Violence, unlike mere force, is a willful act that by design is aimed at inflicting injury or death. Here is how Samuel Mendelsohn puts it:

> The *Talmud* requires that, in order to convict of the crime of murder, violence on the part of the accused must first be proved: an act of touching the body of the victim. But where there is no act of violence: as when one frightens another to death, there is legally no murder … In short the criminal must have put his hand to the deed.[21]

The literal-mindedness of the *Talmud*, where murder requires that touching occur, marks a difference between the legal thought of the Romans and that of the rabbis. As we have seen, the Romans regarded the person who orders or plans for another's killing as guilty of murder just as if that person had actually done the physical act.

Rabbinic ideas about criminality, especially about murder, manifest a strong cautionary discipline. There is much attention given to the question of whether the victim was already dying when struck by the assailant, or whether the assailant's act was sufficient for causing death or injury, not merely one of a set of necessary and jointly sufficient conditions. Indeed, there is a long list of factors that must be satisfied before a person can be convicted of murder or injury.

The *Mishnah* distinguishes manslaughter from murder in various ways that we can begin to see in the following passage that explains when the severe penalty of being forced into exile is to be meted out:

> These must escape into exile: If a man killed a soul unwittingly – if he was rolling [the roof] with a roller and it fell on a man and killed him, or if he was letting down a jar [from the roof] and it fell on a man and it killed him, or if we was coming down a

[20] Ibid., 78a, p. 411.

[21] Samuel Mendelsohn, *The Criminal Jurisprudence of the Ancient Hebrews Compiled from the Talmud and other Rabbinical Writings*, Baltimore, MD: M. Curlander, 1891, pp. 70–71 note 144.

> ladder and he fell on a man and killed him – he must escape into exile; but if he was pulling up a roller and it fell on a man and killed him, or if he was drawing up a jar and the rope broke and it fell on a man and killed him, or if he was going up a ladder and fell down on a man and killed him, he need not go into exile. This is the general rule: he [that causes death] in the course of his coming down must escape into exile, but if not in the course of his coming down, he need not escape into exile.[22]

The language here of going up and going down is somewhat mysterious until one reads how the rabbis understood this in the *Talmud*.

Here is the passage from the Talmud that is meant to explain the difference between manslaughter and murder:

> [This is the governing principle: Whatever happens en route downward – the person goes into exile.] What is the scriptural basis for these distinctions? Said Samuel, "Said Scripture, 'or … he let it fall upon him so that he has died' (Num. 35: 22) – one goes into exile only if something fell in a downward movement." Our rabbis have taught on Tannaite authority: "That kills any person by error … unaware" (Deut. 19: 4) – this excludes one who did so deliberately. "That excludes any person by error – this excludes one who did so intentionally … this excludes one who did so deliberately – that is obvious, Such a one is subject to the death penalty! Said Rabbah, "Say it excludes one who says, 'I thought it was permitted to kill him.'" Said to him Abbayye, "If it is one who says, 'I thought it was permitted,' then he has acted under constraint." He said to him, "I claim, 'he who says, "I thought it was permitted," is close to one who does the deed deliberately.'" … "unaware": this excludes one who kills intentionally.[23]

The puzzle about the downward versus upward movement is partially solved, perhaps, by thinking that if one were already coming down then one is partially responsible for harms that occurred from downward falling objects, but if one were engaged in upward movement, harms occurring by downward falling objects are not criminally liable.

There is something significant about the movement of the person accused of killing – only if your bodily movement is in the same direction as the object that brings about the harm. This seems to be a very narrow way to understand manslaughter and other forms of accidental killing, or more generally harming. Later in the Talmudic account of the examples of manslaughter we learn that the person who is not criminally liable of killing or harming because his movement was not downward can still be seen as civilly liable ("liability to damages"[24]) and made to pay

[22] *The Mishnah, Makkoth*, 2, 1, translated by Herbert Danby, Oxford: Oxford University Press, 1933, p. 403.

[23] The Tractate *Makkoth*, 7a, Vol. 17 of the *Babylonian Talmud*, p. 30.

[24] Ibid., 7b, p. 32.

compensation for the injuries caused. From this line of reasoning we can see that the narrowness of understanding the manslaughter cases is restricted to criminal liability.

Perhaps an easier case discussed by the ancient rabbis in the same section of the *Mishnah* and the corresponding sections of the *Talmud* that we have been examining concerns someone who throws a stone into a public place, injuring a person there. Here is the account in the *Mishnah*:

> If a man threw a stone into the public domain and killed [another], he must escape into exile. Rabbi Eliezier b. Jacob says, "If after the stone had left his hand, the other put out his head and received the stone, he is not culpable. If he threw the stone into his own courtyard and killed another, if he that was injured had the right to enter thither, the other must escape into exile; but if he had not the right, the other need not escape into exile, for it is written, "As when a man goes into the forest with his neighbor" (Deut. 19: 5) – since the forest is a place into which the injurer and the injured have the right to enter, this excludes [from the law of unwitting murder] the courtyard of a householder into which the inured had not the right to enter.[25]

In the corresponding section of the *Talmud* we are told that it is commendable to remove possible danger from the public.[26] And we can see here how the use of the criminal law is aimed at just this goal, along with the related goal of responding to societal outrage.

So, we find very strict requirements for what must be shown in order to convict for criminal liability – where manslaughter calls for exile and murder calls for capital punishment. In both cases, justifying these very extreme penalties is seen to require very strict and highly limiting conditions to be proven. On the other hand, the rabbis treat civil liability for killing or other forms of harming much more leniently in the civil law by reference to monetary fines, not limitations on liberty.

41.5 WHY CRIME IS UNDERSTOOD AS OUTRAGEOUS IN ANCIENT LEGAL THOUGHT

Today, certain crimes are said to shock the conscience, and these crimes are often punished in the most severe way. This is true in both domestic criminal law as well as in international criminal law. The idea is that only certain acts that cause harm are of special interest to the society, as opposed merely to the victim and his or her family. And what makes a difference, now as well as then, is whether the act was deliberate or intentional. When harm is caused deliberately the society is outraged.

25 *The Mishnah, Makkoth*, 2, 1, p. 403.

26 The Tractate *Makkoth*, 8a, Vol. 17 of the *Babylonian Talmud*, p. 34.

In this final section we will attempt to answer the question of why this is so and why outrage is the category that should matter for assigning criminality.

It is perhaps not easy today to see why the direction of the movement of the body should matter for whether society is outraged sufficiently to call for extreme penalties. Indeed, it might help to realize that the more severe penalties were restricted to deliberate and intentional action, not to accidental action. Yet, it is nonetheless interesting to see that for the ancient rabbis, although seemingly not for the Roman jurists, some forms of accidental behavior were sanctioned in criminal law – actions that had something to do with the harm. In the case we examined at the end of the last section, the action (or the movement of the body) had to have some relation to the killing or harming. And this is true even though, for us today, the movement of the body seems irrelevant.

Not all crimes in the Roman Empire involved outrage, principally those that were labeled *injuria* along with several forms of homicide. But the model of crime as involving societal outrage has remained throughout the history of legal thought as an extremely important idea. We have seen earlier ideas that have also proven important such as the idea of crime as a kind of pollution or as an especially worrying danger to the society. These ideas also encompassed large swaths, but not all, of what we today call crime in criminal jurisprudence.

Let us take an example of *injuria* from the Roman Empire. We saw that "writing defamatory matter in prose or verse against" someone was a serious crime. Defamation is often seen, as it was in ancient Rome, as a tort where monetary compensation was owed. But in some extreme cases, as we learned from Gaius' *Institutes*, the matter was seen as such an outrage to the victim that it was subject to criminal punishment. In some contexts a person had the choice of either suing in criminal or civil law, where in the latter only monetary compensation could be sought. As with defamation cases generally, it is often hard to ascertain what precisely the damage to one's reputation was worth in terms of compensation. In that situation, criminal proceedings would make more sense. And this option seems to have been allowed after the Roman Republic, especially if the outrage was sufficiently egregious.[27]

Next we can consider an example from our rabbinic texts that talk about loss of dignity that comes from being the victim of certain crimes. We saw an example of one scribe slapping another scribe with an account book. The reason why the perpetrator is punished severely is because of the public shame that the victim was made to endure. This example is from the *Tosefta*, a rabbinic work from about the same time as the *Mishnah*. Crimes were understood as involving harm to one's dignity and this is seen in that the victim is publicly shamed. It could be that a person's

[27] See Bruce W. Frier, *A Casebook on the Roman Law of Delict*, Atlanta, GA: Scholars' Press, 1989, especially p. 180.

dignity was harmed and yet there was not yet a crime – such a situation is quite similar to that of Roman ideas about outrage as we will see.

Defaming and shaming come to be seen as crimes due to the fact that not only is the victim harmed, but there is also a harm to the good morals of the society or to some other aspect of social cohesion. In earlier times, there were laws against slapping, for instance, and the harm was seen as a kind of shaming. But this idea only seems to have been contemplated when the person slapped was of a higher social status than the one doing the slapping.

As we see the emergence of something like a criminal law that is recognizable today, the social status of the parties has less importance – the victim of a crime is seen as a kind of stand-in for the society, where the indignities suffered or the outrage felt are carried over to other members of the society. Such a transferred indignity or outrage will not occur in minor slights or even physical harms that are perceived as not that important. And here we come to one of the central ideas of criminality going forward.

42

Public Punishment, Penal Prisons, and Police

At the end of the ancient period of legal thought, criminal matters were increasingly handled by public institutions rather than by self-help. And while we have seen some instances of the idea of public punishment in earlier times, it is now becoming common to see self-help disparaged and even outlawed in favor of various forms of public punishment, as well as the use of jails and prisons for punishment and the rise of a rudimentary police force as well. Each of these ideas of public punishment, penal prisons, and police enforcement is controversial but there is evidence that we will examine to support each in the legal thought of the Roman Empire and the ancient rabbinic texts.

In each of the sections that follow we will first look at Roman ideas of public punishment, prisons, and police, and then look at the more meager evidence in rabbinic texts, especially the *Mishnah* and *Talmud*. Then we will attempt to draw some conclusions about why there was this turn in criminal jurisprudence and whether it was indeed an unmitigated positive development. So, in Section 42.1 we discuss the strong evidence for thinking that public punishments were preferred over private penalties in Rome and among the ancient rabbis. In Section 42.2 we look at the evidence for thinking that there were penal prisons and discuss why this institution seemed to arise. And in Section 42.3 we will examine the rather meager evidence for thinking that there was a public police institution arising at this time, especially in the case of the return of runaway slaves – of which there is less evidence in the rabbinic texts than in Justinian's *Digest*. Finally,we will address the question of why these institutions arose and suggest a way to understand these institutions in terms of the legal thought of the time.

42.1 PUBLIC PUNISHMENT

Public beheading and stoning had been employed in earlier times as we have seen, but in the time of the Roman Empire and the ancient rabbinic texts these punishments were employed more often and self-help penalties were increasingly discouraged. Here is how O. F. Robinson describes punishment in the Roman Empire:

> The aggravated forms of death penalty were deliberately brutal; simple death by decapitation seems normally to have been without humiliation or unnecessary pain, as the death of Cyprian evidenced. Deportation or the mines, relegation or forced labor, fines (or loss of rank) or beatings, these made up the normal list of penalties less than death … it is [only] a very modern view to see as cruelty a deserved punishment which involves the deliberate infliction of pain.[1]

Robinson thus expresses and seemingly defends the idea that the intentional infliction of pain was employed throughout the Roman Empire, and that punishments were not only meant to be painful but also meant to be known by the public as a form of deterrence, if not also desert.

The emperor or his agents were seen as responsible for punishing those who had been convicted of serious crimes. And for serious crimes it was mandated that the state punish the guilty quickly:

> As a certain time was granted the defendants, who were convicted by clear evidence, before sentence was passed, the right of petitioning the Emperor as well as the opportunity of evading the penalties incurred by their criminal acts was afforded them; and as in the crime of homicide and other serious offenses punishment should not be deferred, the laws having reference to crime must hereafter be observed, and convicted criminals and malefactors be sentenced without delay.[2]

While the *Twelve Tables* had relied extensively on self-help punishments that would not necessarily be widely known, the Roman thought of the empire period put greater stress on the publicity of punishments, where self-help punishments were discouraged. Yet, the Roman state relied on private captures or at least accusations of serious offenders to begin the process of prosecution. As the Roman Empire proceeded, it became the job of the state then to punish, and to do so in a very public way.[3]

By the time of Justinian, private prisons were outlawed – another clear sign that public punishment was gradually replacing private self-help:

> We order that no one whatsoever shall, under any circumstances be permitted to have a private prison … and we direct the illustrious Augustal Prefect and the distinguished Governors of all the provinces, in the future to use every effort

1 O. F. Robinson, *Penal Practice and Penal Policy in Ancient Rome*, NY: Routledge, 2007, p. 195.

2 Justinian's *Code*, Book 9, Chapter 47, section 18, translated by S. P. Scott in *The Civil Law*, Vol. 15, p. 78.

3 Robinson, *Penal Practice and Penal Policy in Ancient Rome*, pp. 34–36.

> possible to repress the repeatedly mentioned insolence of unprincipled men who are guilty of such an offence … those who have committed a crime of this kind should be subjected to the extreme penalty, not only in accordance with the provisions of the ancient laws and constitutions, but also as guilty of high treason.[4]

The appeal was made to the Emperor, but after then the sentence would be publicly administered.

Despite the fact that punishments were often extreme in the Roman Empire there were also several safeguards and limitations that made these punishments somewhat more humane than might be thought. First, when the sentence was especially harsh there was a mandatory waiting time before execution of the sentence. Justinian's *Code* said:

> If, having in view the circumstances of the case, We, contrary to Our custom, should order any persons to be punished with exemplary severity, We are not willing for the guilty parties to suffer the penalty immediately, or the sentence to be executed without delay; but desire that their fate and fortune shall remain in suspense for the term of thirty days.[5]

And in addition it was stipulated that only the guilty, not their relatives, should be subject to punishment:

> We order that punishment shall be inflicted only upon those who are liable to it, and We exclude all relatives, acquaintances, and companions from the imputation of calumny, as association with criminals does not necessarily render them guilty, and neither affinity nor friendship presumes implication in crime. Therefore, let each one be responsible for the offenses which he himself commits, and let the fear of punishment go no further than the detection of guilt.[6]

The importance of the public deterrence of crime was not sufficient to override the idea that only those who actually commit crime should be publicly punished.

There is little doubt that as the period of the Empire proceeded, the idea of public punishment instead of private means of self-help gained ground. Even those who do not think that there were prisons or police in the Roman Empire have recognized this fact, and as we will see there is evidence for thinking that there were public prisons and police in any event.

4 Justinian's *Code*, Book 9, Chapter 5, section 1, translated by S. P. Scott in *The Civil Law*, Vol. 14, pp. 365–366.

5 Justinian's *Code*, Book 9, Chapter 47, section 20, translated by S. P. Scott in *The Civil Law*, Vol. 15, p. 79.

6 Ibid., section 22.

Turning to the ancient rabbis, we see that the main discussion of punishment in the *Mishnah's Sanhedrin* concerns four types of punishment carried out in public: "stoning, burning, decapitation, and strangulation." And as each of these modes of execution is discussed, it becomes clear that these were meant to be public acts. Consider what is said in the *Mishnah* about stoning:

> The place of stoning was twice the height of a man. One of the witnesses knocked him down on his loins; if he turned over on his heart the witness turned him over again on his loins. If he straightaway died, that sufficed; but if not, the [second] witness took the stone and dropped it on his heart. If he died straightaway, that sufficed; but if not, he was stoned by all Israel.[7]

There is first a determination by the court that a defendant is guilty and should be executed. Then the witnesses are instructed to take stones and attempt to kill the defendant. This is not self-help, for in that situation the witnesses would not need to wait for the court to rule. And the best evidence that this form of punishment was public is that if the witnesses fail to kill the defendant then all of the people at the trial shall cast stones until the defendant is dead.

42.2 PENAL PRISONS

Prisons had been employed in Rome in the Roman Republic, but primarily these prisons were for holding defendants awaiting trial or awaiting the execution of a sentence, not for punishment. Ulpian stated the principle well when he said:

> Governors usually sentence criminals to be confined to prison, or to be kept in chains; but they should not do this, for penalties of this kind are forbidden, as a prison should be used for the safe-keeping of men, and not for their punishment.[8]

Here we have both a description of the historical practice as well as a normative defense of that practice. Julia Hillner claims that this passage from Ulpian is

> the only evidence we have that prohibits the prison penalty outright, against a number of legal sources from the early empire that may point at a legal form of a temporary prison penalty for minor crimes committed by lower-rank people (*humiliores*); for example, for failure by a guardian to draw up an inventory of a warden's property.[9]

7 *The Mishnah, Sanhedrin* 6.4, translated by Herbert Danby, Oxford: Oxford University Press, 1933, p. 390.

8 Justinian's *Digest*, Book 48, Chapter 19, section 8 (9), translated by S. P. Scott in *The Civil Law*, Vol. 11, p. 113.

9 Julia Hillner, *Prison, Punishment, and Penance in Late Antiquity*, Cambridge: Cambridge University Press, 2015, pp. 135–136.

Hillner goes on to argue that there were many literary references to penal prisons in the Roman Empire, indeed so many as to cast doubt on the literal reading of Ulpian's claim.

One question is whether putting people into chalk mines was a kind of penal imprisonment. Ulpian denies this, and does so in the very next section of the text just cited: "these punishments are rather included in that of the mines."[10] Ulpian also excludes various forms of legally sanctioned slavery confinements as penalties which could look like imprisonment, but on his view are not properly so-called: "Where a slave has been sentenced to perpetual or temporary confinement in chains, he continues to be the property of him to whom he belonged before he was convicted."[11]

Ulpian does admit that the law of Rome sanctioned penal slavery where the slave ceased to be the property of his master but was now the property of the owners of the mine. And it seems that if the mine was owned by the state, then the slave sentenced to the mines was in a sense "imprisoned" in the mines. But Ulpian continues to insist that this is the use of slavery as a punishment rather than the use of imprisonment as a punishment.

There is a dispute among historians about how to understand Ulpian, and I will try to reconstruct his thinking about penal imprisonment. Why would he take the normative position, regardless of the descriptive position, that prisons should only be used for "safe-keeping" and not for punishment? This question is especially hard to answer since Ulpian seems to support various forms of quite inhumane forms of capital punishment. What is it about incarceration that is somehow worse than killing a convicted felon?

Ulpian also supported the view, which he attributes to Severus, that "It is better to permit the crime of a guilty person to go unpunished, than to condemn one who is innocent."[12] Given support for this very important normative principle, it would seem that Ulpian should favor penal imprisonment over capital punishment, since the former allows for someone unjustly condemned to be released from his sentence, but not if he is executed. So, we must look to other possibilities. If the capital punishment is quick and relatively painless, then on humane grounds one might support capital punishment over lengthy prison sentences. Unfortunately, there is scant evidence to support this way of reconciling Ulpian's otherwise famous humaneness with his opposition to penal punishment and support for capital punishment.

10 Justinian's *Digest*, Book 48, Chapter 19, section 8(10), in *The Civil Law*, Vol. 11, p. 113.

11 Ibid., section 8 (13), p. 113.

12 Ibid., section 5, p. 110.

One other form of penal imprisonment should be mentioned that is different from what we have discussed so far in this section. As Julia Hillner has claimed:

> The so-called *Sententiae of Paul*, a legal handbook usually dated to the early fourth century and hence thought to reflect Diocletian and Constantinian law, suggested that one reason why offenders would be put into prison was the protection of society and the neutralization of the offender. The offenders in question were soothsayers, corrupters of public mores and exploiters of human credulity, who resisted expulsion from society. Hence other means of controlling them, and impeding the spread of their unwanted teaching, had to be sought, and the prison penalty (*vincula publica*) – provided that forced labor was not meant here – was named as a possible alternative to exile on an island.[13]

This form of public punishment used the prisons in a way that is also true today when certain offenders are incarcerated because they continue to pose a danger to society.

In the *Mishnah* we find an account of a form of punishment that relied on imprisonment – a rare reference to prisons in the rabbinic texts:

> If a man was scourged [and committed again the same transgression] and was scourged a second time [if he transgressed a third time] the court must put him in a prison-cell and feed him with barley until his belly bursts. If a man committed murder but there were no witnesses, they must put him in prison and feed him with the bread of adversity and the water of affliction.[14]

And in the commentary on this passage from the *Mishnah*, the Babylonian *Talmud* has the following exchange:

> So what is at issue.
>
> Said Rabina, "What is at issue is whether there is necessity to give an advance admonition concerning the punishment of imprisonment in a cell."
>
> And what is a cell?
>
> Said Rabbi Judah, "It was the height of the prisoner."[15]

It seems that penal imprisonment, rather than imprisonment while awaiting punishment, is acknowledged here. Yet in the very next section of the *Talmud*, the rabbis quote from Numbers 25: 8 where a man who stole a sacred vessel is punished by self-help when "zealots beat him up on the spot."[16]

13 Hillner, *Prison, Punishment, and Penance in Late Antiquity*, p. 140.

14 *The Mishnah, Sanhedrin*, 9.5, Danby translation, p. 396.

15 The Tractate *Sanhedrin*, 81b, Vol. 16 of the *Babylonian Talmud*, translated by Jacob Neusner, Peabody, MA: Hendrickson Publishers, 2005, p. 425.

16 Ibid., p. 426.

42.3 POLICE ENFORCEMENT

The best evidence of organized police enforcement in ancient times concerns the capture of runaway slaves. These slaves often managed to travel vast distances and there was a serious problem of capturing and returning them. According to Christopher Fuhrmann:

> the self-help model often fails to fit the Imperial era evidence and that state policing significantly expanded in the first three centuries AD. This is especially true of policing on the part of soldiers of the Roman army, who, I maintain were increasingly detached from their legions and outposted among civilians as police in the second and third centuries … The African Christian writer Tertullian could claim circa 200 that "throughout the provinces military stations are assigned the hunting of brigands."[17]

Fuhrmann contends that there was "one issue where Romans made concerted efforts to coordinate every level of police power: recovery of fugitive slaves."[18]

Ulpian provides an account of the myriad of ways that a slave owner could seek help from government officers to seek and return his slave.

> The Divine Pius stated in the Rescript where a party wishes to search for a fugitive slave on the premises of another, he can apply to the Governor for letters to be furnished to him; and, if the case demands it, an officer, also, in order that he may be permitted to enter and make search, and the Governor can also inflict a penalty upon him who does not permit the search to be made. The Divine Marcus, in an address he delivered to the Senate, granted power to parties who wished to search for fugitive slaves to enter upon and search the land of the Emperor, as well as that of Senators and private individuals for fugitive slaves, and to examine the bed-rooms and tracks of those who conceal them.[19]

Notice that the Governor can enlist aid of various forms from government officers to help catch and return runaway slaves.

Ulpian also tells us that "all governors, magistrates, troops and garrisons are obliged to assist persons who are searching for fugitive slaves, and to surrender them if they are found."[20] Paulus, in his *Sentences*, also tells us that:

> Custom house officers and policemen are required to carefully retain fugitive slaves in custody after they have been caught. Municipal magistrates must also send such

[17] Christopher J. Fuhrmann, *Policing the Roman Empire*, Oxford: Oxford University Press, 2012, p. 8.

[18] Ibid., p. 11.

[19] Justinian's *Digest*, Book 11, Chapter 4, no. 3, in *The Civil Law*, Vol. 4, p. 82.

[20] Ibid., no. 1, (2), Vol. 4, p. 81.

> fugitive slaves, after they have been caught, properly guarded to the office of the Governor of the province or the Proconsul.[21]

Here there is a term used that is translated as policemen to signify the officers who are to aid in the search, capture, and return of runaway slaves.

Concerning runaway slaves in the *Talmud*, things are more difficult to understand than in Justinian's *Digest*. According to the *Talmud's Gittin*:

> As to Rabbi Hisda, a slave of his fled to the Samaritans. He sent word to them to return him, "You shall not deliver unto his master a bondman" (Deut. 23:16).
>
> He sent word to them, "But that speaks of a slave who fled from overseas to the Land of Israel, as set forth by Rabbi Ahi b. Rabbi Josiah."
>
> And how come he cited them the statement of Rabbi Ahi b. Rabbi Josiah [and not Rabbi's]?
>
> It is because the sense of the verse would make more sense to them.[22]

So, although there was a general principle in Deuteronomy not to deliver runaway slaves to their owners, the rabbis interpreted this principle "in a narrow fashion … and [Rabbi Hisda] was justified in seeking recovery of his runaway slave."[23]

If rabbis can be enlisted to aid in capture and return of runaway slaves then there is something partially resembling the enlistment of soldiers in this effort in the Roman Empire. Of course the rabbis were not soldiers, but they had an official status in ancient Jewish thought and were those to whom one turned to enforce Jewish law. And while rabbis did not execute the laws, rabbis were responsible for motivating their fellow Jews to enforce Jewish law. Yet, there is scant evidence of how runaway slaves were to be found and returned to their owners in rabbinic writings.

It is worth pausing to consider the idea that all of Jews were supposed to execute the law's punishment of death by stoning. There is here the idea that all Jews were in a sense deputized to enforce the law. But this is not the same as saying that in the Roman Empire soldiers would be deputized to enforce the law. In the Roman case the soldiers could be quasi-permanent police officers whereas in the case of all of Jews being responsible for stoning a law breaker, Jews only took on a quasi-official stance in a very temporary arrangement. In order to talk meaningfully about "police" being recognized in a given society, some specific people would have to be deputized to act for the society or the state in at least a quasi-permanent fashion.

The idea that soldiers or even the whole society could be deputized to aid in capturing or returning runaway slaves can be extended beyond the case of fugitive

[21] Ibid., no. 4, Vol. 11, p. 82.

[22] The Tractate *Gittin*, 45a, Vol. 11 of the *Babylonian Talmud*, p. 186.

[23] Samuel Greengus, *Laws in the Bible and in Early Rabbinic Collections*, Eugene, OR: Cascade Books, 2011, pp. 118–119.

slaves. As we will see in the next section, there is a clear role for the public, not merely for those who were victims of crime, and for the public to act in behalf of the society not merely the victim. The role of punishments, prisons, and police is to provide a way for criminal law to be administered by and for the public.

42.4 PUBLIC INSTITUTIONS AND CRIMINAL LAW

In previous ages and societies we have seen how criminal law arose out of a concern that certain harms were thought to be very serious, affecting the whole society not merely the individual victim. Now what we are seeing especially in the Roman Empire is the rise of public institutions to deal with what were recognized as public harms. And the institutions we have focused on – public forms of punishment, penal imprisonment, and a rudimentary form of police – are meant to distinguish private response to acts of violence and injury from those that rise to the level of public harm.

The increase in public institutions corresponds to the increasing scope and power of the state, best seen in the Roman Empire, and also in the increasing role of rabbinical authority in everyday Jewish life. It is characteristic of the Roman Empire that the scope and power of the state expanded. While some matters were left for local control, serious crimes throughout the Empire became increasingly handled by Rome and its various offices. And it is characteristic of the rabbinic period that there was a need for religious as well as secular law to extend to the reaches of the Diaspora. It seems that as the state or religion expanded, so did the public institutions.

The decline in self-help institutions connected to criminal law is a sign that the state was not willing to grant to the people their own self-enforcement. There were undoubtedly fairness issues responsible for this concern. But it also seems that there was a priority to the consolidation of power to bring crime under control, just as there was a concern about keeping the peace, at the level of interstate activities.

Some have argued that with the Pax Romano especially there was not as much need for soldiers to fight wars and battles so that they could be freed up to do other things for the state such as maintain internal harmony by policing the citizens throughout the Roman Empire. The institution of police probably grew out of the extra time that soldiers had during peacetimes, just as is true today when soldiers are assigned "peace-keeping" missions where what these soldiers do looks very much like what police would do today.

In rabbinic times, as we have seen, the breadth of the Diaspora also created problems with keeping control over serious legal matters where unfairness could easily creep in. And so there was a consolidation of power in the hands of the rabbis in certain key cities as a way to take local control out of the hands of those who might dilute or not enforce the divine law handed down to Moses. It turns out that there was as much attention to keeping the dietary laws undiluted as there was for the civil laws concerning property and homicide for instance. Enforcing the dietary laws was important for keeping the rituals pure, just as was also true of the rituals of the Roman religion and then also of the Christian religion.

One of the consequences of the development of the new public institutions aimed at enforcing the criminal law was a greater involvement in individual lives by the state and also by centralized religious authorities. The new public institutions allowed the central authorities to regulate life across a wide swath of the world. The Roman institutions made it possible for the Roman Empire to expand from Great Britain to Mesopotamia.

Agents of the Roman state, especially soldiers who were now permanently stationed in the furthest reaches of the Empire, enforced the various codes of law, especially those of Constantine, Theodosian, and Justinian. In the Jewish world, the rabbis enforced or recruited people to help enforce the various rules contained in such books as the *Mishnah* and the *Talmud* across the Diaspora. Law was to a large extent now centralized. Issues of equity and fairness became even more important than they were because of the need to take account of local differences, but even these determinations were often made in centralized institutions.

Public institutions have an especially important role to play in criminal law since crime often threatens the very stability and well-being of the society. When crime is punished privately, for instance, the deterrent effect is often only felt locally. Public punishment can be recorded and disseminated across a wide domain, significantly increasing the population that is subject to deterrence.

The justification of punishments is also made easier because of the fact that the laws that define the crime and corresponding punishment are seen as applying nearly to the entire known world. All people living under the Roman Empire are subject to the same punishments according to the Roman laws. All Jews living in the Diaspora are subject to the same punishments according to the rabbinic laws. In a sense there is equality before the law and the punishments for breaking that law are the same. And the fact that the criminal justice institutions are public means that it is transparent to the members of these societies what the punishments are and that they are being administered fairly.

Public institutions of criminal justice are emerging in the first few centuries of the Common Era. In a way this makes sense since crimes had been conceived as public harms since Babylonian times. Now the ways of dealing with crime are also public – there is a match between the nature of the harm and the response to it. The point of especially severe punishment is made clear in a way that could not occur when the response to crime was largely private mainly through self-help measures.

42.5 ASSESSING THE EXPANDING DOMAINS OF ORGANIZED RELIGION AND THE STATE

The use of criminal law to expand the domain of religion and the state is a feature of what we have seen in this chapter. The question I wish to pose at the end is whether we should regard this as a positive or negative value in the legal thought of the first few centuries of the Common Era. It is tempting to see such developments, of which the modern age has also seen much expansion, as an unremitting positive advance on more ancient ways of viewing crime and its enforcement.

The first thing to note is that the infringement on local control over crime seems to have produced a somewhat fairer system of criminal justice. By this I mean that roughly the same penalty was now meted out for the same crime. The principle that each case of a relevantly similar type should be treated the same was perhaps in the background of the justifications for the expansion of the domain of the Empire's jurisdiction over criminal law.

The codification of law and the institutions used to enforce such law also somewhat tried to take account of local variations. In the Roman Empire there were Roman officials posted in each of the areas that Rome had conquered, including as we saw the stationing of troops in those areas. And so there could be local knowledge conveyed to Rome to take account of variations in circumstance throughout the Roman Empire. But the codes of law did not display such variance and it is not clear how seriously the need to take account of such local circumstances was treated.

Second, what we have seen in earlier chapters about the importance of equity now comes to the fore again and causes us to wonder whether the Empire-wide codes could allow for equitable decisions in criminal cases. Local judges could sometimes choose between alternative punishments – such as exile versus capital punishment – but those decisions were reviewable by officials in Rome. In some respects the Empire was just too big for a single code of criminal law to be applied equitably.

There is a conflict that I have noted before between two legal principles: all people should be treated the same before the law, and differences of situation and status should not be overlooked. We can think of these as the principle of equal treatment and the principle of equity of treatment. It is not always fair to treat people all the same. In a very large jurisdiction it is difficult to achieve equality of treatment, as the Romans especially discovered. But leaving criminal matters to local authorities risked a loss of equity or fairness as well. So, it is not clear that a system of law that treated all the same would indeed be better than a system that sought to take account of local differences that were relevant.

Third, it is interesting to note that the various codes, especially Justinian's, gave only relatively short shrift to criminal matters, compared with civil law categories of property and inheritance for instance. The great legal thinkers of the Roman Empire, especially Gaius and Ulpian, did not devote nearly as much writing to criminal law as to civil law. Richard Bauman says: "The criminal law is the poor relation on the Roman legal scene. The jurists, though not ignoring criminal interpretation nearly as much as is generally believed, certainly devoted more attention to private law."[24] And perhaps this shows that the idea of a criminal code was not something that they contemplated for the Roman Empire. So, why would Roman legal theorists not devote as much time to criminal as civil matters? Similar questions can be raised about the ancient rabbis who devoted huge amounts of time to dietary laws as well as to civil law, but relatively little time to criminal law. Why would the ancient rabbis not devote as much time to criminal as civil and dietary matters?

One last issue to consider is that when a code is established covering a wide range of societies and peoples, it is difficult to take account of enough circumstances for the code to be easily applied. In ancient legal thought, codes came to have a kind of pride of place, epitomized as we have seen in Justinian's *Code* as well as the *Mishnah* and *Talmud*. But one problem is that codes often seemingly need to be long, and yet then it is likely that parts of the code will conflict with other parts. Two of the longest codes in US law today – the tax and immigration codes – are notorious for having parts that conflict with other parts – things are added but few things are taken out. The same can be said of especially Justinian's *Digest* and the Babylonia *Talmud*. Why did the jurists and rabbis not seek to reconcile clear contradictions in their codes? And how were people supposed to figure out what is required of them if the codes of law gave contradictory commands?

I do not have a good answer to these questions, but they should give us pause in interpreting Roman and Rabbinic criminal jurisprudence about the codification of crime as significant, as I have been suggesting. In any case these developments in the criminal law might not be developments so much as they were initial attempts that were not fully thought through since they were not debated in the way that matters of civil or private law were a matter of Rabbinic and Roman juridical disputation. One idea to be pursued next is that the universalistic concepts of moral obligation among both Roman jurists and rabbis caused changes in how criminal and private jurisprudence came to be understood. Whether the universalistic jurisprudence is an advance over earlier periods will have to await the next chapter.

What we have seen is the evidence of an expansion of the reach of both political and religious authorities by use of the public enforcement of law. This expansion is crucial for the development of the Holy Roman Empire during the Middle Ages, a topic that I plan to explore in a future work. Indeed, the justification of the

[24] Richard Bauman, *Crime and Punishment in Ancient Rome*, NY: Routledge, 1996, p. 3.

coordination of political and religious authority is a central characteristic feature of Medieval legal thought. In the first few centuries of the Common Era the expansion of these two authorities was not coordinated – certainly not the rabbinic authority in any event, although there was a very serious effort to coordinate the expansion of Christian religious authority with that of the political authority of the Roman Empire.

To a certain extent the development of public institutions that were given wide scope – nearly universal scope – can be seen as a continuation of the cosmopolitan political theories developed at the end of the Roman Republic, which we saw previously in this work, especially in the writings of Cicero, but also Seneca. In the next chapter we will see how the political and legal thought of the early Christian writers such as Augustine adapted cosmopolitan ideals to the legal ideas of the Empire. In addition we will look to the theological and aesthetic writings of Tertullian for guidance about the universality of law. And in the domain of the ancient rabbis we will be especially interested in the universalistic religious doctrines that had such a profound influence on the legal writings at this time. It is to these topics that we will next turn.

SECTION XVI

Universal Law at the End of Ancient Times

43

Universal Law and Human Rights

The Roman jurists and the ancient rabbis shared in common the idea of a universal law. As we saw in Chapter 35, jurists of the Roman Empire such as Gaius and Ulpian believed that there was a law of nature that governed all people and from which criticism of the Roman civil law could be made. The ancient rabbis believed in the existence of God's law and everything that they claimed to be doing was merely interpreting and extrapolating God's universal law for the current Jewish people. In this chapter I will say more about these ideas and attempt to link them to the idea that universal law also has a jurisdictional dimension that is important in understanding, for instance, the debates that we have just rehearsed about criminal law stretching over vast domains of the Roman Empire or the Jewish Diaspora.

The Roman idea of a law of nature is different from the rabbinical idea of a divine law in several important respects. The law of nature is discerned by examining nature and inferring what universal laws were at play. The divine law was also discerned but by looking at what God had revealed to be his law for the human race, or perhaps for the entire natural world. For the Romans, the laws of nature were rational and hence could be discerned by the use of human reason. But for the ancient rabbis, divine law was not necessarily rational, and may in fact be quite chaotic, and hence could not be discerned without examining the word of God. The question of how extensive is the jurisdiction of universal law might receive the same answer for Romans and ancient rabbis but for different reasons, as I will argue in this chapter.

In Section 43.1 we explore the Roman idea of the laws of nature, expanding on what we have seen in Chapter 35. In Section 43.2 we examine the rabbinic idea of divine law. In Section 43.3 we contrast ideas of natural law and divine law with universal law. In Section 43.4 we discuss the emerging idea of human rights in the first centuries of the Common Era. And in the final section we discuss how natural law and divine law support various conceptions of universal jurisdiction for defending human rights.

43.1 ROMAN CONCEPTIONS OF NATURAL LAW

Henry Sumner Maine provides us with a good place to start in examining the emerging ideas of universal law as a basis of jurisdiction in the legal thought of the Roman Empire:

> All ancient communities ran the risk of being overthrown by a very slight disturbance of equilibrium, and the mere instinct of self-preservation would force the Romans to devise some method of adjusting the rights and duties of foreigners who might otherwise – and this was a danger of real importance in the ancient world – have decided their controversies by armed strife. Moreover, at no period of Roman history was foreign trade entirely neglected. It was therefore probably half as a measure of police and half in furtherance of commerce that jurisdiction was first assumed in disputes in which the parties were either foreigners or a native and a foreigner. The assumption of such a jurisdiction brought with it the immediate necessity of discovering some principle on which the questions to be adjudicated upon could be settled …[1]

As the Roman Empire expanded, encompassing more and more previously autonomous states, peace required that the jurisdiction of Roman law also be extended.

Roman lawyers and legal scholars understood that they had to justify the extension of their legal jurisdiction to conquered lands, especially if conquered people were to see themselves as members of the Empire, not merely as subjugated. Here is Maine again:

> The expedient to which they resorted was that of selecting the rules of law common to Rome and the different Italian communities in which the immigrants were born. In other words, they set themselves to form a system answering the primitive and literal meaning of *Jus Gentium*, that is, Law common to all Nations … The *Jus Gentium* was merely a system forced on his attention by political necessity … The crisis arrived when the Greek theory of a Law of Nature was applied to the practical administration of the Law common to all Nations.[2]

The principle that justified expanding jurisdiction was the *jus gentium*, the law common to Rome and the peoples who had been conquered. This was not universal law, although some legal scholars then attempted to link the *jus gentium* to the universal law of nature that had been developed especially by the Greek Stoic philosophers.

We can see the difference between those law scholars who supported the *jus gentium* and those who supported the *jus naturale* principles by examining the work of

[1] Henry Sumner Maine, *Ancient Law*, London: John Murray, 1861, pp. 48–49.

[2] Ibid., pp. 49–52.

Gaius and Ulpian respectively. Turning first to Gaius, we can see his understanding of the *jus gentium* as not necessarily distinct from universal law in the following passage from the beginning of his *Institutes*:

> Every people that is governed by statutes and customs observes partly its own peculiar law and partly the common law of all mankind. That law which a people establishes for itself is peculiar to it, and is called the *jus civile* (civil law) as being the special law of that *civitas* (State), while the law that natural reason establishes among all mankind is followed by all peoples alike, and is called *jus gentium* (law of nations, or law of the world) as being the law observed by all mankind.[3]

Here the *jus gentium*, contrary to what Maine said, is a universal law for all humans. While a person may understand the *jus gentium* by employing reason in looking at what laws are common to all peoples, the successful result of such an endeavor will be to discover the universal law of all peoples.

Ulpian, in his *Institutes*, takes a different tack but in many ways ends up in the same place as Gaius:

> Natural law is that which nature teaches to all animals, for this law is not peculiar to the human race, but affects all creatures which deduce their origin from the sea or the land, and it is also common to birds. From it proceeds the union of male and female which we designate as marriage; hence also arises procreation of children and the bringing up of the same; for we see that all animals, and even wild beasts, appear to be acquainted with the law.
>
> The Law of Nations is that used by the human race, and it is easy to understand that it differs from natural law, for the reason that the latter is common to all animals, while the former only concerns men in their relations with each other.[4]

The law of nature for Ulpian concerns all creatures, not just all humans who are covered by the *jus gentium* – but it is unclear how the conceptions of Gaius and Ulpian would differ in practice in that both lead us to see a law for all upon which a universal jurisdiction can be grounded.

Just to complete this somewhat confusing picture, and returning us to something like what Maine had described as the Roman idea of *jus gentium*, we can turn to Justinian's own *Institutes*:

> The law of nature is that law which nature teaches to all animals. For this law does not belong exclusively to the human race … We see, indeed, that all the other animals besides man are considered as having knowledge of this law.

3 *The Institutes of Gaius*, Book I.1, translated by Francis de Zulueta, Oxford: Oxford University Press, 1946, Part I, p. 3.

4 Ulpian, *Institutes*, Book I.3–4, in Justinian's *Digest*, in *The Civil Law*, translated by S. P. Scott, Cincinnati, OH: The Central Trust Co., 1932, Vol. II, p. 209.

> Civil law is thus distinguished from the law of nations. Every community governed by laws and customs uses partly its own law, partly laws common to all mankind … the law which natural reason appoints for mankind obtains equally among all nations and is called the law of nations, because all nations make use of it.[5]

Justinian seems to pick up Ulpian's idea of *jus naturale* and Gaius' idea of *jus gentium*, and in failing to see that these ideas did not fit together, Justinian failed to see how the *jus naturale* could be applicable to all humans.

In any event, there were two distinct ideas of universal law for the jurists and lawyers of the Roman Empire – the natural law that affected all creatures, including humans, and the law of nations. Both were ascertained by the use of natural reason. The difference was that the laws of nature were discerned by reasoning about what governed all creatures, whereas the laws of nations were discerned by reasoning about what was common in all existing human laws.

Augustine, a Roman jurist and also a Bishop, interpreted natural law in such a way that it came to take on the characteristics of divine law from a Christian perspective. For Augustine, "God, then, created all things in supreme wisdom and ordered them in perfect justice; and in establishing the mortal race of mankind as the greatest ornament of earthly things, he has given to mankind certain good things suitable to his life."[6] And the divine law of God is the cornerstone of justice:

> The peace of body and soul is the duly ordered life and health of a living creature; peace between mortal man and God is an ordered obedience, in faith, in subjection to an everlasting law … the peace of the whole universe … the arrangement of things equal and unequal in a pattern which assigns to each its proper position.[7]

As we will see, the ancient rabbinic doctrines are similar to the Roman, especially the early Roman Christians such as Augustine.

43.2 ANCIENT RABBINIC CONCEPTIONS OF DIVINE LAW

To begin to understand ancient rabbinic ideas of universal law we can follow Remi Brague in distinguishing two ways to think of divine law:

> Greek divine law is divine because it expresses the profound structures of a permanent natural order; Jewish law is divine because it emanates from a god who

5 *The Institutes of Justinian*, Book I, Title II, translated by Thomas Collett Sandars, London: Longmans, Green and Co., 1917, pp. 7–8.

6 Augustine, *The City of God*, Book XIX, Chapter 13, translated by Henry Bettenson, NY: Penguin Books, 1984, p. 872.

7 *The City of God*, Book XIX, Chapter 13, p. 870.

> is master of history. In both cases, it is external to the human and transcends the quotidian.[8]

Universal law is here understood as divine in that it transcends human affairs. But this is also true to natural law, which the Romans were also committed to. So, what was the difference between divine law for the ancient rabbis and natural law for the Greeks and Romans?

The Jewish philosopher, Philo, is important here since he tries to combine philosophical ideas of Stoic nature with Jewish divine law in a manner that is similar to an important strain of ancient rabbinic legal thought when he says that:

> The national laws and ancient ordinances of every people are established for the sake of justice and of every virtue, and what else are laws and ordinances but the sacred words of nature having an authority and power in themselves ...[9]

As Christine Hayes puts it:

> It is Philo of Alexandria who goes the furthest in resolving the cognitive dissonance between the Greco-Roman and biblical conceptions of divine law. He asserts the identity of the two and then labors to demonstrate that the Torah of Moses possesses *all* of the properties and qualities of Greek natural law; it is self- identical with universal truth, which entails its rationality, its immutability, and its unwritten character.[10]

The divine law for Philo was very similar if not identical to the natural law.

Yet, there is this difference between Biblical divine law and natural law – Biblical law could be understood by understanding what God said the law was in his pronouncements to Moses and other Patriarchs, whereas natural law could be understood only by the use of reason in examining the rules of the natural order. The resolution of this issue is that at least some of the ancient rabbis believed that they could discern the divine law by reasoning, albeit reasoning about God's revealed word in the Torah.

There is, though, a clear attempt by the ancient rabbis to make or remake the divine law by reference to their contemporary situation. The word of the Torah allowed for flexible interpretations, where the divine law could even be seen to be in seeming conflict with the word of God conveyed to Moses and the Patriarchs. Hayes tells us:

8 Remi Brague, *The Law of God: The Philosophical History of an Idea*, translated by Lydia G. Cochrane, Chicago, IL: University of Chicago Press, 2007, p. 18.

9 Philo, *The Special Laws* II (13), in *The Works of Philo*, translated by C. D. Yonge, Peabody, MA: Hendrickson Publishers, 1993, p. 569.

10 Christine Hayes, *What's Divine about Divine Law?* Princeton, NJ: Princeton University Press, 2015, p. 111.

> We have already seen Papinian's assertion that one of the functions of the praetor's edict was correction of the *jus civile*. On the Jewish side, the term *taqqanah* – which can mean "correction, repair, improvement" – reflects the same legal notion ... equity and good faith ... It seems plausible that *taqqanot* that improved, repaired, and even on occasion overturned Torah law were largely tolerated in Roman Palestine in the first three centuries of the Common Era, because of the highly visible and parallel phenomenon in the surrounding Roman legal culture, namely, edictal modifications of the civil law.[11]

Divine law for the ancient rabbis, as with natural law for the Romans, was universal law but nonetheless flexible and even changeable in light of contemporary circumstances.

The ancient rabbis believed that they were merely interpreting God's law, not making new law. But it becomes fairly clear in reading the Talmud that the rabbis' means of interpretation are fairly loose, as we have already seen, in that even contradictory interpretations can be each seen as following from a given Biblical passage.

43.3 UNIVERSAL LAW, DIVINE OR NATURAL

Conceptually, universal law can be a function of the natural order which is uniform. Universal law could be a function of having the same source for all humans – a source which is invariant for all people in the universe, or as something much more limited – where divine law does not truly create universal rights but only rights for certain compatriots, whether they be fellow Romans or fellow Jews.

The debate about divine law and its universal scope can be seen in how the ancient rabbis interpreted a passage in Leviticus, 19:18, "Love thy neighbor as thyself." The conceptual problem for ancient rabbis was how to interpret such divine commands in light of the also divine idea that the Jews were supposed to be God's chosen people and hence were supposed to have different privileges, and importantly also different obligations, than non-Jews. Was the idea of treating one's neighbor as oneself supposed to mean that neighbors referred to other Jews or to all people who could be neighbors to the Jews? The first understanding would enshrine divine rights as a form of Jewish privilege; whereas the second would enshrine divine rights as truly universal rights.

There is a similar dispute among the ancient rabbis in the Talmud about whether there is an obligation to save a life "upon whom a building fell down" if the person is not a Jew. Here is a passage from the *Talmud's Yoma*:

[11] Ibid., p. 307.

> He upon whom a building fell down – it is a matter of doubt whether or not he is there, it is a matter of doubt whether [if he is there], he is alive or dead, it is a matter of doubt whether [if he is there and alive] he is a gentile or an Israelite – they clear away the ruins from above him.
>
> What is the point of this statement [of hypothetical cases]?
>
> The intention is to state a series of cases that go without saying, not only is debris removed if one is in doubt as to whether he is there or not, as long as one knows he is alive if he is there; but even if we do not know for sure that he is alive or dead, the debris must be cleared away.
>
> Further, not only if we do not know for sure whether he is alive or dead, so long as we know he is an Israelite, do we clear away debris, but even if we do not know for sure whether he is an Israelite or Samaritan, the debris must be removed.[12]

This text does not address what is to be done if it is clear that the person upon whom a building fell down is not a Jew. But this is addressed in the next portion of the *Talmud* concerning whether to break the Sabbath to save a life – and indeed such questions have met with dispute over the ages, not merely in the ancient rabbinic period.

Here is part of the discussions about whether one must save a life even if this means breaking the prohibitions of the Sabbath.

> Now Rabbi Ishmael, Rabbi Aqiba, and Rabbi Eleazor, were walking on the way … This question was raised to them: How on the basis of Scripture do we know that danger to life overrides the restrictions of the Sabbath? …
>
> Rabbi Simeon b. Menassian says, "'And the children of Israel shall keep the Sabbath' (Ex. 31:16) – the Torah says, 'Desecrate one Sabbath so that Israel may keep many Sabbaths.'"[13]

Here it seems that the Sabbath may be desecrated only if it is done to save the life of a fellow Jew, although again this interpretation has been vigorously debated over the ensuing centuries since the idea of saving the Sabbath for future observance does not clearly mean that the Sabbath can only be broken for the saving of a Jewish life.

In legal theory, some of this was a matter of jurisdiction – over what realm or over what group of people did the "universal" law range? Law could range universally in the sense that specific laws range over all of those who are members of a certain group, or it could range over every person on the planet. In this respect, the idea of universal law is circumscribed by ideas of jurisdiction.

[12] *The Babylonia Talmud*, Tractate *Yoma*, 85A, translated by Jacob Neusner, Peabody, MA: Hendrickson Publishers, 2005, Vol. 5, pp. 331–332.

[13] Ibid., Tractate Yoma, 85A-85B, pp. 333–334.

In the legal thought of the Roman Empire, jurisdiction was distinguished from imperium. Imperium was the right to rule that the emperor or various consuls held to command the army or other branches of the government. Jurisdiction was the right to decide a case of a particular type in a particular region. William Buckland provides us with an understanding of how jurisdiction was understood in matters of Roman civil law:

> Jurisdiction was vested in a variety of officials. In Rome, and later in Constantinople, the *praefectus urbi*, the *vicarius urbis*, and the *praefecti annonae* had civil jurisdiction, in some cases limited to particular affairs, the old praetor having lost jurisdiction long before his name disappeared. In a province the *praeses* had a limited jurisdiction, and in the later Empire, many towns had also a *defensor civitatis*, with similar jurisdiction, concurrent with that of local magistrates. All these were accustomed to act with an assessor or assessors who gave opinions but had no share in the decision, and in the most important courts the best available legal learning was used for this purpose.[14]

What is normally tightly limited jurisdiction was expanded in the legal thought of the Roman Empire. The question arises though of whether the expansion was meant to extend beyond the borders of the Roman Empire and the answer seems pretty clearly to be "no," as was also probably true for the ancient rabbis.

43.4 UNIVERSAL LAW, UNIVERSAL JURISDICTION, AND HUMAN RIGHTS

The ancient Romans and the ancient Jews are credited with promoting the idea of a universal law, not merely with creating laws that were for very specific peoples. In addressing the question of what sort of universal law this was, we have begun to explore the idea of universal jurisdiction, where everyone in the world was subject to the universal law. We will now say more, in specifics, about the connection between universal law and universal jurisdiction, aiming to see whether or not there can be seen the beginnings of the most important idea of universal jurisdiction today, which concerns human rights.

Expanding jurisdiction to cover large swaths of the world is not sufficient to constitute universal jurisdiction; and the rationales for each are different as well. But it is certainly arguable that expanding jurisdiction could be moving toward universal jurisdiction. We can understand such an idea in part by seeing that the Roman Empire initially expanded jurisdiction to cover foreigners who the Romans conquered but not the same jurisdiction as was true for Roman citizens – where the

[14] W. W. Buckland, *A Textbook of Roman Law from Augustus to Justinian*, Cambridge: Cambridge University Press, 1921, p. 663.

courts in Rome were where cases concerning Roman citizens were jurisdictionally located. And for the ancient Jews, the court of the *Sanhedrin* was where matters concerning Jews were jurisdictionally located, although not for those who lived far away in the Diaspora. But it was with the reforms of the second century CE that things changed for the Roman Empire – all people who were citizens of states conquered by the Romans became also citizens of Rome.

There is another way to think of universal law, as we saw was true for the ancient rabbis and for some Roman lawyers like Ulpian, namely, that universal law is a higher law than civil law. Perhaps the first significant treatment of this topic is in Sophocles' *Antigone*. Early in the play there is a discussion, really a debate, between Antigone and her sister, Ismene. Creon, the ruler, has decreed that no one should bury the body of Antigone's brother, since he had fought on the unsuccessful side of the recent civil war. Antigone says she is obligated to bury her brother's remains, contrary to Creon's decree:

ANTIGONE:I shall not prove disloyal [to my brother].
ISMENE:You are mad! When Creon has forbidden it?
ANTIGONE:From mine own. He has no right to stay me.
ISMENE:… Do but consider how most miserably we too shall perish, if despite the law we traverse the behest or power of kings …
ANTIGONE:… Him I will bury. Death, so met, were honor; and for that capital crime of piety – Loving and loved, I will lie by his side. Far longer is there need that I satisfy those nether powers, than powers on earth, for there forever must I lie. You, if you will, hold up to scorn what is approved by Heaven![15]

Antigone appeals to a higher law, a law of heaven, which she believes to override the civil law of King Creon's decree. In the play we have a sense that this higher law is of divine origin, but also that it is a kind of natural law as well.

Antigone believes that she, and everyone else, is governed by a higher law and that that law overrides any civil law governing her and her compatriots such as her sister, Ismene. The appeal to a higher law, a universal law, is today a very common matter – the current nonfiction book that was at the top of the New York Times Best Sellers list is by former FBI director, James Comey, and is called *A Higher Loyalty*, in which he explains that he has loyalties to a higher law than that of the United States.[16] It is much debated today, though, what is the source of this higher universal law. Comey, for his part, associates his idea of a higher loyalty to his own integrity – which blurs the borders of universal law and civil law even more than we have seen in the ancient texts of the Roman Empire and the Talmud.

15 Sophocles, *Antigone*, in *Sophocles: The Theban Plays*, translated by George Young, Mineola, NY: Dover Publications, Inc., 1999, pp. 118–119.

16 James Comey, *A Higher Loyalty*, NY: Flatiron Books, 2018.

Human rights are today seen as one of the most significant battlefields in the war of ideas concerning universal law and universal jurisdiction. In ancient times, human rights were not mentioned in those debates. But as we have seen there were elements of that idea in the emerging ideas of universal jurisdiction based on some conception of a universal law that supercedes or overrides civil law. Indeed, the Universal Declaration of Human Rights asserts just this status for human rights. Yet, there has been a vigorous debate about whether and to what extent these rights are culturally specific and not truly universal at all. Similar things could certainly be said about the natural and divine law's rights and obligations – that they reflected more than people realized the cultural attitudes of the ancient Romans and the ancient rabbis. We next take this idea up in greater detail.

43.5 THE IDEA OF HUMAN RIGHTS

If understood literally, human rights are rights that a person has merely by virtue of being human. In this respect, it would make sense, as we just saw, to link human rights to some conception of universal law that entailed universal jurisdiction. The problem that we have seen is that while there are certain ideas espoused by Roman lawyers and ancient rabbis that seem to move us toward such an idea, the main focus was on how law should treat the members of the Roman Empire and the widespread Jewish Diaspora, respectively in Roman law and rabbinic law. The range of jurisdiction is indeed expanded much farther than in other ancient societies we have discussed, but it is still not clear that this range includes peoples who were not within the domains of the Roman Empire or the Jewish Diaspora, to say nothing of women and slaves.

The legal theorist who is most associated with the idea of human rights in the Roman Empire is, as we saw earlier, Ulpian. Here is how Tony Honore characterizes Ulpian's philosophy:

> The contrast between natural and civil justice and law was a commonplace in both philosophy and law. Ulpian, however, interprets it differently from his predecessors such as Gaius. To them the natural is morally superior to the civil in that the common custom of various peoples, the *ius gentium*, is founded on natural reason and hence has a higher status than the law adopted by a particular state, say Athens or Rome. "Nature" can be used to criticize the narrowness or technicality of the law of a particular state and as an instrument to broaden and simplify the law. Ulpian, however, takes the law of nature not to be embodied in common custom, the *jus gentium*, but to be morally superior to it. In the conditions of his time this was a rational point of view. Roman law had been extended to all the free peoples of the empire, so that the contrast between the civil law and common custom was now of a purely historical interest. Roman law had in effect become the *ius gentium*. The

> role of natural law in justifying some institutions and criticizing others persisted but was wider than the role formerly performed by the *jus gentium*.[17]

For Ulpian, natural law was a universal law from the perspective of which even the nearly universally accepted laws of slavery could be criticized.

In his work, *On Sabinus*, Ulpian gives his understanding of how slaves should be treated according to the civil law as opposed to the law of nature: "So far as the civil law is concerned, slaves are not considered persons, but this is not the case according to natural law, because natural law regards all men as equals."[18] Honore comments on this passage that, for Ulpian, "Slavery is the prime example of an institution contrary to nature but recognized by the *jus gentium* which encroached on (*invasit*) the law of nature."[19] Closely aligned with the idea of the equality of all humans is the idea that each person deserves to be treated with at least minimal respect given their dignity as humans.

Honore's reconstruction of Ulpian as a human rights pioneer is qualified in that Honore sees that:

> It is true that Ulpian recognizes degrees of dignity. Men have more than women. Married women have more than concubines. Slaves, by implication, even have less. All are equal in that they possess dignity, but in contrast with modern thinking, the degree of dignity varies from person to person.[20]

It is indeed hard to see today how all humans could be equal and yet to see such strong disparity in treatment claimed to be consistent with that equality.

Yet it is also true that Ulpian was one of the few theorists in the ancient period to recognize that husband and wife have equal obligations to each other. Ulpian considers the case where "either a husband or wife becomes insane during marriage" and "where the party who is aware of this fact, and of sound mind, gives notice of repudiation of the other who is insane, he will, as we have stated, be to blame for the dissolution of the marriage."[21] So, in at least this case, Ulpian did recognize the equality of married men and women, in keeping with the natural law prescription of equality of rights.

If Ulpian extended the equal treatment of men and women in marriage to all people in all circumstances, then he would be a forerunner of human rights. This is not to say that all people had to be treated the same in all situations, since those situations may call for different treatment based on what the humans in question had

17 Tony Honore, *Ulpian: Pioneer of Human Rights*, second edition, Oxford: Oxford University Press, 2002, pp. 79–80.

18 Ulpian, *On Sabinus*, Book XLIII, quoted in Justinian's *Digest*, in *The Civil Law*, Vol. 11, p. 300.

19 Honore, *Ulpian: Pioneer of Human Rights*, p. 80.

20 Ibid., p. 85.

21 Ulpian, *On the Edict*, Book XXXIII, quoted in Justinian's *Digest*, in *The Civil Law*, Vol. 6, p. 11.

chosen to do. But Ulpian, to a certain extent like Aristotle, saw that a commitment to natural law meant that institutions such as slavery could, and perhaps should, be criticized. The rights and obligations recognized in civil law were not the only, or even the most binding, of legal considerations, when ideas of universal law are taken into account.

Some have also seen the Jewish philosopher Philo as providing a contemporaneous defense of human rights to that provided by the Roman lawyer, Ulpian. Philo talks of a legal order for the whole world when he says:

> And [Moses'] exordium, as I have already said, is most admirable; embracing the creation of the world, under the idea that the law corresponds to the world and the world to the law, and that a man is obedient to the law, being, by so doing, a citizen of the world, arranges his actions with reference to the intention of nature, in harmony with which the whole universal world is organized.[22]

Philo here addresses a world order that is governed by universal law, and he is here influenced by Stoicism much as other cosmopolitans were.

Philo also, in perhaps not so clear a manner as we would have hoped, sees at least some persons, primarily the Patriarchs like Abraham, as a law unto themselves:

> But God adding to the multitude and magnitude of the praises of the wise man one single thing as a crowning point, says that "this man fulfilled the divine law, and all the commandments of God, not having been taught to do so by written books, but in accordance with the unwritten law of his nature, being anxious to obey all healthful and salutary impulses. And what is the duty of man except most firmly to believe those things which God asserts? Such is the life of the first author and founder of our nation; a man according to the law, as some persons think, but, as my argument has shown, one who is himself the unwritten law and justice of God."[23]

This "unwritten law of his nature" that makes Abraham "himself the unwritten law" can be seen, perhaps, as the beginning of the idea that humans are laws unto themselves and hence deserving of respect as right-holders, not for what they have done but simply for who they are.

The idea of human rights is initially hard to fathom since people are so different from each other and seem to follow very different legal and moral rules. One of the most important steps toward seeing that people are governed by universal laws, and also have universal human rights, is to see how law can be extended to cover more and more people in spite of their manifest differences.

[22] Philo, *De Opificio Mundi* (*On the Creation*) 1.3, in *The Works of Philo*, translated by C. D. Yonge, Peabody, MA: Hendrickson Publishers, 1993, p. 3.

[23] Philo, *On Abraham*, 275–276, in ibid., p. 434.

One way to think of the law of humanity is in terms of law for all of the people on the earth. And there were models ready at hand at the end of the ancient period of legal thought – the law of the Roman Empire and the rules of Jewish Diaspora. There was already conceived a universal state that had laws of nature or divine laws to govern it. In a similar vein, the idea that there were citizens of this universal state encompassing all humans is seen at the end of the ancient period of legal thought. Ulpian, and perhaps Philo, began to think of rights of these citizens – rights held by virtue of being members of humanity.

Human rights are best understood within the context of universal law and universal jurisdiction, not in civil law terms. And we have seen in this chapter that the legal thought of the Roman Empire as well as that of the ancient rabbis provides a ground for universal law and jurisdiction so that someone like Ulpian in the Roman tradition, and perhaps Philo in the Jewish tradition of legal thought, can also contemplate the idea of rights attaching universally to all humans.

44

The Origins of the Just War Doctrine

In light of the move toward an acceptance of universal law at the end of the ancient period, we also can find very clear expressions of the Just War doctrine, the view that only some wars were morally justified on very limited grounds, which were spelled out in detail. The Just War doctrine became more than just one doctrine over the centuries as it was employed up until the current time. In the Roman Empire, Augustine of Hippo was the most articulate defender of the Just War doctrine as he attempted to counter the early Catholic Church Fathers who were largely pacifists. And at least some of the ancient rabbis also espoused a view that defended only a limited range of cases where war could be justified on universalist moral grounds. This chapter extends the discussion of Chapter 34 where we had seen the lawyers of the Roman Republic such as Cicero and Seneca already providing support for an idea of a Just War, but not in as fleshed-out a manner as we now will see in the legal thought of the Roman Empire, and to a certain extent of the ancient rabbis.

In Section 44.1 we will discuss the pacifist views of the earliest of the Church Fathers such as Tertullian. In Section 44.2 we will then examine Augustine's response to the early pacifists and his defense of a Just War. In Section 44.3 we will examine the doctrine of the Talmud that the ancient rabbis espoused concerning when war is justified. In Section 44.4 I will argue that to be consistent with a universal morality, there must be humane limits on war. In the final section we will see that there are some aspects of these views of what constitutes a Just War that are nonetheless not as humane as it might appear.

44.1 PACIFISM IN THE EARLY CHRISTIANIZED ROMAN EMPIRE

Often starting from the proposition attributed to Jesus that "one should turn the other cheek," many early Christian lawyers of the Roman Empire espoused a kind of pacifism. In this section we will primarily examine the work of Tertullian. Tertullian wrote only about a century after Seneca but from a very different perspective. Seneca was a noble Roman, whereas Tertullian was a convert to Christianity. Nonetheless they were both pacifists. In an essay on why Christians should accept martyrdom rather than engage in sin, the second-century priest and lawyer, Tertullian, argued that the great evil to be combated by Christians was the devil. Tertullian discusses two kinds of war: war against the devil, and war against one another.

In an essay, "To the Martyrs," Tertullian associates war with the strategy of the devil:

> Do not allow him the good fortune in his own kingdom of setting you against one another, but let him find you fortified by the arms of peace among yourselves, because peace among yourselves means war with him.[1]

And in another essay, "The Chaplet," Tertullian says that the key to leading a good life is to remain untainted by the pursuit of worldly goods that cause one to do what Christ has condemned:

> Keep untainted, therefore, for God … Be you, too, faithful unto death; fight the good fight whose crown the Apostle feels so justly confident … [that you have] advanced in rank in the heavenly army.[2]

For Tertullian, the true army is that of the people of God who can only join God's army by remaining untainted by not doing such things as declaring allegiance to a secular ruler's army.

The early Church Fathers were mainly pacifists who took very seriously Jesus' admonition to turn the other cheek rather than to strike out at those who have harmed them. Tertullian takes this position much farther, and in fact broke with many other Church Fathers who he thought had not properly understood the seriousness of the injunction not to serve false gods. In his view, a person is tainted even by associating with violence and war. And to avoid such taint it was necessary not to serve secular rulers at all since to do so was to place the secular rulers ahead of God. From this perspective, Tertullian argues that all worldly human goods, including intellectual pursuits, should be seen as having diminished importance compared to the goods of religious purity.

Pacifism is here advocated because of its purity. The images of taint and purity are of central importance to Tertullian's belief that any public service was morally wrong. Most especially any military service that was aimed at killing fellow innocent humans, rather than aimed at slaying the devil, could not be countenanced. There were seemingly only two categories: to live life purely in God's service, or

[1] Tertullian, "To the Martyrs," in *Disciplinary, Moral, and Ascetical Works*, translated by Rudolph Arbesmann, Emily Joseph Daly, and Edwin A. Quain, NY: Fathers of the Church, Inc., 1959, pp. 18–19.

[2] Tertullian, "The Chaplet," in ibid., pp. 266–267.

to be tainted by any service or homage to anyone other than God. Here is one of the central strains in traditional pacifism – an insistence that people lead their lives purely and not engage in any activity that would compromise their eternal souls. It should be noted, though, that Tertullian did not restrict his condemnation of worldly matters to a critique of military action. Tertullian condemned all worldly things – including even the study of philosophy. It is positions like this that have given rise to the claim that pacifists were other-worldly and naïve.

In one of his most significant essays, on the soldier's chaplet (a crown composed of laurel), Tertullian gives clear support for the charge of being an extremely unworldly pacifist. Tertullian not only argues that it is against God's law to engage in military service, because all of our efforts should be expended on God's service against the devil. But he goes on to argue that even if military service were abolished, it would still be wrong for anyone to take on the trappings of military life.[3] The symbol of such a life involves accepting such things as crowns of flowers, which are bestowed on those who have sworn allegiance to their rulers. Tertullian devotes an entire treatise to showing that it is wrong to accept such rewards even outside of the domain of an existing secular military.

In particular, Tertullian argues that any complicity with military culture is wrongful:

> Take the annual public pronouncement of vows. What do you think of it? … Is it not a denial of faith? Even though the Christian says nothing on that occasion with his mouth, he makes his response by having the crown on his head. The wearing of the laurel crown is likewise enjoined … Idolater! … You cannot serve God and mammon.[4]

For Tertullian, even attending a public ceremony where vows of patriotism are taken produces the kind of taint that should be completely avoided.

Tertullian's explicit rejection of all military service for Christians is framed in the starkest of terms:

> For Military service offers neither exemption from punishment of sins nor relief from martyrdom. The Gospel is one and the same for the Christians at all times whatever his occupation in life. Jesus will deny those who deny Him … He will destroy the one who has been gained against His Name.[5]

As can be seen here, Tertullian advocates that those who are conscripted should refuse to serve even if the alternative is death. He sees such death as "martyrdom" and even argues that it is wrong to run from persecution.[6]

3 Ibid., pp. 258–259.
4 Ibid., p. 260.
5 Ibid., p. 257.
6 Tertullian, "Flight in Time of Persecution," in ibid., p. 282.

Tertullian argues that each of the activities involved in military service are proscribed explicitly by the word of God:

> Is it likely that we are permitted to carry a sword when our Lord said that he who takes the sword will perish by the sword? Will the son of peace who is forbidden to engage in a lawsuit, espouse the deeds of war? Will a Christian taught to turn the other cheek when struck unjustly, guard prisoners in chains and administer torture and capital punishment? ... Will he protect at night those very demons whom in the daytime he has put to flight by his exorcisms, leaning on a lance such as pierced the side of Christ?[7]

Tertullian's rejection of all aspects of military life is the kind of pacifism that traditionally has been seen as an uncompromising position not contingent on any current situations or developments in practical life.

Tertullian's absolutism highlights the type of pacifism that has been widely criticized over the intervening centuries, where it is sometimes said that the pacifist cares more about symbolism than reality. But it seems to me that Tertullian and some of the other Church Fathers were following ancient Greek and Roman conceptions of morality where what mattered most was that one not do or associate with wrongdoing of any sort. Again the idea is to be pure rather than tainted in any way. In some sense, it was the "touching" of wrong, not necessarily the doing of wrong, that conveyed a stain, hence taint, to the person who touches it.[8]

In another essay, Tertullian warns against the "perversion of conscience leading to self-deception."[9] Being tainted and having one's conscience perverted are also important themes in Greek ethics as well since such an ethic focuses on character more than action. For Tertullian, it is the purity of soul that is of most concern where that means that how one behaves takes precedence over what one brings about or could bring about. In order to attain heaven, one must have had a purity of soul that is untainted by compromise or complicity with wrongdoing. In some respects this is an admirable way to think about morality, as a staunchly principled guide to action. But this is also not a view that many people think is consistent with common sense.

The idea of moral purity is central to the early Christian conceptions of pacifism. In addition, early conceptions of pacifism focused on the innocence of those who were most likely to be killed or wounded during battle. In the hands of Tertullian, pacifism is a moral, religious, and also legal doctrine.

7 Tertullian, "The Chaplet," in ibid., p. 256.

8 See Arthur Adkins, *Merit and Responsibility: A Study in Greek Values*, Oxford: Oxford University Press, 1960.

9 Tertullian, "Spectacles," in *Tertullian: Disciplinary, Moral, and Ascetical Works*, op. cit., p. 48.

44.2 AUGUSTINE'S DEFENSE OF THE JUST WAR

The Just War tradition is normally traced back to Augustine, although there are surely similar ideas expressed already in Cicero and even Plato. In Augustine's writings we find explicit discussion of "laws of war": rules concerning the initiation of war as well as rules that prevent the commission of wrongs during war.[10] Augustine stipulates that "concern for the interests of others" not "lust or domination" must be the grounding of just wars.[11] The justification of wars grounded in concern for the interests of others follows from the two main principles of morality that Augustine articulates: "First, to do no harm to anyone; and secondly, to help everyone wherever possible."[12] Typically, killing someone does them harm and must be prohibited. But in rare cases in order to help others and prevent graver injustice, it may be necessary to kill during war. It is for this reason that it is possible for some wars to be "just wars."[13]

In a famous passage from his *City of God*, Augustine sets the main impetus for a doctrine of the Just War:

> Those wars are now past history; and yet the misery of these evils is not yet ended … If I were to try to describe, with an eloquence worthy of the subject, the many and multifarious disasters, the dour and dire necessities, I could not possibly be adequate to the theme, and there would be no end to this protracted discussion. But the wise man, they say, will wage just wars. Surely, if he remembers that he is a human being he will rather lament the fact that he is faced with the necessity of waging just wars; for if they were not just, he would not have to engage in them, and consequently there would be no wars for a wise man. For it is the injustice of the opposite side that lays on the wise man the duty of waging wars; and this injustice is assuredly to be deplored by a human being since it is the injustice of human beings, even though no necessity for war should arise from it.[14]

Here we see that wars are just insofar as they are necessary to confront injustice. So even though war is lamentable and to be undertaken rarely, it can be justified to wage war in response to injustices that cannot be prevented in any other way.

In another important passage from Augustine's *City of God*, we find a striking comment on the types of injustice and the priority of confronting them:

[10] Augustine, *The City of God* (*De Civitate Dei*), translated by Henry Bettenson, London: Penguin Books, 1972, 1984, p. 874.

[11] Ibid., p. 862.

[12] Ibid., pp. 873–874.

[13] Ibid., p. 861.

[14] Augustine, *City of God* (*De Civitate Dei*), Book 9, Chapter 7, translated by Henry Bettenson, London: Penguin Books, 1972, 1984, pp. 861–862.

> Now God, our master, teaches two chief precepts, love of god and love of neighbor; and in them man finds three objects for his love: God, himself, and his neighbor … For this reason he will be at peace, as far as lies in him, with all men, in that peace among men, that ordered harmony; and the basis of this order is the observance of two rules: first, to do no harm to anyone, and secondly, to help everyone whenever possible. To begin with, therefore, a man has a responsibility to his own household … This is where domestic peace starts, the ordered harmony about giving and obeying orders among those who live in the same house. For the orders are given by those who are concerned for the interests of others … they do not give orders because of a lust for domination, but from a dutiful concern for the interests of others, not with pride in taking precedence over others, but with compassion in taking care of others.[15]

From this it follows that war can be justly waged for either defense of self or defense of others – where the latter seems to have priority over the former. And in both cases the wars must satisfy a necessity or last resort condition since the violence that is perpetrated during war is in need of a specific and powerful justification – that harm to others can be prevented in no other way.

Whether fought for self-defense or defense of others, a just war is one fought to oppose injustice. And the moral demand to oppose injustice, for Augustine, is grounded in God's universal law.

> The peace of body and soul is the duly ordered life and health of a living creature; peace between mortal man and God is an ordered obedience, in faith, in subjection to an everlasting law; peace between men is an ordered agreement of mind with mind; the peace of a home is the ordered agreement of those who live together about giving and obeying orders; the peace of the Heavenly City is a perfectly ordered and perfectly harmonious fellowship in the enjoyment of God; the peace of the whole universe is the tranquility of order …[16]

For Augustine, there are laws or rules of war that dictate how humans should behave toward each other during war. Such rules are rules of universal justice: "God then created all things in supreme wisdom and ordered them in perfect justice."[17]

Because of his discussion of "just wars" Augustine is considered the founder of Just War theory, the theory that some wars can be morally justified in order to prevent consequences that are themselves worse than the violence of war itself. Augustine develops his doctrine in reaction to the early Church Fathers who were largely pacifists. Thinkers like Tertullian had argued that all wars were immoral, at least for

[15] Ibid., Book 19, Chapter 14, pp. 873–874.
[16] Ibid., p. 870.
[17] Ibid., p. 872.

those who are Christian.[18] It is not implausible to think of war as always unjustified, given the horrors of war. Even for Augustine, there will be few wars that meet his standards of justification. Most wars have been fought for territorial expansion, and these wars would generally not be justified on the theory of the Just War. But when wars are fought for attaining peace, or for preventing peace from deteriorating, they might be justified. And Augustine initiates a long historical line of theorizing by claiming that the best justification is framed in terms of the interests of others, rather than even the intuitively plausible self-defensive wars.

44.3 ANCIENT RABBINIC IDEAS OF A JUST WAR

Here is a portion of the *Talmud* that provides some of the ideas of a Just War similar to those ideas espoused by Roman lawyers:

> They station warriors at their head and others behind them, and iron axes are in their hand.
>
> And whoever wants to retreat – he has the power to break his legs.
>
> For the start of defeat is falling back, as it is written, "Israel fled before the Philistines and there was also a great slaughter among the people" (1 Sam. 31:1).
>
> Under what circumstances [do the foregoing rules apply]?
>
> In the case of an optional war.
>
> But in the case of a war subject to religious requirements, everyone goes forth to battle – even a bridegroom from his chamber, and a bride from her marriage- canopy.
>
> Said Rabbi Judah, "Under what circumstances? In the case of a war subject to religious requirement.
>
> "But in the case of an obligatory war, everyone goes forth into battle …"[19]

Here an important distinction is made between optional and obligatory wars.

In these passages from the *Talmud* there is then a dispute about how to characterize wars of conquest – were they optional or obligatory? One side to this debate says that if the war was to prevent idolaters from striking against Israel, then the war should be seen as obligatory. Another opinion is that all wars of conquest are also to be seen as obligatory because they were divinely sanctioned. But other rabbis argued that wars of conquest, insofar as they were not necessary for the preservation of Israel, should be seen as optional, not obligatory. The *Talmud*'s discussion ends with this inconclusive statement: "One authority regards it as a war fought as a

[18] Tertullian, "The Chaplet" (c. 210), Chapter 11 and 12 in *Disciplinary, Moral, and Aesthetic Works*, pp. 255–260.

[19] *The Babylonia Talmud, Tractate Sotah*, 44A-B, translated by Jacob Neusner, Peabody, MA: Hendrickson Publishers, 2005, Vol. 11, pp. 214–215.

religious obligation, and another authority regards such a war as an optional war."[20] Here we see the ancient rabbis attempting to understand what was to be called the condition of last resort or necessity – wars are only just if they are necessary for the self-defense of a nation – or perhaps for the defense of an innocent nation that is not one's own (although this is only hinted at in the passages from the *Talmud* we are here considering).

One commentator says that the difference between Roman and Rabbinic doctrines was that the former talked in terms of just and unjust wars, whereas the latter talked in terms of obligatory and optional wars. And while clearly these category pairs are very different, it seemed to some commentators that there was movement toward recognizing some of the same ideas about what would justify war and what would call for war being declared unjustified.[21]

The Just War principle of proportionality can also be seen in certain passages in the Talmud's *Sanhedrin*:

> Rabbi Jonathan b. Saul says, "If there is one in pursuit, who was pursuing his fellow so as to kill him, and one can save him [from the sin] at the cost of one of his limbs [rather than by killing him] and one did not do so, he is put to death on this account." …
>
> "Now if you maintain that if one can save [the pursuer from committing sin] by taking away one of his limbs, it is not permitted to save him at the cost of his life."[22]

This account is in the context of killing in domestic settings but can also apply to situations of war. And the account employs a clear-cut principle of proportionality that could apply *ad bellum* or *in bello*.

It is also clear that various Jewish sources at the end of the ancient period recognized the immunity from being attacked of those who were noncombatants – hence recognizing something like the principle of discrimination (or distinction). Philo is often cited in this respect:

> Let them, therefore, at once send out heralds to invite the enemy to an agreement, and at the same time let them display the power and considerable force which is encamped … But if they persevere in their folly, and push it further, acting with arrogance, then let our people display vigorous confidence, relying also on the invincible alliance of justice, and so let them advance … But let them suffer the maidens and the women to go free, inasmuch as they did not expect to suffer any

[20] Ibid., p. 216.

[21] See Norman Solomon, "The Ethics of War: Judaism," in *The Ethics of War: Shared Problems in Different Traditions*, edited by Richard Sorabji and David Rodin, Aldershot: Ashgate Publishing, 2006, pp. 108–137, especially p. 111.

[22] *The Babylonia Talmud, Tractate Sanhedrin*, 74A, translated by Jacob Neusner, Peabody, MA: Hendrickson Publishers, 2005, Vol. 16, p. 389.

> of the evils which war brings upon men at their hands, as they are exempt from all military service through their natural weakness … for to be eager to slay all men, and even those who have committed slight offences, or no offences, at all against one, I should call the conduct of an inhuman and pitiless soul, as it would be also to treat women as if they were an addition to the men who carry on war; when their way of life is naturally peaceful and domestic.[23]

Here it is clear that people who do not pose a threat to soldiers are not to be attacked according to Philo's view of the moral constraints on war.

The ancient rabbis did not develop a systematic account of what constitutes a just war, but many of the elements of the Just War that we have seen in the more systematic accounts of Augustine are also to be found in these rabbinic legal writings. And the ideas we have seen in ancient rabbinic texts are clearly related to the universalistic ethics espoused by the same sources that we examined in Chapter 43. The law relating to war was an extension and application of the law of the *Torah*, as understood in the *Mishnah* and especially in the *Talmud*. Such a law was especially binding on Jews because of their special relationship with God, but it is also clear that these laws and rules were also meant to apply to all people as well as also seems to be true of the Just War doctrine of the Roman lawyers such as Augustine.

44.4 UNIVERSAL LAW AND LIMITATIONS ON WAR

One of the central ideas in Augustine's articulation and defense of the Just War is that the universe is a kind of city or nation that must be governed by rules of justice as is true for all other kinds of cities or nations. Indeed, Augustine believed that if a city or nation was not administered according to justice there could be no conception of "right" and no sense in which that entity could be a republic, a thing of the people, an entity serving the interests of the people who were subjects in it. "And because God does not rule there the general characteristic of that city is that it is devoid of true justice."[24] Even during war, cities and nations must act justly or they risk alienating themselves from God and his universal laws.

The theorists we have been examining believe that war must be seen as limited by considerations of justice. In this sense, war is governed by a universal law – there are "laws of war," as Augustine put it. Let us consider what it means to say that there are "laws" of war. As I have presented these views so far, it should be clear that the "laws" in question are not civil laws but universal laws, either divine or natural. There is a sense in which these are "international" laws in that the laws in question govern the

[23] Philo, *The Special Laws* IV, 221–224, in *The Works of Philo*, translated by C. D. Yonge, Peabody, MA: Hendrickson Publishers, 1993, p. 638.

[24] Augustine, *City of God*, Book 19, Chapter 24, p. 891.

relations of nations and cities, not the people within those jurisdictions. These are higher laws that can override civil laws in some respects. What Augustine, and to a certain extent Philo, seem to have in mind is that there are universal laws of war that when violated make the act of war, no matter how praiseworthy in other respects, unjust and failing to manifest rightness.

Universal law, especially divine law, is employed to justify limitations on war that might indeed adversely affect the efficacy of war. Among other ideas, we have the thought that the hand of vengeance should be stayed. But there is still a wide gap between not pursuing vengeance and actually pursuing justice during war. Most of the legal theorists of the ancient period were not pacifists but nonetheless argued for certain restraints during war.

Laws or rules of war are introduced by the Just War doctrine so that warriors do not have to guess or use their disparate intuitions to decide about whether their proposed actions would be considered just or unjust. Today we separate the justice and laws of war into three categories: laws concerning the initiation of war (*jus ad bellum*), laws concerning the conduct of war (*jus in bello*), and laws concerning the end of war (*jus post bellum*). It is no accident that the Latin terms remain in use in international legal and moral theory today – for these categories have clear roots in the Roman era, especially due to Augustine, as well as to Cicero and Seneca.

The laws of war thus serve several purposes: first, there is a humane purpose in so far as unnecessary suffering during war is limited, and second, another humane purpose that gives soldiers who restrain themselves a certain kind of right that would not normally be seen except for the bastardized "right of the stronger." This is arguably what all laws do: they restrain people in terms of what they would normally feel free to do, and they provide to those who act within law's restraints a right so to act.

The authority of law, whether of the city or the cosmopolis, provides obligations and rights. In the context of war, law is seen as doing the same as what law does in the city or nation, at least in Augustine's account. To claim that war is governed by laws is not necessarily to be merely speaking metaphorically. Indeed, there is a sense in which Augustine and Philo, for instance, see God's universal law as the model for the law of the city, not the other way around.

Augustine calls his work *Civitas Dei* (*City of God*), and conceives of that city as overlapping with the city of humans. In the preface to his work, Augustine says: "I treat it [the city of God] both as it exists in this world of time, a stranger among the ungodly, living by faith, and as it stands in the security of its everlasting seat."[25] When he spoke of the laws of war he was speaking of the laws of God applied to war, just as he saw the laws of God applied to the dealing within the city as well. In the idea of the *City of God* was the regulating idea of the law of war.

[25] Augustine, *City of God*, Book 1, Preface, p. 5.

It is of course of great interest that Augustine did not think that when God's universal law was applied to war the law would simply outlaw war. And here we can see the idea again that it might be possible to act from love and yet engage in violence. This will remain the great puzzle or paradox of the doctrine of the Just War – that love for the interests of others could call for, or at least permit, the killing or maiming of others. As we will next see, there are residual problems concerning humaneness that result from the permission to use violence even in a just cause. But we are now thoroughly within the confines of the doctrine of the Just War even to formulate the problem as one of acting for the other while also seeking the destruction of another.

44.5 SOME REMAINING WORRIES ABOUT WAR'S INHUMANENESS

Actual wars fought during the end of the ancient period are not known for their humaneness, despite the views of the legal theorists we have been rehearsing. Indeed, Roman armies were notorious for their brutality. In addition, there are many instances of brutality in the *Torah* and these are not disavowed by the ancient rabbis – seemingly thinking that God has dictated that Jews were to vanquish their foes by whatever means were at their disposal. In this sense it is the justice of the way wars are fought, not necessarily the justice of the decision to fight war, which is most in need of being addressed at the end of this final chapter of our long saga through 3,000 years of ancient legal thought.

Universal law, especially when it is divinely inspired, can be highly discriminatory if there are some people under universal law who are more valued than others. Indeed, our contemporary rules of war call for all noncombatants to be treated the same – with a high degree of humaneness. There is also the *jus in bello* idea of proportionality that is not well supported in practice even though it was supported in some of the Talmudic texts, for instance.

One idea that we have not given enough attention to that is highly relevant now is that the Jews saw themselves as God's chosen people and that the Romans saw themselves as destined to be the greatest rulers – in both cases there is a kind of special status to the Jews and Romans not also attributed to those with whom they fought their wars. The universal laws of war, even those calling for humane treatment, can be differently applied if some of the people in question are thought to be more righteous than others. This chosen or special status of the Jews and Romans did lead some theorists to think that there were different obligations and rights during war based on this differential status.

For war to be pursued effectively there is the question of whether it can also be pursued justly. And this is the concern especially of nations that feel they are in the right when waging war. The rightness of the cause is thought to carry over into the rightness of the employment of the terrible forces of war. Nearly everyone believes that after war is over the implements of war should be beaten "into ploughshares" as we find in the famous passage from Isaiah 2:4. But few, except the most extreme pacifists, would argue that weapons should be beaten into ploughshares during war or that tactics should be employed that would not be effective in pursuing a truly just cause.

It is important to note that the newly emerging doctrine of the Just War was seen as contrasted to the pacifism of theorists such as Tertullian. Pacifism puts great stress on the idea of humaneness – seeing war as the epitome of intentional acts of inhumane treatment, where killing and plundering are tactics nearly indispensable to most war efforts. In this context, the doctrine of the Just War seemingly moves away from the most humane position and is not clearly morally progressive.

Augustine is forthright in recognizing this argument concerning the inhumane character of war. Indeed, Augustine reminds us that every person should abhor war. Yet, Augustine points out that sometimes war can be more humane than the alternative – if the alternative involves allowing innocent people to be killed, for instance. So, in this respect at least Augustine's position seems to be a "lesser evil" position – war is seen as an evil, but in a few cases not engaging in war produces a worse evil, namely allowing innocent others to be killed. As we have seen, it is noteworthy that Augustine thinks that war aimed at the defense of innocent others is more justifiable than war aimed at defense of self.

Once pacifism's strictures are breached there is the possibility, even likelihood, that inhumane treatment of one's "enemies" will become acceptable. The problem is that there is little appetite for behaving humanely when it is thought that justice and universal law are on one's side and that the enemy is on the side opposed to justice and universal law.

CONCLUDING THOUGHTS FOR PART D

The development of the doctrine of the Just War does provide a nice ending to our exploration of ancient legal thought. Here we find a humanizing effort to mitigate the most horrible effects of war, both in terms of initiating war and conducting war. This is a progressive development over those times when war was waged without constraints. Yet, when compared to the pacifist position taken in the centuries before Augustine, it is not so clear that the Just War doctrine is indeed an advance in terms of humaneness.

To claim that there is a domain for universal law is already to suggest a parallel between laws of the city or nation, on the one hand, and laws of the world (cosmos), on the other hand. Indeed, the ancient Greek Stoics already espoused the idea of a cosmopolitan order that was governed by law. Augustine's development of this idea is to suggest a tri-partite parallel: the laws of the household, of the city, and of the universe. But while there is a clear parallel here in some respects we still need to understand what kind of law the universal law is.

Law is a rule or regulation of a certain kind of order. When theorists speak of universal law they are clearly contemplating an order of the universe. And when that universal law is applied to the field of war there is the idea that soldiers are bound to act in certain ways and to refrain from acting in other ways so as to place themselves in a situation where they do not have to see themselves as murderers even though they intentionally kill.

The experience of legal thinkers in the Roman Empire was that law was already extended over most of the world. And within short order the idea surfaced that these people could all be seen as citizens of the Roman Empire. Rabbis and other Jewish legal thinkers also had experience of a somewhat similar sort in seeing the Diaspora extend out to cover almost the same terrain as the Roman Empire. If laws can rule over people so widely distributed across the world, then perhaps a system of rights can do so as well.

But as wave after wave of Germanic invasions occurred in the Roman Empire, the idea of a Just War did not get much purchase if that meant giving in to the invaders who did not seem to care about justice or righteousness during battle. This is one of the first topics I will take up in a new work on the legal thought of Medieval and Renaissance times.

PART E

Final Thoughts

45

Final Thoughts on Equity, Justice, and Humaneness

A legal system expresses humaneness through how it treats those who are suffering, in need, or oppressed. The chief characteristic of a legal system that expresses humaneness is that in some sense compassion and respect are displayed to all of the citizens or subjects of a society. Some of the most humane legal systems are those that see concern for the widows, orphans, poor, and aliens not as a matter of charity but as a requirement of good law-making and judging. From ancient times until today humaneness of a legal system is seen in the way that justice is meted out, and in the way that equity is seen as an amelioration of strict justice.

Equity and justice are concepts that sit at the intersection of law and morality. Justice, as a legal concept, dictates that we "treat like cases alike … and treat different cases differently."[1] There is a strong sense of moral equality in this concept of justice. But in many ways, the morality here is largely procedural – regardless of outcomes, justice dictates that all cases of a certain kind should be treated the same. And what is importantly ruled out is that people are discriminated against, for instance, "by reference to such matters as color and race."[2]

Equity, as a legal concept, dictates that "for every wrong there ought to be a remedy."[3] As H. L. A. Hart says, some laws "might also be unjust in quite a different way: for while making no unfair discriminations they might fail altogether to provide a remedy for certain types of injury."[4] Lord Kames and others go further and say that equity can apply beyond "what even in a proper sense may be termed the injustice of the common law" in that equity "boldly undertakes to correct or mitigate" (moral) wrongs that are not injustices.[5] Such considerations have led some to say that equity

1 H. L. A. Hart, *The Concept of Law*, Oxford: Oxford University Press, 1961, p. 155.
2 Ibid., p. 158.
3 Henry Home, Lord Kames, *Principles of Equity*, London: Alex, Lawrie, and Co., 1765, p. 27.
4 H. L. A. Hart, *The Concept of Law*, p. 160.
5 Lord Kames, *Principles of Equity*, p. 10.

is best understood as a form of mercy or closely related to it.[6] But the reference to wrongs belies this position. Correcting wrongs is not a matter of leniency or mercy (as a form of charity), but of fairness as we will see in this chapter.

Equity, as a legal concept, is often associated with a certain form of mercy – treating people not on the basis of what they deserve but somehow better than that, more leniently, perhaps out of pity. In this chapter I argue that equity is different from this form of mercy and not necessarily linked to it. Equity is a kind of fundamental fairness that is deserved as something obligatory and takes account of uniquely relevant circumstances. As we know from Aristotle, equity is different from at least strict justice – because there is room for creative remedies that are not mandated by, and even at odds with, strict adherence to legal rules. Yet for this reason equity has problems with the rule of law; but I argue that it is mostly better than justice for establishing a humane legal system.

In the first section of this concluding chapter I briefly review what we have seen about ancient conceptions of equity and justice. In Section 45.2 I consider a few historical examples of equity. In Section 45.3 I talk about equity's relation to mercy. In Section 45.4 I explain how equity can provide a limit on discretion of judges and at least partially respond to the worries about the rule of law. Throughout this chapter I argue that a proper understanding of equity, which we can find in ancient times, makes clear why equity is probably even more important than justice for establishing a humane legal system.

45.1 ANCIENT CONCEPTIONS OF EQUITY AND JUSTICE

In our examination of ancient Mesopotamian law, we first encountered the idea of equity in the debt forgiveness Laws of Hammurabi and the kings that followed him in Babylonia. Equity was appealed to in order to alleviate suffering from the heavy debt of large portions of the population. Strict justice would have dictated that debt was to be repaid even if it meant debt enslavement for the debtor. Hammurabi uses the term *misarum* (equity) in his account of why he promulgated edicts for debt cancellation. Somewhat later there were similar edicts in Egypt, and the Bible makes reference to some as well.[7]

There are several types of consideration underlying ancient debt forgiveness edicts that one can see operating in ancient Babylonia, Egypt, and in the Bible. The first is a kind of justice that demands equal treatment of the laws – all debts must

6 See Martha Nussbaum, "Equity and Mercy," *Philosophy & Public Affairs*, Vol. 22, number 2, Spring 1993.

7 See Deuteronomy 15.1–2. On the connection between debt slave forgiveness and other forms of relief of slavery in the Bible see N. P. Lemche, "The Manumission of Slaves – The Fallow Year – The Sabbatical Year – The Jobel Year," *Vetus Testmentum*, Vol. 26, Fasc. 1 (Jan. 1976), pp. 38–59.

be repaid, and the law treats all debtors the same. The second is a kind of equity that calls for considering the effects of equal enforcement of the law, and called for undoing wrongful suffering. Equity in very ancient times was already conceived as different from justice. The need for equitable fairness came from the rise of written law which seemingly gave judges little room for discretion – the law was plainly recorded and need only be consulted to know how the judge should rule. Indeed, Hammurabi states this explicitly in the preface to his code of laws, even as he also recognized the need for equity in a few cases. In Egypt, though, there was not, as far as we can tell, much in the way of written laws. Here the idea of *Maat* bridged the ideas of justice and equity as well as the truth sought by the pharaoh in trials where the judge was not much limited by strict justice since there was not much written law.

In our examination of ancient Greek legal thought, we encountered the first sustained theoretical account of equity. In his *Nicomachean Ethics*, Aristotle defined equity to be "a correction of law where it is defective owing to its universality."[8] Justice often did not allow for consideration of the particularities of a given case – so that the strict application of justice created a wrong that considerations of equity could correct. Aristotle saw equity as a kind of justice, but not strict justice – something that sought to express what the lawmaker would have said about a given case if confronted by it – this made equity a kind of fairness.

It also became clear that Aristotle was struggling with the idea of mercy and its relation to equity, especially in his *Rhetoric*.

> Equity bids us to be merciful to the weakness of human nature; to think less about the laws than about the man who framed them, and less about what he said than about what he meant; not to consider the actions of the accused so much as his intentions, nor this or that detail so much as the whole story; to ask not what a man is now but what he has always or usually been.[9]

Mercy also moved the judge to be like an arbitrator in looking more to the spirit rather than the letter of the written law.

In ancient China, as in Egypt, written law was not often appealed to and so there was no need to separate the justice of the written law from the considerations of equity. Yet we also found the most explicit reference to humaneness, in the writings of Confucius and especially Mencius. If people acted humanely toward each other there was actually little need for formal law or even for judges.[10] Treating one another

8 Ibid., 1137b27.

9 Aristotle, *Rhetoric*, 1374a18–1374b22, translated by W. Rhys Roberts, in *Basic Works of Aristotle*, edited by Richard McKeon, NY: Random House, 1941, p. 1372.

10 See *Mencius*, translated by Irene Bloom, NY: Columbia University Press, 2009.

fairly was the hallmark of humaneness and while not explicitly named equity, was in a sense elevated even over justice.

In our examination of the legal systems of the Roman Republic and India we saw equity institutionalized in various significant ways, and we also saw equity linked to emerging ideas of natural law. Cicero was the outstanding adapter of Aristotelian ideas of equity, but also from a practitioner's standpoint he raised serious questions about the coherence of the idea of equity. Cicero said:

> accepting an excuse is nothing more than repealing the law, because when once an excuse is taken into consideration there is no point in weighing it with reference to the law, seeing that it is not written into the law. And if this principle is set up, all men will be given a reason and opportunity for violating the law, when they know that you are deciding the case by the character of the man who broke the law rather than by the law which you are sworn to uphold.[11]

Nonetheless, Cicero saw positive value in equity and linked equity to natural law ideas.

We also saw that in India equity emerged as deeply related to religious legal texts, especially the Code of Manu, where considerations of basic fairness were paramount. And in the *Narada*, *dharma*, understood as the ancient truth, is said to be one of the four feet of legal procedure, and while the king's edicts can "overrule" *dharma* it must be taken into account, just as is true of custom. "The four feet of legal procedure are *dharma*, legal procedure, custom, and the king's decree: each latter one overrules the former."[12]

In our examination of legal thought of the Roman Empire and the ancient rabbis, we saw that equity became solidified in the Roman Empire – through the office of the Praetor, and also in rabbinic legal thought, conceptions of equity were linked to divine law. But we also saw that the discretion of equity was problematic when a legal system stretched over vast geographical areas – the more discretion, the more potential confusion about what the law called for, especially in the furthest reaches of the Empire or of the Diaspora.

Nonetheless, we saw that equity in the Roman Empire and the rabbinic law was the crucial component of what made these legal systems humane. Seneca saw equity as deeply dependent on mercy, but it was a mercy that was different from simple pardoning. Ulpian, writing in the second century CE, saw equity as a more straightforward form of basic fairness that it was the duty of the judge to consider. Ulpian argued that equity was best understood as closely connected to the principle

[11] *De Inventione*, II.XLV.130–131; p. 299.

[12] *The Naradasmrti*, Prolegomena, paragraph 10, translated by Richard W. Lariviere, Delhi: Motilal Banarsidasss Publishers, 2003, p. 256.

of humanity.[13] If equity is so understood then it is easier to see that equity would tend to favor those who are poor or less powerful,[14] although all people should be able to benefit from principles of humanity since all people are humans and should be treated equally.

There was not, though, a straight progressive path from Hammurabi and the Pharaohs to Justinian and the Talmud. Indeed, in terms of moral progress what we saw was a forward-and-backward path, where both justice and equity were recognized as crucial for the humaneness of a legal system, although some saw equity as a matter of fairness and others saw it as closely related to mercy. Even when equity was linked to mercy, though, it was not mercy seen as mere charity but as something obligatory for judges to consider.

45.2 SOME CASES OF EQUITY

When we move into the Medieval period, equity again takes center stage for several important legal theorists, culminating in the sixteenth century CE with the preeminent theorist of equity, Christopher Saint Germain. Here is the first of the cases he employed to educate students about the importance of equity:

> I have heard say, that if a man is bound in an obligation [to] pay the money, but he taketh no acquittance, or it he take one, and it happeneth him to lose it, that in that case, he shall be compelled by the laws of England to pay the money again. And how may it be said that the law standeth with reason and conscience? For it is grounded upon the law of reason, that debts ought of right to be paid: so it is grounded upon the law of reason (as it seemeth) that when they be paid, that he that paid them should be discharged.[15]

In this case, the sixteenth century CE law required that a debtor have a receipt for payment of the debt to establish that the debtor was no longer obligated to pay the creditor. Yet, it seemed unfair or unreasonable not to recognize other evidence for such debt repayment, and hence to require a debtor to repay the debt a second time merely for lack of a receipt. Equity was appealed to by the debtor to get relief from the obligation.

[13] See D. H. van Zyl, *Justice and Equity in Greek and Roman Legal Thought*, Pretoria: Academica Press, 1991, pp. 134–135.

[14] See Martha Nussbaum, "Equity and Mercy," *Philosophy & Public Affairs*, Vol. 22, no. 2 (Spring 1993), pp. 83–125.

[15] Christopher Saint Germain, *Doctor and Student: Or Dialogues between a Doctor of Divinity and a Student in the Laws of England Containing the Grounds of those Laws together with Questions and Cases Concerning Equity thereof* (1518), London: A. Strahan and W. Woodfall, 1787, p. 37.

And then Christopher Saint Germain also provides us with a slightly more complicated case, which is a variation of a case we saw that Cicero also discussed 1,600 years earlier:

> And if a law were made in a city, that no man under the pain of death should open the gates of the city before the sun-rising: yet if the citizens before that hour flying from their enemies, come to the gates of the city, and one for saving of the citizens openeth the gates before the hour appointed by the law, he offendeth not the law, for that case is excepted from the said general law by equity ...[16]

In this second case, the law fails to recognize an excuse of necessity when saving a life is at stake. Yet it seems unfair to penalize a person for doing something necessary to save a life when his failure to follow the law was much less significant.

In a sense, these two equity cases involve a gap in the law that creates a wrong in need of being remedied. In the first case of debt, the law only recognizes discharge when there is a receipt – but if the receipt was withheld or was lost, discharge is not recognized even if full payment of the debt has been made. The strictness of the law – demanding evidence of a receipt in order to recognize discharge of a debt – creates a wrong in the case where there has been full payment but no receipt is available to prove it. There may be witnesses that will testify that the debt has been repaid but the testimony is not allowed – only the receipt is admissible. It is surely a wrong for a debtor to have to pay twice to discharge his or her debt yet the strict justice of the law cannot acknowledge the wrong. For Saint Germain, equity is the concept that calls for this wrong to be remedied.

In the second case of the closed gate, the law only recognizes the rising of the sun as a legitimate reason to open the gate – even if there are extenuating circumstances that would override the strict application of the law. The gatekeeper, who opens the gate at night to admit fellow citizens fleeing for their lives from the enemy, is subject to punishment when the law is strictly applied – yet there is a wrong done to the gatekeeper when the extenuating circumstances are not seen as relieving the gatekeeper of the obligation not to open the gate until the rising sun. The strict application of the justice of the law creates a wrong upon the gatekeeper.

In both of these cases, there is a form of unfairness resulting from the strict application of the law. It is not an *optional* matter of mercy that the law not be strictly applied. Rather the party wronged is *due* a remedy lest unfairness occur. The unfairness in both cases involves a suffering, even though there is good reason not to be made to suffer. In a sense there are two somewhat different kinds of unfairness in these two cases. In the debt case, there is no remedy for a person forced by the law

[16] Ibid., p. 46.

to pay twice what is due. The law creates a situation where by its strict application, unfairness in the form of a wrong is the result. In the second closed gate case, there is a gap in the law, where a certain type of reasonable excuse is not recognized.

Equity enters into the picture to cure the unfairness of the strict application of the law, either because its application creates a wrong, or because its application offers no remedy for a wrong. To see how the strict application of the law can create a wrong we can turn to a nineteenth century CE case for our third example made famous by Ronald Dworkin. Here is Dworkin's description of the case of *Riggs v. Palmer* from 1889:

> Elmer murdered his grandfather – he poisoned him – in New York in 1882. He knew that his grandfather's existing will left him the bulk of the estate, and he suspected that the old man, who had recently remarried, would change the will and leave him nothing. Elmer's crime was discovered; he was convicted and sentenced to a term of years in jail ...[17]

The judges had to decide whether to follow justice and apply the statute law strictly, which made no exceptions to who could benefit based on the commission of a crime, or whether to follow equity and not allow the grandson to profit from his own wrongdoing.

In this nineteenth century CE case, the strict application of the law created two wrongs. On the one hand the grandson unjustly enriched himself, and on the other hand the daughters were deprived of their inheritance. Appealing to equity remedies these wrongs – the grandson is disinherited, and the daughters are pronounced inheritors. As a matter of equity, a judge should have the discretion to remedy these wrongs. But it is a mistake to say that the judge has discretion to show mercy, here understood as a form of charity that is not owed to anyone. Rather, the judge is under an obligation (at least quasi-moral) to remedy the wrongs that would result from the strict application of the law. Indeed, equity requires that no mercy be paid to the grandson.

Justice, or at least justice strictly applied, requires that the grandson inherit since this is what the strict adherence to the terms of the extent will require. For a judge to make an exception in this case is to fail to treat the grandson as deserving of being treated like other inheritors. In this case, justice, or at least strict justice, creates a wrong. In this sense, equity opposes justice in obligating the judge to remedy the wrong created by the strict application of justice. But like justice, equity does obligate the judge to act in certain ways – whereas mercy is generally not conceived in terms of one's obligations.

[17] Ronald Dworkin, *Law's Empire*, Cambridge, MA: Harvard University Press, 1986, pp. 15–16.

45.3 MERCY AND EQUITY

Christopher St. Germain is also one of the most important Medieval theorists to link equity to mercy. Here is his definition of equity:

> Equity is a right wiseness that considereth all the particular circumstances of the deed, the which also is tempered with the sweetness of mercy. And such an equity must always be observed in every law of man, and in every general rule thereof: and that knew he well that said thus, Laws covet to be ruled by equity … in some cases it is necessary … to temper and mitigate the rigor of the law.[18]

Mercy is posited as linked with equity as what motivates judges to mitigate the harshness of strict adherence to law. But in some cases, Saint Germain admits, it is *necessary* to be merciful and follow equity – equitable considerations in at least some cases are not optional.

Another legal theorist seemingly to embrace the connection between equity and mercy or pity was the early twentieth century law scholar, Frederic Maitland.

> I do not think that in the fourteenth century the Chancellors considered that they had to administer any body of substantive rules that differed from the ordinary law of the land. They were administering the law but they were administering it in cases which escaped the meshes of the ordinary courts … In this period one of the commonest of all the reasons the complainants will give for coming to the Chancery is that they are poor while their adversaries are rich and influential – too rich, too influential to be left to the clumsy process of the old courts and the verdicts of juries.[19]

In effect, the complainant in equity cases asked the Chancellor to take pity on them and aid them because they were powerless against the rich and influential.

Yet, there are then questions about how best to understand equity in a case involving acts of complicity, which are not recognized as illegal, but instead immoral, acts. In an ancient Babylonian case we examined in some detail, the court seems to act on the basis of a moral judgment about the character of the wife of the victim – holding her to a higher standard because of her wifely duties. Here we come to an issue of how equity relates to morality. Yet, here we also have an example of where conscience or morality and mercy diverge. It should be noted that the conception of equity employed in ancient legal thought does not always track mercy.

There is a disconnect between equity and the idea of mercy. When juries *acquit* despite the law, this is often due to considerations of mercy for the defendant. But

[18] Christopher Saint Germain, *Doctor and Student*, p. 45.

[19] F. W. Maitland, *Equity: A Course of Lectures*, Cambridge: Cambridge University Press, 1909, 1936, pp. 5–6.

when juries *convict* despite the law, equity is differently understood than as a concept closely related to mercy.[20] For it must be recognized that taking account of the particularities of the parties before the law does not always result in a merciful decision by the jury or judge.

At this point it is worth briefly considering a 1993 CE essay by Martha Nussbaum that also tracks conceptions of equity from ancient times. Nussbaum argues that "From the beginning the idea of flexible particularized judgment [of equity] is linked with leniency."[21] Nussbaum does not trace the history of equity back to Mesopotamia, but to ancient Greece. And in that respect she argues that:

> the original and real etymology of the word *epieikeia* – from *eikos*, the "plausible" or "appropriate," is being supplemented by a popular derivation of the term from *eiko*, "yield," "give way." Thus even in writing the history of the term, Greek thinkers discover a connection between appropriate judgment and leniency. The puzzle lies, as I have said, in the unexplained connection between appropriate situational judgment and mercy.[22]

Indeed, Nussbaum goes on to admit that "we might expect that the equitable will sometimes be more lenient than the generality of law, but sometimes harsher."[23]

Nussbaum argues that equity stands somehow opposed to what she calls "the retributive idea" which is characterized by a "neglect of the particulars."[24] Wrongs must be made up, Nussbaum says, and this often involves neglecting the possibly good character of the wrongdoer. Oedipus commits parricide and must be avenged even though he was ignorant that the person he slew was his father. For Nussbaum, this model of retribution stands at odds with the model of equity that calls for leniency in such cases when we focus on the particularities of the person who is Oedipus the wrongdoer.[25]

Yet as Nussbaum has admitted, things could go the other way – it may be that attention to the particulars of the case call not for leniency, but for even more harsh treatment. I would argue that paying attention to the particulars of the person and situation will not always amount to leniency but will track a certain kind of fairness, which is necessary for humaneness, even if not involving mercy. Indeed, humaneness is best seen as a requirement rather than something optional (as would normally be true of mercy).

20 See Alan W. Scheflin and Jon M. Van Dyke, "Merciful Juries: The Resilience of Jury Nullification," *Washington and Lee Law Review*, Vol. 48, 1991, p. 165.

21 Martha Nussbaum, "Equity and Mercy," *Philosophy & Public Affairs*, Vol. 22, no. 2 (Spring 1993), p. 86.

22 Ibid., pp. 86–87.

23 Ibid., p. 87.

24 Ibid., p. 89.

25 See ibid., pp. 91–92.

45.4 HUMANENESS, DISCRETION, AND EQUITY

Concern for the plight of "widows, orphans, and the poor" or for those who are aliens has been a characteristic of humane legal systems. On its face, this looks like an easy way to see equity connected to mercy as a kind of charity. But the result is to see that the widows, orphans, poor, and aliens are to be subject to the whim of the judge – good judges will feel moved to help them, but this in no way translates into an obligation. Yet, when there is no obligation, the judge will only respond leniently to these people if he or she is indeed so moved.

There is another problem with equity understood as connected to mercy, and it is that, as we saw above, a judge will be given discretion that is not limited and thus will be open to abuse – a judge might only help those poor people who were of his same racial group, for instance. But if equity is disconnected from mercy, then how do we account for the discretionary aspect of equity? If equity is a matter of obligation, not "charity," then what sense is there to the idea that equitable considerations like "no man should profit from his own wrongdoing" are discretionary? One idea, suggested by Ronald Dworkin, is to see equity as providing principles not rules, and that principles obligate only in the sense that they must be taken into account, not in the sense that they must be satisfied.[26]

Why would following principles of equity make for a more humane legal system than merely following rules of justice? One explanation is that equity is really only a supplement to justice considerations. Equity does not and really cannot completely replace justice – people should still feel that by and large they should follow the justice rules of the law. In this sense, equity is a limitation on justice – something that judges must take into account, and that is not mere charity toward the parties to a law suit.

But what of those cases where a judge exercises equitable discretion by being more severe to one of the parties to a suit than following strict justice would call for? Even in this case, the attention to the particulars of the facts of the case and the people involved is a sign of humaneness. Taking into account a defendant's poverty is simply to respond to this person as a whole person who has distinct characteristics and who is in distinct circumstances. Treating this poor defendant with respect for who he is does not translate well into pitying him or her.

There is a conflict that I have noted before between two legal principles: all people should be treated the same before the law, and differences of situation and status should not be overlooked. We can think of these as the principle of equal treatment and the principle of equity of treatment. It is not always fair to treat people all the same. In a very large jurisdiction it is difficult to achieve equality of treatment, as

[26] See Ronald Dworkin, *Law's Empire*, Cambridge, MA: Harvard University Press, 1986.

the Romans and ancient rabbis especially discovered. But leaving criminal matters to local authorities risked a loss of equity or fairness as well. So, it is not clear that a system of law that treated all the same would indeed be better than a system that sought to take account of local differences that were relevant.

We need to think more clearly about what humaneness itself consists of. One crucial factor in humaneness is that people are treated as individuals and not as instances of a collectivity – whether ethnic, religious, racial, or national.[27] Another crucial factor is that people who are more powerful or wealthy should not be able to use the legal system to take advantage of those who are weak or poor.

In order to accomplish the objective of fairness and humaneness it is important that equity not warrant such discretion that the rule of law is adversely affected. A humane legal system also involves transparency and predictability so that people know what to expect of the law. If elevating equity over strict justice meant that law became too difficult to predict then humaneness would also suffer. There is thus a sense that a humane legal system does not allow so much discretion that judges are allowed to overrule the law whenever they are so moved to do so. If equity was closely associated with mercy as a form of charity, such a result could occur.

We have seen the back-and-forth development of ideas of equity, from the earliest recorded writing about law, which understood equity as providing judges with discretion to correct the law when injustices or wrongs would arise with a too strict justice. Humaneness and equity thus came to have a close relationship. And while sometimes equity is linked to mercy, it is not necessarily so. In my projected next volume on Medieval legal thought, many of these issues will get addressed in much detail and sophistication, but we will again see that there is no straightforward progressive line from older to newer legal texts and ideas.

[27] These are the prohibited categories of treatment which the 1948 genocide treaty criminalizes.

Bibliography

Acilian Law on the Right to Recovery of Property Officially Extorted (122 BCE), in *Ancient Roman Statutes*, translated and edited by Allan Johnson, Paul Coleman-Norton, Frank Bourne, and Clyde Pharr, Austin: University of Texas Press, 1961, 2012.

Adkins, Arthur. *Merit and Responsibility: A Study in Greek Values*, Oxford: Oxford University Press, 1960.

Aeschylus, *Eumenides*, in Aeschylus, *The Orestaian Trilogy*, translated by Philip Vellacott, NY: Penguin Books, 1956.

Allam, S. "Egyptian Law Courts in Pharaonic and Hellenistic Times," *The Journal of Egyptian Archeology*, Vol. 77, 1991, pp. 109–127.

Allen, Danielle. *The World of Prometheus: The Politics of Punishing in Democratic Athens*, Princeton, NJ: Princeton University Press, 2000.

Ancient Egyptian Literature, 2 volumes, edited by Miriam Lichtheim, Berkeley: University of California Press, Vol. 1, 1973.

Ancient Greek Laws: A Sourcebook, edited by Ilias Arnaoutoglou, NY: Routledge, 1998.

Ancient Records of Egypt, 5 volumes, translated and edited by James Henry Breasted, Chicago, IL: University of Chicago, 1906.

Ancient Roman Statutes, translated and edited by Allan Johnson, Paul Coleman-Norton, Frank Bourne, and Clyde Pharr, Austin: University of Texas Press, 1961, 2012.

Andocides. *Against Alcibiades*, in *Minor Attic Orators I*, translated by K. J. Maidment, Cambridge, MA: Harvard University Press' Loeb Classical Library, 1941.

Anscombe, G. E. M. "War and Murder," in her *Ethics, Religion, and Politics, Collected Philosophical Papers*, Vol. III, Minneapolis: University of Minnesota Press, 1981.

Antiphon. *Third Tetralogy*, in *Minor Attic Orators*, translated by K. J. Maidment, Cambridge, MA: Harvard University Press' Loeb Classical Library, 1941.

On the Murder of Herodes, in *Antiphon and Andocides*, translated by Michael Gagarin, Austin: University of Texas Press, 1998.

Second Tetralogy, translated by Michael Gagarin, in *Antiphon and Andocides*, edited by Michael Gagarin and Douglas M. MacDowell, Austin: University of Texas Press, 2006.

Third Tetralogy, translated by Michael Gagarin in *Antiphon and Andocides*, Austin: University of Texas Press, 2006.

First Tetralogy, in *Speeches from Athenian Law*, edited by Michael Gagarin, Austin: University of Texas Press, 2011.

The *Apastamba*, in *Dharmasutras: The Law Codes of Apastamba, Gautama, Baudhayana, and Vasistha*, translated by Patrick Olivelle, Delhi: Motilal Banarsidass, 2000.

Arendt, Hannah. "What is Authority?" in *The Portable Hannah Arendt*, edited by Peter Baehr, NY: Penguin Books, 2000.

Aristotle. *Nicomachean Ethics*, in *Aristotle XIX*, translated by H. Rackham, Loeb edition, Cambridge, MA: Harvard University Press, 1926.

Politics, translated by H. Rackham, Loeb Library, Cambridge, MA: Harvard University Press, 1932.

Eudemian Ethics, translated by R. Hackman, Loeb edition, Cambridge, MA: Harvard University Press, 1935.

Nicomachean Ethics, in *The Basic Works of Aristotle*, translated by W. D. Ross, edited by Richard McKeon, NY: Random House, 1941.

Physics, in *The Basic Works of Aristotle*, translated by R. P. Hardie and R. K. Gaye, edited by Richard McKeon, NY: Random House, 1941.

Rhetoric, in *The Basic Works of Aristotle*, translated by W. Rhys Roberts, edited by Richard McKeon, NY: Random House, 1941.

Politics, in *The Basic Works of Aristotle*, translated by Benjamin Jowett, edited by Richard McKeon, NY: Random House, 1941.

The Constitution of Athens, translated by J. M. Moore, Cambridge: Cambridge University Press, 1966.

The Constitution of Athens, translated by F. G. Kenyon, in Aristotle, *The Politics and the Constitution of Athens*, edited by Stephen Everson, Cambridge: Cambridge University Press, 1996.

Askowith, Dora. *The Tolerance and Persecution of the Jews in the Roman Empire*, NY: Columbia University, 1915.

Assmann, Jan. "When Justice Fails: Jurisdiction and Imprecation in Ancient Egypt and the Near East," *Journal of Egyptian Archeology*, Vol. 78, 1992, pp. 149–162.

Associated Press. "Lawsuit: Court Illegally Jails People Who Can't Pay Fines," October 13, 2015.

Augustine. *The City of God* (*De Civitate Dei*), translated by Henry Bettenson, NY: Penguin Books, 1972, 1984.

Avalos, Hector. "Legal and Social Institutions in Canaan and Ancient Israel," in *Civilizations of the Ancient Near East*, edited by Jack M. Sasson, NY: Charles Scribner's Sons, 1995.

The Babylonian Talmud: Tractate Berakhot, translated by A. Cohen, Cambridge: Cambridge University Press, 1921.

The Babylonian Talmud, 22 volumes, translated by Jacob Neusner, Peabody, MA: Hendrickson Publishers, 2005.

Baier, Annette. "Trust and Antitrust," in her *Moral Prejudices*, Cambridge, MA: Harvard University Press, 1994.

Baker, H. D. "Degrees of Freedom: Slavery in Mid-First Millennium BC Babylonia," *World Archeology*, Vol. 33, no. 1, June 2001, pp. 18–26.

Barmash, Pamela. *Homicide in the Biblical World*, NY: Cambridge University Press, 2005.

Bassiouni, M. C. and E. M. Wise. *Aut Dedere Aut Judicare*, Dordrecht: Martinus Nijhoff Publishers, 1995.

The Baudhayana, in *Dharmasutras: The Law Codes of Apastamba, Gautama, Baudhayana, and Vasistha*, translated by Patrick Olivelle, Delhi: Motilal Banarsidass, 2000.

Bauman, Richard A. *Crime and Punishment in Ancient Rome*, NY: Routledge, 1996.

Beard, Mary, John North, and Simon Price, *Religions of Rome*, 2 volumes, Cambridge: Cambridge University Press, 1998.
Beckman, Gary. *Hittite Diplomatic Texts*, second edition, Atlanta, GA: Scholars' Press, 1999.
"International Law in the Second Millennium: The Late Bronze Age," in *A History of Ancient Near Eastern Law*, Vol. 1, edited by Raymond Westbrook, Leiden: Brill, 2003.
Bedau, Hugo. "Egalitarianism and the Idea of Equality," in *Nomos IX – Equality*, edited by J. Roland Pennock and John W. Chapman, NY: Atherton Press, 1967.
Bederman, David J. *International Law in Antiquity*, Cambridge: Cambridge University Press, 2001.
Bentham, Jeremy. *Introduction to the Principles of Morals and Legislation (1789)*, edited by J. H. Burns and H. L. A. Hart, Oxford: Oxford University Press, 1970.
Bleiberg, Edward. "Loans, Credit and Interest in Ancient Egypt," in *Debt and Economic Renewal in the Ancient Near East*, edited by Michael Hudson and Marc Van De Mieroop, Bethesda, MD: CDL Press, 2002.
Blum, Gabriella. "The Dispensable Lives of Soldiers," *Journal of Legal Analysis*, Vol. 2, 2010.
Blundell, Sue. *Women in Ancient Greece*, Cambridge, MA: Harvard University Press, 1995.
Bodde, Dirk and Clarence Morris. *Law in Imperial China*, Cambridge, MA: Harvard University Press, 1967.
Boecker, Hans Jochen. *Law and the Administration of Justice in the Old Testament and Ancient East*, translated by Jeremy Moiser, Minneapolis, MN: Augsburg Publishing House, 1980.
Bonner, Robert J. and Gertrude Smith. *The Administration of Justice from Homer to Aristotle*, 2 volumes, Chicago, IL: University of Chicago Press, 1938.
Booth, Charlotte. *Horemheb: The Forgotten Pharaoh*, Stroud, Gloucestershire: Amberley Publishing, 2009, 2013.
Bottero, Jean. *Mesopotamia: Writing, Reasoning, and the Gods*, translated by Zainab Bahrain and Marc Van De Mieroop, Chicago, IL: University of Chicago Press, 1992.
Everyday Life in Ancient Mesopotamia, translated by Antonia Nevill, Baltimore, MD: Johns Hopkins University Press, 1992, 2001.
Brague, Remi. *The Law of God: The Philosophical History of an Idea*, translated by Lydia G. Cochrane, Chicago, IL: University of Chicago Press, 2007.
Breasted, James Henry. *A History of Egypt, From the Earliest of Times to the Persian Conquest*, NY: Charles Scribner's Sons, 1912.
Brennan, T. Corey. *The Praetorship in the Roman Republic*, 2 volumes, Oxford: Oxford University Press, 2000.
Brownmiller, Susan. *Against Our Will*, NY: Simon and Schuster, 1975, pp. 18–19.
Buckland, William Warwick. *The Roman Law of Slavery*, Cambridge: Cambridge University Press, 1908.
Equity in Roman Law, London: University of London Press, 1911.
A Textbook of Roman Law from Augustus to Justinian, Cambridge: Cambridge University Press, 1921.
Calhoun, George Miller. *The Growth of Criminal Law in Ancient Greece*, Berkeley: University of California Press, 1927.
Campbell, James E. "A Cuneiform Legal Presence in 'The Report of Wenamun,'" *Journal of Ancient Egyptian Interconnections*, Vol. 1, no. 3, 2009, pp. 1–10.
Campbell, Tom. *Rights: A Critical Introduction*, NY: Routledge, 2006.
Carawan, Edwin. *Rhetoric and the Law of Draco*, Oxford: Oxford University Press, 1998.

The Athenian Amnesty and Reconstructing the Law, Oxford: Oxford University Press, 2013.

Castor, Helen. *Joan of Arc*, NY: Harper, 2015.

Charpin, Dominique. *Writing, Law, and Kingship in Old Babylonian Mesopotamia*, translated by Jane Marie Todd, Chicago, IL: University of Chicago Press, 2010.

Chattopadhyaya, Annapurna. "Studying the Economic Position of *Women in the Dharmasastras*: Perspectives in Occupation, *Stridhana*, Property, and Inheritance," in *Women in Dharmasastras*, edited by Chandrkala Padia, New Delhi: Rawat Publications, 2009.

Chrysippus. *De Jure et Lege*, from *Stoicorum Veterum Fragmenta*, in *Greek and Roman Philosophy after Aristotle*, translated by Jason L. Saunders, edited by Hans von Arnim, NY: Free Press, 1966.

Cicero. *On the Consular Provinces*, translated by C. D. Yonge in *The Orations of Marcus Tullius Cicero*, London: George Bell & Sons, 1891.

Pro Flacco, in *The Tolerance and Persecution of the Jews in the Roman Empire*, Part I, translated by Dora Askowith, NY: Columbia University Press, 1915.

De Legibus, in *Cicero* XVI, translated by Clinton Walker Keyes, Cambridge, MA: Harvard University Press' Loeb Classical Library, 1928.

De Re Publica, in *Cicero* XVI, translated by Clinton Walker Keyes, Cambridge, MA: Harvard University Press' Loeb Classical Library, 1928.

De Inventione, in *Cicero* II, translated by H. M. Hubbell, Cambridge, MA: Harvard University Press' Loeb Classical Library, 1949.

On Duties (*De Oficiis*), edited and translated by M. T. Griffin and E. M. Atkins, NY: Cambridge University Press, 1991.

Cline, Eric H. *1177* BC: *The Year Civilization Collapsed*, Princeton, NJ: Princeton University Press, 2014.

Cohen, Boaz. *Jewish and Roman Law: A Comparative Study*, 2 volumes, New York: Jewish Theological Seminary, 1966.

Cohen, David. *Law, Sexuality, and Society: The Enforcement of Morals in Classical Athens*, Cambridge: Cambridge University Press, 1991.

Combs, Nancy. *Fact-Finding Without Facts: The Uncertain Evidentiary Foundations of International Criminal Convictions*, Cambridge: Cambridge University Press, 2010.

Comey, James. *A Higher Loyalty*, NY: Flatiron Books, 2018.

Confucius. *Analects*, in *The Confucian Analects, The Great Learning, and the Doctrine of the Mean*, translated by James Legge, NY: Cosmo Classics, 2009.

Cook, Stanley. *The Laws of Moses and the Code of Hammurabi*, London: Adam and Charles Black, 1903.

Cooper, Jerrold. "International Law in the Third Millennium," in *A History of Ancient Near Eastern Law*, Vol. I, edited by Raymond Westbrook, Leiden: Brill, 2003.

Cornford, F. M. *From Religion to Philosophy: A Study in the Origins of Western Speculation* (1912), New York, NY: Harper & Row Publishers, 1957.

Cornelian Law on Murderers and Poisoners or Magicians, in *Ancient Roman Statutes*, translated and edited by Allan Johnson, Paul Coleman-Norton, Frank Bourne, and Clyde Pharr, Austin: University of Texas Press, 1961, 2012.

Crawford, Harriet. "An Exploration of the World of Women in Third-Millennium Mesopotamia," in *Women in the Ancient Near East*, edited by Mark W. Chavalas, NY: Routledge, 2014.

Crook, J. A. *Law and Life of Rome, 90 B.C.–A.D. 212*, Ithaca, NY: Cornell University Press, 1967.
The Cyrus Cylinder, edited by Irving Finkel, London: I. B. Tauris and Co. Ltd, 2013.
Daube, David. *Studies in Biblical Law*, Cambridge: Cambridge University Press, 1947.
Decree of the Senate on the Bacchanalia (186 BCE), in *Ancient Roman Statutes*, translated and edited by Allan Johnson, Paul Coleman-Norton, Frank Bourne, and Clyde Pharr, Austin: University of Texas Press, 1961, 2012.
Decree of the Senate on Philosophers and Rhetoricians (161 BCE), in *Ancient Roman Statutes*, translated and edited by Allan Johnson, Paul Coleman-Norton, Frank Bourne, and Clyde Pharr, Austin: University of Texas Press, 1961, 2012.
Demosthenes. *Against Androtion*, in *Demosthenes III*, translated by J. H. Vince, Cambridge MA: Harvard University Press' Loeb Classical Library, 1935.
Against Meidias, in *Demosthenes III*, translated by J. H. Vance, Loeb Classical Library, Cambridge, MA: Harvard University Press, 1935.
Against Conon, in *Demosthenes VI: Orations*, translated by A. T. Murray, Loeb Classical Library, Cambridge, MA: Harvard University Press, 1939.
The Digest or the Pandects of Justinian, in *The Civil Law*, translated by S. P. Scott, Cincinnati, OH: The Central Trust Co., 1932.
Dinstein, Yoram. *War, Aggression, and Self-Defense*, third edition, Cambridge: Cambridge University Press, 2001.
Diodorus of Sicily. *The Library of History*, Vol. I, translated by C. H. Oldfather, Cambridge: Loeb Classical Library of Harvard University Press, 1933.
Dobbs, Dan B. *Handbook on the Law of Remedies: Damages, Equity and Restitution*, St. Paul, MN: West Publishing Co., 1973.
Douglas, Mary. *Purity and Power: An Analysis of the Concept of Pollution and Taboo*, NY: Routledge, 1966, 2002.
Driver, Godfrey Rolles and John C. Miles, *The Assyrian Laws*, Oxford: Clarendon Press, 1935.
Driver, Godfrey Rolles and J. C. Miles, *The Babylonian Laws*, 2 volumes, Oxford: Oxford University Press, 1952.
Dworkin, Ronald. *Law's Empire*, Cambridge, MA: Harvard University Press, 1986.
The Edicts of Asoka, edited and translated by N. A. Nikam and Richard McKeon, Chicago, IL: University of Chicago Press, 1959.
Edict of the Curule Aediles (129 CE), in *Ancient Roman Statutes*, Document 245, translated by Allan Chester Johnson, Paul Robinson Coleman-Norton, and Frank Card Bourne, Austin: University of Texas Press, 1961, 2012.
The Egyptian Book of the Dead: The Book of Going Forth by Day, translated by Raymond O. Faulkner and Ogden Goelet, Jr., edited by Eva von Dassow, San Francisco, CA: Chronicle Books, 1994.
Eliot, Carl. *The Rules of Moral Insanity: Moral Responsibility and the Mentally Ill Offender*, Albany: State University of New York Press, 1996.
The Epic of Gilgamesh, translated by Andrew George, NY: Penguin Books, 1985.
Euripides. *Children of Heracles*, Euripides, *Children of Heracles*, in *Euripides III*, translated by David Kovacs, Cambridge, MA: Harvard University Press' Loeb Classical Library, 1995.
Evans, D. G. "The Incidence of Labor-Service in the Old Babylonian Period," *Journal of the American Oriental Society*, Vol. 83, no. 1, Jan.–Mar., 1963, pp. 20–26.
Falk, Ze'ev W. *Hebrew Law in Biblical Times*, Provo, UT: Brigham Young University Press, 2001.

Feinberg, Joel. *Harm to Others*, Oxford: Oxford University Press, 1984.
Feizi, Han. *Basic Writings*, edited and translated by Burton Watson, NY: Columbia University Press, 2003.
Fensham, F. Charles. "Widow, Orphan, and the Poor in Ancient Near Eastern Legal and Wisdom Literature," *Journal of Near Eastern Studies*, Vol. 21, no. 2, April 1962, pp. 129–139.
Fingarette, Herbert. *Confucius: The Secular as Sacred*, NY: HarperCollins, 1972.
Finkelstein, J. J. "Amisaduqa's Edict and the Babylonian 'Law Codes'," *Journal of Cuneiform Studies*, Vol. 15, 1961, pp. 91–104.
Finkelstein, Jacob. "The Edict of Ammisaduqa," in *Ancient Near Eastern Texts Relating to the Old Testament*, third edition, edited by J. B. Pritchard, Princeton, NJ: Princeton University Press, 1969.
Finkelstein, J. J. "The Ox that Gored," *Transactions of the American Philosophical Society*, Vol. 71, part 2, 1981, pp. 1–89.
Fish, Morris. "An Eye for an Eye: Proportionality as a Moral Principle of Punishment," *Oxford Journal of Legal Studies*, Vol. 28, no. 1, 2008, pp. 57–71.
Fisher, N. R. E. *Hybris: A Study in the Values of Honor and Shame in Ancient Greece*, Warminster: Aris & Phillips, 1992.
Slavery in Classical Greece, second edition, London: Gerald Duckworth and Co., 2001.
Flannery, Kent and Joyce Marcus, *The Creation of Inequality: How Our Prehistoric Ancestors Set the Stage for Monarchy, Slavery, and Empire*, Cambridge, MA: Harvard University Press, 2012.
Fleming, Daniel E. *Democracy's Ancient Ancestors: Mari and Early Collective Governance*, NY: Cambridge University Press, 2004.
Fletcher, George. *Basic Concepts of Legal Thought*, NY: Oxford University Press, 1996.
Basic Concepts of Criminal Law, NY: Oxford University Press, 1998.
Fordyke, Sara. *Exile, Ostracism, and Democracy*, Princeton, NJ: Princeton University Press, 2005.
Forester, Benjamin. "Water Under the Straw: Peace in Mesopotamia," in *War and Peace in the Ancient World*, edited by Kurt A. Raaflaub, Oxford: Blackwell Publishing, 2007, pp. 66–80.
Foster, Benjamin. *The Age of Agade: Inventing Empire in Ancient Mesopotamia*, NY: Routledge, 2016.
France, Anatole. *Le Lys Rouge* 1894 [*The Red Lilly*], Paris: Calman-Levy, 1906.
Frankfort, Henri and H. A. Frankfort. *Before Philosophy: The Intellectual Adventure of Ancient Man*, Baltimore, MD: Penguin Press, 1949.
Frier, Bruce W. A *Casebook on the Roman Law of Delict*, Atlanta, GA: Scholars' Press, 1989.
Fuhrmann, Christopher J. *Policing the Roman Empire*, Oxford: Oxford University Press, 2012.
Gadd, C. J. "Hammurabi and the End of his Dynasty," in *Cambridge Ancient History*, third edition, edited by: I. E. S. Edwards, C. J. Gadd, N. G. L. Hammond, and E. Sollberger, Vol. 1, part 1, Cambridge: Cambridge University Press, 1973.
Gaius. *The Institutes of the Civil Law*, in *The Civil Law*, translated by S. P. Scott, Clark, NJ: The Law Book Exchange, [1932] 2001.
Ganley, Andrew H. "The Case of Sobekhotpe and Tjau – Principle, Practice, and Legal Procedure in the Sixth Dynasty," *Discussions in Egyptology*, Vol. 53, 2002, pp. 30–37.
Gardner, Jane F. *Women in Roman Law and Society*, Bloomington, IN: Indiana University Press, 1986.

Ghoshal, Pranati. "Women's Education in Vedic India," in *Women in Dharmasastras*, edited by Chandrakala Padia, New Delhi: Rawat Publications, 2009.
Ghoshal, Upendra Nath. *A History of Indian Political Ideas*, Oxford: Oxford University Press, 1959.
Gillespie, Alexander. *The Causes of War: Vol. I: 3000 BCE to 1000 CE*, Oxford: Hart Publishing, 2013.
Goetze, Albrecht. "The Laws of Eshnunna," *The Annual of the American Schools of Oriental Research*, Vol. 31, 1951–1952, pp. 1–197.
Goldsworthy, Adrian. *Pax Romana*, New Haven, CT: Yale University Press, 2016.
Good, Edwin M. "Capital Punishment and its Alternatives in Ancient Near Eastern Law," *Stanford Law Review*, Vol. 19, no. 5 (May, 1967), pp. 947–977.
Goody, Jack. *The Logic of Writing and the Organization of Society*, Cambridge: Cambridge University Press, 1986.
The Gortyn Code, in *The Laws of Ancient Crete c. 650–400 BCE*, edited by Michael Gagarin and Paula Perlman, Oxford: Oxford University Press, 2016.
Greek Elegiac Poetry, translated by Douglas E. Gerber, Loeb Classical Texts, Cambridge, MA: Harvard University Press, 1999.
Greek Sacred Law, second edition, edited and translated by Eran Lupu, Leiden: Brill, 2009.
Greengus, Samuel. "Legal and Social Institutions of Ancient Mesopotamia," in *Civilizations of the Ancient Near East*, edited by Jack M. Sasson, NY: Charles Scribner's Sons, 1995.
Laws in the Bible and in Early Rabbinic Collections, Eugene, OR: Cascade Books, 2011.
Greenidge, A. H. J. *Infamia: Its Place in Roman Public and Private Law*, Oxford: Oxford University Press, 1894.
The Legal Procedure of Cicero's Time, Oxford: Oxford University Press, 1901.
Grote, George. *History of Greece*, 10 volumes, London: John Murray, 1888.
Grotius, Hugo. *De Jure Belli ac Pacis (On the Law of War and Peace)* (1625), translated by Francis Kelsey, Oxford: Clarendon Press, 1925.
The Guatama, in *Dharmasutras: The Law Codes of Apastamba, Gautama, Baudhayana, and Vasistha*, translated by Patrick Olivelle, Delhi: Motilal Banarsidass, 2000.
Hammer, Dean. *Roman Political Thought: From Cicero to Augustine*, NY: Cambridge University Press, 2014.
Handbook of Epictetus, translated by Nicholas White, Indianapolis, IN: Hackett Publishing Co., 1983.
Hansen, Mogens Herman. *The Athenian Democracy in the Age of Demosthenes*, Oxford: Blackwell, 1991, p. 178.
Hanson, Victor David. *The Western Way of War: Infantry Battle in Classical Greece*, Berkeley, CA: University of California Press, 1994.
Hardy, E. G. *Studies in Roman History*, London: S. Schonschein, 1906.
Harries, Jill. *Law and Crime in the Roman World*, Cambridge: Cambridge University Press, 2007.
Harrison, A. R. W. *The Law of Athens*. 2 volumes, Oxford: Oxford University Press, 1968.
Harrison, Jane Ellen. *Themis: A Study of the Social Origins of Greek Religion*, Cambridge: Cambridge University Press, 1927.
Hart, H. L. A. *The Concept of Law*, Oxford: Oxford University Press, 1961.
Punishment and Responsibility, Oxford: Oxford University Press, 1968.
Hart, H. L. A. and A. M. Honore, *Causation in the Law*, Oxford: Oxford University Press, 1959.
Hartland, E. Sidney. *Primitive Law*, London, Kennikat Press, 1924.

Hayes, Christine. *What's Divine About Divine Law?* Princeton, NJ: Princeton University Press, 2015.

"Law in Classical Rabbinic Judaism," in *The Cambridge Companion to Judaism and Law*, edited by Christine Hayes, Cambridge: Cambridge University Press, 2017.

Henningsen v. *Bloomfield Motors*, 32 N.J. 385, 161 A. 2d 69 (1960).

Hiers, Richard H. *Justice and Compassion in Biblical Law*, NY: Continuum Publishers, 2009.

Hillner, Julia. *Prison, Punishment, and Penance in Late Antiquity*, Cambridge: Cambridge University Press, 2015.

Hoebel, E. Adamson. *The Law of Primitive Man*, Cambridge, MA: Harvard University Press, 1954.

Home, Henry (Lord Kames). *Principles of Equity*, London: Alex, Lawrie, and Co., 1765.

Honore, Tony. *Ulpian: Pioneer of Human Rights*, second edition, Oxford: Oxford University Press, 2002.

Hopkins, E. Washburn. "The Growth of Law and Legal Institutions," in *The Cambridge History of India, Vol. 1: Ancient India*, edited by E. J. Rapson, Cambridge: Cambridge University Press, 1922.

"Family Life and Social Customs as They Appear in the Sutras," in *The Cambridge History of India*, Vol. 1, edited by E. J. Rapson, Cambridge: Cambridge University Press, 1922.

Hsu, Cho-yun. "The Spring and Autumn Period," in *The Cambridge History of Ancient China: From the Origins of Civilization to 221 BC*, edited by Michael Lowe and Edward Shaughnessy, Cambridge: Cambridge University Press, 1999.

Hudson, Michael. "Reconstructing the Origins of Interest-Bearing Debt and the Logic of Clean Slates," in *Debt and Economic Renewal in the Ancient Near East*, edited by Michael Hudson and Marc Van De Mieroop, Bethesda, MD: CDL Press, 2002, pp. 7–58.

Hulsewe, A. F. P. *Remnants of Ch'in Law*, Leiden: Brill, 1985.

Hume, David. *Treatise*, Selby-Bigge edition, Oxford: Oxford University Press, 1968.

The Institutes of Gaius, 2 volumes, translated by Francis De Zulueta, Oxford: Oxford University Press, 1946.

The Institutes of Justinian, translated by Thomas Collett Sandars, London: Longmans, Green and Co., 1917.

Isocrates. *On the Peace*, in *Isocrates II*, translated by George Norlin, Cambridge, MA: Harvard University Press' Loeb Classical Library, 1929.

Jackson, Samuel. *A Comparison of Ancient Near Eastern Law Collections Prior to the First Millennium BC*, Piscataway, NJ: Gorgias Press, 2008.

Jacobsen, Thorkild. "Primitive Democracy in Ancient Mesopotamia," *Journal of Near Eastern Studies*, Vol. 2, 1943, pp. 159–172.

"Early Political Development in Mesopotamia," *Zeitschrift fur Assyriologie*, Vol. 18, 1957, pp. 91–140.

"Ancient Mesopotamian Religion: The Central Concerns," in his *Toward the Image of Tammuz and Other Essays on Mesopotamian History and Culture*, edited by William L. Moran, Cambridge, MA: Harvard University Press, 1970.

"An Ancient Mesopotamian Trial for Homicide," in Thorkild Jacobsen, *Toward the Image of Tammuz and Other Essays on Mesopotamian History and Culture*, edited by William L. Moran, Cambridge, MA: Harvard University Press, 1970.

Jaeger, Werner. *Paideia: The Ideals of Greek Culture*, 3 volumes, translated by Gilbert Highet, Oxford: Oxford University Press, 1945.

Jasnow, Richard. "Pre-Demotic Pharaonic Sources," in *Security for Debt in Ancient Near Eastern Law*, edited by Raymond Westbrook and Richard Jasnow, Leiden: Brill, 2001.

Jaspers, Karl. *Confucius*, in *Socrates, Buddha, Confucius, and Jesus*, translated by Ralph Manheim, NY: Harcourt Brace and Company, 1957, 1962.

Johns, C. H. W. *Babylonian and Assyrian Laws, Contracts and Letters*, Edinburgh: T & T Clark, 1904.

Jones, A. H. M. *The Criminal Courts of the Roman Republic and Principate*, Oxford: Basil Blackwell, 1972.

Jones, J. W. *The Law and Legal Theory of the Greeks*, Oxford: Oxford University Press, 1956.

Josephus, Flavius. *Against Apion*, in *Josephus: The Complete Works*, translated by William Whiston, Nashville, TN: Thomas Nelson Publishers, 1998.

Joshel, Sandra R. *Slavery in the Roman World*, Cambridge: Cambridge University Press, 2010.

The Code of Justinian, Book IX, Chapter 9, no. 20, translated in *The Civil Law*, translated by S. P. Scott, Vol. II, Cincinnati, OH: The Central Trust Co., 1932.

Kamen, Deborah. *Status in Classical Athens*, Princeton, NJ: Princeton University Press, 2013.

Kautilya. *Arthashastra*, Book IV, Ch. IV, translated by R. Shamasastry, 1915, NY: reprinted by Bottom of the Hill Publishing, 2010.

Kim, Chin and Theodore R. LeBlang. "The Death Penalty in Traditional China," *Georgia Journal of International and Comparative Law*, Vol. 5, 1975, pp. 92–93.

King, L. W. editor and translator, *The Letters and Inscriptions of Hammurabi*, Vol. 3, London: Luzac and Co., 1900.

Kirk, G. S. and J. E, Raven, *The Presocratic Philosophers*, Cambridge: Cambridge University Press, 1957.

Kirschenbaum, Aaron. *Equity in Jewish Law*, 2 volumes, Hoboken, NJ: Ktav, 1991.

Kitchen, Kenneth A. and Paul J. N. Lawrence. *Treaty, Law, and Covenant in the Ancient Near East*, 2 volumes, Wiesbaden: Harrassowitz Verlag, 2012.

Krutschten, Jean-Marie. "Law," in *The Oxford Encyclopedia of Ancient Egypt*, Oxford: Oxford University Press, 2001, pp. 277–282.

Kupperman, Joel. *Classical Asian Philosophy*, NY: Oxford University Press, 2007.

LaFave, Wayne R. and Austin W. Scott, Jr., *Criminal Law*, second edition, St. Paul, MN: West Publishing Co., 1986.

Lafont, Bertrand. "International Relations in the Ancient Near East: The Birth of a Complete Diplomatic System," *Diplomacy & Statecraft*, Vol. 12, no. 1 (March 2001), pp. 39–60.

"The Ordeal," in *Everyday Life in Ancient Mesopotamia*, translated by Antonia Nevill, edited by edited by Jean Botero, Baltimore, MD: Johns Hopkins Press, 2001.

Langbein, John. *The Origins of the Adversary Criminal Trial*, Oxford: Oxford University Press, 2003.

The Law Code of Visnu, translated by Patrick Olivelle, Cambridge: Harvard University Press, 2009.

Law Collections from Mesopotamia and Asia Minor, second edition, translated by Martha T. Roth, Atlanta, GA: Scholars' Press, 1997.

Law of the Kings: Numa Pompilius, in *Ancient Roman Statutes*, translated by Allan Chester Johnson, Paul Robinson Coleman-Norton, and Frank Card Bourne, Austin: University of Texas Press, 1961, 2012.

Laws of the Kings: Romulus, in *Ancient Roman Statutes*, translated by Allan Chester Johnson, Paul Robinson Coleman-Norton, and Frank Card Bourne, Austin: University of Texas Press, 1961, 2012.

Law of the Kings: Servius Tullius, in *Ancient Roman Statutes*, edited and translated by Allan Chester Johnson, Paul Robinson Coleman-Norton, and Frank Card Bourne, Austin: University of Texas Press, 1961, 2012.

The Laws of Ancient Crete c. 650–400 BCE, edited and translated by Michael Gagarin and Paula Perlman, Oxford: Oxford University Press, 2016.

Laws of Eshnunna, Law Collections from Mesopotamia and Asia Minor, second edition, translated by Martha Roth, Atlanta, GA: Scholars' Press, 1997.

Laws of Hammurabi, in *Law Collections From Mesopotamia and Asia Minor*, second edition, translated by Martha T. Roth, Atlanta, GA: Scholars' Press, 1997.

Laws of Lipit-Ishtar, in *Law Collections From Mesopotamia and Asia Minor*, second edition, translated by Martha T. Roth, Atlanta, GA: Scholars' Press, 1997.

Laws of Ur-Namma [LU], *Law Collections from Mesopotamia and Asia Minor*, second edition, translated by Martha Roth, Atlanta, GA: Scholars' Press, 1997.

Lemche, N. P. "The Manumission of Slaves – The Fallow Year – The Sabbatical Year – The Jobel Year," *Vetus Testmentum*, Vol. 26, Fasc. 1 (Jan. 1976), pp. 38–59.

Levi, Edward H. *An Introduction to Legal Reasoning*, Chicago, IL: University of Chicago Press, 1949.

Lewis, Mark Edward. *The Early Chinese Empires: Qin and Han*, Cambridge, MA: Harvard University Press, 2007.

Li Feng. *Early China: A Social and Cultural History*, Cambridge: Cambridge University Press, 2013.

Linder, Amnon. *The Jews in Roman Imperial Legislation*, Detroit, MI: Wayne State University Press, 1987.

Lindgren, James. "Why the Ancients May Not Have Needed a System of Criminal Law," *Boston University Law Review*, Vol. 76, February/April 1996, pp. 29–57.

Lingat, Robert. *The Classical Law of India*, translated by J. Duncan and M. Derrett, Oxford: Oxford University Press, 1973.

Livy. *History of Rome*, translated by B. O. Foster, Loeb edition, Cambridge, MA: Harvard University Press, 1926.

Lorton, David. "Legal and Social Institutions of Pharaonic Egypt," in *Civilizations of the Ancient Near East*, edited by Jack M. Sasson, NY: Charles Scribner's Sons, 1995, Vol. 1, pp. 345–362.

Lowe, Michael. "The Heritage Left to the Empires," in *The Cambridge History of Ancient China: From the Origins of Civilization to 221 BC*, edited by Michael Lowe and Edward L. Shaughnessy, Cambridge: Cambridge University Press, 1999.

MacDowell, Douglas M. *Athenian Homicide Law in the Age of the Orators*, Manchester: Manchester University Press, 1963.

The Law in Classical Greece, Ithaca, NY: Cornell University Press, 1978.

MacLachlan, Bonnie. *Women in Ancient Rome: a Sourcebook*, NY: Bloomsbury Academic, 2013, p. 120.

Mackie, J. L. *Ethics: Inventing Right and Wrong*, NY: Penguin Books, 1977.

Maine, Henry Sumner. *Ancient Law*, London: John Murray, 1861.

Maitland, F. W. *Equity: A Course of Lectures*, Cambridge: Cambridge University Press, 1909, 1936.

Mancini, Anna. *Maat Revealed: Philosophy of Justice in Ancient Egypt*, Paris: Buenos Books, 2004.

Manu's Code of Law, translated by Patrick Olivelle, Oxford: Oxford University Press, 2005.

Marcianus. "Institutes," in Justinian's *Digest*, in *The Civil Law*, translated by S. P. Scott, Cincinnati, OH: The Central Trust Company, 1932.

May, Larry. "Vicarious Agency and Corporate Responsibility," *Philosophical Studies*, Vol. 43 (1983), pp. 69–82.

War Crimes and Just War, NY: Cambridge University Press, 2007.

Aggression and Crimes Against Peace, NY: Cambridge University Press, 2008.

After War Ends, Cambridge: Cambridge University Press, 2012.

Contingent Pacifism, Cambridge: Cambridge University Press, 2015.

May, Larry and Elizabeth Edenberg. *Jus Post Bellum and Transitional Justice*, NY:Cambridge University Press, 2013.

May, Larry and Andrew Forcehimes. *Morality, Jus Post Bellum, and International Law*, NY: Cambridge University Press, 2012;

May, Larry and Shannon Fyfe. *International Criminal Tribunals: A Normative Defense*, NY: Cambridge University Press, 2017.

McMahan, Jeff. *Killing in War*, Oxford: Oxford University Press, 2009.

The Meditations of Marcus Aurelius Antoninus, in *Great Books of the Western World*, translated by George Long, edited by Robert Maynard Hutchins, Chicago, IL: University of Chicago Press, 1952.

Mencius, translated by Irene Bloom, NY: Columbia University Press, 2009.

Mendelsohn, Isaac. *Slavery in the Ancient Near East*, NY: Oxford University Press, 1949.

Mendelsohn, Samuel. *The Criminal Jurisprudence of the Ancient Hebrews*, Baltimore, MD: M. Curlander, 1891.

Meyer, Elizabeth. *Metics and the Athenian Phialai-Inscriptions*, Stutgart: Franz Steiner Verlag, 2010.

Middle Assyrian Laws, in *Law Collections From Mesopotamia and Asia Minor*, second edition, translated by Martha T. Roth, Atlanta, GA: Scholars' Press, 1997.

Milgrom, Jacob. "Lex Talionis and the Rabbis," *Bible Review*, Vol. 12, no. 2, 1996, pp. 16–25.

Mill, John Stuart. *On Liberty* (1859), edited by Stefan Collini, Cambridge: Cambridge University Press, 1989.

Mill, John Stuart and Harriet Taylor, *The Subjection of Women* (1969), Indianapolis, IN: Hackett Publishing company, 1988.

The Mishnah, translated by Herbert Danby, Oxford: Oxford University Press, 1933.

Mommsen, Theodor. *The History of Rome*, Oxford: Benediction Classics, 2001.

Morrow, Glenn. *Plato's Cretan City*, Princeton, NJ: Princeton University Press, 1960.

Mozi. *Basic Writings*, translated by Burton Watson, NY: Columbia University Press, 2003.

Murphy v. *McNamara*, 38 Conn. Super. 183, 416 A. 2d 170 (1975).

Murphy, Jeffrey. *Getting Even: Forgiveness and its Limits*, Oxford: Oxford University Press, 2004.

Murphy, Jeffrey and Jean Hampton. *Forgiveness and Mercy*, Cambridge: Cambridge University Press, 1988.

The Naradasmrti, translated by Richard W. Lariviere, Delhi: Motilal Banarsidass Publishers, 2003.

Neufeld, E. *The Hittite Laws*, London: Luzac and Co. Ltd, 1951.

Newton, Michael and Larry May. *Proportionality in International Law*, NY: Oxford University Press, 2014.

Nippel, Wilfried. *Public Order in Ancient Rome*, Cambridge: Cambridge University Press, 1995.

Noortmann, Matt. *Enforcing International Law: From Self-help to Self-contained Regimes*, Burlington, VT: Ashgate Publishing, 2005.

Novel Constitutions of Justinian, *The Civil Law* translated by S. P. Scott, Vol. II, Cincinnati, OH: The Central Trust Co., 1932.

Nussbaum, Arthur. *A Concise History of the Law of Nations*, NY: The Macmillan Company, 1953.

Nussbaum, Martha. "Equity and Mercy," *Philosophy & Public Affairs*, Vol. 22, no. 2 (Spring 1993), pp. 83–125.

Ober, Josiah. "'I besieged that Man': Democracy's Revolutionary Start," in *Origins of Democracy in Ancient Greece*, edited by Kurt A. Raaflaub, Josiah Ober, and Robert W. Wallace, Berkeley: University of California Press, 2007, pp. 83–104.

Ohlin, Jens and Larry May. *Necessity in International Law*, NY: Oxford University Press, 2016.

Okin, Susan Moller. *Women in Western Political Thought*, Princeton, NJ: Princeton University Press, 1979.

Ostwald, Martin. *Nomos and the Beginnings of the Athenian Democracy*, Oxford: Oxford University Press, 1969.

The Palestinian Talmud, Sanhedrin, translated in Samuel Greengus, *Laws in the Bible and in Early Rabbinic Collections*, Eugene, OR: Cascade Books, 2011.

Parker, Robert. *Miasma: Pollution and Purification in Early Greek Religion*, Oxford: Oxford University Press, 1983.

Patterson, Orlando. *Slavery and Social Death*, Cambridge MA: Harvard University Press, 1982.

Freedom, Vol. I: Freedom in the Making of Western Culture, NY: Basic Books, 1991.

The Opinions of Julius Paulus, Book V, Chapter 22, section I, translated by S. P. Scott, in *The Civil Law*, translated by S. P. Scott, Vol. II, Cincinnati, OH: The Central Trust Co., 1932.

Peet, T. Eric. *The Great Tomb-Robberies of the Twentieth Egyptian Dynasty*, Oxford: Clarendon Press, 1930.

The Permanent Edict of the Urban Praetor, *Ancient Roman Statutes*, translated by Allan Chester Johnson, Paul Robinson Coleman-Norton, and Frank Card Bourne, Austin: University of Texas Press, 1961, 2012.

Pettit, Philip. *Republicanism: A Theory of Freedom and Government*, Oxford: Oxford University Press, 1997.

Philo. *De Opificio Mundi*, in *The Works of Philo*, translated by C. D. Yonge, Peabody, MA: Hendrickson Publishers, 1993.

On Abraham, in *The Works of Philo*, translated by C. D. Yonge, Peabody, MA: Hendrickson Publishers, 1993.

The Special Laws II, in *The Works of Philo*, translated by C. D. Yonge, Peabody, MA: Hendrickson Publishers, 1993.

The Special Laws IV, in *The Works of Philo*, translated by C. D. Yonge, Peabody, MA: Hendrickson Publishers, 1993.

Pfluger, Kurt. "The Edict of King Haremhab," *Journal of Near Eastern Studies*, Vol. 5, no. 4, October 1946, pp. 260–276.

Phillipson, Coleman. *The International Law and Custom of Ancient Greece and Rome*, 2 volumes, London: Macmillan and Company, 1911.

Plato. *Euthyphro*, in *Plato I*, translated by Harold North Fowler, Cambridge, MA: Harvard University Press' Loeb Classical Library, 1914.

Phaedo, in *Plato* I, translated by Harold North Fowler, Loeb edition, Cambridge, MA: Harvard University Press, 1914.
Statesman, Loeb edition, *Plato* VIII, translated by Harold Fowler, Cambridge, MA: Harvard University Press, 1925.
Republic, translated by Paul Shorey, in *Plato's Collected Dialogues*, edited by Edith Hamilton and Huntington Cairns, Princeton, NJ: Princeton University Press, 1961.
The Laws, translated by Thomas Pangle, NY: Basic Books, 1980.
Crito, in Plato, *The Trial and Death of Socrates*, translated by G. M. A. Grube, Indianapolis, IN: Hackett Publishing Co., 1986.
Pope Francis. *The Name of God is Mercy*, NY: Random House, 2016.
Plutarch. *Life of Lycurgus*, translated by Bernadotte Perrin, Cambridge, MA: Harvard University Press, Loeb edition, 1914.
Lives, Solon 18. i–ii. Quoted and translated by Delfim F. Leao and P. J. Rhodes, *The Laws of Solon*, London: I. B. Tauris, 2015.
Price, Simon. *Religions of the Ancient Greeks*, Cambridge: Cambridge University Press, 1999.
Rangju, Sima. *Methods of War*, in *Military Strategy Classics of Ancient China*, translated by Chen Song, NY: Special Editions Books, 2013.
Redford, Susan. *The Harem Conspiracy*, Dekalb: Northern Illinois University Press, 2002, 2008.
Rhodes, P. J. *A Commentary on the Aristotelian Athenaion Politeia*, Oxford: Oxford University Press, 1981, 1992.
Riggsby, Andrew. *Roman Law and the Legal World of the Romans*, Cambridge: Cambridge University Press, 2010.
Robinson, O. F. *The Criminal Law of Ancient Rome*, Baltimore, MD: Johns Hopkins University Press, 1995.
Penal Practice and Penal Policy in Ancient Rome, NY: Routledge, 2007.
Rosenstein, Nathan. "War and Peace, Fear and Reconciliation at Rome," in *War and Peace in the Ancient World*, edited by Kurt A. Raaflaub, Oxford: Blackwell Publishing, 2007.
Ross, W. D. *Aristotle's Physics: A Revised Text with Introduction and Commentary*, Oxford: Oxford University Press, 1936.
Roth, Martha. "Mesopotamian Legal Traditions and the Laws of Hammurabi," *Chicago-Kent Law Review*, Vol. 13, 1995–1996, pp. 13–39.
Roth, Martha T. "Reading Mesopotamian Law Cases PBS 5 100: A Question of Filiation," *Journal of the Economic and Social History of the Orient*, Vol. 44, no. 3, 2001, pp. 243–292.
Roy, Devapriya. "My Hours with Manu and Some Unlikely Answers," in *Women in Dharmasastras*, edited by Chandrakala Padia, New Delhi: Rawat Publications, 2009.
Saggs, H. W. F. *The Greatness That Was Babylon*, NY: Hawthorn Books, 1962.
Saint Germain, Christopher. *Doctor and Student: Or Dialogues between a Doctor of Divinity and a Student in the Laws of England Containing the Grounds of those Laws Together with Questions and Cases Concerning Equity thereof (1518)*, London: A. Strahan and W. Woodfall, 1787.
Sarna, Nathum M. *The JPS Commentary on Genesis*, Philadelphia, PA: The Jewish Publication Society, 1989.
Saunders, Trevor. *Plato's Penal Code*, Oxford: Clarendon Press, 1991.
Schabas, William A. *The Abolition of the Death Penalty in International Law*, Cambridge: Cambridge University Press, 1997.

Scheflin, Alan W. and Jon M. Van Dyke. "Merciful Juries: The Resilience of Jury Nullification," *Washington and Lee Law Review*, Vol. 48, 1991, pp. 165–183.

Schurer, Emil. *A History of the Jewish People in the Time of Jesus Christ*, 5 volumes, translated by Sophia Taylor and Rev. Peter Christie, Edinburgh: T & T Clark, 1890.

Sen, Amartya. *Inequality Reexamined*, Cambridge, MA: Harvard University Press, 1992.

Seneca. *De Clementia (On Mercy)*, in *Seneca I: Moral Essays I*, translated by John W. Basore, Cambridge, MA: Harvard University Press' Loeb Classical Library, 1928.

On Mercy (De Clemntia), in *Seneca: Moral and Political Essays*, translated by John M. Cooper and J. F. Procope, Cambridge: Cambridge University Press, 1995.

The Book of Lord Shang, translated by J. J. L. Duyvendak, NY: Create Space, 2016.

Shaughnessy, Edward L. "Western Zhou History," in *The Cambridge History of Ancient China: From the Origins of Civilization to 221 BC*, edited by Michael Lowe and Edward L. Shaughnessy, Cambridge: Cambridge University Press, 1999.

Singh, Preeti. "Re-reading Dharmasastras through Indian Eyes: A Feminist Perspective," in *Women in Dharmasastras*, edited by Chandrakala Padia, New Delhi: Rawat Publications, 2009.

Sistare, Christine. *Responsibility and Criminal Liability*, NY: Springer Verlag, 1989.

Skinner, Quentin. *Liberty before Liberalism*, Cambridge: Cambridge University Press, 1998.

Smith, Brian K. *Classifying the Universe: The Ancient Indian Varna System and the Origins of Caste*, Oxford: Oxford University Press, 1994.

Solomon, Norman. "The Ethics of War: Judaism," in *The Ethics of War: Shared Problems in Different Traditions*, edited by Richard Sorabji and David Rodin, Aldershot: Ashgate Publishing, 2006, pp. 108–137.

Solomon, Richard. "Ancient India: Peace Within and War Without," in *War and Peace in the Ancient World*, edited by Kurt A. Raaflaub, Oxford: Blackwell Publishing, 2007.

Sophocles. *Ajax*, in *Sophocles I*, translated by Hugh Lloyd-Jones, Loeb edition, Cambridge, MA: Harvard University Press, 1994.

Antigone, in *Sophocles II*, translated by Hugh Lloyd-Jones, Cambridge MA: Harvard University Press' Loeb Classical Library, 1994.

Oedipus Tyrannus, in *Sophocles I*, translated by Hugh Lloyd-Jones, Loeb edition, Cambridge, MA: Harvard University Press, 1994.

Oedipus at Colonus, in *Sophocles II*, translated by Hugh Lloyd-Jones, Loeb edition, Cambridge, MA: Harvard University Press, 1994.

Antigone, in *Sophocles: The Theban Plays*, translated by George Young, Mineola, NY: Dover Publications, Inc., 1999.

Sorabji, Richard. *Necessity, Cause, and Blame: Perspectives on Aristotle's Theory*, London: Duckworth, 1983.

Speiser, E. A. "The *Muskenum*," *Orientalia*, Vol. 27, no. 1 (1958), 19–28.

Stalley, R. F. *An Introduction to Plato's Laws*, Indianapolis, IN: Hackett Publishing Co., 1983.

Steele, Francis. *The Code of Lipit-Ishtar*, Philadelphia: The University Museum of the University of Pennsylvania, 1948.

Steinkeller, Piotr. "Money-Lending Practices in Ur III Babylonia: The Issue of Economic Motivation," in *Debt and Economic Renewal in the Ancient Near East*, edited by Michael Hudson and Marc Van De Mieroop, Bethesda, MD: CDL Press, 2002.

Stroud, Ronald. *Drakon's Law on Homicide*, Berkeley: University of California Press, 1968.

Tallqvist, Knut Leonard. "Old Assyrian Laws," *Oversikt av Finska Vetenskaps-Societetens Forhandlingar*, Vol. LXIII, no. 3, 1920–1921, pp. 1–41.

Tanakh: The Holy Scriptures, Philadelphia, PA: The Jewish Publication Society, 1985.
Ten, C. L. *Crime, Guilt, and Punishment*, Oxford: Oxford University Press, 1987.
Tertullian. *The Chaplet*, in *Disciplinary, Moral, and Aesthetic Works*, translated by Rudolph Arbermann, Emily Joseph Daly, and Edwin Quain, NY: Fathers of the Church, Inc., 1959.
Flight in Time of Persecution, in *Disciplinary, Moral, and Ascetical Works*, translated by Rudolph Arbesmann, Emily Joseph Daly, and Edwin A. Quain, NY: Fathers of the Church, Inc., 1959.
Spectacles, in *Disciplinary, Moral, and Ascetical Works*, translated by Rudolph Arbermann, Emily Joseph Daly, and Edwin Quain, NY: Fathers of the Church, Inc., 1959.
To the Martyrs, in *Disciplinary, Moral, and Ascetical Works*, translated by Rudolph Arbesmann, Emily Joseph Daly, and Edwin A. Quain, NY: Fathers of the Church, Inc., 1959.
Tetlow, Elizabeth Meier. *Women, Crime, and Punishment in Ancient Law and Society*, NY: Continuum, 2004.
The Theodosian Code, translated by Clyde Pharr, Princeton, NJ: Princeton University Press, 1952.
Theodorides, Aristide "The Concept of Law in Ancient Egypt," in *The Legacy of Egypt*, edited by J. R. Harris, Oxford: Oxford University Press, 1971.
Thompson, J. A. *The Ancient Near East Treaties and the Old Testament*, London: The Tyndale Press, 1963.
Thucydides. *History of the Peloponnesian War*, translated by Charles Forster Smith, Loeb Library, Cambridge, MA: Harvard University Press, 1919.
History of the Peloponnesian War, translated by Crawley, NY: The Modern Library, 1951.
Tiwari, Pushpa. "Social Dimensions of the Discourse on Women and Sex as Reflected in Manusmrti – The Earliest Known Indian Code of Law," in *Women in Dharmasastras*, edited by Chandrakala Padia, New Delhi: Rawat Publications, 2009.
The Tosefta, Baba Qamma, translated by Samuel Greengus, in *Laws in the Bible and in Early Rabbinic Collections*, Eugene, OR: Cascade Books, 2011.
Treaty between Niqmepa of Alakh and Ir-Adad/Tesup of Tunip (c. fifteenth century BCE), translated in *Treaty, Law, and Covenant in the Ancient Near East*, edited and translated by Kenneth A. Kitchen and Paul J. N. Lawrence, Wiesbaden: Harrassowitz Verlag, 2012.
Treaty Between Rome and Carthage (509 BCE), in *Ancient Roman Statutes*, translated by Allan Chester Johnson, Paul Robinson Coleman-Norton, and Frank Card Bourne, Austin: University of Texas Press, 1961, 2012.
Treston, Hubert J. *Poine: A Study in Ancient Greek Blood-Vengeance*, London: Longmans, Green and Co., 1923.
Trial from December 1, 513 BCE, translated by Shalom E. Holtz in his book, *Neo-Babylonian Trial Records*, Atlanta, GA: Society of Biblical Literature, 2014.
Tritle, Lawrence A. "'Laughing for Joy': War and Peace among the Greeks," in *War and Peace in the Ancient World*, edited by Kurt A. Raaflaub, Oxford: Blackwell Publishing, 2007.
T'ung-Tsu Ch'U. *Law and Society in Traditional China*, Paris: Mouton & Co., 1965.
The Twelve Tables, in *The Civil Law*, translated by S. P. Scott, Cincinnati, OH: The Central Trust Co., 1932.
The Twelve Tables, in *Ancient Roman Statutes*, translated by Allan Chester Johnson, Paul Robinson Coleman-Norton, and Frank Card Bourne, Austin: University of Texas Press, 1961, 2012.

Ulpian. *Institutes*, in Justinian's *Digest*, in *The Civil Law*, translated by S. P. Scott, Cincinnati, OH: The Central Trust Co., 1932.

On Adultery, in Justinian's *Digest*, in *The Civil Law*, translated by S. P. Scott, Cincinnati, OH: The Central Trust Co., 1932.

On Sabinus, in Justinian's *Digest*, in *The Civil Law*, translated by S. P. Scott, Cincinnati, OH: The Central Trust Co., 1932.

On the Edict, in Justinian's *Digest*, in *The Civil Law*, translated by S. P. Scott, Cincinnati, OH: The Central Trust Co., 1932.

Ulpian, *The Rules*, in Justinian's *Digest*, in *The Civil Law*, translated by S. P. Scott, Cincinnati: The Central Trust Co., 1932.

Uniacke, Suzanne. *Permissible Killing: The Self-Defense Justification of Homicide*, Cambridge: Cambridge University Press, 1994.

Van de Mieroop, Marc. *Cuneiform Texts and the Writing of History*, London: Routledge, 1999.

Van De Mieroop, Marc. "Credit as a Facilitator in Old Babylonian Mesopotamia," in *Debt and Economic Renewal in the Ancient Near East*, edited by Michael Hudson and Marc Van De Mieroop, Bethesda, MD: CDL Press, 2002, pp. 163–173.

"A History of Near Eastern Debt?" in *Debt and Economic Renewal in the Ancient Near East*, edited by Michael Hudson and Marc Van De Mieroop, Bethesda, MD: CDL Press, 2002.

King Hammurabi of Babylon, Oxford: Blackwell Publishing, 2005.

A History of the Ancient Near East c. 3000–323 BC, second edition, Oxford: Blackwell Publishing, 2007.

A History of Ancient Egypt, Oxford: Blackwell Publishing, 2011.

Philosophy Before the Greeks, Princeton, NJ: Princeton University Press, 2016.

VanDrunen, David. "Natural Law, The Lex Talionis, and the Power of the Sword," *Liberty University Law Review*, Vol. 2, 2008, pp. 945–967.

Van Zyl, D. H. *Justice and Equity in Greek and Roman Legal Thought*, Pretoria: Academica Press, 1991.

The Vajnavalkya Smrti, translated by B. S. Best, Delhi: Chaukhamba Sanskrit Pratishthan, 2004.

The Vasistha, in *Dharmasutras: The Law Codes of Apastamba, Gautama, Baudhayana, and Vasistha*, translated by Patrick Olivelle, Delhi: Motilal Banarsidass, 2000.

The Vedas, translated by Ralph T. H. Griffith, Delhi: Kshetra Books, 1914, 2017.

Veenhof, Klaas R. "Old Assyrian Period," in *A History of Ancient Near Eastern Law*, edited by Raymond Westbrook, Leiden: Brill, 2003.

Veenker, Ronald and J. Cale Johnson, "The Appellate Process in the Legal Record [di til-la] from Ur III Umma," *Altoriental Forsch*, Vol. 36, no. 2, 2009, pp. 349–364.

VerSteeg, Russ. *Early Mesopotamian Law*, Durham, NC: Carolina Academic Press, 2000, p. 127.

Viswanatha, S. I. *International Law in Ancient India*, Bombay: Longmans, Green & Co., 1925.

Von Hirsch, A. "Censure and Proportionality," in *A Reader on Punishment*, edited by Antony Duff and David Garland, Oxford: Oxford University Press, 1994.

Waldron, Jeremy. "Lex Talionis," *Arizona Law Review*, Vol. 34, 1992, pp. 25–51.

Walker, Thomas A. *A History of the Law of Nations*, Cambridge: Cambridge University Press, 1899, Vol. 1.

Walzer, Michael. *Just and Unjust Wars*, NY: Basic Books, 1977.

Weinfeld, Moshe. "Covenant Making in Anatolia and Mesopotamia," *Janes* 22 (1993), pp. 135–139.

Wertheimer, Alan. "Unconscionability and Contracts," *Business Ethics Quarterly*, Vol. 2, no. 4, 1992, pp. 479–496.

Westbrook, Raymond. "Social Justice in the Ancient Near East," in *Social Justice in the Ancient World*, edited by K. D. Irani and Morris Silver, London: Greenwood Press, 1995.

Westbrook, Raymond M. *A History of Ancient Near Eastern Law*, 2 volumes, Leiden: Brill, 2003.

Westbrook, Raymond. *Ex Oriente Lex: Near Eastern Influences on Ancient Greek and Roman Law*, edited by Deborah Lyons and Kurt Raaflaub, Baltimore, MD: Johns Hopkins University Press, 2015.

Wilcke, Claus. "Early Dynastic and Sargonic Periods," in *A History of Ancient Near Eastern Law*, edited by Raymond M. Westbrook, Leiden: Brill, 2003.

Williams, Bernard. *Shame and Necessity*, Berkeley: University of California Press, 1993.

Whitman, James Q. *The Origins of Reasonable Doubt*, New Haven, CT: Yale University Press, 2008.

Williams v. *Walker-Thomas Furniture Co.*, 350 F.2d 445 (1965).

Wilson, John A. *The Culture of Ancient Egypt*, Chicago, IL: University of Chicago Press, 1951.

The Works of Philo, Complete and Unabridged, translated by C. D. Yonge, Peabody, MA: Hendrickson Publishers, 1993.

Wright, David P. *Inventing God's Law: How the Covenant Code of the Bible Used and Revised the Laws of Hammurabi*, Oxford: Oxford University Press, 2009.

Xenophon. *Cyropaedia (The Education of Cyrus)*, translated by Walter Miller, Cambridge, MA: Harvard University, Loeb Classical Library, 1914.

Oeconomicus, in *Xenophon's Memorabilia and Oeconomicus*, translated by O. J. Todd and revised by Jeffrey Henderson, Cambridge, MA: Harvard University Press' Loeb Classical Library, 2013.

Xunzi, *Basic Writings*, translated by Burton Watson, NY: Columbia University Press, 2003.

Yaron, Reven. *The Laws of Eshnunna*, Jerusalem/Leiden: The Magnes Press, E. J. Brill, second revised edition, 1988.

Ziegler, Karl-Heinz. "Conclusion and Publication of International Treaties in Antiquity," *Israel Law Review*, Vol. 29, nos. 1–2, 1995, pp. 233–249.

Ziskin, Jonathan. "When Two Men Fight: Legal Implications of Brawling in the Ancient Near East," *Revue Internationale des Droits de l'Antique*, 1997, pp. 13–42.

Zucrow, Solomon. *Women. Slaves, and the Ignorant in Rabbinic Literature*, Boston, MA: The Stratford Company, 1932.

Index